MANAGERIAL FINANCE

MANAGERIAL

FINANCE

SALOMON J. FLINK
RUTGERS—THE STATE UNIVERSITY

DONALD GRUNEWALD
SUFFOLK UNIVERSITY

John Wiley & Sons, Inc.

New York · London · Sydney · Toronto

𝒬 26752

Preface

The science of management has made significant progress in the past two decades. The science of financial management has shared in this evolution. Old techniques have been improved and new techniques have been introduced.

But management, in general (and financial management, in particular), is both a *science* and an *art*. Whereas science is quantitative and objective, art is qualitative and subjective. For example, an evaluation of the past performance of the firm involves essentially a quantitative analysis of the relevant statistical facts and financial data. However, policy formulation and decision making involve, in addition to a quantitative determination, subjective value judgments by top management. The decision to buy or rent a new plant calls, first, for an objective scientific calculation of the relative annual costs of each alternative. The final decision, however, rests on the answers to such questions as: Are construction costs likely to go up or down in the next few years? Are interest rates on mortgages likely to rise or fall? How strong is the liquidity preference of management? The answers to these and similar questions call for subjective value judgements by top management. Financial management thus combines the application of scientific techniques and the art of qualitative judgments.

The central aim of this book is to define the problems and to analyze the functions of financial management in the decision-making process of the firm. The 1950's and 1960's have witnessed many significant changes in the financial community. New institutions have emerged as additional sources of funds, especially for small firms: the Small Business Administration and small business investment companies. The phenomenal growth of pension funds in the past two decades has provided a potential source of funds for medium-sized firms. At the same time, the traditional sources of funds, such as commercial banks, finance companies, and insurance companies, have added new dimensions to their lending and investment policies.

These external, institutional changes have been paralleled by important internal changes in the financial planning of firms. The increased range of alternative external sources of funds calls for greater skill in the application of value judgments in the selection of the "best" choice of either one single source or a combination of several sources, that is, a "package" deal. Top management has also become increasingly aware of the various alternatives that make possible a more efficient use of the funds within the firm. Thus financial management has a dual function. It attempts to maximize the utilization of the funds employed by the firm and to minimize the burdens imposed by recourse to external sources.

The effective performance of these interrelated functions has grown in complexity. New techniques of inventory control, in operations research, ratio analysis, and short-term financing present a variety of alternatives which must be evaluated in relation to each other and to the specific needs of the firm. Similarly, intermediate and long-term financing offer a wide variety of alternative sources of funds.

This book provides the student, first, with the broad theoretical frame of reference within which finance performs its function as a managerial policy guide. Second, it alerts the student to the real-life complexity of managerial finance. The book also has a practical orientation. It gives many examples of how-to-do-it in practice.

In addition to the material covered in other currently available texts, this book offers several new features. Material has been added in the areas of ratio analysis, operations research, intermediate term financing and equity financing of small firms, valuation in merger negotiations, and the impact of inflation on financial management. The inclusion of questions, short problems, and a case tailored to each chapter provides a complete package of instruction in one text. The questions at the end of each chapter serve the traditional purpose of highlighting the major points in the chapter. The problems give experience in the use of the quantitative tools of finance. Each chapter's case presents a real-life situation that challenges the student to apply his acquired general knowledge to a specific situation.

In recent years, there has been an increasing divergence between financing the large business enterprise and financing the small business. Both of us have had experience as consultants to both large and small businesses in the area of finance. One of us has been a consultant to the Small Business Administration and to several small business investment companies. Based on this experience, we have included extensive new material on the sources of funds and other financial problems that have special significance for small business firms. Thus, the text will be useful to those wishing to enter small business as well as to those who plan a career with a large corporation.

In every business firm, short-term financing is a continuing concern of top management. The need for intermediate term financing arises at irregular intervals in the lifetime of the firm. The problem of long-term financing is, in turn, an issue that calls for decision making still less frequently. Each of these three facets of financial management is treated as a distinct problem area. At the same time, however, the student is alerted to the fact that there are significant interrelationships between these several types of financial needs.

The volume is designed for a one-semester introductory course; either on the upper level of an undergraduate curriculum or the first year of an M.B.A. program. We have used the material, problems, and cases in our classes, both undergraduate and graduate, over the past five years. Although there have been differences in the business-educational background of graduate students compared with their undergraduate counterparts, both groups responded with equal effectiveness. The problems and cases have proved a highly valuable link between theoretical principles and the dynamics of real-life situations.

With the growing stress by schools of business on the managerial approach, we believe that the present volume will meet the needs of instructors and students. Hopefully, the book will also stimulate student interest in the further study of finance and the opportunities in financial management as a profession.

Salomon J. Flink
Donald Grunewald

Acknowledgements

Many persons have had a hand in the successful completion of this book. First, we gratefully acknowledge the contribution of Professor George Steinlieb of Rutgers University. Dr. Steinlieb was active in the initial planning of the book and contributed many ideas, particularly to the section on short-term financing.

We thank Professor William J. Carroll of Rutgers for his share in the writing of "The General Inventory Problem Under Uncertainty" (Appendix A to Chapter 7). The kind contribution by Professor Hal P. Eastman of Rutgers University of the problem to Chapter 7 and permission to include his "Romac Appliance Company" case in Chapter 7 is gratefully acknowledged.

We express our appreciation to the *Harvard Business Review* and the authors for permission to reproduce "How to Evaluate New Capital Investments" by John G. McLean and "Risk Analysis in Capital Investment" by David B. Hertz as appendices to Chapter 9 and 10. The former article was first published in the November–December 1958 issue of the *Harvard Business Review* and the latter article appeared in the January–February 1964 issue. Dun & Bradstreet graciously granted permission to reprint their 1966 Table of Business Ratios.

We acknowledge the contributions to the field of finance of the American Accounting Association and to Ralph Jones for his excellent study, "Price Level Changes and Financial Statements—Case Studies of Four Companies." An excerpt of his study has been reprinted in Chapter 21.

The courtesy of our colleagues at Rutgers University and at Suffolk University in answering our numerous queries for information is much appreciated. The late Professor Erich Otto of Rutgers read all of the material on capital budgeting. His criticism was very helpful.

We also acknowledge our great debt to the many firms, individuals, businessmen, and government agencies who gave us valuable time and information both for the text and the cases. These individuals and organizations deserve much credit for their contributions to business education. Unfortunately, the lack of space and the need to preserve anonymity in some cases precludes individual acknowledgements of all of this help and encouragement.

We especially acknowledge the contribution of these professors who independently reviewed the manuscript in varying stages:

Richard E. Ball
University of Cincinnati
Cincinnati, Ohio

James F. Jackson
Oklahoma State University
Stillwater, Okla.

Robert S. Carlson
Harvard University
Graduate School of Business
Boston, Mass.

Sidney L. Jones
University of Michigan
Ann Arbor, Mich.

Albert H. Clark
Georgia State College
Atlanta, Ga.

Alexander A. Robichek
Stanford University
Stanford, Cal.

Paul T. Hendershot
Assistant Dean
East Carolina College
Greenville, N. C.

Glenn A. Wilt, Jr.
Arizona State University
Tempe, Ariz.

Their valuable comments and suggestions are greatly appreciated. We also express our thanks to our post-graduate and undergraduate students at both Suffolk and Rutgers universities for serving as guinea pigs and for their helpful ideas, suggestions, and constructive criticism.

We acknowledge the kind help and cooperation of the publishing and editorial staff of John Wiley and Sons. We especially thank John Young for his advice and encouragement.

Mrs. Eleanor Yurkutat and Miss Jeanne Chevoor typed the bulk of the manuscript in various drafts. We gratefully acknowledge their meticulous work and splendid cooperation in this difficult task. Mrs. Irene Kay, Miss Lilian A. Shaw, Miss Nancy Hall, and Miss Susan Schaufenbil also helped with some of the clerical and typing tasks.

Finally, we thank our families for their help and understanding cooperation.

We, of course, accept the blame for all errors and omissions in the text. All cases, problems, examples, and questions in this book have been prepared for class discussion instead of for the purpose of illustrating either effective or ineffective handling of administrative situations.

S. J. F.
D. G.

Contents

MANAGERIAL FINANCE

Part I

Short-Term Financing

~~~~~~

Chapter One

The Function of the Financial Manager

The major objective of any business firm is to make a profit for its owners by producing goods or services for sale in the market place. To reach this goal, the firm purchases the factors of production and with them produces the output it sells. The central feature of financial management is its formulation of the firm's strategy in determining the most effective use of the funds currently at the disposal of the company and in selecting the most favorable sources of additional funds that the enterprise will need in the foreseeable future.

As we shall view him, the financial manager performs an operational function. He is the member of a firm's top management charged with the responsibility of planning, organizing, effectuating, and controlling the financial affairs of the enterprise. In a large concern he is usually an officer who carries the title of vice president for finance, controller or treasurer. In smaller firms, this function generally resides with the president of the corporation or the owner of an unincorporated business in addition to his other burdens. How well the financial manager meets this challenge determines whether the enterprise will prosper or fail.

I. FUNCTIONS OF THE FINANCIAL MANAGER

The responsibility of the financial manager encompasses five major functions.

1. An in-depth financial analysis of the accounting statements and records.
2. Estimating the prospective inflow and outflow of funds in the next quarter or year, in order to determine the prospective liquidity of the firm.

3. Selecting the most desirable temporary investment for the excess cash and near-cash resources of the firm.
4. Providing top management with information on current and prospective financial conditions of the business as a basis for policy decisions on purchases, marketing, and pricing.
5. Finally, and the most important single function, preparing the detailed financial plan for the procurement (sources) and allocation (uses) of funds by the firm, both short-term and long-term. It is the responsibility of the financial manager to evaluate the prospective cost of funds as against the anticipated profit from the use of these funds by the operating units to which they are to be allocated.

Accounting Data   The accountant records the results of the firm's economic activities. He lists all revenues, the explicit (or observable) expenditures, and profit or loss. The financial manager considers all these and also the implicit (or unobservable) costs. Unlike the accountant who records only those changes in the value of assets that are "in accordance with accounting principles," the financial manager recognizes the importance of other factors that may have an effect on the firm's credit rating, its borrowing power, and its evaluation in case of merger or sale. The financial manager is also very much concerned with the specific causes of the firm's profit or loss. For instance, he may question whether the profits were due to superior efficiency or to mere "luck" because major competitors were subject to a prolonged shutdown as a result of a strike, fire, or some other temporary disturbance. Then, too, he attempts to project the firm's financial conditions and needs in the months ahead through the use of recent sales and profit or loss figures.

Flow of Funds   The financial manager must estimate the cash inflow from sales and the outflow for wages, services, goods, taxes, etc. This flow of funds is projected either on a weekly or monthly basis. It provides a foundation for determining whether the firm will have to borrow funds to meet a cash deficit and, if so, how long it will require such loans. The financial manager also has the responsibility of evaluating the financial advantages of alternatives to borrowing. For example, should the firm purchase goods and supplies in smaller quantities, if and when needed, without a quantity discount rather than make a single large purchase? Or should it take full advantage of the credit extended by suppliers instead of gaining the discount for payment within a few days of receipt of goods?

Excess Cash It is a common experience for a firm, especially a large establishment, to have a substantial cash balance in excess of its scheduled requirements. Such a situation arises periodically as a consequence of seasonal influences, i.e., in the "slow" season of output and/or sales. Excess cash balances are also generated if the firm sells a fixed asset or floats an issue of stocks or bonds. While these funds may be subsequently invested in new fixed assets they constitute excess cash until disbursed. It is the function of the financial manager (1) to estimate the length of time during which the firm will have at its disposal such excess cash, and (2) to select the temporary investment(s) into which such excess cash can be channeled. Such investment could be, among others, a savings deposit, a Certificate of Deposit, or short-term government obligations, each of which possesses a high degree of liquidity, yields interest, and involves a minimum of risk.

Financial Outlook Within the firm, the several members of management have specified areas of supervision, planning, and decision making, and all their actions have a direct impact on the financial resources of the enterprise. It is the financial manager's task to evaluate the effects of such actions on the financial conditions of the firm and to communicate his findings to the other members of the management team. Whereas the production manager or the purchasing agent thinks primarily in terms of his own sphere of responsibility, the financial manager views the contemplated action from the perspective of the whole firm. An expenditure which may be profitable from the standpoint of one department may deprive another department of the funds it requires for effective operation.

Financial Planning Last, but by no means least, top management must at regular intervals, or sporadically, make decisions on when, where, and how to raise funds to finance either an increase of current output or an expansion of plant, if not both. It behooves the financial manager to evaluate the alternative sources of funds, their respective costs, and the extent to which the procurement of funds from a given source may affect future dividend policy, borrowing capacity, or the decision making powers of top management.

Summary The first three functions are basically financial in nature. Their effective execution requires financial proficiency and analytical know-how. They do not involve major decisions by the top officer of the firm and approval by the board of directors. By contrast the last two functions call for decisions from the top. This is particularly true of financial planning. A decision to procure long-term funds by means of the sale of stock or bonds needs not only the approval of the board of directors but often also the approval of stockholders. The financial manager prepares the proposal and the supporting facts and arguments, but the ultimate decision is beyond his scope of authority.

Types of Capital Assets It is axiomatic, in accounting as well as in finance, that every asset of the firm automatically generates a liability. Whatever the firm owns it must owe a corresponding amount of dollars to somebody whether it be a creditor or the owners of the business.

The assets of the firm are usually divided into two broad categories: current assets and fixed assets. Financial management deals with the problem of how to procure the funds for the ownership or use of assets by the firm at least cost. In the case of current assets, the firm disburses funds for the purchase of materials, supplies, services, salaries, and wages. These expenditures are a function of anticipated sales which, in turn, are affected by seasonal factors and cyclical influences. These expenditures are called the *variable cost* of the firm. The net effect is that the amount of funds and the time interval for which they will be needed will fluctuate from month to month and, in many cases, even on a day-to-day basis. The relevant decision of the financial manager—source of and use of funds—are therefore of a short-term nature.

By contrast, the fixed assets of the firm become an integral part of the enterprise until the particular asset has reached the end of its usable life span. The cost of the fixed asset—wear and tear (depreciation), maintenance, and repairs—are fixed. If the fixed asset(s) have been purchased with funds obtained from others than the owners, e.g., stockholders, of the firm the fixed costs also include the interest on the debt.

Capital assets, in any form, are the lifeblood of the business. They permeate each facet of the firm's anatomy. Accordingly, there is a close relationship between the financial manager and every division of the firm. The financial manager must be willing and able to communicate with the other members of top management both in the formulation and implementation of the financial program.

Allocation of Funds Unlike the other officers of the firm, the financial manager measures the success of his operation in terms of the business as a whole. The manager of the production department can point to the level of output and the cost per unit as a yardstick of his competence and efficiency. The sales manager can use sales volume as his measure of success. The director of research and development can refer to product improvements or new designs and innovations generated by his department as evidence of his specific share in the firm's progress.

In contrast, the contribution of the financial manager is not confined to a specific and readily identifiable segment of the enterprise. His function and responsibility touch all operations of the firm. It is his task to measure, in terms of money, the performance of each department or division in relation to its specific objectives. At the same time, he must evaluate the financial impact of a given department's operation on the funds required by other departments. And finally, he must appraise the performance of the firm as a whole.

Suppose a retail firm or a manufacturing company has three major divisions: A, B, and C. Assume that, based on sales forecasts, the manager of division A requests a substantial increase in funds for expanded inventory and an aggressive promotion campaign, while divisions B and C project no appreciable change in their respective sales volumes. Suppose, however, that the financial manager finds it impossible to raise additional funds to meet the request of division A. Should he approve the request? If the answer is affirmative, should the adjustment in allocation of funds be made in B, C, or both; and to what extent? How will the cutback affect the profit of the curtailed division(s), and what effect will it have on the firm as a whole? Is the cutback in B and/or C going to hurt the "image" of the firm? Will it antagonize customers who ordinarily buy in all three divisions but who will curtail their purchases in A if B and C no longer offer a complete line?

From the standpoint of the financial manager, the individual division is but part of an integrated entity called the firm. Whereas the manager of each division is concerned with the profitability of his particular segment of the enterprise, the financial manager—and the same holds true of top management—must view the division in relation to the total firm.

The financial manager prepares the analysis which serves as a basis for top management's allocation of funds to the individual divisions or departments of the firm. Each element of the firm's operation requires funds and is expected to contribute to the overall profit of the enterprise. But the funds available may be limited. To insure the most profitable employment of funds, the financial manager must weigh the several uses to which the funds can be allocated. If additional funds are to be allocated, say, to research and development, this decision reduces the amounts available for the other divisions of the firm. Or let us suppose that the company has $100,000 in available funds for capital expenditures. Top management has given serious thought to (1) the expenditure of $50,000 to acquire its own fleet of delivery trucks, which are expected to yield an appreciable saving over the present cost of trucking services provided by an outside firm; (2) the purchase of $50,000 worth of new machinery to replace less efficient equipment; (3) an expenditure of $30,000 for a modern air conditioning and heating installation that will raise the efficiency of the labor force; and (4) the installation of a modern bookkeeping and control system at a cost of $20,000. These requirements add up to $150,000 whereas the firm has only $100,000 at its disposal. Someone within top management must decide who should get how much of the limited funds. The financial manager has to estimate and compare the relative profitability of each course and recommend to top management the most promising allocation of the funds among the competing demands.

In fact, an essential task of the financial manager is to weigh competing uses for the funds employed in the firm. His aim is to make sure that the company "gets maximum mileage" out of every dollar used in its day-to-day operations as well as out of the funds invested in fixed assets such as plant, equipment, machinery, and other assets.

Source of Funds   The funds that the financial manager can allocate to the several departments of the firm flow from two sources. The primary source consists of the capital invested by owners of the firm and reinvested profits. In addition, the typical firm has access to a variety of *external sources*. These include the credit extended by its suppliers; loans obtained from financial institutions, private lenders, or governmental lending agencies; and the proceeds from the sale of debt securities (bonds, debentures) or the sale of new stock issues.

The decision to use external sources generally involves borrowing and thus generates costs in the form of interest payments. In addition, borrowed funds are obtained for a given period of time and frequently call for specified repayment installments at certain time intervals. This requires the financial manager to determine that the use of external funds will, with reasonable probability, generate a gross profit in excess of their cost. Furthermore, he must estimate the likelihood that the firm will have the money to repay the loan, or the loan installments, on the due dates.

External suppliers of funds offer a range of interest rates and differences in the length of time for which they are willing to extend credit or make loans, and in the amount of the loan (or credit) they are willing to extend to a firm of given size. Moreover, the lending policies and criteria do not remain constant over a period of time. Even within a given group of lenders some institutions may curb their loans during a particular period, while other banks maintain a "liberal" policy. Each potential supplier and lender thus presents one of several sources of external short- or long-term funds.

The selection of the most favorable external source of funds among those available to the firm is another major task of the financial manager. The effective execution of this task calls first for adequate familiarity with the policies and terms of the various types of external sources. Second, it demands an evaluation of the financial effects of several competing methods of procuring funds from these external sources, their relative costs, and the repayment burdens assumed by the firm. For example, the use of debt will affect the availability and the cost of equity financing, i.e., the sale of common stock.

At times, there is the additional problem of choosing between internal and external sources. This issue arises usually in conjunction with the determination of dividend payments at a time when the firm contemplates substantial expansion. If the company decides to omit the dividend payment and instead, to reinvest the earnings into additional plant facilities, it will save the cost of borrowing funds and will not be obligated to make periodic repayments of the loan. On the other hand, the omission of dividends may have an adverse effect on stockholders and cause the price of the stock to decline. Thus, it becomes a problem of choosing the best of several courses of action.

II. OBJECTIVES OF FINANCIAL MANAGER

The goal of the firm is the maximization of the wealth invested by the owners of the firm. Under most conditions, this objective can be obtained by pursuing a policy of maximizing the profit. However, alternative decisions on product, output volume, and price may involve potential results with a wide range of risk. An alternative that promises maximum profit may not lead to a maximization of wealth if the results do not live up to the expectation. Since it is the function of the financial manager to plan the allocation of funds, he must evaluate not only the expected rate of profit from alternative uses of funds by the several operating divisions of the firm, but he must also estimate the relative probabilities of obtaining the anticipated profit. This problem will be analyzed in greater detail in subsequent chapters.

Another basic objective, particularly in relation to the short-term operations of the firm, is the maintenance of adequate liquidity. The firm must have the cash funds to pay wages and salaries, to meet its obligations to suppliers of goods and services in accordance with the terms of purchase, and to pay its taxes when due. The firm may have assets with a value far in excess of such liabilities. But if these assets consist of buildings, machinery, equipment and the like the firm will be "solvent"—i.e., it has total assets in excess of its total liabilities to creditors—though it is "illiquid" since it cannot meet its current obligations when due.

Maximizing Profit   One basic approach is the single-cycle concept. From this standpoint the firm's price and profit policy is focused solely on the immediate selling cycle, i.e., the present sales season. Top management wants to obtain maximum profit in the current market with little, if any, attention given to the next season. This situation prevails, for example, among producers of low-priced garments, such as underwear, and among wholesalers of fresh fruits and vegetables.

A second approach may be called the stepping-down price and profit policy. The product is sold first at a top price in a limited market. This is followed by a sequence of price reductions, each of which is directed at a progressively wider segment of the total market. This approach is best illustrated by the film industry. A prospective "hit" will be shown first in a limited number of theatres at fairly high admission prices. After the special "run" of several months it will then be released to so-called first-run theatres at advanced prices. One or two years after the "premiere," it may be released for showing in every theatre at regular prices. Works by well-known authors are usually published first in hardback and subsequently in paperback editions at a fraction of their former price.

A third approach calls for maximum penetration of the market at a price which will yield a uniform predetermined rate of profit; for example, 10%. In establishing the anticipated rate of profit, top management wants to procure for the firm its portion of the total market not merely for a single season but for an indefinite series of selling cycles.

The firm exists to earn profits for its stockholders—more particularly, for its common stockholders. Hence, the best profitability goal for management to select is maximization of profits for the firm's common stockholders in the long run. Short-run profit maximization may lead to customer reaction that could jeopardize the long-range existence of the firm. A more moderate profit objective during a period of supply shortages, for example, is likely to retain customer goodwill and loyalty after the period of shortages ends, whereas a policy of charging all that the market will bear may yield large profits in the short run but loss of business ultimately.

Explicit and Implicit Cost of Funds   As a scarce resource, capital employed in the enterprise has an economic value. In the marketplace this value is expressed as interest payment. In the case of borrowed funds, the agreed-upon rate of interest is the *explicit cost* of capital. Accounting practice acknowledges such explicit costs which are recognized by tax legislation as a deductible expense in calculating the taxable income (profit) of the firm.

But what about the capital invested by the owners or stockholders? The tax authorities do not allow them to charge their capital against the income of the firm. The accountant following the rules of the Internal Revenue Services therefore does not charge the cost of the owner's capital to the firm.

From the viewpoint of the firm as a taxpayer this procedure is logical. Assume that the firm has total receipts of $500,000 and total expenses, exclusive of the cost of the owner's capital, of $350,000. Thus it has a profit of $150,000. Assume further that the owners invested $500,000 which could have earned 6% in a reasonably safe investment. If the accountant were to charge 6% or $30,000 as expense, the profit would be only $120,000. However, the taxable income of the firm would be $120,000 (profit) + $30,000 = $150,000. The tax authorities do not distinguish between "profit" and "interest" as far as the tax liability is concerned, since the latter is a tax on *income* rather than on economic profit.

The financial manager is concerned with the *profit* of the firm. In addition to the explicit costs he also makes full allowance for all *implicit costs* which the firm incurs in employing the factors of production. Such implicit costs include, for example, the market value of the services performed by the single proprietor or the partners in a partnership, the rental value of buildings or equipment owned by the proprietor or partners of the firm, and the interest which could have been earned on the cash funds invested by the owners.

The importance of implicit cost becomes readily apparent if a business is to be sold. Suppose two firms in the same line of business show at the end of the year sales of $1,000,000 each. The profit before tax for firm A is $60,000 while firm B shows a profit before tax of $90,000. Assume that firm A is incorporated, it rents the premises in which it is located for $20,000 per year, and the president draws a salary of $15,000. Both items, rent and salary, are tax deductible expenses and are therefore entered by the accountant as explicit costs. Next, assume that firm B is an individual proprietorship. Its owner drew $15,000 as his salary, he owns the property in which the firm is located, and these premises have a rental value of $20,000.[1] In this instance, the accountant will enter as expenses only the depreciation of the property, local taxes, costs of maintenance, insurance, and (if the property is mortgaged) interest payments. Suppose that these several items total $10,000. In this instance, the profit of $90,000 by firm B ignores the implict costs of $15,000 withdrawn by the owner as salary and the net rental value of the property of $20,000. If these two items are deducted from the $90,000 profit shown by the accountant, it will be evident that firm B earned $5,000 less than firm A.

Aside from the special case of sale or merger, the determination of the profit of the firm, as distinct from the income, plays an important role in such managerial issues as: the profitability of the firm in comparison with competitors of comparable size, the relative profitability of the several products manufactured or distributed by the firm, the desirability of adding a new product or discontinuing a product.

Liquidity versus Profitability The financial manager must be on constant guard to insure the *liquidity* of the firm. In a literal sense the typical business establishment is a constant "debtor." It purchases supplies on credit. It borrows from financial institutions. Its operating facilities may be rented and some of its equipment leased from other firms. As it operates, it builds up a tax obligation to local, state and

[1] For the sake of simplicity, it assumed that the first firm pays a rental of $20,000 and agrees to pay the taxes, insurance, and maintenance of the property amounting to $10,000 per year and that these expenses are the same for the property of the second firm.

federal authorities. If it manufactures or distributes goods under a license or franchise, it incurs a debt for royalties. Whatever the nature and source of these debts, they fall due on certain dates. Unless payment is made at the maturity of the particular debt, the firm is "delinquent." At best, the reputation of the firm is tarnished; at worst, the creditor may force the firm to terminate its business.

By its very nature, liquidity represents funds that are not used in the operations of the firm. In effect, the financial manager "trades" profitability for liquidity. If he overstresses liquidity the firm foregoes profitable opportunities. If he overemphasizes profit, he endangers the firm's ability to meet bills and notes when payment is due. The ratio of cash and cash equivalents to short-term liabilities reflects the financial manager's ability to maintain an effective balance between liquidity and profitability.

It is the function of the financial manager to "manage" the financial affairs of the firm in such a manner that funds will be available to meet not only the internal requirements—payrolls, salaries, and commissions—but also the external obligations. If the financial manager succeeds in this task, the firm is said to be in a liquid position. It is able to meet its financial obligations to the outside world. Failure to pay bills when due has an unfavorable effect on the firm's credit rating. Prolonged delinquency in meeting overdue obligations may lead to bankruptcy proceedings.

III. THE DIMENSIONS OF FINANCIAL MANAGEMENT

The financial manager is concerned with the performance of the firm both in the past and in the future. He reviews the financial record of the company for the past year, quarter, or month, as the case may be, and prepares a preview of the company's probable financial conditions in the course of the next month, quarter, year, or several years.

The review function, which is essentially an analytical one, involves an analysis of the flow of funds: payments to suppliers or money received from customers, payroll, tax returns, and the like. The financial manager's primary and major task—the core of financial management—centers on *planning*. He evaluates the fund needs, present and future, the several departments, the extent to which they are likely to generate an inflow of funds, the available sources and costs of funds, the alternative means of procuring funds from outsiders, and related problems.

These matters will be discussed in detail in various chapters of this book.

Planning must, however, be complemented by *control*. The result must be measured concurrently against projections. For example, are the actual sales keeping pace with the projected level for the period? If not, how will the firm meet its obligations to suppliers? Assuming that sales reach the expected volume, are the customers paying their bills at the anticipated rates? Are the costs of production within the projected range? Is the firm accumulating a larger inventory than is required by its sales? These and many other questions are bound to arise at one time or another. In each instance, the effect may be to throw off balance the initial financial plans for the period. The only way to restore the balance between the outflow and inflow of funds is to apply an adequate control over expenditures and revenues.

Profitability   Both control and planning have one common denominator—profit. It is the duty of financial management to examine at frequent intervals—usually monthly and quarterly—whether the firm is operating at a profit. And, if so, whether the rate of profit is adequate and satisfactory. In the last analysis, the performance of the firm during the previous quarter, for example, either exceeded, equalled, or fell short of management's target for that period. The review of the past quarter is thus a retrospective appraisal of the plans for and the achievements of the firm during that interval. Similarly, in examining the estimated future needs for funds by the several divisions, the financial manager evaluates (1) the projected profitability, (2) the adequacy of the anticipated rate of profit, and (3) the financial cost of making the funds available.

Whether a given firm entrusts planning and control to a single individual or divides the two tasks among two or more members of management is a matter of organization. In either case, the basic objective of financial management remains unchanged, to make the most effective use of the funds employed in the operations of the firm. In performing the dual task of planning and control, the financial manager looks at three time intervals or dimensions: past and present, immediate future or short run, and the more distant future or long run.

1. Diagnosis   As pointed out earlier in this chapter, the financial manager is charged with the job of procuring and allocating funds for the day-to-day operations of the firm. In order to discharge this task effectively, he must first ascertain the funds presently at the disposal of the business. Next, he must estimate the probable inflow and outflow of funds in the days, or weeks, ahead. Thus, past, present, and future merge into a continuous flow of financial sources and uses of funds. But, although the flow is continuous, it is also uneven. In a given time period, say a week, the cash received from sales may be substantially in excess of the payments that have to be made to suppliers, employees, and others from whom the firm purchases goods and services. The reverse may be true of the following time period.

To determine the significance of these fluctuations in the cash flow and their probable impact on the liquidity of the firm, the financial manager prepares a prospective cash flow for, say, one year. This, in turn, is broken down into monthly (and sometimes even weekly) figures of anticipated positive (excess cash) and negative (insufficient cash) inflow. Subsequently, the financial manager measures the actual experience against the original forecast. If he finds a substantial deviation of the actual from the projected, he must determine whether these differences arc symptomatic of developments which had not been considered in the original projection.

In setting up the cash-flow forecast, the financial manager uses, as a point of departure, the most recent financial statements of the firm: the balance sheet and the income statements. The balance sheet is analogous to the physical measurements, age, and sex of a patient that the physician requires as a point of departure. The income statement is analogous to the several tests of pulse beat, respiration, blood pressure, and the like that give the physician some insight into the patient's anatomy as a functioning organism.

However, the financial manager cannot be satisfied by merely looking at the balance sheet and income statement and accepting these documents as the complete picture of the company's present state of health. Like the doctor, the financial officer must next look into the past history. He must *interpret* the accountant's facts in the light of the various elements that influenced the company's operations favorably or adversely and that produced the results shown in the financial statements.

2. Interpretation   The second question is this: Does the past performance record of the firm provide a solid basis for the anticipated operations in the next six or twelve months? In the last analysis, the financial statements reflect the *results* of past operations. They are inadequate for determining the specific *causes* that produced these results. It is the responsibility of the financial manager to look behind the figures and to pinpoint the specific factors that account for the present status of the firm.

Suppose that Company XY shows a substantial profit for the past year. Upon a closer examination of the facts behind the figures, the financial officer discovers that sales and earnings of XY rose sharply because its major competitor, L. M., Inc., had cut back its output and sales for several months owing to a prolonged strike in the plant of its major supplier. The loss in sales affected adversely the profit picture. At this moment of time, at the end of the last fiscal year for both companies, XY looks healthy and vigorous while L. M., Inc. appears relatively weak and shaky. But looking ahead to the next few months, it is conceivable that XY's level of sales and rate of profit may decline while L. M., Inc. can look forward to the resumption of sales, output, and adequate profit.

3. Planning   Financial management is concerned not only with the market prospects for and the financial needs of the next few weeks or months. From time to time, top management must think in terms of years. Decisions have to be made that create obligations and commitments for a span of many years. The consummation of a lease for the plant, store, or office usually involves a period of five, ten, or more years. A lease is only an alternative to the purchase of an existing plant or the construction of a new plant. It is the function of the financial manager to estimate the financial consequences of each of these alternatives. If the company buys an existing plant, the annual cost of taxes, repairs, and insurance, plus interest on and repayment of the mortgage are likely to be less than the annual rental for a comparable building. However, the purchase of a plant usually means that the firm will have to invest some money, i.e., the difference between the purchase price and the amount of the mortgage. This investment in the plant means a diversion of funds that would otherwise be available for use in the several operations of the firm. If the company cannot spare the money for the downpayment (purchase price minus mortgage), without running short of cash, the economy of plant acquisition over rental may be more than offset by the diseconomy of insufficient funds for production, marketing, or other operations. But even if the firm has enough in idle funds to afford the downpayment, other questions arise that need to be answered by the financial manager before a rational decision can be reached.

The same basic issues arise in the long-range planning of expansion of production facilities by either acquiring new machinery, leasing it, or subcontracting with outside firms to produce all or part of the added output. In product research and development, the firm has similar alternatives of setting up its own facilities or contracting with an outside firm for the performance of this task.

The results of the long-range spending program are embodied in the *Capital* Budget. This budget shows, in detail (1) the proposed expenditures for each of several capital assets (e.g., plant improvement, machinery, and equipment); (2) the time schedule for each expenditure; (3) the revenues that each investment is expected to generate; (4) the cost of the funds that will be invested in these assets; and (5) the net profit, before taxes, that the firm will derive from the proposed investments.

IV. FINANCIAL MANAGEMENT IN DECISION-MAKING

A financial program, like any plan, is no better than the people entrusted with its execution. After the financial manager prepares the program, top management must then approve it before it can become effective. The several department heads then must translate the program into appropriate courses of action. This is frequently more easily said than done.

A. Desirability versus Feasibility

In analyzing past performance and preparing the financial program for the future, the financial manager thinks primarily in terms of costs and profit. He translates past and future actions into dollars. Alternative policies are similarly treated and expressed as prospective money incomes, money expenditures, and money profit. In other words, the financial manager tells top management how much money is involved in each of several proposals, or alternatives, the cost or difficulty of raising these sums, and how much profit is expected to be attained.

Basically, therefore, the financial manager's recommendations are intended to be impersonal, objective, and rational. He seeks that solution which promises the largest return (profit) of dollars while, at the same time, assures that the firm will remain liquid. The latter also is measured in dollar terms. Having to choose, for example, between the alternative of buying finished components or making them in the plant, the financial manager's questions will be: How much will we save, and thus add to profit, if we produce the parts? How much will it cost us to borrow the money, if we do not have the money for additional payroll and supplies? If the manufacturing cost plus the cost of borrowing is less than the price paid for finished components, the arithmetic answer is clear (unless there are other factors of weight) : produce the goods rather than buy them. On an impersonal *quantitative* basis, this then represents the most desirable alternative from a financial point of view.

Qualitative Factors   There is another equally important side to this matter: the *qualitative* element in business. The arithmetic equation (revenues minus cost equals profit) does not readily reflect the human factor. Whereas the financial manager deals, initially at least, with dollar figures, the department heads must deal with human relations. Customers, suppliers, employees, labor union officials, and the officers themselves are human. They have emotions, attitudes, preferences, and prejudices which enter into their economic behavior within the firm or in the market. These attitudes add a qualitative dimension which creates the problem of feasibility as against desirability. Although a particular plan may be most desirable from the standpoint of prospective profits, it may not prove feasible for any one of a number of reasons.

The following simplified case illustrates a situation in which desirability comes into conflict with feasibility. The financial manager of a company with annual sales of about $3 million concludes that the firm is too liberal in the extension of credit to its customers. Too much money is tied up in receivables and a substantial portion of the receivables represents overdue accounts. He therefore recommends to top management that customers who are in arrears in paying their bills at the end of the stipulated credit period should not receive any merchandise until the overdue bills are paid. He also urges that prompt payment be insisted upon in accepting future orders from these delinquent accounts.

On the surface, this recommendation may appear to be rational and sound. But suppose the sales manager presents the following arguments. First, these delinquent accounts represent customers of long standing with a previously fine record of prompt payment. Unfortunately, for these customers, a sharp drop in the local employment level or some other unfavorable development, such as abnormal seasonal weather, has temporarily caused a sharp drop in collections from these customers. To cut off further deliveries would aggravate rather than improve the business outlook of the firm. Second, the sales manager calls attention to the fact that the firm's competitors have liberalized their terms of credit. To tighten credit terms at this stage would cause a substantial loss of sales. Finally, he may stress the fact that a change in the credit policy is bound to have a demoralizing effect on the sales force which stands to lose the commissions on sales to established accounts.

These arguments by the sales manager can, and should, carry some weight with top management. Top management must then attempt to find an alternative which offers the best combination of what is desirable and what is feasible.

B. Flexibility, Not Rigidity

Before arriving at a final financial decision, top management must evaluate all elements involved in the operation of the several divisions of the firm. A sound decision, therefore, requires great flexibility.

Although it is important for the firm to maintain liquidity, for example, this objective is not inflexible. Various subjective and market factors often necessitate modification of iron-clad rules. In the previous illustration, the firm would endeavor to bridge the gap between its bills due and accounts receivable by one of several courses of action. It might ask its suppliers to extend the due date on accounts payable for the reasons cited by the sales manager. Or it might try to obtain a short-term loan from a bank and absorb its cost. Alternatively, it might decide to acquire the funds from a finance company at a higher rate of interest than it would have to pay a bank. Any of these actions, if it succeeded, would preserve customer goodwill, particularly of customers who are temporarily in a nonliquid condition. It would also sustain the morale of the sales force, a fact of great significance to top management.

Flexibility also helps in the coordination of top management effort. Often the best-laid financial plans may go astray and threaten the relationships between departments. This problem may be averted by conferences before and after the plan has been prepared by the financial manager. A plan can be effectively executed only if the individuals who share its responsibility (1) clearly *understand* the objective and its basic reason, (2) are *willing* to play their respective parts, and (3) are *able* to perform their assignments.

C. The Give-and-Take of Planning

Let us assume that no one individual in the firm is an expert in all phases of its operation. If we accept this premise, it follows that each member of management can make a significant contribution to the formulation of an overall financial program. And we may conclude that each team member is likely to obtain a better understanding of his specific role if he can see himself and his task from the standpoint of the firm as a whole. This process of going from the specific to the general, then from the general to the specific, is analogous to what modern technology calls *feedback:* a constant two-way flow designed to achieve a balance among the component parts.

Within this process of management feedback, it is the function of the financial manager to prepare and submit his objective financial analysis as a means of communication between the several functional areas of the firm.

The Feedback Process: An Illustration   The following case history illustrates the nature and application of feedback to a major financial problem.

Company **XY** manufactures office equipment ranging in price from $500 to $10,000. Its customers are government agencies, large business firms, educational institutions, and commercial printing establishments. Its sales in the last fiscal year amounted to about $2.5 million. Sales in the current fiscal year are running about 20% above last year. Top management wants a projection of output, sales, and financial requirements for the next fiscal year. At a management meeting, each division head submits his tentative views on the prospects for the coming twelve months.

The sales manager is confident that he can raise sales by another 20%. The production chief reports that existing equipment can handle the larger output through about 5 hours of overtime per week. Naturally, the overtime wage rate of one and one-half times the standard hourly wage rate prevails. As an alternative to overtime, the production chief can increase output by 20% if he can expand the labor force by 10% and add two new machines. The personnel manager reports that the labor supply in the market may present a problem in recruiting the needed workers, and that the cost of the necessary in-plant training of new workers would average an amount equal to 3 weeks wages per worker. The shipping department states that some outside space would have to be rented to store a portion of the additional inventory of raw materials and parts as well as for the larger volume of finished items.

Several questions must be resolved before the financial manager can start on his task. These questions are: (1) Will the present workers and their union go along with overtime for many weeks? (2) How much will two new machines cost? (3) How soon can the personnel manager give assurance that, if necessary, the new workers can be recruited? (4) Is outside rental space available in a desirable location and what are the monthly charges?

Each of the participants accepts the assignment to provide his share of the answers to these questions at the next conference a week later. On that date, the financial manager receives the desired information and cost estimates. He then prepares a series of schedules showing the various costs and financial requirements.

An expanded sales volume of plus 20%, the financial manager shows, requires additional funds ranging from a low of $75,000 to a high of $125,000 to finance the increase of space, inventory, payroll, and so forth. He is of the opinion that it would be difficult to obtain from outside sources a loan in excess of $50,000. He now requests another conference. On this occasion, he recommends the following alternatives for consideration by the appropriate department heads: (1) revise the purchasing schedule of raw materials in order to carry a smaller stock-on-hand; (2) carry a smaller supply of finished goods; (3) cut down on existing inventory, which is tying up funds, by promoting a special sale below the regular price; or (4) obtain more liberal credit terms from suppliers. Once more, the feedback goes into operation. This time it flows from the financial manager to the several department heads. Their responses represent another phase of the feedback process. This give-and-take continues until a meeting of minds is reached.

D. The Decision-Making Process

Whether or not agreement is reached, the final decision rests either with the president of the firm or the board of directors, or both. In matters of lesser significance, this final managerial responsibility may be delegated to lower ranking officers. However, on issues of major concern, the top officer usually has the final word.

Let us assume therefore that the program advocated by the financial manager—at the end of a series of conferences—calls for: (1) the purchase of two new machines, and (2) a bank loan of $50,000. As far as (2) is concerned, the negotiation for the loan is usually the function of the president of the firm. If the loan is granted, the president and one or more of the authorized officers of the corporation must sign the debt instrument—a promissory note—on behalf of the company. The president will have to decide whether he wants to approve this investment which will tie up a portion of the firm's resources for several years.

1. Evaluating the Sales Forecast   What are some of the factors that the president will consider in this case? First, he must decide whether to accept the sales manager's optimistic forecast. Every forecast contains an element of uncertainty. Also, it is based on specific assumptions about the prospective general level of business activity, either in the economy as a whole or in this particular line of business, or both. Is the president prepared to accept these assumptions? Do they coincide with his own judgment of the future outlook? If not, are they sufficiently persuasive to make him change his own views?

Second, the president has to weigh the results of this forecast if events turn out less favorably than anticipated. What is the extent of fixed financial commitments, e.g., one year's rental of warehouse space? Are there alternatives that will reduce the risk even at a price? For instance, is it more advisable to lease the space on a month-to-month basis and pay a higher monthly rental than under an annual lease?

2. Weighing the Tax Advantages   Third, what are the tax advantages or drawbacks of the several courses? It would exceed the limits of an introductory chapter to discuss this complex subject at length. However, one simple set of alternatives will suffice as an illustration.

If the firm borrows the funds and purchases the machines it will be obliged to pay back the loan and interest in lump-sum or periodic payments. These repayment installments will have to be met whether machines are fully utilized or operated at a fraction of their capacity. Under a lease, it is conceivable that the firm will be given the right to terminate the rental with three months notice. The rental of machines usually involves a higher monthly payment than the installments under outright purchase.

As pointed out earlier in this chapter, the higher cost of rental over purchase—if the machines are used for the projected full lifetime—is partly offset by tax savings. In the present example, the firm can either purchase the two machines at a price of $50,000 or pay an assumed rental of $15,000 per annum. For simplicity, we shall assume that the firm has a cash surplus of $50,000 which it could invest in the machines. The alternatives are as follows:

1. Invest $50,000 in two machines that have an estimated lifetime of five years, without salvage value at the end of the period, and recover $10,000 each year through depreciation.

2. Lease the two machines and pay five years annual rental of $15,000.

Under (1) the firm will have $5,000 less expenses per year and, assuming that the firm earns a profit subject to a 50% tax rate, pay an income tax of $2,500 per year on this saving of $5,000. The net difference in terms of profit after taxes is therefore $2,500 if the machines are purchased rather than rented. On the other hand, if (2) is selected, the firm will have the $50,000 available for any future needs that are now not foreseen.

A Note of Caution. In the preceding case we have discussed the role of the financial manager and that of the president of the firm *as if* they were two distinct individuals. This may or may not be the situation. It will vary among firms. In some firms the president will assume both functions. In other companies, the task of financial planning is delegated to one officer while the president reserves the ultimate right to reject, modify, or accept his suggestions.

V. SUMMARY

Managerial finance performs the dual function of control and planning. It is a major instrument in the formulation of the firm's operational policies. In the execution of his tasks the financial manager uses, as a point of departure, the financial statements prepared by the accountant(s) of the company. The diagnosis of these statements is intended to bring to the surface the reasons, favorable and unfavorable, that account for the firm's performance in the past. Whereas the balance sheet provides insights into the resources (assets) and obligations (liabilities) of the business, its income (profit and loss) statement discloses whether the past operations have been profitable.

The diagnosis of past performance is followed by an interpretation of the firm's present position. The central question here is: Where does the company stand now and how does it compare with other companies of similar size in the same industry and operating in the same market? Such interpretation is both absolute and relative. It is absolute in the sense that it aims to establish whether the firm is currently in a sound financial position. The interpretation is also designed to point up whether, and to what extent, the firm compares favorably or unfavorably with its competitors. The central feature of financial management is the formulation of the firm's strategy in determining the most effective use of the funds currently at the disposal of the company and selecting the most favorable source of additional funds that the enterprise will need in the foreseeable future.

Both diagnosis and interpretation form the background for the future plans of the firm. In preparing the estimate of the company's financial requirements in the months or years ahead, the financial manager must work closely with the several department heads of the company, both individually and collectively. This process must entail managerial feedback. He must first translate the anticipated level of operations of each department into dollar figures. By comparing the projected monthly cash receipts with the projected expenditures for each month—in the form of a cash-flow forecast—the financial manager estimates the probable excess or shortage of funds in any given month. He must then weigh alternatives of bridging the gap between the inflow and outflow of funds. One group of alternatives is exemplified by adjustment of any of the following operations: size of inventory, length of credit terms from suppliers and to customers, or the size of the minimum cash balance of the firm. Another alternative is to obtain a loan from a financial institution.

From time to time, a firm will consider the need to expand its physical facilities in the form of building, machines, and equipment. In the case of machines and equipment the financial manager deals with investments that usually have an estimated lifetime of three to ten years or longer. These involve intermediate-term financing. Buildings have a life expectancy of several decades. Such investments are financed by means of long-term instruments: stocks, bonds, or debentures. These instruments are at times also used in procuring intermediate-term funds.

The ultimate approval, modification, or rejection of the plan(s) submitted by the financial manager rests with the top officer of the firm. The firm's chief executive has to make the final decision with or without the approval of the board of directors. This depends on the scope of the proposals and the authority vested in the president of the corporation by the board. In any event, to be truly effective, top management must have financial competence.

The analysis by the financial manager serves also as a highly valuable instrument of communications between the several departments of the firm. It provides a common denominator (money) and a uniform yardstick (cost of funds and yield). In addition, the financial analysis furnishes top management with a tool for the evaluation of past performance and future plans.

Appendix A

I. THE CORPORATION

The objectives of managerial finance are the same whether the firm is organized as an individual proprietorship, partnership, or corporation: to maximize profits. However, the resources available to a firm of a given size depend in large measure upon the form of organization. This is especially true in the case of intermediate- and long-term financing. It is here that the corporate form plays a prominent role. Table 1-1 shows the relative importance of the three forms of business organization as measured by sales and profits.

Legal Character

The corporation is a creation of the law. Each state has adopted legislation regulating the issuance of charters for the organization of corporations. Although differing in details, these laws show substantial uniformity on the structural organization, rights, and duties of the corporation. As a creation of the law, the corporation is a legal person. That is to say, the corporation can sue and be sued in court, it can assume obligations and acquire claims. It should be pointed out, however, that every state has adopted special laws for the chartering of banks, other financial institutions, insurance companies, and public utilities.

Structure

The corporate organization consists of stockholders, directors, and officers.

The *stockholders* are the legal owners of the corporation. They provide the capital of the business. Ownership in the corporation is evidenced by common stock issued by the corporation in exchange for the stipulated price. If the price is fixed in the charter at a given dollar figure, this stock is known as *par value* stock. For example, a $10 par value stock presumably signifies that the original or first purchaser of the stock paid ten dollars in cash or the equivalent in physical assets or services for each share of stock issued by the corporation. However, in real-life—with the exception of banks, insurance companies, and public utilities—the par value is frequently a nominal rather than an actual price. This results from the fact that the organizers of the corporation have considerable leeway in

TABLE 1-1. Sales and Net Profit in 1962 for Sole Proprietorships, Partnerships, and Corporations

	Sales In Millions of Dollars	Net Profit In Millions of Dollars	Net Profit As A Percent of Sales
Sole Proprietorships			
All Industries	178,420	23,895	13.4
Agriculture, forestry and fisheries	30,200	3,696	12.2
Mining	987	64	6.5
Construction	15,539	2,108	13.6
Manufacturing	6,710	654	9.7
Transportation, communication, electric, gas and sanitary services	4,241	642	15.1
Wholesale trade	16,953	1,453	8.6
Retail trade	68,440	4,187	6.1
Finance, insurance, & real estate	5,172	1,638	31.7
Services	26,079	9,289	35.6
Partnerships			
All Industries	72,304	8,513	11.8
Agriculture, forestry and fisheries	4,983	655	13.1
Mining	912	4	.4
Construction	6,805	594	8.7
Manufacturing	6,654	595	8.9
Transportation, communication electric, gas and sanitary services	995	124	12.5
Wholesale trade	12,357	573	4.6
Retail trade	23,227	1,564	6.7
Finance, insurance, and real estate	4,976	952	19.1
Services	10,380	3,394	32.7
Corporations			
All Industries	895,120	49,606	5.5
Agriculture, forestry and fisheries	5,978	161	2.7
Mining	11,955	794	6.6
Construction	40,311	617	1.5
Manufacturing	399,660	25,351	6.3
Transportation, communication, electric, gas and sanitary services	71,092	8,011	11.1
Wholesale trade	142,730	2,421	1.7
Retail trade	143,687	2,640	1.8
Finance, insurance and real estate	46,295	8,691	18.7
Services	26,608	833	3.1

Source. Statistical Abstract of the United States, 86th Edition, 1965, p. 490.

evaluating the physical assets or services that the corporation accepts in lieu of cash from stockholders. Another reason is that, in many states, the tax laws on securities make a nominal or no-par value stock a more attractive instrument. *No-par value* stock does not carry a price tag on the stock certificate. It can be sold by the corporation at whatever price the organizers set for the stock.

The rights of the stockholders are basically as follows. As the owners of the corporation, they are the beneficiaries of the profits earned by the business. These earnings may be retained in the firm or distributed as dividends. In case of liquidation or sale of the business, they have a claim to whatever is left after all creditors of the corporation have been paid off. Since the corporation is a separate legal person, the stockholders have no personal liability for the debts of the firm. Typically, the stockholders also have the right to elect the board of directors.

The *board of directors,* usually elected at the annual meeting of the stockholders, functions as the representative body in behalf of the stock-holders. It is charged with the task of overseeing the operations of the corporation and reporting to the owners at the annual meeting. In addition, it has the authority to engage the employees of the corporation and to enter into contracts within the provisions of the corporation's charter. In regard to employees, the board of directors confines itself to the appointment of the top officers and delegates to them the authority to engage the other employees of the firm.

The *officers* are generally composed of the president, one or more vice-presidents, a secretary, and a treasurer. In smaller firms, one individual may fill two of these positions: for example, secretary and treasurer.

II. SOME FACTS ABOUT SMALL FIRMS

In form, the corporation shows the same features in the small corpora-tion as in the large corporation. However, this is not true of the substance. For example, the role of the stockholders may change. Many of the large corporation number their owners-stockholders in the thousands, tens of thousands, or even millions. Most of these shareholders own but a small fraction of the stock issued by the corporation. The individual small share-holder has neither the time, the financial stake, nor the opportunity to keep himself informed about the operations of the corporation. As a matter of fact, only an insignificant percentage of stockholders in large corporations find it feasible or vital to attend the annual meetings. By and large, the stockholders in a large corporation are *absentee* owners of the business.

The situation is quite different in a small corporation. In most of these firms, either the total stock issue or a majority of it is held by a few individuals. These same individuals customarily elect themselves as the directors of the corporations. Acting as directors, they appoint themselves as the officers of the business. Thus, the same individuals combine within themselves the three functions of owners, directors, and officers. In consequence, these stockholders-owners are familiar with the operations of the firm, its problems, plans, and prospects. The owners can, therefore, adopt those policies that they believe to be in their best interest. As officers, they execute these policies. And as directors they approve, for the record of the corporation, whatever course of action they have decided on as stockholder-officers of the corporation.

In a large corporation, the board of directors plays an important role. Its members, often drawn from a variety of business fields, provide the large company with a considerable breadth of business experience and knowledge. Frequently, one or more of the directors are identified with a large bank or insurance company. Their knowledge of finance becomes a valuable source of contacts and advice for the officer in charge of financial planning.

By contrast, it is the exception for a small corporation to number among its directors a member who has substantial experience and who is not an officer and co-owner of the business. The absence of an impartial expert among the directors places an additional burden of responsibility on the financial manager of the small firm. It deprives him of the opportunity to obtain advice from or to consult with a director who has the know-how about the practices and polices of financial institutions. To make up for this lack within the (small) corporation, the financial manager must establish his own contacts with lending institutions and attempt to keep abreast of changes in their practices and/or policies.

Appendix B   BIG BUSINESS AND SMALL BUSINESS: ESSENTIAL DIFFERENCES

As was shown in Appendix A, the actual operation of a small corporation is quite dissimilar in substance although not in legal form from the large corporation. A similar situation prevails in regard to financial management in general and the financial manager in particular. In the following pages, we shall trace the major dissimilarities that are in large measure a function of the size of the firm.

Big Business

In a large company with assets running into many millions of dollars, the principle of division of labor is applied to management. The functions of management are broken down into a series of specialized positions. Each of these is assigned to an individual whose task and responsibilities are clearly identified by his title. Some of the more common management functions are: production, sales, promotion or marketing, public relations, research and development, labor relations, personnel. It is customary to reflect the importance of these functions by the title of vice-president or director in charge of a given department or division. The function of financial management is assigned to an individual who is designated either as vice-president in charge of finance, treasurer, or controller.

As pointed out previously, every officer (except the one in charge of finance) is not only identifiable by his title but is also limited to a specific area of the company's overall operations. Thus, the vice-president in charge of production is concerned primarily with planning, scheduling, and supervising the manufacturing activities in his division. This does not mean, however, that he is disinterested in the operations of other divisions within the firm. In fact, he is fully aware of the interdependence of all departments or divisions in assuring maximum efficiency in any one department. But as vice-president of production, he has neither responsibility for nor a voice in the running of the other divisions. To be sure, he will meet with the other department heads at the periodic meetings of top management. On these occasions, the several vice-presidents discuss their respective problems and plans in terms of the firm as a whole. But each vice-president speaks essentially from his own vantage position. He tends to press for what he considers essential for the future growth of his particular orbit of operations.

On the other hand, the financial manager, whatever his official title, has no such special interest. His area of operations is financial management. He examines the operations, current and projected, of all major divisions of the company, first, in terms of liquidity and profitability, second, in relation to the sources of funds, and third, in terms of allocation of funds. Frequently, a large company divorces the control function from the finance officer and assigns it to the controller or treasurer.

The Small Firm

What constitutes a "small" firm? Where is the dividing line between small, medium-sized, and large? The answer is not easy. There is some difference of opinion on the definition of a "small" firm. For the purposes of this book, the following criteria will be employed. A firm will be regarded as small if (1) as a manufacturing company, it employs between 25 and 250 people, (2) as a wholesaler, it has an annual sales volume between one million and five million dollars, and (3) as a retailer, its sales range between $500,000 and $2,500,000.[1]

Firms that fall into the above categories usually have two common characteristics. First, their size reflects a history of growth and expansion. Such a process of development, as a rule, generates problems of financial management in terms of balancing the current needs of the several departments against the available funds. Second, the process of growth generates a constant need for funds to finance the expansion of the firm's operations.

The typical small firm assigns the financial function to the controller or treasurer. In turn, in most cases the controller or treasurer of a small firm restricts his function to those tasks that constitute the minor function of the finance officer in a large company: control and supervision over the daily financial operations. The major function (financial evaluation and planning) is retained by the president of the firm.

Financial Illiteracy in Small Business

In theory, this division of the finance function between controller and president will appear sound and efficient. The president is usually the driving force behind the rapid expansion of the small firm. He is in close touch with every important facet of its operations. He has to make frequent

---

[1] This delineation differs from the definition of small business by the Small Business Administration, which identifies a business as small, if (a) its total assets do not exceed $5 million, (b) its net worth is not more than $2.5 million, and (c) it did not have a net average income, after taxes, of more than $250,000 in the last two years. The United States Census defines a business as small if (a) it employs less than 250 people (manufacturing firm), (b) as a wholesaler, it has annual sales of less than $5,000,000, and (c) as a retailer, its sales do not exceed $2,500,000. Neither of these two definitions sets a minimum. Realistically, the family-operated grocery store, gasoline station, and machine shop are literally too small to require more than a few simple principles of financial management. For this reason, firms that fall below the above stated minimum levels have been excluded from the definition of small business.

decisions on major matters, each of which has financial implications not only for the present but also for the future of the firm.

In real life, however, the theoretical advantages of centralized control are frequently more than offset by a lack of financial know-how. The president and his fellow officers are, as a rule, competent and experienced specialists in the operational spheres of business. The background of the officers-owners of the small firm may have been in merchandising, selling, and production. These are also their special fields of responsibility in the small firm. It is rare, however, for an officer of a small company to possess, in addition to his specialized operational knowledge, training and experience in the complex field of financial management. (See Appendix A for a summary of the effects of poor financial management by small companies.)

Questions

1. The personnel manager deals with the product factor labor while the financial manager is concerned with the product factor capital. How do you explain the fact that the financial manager plays a far more important role in the planning and decision-making process of the firm than the personnel manager?

2. Discuss the basic objectives of financial management.

3. What are the major responsibilities of the top financial officer of a firm?

4. "A high rate of profit is not an automatic assurance of high liquidity." Do you agree? State your reasons.

5. Differentiate between internal and external sources of funds.

6. What are the major differences between an accountant and the financial manager in looking at (a) the balance sheet and (b) the income statement of a firm?

7. Explain the usefulness of a cash-flow forecast. Why is the cash-flow forecast a major planning tool for the financial manager?

8. Give an example of a conflict between the desirability of a particular project and its feasibility from the viewpoint of the financial manager.

9. "Effective financial planning calls for managerial feed-back." Explain and illustrate this statement.

10. Identify the major operational differences between a large corporation and a small corporation in regard to the respective roles of stockholders, officers, and the board of directors.

11. What are the differences in the managerial structure and functions of a large firm compared with a small firm?

12. How do you explain the fact that so many small firms suffer from "financial illiteracy"?

Case: CAPTAINS ACRES HOMES

Mr. Russell Elga is assistant treasurer of a large appliance wholesaler in Providence, Rhode Island. He has been with the firm since receiving his M.B.A. six years ago and is currently earning $15,000 per year. Mr. Elga spends every July with his wife and three children in a small Cape Cod town, at a house left to him by his aunt. He rents the house every August for $750.

Ten days after his arrival on the Cape this July, Mr. Elga was approached by a neighbor, Charles Anderson, who is a permanent resident of the town. Mr. Anderson, who retired from medical practice last year at age 55, owns 57 acres of undeveloped land eight minutes' drive from the center of town. He bought this land in the 1930's at a low price. Similar undeveloped land is selling currently at approximately $2000 per acre. Anderson is bored with retirement and would like to try his hand in business. Anderson would like to eventually develop his land into a retirement community of approximately 100 homes.

Mr. Vermont Lubis, 38, who has worked all his life in the building business for local builders and, in the last three years, as an independent builder, wants to join with Mr. Anderson in developing the acreage, which they have tentatively decided to name Captains Acres Homes.

Mr. Anderson would like Mr. Elga to act as financial consultant to the project and, hopefully, would like Mr. Elga to join the proposed venture as treasurer and controller. Mr. Anderson, who is in good health, and has an outgoing personality, would handle the sales end of the venture. Mr. Lubis would abandon his independent building activities to supervise the planning and building of the homes. Mr. Elga knows that both of these men have good personal reputations in the town. Mr. Lubis is a very competent builder. However, like many builders, he has little financial know-how.

One of the questions to be decided is how the two principals (three if Mr. Elga decides to join the venture) should share ownership and be compensated for their services. It is planned to incorporate the venture and issue shares of stock to the principals. Mr. Anderson will deed over his acreage to the corporation in exchange for stock. Mr. Lubis will invest $10,000 cash in the venture in exchange for stock. Mr. Elga could mortgage his summer home for $10,000 to invest in the venture. Mr. Elga would want, however, to have a bigger share of ownership than he could immediately afford if he decides to go into the venture. So would Mr. Lubis. Consequently, some plan of stock purchase would have to be worked out that would be equitable to all three individuals.

Mr. Elga must plan also for the financial management of the firm. The land could be mortgaged on a three year basis at a local bank for $40,000, at an interest rate of 7%. Interest would be paid quarterly. A model house would be built at an expected cost of $9000. Roads and other improvements during the first year would cost about $20,000. Construction loans can be secured from the bank as houses are built for 80% of their wholesale value. They hope to sell houses, on the average, for $15,000 net of real estate commissions. It is expected that the cost of the average house (construction and materials and land) would be approximately $10,000. This would leave a margin of about $5000 per house for promotion expenses, general improvements, salaries of the three principals, and for profit. Mr. Anderson believes that between 15 and 25 houses can be sold per year at about $15,000 per average house. Mr. Anderson believes more land can be purchased nearby, if the venture is a success, so that the business can be continued.

Case Questions:

1. As Mr. Elga, be prepared to describe to Mr. Anderson what the treasurer's function will be in the proposed company.
2. What overall financial advice would you give to Mr. Anderson? What financial pitfalls, if any, do you see for the company?
3. How much compensation should each of the three principals receive in the form of salary?
4. What would be a fair method of dividing the ownership of the company?
5. If you were Mr. Elga, would you join the proposed firm as treasurer? Why or why not?

~~~~~~

Chapter Two

The Financial Statements

What are the firm's financial resources? How much and to whom is it in debt? Is the business profitable? Are the pricing policies and the marketing strategies paying off in profits? Can the firm sustain the stress of future growth without recourse to external sources? The answers to these questions play a dominant role in setting the framework of management decision making. To provide aids in analyzing these problems, a variety of financial tools have evolved. Their use is not confined to internal analysis alone, but also most significantly to the external relationship of the firm. Suppliers, financial institutions, investors, and speculators all have a vital interest in the health of the company as potential creditors or investors. At times, even customers of the firm examine the firm's statements; for example, public authorities and large corporations frequently insist that potential suppliers soliciting sizable orders be financially in a position to assure delivery of the order.

Six Basic Tools

This chapter describes six of the principal tools used in financial analysis by the financial manager, the financial analyst, investors, creditors, and others interested in the financial condition of the firm as follows.

1. *The Balance Sheet.* This is the principal guide to the first question—"How do we stand?" *It gives management a snapshot view at a moment in time. It tells how the company as of a particular date looks from a financial point of view.*

2. *The Income Statement (Profit and Loss Statement).* Have our strategies paid off in profits? Are there costly or weak areas in our operations? The income statement provides a description of the dollar-profit

success of our business in the course of a specific period of time, usually an interval of months, rarely more than a year. *The income statement is a measure of past performance.*

3. *The Source and Application of Funds Statement.* In analyzing the past, it is essential to be able to pinpoint how the financial resources of the firm were utilized. As a first approach to answering this question, we compare the balance sheet at the beginning and at the end of the period under study. *The source and application of funds statement is used to indicate the flow of funds as reflected by changes in the firm's assets and liabilities.*

4. *The Cash-Flow Budget.* In the course of our projected future business, will we run into periods of cash shortages; into times when obligations become due while the cash with which to meet them is, for one reason or another, not yet available? It is essential that we forecast our cash requirements and sources of funds in order to answer this question. *The cash-flow budget is used to project cash needs; to identify cash surpluses and to highlight possible critical points in the income and outgo of cash.*

5. *The Pro Forma (Projected) Income Statement.* What success do we anticipate in the near future? Based upon past income performance and the vision of things to come, management continually attempts to project anticipated business and profits. *The pro forma income statement is used to quantify the future prospects of the planned operations.*

6. *The Pro Forma (Projected) Balance Sheet.* When enough information is not available to prepare a complete cash-flow budget, the financial manager will prepare a pro forma balance sheet to determine the needs for funds on a specific date based on a specific forecast. *The pro forma balance sheet pinpoints the firm's need for funds on a specific date.*

A word of caution is in order before the construction and detailed application of the tools listed above is examined. It must be kept in mind that these tools are take-off points for more detailed investigations rather than complete answers in themselves, serving to narrow the range of more detailed analysis rather than supplanting the need for it. The lean, hard look of dollar signs sometimes beguiles the student—and the financial manager—into forgetting that these seemingly clear-cut indicators can conceal, as well as reveal, the realities of the business. The greatest value of these financial tools is not in providing clear-cut answers to the company's problems, but rather in indicating potential trouble spots. Intensive research costs money and manpower. Financial statements and tools are used to highlight the areas that are *most* in need of more detailed analysis.

With this admonition in mind, let us turn to the specifics of the tools described briefly above.

I. THE BALANCE SHEET

The balance sheet is a simple listing of the firm's resources such as cash, monies due from customers (accounts receivable), inventories, plant, machinery, equipment and furnishings on the one hand, and the claims against those assets on the other, such as money owed creditors and the investment in the company. Bear in mind that this is a listing of monetary values only. If we looked at the balance sheets of Coca Cola or of the Kellogg Company for example, we should not find included there the enormous value of their respective brand names, although these are probably the single most valuable possessions of the two companies.[1] Suppose we have before us the similar balance sheets of two aircraft manufacturers. One might have developed an extensive capability in advanced electronics for missile work. The other manufacturer conceivably would be finishing up the last of its jet plane contracts with little in the way of future business in sight. While their balance sheets might match, their value as going concerns would obviously differ sharply.

Or, take the case of two pharmaceutical companies of about the same size. Company No. 1 occupies rented quarters; Company No. 2 owns its plant and substantial land acreage which it acquired many years ago. This land has increased in value many times the original price and much of it is not required by the company. The balance sheet reflects only the acquisition price. Clearly, Company No. 2 possesses an "invisible" asset that can easily yield a substantial profit. Even if the company does not intend to sell the land, its substantially increased current value adds significantly to the borrowing power of the firm and its credit rating with suppliers.

---

[1] Some firms list "goodwill" and other intangible values on their balance sheets at a nominal value of $1.

Despite the limitations of the balance sheet, it is the first essential port of call for internal management and the external analyst. As the balance sheet's name indicates, the two major listings (assets versus liabilities plus capital) must balance. A simple reminder is that all "good" things must be paid for. All increases in assets or repayment of debts require funds.[2] The latter are secured by increasing liabilities and capital. Whenever the firm makes a purchase of goods or services either cash on hand is reduced or accounts payable are increased; or the firm obtains a loan and uses the proceeds to pay for the purchases.

It is the relationship between these factors that give a fast check on the company's financial status both to management and to outsiders, whether the latter are suppliers, potential lenders, or investors. Do the firm's assets safely cover the claims of creditors? Will it be able to repay the latter? Or is the status of the company's financial position insecure, with obligations in excess of financial resources? While additional funds may be secured from future profitable operations, these are conjectural and first dependence is always placed on resources at hand in relationship to the call on them. It is not enough, however, to state the company's financial position as a simple ratio between assets and liabilities. The financial manager must take into account the relative liquidity of the assets, how quickly they can be made available, and the degree of urgency of the liabilities and how soon they must be paid. He must also consider the availability of alternative sources of funds external to the firm.

The New England sportswear store with all of its $10,000 of assets tied up in swim suits as of Labor Day will not be able to pay its $500 monthly rent bill without horrendous markdowns. The same store, with the same position on Memorial Day, in all probability, is in a more reasonable financial position *although the balance sheets may differ in the date only*. This will surely be the case if the landlord in the latter situation is willing to extend the payment date of the rent for a month or two. On the other hand, if the $10,000 in assets as of Memorial Day is comprised substantially of cash there will be no problem in meeting the rent bill—but a substantial degree of difficulty in keeping the store's clientele interested in a retailer without merchandise.

[2] The familiar accountants phrase of "debits and credits" hinges on this fact. The first defines any increase in the firm's asset picture or decrease in liabilities. The latter refers to the sources of the funds which make the change possible.

If our over-inventoried retailer secures a loan for 30 days to pay his rent, the financial analyst would note this as a potential strain that would be felt fairly soon. On the other hand, if he was able to secure a longer term loan, repayable perhaps in a year, the firm would obviously have more breathing space. In the latter case however, the firm would still have interest payments to make that could conceivably strain the store's resources. As a third alternative, a partner could be secured bringing in additional investment. Although this equity investment bears no fixed rate of interest and does not require repayment and, therefore, strengthens the financial position of the company, it entails a new claim on its earnings.

Management must continually weight the needs of the company for the *means* of doing business: inventories, machines and so on, with the cost and risk of those means: borrowing of various kinds as well as securing additional equity investment. We turn to the balance sheet to tell us not only the ratio between aggregate assets and aggregate liabilities, but also the makeup of these elements. Since long-term strategy is contingent on short-term survival, we focus first upon these resources, and demands against them, that are most current.

A. Assets

The assets of a business are divided by accounting convention into two broad categories:

a. Current Assets. These are assets that are either cash or close enough to cash as to be easily available for meeting the company's financial obligations. Included under these headings are cash, marketable securities, money owed to us by customers (accounts receivable), inventories, and other items, all of which usually have in common the fact that in the normal course of business they will be converted into cash within the course of a year. They are, therefore, the firm's most liquid (nearness to cash) possessions or assets.

b. Fixed Assets. These are assets of the company that will, at least in theory, take more than one year to convert into cash. Machinery and plant usually bulk largest under this heading. Generally, special installations (power plant and air conditioning) are assets whose life expectancy is counted in decades rather than a few years. Although a plant, equipment, and machinery may be saleable or serve as collateral for a loan, in the normal course of business their value is least available for meeting immediate cash needs.

This differentiation between current and fixed assets is an accounting convention that usually, but not always, mirrors life. At this writing, Xerox, the electrostatic copying machine company, for example, on the average receives an income from the lease of its "914" machine to customers which, in less than a year, equals the cost of the unit. The machine is still listed, however, as a fixed asset. Conversely, the whiskey that is aging in the distiller's warehouse is classified as a current asset (inventory) although it may be kept in storage for several more years to attain its proper "age." These exceptions to the rule are intended to point up the risk or folly of failing to treat each situation on its own merits.

Accounts receivable (particularly if they are small and numerous) may be less useful as a ready source of cash than the resale of a general purpose machine tool, and the same thing is often true of out-of-season inventory. While these exceptions should be noted, in general, the comparison of the relative magnitude of current and fixed assets is useful as a basic rough measure of financial liquidity.

The relative size and variety of company assets will vary considerably depending on the industry and on the specific operational strategy of the particular firm within it. The balance sheet of IBM or Xerox, both of whom lease rather than sell the bulk of their equipment, will be quite different from that of a supermarket chain selling for cash. The inventory of the DuPont dye division with a six months production cycle will certainly be greater in proportion to sales than the typical inventory of a fuel oil distributor whose usual time between receipt and dispatch of merchandise is less than one week. The principles behind their balance sheets and the equivalent listing for a corner drug store, however, are the same. Therefore, by studying one balance sheet in detail, the financial analyst can gain insight that is not limited to the specifics of a particular company. Table 2-1 is the balance sheet of a small southwestern electronics manufacturer. Let us examine first the assets of the operation and then the liabilities and ownership claims that have been the means of securing the assets. Before doing so, note that the balance sheet has a specific date. In the example used, it is a picture of the firm's financial structure as of December 31, 1966. There is no assurance that it was similar a month before or even a day before or that it may not be markedly dissimilar in the future.

1. Cash   The most current, i.e., the most immediately liquid asset in any business, is cash. Therefore, it is listed first. All other assets must first be converted into cash, the medium of exchange, before being utilized to pay bills. This conversion process can take a considerable period

TABLE 2-1. Y. G., Inc., Balance Sheet as of December 31, 1966 (Figures Are Rounded to the Nearest $1000)

Assets			
Current assets			
Cash	$ 603		
Accounts receivable	1468		
Inventories	2610		
Prepayments	19		
Total current assets			$4700
Fixed assets			
Machinery	742		
Less: depreciation	132	610	
Leasehold improvements	339		
Less: depreciation	43	296	
Total fixed assets			906
Total assets			$5606
Liabilities			
Current liabilities			
Accounts payable	$ 633		
Notes payable to bank	675		
Accruals	433		
Federal income tax	459		
Total current liabilities			$2200
Long-term debt			
5% debentures due 1983			700
Owners equity (net worth)			
Common stock ($1 share)	612		
Retained earnings	2094	2706	
Total liabilities and equity			$5606

of time (witness the sportswear shop earlier cited, that may have to wait until spring to sell its bathing suits unless willing to sell them at a sharply reduced price). For this reason, the financial manager of the firm must always look first at the cash position of the company. On the other hand, cash in itself is the least productive of assets. It earns no profit if kept idle in the business; it earns no interest in the checking account and a moderate rate on the savings account or in certificates of deposit. The financial manager, therefore, must always attempt to strike a happy balance between the risk of running out of cash and the lost income from carrying excess cash balances. Immediately after cash, the closest to cash are listed on the balance sheet.

2. Accounts Receivable   (A/R) Customers owe Y. G. Inc. money. Chapter Five will discuss some of the managerial strategies that cause the volume of receivables to vary with a given volume of business. At this stage, however, the reader should keep in mind that sales normally generate accounts receivable—not cash, and it is only with cash that the company can pay its own bills. The length of time that the company will have to wait to collect cash on these receivables will vary depending on the industry's usual terms, and management's own collection policies, Although there are lenders who specialize in making cash immediately available on the strength of receivables, this can be an expensive process. Some of the accounts receivable may never be paid. Most firms anticipate this experience and deduct a given percentage on sales, based on past history, as a reserve against bad debts or doubtful accounts. This reduces the accounts receivable on the balance sheet.

3. Inventories   The stock of goods on hand, or inventory, is yet another stage back in the cash-generating process. Frequently, this item is subdivided in the order of its normal proximity to the ultimate sales transaction into finished goods, goods in process, and raw material. In simpler terms, raw materials and inventories must be processed and sold *before* a receivable is generated. In addition, generally speaking it is easier to borrow money using accounts receivable as collateral than using inventories.[3] Given this relative inflexibility, should not the financial manager attempt to minimize inventories? From a shortsighted financial point of view, this may be an appropriate viewpoint. However, the businessman views inventories on hand as a means of speeding deliveries and, thus, satisfying customers, of minimizing production delays, and guarding against price increases. Consideration of quantity discounts, freight costs and availability of goods also must be acknowledged. Chapter Six will examine these elements in some detail.

4. Prepayments   At the end of the company's list of current assets are the prepayments. These usually represent supplies and services already paid for which will be utilized in the future operations of the firm. They might include such things as a forward payment of liability insurance or an advance to a supplier.

[3] This observation is open to an enormous number of exceptions depending upon the collectability of the receivables and on the salability of the inventories.

Proceeding down the list of the company's assets we come to a second category, those assets that will not be absorbed into the flow of sales within the short run, but rather have a life of one year or more.

5. Machinery and Depreciation   When a company buys machinery, it has converted one form of asset, cash, into another asset: machinery. Depending on the type of equipment involved, the useful life of the item within this account may be as much as twenty or more years. However, if the financial manager does not make allowance for the fact that, ultimately, the equipment must be replaced, the annual profit of the company will be overstated. For example, assume that upon graduation you take a job as a salesman. The job requires you to own an automobile. Assume the car is usable for five years. In each of those years, you are using up part of your asset. Certainly the car is worth less at the end of the period than at its beginning. If you do not save part of your income to buy a new vehicle you will be "out of business" all too shortly. The calculations, assuming an original cost of $2500 and a value at the end of the period of $500, might be something like that shown in Table 2-2. Another approach to depreciating the car would be to analyze the reduction in its market value each year. This, typically, is far from the *straight line* depreciation illustrated above. i.e., total loss of value divided by the number of years. A car suffers its greatest loss of value the first year with smaller losses for successive periods. For tax purposes, the government permits a variety of forms of *accelerated depreciation*. One form that might be used in this case is the *sum of the years digit*. Here we should add up the number of years of expected life $(1 + 2 + 3 + 4 + 5 = 15)$ and use the figure

TABLE 2-2.   Straight Line Depreciation

Period	Formula ($)	Depreciation ($)	Cumulative Depreciation ($)	Balance Sheet Value of Asset at End of Period ($)
1st year	$\frac{1}{5} \cdot 2000$	400	400	2100
2nd year	$\frac{1}{5} \cdot 2000$	400	800	1700
3rd year	$\frac{1}{5} \cdot 2000$	400	1200	1300
4th year	$\frac{1}{5} \cdot 2000$	400	1600	900
5th year	$\frac{1}{5} \cdot 2000$	400	2000	500

TABLE 2-3.   Sum of the Digits Depreciation

Period	Formula ($)	Depreciation ($)	Cumulative Depreciation ($)	Balance Sheet Value End of Period ($)
1st year	$\frac{5}{15}$ · 2000	667	667	1833
2nd year	$\frac{4}{15}$ · 2000	533	1200	1300
3rd year	$\frac{3}{15}$ · 2000	400	1600	900
4th year	$\frac{2}{15}$ · 2000	266	1866	634
5th year	$\frac{1}{15}$ · 2000	134	2000	500

15 as a denominator of the fraction of value lost each year. The numerator is the inverse of the sequence of years listed above. Our calculations would be as shown in Table 2-3.

Another approach is known as the double-declining balance method. In this case, the percentage used under the straightline method is doubled and applied to the balance at the end of each year. In our simple illustration, the straight line percentage was 20%. Under the double-declining balance method, we would take 40% of $2000 in the first year, 40% of the "balance" at the end of the second year, and so forth; as shown in Table 2-4.

The operating income before allowing for depreciation will not be altered in any case. The post-depreciation income however, will be quite different. If we asume that you make $6000 a year before depreciation, the result would be as shown in Table 2-5.

TABLE 2-4.   Double-Declining Balance Depreciation

Period	Percentage	Depreciation ($)	Balance ($)	Balance Sheet Value ($)
1st year	40%	800	1200	1700
2nd year	40%	480	720	1220
3rd year	40%	288	432	932
4th year	40%	93	339	839
5th year	balance	339	—	500

TABLE 2-5. Effects of Alternative Methods of Depreciation

Period	Income Before Depreciation ($)	Income After Straight Line Depreciation ($)	Income After Sum of the Years Digit Depreciation ($)	Income After Declining Balance ($)
1st year	6000	5600	5337	5200
2nd year	6000	5600	5467	5520
3rd year	6000	5600	5600	5712
4th year	6000	5600	5734	5907
5th year	6000	5600	5866	5661

In none of the five years is the reported income net of depreciation the same! The use of accelerated depreciation will tend to decrease *taxable* income in the near future and increase it in later years after the depreciation charges have expired. Therefore, the financial analyst or potential investor should be aware of the kind of depreciation formula being used by the firm that he is appraising.

Suppose that, at the end of the depreciation period, automobiles have increased in cost beyond the reserve that has been set up for replacement or that the residual value of the automobile has diminished. Depreciation formulas do not allow for these changes. It must be remembered that depreciation in itself does not *generate cash*. Depreciation is basically an adjustment of values on the books of the company. The dollar amount of this adjustment—i.e., depreciation—may have been channeled by the firm into any one or several of the current asset items. This noncash nature of the depreciation reserve becomes clear if it is borne in mind that the entry for the depreciation is made at the end of the accounting period.

6. Leasehold Improvements   Although Y. G., Inc. leases its facilities, major improvements have been made at company expense. These investments usually are depreciated over the life of the lease, assuming that they will have no value after the lease has come to an end. The handling of this entry is the same as that of the machinery described above. In this fashion, the company recovers *the dollar* total of capital investments. In short, the accountant allocates the expense over the proper revenue periods. The recovery of the dollar investment does not mean that the firm will actually be able to replace the used up asset with a new asset of the same capacity. Inflation over a period of years can play havoc with the depreciation reserve in terms of the actual replacement cost of an asset.

B. Liabilities (The Source of Funds)

The firm has obtained its assets from a variety of sources. Some are the result of bills that have not yet been paid. Few, if any, firms pay for goods immediately upon receipt but, instead, normally take as much as thirty days or more to make payment. Similarly, the company's work force, if not paid in advance, would usually be a "creditor" of the firm. Other liabilities are the results of more formal borrowing procedures. The company may have borrowed money from banks or other lending institutions. Perhaps the company has a long-term debt outstanding (for instance, a bond issue). The liabilities section first lists external sources of funds that have been used by the firm. Liabilities differ from owners contributions in that liabilities are obligations with definite terminal dates on or before which they are repaid.

The liabilities of the firm are usually classified into three groups on the basis of how soon they are due.

1. Current Liabilities   Current liabilities are those obligations of the firm that must be met within one year. Because of their short maturity, they are a quick checkpoint on the financial health of the firm. Funds must be available in short order with which to repay this category of debt. Table 2-6 shows the growth and composition of current assets and current liabilities of all nonfinancial corporations in the United States during the period 1958–1966.

2. Long-Term Obligations   As the name suggests, these are debts owed by the company that do not have to be repaid within the year. The company, therefore, has more breathing space with which to deal with these debts.

3. Owners' Investment and Retained Earnings   The original source of the company's resources is usually equity, the stockholders investment. If the firm makes profits, not all of these are customarily paid out to the stockholder as dividends. Usually, a proportion of earnings are reinvested in the firm. This portion is called earned surplus or retained earnings. It represents a plowing back of earnings by the stockholders. As these sources of company funds do not have to be repaid until the firm's dissolution, they are listed last. Because the investment of stockholders has a low order of priority in repayment, coming *after*

TABLE 2-6. Current Assets and Liabilities of Corporations (In Billions of Dollars)

End of Period	Net Working Capital	Current Assets							Current Liabilities				
		Total	Cash	United States Government Securities	Notes and Accounts Receivable		Inventories	Other	Total	Notes and Accounts Payable		Accrued Federal Income Taxes	Other
					United States Government[a]	Other				United States Government[a]	Other		
1961	148.8	304.6	40.7	19.2	3.4	133.3	95.2	12.9	155.8	1.8	110.0	14.2	29.8
1962	155.6	326.5	43.7	19.6	3.7	144.2	100.7	14.7	170.9	2.0	119.1	15.2	34.5
1963	163.5	351.7	46.5	20.2	3.6	156.8	107.0	17.8	188.2	2.5	130.4	16.5	38.7
1964	172.3	372.6	47.1	18.8	3.4	170.6	114.0	18.8	200.3	2.7	139.6	17.2	40.7
1965													
I	175.1	378.4	44.4	18.3	3.3	174.6	117.1	20.6	203.2	2.8	141.1	16.8	42.5
II	177.7	386.3	45.8	16.1	3.2	179.9	119.4	21.9	208.6	2.9	145.8	16.2	43.8
III	180.7	395.4	45.6	15.8	3.6	185.2	123.1	22.1	214.6	3.1	150.0	17.2	44.3
IV	183.4	407.9	49.2	16.7	3.9	189.6	126.3	22.1	224.5	3.1	157.2	19.2	45.0
1966													
I	186.0	413.7	46.9	16.9	3.9	192.5	130.2	23.4	227.7	3.8	157.5	19.1	47.3
II	190.4	423.6	47.7	15.3	4.0	198.4	134.4	23.7	233.1	3.9	163.4	16.7	49.1
III	191.5	431.4	46.9	14.6	4.2	202.8	139.4	23.5	239.9	4.4	167.1	17.9	50.4

[a] Receivables from, and payables to the United States Government exclude amounts offset against each other on corporations' books.
Note.—Securities and Exchange Commission estimates; excludes banks, savings and loan associations, insurance companies, and investment companies.
Source: Federal Reserve Bulletin, February 1967, p. 285.

other forms of debt, it provides security for the repayment of the debts. Therefore, the financial manager must always be concerned over the balance between debt and equity as a condition of future success in borrowing. Present and potential lenders view the stockholders' investment as a cushion for their loans.

Reference to Table 2-1 will show the specific means whereby Y. G., Inc. maintains its assets structure becomes clear.

a. Accounts Payable. Y. G., Inc. owes money to companies who have sold them goods for which $633,000 are still due. The speed with which a company has to make payment to its vendors varies among industries. The usual range is between 30 and 60 days. Occasionally, special lengthy terms are arranged for out-of-season purchases (a retailer who will take deliveries of toys in March may not have to pay for them until September) or for special promotions. The rapid expansion of the checkout discount stores was greatly helped by their suppliers who shipped goods to new stores and waited for payment until well after the opening of these stores. On the other hand, in most industries incentives, usually in the form of discounts, are offered to secure more rapid payment.

b. Notes Payable to Bank. Y. G., Inc. owes $695,000 on a loan from the bank. The balance sheet does not indicate whether this is on a secured basis (i.e., with specific collateral pledged to the lender) or on an unsecured basis (secured by the general credit of the firm). In general, this depends on the size and vigor of the borrower and his relationship with the lending bank. (The student might well put himself in the role of a banker at this stage and ponder the question in terms of the Y. G. balance sheet.) Since the notes payable are listed under current liabilities, they are due to be paid within one year. Loans from banks for periods of more than one year would be listed with other long-term liabilities except for the portion of the long-term debt payable within one year beyond the date of the balance sheet.

c. Accruals. Just as the company had prepayments classified as one of the assets, it also has obligations for services already rendered to the firm, but not yet paid for. Accruals usually include salaries and wages for work done by employees, but not yet paid for, as well as services (electricity, heat, accounting services, etc.). The balance sheet attempts to mirror a business on a specific date. The firm does not close down the operation and so there are many loose ends grouped under the accrual heading.

d. Federal Income Tax.   The year ending December 31, 1964 has been a profitable one. Y. G. Inc., therefore owes a considerable amount in taxes that must be paid.

Notice that, as long as the business remains at least equally profitable, the taxes owed will be a temporary source of funds. In other words, assuming constant tax rates, the operations of the company will continue to generate taxes equal to or greater than those of the previous years. At each year's end, Y. G., Inc. will continue to owe the government tax payments of at least $459,000. But suppose that the company has a poor year in which its profit drops to a few thousand dollars. It will then have to pay the taxes due for the previous year without generating the profit, including the tax liability, of about $460,000.[4]

e. Long-Term Debt.   In addition to funds that must be repaid within the year, Y. G., Inc. has borrowed $700,000 at a cost of 5% annually, which is not due until 1983. At a minimum, these loans usually involve a limitation on dividends (that part of the company's earnings given to the owners of the company rather than reinvested in its operations) as well as strictures on the minimum current-asset position. In return, however, the management of Y. G., Inc. has the use of the funds over a long period of time at a *fixed percentage cost*. If management can succeed in making more than 5% on the money borrowed, this excess will accrue to the benefit of the company and its equity investors—not to the lenders. On the other hand, if losses should be incurred, the lenders are guaranteed their fixed return and must be paid. The debtor, although he may have a ceiling on his income, also has a floor to sustain his loan. This is not true of the stockholders in this company.

f. Common Stock.   The primary risk capital in Y. G., Inc. is provided by the owners of the business, the stockholders, who have purchased $612,000 in common stock. In addition, over $2 million in company earnings have been plowed back into the business (called retained earnings or surplus). Since the stockholders' claims in liquidation come after all lenders if the company is dissolved, the owners assume the highest degree of risk. The potential lender appraising Y. G., Inc. views

---

[4] In the now historic squeeze-out of small "growth" companies in 1962, this factor played a major role. Lack of confidence destroyed the borrowing power of many of these companies. When business dipped slightly, the taxes owed, which many of them had been leaning on, had to be paid without new income to replenish them. The resulting cash shortage served to compound their problems.

the *equity capital* or net worth (the owner's original investment plus retained earnings) as a guarantee of his loan. In return for giving up this priority of repayment to lenders, however, as the company's profits grow, the owners' dividends and investment will increase.

In return for working his way through the complexities of the asset and liability listing of a company such as Y. G. Inc., the potential investor or financial manager can secure a wealth of insight into the company's financial health. Are there enough cash and near-cash holdings to balance the short-term obligations of the business?[5] What proportion of the company's assets are tied up in relatively fixed forms? In machinery and plant improvements? Is there a proper balance between the company's total debt and its owners' equity? Does it have too much in the way of inventory or accounts receivable? For that matter, should it have more invested in interest-bearing notes rather than nonproductive cash?

Questions like those above are at the core of financial analysis. To answer them, the financial manager must secure an adequate grasp of the company's operational needs. Accounts receivable, for example, are a result of company sales and the speed with which its customers pay for their purchases. If the receivables are inordinately high, the customers are probably not paying promptly. But how does the financial manager judge whether the receivables are "inordinately" high? Similarly, is the company's cash position high or low? As was stated earlier, the balance sheet gives the financial manager a snapshot of the company as a fiscal unit. It must be supplemented by an analysis of the operational characteristics of the firm if the conditions of the latter are to be properly interpreted. To do this, we turn to the income statement, often known as the profit and loss statement, or the statement of operations.

II. INCOME STATEMENT

The condensed income statement of Y. G., Inc. for the year ending December 31, 1966 is shown in Table 2-7. (Usually, management would have, in addition, a series of three-months statements and, not infrequently, operating results for even shorter periods.) By turning to the details of the income statement and by integrating the elements

[5] The analyst must be careful not to place too much weight on static financial statements to determine the adequacy of cash. The analyst must also look to the plans for cash spending and cash receipts as developed in the cash budget.

into the knowledge that has been secured from the balance sheet, a more dynamic picture of the company's operations is made possible.

A. Net Sales and Net Income After Taxes

From the balance sheet of Y. G., Inc., the analyst knows that the stockholders have $2,706,000 book value invested in the company. Y. G., Inc. is using this investment as a base in generating nearly $10,000,000 in net sales (after taking into account merchandise returns and allowances) and an after-tax profit of $449,000. How does the financial analyst evaluate these figures? A primary step is to compute sales per dollar of equity investment and the return on investment (i.e., net profit after tax) as a percentage of equity. Y. G.'s management is generating nearly four dollars of sales for every dollar invested in the business. Does this mean the company is over-extended—that it is doing too much business with too little in the way of funds? A glance at the balance sheet is reassuring. Y. G., Inc. has more than twice as much in current assets as in equivalent liabilities, and the company's total debt is more than matched by its equity. The company is earning 16.6% after taxes on owners' equity (common stock plus retained earnings). This provides the analyst with a measure of the management's efficiency in administering the stockholder's money.

The analyst could, perhaps, turn to the previous year's sales and earnings to gauge the company's growth. This will not tell the analyst, however, how this compares with equally risky alternative investment outlets or how Y. G., Inc. is doing compared with competitors. Is Y. G., Inc. keeping pace with comparable firms? If we turn back again to the analysis of the financial standing of the firm, integrating the income statement's information into the balance sheet provides many suggestions of areas worthy of more concentrated attention. For example: How "current" are the two principal current assets? The analyst might turn first to the *accounts receivable*. An analysis of accounts receivable is much more fruitful if looked at from the viewpoint of sales. The primary question to be asked is whether the accounts receivable are overdue, thus showing signs of being either difficult or impossible to collect. How old are they? One approach is to view the receivables as a function of sales. If a year's sales are $9,995,000, how many days of sales are reflected in the company's receivables? On an average day of the year, 1966, Y. G., Inc. generated sales of roughly $27,000

(9,995,000/365). Since Y. G., Inc. has $1,468,000 in receivables, these are equal to 53 days' worth of sales. However, there might be a seasonal pattern to the company's sales. If, instead of a level pattern of sales, the volume of sales reaches a peak in December (this would be true

TABLE 2-7.   Y. G., Inc. Income Statement for Fiscal Year Ending December 31, 1966. (Figures are rounded to the nearest $1000.)

	Dollars	Percent
Net sales	9995	100.00
Cost of goods sold	6643	66.46
Gross margin	3352	33.54
Selling expense:		
Advertising	185	
Shipping	74	
Salesmen salaries and commissions	442	
Field servicing	510	
Total selling expense	1211	12.12
Research and development	671	6.71
Administrative expense:		
Officers salaries	185	
Administrative overhead	342	
Total administrative expense	552	5.52
Interest expense	10	
Net income before taxes	908	9.08
Less: taxes	459	
Net income after taxes	449	4.49
Dividends	61	
Increase in retained earnings	388	

of most retailer's sales, for example) then the company's receivables would be more current than the above computation would indicate. Since the balance sheet reflects the company's position as of December 31, 1966, the receivables, in this case, would be the equivalent of relatively few days of sales. On the other hand, if this were a road materials company whose sales are at their lowest in the winter, the financial analyst would immediately know that receivables averaged even more than 53 days of sales.

What is the next step of the financial manager, assuming that after checking the company's sales he finds that the firm actually has 53 days worth of sales in accounts receivable? If we know that, normally, bills are paid in this industry within 30 days, for example, we would immediately be aware that a substantial portion of our receivables are overdue. We should, then, possibly analyze each account individually, seeking the cause. Some of the questions we should address to management would include the following.

Are we being too lenient in our collection policies? Are we giving our customers unusually long credit terms? If we are borrowing money from a finance company at $\frac{1}{20}$ of 1% per day and part of this money is supporting our customers, the length of this credit to the customers is costly. For example, by lowering our average of 53 days' worth of receivables to 40 days, we could reduce the funds required to "carry" them by $\frac{15}{20}$ of 15%. Thus if our receivables averaged $1,468,000 we would save $9,114 a year. The credit terms that account for this excess may be the optimum way of securing business, but they must be weighed against equally costly and, perhaps, more productive alternatives (for instance, price reductions, more sales effort, and the like).

Are there uncollectable items listed in the receivables? The financial manager might want to review the credit standing of the company's customers and, possibly, stop doing business with the tardiest and least stable of them.

Are new credit arrangements for our customers in order? If our receivables are tending to stretch out, perhaps we should consider new terms of sale. Giving discounts for prompt payments is one approach. Conceivably, in some businesses the setting up of installment purchasing arrangements might be worthwhile.

The financial manager's appraisal will be influenced by the pattern or relationship between sales and receivables over time. He would look at data for years past to see whether the company was dealing with a growing problem. Certainly, a pattern of increased time lag between sales and collection would be an immediate red flag for investigations. However, this cannot be an exclusively "financial" investigation; the financial manager must also consider corporate strategy and selling problems. In spite of the apparently slow collection, the company may decide to continue its present credit policies, but only after knowledge of their cost has been aired and weighed against the incremental profits derived from the liberalization of credit.

B. Cost of Goods Sold (Sometimes known as Cost of Sales)

This is the estimated cost of the merchandise incurred by the company up to the time when the goods leave the factory, but before the costs of selling and running the administrative and sales end of the business are added on. Since inventories will ultimately be reflected in sales, it gives the financial manager a crude gauge on their amplitude. Assume that management predicts sales of $12,000,000 in 1967. Based on 1966, some two-thirds of this figure (or $8,000,000) reflects the costs of goods sold. Therefore, the company's inventories of $2,160,000 represent, arithmetically, a little more than four months of prospective sales. But is this rough and ready calculation adequate? To answer that question, the financial manager has to look more closely at the makeup of the inventories.

C. Types of Inventory

In a manufacturing operation, inventories are typically classified into finished goods, goods in process (work in process), and raw materials. The last two will both require additional inputs of labor and, possibly, of materials before they become finished goods. Finished goods, in turn, represent perhaps only two-thirds of a sales dollar since sales expenses, overhead, profit, and several other expense items must be added on in arriving at the typical sales price.

Few businesses have only one product line. In Y. G.'s case, there are three product lines. Inventories useful for one product may have no function in the production of another product. Although the sales total is expected to increase, some products will undoubtedly do better than others. With these factors in mind, an analysis along the lines of Table 2-8 is in order.

This type of analysis enables the financial manager to see that the amounts of inventory the company has on hand *is a function of sales of those specific inventories that vary considerably between product lines.* Product A, for example, should be absorbed in 3 to 4 months. In contrast, Product C (assuming that our anticipated sales figures will be attained) may require over 16 months before it is sold. Unless there is some specific reason for this bulge, it looks as if the financial manager should consider strategies for reducing the inventory of this item. Assume

TABLE 2-8.   Y. G. Inc. Inventory Evaluation[a]

Product Line:	Inventories ($)		Average Degree of Completion (Percent)	Ultimate Value In Cost of Goods Sold = 100% (Percent Completion) ($)	Sales Required to Absorb Inventory (Cost of Goods Sold × 3⁄2) ($)
A	Finished	600	100	600	900
	In process	425	75	633	950
	Raw material	275	50	550	825
Total sales required					$2675
Anticipated annual sales of product A					$8400
Period required to absorb inventory at anticipated sales levels					3 to 4 months
B	Finished	500	100	500	750
	In process	200	75	267	400
	Raw material	100	50	200	300
Total sales required					$1450
Anticipated annual sales of product line B					$2900
Period required to absorb inventory at anticipated sales levels					6 months
C	Finished	200	100	200	300
	In process	160	75	213	320
	Raw material	150	50	300	450
Total sales required					$1070
Anticipated annual sales of product line C					$ 700
Period required to absorb inventory at anticipated sales levels					16 months

[a] It is assumed that the firm employs the same markup on its entire product line. All figures are rounded to the nearest $1,000.

that, based on deliveries and optimum lot size, an inventory of C equal to 4-months' sale is adequate, then the company is carrying three times the amount of inventory required. The cost of excessive borrowing ($510,000 for a year's inventory requirements) is obviously greater than the cost of borrowing $127,000 to carry on for 4 months. In addition, the risks of inventory obsolescence, although perhaps less quantifiable, are perhaps even more onerous. The more *time* required to sell the inventory, the more vulnerable that inventory is to changes in consumer wants. The validity of future-demand projections varies inversely with the time these projections cover. For that reason, when Y. G. carries a 12-month inventory rather than a 4-month inventory, the risks of product obsolescence are far more than four times as great.

In this case, the financial manager has not told the production supervisor how much inventory to carry but, instead, has highlighted the costs and dangers of present inventory policy; the production manager may still justify the inventory coverage of product line C but he will do so knowing the costs of the policy. It is the financial measuring stick that enables management to equate competing internal demands on the company's limited resources.

One other point should be touched on before moving on to the other elements of the income statement. This is the ratio between the cost of goods sold and the net sales. Often, the financial manager must accept the company's selling price and the efficiency of the company's production technique. If the gross margin (the difference between net sales and cost of goods sold) begins to drop, therefore, the financial manager must defer to management for remedial action, if possible. The income statements, when studied for a period of time, can signal these weak spots to management for more intensive investigation, with declining margins perhaps calling for investment in more efficient production facilities—or even for a change in product line. In the semiconductor business, for example, declining gross margins caused a number of firms to automate their production facilities and, thus, lower the cost of goods sold. Other managements saw the decline in margins as a signal to turn their attention to other less competitive areas. In any case, declining gross margin is often the first danger signal that an industry is becoming overly competitive; that the relationship between demand and productive capacity has taken a turn for the worse.

D. Selling Expense

The total cost of Y. G.'s sales effort was 12% of sales. Is this a high or low figure? If Y. G. is in an industry in which expense date for a number of comparable firms is available similar to the ratios covered in the next chapter, the question is easily answered. Without these aids, the financial manager must turn to a year-to-year comparison of the company's expenditure patterns. Again, more intensive investigation of the elements within the selling expense heading (advertising, salesmen's reimbursements, and the like) may be called for.

E. Research and Development

From the financial manager's point of view, this is one of the most difficult areas to appraise. Decrying research and development expenditures, in some industries at least, is the equivalent of decrying the morality of patriotism. In the drug and chemical fields, for example, most companies proudly list the proportion of their total sales that is expended in research and development. The results of the research and development dollar input may take several years, at best. In any one year, therefore, it is difficult to evaluate what the company is securing through its research and development effort. However, the financial manager can restate alternate forms of business investment in a fashion that makes these forms comparable to research and development investment in the eyes of top management. For example, the $676,000 research and development expense indicated on the Y. G. income statement could have doubled the company's advertising and sales force or increased the field servicing by an equivalent factor. As an alternative, sales prices could have been reduced by more than 6%. By comparing research and development expenditures against these comparable alternative forms of investment, the financial manager can help clarify top-level decision making.

Management may well decide to maintain the research and development expenditures, or even increase them. But this will be done with an awareness of the alternatives made possible through the common denominator—the dollar figures of the income statement.

F. Administrative Expense

Administrative expense is generally referred to as a relatively fixed overhead element. Within some limit of additional volume, Y. G.'s administrative staff may be adequate to handle increased business without increased expense, while the cost of goods sold category tends to vary more directly with volume. Therefore, if it is assumed that all other costs of doing business as a *percentage* of sales remained constant while the *dollar total* of company administrative expenses was constant, additional volume could be much more profitable than was the case of the average sales dollar in 1966. For example, if Y. G., Inc. generates

$12,000,000 in sales, as planned for 1967, at a percentage margin comparable to that enjoyed in 1966, without increasing its administrative expenditures, the additional $2,000,000 will result not in 9% profit before taxes, but rather in 9% + 5.5%. The additional 5.5% reflect the fact that the incremental business does not require additional administrative expenditures—i.e., the president of the company received the same salary as the previous year, administrative office facilities are not increased, and so on.

The basic principal of *fixed expense* is the same whether it refers to administrative expense or to a plant whose basic costs will remain the same at different levels of output. The corner drugstore paying a fixed rent of $500 a month and doing $5000 a month in volume may return 10% on the average sales dollar. If volume is doubled while the rent remains the same, and all other expenses as a percent of volume are constant, the additional sale will return 20% in incremental profits.

To the banker or potential investor, administrative expenses are a check point in determining the efficiency with which businesses are run. In addition, with the separation of ownership and management that characterizes so much of American industry, it provides a check on the salary structure of the administrators.

G. Interest Expense

Y. G. must pay for the money that it borrows. Notice however, that this expenditure is, in effect, absorbed partly by tax savings, assuming the company is operating at a profitable level. *Interest expenses are paid before taxes.* With corporation income taxes roughly half of income, half of Y. G.'s expenditures in borrowing money are essentially covered by the government. Since considerable penalties are usually the rule for nonpayment of interest charges, both management and lenders are interested in the relationship of company earnings to its debt charges. This is often referred to as the coverage ratio.

Some firms distinguish between operating income and expenses and nonoperating income and expenses. The distinction is generally made on the basis of what is the firm's main line of business. A railroad, for example, may choose to regard oil royalties on its right-of-way land as a nonoperating source of income. Interest expense may be regarded as a nonoperating expense if the money is borrowed for other purposes than to carry out the firm's major operations. For example, if Y. G., Inc. borrowed money to help finance a building to be rented to other tenants as well as used by Y. G., that portion of the interest expense used to help finance space rented to other tenants should not be charged as an operating expense against Y. G.'s main line of business, since this expense was not required by normal operations. Similarly, income realized by Y. G., Inc. from renting space should not be credited to operating income, since it was not generated from normal operations of the firm. Such income should be listed on the income statement as nonoperating income.

H. Dividend

In order to attract stockholders (i.e., equity investors in the business) the firm pays a dividend. Unlike interest expense, this dividend is paid out of post-tax earnings and, therefore, Y. G.'s pretax earnings must be more than $120,000 in order to maintain a $61,000 dividend. In addition, if Y. G. has to pay as high a dividend rate to attract equity investment as interest to secure loans, in attracting a similar amount of funds under current tax rates, the latter will require little more than half as much in pre-tax dollars. *A dollar in dividends requires nearly twice as many pre-tax dollars as a dollar of interest.* As will be seen later, this fact has had a significant effect in shaping the capital structure of American corporations.

I. Increase in Retained Earnings

Part of Y. G.'s earnings have been reinvested in the business rather than dispersed to the stockholders. Each year, the residue of the post-tax earnings after dividends shown in the operating statement is reflected by the retained earnings or the earned surplus account in the balance sheet. This measures the plowing back into the business of earnings generated by it. Notice that this reinvestment serves as a principal source of funds for the company's activities.

Tables 2-9 and 2-10 show the composite income statement and balance sheet of all manufacturing corporations (except newspapers) in the first quarter of 1966 both in absolute dollar figures and in percentages. It should be noted that earned surplus and surplus reserves constituted 38.5% of total liabilities and stockholders' equity compared with 21.8% for capital stock and capital surplus. To put it differently, the accumulated retained earnings equalled approximately 1.75 times the capital stock and capital surplus.

TABLE 2-9. Financial Statements for All Manufacturing Corporations (except Newspapers), First Quarter, 1966 (in Millions of Dollars)

INCOME AND SURPLUS

Sales (net of returns, allowances, and discounts)	$129,911
Deduct: Costs and expenses (net of purchase discounts)	117,666
Net profit from operations	12,245
Add: Other income or deductions (net)	121
Net profit before Federal income taxes	12,366
Deduct: Provision for Federal income taxes	5,137
Net profit after taxes	7,229
Deduct: Cash dividends charged to surplus	3,040
Net profit retained in business	4,189
Add: Earned surplus and surplus reserves at beginning of period	138,982
Add: Other direct charges or credits to surplus (net)	−1,180
Earned surplus and surplus reserves at end of period	$141,991
Depreciation and depletion included above, including accelerated amortization of emergency facilities	$ 4,146

ASSETS

Cash on hand and in bank	20,097
U.S. Government securities, including Treasury savings notes	9,345
Total cash and U.S. Government securities	29,442
Receivables from U.S. Government, excluding tax credits	3,572
Other notes and accounts receivable (net)	61,764
Total receivables	65,336
Inventories	87,535
Other current assets	13,239
Total current assets	195,552
Property, plant, and equipment	283,761
Deduct: Reserve for depreciation and depletion	140,013
Total property, plant, and equipment (net)	143,749
Other noncurrent assets	29,733
Total assets	$369,035

TABLE 2-9. (*Continued*)

LIABILITIES AND STOCKHOLDERS' EQUITY

Short-term loans from banks (original maturity of 1 year or less)	$12,436
Advances and prepayments by U.S. Government	3,666
Trade accounts and notes payable	29,983
Federal income taxes accrued	13,482
Installments, due in 1 year or less, on long-term debt	
(*a*) Loans from banks	1,172
(*b*) Other long-term debt	1,998
Other current liabilities	23,990
Total current liabilities	86,727
Long-term debt due in more than 1 year (*a*) Loans from banks	9,505
(*b*) Other long-term debt	40,212
Other noncurrent liabilities	10,198
Total liabilities	146,642
Reserves not reflected elsewhere	—
Capital stock, capital surplus, and minority interest	80,402
Earned surplus and surplus reserves	141,991
Total stockholders' equity	222,393
Total liabilities and stockholders' equity	$369,035

NET WORKING CAPITAL

Excess of current assets over current liabilities	$108,825

Source: FTC-SEC, Quarterly Financial Report for Manufacturing Corporations, First Quarter, 1966, p. 34.

III. SOURCE AND APPLICATION OF FUNDS

What did the company invest in during the course of the last period and where did it get the funds? The answers to these questions give management a quick insight into the changes within the firm. In order to secure this information, it is necessary to compare balance sheets at the beginning and at the end of the period studied. Every increase in an asset or decrease in a liability must be paid for. Whether it is increasing inventory or decreasing the amount owed people who have sold the company goods, money is needed. Conversely, when the company borrows money or uses up an asset it generates funds. By formally indicating the changes in company balance sheets over time, the financial manager can envision the flow of funds during the period for which

TABLE 2-10. Financial Statements for All Manufacturing Corporations (except Newspapers), First Quarter, 1966 (in Percentage and Ratio Form)

INCOME	percent of sales
Sales (net of returns, allowances, and discounts)	100.0
Deduct: Costs and expenses (net of purchase discounts)	90.6
Net profit from operations	9.4
Add: Other income or deductions (net)	0.1
Net profit before Federal income taxes	9.5
Deduct: Provision for Federal income taxes	4.0
Net profit after taxes	5.6
Depreciation and depletion included above, including accelerated amortization of emergency facilities	3.2

ASSETS	percent of total assets
Cash on hand and in bank	5.4
U.S. Government securities, including Treasury savings notes	2.5
Total cash and U.S. Government securities	8.0
Receivables from U.S. Government, excluding tax credits	1.0
Other notes and accounts receivable (net)	16.7
Total receivables	17.7
Inventories	23.7
Other current assets	3.6
Total current assets	53.0
Property, plant, and equipment	76.9
Deduct: Reserve for depreciation and depletion	37.9
Total property, plant, and equipment (net)	39.0
Other noncurrent assets	8.1
Total assets	100.0

the balance sheets serve as boundaries. The method that is used is to compare all the elements in the balance sheets and to indicate their dollar changes from the beginning to the end of the period in question.

As can be seen from Table 2-11, Y. G., Inc. has expanded its inventories and accounts receivable as well as its investment in machinery. The sources of funds have been, in part, some of the cash the company started the period with. A contribution was made by depreciation of the old equipment (i.e., the increase in costs and therefore, the charge to profit that was made to reflect the allowable decline in value on

Table 2-10. (*Continued*)

LIABILITIES AND STOCKHOLDERS' EQUITY

Short-term loans from banks (original maturity of 1 year or less)	3.4
Advances and prepayments by U.S. Government	1.0
Trade accounts and notes payable	8.1
Federal income taxes accrued	3.7
Installments, due in 1 year or less, on long-term debt	
(*a*) Loans from banks	0.3
(*b*) Other long-term debt	0.5
Other current liabilities	6.5
Total current liabilities	23.5
Long-term debt due in more than 1 year (*a*) Loans from banks	2.6
(*b*) Other long-term debt	10.9
Other noncurrent liabilities	2.8
Total liabilities	39.7
Reserves not reflected elsewhere	—
Capital stock, capital surplus, and minority interest	21.8
Earned surplus and surplus reserves	38.5
Total stockholders' equity	60.3
Total liabilities and stockholders' equity	100.0

OPERATING RATIOS

	percent
Annual rate of profit on stockholders' equity at end of period—	
Before Federal income taxes	22.2
After taxes	13.0
	times
Current assets to current liabilities	2.25
Total cash and U.S. Government securities to total current liabilities	0.34
Total stockholders' equity to debt	3.40

Source: FTC-SEC, Quarterly Financial Report for Manufacturing Corporations, First Quarter, 1966, p. 12.

Y. G.'s facilities). The largest part of the funds was secured through borrowing: Y. G. has increased its obligations to the bank in the form of notes, to its vendors in the form of accounts payable, and to its long-term debt holders in the form of debentures. In addition, the taxes owed to the Federal Government have increased. The use of the source and application statement as a tool of *communication* should not be forgotten. It clearly defines the past flow of funds and gives insight into the evolution of the present situation. The financial manager of the company, therefore, uses it to spotlight the causes of present financial

Table 2-11. Y. G. Inc. Balance Sheet. (Figures are Rounded to the nearest $1000)

	December 31, 1966 (Dollars)		December 31, 1965 (Dollars)	
	(1)	(2)	(3) Source	(4) Application
Assets				
Current Assets				
Cash	603	812	209	
Accounts receivable	1468	975		493
Inventories	2610	1650		960
Prepayments	19	19		
Total current assets	4700	3456		
Fixed assets				
Machinery	742			300
Depreciation	132	60	72	
	610	382		
Leasehold Improvements	339	228	20	111
Depreciation	43	23		
	296	205		
Total fixed assets	906	587		
Total assets	5606	4043		
Liabilities				
Current liabilities				
Notes payable to bank	675	507	168	
Accounts payable	633	530	103	
Accruals	433	313	120	
Federal income tax	459	375	84	
Total current liabilities	2200	1725		
Long-term debt				
5 percent debentures due 1983	700		700	
Owners' equity				
Common stock ($1 share)	612	612		
Retained earnings	2094	1706	388	
	2706	2318	1864	1864
Total liabilities and equity	5606	4043		

strain, to answer the question of "Where have our resources been moving?" From the static picture of the balance sheet (giving the situation of the company at a moment of time) through the use of the income statement, we have advanced to a dynamic picture: the flow of funds over time. But it is not the past and present alone with which management must be concerned. While the financial manager hopefully looks to them for general lessons in meeting future challenges, it is to the specific shape of the future that he must turn.

IV. THE CASH-FLOW BUDGET

A prime responsibility of the financial manager is to make sure that the firm will never be embarrassed by not having enough cash on hand to meet its bills. In order to properly anticipate the financial stresses of the future, the financial manager usually works with a projection of the *cash* needs of the firm. Notice the emphasis on cash in that statement. Generally, the financial manager cannot easily pay bills with accounts receivable nor, when pay day comes, can Y. G. satisfy its workers with their pay in the form of company products such as transistors! In addition, banks and other lending institutions, in extending funds, tend to be much more sympathetic to prepared statements of future financial needs than they are to a firm's immediate need to meet unanticipated cash requirements.

How does the financial manager set up the cash-flow budget? Usually this is a projection for a 12-month period for which he lists the anticipated cash flow into and out of the firm. It obviously requires evaluation of the shape of the business to come and of the cash needs of the company during the period. The volume and timing of sales are prime considerations. If there were no seasonal peaks of volume, if goods were paid for when delivered and if production costs did not precede sales income, the prediction would be simpler. But these conditions and many others do persist. Because of these complications, the company's cash budget is a very important tool for avoiding future pitfalls. The following is an example of a typical cash budget for a small manufacturing business. Although the particular stress elements may vary from business to business, the basic principles of this kind of analysis are the same. Suppose that the firm has $5000 in cash on hand, anticipates sales of $50,000 in each of the next two months, and that its terms of sale are 1% discount for payment upon-receipt of the goods by the customer or net (i.e., full invoice) price if payment is made 30 days after receipt of merchandise. Assume that there are no accounts receivable outstanding. Assume, further, that the firm ships all goods during the last five days of the month and that these are received by the customers between the first and the fifth of the following month. Finally, assume that customers who account for one-half of all sales habitually take advantage of the cash discount and that the others wait until the expiration of the 30-day credit period.

The first two months' figures will then appear as follows:

	First Month	Second Month
Sales of goods	$50,000	$50,000
Collections	—	24,750
Total Receipts	—	24,750

On the other side of the coin are the *actual* monthly expenditures for wages and salaries, supplies, power, heat, and the like. It must be emphasized that the cash-flow budget does not show any entry for invisible costs or obligations that occurred in any one month but that were not paid out in that month. For example, a firm may have a license under a patent and agrees to pay the inventor a royalty of $5 per unit produced with payment to be made annually. The cash-flow budget would not reflect this, except in the month the payment was actually made. In the case of depreciation, the cash-flow budget would not show this cost item at any time since depreciation is not an actual payment, in cash or check, but merely a debit entry on the books of the firm, to reflect wear and tear on machinery and plant.

After entering the actual scheduled expenses for each month, the financial manager then subtracts the outflow of funds from the anticipated inflow of the first month. If the outflow is less than the inflow, the budget will show a cash deficit at the end of this month. If the same is true of the second month, the financial manager will add the cash deficit from the first month to that of the second month and show the cumulative deficit at the end of the second month. Assuming that the inflow in the third month exceeds the outflow, the cumulative deficit at the end of the third month will be reduced by the excess of inflow over outflow. In summary form the picture might be as shown in Table 2-12.

Since the company started with $5000 in cash, its needs will be decreased by $5000 for each of the periods, and the final net-cash bal-

TABLE 2-12.   Cash-Flow Budget Work Sheet (Dollars)

	Month 1	Month 2	Month 3	Month 4
Sales	50,000	50,000	50,000	50,000
Collections		24,750	24,750	24,750
			25,000	25,000
Total receipts	0	24,750	49,750	49,750
Disbursements				
Payments on Accounts Payable	0	20,000	20,000	20,000
Wages	10,000	10,000	10,000	10,000
Direct factory expenses	3,000	3,000	3,000	3,000
Administrative expenses	800	800	800	800
Selling expenses	1,200	1,200	1,200	1,200
Payments for equipment	0	0	0	500
Total Disbursements	15,000	35,000	35,000	35,500
Net monthly cash gain (loss)[a]	(15,000)	(10,250)	14,750	14,250
Cumulative cash gain (loss)	(15,000)	(25,250)	(10,500)	3,750

[a] Total receipts less total disbursements.

ance will be increased equally. Projecting cash needs in advance makes it possible to explore alternative means to cut the deficit. In this case, perhaps an arrangement could be made with the company's supplier to delay payment for goods longer than the standard thirty days. Alternatively, the discount given to the company's customers could be increased in the hope of shortening the delivery-payment gap, and so on. If internal means prove inadequate to supply the additional funds or reduce their need, the company must turn to external sources. In shopping among the latter, the cash-flow statement is extremely useful as a means of communication permitting the possible lender or investor to clearly see the need and its duration.

Often the cash-flow statement is only a way station toward a more comprehensive forecast of projected income.

V. PROJECTED-INCOME STATEMENT

In the cash-flow analysis, the financial manager is concerned only with the elements that affect the company's cash picture. For example, a sale from inventory that is not paid for until after the projected period does not enter into the cash analysis, although it may be most significant in terms of profits. In going from the cash-flow budget to the projected income statement, the financial manager takes cognizance of the noncash items that affect the financial operations of the firm.

A. Postponed Payments

To the total of costs, the company must add several items that had been omitted in the cash budget. First, any obligations to third parties that will accrue during the period under consideration will be included, even though they may not have to be paid until a later date. For example, local real estate taxes or interest on the mortgage may not be due for one month or more after the end of the fiscal period. However, the proportionate share of these expenses must be allocated to the fiscal period and is shown as a part of costs or operations during this period. Fixed annual payments to a pension fund, insurance premiums, installment payment on equipment, and the like will be shown on a pro rata basis in the income statement, while they appear in the cash budget only if payment is made and then with the full amount in the month in which they are disbursed.

B. Depreciation

Second, the financial manager will allocate to the expenses a sum which equals the estimated depreciation of fixed assets during the fiscal period. Plant, machinery, equipment, furnishings, and similar assets decrease in value over a period of time. This is due partly to wear and tear, partly to the fact that it is "used" or "old" and, partly, because new models make their appearance in the market. As has been noted, there are several methods of calculating depreciation. Whichever method is selected, the financial manager will calculate the amount of such depreciation and charge it as a cost, technically known as "expensing" depreciation.

C. Advantages

The projected-income statement serves as an important tool in the planning by management. The profit forecast, although only an estimate and not certain, enables management to decide whether to go ahead with planned sales and output or to consider alternative output, merchandising, or pricing policies. Many companies, large as well as small, have several product lines or merchandise departments. Frequently, the financial manager is asked to prepare, in addition to the overall income statement, departmental or product statements. If the financial manager has prepared such separate income statements, top management may well decide to reapportion funds and manpower from the prospectively less profitable products or departments to those with better prospects.

The income projection is frequently used as a guide to the funds available to the company for long-range projects. These, in turn, are appraised and ascribed priority by the collection of techniques referred to as capital budgeting.

VI. PRO FORMA BALANCE SHEET

The purpose of a pro forma balance sheet (also called a projected balance sheet) is to make a rough forecast when enough information is not available to make a detailed cash-flow budget. This tool is used to estimate needs for cash funds as of a specific balance sheet date only. This is the major limitation of a pro forma balance sheet since company cash needs may fluctuate radically from month to month or even more frequently. The date picked for the pro forma balance sheet should, therefore, be the date of maximum estimated cash needs.

Basically, a pro forma balance sheet is a forecast of the dollar size of the items making up the balance sheet for any future selected date. For the financial manager to prepare a pro forma balance sheet, it is necessary to first prepare sales, purchasing, manufacturing, and profit estimates for the period ending on the date of the pro forma balance sheet.

Generally, the financial manager first estimates the expected level of accounts receivable on the date of the pro forma balance sheet. From the past experience with the relationship between sales and receivables, such an estimate can be prepared based on the forecast sales for the period ending on the date of the projected balance sheet. Changes can be made in this figure based on anticipated changes in credit terms. A similar figure can be prepared for inventory based on the relationship of past sales to inventory and anticipated sales levels.

The minimum cash balance that the company expects to carry is estimated by the financial manager based on past experience as is the investment (if any) in such near cash assets as government bonds or securities in other companies.

Fixed assets on the pro forma balance sheet date can be forecast by adding planned additions of new plant, property, and equipment to present fixed asset items and by subtracting out forecasted depreciation. Similar forecasts are used for any other asset items on the balance sheet.

Figures are derived for the liability side of the pro forma balance sheet in a similar manner. Accounts payable for the forecast date are estimated based on the past relationship between sales and purchases and the expected volume of purchases for the forecast period. Adjustments should be made for expected changes in terms of purchase and/or payment of bills.

Accrued income tax can be forecast based on the expected level of profit before taxes, provided income tax rates are known. These accrued taxes are added to the present balance of accrued income taxes and expected payments on this balance due before the pro forma balance sheet date are deducted. Similar estimates are made for other accrued expenses such as accrued salaries and wages based on forecasts of the size of workforce and other expected expense items.

The stockholders equity figure is adjusted for sales or repurchases of stock or any other expected changes. Retained earnings are estimated by adding forecasted profits after taxes to present retained earnings and deducting planned dividends.

When all this is done, both the assets and the liabilities are totaled. Generally, at this point, the financial manager finds that there are more assets than liabilities. The difference, often referred to as the "plugged figure" or the balancing figure, represents the additional funds necessary to achieve the planned investment in assets. These funds must be secured from lenders or the owners or the amount of assets planned must be reduced to equal the expected amount of funds available.

The pro forma balance sheet is often used when enough information is not available to prepare a complete cash flow budget. The pro forma balance sheet can also be used as a supplement to the cash flow budget since the information needed to prepare the cash budget can be used to prepare the pro forma balance sheet. The estimates of cash needed on the pro forma balance sheet date should be the same as for the same date on the cash flow budget, provided the same assumptions were used in preparing both tools.

SUMMARY

The financial manager has six basic tools to aid him in the financial analysis of the firm. The balance sheet tells how the company looks from a financial point of view as of a particular date. The balance sheet simply lists the resources of the firm and the claims against these assets. The two sides of the balance sheet must balance. An examination of each type of asset and liability is neccessary to give a quick check on the company's financial status both to management and to outside.

The income statement is a measure of past performance in the key area of profitability. It gives a picture of the operational characteristics of the firm for a period of time such as a year. The income statement begins with the firm's sales and ends with a statement of net profit (or loss). An examination of each item on the income statement reveals much of what has happened to the firm financially during this period of time.

The source and application of funds statement is used to indicate the flow of funds as reflected by changes in the firm's assets and liabilities. The cash flow budget is used to project cash needs and to identify cash surpluses or shortages to highlight possible critical points in the income and outgo of cash. The pro forma income statement quantifies the future prospects of the planned operations. The pro forma balance sheet pinpoints the firm's need for funds on a specific date. The greatest value of these six financial tools of analysis is not in providing clean-cut answers to the problems of the company, but rather in indicating potential trouble spots, which then can be subjected to more detailed analysis.

Questions

1. What is the chief value of such tools as the balance sheet and the income statement to the financial manager?
2. It is often stated that cash is the least productive of assets. Why is this true?
3. What is the purpose of depreciation?
4. Why is owners' equity listed on the liability side of the balance sheet?
5. Explain how income taxes owed to the government may be a source of funds to the firm.
6. What can a company do if its accounts receivable are too high?

7. Why is it important for the financial manager to evaluate inventory levels?

8. What does a decline in the gross margin mean to the financial manager?

9. Why is it so difficult for the financial manager to appraise the results of research and development expenditures?

10. What is the purpose of the cash-flow budget?

11. What are the advantages of a projected-income statement? What are its limitations?

Problems

1. Alpha Company has purchased a machine for $12,500. It is expected that the machine will be scrapped in 6 years. Its scrap value is estimated at $500. Prepare schedules of depreciation and balance-sheet values for this machine under the three alternative methods of depreciation.

2. Fenton Company had sales of $5,573,028 in 1966. The balance sheet for the company shows $1,528,350 in accounts receivable. Bills are normally paid in this industry in 30 days. How does Fenton stand compared to its industry average?

3. Company A has a capital structure consisting of 5% bonds $50,000 and common equity $70,000. Company B has no bonds and common equity $120,000.

   a. What is the net profit after taxes for each company assuming a 50 percent tax rate for each of the following years, when net income before interest and taxes was:

Year One:	$ 7,000
Year Two:	3,000
Year Three:	18,000
Year Four:	500

   b. What is the rate of return after taxes on the total common equity for each company?

4. Prepare a cash-flow budget for Ajax Corporation for January through June 1967. Sales of Ajax Corporation were $75,000 in December, 1966, and are expected to run at the rate of $75,000 per month through March, 1967. Sales will be at the level of $90,000 per month in April through June. 25% of receipts are collected in the month of sale, the balance the following month. The company purchased $60,000 worth

TABLE 2-13. Basso Semiconductor Corporation: Income Statements (Dollars)

	For the Year Ended	
	December 31, 1966	December 31, 1965
Net Sales	436,369	327,579
Operating expenses and costs:		
Cost of goods sold	308,023	230,388
General, administrative, and mailing expenses	62,515	49,005
Employees profit-sharing and retirement plans	19,364	13,478
Total operating expenses and costs	389,902	292,871
Profit from operations	46,273	34,708
Other income (expenses)	(194)	(149)
Net income before taxes	46,273	34,857
Federal income taxes	21,434	16,816
Net income	24,839	18,041

TABLE 2-14. Basso Semiconductor Corporation: Statement of Retained Earnings Reconciliation (Dollars)

	For the Year Ended	
	December 31, 1966	December 31, 1965
Net income	24,839	18,041
Retained earnings at beginning of year	93,730	80,953
Cash dividends paid	(5,046)	(5,264)
Retained earnings end of year	113,523	93,730

of raw materials in December, 1966. It will purchase $60,000 per month in January and February and $30,000 per month thereafter. Payments on accounts payable are made 30 days after purchase. Wages will be at the rate of $15,000 per month in January and February and $18,000 per month thereafter. Direct factory and administrative expenses are expected to total $5000 per month. Selling expenses are expected to be at the rate of $1500 per month. A federal income tax payment of

TABLE 2-15   Basso Semiconductor Corporation: Balance Sheets (Dollars)

	December 31, 1966	December 31, 1965
Assets		
Cash	59,594	41,385
Accounts receivable	73,221	46,308
Inventories	64,751	44,818
Prepaid expenses	3,162	1,904
Total current assets	200,728	134,415
Property, plant, and equipment at cost	141,707	107,635
Less depreciation	59,806	50,626
Net property, plant, and equipment	81,901	57,009
Other assets	2,490	347
Total assets	285,119	191,771
Liabilities		
Loans payable	3,490	4,830
Accounts payable	27,953	17,892
Income taxes payable	22,010	18,384
Contract progress billings	14,661	10,915
Accrued retirement contributions	19,360	13,558
Accrued expenses	14,343	9,706
Dividends payable	1,262	1,256
Total current liabilities	103,079	76,541
Long-term debt	48,708	3,937
Deferred incentive compensation	1,082	—
Total liabilities	152,869	80,478
Common stock, par value $1 per share	5,058	5,024
Capital surplus	13,669	12,539
Retained earnings	113,523	93,730
Total liabilities and equity	285,119	191,771

$5000 will be made on April 15, 1967. The company has ordered a new stamping press, which is expected to be delivered in April. Payment of $2000 will have to be made in May on this equipment. The balance of $8000 will be paid in July. Depreciation of current equipment is at the rate of $1800 per month. The company has a cash balance (December 31, 1966) of $4000.

5. On the basis of your cash-flow budget, prepare a proforma income statement for Ajax Corporation for the period January 1 through June 30,

1967. Assume a federal tax rate of 50%. Do not begin depreciating the new stamping press during this period. Assume also that raw material purchases made from December, 1966, through May, 1967, are used to manufacture goods sold in the period January to June, 1967.

Case: Basso Semiconductor Corporation

Basso Semiconductor Corporation is a midwest manufacturer of semiconductors and related products. Balance sheets and income statements for 1966 and 1965 (Tables 2-13 to 2-15) show rapid company progress in several areas. The year 1966 resulted in some substantial changes in the working capital position of the company.

Case Questions:

1. Prepare a statement of sources and applications of funds for the company.
2. If expansion continues at the same rate in 1967, what financial problems are likely to occur?

~~~~~~

Chapter Three

Analysis of Financial Statements

One major fact emerges from the discussion in the preceding two chapters. Financial management is an all-encompassing function. Its objective is first to select the pieces of financial information that are relevant to a particular problem and second, to fit these pieces into a coherent picture of the problem in relation to the firm's aims and financial resources. The final objective of financial management is to suggest alternative solutions to the problem.

A major analytical tool is the construction of financial ratios. The financial or accounting statements are expressed in absolute dollar figures. Although they classify the various items under specific headings (for instance, current assets, capitalization, ect.), they do not point up the *relative* importance of these items. This task is aided by the use of ratios.

The Concept of Ratios

Balance sheet items that have a functional relationship are paired and their respective absolute dollar figures are reduced to a proportion or ratio. For example, the current assets provide, in principle, the means with which to meet the current liabilities. By reducing the corresponding dollar figures to a ratio, the financial manager determines that this ratio is, for instance, 2:1. This tells him that the firm has two dollars of current assets for every dollar of current liabilities. Furthermore, it enables him to compare this ratio (2:1) with the ratio prevalent among other firms in the same line of business, regardless of their size, since he compares ratios rather than absolute figures. Moreover, the analyst can also compare easily and effectively changes in this ratio of his firm over a period of time; e.g., the ratio at the end of each of the last four quarters, or years, or any other time interval that he selects.

Every major item in the balance sheet, as well as in the income statement, has a functional relationship to one or more other items. For example, the absolute level of the current assets must be appraised in the light of the immediate need to pay off some of the current liabilities. In practice, therefore, the financial manager examines a series of ratios, not only at a given point of time but also for a series of time intervals. A comparison of absolute figures would be, at best, difficult and confusing whereas ratios are "manageable."

The use of ratio analysis is not confined to the financial manager. The credit officer of a supplier, of a bank, or of other types of lender, the financial analyst of an investing institution, and the experienced investor use ratio analysis as their initial tool in evaluating the firm as a desirable borrower or as a potential investment outlet. Ratio analysis functions as a sort of health test. There is no assurance that the firm, having passed this test, will automatically make good in the future; i.e., meet its obligations as they fall due and operate at a profit. On the other hand, failure to meet this test of past and present performance indicates a strong probability that the firm is not likely to make good in the future. This suggests a need for further analysis in depth.

In a similar vein, the financial manager looks upon ratio analysis as a measuring instrument that shows whether the firm is *at present* financially healthy. However, the fact that the firm passes the health (i.e., ratio) test does not terminate the financial manager's job, even though outsiders may be satisfied. The firm's objective is not merely to be "healthy" but to maximize profits. That means, the financial manager must still explore the feasibility of minimizing the current and prospective cost of using funds and, thus, of maximizing the firm's profitable employment of its own financial resources as well as of those obtained from outside sources. If the firm does not pass the health (ratio) test, the need for further exploration in depth becomes that much more imperative.

The first step in ratio analysis consists of a detailed examination of the data in the financial statements of the firm. In addition to such internal ratio analysis, the financial manager can frequently utilize industry-wide ratios as a yardstick of comparison. The methodology of using these industry statistics and the sources of this information will be taken up in the second and third sections of this chapter. The last section of this chapter examines the use of other internal data of the firm, not contained in the financial statements, which serve as a valuable complement to ratio analysis.

I. TYPES OF RATIOS

The process of ratio analysis involves three steps. First, the financial manager selects from the financial statements—balance sheet and/or income statement—those sets of data that are relevant to his immediate objective. He may be concerned with the *solvency* of the firm; i.e., whether its total assets are equal to, greater than, or less than the obligations of the firm to its creditors. An excess of assets over liabilities constitutes the net worth of the firm and represents the *equity* of its owners. In a corporation, this would be expressed as the book value of the capital stock, paid-in surplus, retained earnings, and various contingency reserves. The ratio of net worth or equity to liabilities plays an important role in the credit rating of the firm.

Or the financial manager may be concerned with the *liquidity* of the firm; i.e., its ability to meet its current obligations to suppliers, banks, and other short-term creditors as these obligations fall due in the near future. In this case, his focus is on the current ratio, which will be discussed in detail in the next pages. Other objectives of the analyst, within or outside the firm, and the relevant ratios will be taken up in subsequent sections.

The second step calls for a comparison of the firm's ratio(s) with those of other firms in its industry or with industry in general. This enables the financial manager to evaluate the relative financial conditions of his firm in terms of the industry and, thus, to determine whether it ranks, on a given ratio test, above or below the industry average.

The third step involves a comparison, both internal and external, over a period of time.

A. Liquidity Ratios

Liquidity is the ability of the firm to meet its current obligations as they fall due. Since liquidity is basic to continuous operation of the firm, it is necessary to determine the degree of liquidity of the firm. In this instance, the financial manager analyzes not one but as many as five sets, or pairs, of ratios. These are known as (1) current ratio; (2) quick ratio or acid-test ratio; (3) cash-position ratio; (4) daily cash-payments ratio; and (5) inventory ratio. Each of these ratios highlights a specific facet of the firm's current level of liquidity.

1. Current Ratio This is a *general* measure of liquidity. It represents the ratio of all current assets to all current liabilities. The arithmetic is simple. Current assets are divided by current liabilities:

$$\text{Current ratio} = \frac{\text{Current assets}}{\text{Current liabilities}}$$

If the result is greater than 1, the firm *presumably* has sufficient current assets to meet its current obligations. For example, a ratio of 2:1 indicates that the firm has two dollars in current assets for every one dollar of current liabilities.

As a barometer of liquidity, the current ratio suffers from two defects. In the first place, it treats all current asset items alike. No distinction is made—in the ratio—between such current assets as cash, receivables, and inventory. As a practical matter, receivables represent a definite fixed dollar amount of claims of the firm against its customers. Barring bankruptcy by the latter, the firm can be reasonably certain of collecting the dollar amounts stated in the item "receivables."

The same is not true of inventory. There is no assurance that these goods will be saleable at some future date for the amount of dollars at which the inventory is shown on the books. Future market conditions and prices are, as a rule, unpredictable. The uncertainty of future price is still more pronounced for that portion of inventory that is partly processed; or, in the case of finished goods, if the goods are subject to seasonal fashion and style changes. On the other hand, cash, whether in the vault of the firm or in a demand deposit with a bank, represents perfect liquidity since it is the medium of exchange. The item "cash equivalent"—consisting of government securities, municipal or state bonds—can be sold at any time in the market, although bonds are subject to some price fluctuations.

The second reason for the inadequacy of the current ratio is to be found in the accountant's treatment of "current." Basically, the accountant will treat an asset, or liability, as current if it matures within the next twelve months. The underlying reason for the selection of this time interval is that the balance sheet is usually an annual statement; although monthly statements are customarily prepared as interim reports.

From the viewpoint of financial management, it is of little consolation to know that the receivables will be collected in 90 days or that the inventory will be sold for cash in six or nine months if the obligations to suppliers will mature in thirty or sixty days. In this type of situation, the firm is technically solvent but it is not liquid, even though the dollar amount of current assets exceed the current liabilities.

It is for the above two reasons that many financial analysts look with suspicion at a current ratio of less than 2:1. This ratio is a so-called rule of thumb. However, in some lines of business, a ratio of 1.5:1 may be highly satisfactory; e.g., the current assets may consist of receivables from leading companies that can be readily financed with a loan from a bank and an inventory that enjoys fairly stable prices and has a high rate of turnover. By the same token, in some lines of business, a ratio of 3:1 or even 5:1 may represent the minimum level of reasonable liquidity.

Many vending machine companies have a current ratio of less than 2:1 and yet enjoy high liquidity. This is explained by the fact that their bills to suppliers are due 30 days after receipt of the merchandise while the latter has a turnover of more than once a month. These companies are, therefore, in a position to sell their merchandise within a few days after receiving it, to collect the proceeds from the vending machines, and to pay their bills within, for instance, 10 days and obtain the customary discount for cash payment.

Current ratios differ not only among industries but also between manufacturers and retailers in the same line of business. This is strikingly illustrated in Table 3-1 which shows the current ratios of the median firms in five selected industries.

Among the manufacturing firms in the five industry groups, the median firm—i.e., the firm that ranked in the middle between the highest and lowest ratios from Dun and Bradstreet in its line of business—had

TABLE 3-1. Current Ratios in Selected Industries

	Manufacturers	Wholesalers	Retailers
Furniture	2.62	2.06	3.19
Lumber and building materials	2.47	2.24	3.72
Shoes	2.19	2.11	3.12
Household appliances	2.65	2.23	2.21
Hardware	2.95	2.98	3.62

Source: *Key Business Ratios* in 125 Lines 1965, Dun and Bradstreet, New York, 1966.

ratios that ranged between 2.19:1 and 2.95:1. Among the retailers in these same five lines of business, the lowest current ratio of a median firm was 2.21 while the highest current ratio was 3.62. It must be emphasized that each of these firms, both in the manufacturing and retailing group, represented a good credit risk.

2. Acid-Test This ratio is sometimes known as the "quick ratio." In this ratio, the inventory is removed from current assets and the remainder is divided by the current liabilitities. Therefore, this ratio shows the proportion of cash, cash equivalents, plus receivables to all current liabilities.

$$\text{Acid-Test Ratio} = \frac{\text{Current Assets minus Inventory}}{\text{Current Liabilities}}$$

In every case, the acid-test ratio will, thus, be smaller than the current ratio. In this analysis, we are ignoring those rare instances in which a firm does not carry any inventory but sells on the basis of samples and, upon receipt of an order, transmits the same to its supplier for direct shipment to the customer. In these special cases, the firm's current assets consist mostly of cash and receivables. Suppose Company A has current assets of $400,000 with an inventory of $250,000. Its current liabilities total $200,000. The current ratio is 2:1 (400,000 ÷ 200,000 However, its acid-test ratio is 0.75:1 ($400,000 — $250,000 ÷ $200,000.)

An acid-test ratio of 1:1 or better generally indicates that the firm will be able to meet its current obligations without depending upon an early sale (for cash) of a portion of its inventory. On the other hand, an acid-test ratio of less than 1:1 often points up the following fact. The firm's inventory must be readily marketable if the current liabilities are to be met at maturity, unless the firm can obtain an extension of the due date from the suppliers or a loan from a financial institution. *In essence, the acid-test ratio is a measure of the firm's dependence on its inventory for liquidity.*

This question of inventory liquidity plays a particularly important role in a line of business that is subject to seasonal variations of a substantial magnitude. In a highly seasonal market, the financial manager must then face this question. How liquid, or nonliquid, is the inventory? That is to say, how stable is the market price for the inventory if it is found necessary to dispose of part or most of it in a few days or weeks? Assume that the inventory of a firm, a retailer in New York, consists of air conditioners, and the analysis is made in January. It will be readily conceded that this retailer is going to find it difficult to liquidate even a portion of his inventory at anything but a very sharp reduction in prices; probably only at a price significantly below his purchase cost. By contrast, assume that the same situation—air conditioners in January—confronts a retailer in southern Florida. In all likelihood, he will have little trouble in selling a portion of this inventory at a modest reduction from the regular retail price.

3. Cash-Position Ratio   This ratio is obtained by subtracting both the inventory and the receivables from the current assets. Cash plus government securities plus other cash equivalents are expressed as a proportion of current liabilities.

$$\text{Cash-Position Ratio} = \frac{\text{Current Assets} - (\text{Receivables} + \text{Inventory})}{\text{Current Liabilities}}$$

or

$$\text{Cash-Position Ratio} = \frac{\text{Cash plus Marketable Securities}}{\text{Current Liabilities}}$$

Realistically, few firms would be expected to, or care to, have a ratio of 1:1. Such a ratio would imply that the firm has enough cash on hand to meet all current liabilities.

The significance of a relatively high, or low, cash-position ratio depends in large measure on the seasonal nature of purchases and sales. Let us first assume that the firm has maintained consistently a cash position ratio of 1:1, or better, throughout the past year. This would indicate that the company had, at all times, enough cash on hand to meet its accounts payable. This high liquidity, in turn, would usually reflect an unwillingness on the part of the firm to maximize the credit available from suppliers, banks, or both and would indicate a relatively unaggressive management.

However, the picture is different if the cash-position ratio is close to or better than 1:1 only over a period of a few weeks or months in the course of the year. Such a situation is, in fact, found in many industries. For example, a company that is subject to strong seasonal changes in sales may show the following variations in the course of the year. In the first quarter of its fiscal year, the firm buys heavily from its suppliers in preparation for the second quarter that represents the peak of its sales during the year. The third quarter shows a seasonal decline in sales and the fourth quarter produces only a modest seasonal volume of business. The cash-position ratio of this firm might show the changes in Table 3-2 in the course of the four quarters.

TABLE 3-2.

	First Quarter	Second Quarter	Third Quarter	Fourth Quarter
Cash	$ 50,000	50,000	150,000	200,000
Inventory	250,000	150,000	100,000	50,000
Receivables	100,000	250,000	150,000	150,000
Liabilities (current)	250,000	200,000	150,000	100,000
Cash-position ratio	0.2:1	0.25:1	1:1	2:1

The above schedule is an over-simplified illustration of the impact of a seasonal product on the cash-position ration. But it is sufficient to point up the function if this ratio. First, it indicates the immediate liquidity position of the firm at a given point of time, e.g., the end of the second quarter. Second, it reflects the dependence of the firm's liquidity position on the prospective volume of business in the next quarter. Suppose the firm's peak sales extend over two quarters rather than over one, i.e., over the second and third quarters. Clearly the company's cash-position ratio would remain below 1:1 for three successive quarters—the build-up of inventory in the first quarter and the heavy volume of sales in the next two quarters—and then go 2:1 in the course of the last quarter.

By the same token, it follows that, in our example, the ratio of 2:1 at the end of the fourth quarter is likely to disappear within the next few months.

The foregoing observations point up sharply an important facet of ratio analysis: no single ratio in itself gives an adequate picture of the liquidity of the firm. Each ratio focuses on a particular facet of the financial components of the firm. The broad picture emerges only after the several ratios have been analyzed separately and are then put together into one overall mosaic of the business.

4. Daily Cash-Payments Ratio   A comparison of the level of cash and near-cash accounts (marketable securities) with average daily cash payments provides another tool of assessing liquidity.

$$\text{Daily Cash Payments Ratio} = \frac{\text{Cash} + \text{Marketable Securities}}{\text{Average Daily Cash Payments}}$$

This ratio can seldom be computed by financial analysts outside the firm since figures for daily-cash outflows are not released by companies. Companies with strong lines of credit with banks or trade creditors can operate with a lower cash balance than can those firms without such reserves in case of unusual cash stringencies. Changes in this ratio may indicate to the financial manager a need to develop lines of credit or to otherwise search for greater liquidity.

5. Net Working Capital   If we subtract current liabilities from current assets, we obtain the *net working capital* of the firm. This represents the funds that the firm has put into its current operations. It does not matter at this point whether these funds have been supplied by the owners or whether a portion, or all of it, has been furnished by long-term creditors in the form of mortgages, mortgage bonds, or debentures. In either event, the amount represented by net working capital can be used by the firm in its current operations without creating a short term liability.

Net Working Capital = Current Assets − Current Liabilities

6. Inventory Ratio   The inventory ratio measures the extent to which the net working capital is financing a current asset item (inventory) which shows generally the least liquidity. Thus, an inventory ratio of less than 1 indicates that the working capital of the firm is greater than the inventory. In this situation, the remainder of the current assets (cash and receivables), including the excess of net working capital over inventory, are available to meet the current liabilities.

The reverse is also true. If the inventory ratio is greater than 1, it follows that (1) a portion of the net working capital is tied up in inventory, and (2) that the excess of inventory over net working capital has been financed by outside sources.

$$\text{Inventory Ratio} = \frac{\text{Inventory}}{\text{Net Working Capital}}$$

$$\text{or} \quad \frac{\text{Inventory}}{\text{Current Assets} - \text{Current Liabilities}}$$

The schedule shown in Table 3-3 illustrates these two situations.

TABLE 3-3.

	Company A	Company B
Current assets		
Cash	$ 50,000	$ 50,000
Receivables	100,000	200,000
Inventory	150,000	50,000
	$300,000	$300,000
Current liabilities		
Payables	$150,000	$150,000
Notes due to banks	50,000	50,000
	$200,000	200,000
Working capital	$100,000	$100,000
Inventory ratio	1.5:1	0.50:1

For the purpose of comparability, assume that both firms are engaged in the same line of business. Company A, with a working capital of $100,000 and an inventory of $150,000, has cash and receivables totalling $150,000 against current liabilities of $200,000. It must therefore reduce (i.e., liquidate) $50,000 worth of inventory to meet its current obligations. On the other hand, Company B has $250,000 in cash and receivables and, thus, it has more than is required to meet its liabilities of $200,000. The working capital of Company B has not only financed its inventory of $50,000 but has supplied $50,000 of funds that went either into cash or receivables or both.

B. Profit Ratios

The income statement of the firm shows the total profit earned during the preceding fiscal period. This profit figure has, however, different meanings to different groups of individuals. Stockholders look upon it as a source of dividends and as a measure of the profitability of their investment in the company. Lenders view the same figure as an indicator of whether or not the firm earns substantially more than it pays in interest for the use of the borrowed funds and whether the ultimate repayment of their credit appears reasonably certain. Suppliers regard it as a clue to the success of the firm in selling its goods at a price in excess of costs. Long-term creditors such as bondholders, in turn, take a somewhat different view. They are concerned with the excess of profits over interest payments as a barometer of the ability of the firm to maintain the stipulated rate of interest on the long-term debt over the lifetime of the debt.

In each of the above mentioned cases, the profit in the income statement of the firm is related to, or paired with, a specific debit item in the balance sheet. This section briefly describes some of these ratios. A more detailed analysis will be given in later chapters.

1. Profit on Sales   This ratio highlights the success of the firm to obtain a price for its products above the total cost of making and/or selling the goods. This ratio represents the net operating margin. As such, it indicates the strength or weakness of the firm's market position as compared with other firms in the industry, at least during the preceding fiscal period.

The ratio of profit to sales plays an important role in two management areas. In the area of financial management, the ratio serves as a valuable indicator of the firm's ability to utilize effectively (i.e., profitably) outside sources of funds. Suppliers and lenders are more readily inclined to extend credit to a company that shows a high profit per dollar of sales than to another company in the same line of business with a less favorable ratio.

The profit ratio also serves as an important tool in shaping the pricing policy of the firm. A high ratio of profit on sales shows that the firm could, if necessary, lower its market price in the next fiscal period and, if sales volume does not decline, still operate at a profit, although the latter would be less than in the preceding period unless the lower prices stimulated demand sufficiently to result in a greater total profit. Conversely, a low profit-on-sales ratio would serve as a warning that even a modest decline in sales might wipe out the prospect for profit. Parenthetically, it should be stressed that a reduction in price, even on an industry-wide basis, does not necessarily mean less profit for the firm. The price cut may be accompanied by a substantial rise in sales. The net effect would be greater total profit although unit profit (i.e., profit per dollar of sales) declines.

2. Profit on New Worth   This ratio shows the rate of profit— after interest payment and taxes—on the equity of the stockholders. A ratio of 10%, for example, means that the firm has earned a net profit of 10 cents for every dollar of equity capital. The stockholder, or a potential investor, then determines whether or not this rate of earnings is adequate, compared with the past performance of the company and of the industry and with other investment alternatives. A refinement of the profit on net worth ratio would be: profit *minus* dividends on preferred stock *divided* by common stock equity *plus* retained earning. This ratio relates the profit available for common stock to the total equity of these stockholders.

Profit on net worth is frequently used as a yardstick of the "maturity" of an industry. Generally, as an industry emerges from its infancy, competition among the early pioneers and from new entries generates a process of price cutting. For example, the computer industry, which had grown at a very fast pace in the 1950s and early 1960s, experienced a wave of price cutting beginning in 1964. As a result, the profits of most companies, old and new, declined sharply. Investment companies and individual large investors suddenly took a more cautious look at the prospective future profits and the value of the stock.

3. Profits on Total Assets   This ratio shows the rate of profit on the total assets of the firm:

$$\text{Profit of Assets Ratio} = \frac{\text{Net Profit after Taxes}}{\text{Total Assets (End of Year)}}$$

This ratio is useful to show the analyst how well the firm employs its assets in the business. It is most significant when comparing different companies in the same industry, as one indication of the ability of management to use assets profitably in the business.

Financial Leverage

Many financial analysts are interested in the relative use of debt and equity in the firm. One way to show the total extent of use of debt is to compare total debt to assets.

$$\text{Debt/Asset Ratio} = \frac{\text{Current Liabilities} + \text{Other Liabilities}}{\text{Total Assets (End of Year)}}$$

Another way of highlighting the relationship between debt and ownership is the net worth to debt ratio.

$$\text{Net Worth to Debt Ratio} = \frac{\text{Total Net Worth}}{\text{Total Debt}}$$

Certain special industries (for instance, railroads and many public utilities) prefer to show debt as a percentage of total capitalization. This ratio is the same as the debt/asset ratio except that current liabilities are deducted from both total debt and total assets as follows:

Debt as a percentage of total capitalization =

$$\frac{\text{Total Debt} - \text{Current Liabilities}}{\text{Total Assets} - \text{Current Liabilities}}$$

Creditors generally prefer as low as possible a percentage of debt to total assets. A company with a debt amounting to 10% of assets could obviously afford a much greater shrinkage of assets in event of liquidation or heavy operating losses in a given year than the company with debt at 75% of assets. Creditors regard assets as a protection against loss.

D. Other Ratios

The accounting records of the firm also provide useful data for the measurement of the company's level of activities. A brief description of these ratios follows.

1. Rate of Turnover   This ratio measures the effectiveness of the firm's sales efforts. Turnover is the number of times that the finished inventory of the campany is sold in the course of the year. The arithmetic calculation involves two steps. First, it calls for the determination of inventory at the start of the year plus the closing inventory at the end of the year divided by two. The second step is to divide this average inventory into total sales or cost of goods for the year.

$$\text{Rate of Turnover} = \frac{\text{Annual Sales}}{(\text{Opening plus Closing Inventory}) \div 2}$$

Some analysts use cost of goods sold instead of annual sales in computing this ratio. Suppose a company's record shows the following data:

Opening Inventory	$ 70,000
Closing Inventory	$ 90,000
Annual Sales	$400,000

Applying the above formula using annual sales, we obtain $400,000 ÷ [(70,000 + 90,000)/2] = 400,000 ÷ 80,000 = an inventory turnover of 5.

The inventory turnover ratio of 5 indicates that it took almost $2\frac{1}{2}$ months for the average inventory to be sold. In other words, the firm's inventory turned over completely five times in the course of the year. This can also be demonstrated by dividing the annual sales of $400,000 by 12 giving average monthly sales of $33,333; and sales in $2\frac{1}{2}$ months of about $80,000 compared with an average inventory of $(70,000 + 90,000 \div 2) = 80,000$.

There is no rule of thumb for the turnover ratio. Each field and kind of business has its own market conditions. For example, in a recent year the median firm in the manufacture of automotive parts and accessories had a turnover rate of 7.3 times compared with 20.3 times for large bakeries, 5.3 times for cotton mills, 26.7 for meat packers, and 4.7 times for drug manufacturers. Among wholesalers, the turnover ratio ranged from as high as 48.3 times (fruits and produce) to a low of 4.3 times for hardware wholesalers.

The turnover ratio is of special significance in a comparative analysis of the performance of the individual firm when measured against its specific industry ratio. It shows whether the firm has been able to do a more effective selling job in the market, with a given volume of inventory, than its competitors. It serves also as a warning of a possible unbalanced or unsaleable inventory position. In either event, it calls for a reevaluation of the firm's inventory policies.

2. Average Collection Period This figure shows the average number of days that elapsed between the receipt of the invoice by customers and the actual payment of the invoice. When measured against the credit term obtained from suppliers, the average collection period shows the length of time during which the firm is financing the accounts receivable either with its own funds or borrowed funds.

The computation of the average collection period requires two steps. In the first step the annual credit sales are divided by 365. This shows the average daily volume of credit sales:

$$\text{Average Daily Credit Sales} = \frac{\text{Annual Credit Sales}}{365}$$

In the next step, the total of accounts and notes receivable, as shown on the balance sheet, is divided by the average credit sales. If the firm received notes from customers and discounted these notes with a bank or finance company, the total of such discounted notes (which is not shown on the balance sheet) must be added to the item of notes receivable.

$$\text{Average Collection Period} = \frac{\text{Accounts + Notes Receivable}}{\text{Average Daily Credit Sales}}$$

The result shows the average number of days that elapsed, in credit sales, between receipt of invoice and payment by customers.

3. Net Sales to Working Capital   This ratio reflects the turnover of the firm's net working capital in the course of the year. The ratio is obtained by dividing net working capital into total sales:

$$\text{Working Capital Turnover} = \frac{\text{Net Annual Sales}}{\text{Net Working Capital}}$$

II. INDUSTRY RATIOS

The ratios shown by a given firm require some standard for evaluation; for example, what does a current ratio of $2:1$ actually mean? Is this ratio high, low, or fair? The answer depends, in large measure, on the market in which the firm sells its product, since the latter determines the price risk of the inventory. It also depends on the quality of its accounts receivable which, in turn, is affected by competition, style and fashion, terms of sale, and other market influences. To make a detailed analysis of these factors would exceed the resources of most companies.

E. Nature of Industry Ratios

Fortunately, in most cases there is no need for such analysis. Several private organizations prepare and publish at regular intervals series of ratios for entire lines of business. These ratios are calculated from representative samples of statements published by firms in these different industries. The data obtained from each firm in a given industry are arranged in a graduated series with the largest ratio at the top and descending to the lowest ratio at the bottom. From this array are then calculated specific positional ratios. Dun and Bradstreet, for instance, use three such positions: (1) the median representing the ratio of the firm above which are as many firms with higher ratios as there are firms below with lower ratios; (2) the upper quartile ratio which represents the firm one-quarter down from the top firm; and (3) the lower quartile which stands for the firm one-quarter above the firm with the bottom or lowest ratio. The three positional ratios provide a useful tool of comparison. Expressed in qualitative terms, the median, for example, may be regarded as satisfactory or fair. Similarly, the upper quartile ratio may be equated with good and the lower quartile with poor. By substituting these qualitative terms for the corresponding industry ratios and projecting the firm's own ratio(s) against these guideposts, the management can assess with reasonable assurance its performance vis-à-vis its competitors.

1. Sources of Industry Ratios   The financial manager can obtain industry ratios from a variety of sources, both private and public.

Dun & Bradstreet is probably the best-known private organization which, in addition to an extensive credit-rating service, publishes annually a series of fourteen ratios covering 125 lines of business activity. These include 72 manufacturing industries, 29 fields of wholesaling, and 24 lines of retail business. Table 3–4 (pages 92–93) illustrates the ratios shown by D & B for some of the 125 lines of business in 1966.

The Accounting Corporation of America publishes twice a year a Barometer of Small Business which supplies the major financial ratios of small firms in 51 lines of business, broken down into groups such as food, apparel, automotive, building materials, etc.

Robert Morris Associates, a national association of bank loan officers, publishes for its members an annual Statement Studies. These contain calculations of eleven ratios for over 150 lines of business. Unlike the ratios published by the Accounting Corporation, those compiled by Robert Morris Associates are focused primarily on the larger firms.

Larger trade associations also compile and distribute to their members ratio information for their respective industries. Unlike the sources previously mentioned, a trade association confines itself to its own specific line of business. Such information is particularly useful to the financial manager in those cases in which the association provides not only the ratios but also valuable background comments and explanations.

In addition to the private sources, the financial manager also has available the periodic publications of various governmental agencies which provide useful general financial data about corporations. A widely used source of the information is supplied by the joint quarterly publication of the Federal Trade Commission and the Securities and Exchange Commission.

2. How to Use Industry Ratios   Whether the financial manager is analyzing three, ten, or more ratios of his firm depends on the objectives that he has in mind. Since each ratio, or group of ratios, deals with a specific facet of the firm, the financial manager will, in the course of time, have occasion to make a periodic comprehensive study of more rather than fewer ratios. In either case, the methodology of comparing a specific series of ratios with those of the industry is the same. In the following illustration, we shall assume that the financial manager is, at the moment, concerned with the question of liquidity. Accordingly, he has calculated for his firm the following ratios:

Current Ratio	2:1
Acid Test	1:1
Cash Position	0.50:1
Inventory to Working Capital	1.50:1

Consulting one or more of the several sources previously mentioned, he then records the ratios for the industry and those of the firm (Table 3-5).

TABLE 3-5.   Comparison of Firms and Industry Ratios

Ratios	Position	Industry	Firm
Current	Upper quartile	3.2:1	
	Median	2.1:1	2:1
	Lower quartile	1.4:1	
Acid test	Upper quartile	1.1:1	1:1
	Median	0.7:1	
	Lower quartile	0.5:1	
Cash position	Upper quartile	0.8:1	
	Median	0.5:1	0.5:1
	Lower quartile	0.3:1	
Inventory	Upper quartile	0.5:1	
	Median	1.0:1	
	Lower quartile	1.5:1	1.5:1

A comparison of the last two columns points up the following facts. In one of the four tests (acid test), the firm ranks close to the upper quartile. In two tests, it stands in a median position and, in the fourth ratio, it ranks with the lower quartile. The first and immediate conclusion is that some effort should be made to rectify the weakness revealed in the inventory ratio. Conceivably, this may be a temporary situation

Table 3-4. Selected Business Ratios[a]

RETAILING

Line of Business (and number of concerns reporting)	Current Assets to Current Debt	Net Profits on Net Sales	Net Profits on Tangible Net Worth	Net Profits on Net Working Capital	Net Sales to Tangible Net Worth	Net Sales to Net Working Capital	Collection Period	Net Sales to Inventory	Fixed Assets to Tangible Net Worth	Current Debt to Tangible Net Worth	Total Debt to Tangible Net Worth	Inventory to Net Working Capital	Current Debt to Inventory	Funded Debts to Net Working Capital
	Times	Percent	Percent	Percent	Times	Times	Days	Times	Percent	Percent	Percent	Percent	Percent	Percent
5511 Automobile Dealers (127)	2.37	2.03	18.49	26.86	13.65	18.84	*	10.6	7.8	47.0	94.3	104.7	70.2	11.8
	1.77	1.17	8.93	14.02	8.89	14.20	*	8.0	19.5	93.3	144.6	151.6	86.5	34.0
	1.47	0.60	5.33	7.88	5.50	8.72	*	6.5	41.5	145.8	214.1	223.7	95.6	63.4
5311 Department Stores (205)	5.46	3.37	12.58	15.88	4.38	5.74	*	6.9	10.6	17.7	45.9	56.7	35.8	13.5
	3.16	2.33	6.94	8.67	2.97	3.85	*	5.4	22.3	33.5	72.7	73.9	66.8	32.3
	2.17	1.25	3.82	4.39	2.24	2.93	*	4.0	44.8	58.3	125.6	103.1	93.6	60.5
Discount Stores (145)	2.39	2.73	19.80	26.37	10.86	14.29	*	4.6	12.2	58.3	96.8	118.9	58.7	13.3
	1.73	1.90	12.96	15.60	7.40	8.95	*	5.3	25.5	116.8	173.0	198.0	76.8	33.4
	1.40	0.81	7.99	10.20	4.57	5.49	*	3.7	52.8	189.0	284.4	244.8	102.8	73.7
5712 Furniture (191)	5.90	5.25	11.12	11.69	4.25	5.05	53	6.7	4.7	19.5	46.5	31.8	53.0	10.3
	2.87	2.87	7.21	7.93	2.32	2.49	124	4.8	11.0	47.4	92.4	60.7	90.8	28.7
	1.90	1.26	3.28	3.77	1.50	1.52	220	3.5	29.4	97.7	183.8	108.5	151.4	48.8
5541 Gasoline Service Stations (71)	3.59	5.49	15.12	38.84	5.15	9.19	*	20.4	30.0	15.9	44.9	45.0	68.2	23.8
	2.20	2.68	9.85	25.01	3.34	6.59	*	10.7	47.0	32.8	74.5	70.3	100.6	50.7
	1.61	1.36	4.99	10.06	2.16	4.64	*	5.4	67.0	62.0	104.3	117.0	182.3	102.4
5211 Lumber Yards (136)	8.05	3.48	8.30	11.10	3.57	4.55	41	4.6	11.7	13.2	38.3	48.7	25.5	7.4
	4.28	1.57	4.97	5.76	2.28	3.06	58	3.5	19.6	23.6	66.0	67.5	55.3	22.2
	2.42	0.47	1.12	1.26	1.70	2.03	78	3.5	33.6	57.9	110.0	87.7	96.3	39.8
5722 Household Appliances (96)	2.93	3.59	14.04	20.24	6.90	10.60	22	8.6	6.4	41.4	57.0	62.0	71.9	8.0
	2.05	1.89	8.68	10.41	4.29	5.96	39	5.9	17.2	71.2	113.0	101.2	101.5	27.7
	1.57	0.87	3.99	6.31	2.89	3.87	60	4.3	36.9	119.2	258.8	146.4	134.5	52.7

WHOLESALING

Line of Business (and number of concerns reporting)	Current Assets to Current Debt	Net Profits on Net Sales	Net Profits on Tangible Net Worth	Net Profits on Net Working Capital	Net Sales to Tangible Net Worth	Net Sales to Net Working Capital	Collection Period	Net Sales to Inventory	Fixed Assets to Tangible Net Worth	Current Debt to Tangible Net Worth	Total Debt to Tangible Net Worth	Inventory to Net Working Capital	Current Debt to Inventory	Funded Debts to Net Working Capital
	Times	Percent	Percent	Percent	Times	Times	Days	Times	Percent	Percent	Percent	Percent	Percent	Percent
5022 Drugs & Drug Sundries (111)	3.42	2.81	14.85	19.58	8.66	9.22	27	8.2	5.8	38.4	68.5	72.5	61.5	16.2
	2.33	1.34	9.16	11.06	5.88	6.38	36	7.0	13.9	63.3	117.2	93.3	82.0	27.6
	1.71	0.68	4.79	5.35	4.03	4.73	48	5.5	31.0	116.9	189.2	135.4	109.1	49.9
5032 Dry Goods (134)	3.24	1.96	14.89	15.41	9.36	10.67	25	8.1	2.0	39.6	88.9	66.6	61.4	14.8
	2.06	1.21	6.95	7.94	5.40	5.65	44	6.1	5.2	93.5	131.8	97.9	92.3	26.2
	1.51	0.33	3.13	3.24	3.48	3.53	64	4.7	10.2	177.5	226.5	152.3	134.5	41.5
5062-63 Electrical Parts & Supplies (157)	2.80	2.89	17.46	19.36	8.52	9.97	34	10.0	4.2	49.2	85.8	85.9	77.1	13.4
	2.08	1.57	10.83	11.52	6.04	6.65	43	7.3	10.5	81.0	146.5	64.9	108.0	21.4
	1.65	1.00	5.44	6.55	4.17	4.69	56	5.4	22.7	144.3	219.8	115.8	150.0	42.7

The following table presents three sets of figures for each group of ratios in each industry (top = upper quartile, center = median, bottom = lower quartile). The 14 ratio columns are numbered 1–14 for reference; no column headings are printed on this page.

Industry	1	2	3	4	5	6	7	8	9	10	11	12	13	14
5065 Electronic Parts & Equip. (56)	3.24	4.55	16.15	16.21	6.85	7.86	33	5.2	5.5	44.2	73.5	88.6	50.5	7.9
	2.34	2.97	11.09	11.35	4.43	4.46	42	4.0	11.3	74.5	124.5	102.7	67.6	33.8
	1.69	1.73	7.95	8.03	3.03	3.33	53	3.4	27.4	118.7	173.8	149.5	97.2	48.2
5083 Farm Machinery & Equipment (55)	3.78	3.56	15.72	23.38	6.62	6.81	30	6.7	6.2	32.1	46.6	67.7	47.2	9.3
	2.48	1.73	8.65	10.52	4.07	5.40	45	5.5	12.9	54.6	89.3	94.4	77.0	20.6
	1.76	0.95	4.69	4.86	3.07	3.54	65	4.1	32.3	88.4	136.3	136.2	104.8	38.7
5098 Lumber & Bldg. Materials (166)	4.47	2.70	12.01	17.40	7.17	9.62	32	11.7	10.5	21.1	58.1	57.7	46.8	9.2
	2.54	1.53	8.56	7.75	4.40	6.05	44	7.0	21.6	52.0	103.0	88.7	89.2	28.2
	1.71	0.67	4.36	3.18	2.83	3.63	60	4.7	42.4	102.6	151.2	118.8	139.0	49.0
5092 Petroleum Products (81)	2.84	4.17	34.22	21.27	4.02	14.08	22	34.9	27.7	21.8	42.5	28.0	110.8	24.0
	2.09	1.81	15.26	8.85	2.58	8.65	33	19.0	53.6	42.2	77.9	47.8	191.9	48.0
	1.44	0.92	8.52	4.34	1.92	5.80	53	11.2	92.6	66.2	172.1	79.1	335.3	134.0
5095 Wines & Liquors (86)	3.08	1.93	16.34	27.23	10.92	17.81	9	14.6	5.0	31.2	75.5	78.4	62.0	9.8
	2.23	0.80	7.68	10.23	7.40	10.61	21	9.4	15.1	65.5	159.0	99.2	90.7	29.3
	1.52	0.45	3.76	5.37	5.32	7.33	41	6.7	32.3	140.3	294.7	164.5	141.1	82.8

MANUFACTURING AND CONSTRUCTION

Industry	1	2	3	4	5	6	7	8	9	10	11	12	13	14
3714 Automobile Parts & Accessories (84)	3.77	6.75	18.89	32.11	3.89	6.54	35	8.0	25.7	23.5	47.3	60.5	56.5	14.6
	2.58	4.59	14.60	20.32	2.99	4.63	42	5.3	39.6	38.0	77.8	86.2	79.7	41.6
	2.03	3.22	8.65	14.09	2.19	3.23	51	4.2	55.5	63.4	116.9	100.5	113.7	59.9
2331 Blouses & Waists (72)	2.24	1.78	14.88	19.29	13.56	15.09	28	19.8	3.1	70.5	102.4	56.8	112.4	3.5
	1.77	0.78	8.63	11.91	9.03	10.80	37	11.8	7.8	105.0	133.1	83.1	152.2	16.3
	1.46	0.19	1.47	3.56	6.47	7.51	47	8.0	14.3	177.9	187.3	121.7	241.2	30.5
3712-13 Bodies: Auto, Bus & Truck (41)	4.84	3.62	13.63	20.31	6.47	7.06	32	9.6	17.0	16.2	56.9	55.5	49.7	17.7
	2.32	2.77	7.75	13.20	5.06	5.33	43	6.8	37.9	50.4	91.2	88.6	94.1	33.5
	1.69	1.34	5.35	7.33	3.89	3.33	53	4.0	56.1	110.7	139.9	144.1	127.0	55.5
2851 Paints, Varnishes & Lacquers (127)	5.03	5.41	16.05	26.72	3.87	6.16	33	8.8	18.6	16.7	31.4	47.8	42.6	7.2
	3.25	3.07	9.81	17.52	2.57	4.57	41	6.9	32.3	26.9	55.4	66.5	74.4	19.7
	2.21	1.22	4.28	6.49	2.07	3.16	53	5.3	46.8	42.4	83.9	89.2	107.5	57.0
264 Paper Products, Converters (51)	3.85	6.05	17.26	31.29	4.66	8.59	27	11.7	34.3	21.2	37.7	56.0	65.9	23.0
	2.44	4.48	13.51	25.08	2.68	4.93	40	6.9	53.3	33.5	75.4	71.8	97.4	50.8
	1.58	2.89	9.13	11.75	2.10	3.79	49	5.6	75.9	72.6	126.2	128.3	126.4	90.3
2911 Petroleum Refining (62)	1.83	7.56	13.35	60.23	3.16	13.94	24	24.5	10.9	10.9	8.5	62.2	100.0	83.4
	1.37	4.63	8.86	28.56	1.77	6.96	41	11.5	51.5	31.9	46.7	93.5	132.8	149.9
	1.00	2.05	4.54	12.82	1.15	5.74	53	8.0	96.1	52.0	93.2	137.8	209.5	197.2
3811 Scientific Instruments (39)	4.74	6.31	19.67	35.36	3.75	4.68	38	6.5	15.4	20.9	57.0	51.8	50.7	22.4
	2.93	4.61	12.41	17.18	2.48	3.15	51	4.4	32.6	44.5	89.8	79.6	70.5	45.4
	2.24	1.69	5.84	7.78	1.95	2.36	77	3.2	53.8	73.0	231.7	117.2	109.3	96.5

a In the ratio tables each group of ratios in each industry carries three sets of figures. The top figure is the upper quartile, the center figure is the median, and the bottom figure is the lower quartile. They are calculated as follows: Year-end financial statements are selected from a sampling of corporations whose tangible net worth, with few exceptions, exceed $35,000. The financial statements are those appearing in the Dun & Bradstreet credit reports on these businesses. Statement copies are referred to statisticians who compute each of the "14 Ratios" on each of the concerns. The ratios are then punched on data processing cards, and arranged into industry groups. After this, ratio figures are arranged so that the best ratio figure is at the top, the weakest at the bottom. The figure which falls just in the middle of this series becomes the median for that ratio in that line of business. The figure halfway between the median and the highest term of the series is the upper quartile; and the term halfway between the median and the bottom of the series is the lower quartile. The purpose of these interquartile ranges is to show an upper and lower limit area without reflecting the extremes either at the top or the bottom of the series. After the first of the "14 Ratios" has been compiled for a particular industry, the identical process is followed for the remaining 13 ratios in this industry group, and then for remaining industry groups.

Source: Dun and Bradstreet, Inc. Key Business Ratios in 125 lines; 1966.

that is expected to remedy itself in the near future. Perhaps special circumstances confronting this firm account for the high inventory ratio. Whatever the reasons or circumstances, the financial manager must ascertain the facts that lie behind this ratio.

The examples of the inventory ratio demonstrates both the usefulness and the limitation of ratio analysis. Its usefulness to management lies in the following fact. In the case of inventory, its composition (raw materials, semifinished goods, finished goods) and size ordinarily reflect the estimated requirements of the production and/or sales departments. Suppose management were to confine itself merely to an examination of whether or not the inventory is in excess of these requirements. Assume that this analysis reveals no excessive inventory. Does this automatically mean that the firm faces no inventory problem? From the viewpoint of the firm's overall liquidity, the answer in the present case is that such a problem may exist. Thus, the ratio analysis puts into focus the relationship of a particular asset or liability (in this instance, it is inventory) to the liquidity of the firm.

On the other hand, ratio analysis does not indicate how this situation has arisen, whether it represents a temporary imbalance, and what, if any, remedies can be applied. To answer these questions, the ratio analysis must be followed by a probe in depth. That is to say, the financial manager must proceed with a detailed examination of the composition and size of the inventory, the purchasing policy of the firm, its sales program, and other related factors. These questions will be covered in Chapter Six.

In summary, the financial manager's diagnosis of the several ratios serves two useful purposes. First, it becomes a useful gauge in measuring the need for an examination of inventory policy. And, second, it enables the firm to explain to the loan officer of a bank, or to the credit manager of a supplier, either the temporary nature of an unfavorable ratio, compared with that of the industry, or the remedial steps that the firm plans to initiate.

In the above example, a series of four ratios was used. At times, the financial manager may find it desirable to include in a comparison not four but seven, ten, or more ratios. In either event, he is then confronted by a basic question that arises whenever a series composed of several ratios is compared. The question may be stated as follows: Is each ratio of the same importance as the others? If the answer is negative, the analyst must attach greater importance to those ratios that he regards as more significant. This is known in statistics as the assignment of relative weights to each item in the series. Applying this principle to our example, the financial manager will assign to each ratio a weight-factor that reflects its relative importance within the series of ratios that he analyses.

An analysis of a series of ratios, even if weighted, is usually a cumbersome task, since the analyst must constantly bear in mind the individual weights. There is always the risk that the analyst may lose sight of the forest as a whole because he is checking the individual trees. To overcome this risk the device of a composite index—*the ratio index*—can be used effectively in a comparative ratio analysis.

F. The Ratio Index

The objective of this index is to present, in a single figure, the *ratio profile* of the firm as compared with that of the industry. With the aid of this tool, the financial manager can obtain a yardstick with which to measure the *overall* financial health of the company. His analysis then involves three phases. In the first phase, the financial manager compares the ratio profile of the firm either with that of the industry, or with that of the firm itself over a period of time, or with both, industry and firm, over a period of time. The second phase involves an examination of the individual components of the profile. And the final phase is the internal probe in depth previously mentioned.

1. Determination of Weights   The allocation of degrees of relative importance to each of the several ratios in the index is essentially a matter of judgment. Suppose the index to be constructed is made up of the four ratios: current ratio, quick ratio, cash position, and inventory ratio. Their combined importance, or weight, is 1 or 100%. How much of the 100% should be assigned to the current ratio? Or to the inventory ratio?

The answer to this question of weight allocation will differ among lines of business and also between manufacturers, wholesalers, and retailers in a particular line of business. Moreover, this allocation involves qualitative rather than quantitative determination. In the case of a price index, it is possible to determine the weight of each product price by using the quantities of such products purchased during a fixed period of time, e.g., the base period of the index.

The financial manager has no simple quantitative yardstick, as in the case of the price index, by which to measure the relative weights of the several financial ratios. Instead, he must rely largely on personal subjective judgment. One of the factors to be considered is the past-experience record of the firm in regard to the liquidity, first, of receivables and, second, of inventory. The acid-test ratio—consisting of cash plus receivables divided by current liabilities—plays an important role. The primary importance of the receivables as a source of liquidity is not diminished by the fact that, for example, the receivables total $150,000 and inventory amounts to $200,000.

Let us assume that the financial manager allocates the largest single weight to the acid-test ratio, next, to inventory, and so forth, with the result that he gives to the four ratios, which together measure liquidity, the following weights: current ratio: 10; acid-test ratio: 40; cash position: 20; inventory ratio: 30; or a total of 100%.

2. Construction of the Index   The next step calls for the evaluation of the several positional ratios of the industry. In allocating a value, or weight, to each of the three positions, the top value clearly must go to the firm ranked as the upper quartile, with a lower value to the median, and the lowest value to the firm in the lower quartile position. This allocation can be on the basis of 75, 50, and 25 points, respectively, out of a possible perfect score of 100 for the (unknown) best firm. In turn, the figures 75, 50, and 25 can be expressed as 0.75, 0.50, and 0.25. Or, the financial manager can value the upper quartile firm at 1.0—representing the "norm" of a financially well managed firm—with a score of 0.70 for the median, and 0.5 for the lower quartile firm. This scoring system has been used in Table 3-6.

The ratios shown in the first line of each group are the same as those in Table 3-5. The weight of each ratio is the same for every firm whatever its rank (upper or lower quartile). The positional value of the three industry firms remains unchanged. However, the positional value for each ratio of Firm X is calculated by interpolation. For example, the firm's current ratio (2:1) is slightly below that of the median firm (2:1:1). Since the latter has a positional value of 0.7, the value of 2:1 is slightly lower (0.67).

When adding the weight-position figures for each group, it will be noted that the upper quartile firm had a rating of 100 while Firm X rated 72.5 or moderately above the level of the median company.

What does the index figure of 72.5 for this firm convey to the financial manager? In the first place, it points up the firm's overall liquidity position in relation to the industry. Top management can quickly identify

Table 3-6.   A Weighted Ratio Index

| | Industry | | | |
	Upper Quartile	Median	Lower Quartile	Firm X
Current ratio	3.2:1	2.1:1	1.4:1	2:1
Weight	10	10	10	10
Positional value	1	0.7	0.5	0.67
Weight position	10	7	5	6.7
Acid test	1.1:1	0.7:1	0.5:1	1:1
Weight	40	40	40	40
Positional value	1	0.7	0.5	0.92
Weight position	40	28	20	36.8
Cash position	0.8:1	0.5:1	0.3:1	0.5:1
Weight	20	20	20	20
Positional value	1.0	0.7	0.5	0.7
Weight position	20	14	10	14.0
Inventory ratio	0.5:1	1.0:1	1.5:1	1.5:1
Weight	30	30	30	30
Positional value	1.0	0.7	0.5	0.5
Weight position	30	21	15	15.0
Index	100	70	50	72.5

its *liquidity profile* as being slightly better than that of the median firm but significantly below that of the upper quartile firm. Or, to put it differently, top management may conclude: "We are, generally, in a better liquidity position than over 50% of all firms. However, close to 50% of all firms show a better liquidity profile than we have. Where do we fall down?"

To answer the last question, the financial manager then proceeds to an examination of the individual ratios in the index. For this purpose, he compares, horizontally, the figures in the last row of each ratio. Thus, in checking the current ratio, he finds that his company scored 6.7, compared with 7.0 for the median firm and 10 for the upper quartile company. In this instance, his firm did not even equal the median. He does the same with the three other ratios. As a result, the financial manager can pinpoint the weakness(es) of the firm both in terms of a particular ratio as well as in terms of the relative importance of a given ratio. Again, looking at Table 3-6, it will be seen that the firm's cash position which had the largest single weight came rather close to that of the upper quartile firm. On the next important ratio, inventory, the firm only equalled the performance of the median firm.

The usefulness of the index increases with the number of ratios that are included in the analysis. While it is not too difficult to make comparisons of three or four ratios, the task becomes quite complex with eight or more. A composite index then serves as a major guidepost to the financial evaluation of the firm.

3. Trend Analysis Up to this point, the discussion was confined to the use of ratio analysis on the basis of the most recent financial statements of both the firm and the industry. But time does not stand still. Nor does the individual firm maintain the same relationships between the different components that make up the several ratios. For example, the ratio of inventory to total current assets will hardly remain unchanged over a period of years or even a week, for that matter. Similarly, the proportion of working capital to receivables will either go up or down in successive years. In general, it can be stated that the change in the percentage of one item is more likely than not to be accompanied by percentage, or ratio, changes in several other items. Thus, the ratios for several series or groups of paired items will show variations over a period of time.

A similar situation exists in the industry at large. To some extent, this is the result of the business cycle. In part, it is the consequence of technological innovations, the development of new raw materials or finished products, shifts in the buying habits of consumers, opening of new markets, and other forces that make for a dynamic economic society.

a. Usefulness. Changes in the ratios which have occurred over the past few years are more than a mere measure of past performance. Quite frequently, they are also indicative of a trend within the firm and the industry. By examining the changes over a period of time, the analyst may discover that there is a distinct pattern, or direction, of change. For example, the acid-test ratio may have become progressively smaller in each of the last three years. Does this trend reflect a pattern of sales to customers who are less and less prompt in making payments? Is management aware of this fact? What will happen to the firm next year if it permits this trend to continue? Will it be able to stand this strain on its current resources? And what has happened to the competitors? Have they been exposed to the same trend? And if so, to what extent; i.e., as much as or less than our firm?

A trend analysis covering a period of years will point up to the financial manager (1) whether the firm has been able to improve its financial conditions relative to other firms in the same line of business; (2) the degree to which the firm's position has moved up or down; and (3) whether and to what extent specific components of the index have grown better or worse.

b. Construction of Composite Index.   To make this trend analysis, the financial manager first constructs a series of annual composite indices. He then sets up a second summary schedule as illustrated in Table 3-7.

Each figure in the above table represents the weighted positional value of the firm at the end of a given year. The figures in the last column (Year Four) are the same as those in the last column of Table 3-6. The annual composite index shows that the firm's overall liquidity position moved up significantly in Years Two and Three but dropped sharply in Year Four. Looking then at the individual ratios, the financial manager discovers that the decline in the inventory ratio was the major cause. The acid test ratio, on the other hand, shows a steady improvement over the four-year span. The current ratio and the cash-position ratio went down moderately but still merit some attention. However, it is the inventory ratio that calls for close scrutiny.

The financial manager next turns to the worksheet for each of the four years. These worksheets are similar to Table 3-6. In this case, the worksheet (see Table 3-6) for Year Four shows that the upper quartile firm had an inventory ratio of 0.50:1 compared with, our firm's ratio of 1.5:1. By looking next at the worksheet for Year Three, the financial

TABLE 3-7.   Trend of Composite Ratio Index

	Year One	Year Two	Year Three	Year Four
Current ratio	7.5	8.2	7.1	6.7
Acid test	29.5	32.5	33.5	36.8
Cash position	15.0	16.0	16.0	14.0
Inventory ratio	20.0	27.0	30.0	21.0
Composite index	72.0	83.7	86.6	78.5

manager can determine the respective inventory ratios of the upper quartile firm and of our firm. Suppose, for example, that the figures in Year Three were 1.2:1 for the upper quartile and 1.2:1 for our firm. In that case, our firm had a rating of 30 points on this item. Now in Year Four, the upper quartile improved its ratio to 0.5:1 while our firm had the opposite experience, a rise to 1.5:1.

III. PROBING IN DEPTH

Ratio analysis provides a coordinated frame of reference for the financial manager. It furnishes an overview of the dynamic relationships between the several components that make up the financial performance record of the firm. It reveals existing imbalances and weaknesses in the financial structure of the business and, when viewed over a period of time, whether these adverse conditions have worsened or improved. However, it must be borne in mind that the ratio analysis only provides an overview. As such, it serves as a point of departure for an examination in depth of those components that reflect a significant degree of weakness.

A. The Problem

The financial statements show the total dollar amounts for the various categories. In the case of the item "cash," there is no room for difference of opinion. It does not matter whether the firm has ten $100 bills, fifty $20 notes, or one hundred $10 notes, or a bank balance of $1000. The sum is always $1000 and each of these units is equally liquid.

The same is not true of the noncash items. The units that make up the aggregate of a balance sheet item are usually not homogeneous. For example, the statement shows that the accounts receivable totaled a certain sum of dollars. Suppose that, in a given case, these receivables are due from governmental bodies, department stores, and small retail firms. In terms of credit risk, these receivables are anything but uniform or homogeneous. Some of these customers, like governmental bodies, represent practically no credit risk, while the smaller retailer's account involves some degree of risk. Qualitatively, therefore, the receivables are heterogeneous. As a consequence, the ability of the firm to obtain, for example, a bank loan against its receivables will depend in large measure on the quality of the receivables.

Let us consider another item: the average collection period. Suppose the ratio shows an average collection period of 60 days while the terms of sale call for payment 30 days after receipt of the merchandise. Does the 60-day interval indicate that many or most customers are poor credit risks? Superficially, this would seem to be the fact. As will be shown later in this section, such is frequently not the case.

Another example is the item inventory. The balance sheet typically shows the dollar value of the inventory calculated by the accountant on the basis of invoice price or market price, whichever is lower. Suppose the inventory consists of raw materials, components in various stages of completion, and finished goods, some of which are subject to seasonal market forces while others are closely tied to rapidly changing fashions. One portion of the inventory, finished or unfinished, is exposed to keen competition in price, while another portion enjoys reasonable stability of price. While the accountant does not look beyond the closing date of the fiscal period that is covered by the statement, the financial manager must look ahead. In doing so, he may be aware of the fact that a portion of the inventory—if the company is heavily overstocked—may have to be sold in the near future below the dollar value at which it is carried on the books and at less than the present market value. Of course, this future event will not affect the profit (or loss) for the *past* fiscal period. Therefore, the accountant is correct insofar as the past is concerned. But the financial manager must plan for the impending future. Viewed from the perspective of things to come he must, therefore, reappraise the inventory in terms of probable market value in the next fiscal period when the inventory must be sold. A similar situation exists in regard to most other items both among the assets and the liabilities.

Basically, the financial manager is confronted by the following question: Is the *quality* of the individual item in the financial statements of such a calibre that the quantity (dollar figure) shown by the accountant is a true reflection of the future liquidity and money value of the item?

Significance   The technique of an analysis or probe in depth will be illustrated in conjunction with the item "earnings" or profit. But before proceeding with this demonstration, it is necessary to emphasize strongly the following point. A depth analysis of each category or major item in the financial statement plays a major role in financial management. It brings to the surface weaknesses and strengths of the firm's operations that must be faced by top management since they affect either the current or future financial health of the company. Without this information at its disposal, top management is not in a position to formulate financial plans that will maximize profits and preserve the firm's financial liquidity.

Attention must also be called to the fact that the methodology of a probe in depth is not the same for all items in the financial statements. The relevant technique or methodology applicable to a particular item will be discussed in the following chapter, which deals in detail with the several components of the current assets. In this manner, the technique will be treated as an integral part of the financial manager's analysis of the item—for example, inventory, receivables, machinery, plant—and the selection of the best alternative for financing this particular facet of the firm's operations.

B. The Basic Approach

The financial manager's approach to a depth analysis can be illustrated, using the item "receivables."

Although receivables are customarily regarded as a liquid item, it is, at the same time, recognized that an account receivable is not actually liquidated—i.e., cash—until the amount due is paid by the customer. In the interval, an account receivable represents a claim that is *expected* to become liquid in the near future, either on or shortly after the expiration of the credit term.

From the viewpoint of the financial manager, the liquidity of receivables—i.e., the receipt of payment on the due date of the invoice—depends on (a) the credit risk of the account(s), and (b) whether the individual account has a record of paying its bills as they fall due. Some purchasers, in spite of top credit rating, are notoriously "slow" payers of bills. Large municipalities frequently fall into this category. This is also true of some branches of the federal government and of many state governments. The reason is simple. Orders are placed and the goods are received by a political subdivision that was authorized to make these purchases. When the invoice is received, it must pass through a maze of bureaus before the paying officer finally gets around to approve payment. It then returns to the "assembly line" in the disbursement office where the check is processed. Similar delays also occur in some large private corporations and in many nonprofit institutions.

The net effect is that, on the record at least, the *average* collection period on such accounts may appear unduly long. On the books, these receivables will show up as "overdue" and, thus, appear to have a doubt-ful liquidity value. An overdue receivable generally implies a poor credit risk; the customer seems to have some difficulty in meeting his obliga-tions. Yet these accounts receivable enjoy a high liquidity rating. This paradox is explained by the fact that the financial manager has less trouble in "discounting" these receivables; i.e., borrowing from a bank against these accounts at the same or at lower interest rates than the lender charges for a loan against receivables from private firms that pay on time.

In order to obtain a realistic picture of the quality of receivables, the financial manager, therefore, must analyze the internal sales records of the firm. Accounts are then classified by (1) type of accounts, for instance, government (federal, state, municipal), institutional customers, manufacturers, commercial firms, etc.; and (2) collection period or range of days between date of billing and date of payment for each type of account. The details of this type of breakdown and its interpreta-tion by the financial manager will be presented in the next chapter, which deals with the problem of receivables.

1. Profit: A Probe in Depth   The income statement of the firm shows the earnings, both before and after taxes, reported at the close of the fiscal period. Profit, or loss, is the *result* of performance. As shown in the income statement, the earnings reflect the aggregate performance of the firm. However, from the viewpoint of top management, and bear-ing in mind its objective of maximizing profits, it is not enough to know that the total profit for the past fiscal period was satisfactory. It is equally important for top management to know whether each group of products has earned a profit.

The depth probe of earnings, therefore, serves two purposes. First, it reveals the rate of profit earned on each group of items that, together, make up the firm's product line. Usually, it will be found that there exists a considerable range of profit per dollar of sale among the several items.

Many of the larger discount stores operate on the principle of con-centrating on low markup items only. Some food chains are periodically featuring loss-leaders. Most department stores carry a great variety of items in order to offer maximum selectivity to customers. Manufacturing companies, too, may choose one of these alternatives as a matter of policy. It then becomes a matter of company policy to decide whether (a) to shift sales efforts to the more profitable lines, (b) to discontinue the low-profit items, (c) to carry some items as loss-leaders as a means of attracting customers to the more profitable items, or (d) to carry low-profit items as a service to customers who will, thus, have a full line from which to chose. The composite of the company's sales strategies, in any case, must yield an appropriate return.

2. A Brief Case History   Company L. W. started with the manufacture of one product: aluminum windows. Its product line initially consisted of two items: a medium-priced and a low-priced window. In the second year, a third item was added: high-priced, custom-made windows. Other items were added in subsequent years. The firm's price policy was to charge as much as it believed the traffic would bear. Whenever it introduced a new item ahead of its competitors, the firm would add a substantial profit margin to its cost of production. As soon as competition caught up with the new item, the firm would cut the price to meet the lower price quoted by competitors.

Every addition of a new item, or the introduction of an item of better quality and higher price, resulted in a shift in the relative importance of each item in total sales. For example, the two items aluminum windows constituted 100% of total sales in the first year of operations. In the last year, they accounted for only 10% of total sales, although the absolute dollar volume of windows sold in the last year was greater than in the first year.

a. The Breakdown.   Table 3-8 shows the breakdown of the firm's product line and profit makeup during a period of six years.

The figures in column 1 were obtained from the sales records of the firm; column 2 was derived from the selling price of the individual item minus the total unit cost of the item as shown in the cost accountant's calculations by item produced. The figures in column 4 were obtained by multiplying, for each period, columns 1 and 2 and then averaging the total. For example, in March, 1958 there were two items. Thus, the average profit per dollar of sale was $(15¢ \times 0.6 + 12¢ \times 0.4) = 13.8¢$. For January, 1959, the average profit was $(10¢ \times 0.40 + 12¢ \times 0.40 + 12¢ \times 20) = 11.2¢$. Column 3 involved the following step. Multiply the figures in columns 1 and 2 and express the total as a percentage of the figure in column 4. For instance, in March, 1958, for the low-price window: $(15 \times 0.60) \div 13.8 = 9 \div 13.8 = 65.2\%$ and, for the next item: $(12 \times 0.40) \div 13.8 = 4.8 \div 13.8 = 34.8\%$.

The time- and product-profit schedule in Table 3-8 shows, at a quick glance, the specific time(s) when the company decided to introduce a new item, or to discontinue an item. It also shows whether and to

Table 3-8.   Shifts in Product Mix of an Aluminum Window Company

Date	Item	Price Bracket	Percent of Total Output (1)	Per Dollar of Sales of Item (2)	Percent of Total Profit of Firm (3)	Profit of Firm per Dollar of Total Sales (4)
	Item				Profit	
March, 1958	Windows	Low price	60	15¢	65.2	13.8¢
	Windows	Medium price	40	12	34.8	
January, 1959	Windows	Low price	40	10	35.7	
	Windows	Medium price	40	12	42.8	11.2
	Windows	Custom-made	20	12	21.4	
April, 1959	Windows	Low price	20	10	17.2	
	Windows	Medium price	35	11	33.0	11.65
	Windows	Custom-made	25	12	25.7	
	Doors	Medium price	20	14	24.1	
June, 1960	Windows	Low price	10	10	7.6	
	Windows	Medium price	30	11	25.2	
	Windows	Custom-made	25	13	24.8	13.1
	Doors	Medium price	20	15	22.8	
	Awnings	Medium price	15	17	19.6	
October, 1961	Windows	Low price	Discontinued			
	Windows	Medium price	20	10	14.1	
	Windows	Custom-made	15	13	13.8	
	Doors	Medium price	20	15	21.2	
	Awnings	Medium price	20	17	24.0	
	Extrusions: Item A		5	12	4.2	14.15
	Item B		5	10	3.5	
	Item C		10	20	14.1	
	Item D		5	14	5.1	
October, 1963	Windows	Medium price	10	10	6.4	
	Windows	Custom-made	Discontinued			
	Doors	Medium price	15	12	11.5	
	Awnings	Medium price	15	12	11.5	
	Extrusions: Item A		10	15	9.6	
	Item B		15	13	11.8	15.65
	Item C		15	18	17.9	
	Item D		20	25	31.3	

what extent these shifts in the product-mix resulted in a rise or decrease in the contribution of a given item to the total profit. For instance, the addition of custom-made windows in January, 1959, resulted in a *relative* decline in the share of low-priced windows in total sales that dropped from 60% of the total output to 40%. It also shows that this item's contribution to total profits dropped from 65.2% in March, 1958, to 35.7% in January, 1959. It will also be noted that the profit per dollars of sales of the low-price windows dropped from 15¢ to 10¢. The newly introduced custom-made windows showed a profit of 12¢; thus compensating in part for the declining rate of profit on the low-priced item.

In 1960, further shifts occurred when again one new item was introduced. The 15% slice captured by awnings equalled the drop of 10% in the share of low-priced windows and of 5% in the share of medium-priced windows. At the same time, however, the profit on awnings of 17¢ per dollar of sales was substantially in excess of the 10¢ and 11¢ respectively earned by the first two items. As a result, the average profit on all sales was raised to 13.1¢ compared with 11.65¢ during the preceding period.

Similar shifts occurred in 1961 and in 1963 as a result of the introduction of new items, the discontinuance of two old items, and the rise in the sale of the new items.

b. Interpreting the Product-Profit Shifts. The usefulness of a breakdown of the product-profit mix can best be demonstrated by the action taken by top management of Company L.W.

The firm's fiscal year ended on December 31. Its rate of profit on sales for the period October to December, 1963, was 15.65%. For the first nine months, the rate of profit had been 14.15%. The income statement for fiscal 1963, therefore, reflected only in part the increased rate of profit in the last quarter.

Looking ahead at 1964, the firm projected for that year a rate of profit of 15.65% on the anticipated volume of sales. Moreover the company's projection for 1964 included a substantial increase in the share of the four extrusion items in total sales. On this basis, the anticipated overall rate of return of 15.65% appeared conservative.

However, the projected increase in total sales combined with the anticipated rise in the sale of the new items necessitated a reappraisal of the firm's financial resources. Although each item in the product line yielded a profit, the company lacked the funds to support the expanded line at the increased volume. Furthermore, the rate of turnover—and, thus, the average inventory per dollar of sales—varied substantially among the several items. After a careful appraisal of the financial requirements and of each item in the product line and its relative importance as a source of profit, the firm decided to discontinue the window and awning lines and to concentrate, in 1964, on awnings and extrusions.

These facts were stressed by top management in its negotiations with the bank for an increased loan to carry the larger volume of receivables that was expected to accompany the projected rise in sales for fiscal 1964.

The five-year breakdown of the product-profit mix served two purposes in conjunction with the application for a larger bank loan. The lender, as happens quite frequently in the case of a relatively large loan, asked not only for the most recent financial statements, but also for those of the preceding four years. Thus, the product-profit breakdown became a useful supplement to the accountant's statements by disclosing, first, the contribution of each product item to total profit and its share in total sales. And, second, it demonstrated the fact that the management of the company responded effectively to rising competition by shifting into new items with greater promise of profit.

SUMMARY

A major analytical tool in financial management is the construction of ratios. Most financial statements are expressed in absolute dollar figures. The use of ratios aids the financial manager and other analysts, such as bank lending officers, in pointing up the relative importance of the various items found on the financial statements. Each major item in the balance sheet and the income statement has a relationship with one or more items in either or both statements, which often can be expressed in a ratio or percentage. By use of ratios, comparisons with financial statements of other firms are facilitated and comparisons of a firm's performance can be made over a period of time.

Ratio analysis involves three steps. First, the financial manager selects from the financial statements those sets of data which are relevant to his immediate objective and calculates appropriate ratios for the firm. The second step calls for a comparison of the firm's ratios with those of other firms in its industry or with industry in general. The third step involves a comparison of ratios, both internal and external, over a period of time.

Ratios often used include liquidity ratios (such as the current ratio, acid test ratio, and cash position ratio); profit ratios (such as profit on sales, profit on assets, and profit on net worth); ratios concerned with financial leverage (such as the debt asset ratio, and debt as percentage of total capitalization); and other ratios (such as the rate of turnover, average collection period, and net sales to working capital).

Ratio analysis provides an overview of the dynamic relationships between the several components that make up the financial performance record of the firm. It provides a coordinated frame of reference for the financial manager. However, ratio analysis only provides an overview. It must be followed up by an analysis in depth of those components that reflect weakness in the financial position of the firm.

Questions

1. Why does the financial manager use ratios?
2. Which ratios are most useful to test the firm's liquidity? Why?
3. Explain the differences in the liquidity of cash, marketable securities, accounts receivable, and inventory.
4. Is it possible for a company to have a current ratio of 2:1 and be unable to pay its bills on time? Why?
5. Which ratios are most useful to indicate the firm's profitability? Why?
6. How can the financial manager compare the use of debt and equity in a firm? Why are the ratios significant?
7. What are the sources of industry ratios?
8. How are industry ratios useful to the financial manager?
9. What are the limitations of ratio analysis?
10. Give an example of how the financial manager uses the techniques of probing in depth.
11. What purposes does a probe in depth of earnings serve?

Problems

1. Prepare the following information from the latest annual reports of International Business Machines, Erie-Lackawanna Railroad, American Telephone and Telegraph Co., and First National City Bank. (Relevant financial information from the annual reports of these companies may be found in financial services such as Moodys & Standard Poor's).
   (a) Compute the following ratios for each of the companies: current ratio and acid-test ratio, inventory ratio, profit on sales, profit on net

worth, profit on net assets, debt/asset ratio, ratio of turnover, average collection period, working capital turnover.

(b) Explain why there arc differences in the various ratios among the above companies. Are there any similarities? Why? Are any of the ratios meaningless and/or impossible to compute for any of the above companies? Why?

2. The Elite Gift Shoppe had an inventory of $12,500 on January 1, 1966, and $14,000 on January 1, 1967. Net sales during 1966 were $62,500. Compute the rate of turnover. The Elite Gift Shoppe had an inventory of $13,000 on January 1, 1965, and a rate of turnover of 5.14. What were net sales in 1965?

3. The Montclair Maternity Shop has cash of $8000, United States Government bonds of $2000, accounts receivable of $15,000, inventory of $19,000, and current liabilities of $22,000. Compute the effect of each of the following transactions on the current ratio, the acid-test ratio, and the cash-position ratio. View each transaction separately, i.e., do not cumulate results.

(a) $10,000 is borrowed on a three year mortgage on a vacant lot next door to the shop.

(b) Allowance for depreciation of fixtures is increased $2000.

(c) $5000 of merchandise is purchased from suppliers on trade credit.

(d) The company sells a $500 United States Government bond for $500 cash (at par).

(e) The owner invests $3000 more cash in business.

(f) A delivery van is purchased for $2500 in cash.

(g) Payment of $3000 cash is made on accounts payable.

(h) A supplier is given a one-year note for $2000 as payment on accounts payable.

4. Prepare a weighted ratio index for the Vladmir Company. The company is in the same industry as shown in Table 3-5.

Vladmir Company Balance Sheet (000 Omitted) December 31, 1966

Cash	$ 28	Accounts payable	$ 56
Marketable securities	27	Income taxes payable	23
Receivables	65	Short-term bank loans	30
Inventory	129	Fixed liabilities	164
Fixed assets	163	Net worth	139
	$412		$412

As financial manager of Vladmir, examine the strengths and weaknesses of the company as indicated by the weighted ratio index.

Case: Banzai Rivet Corporation

As an independent financial consultant, you have been asked to evaluate the decline in the efficiency of the Banzai Rivet Corporation, a West Coast manufacturer and wholesaler of rivet equipment (see Tables 3-9, 3-10, and 3-11).

TABLE 3-9. Banzai Rivet Corporation: Balance Sheet (in Thousands of Dollars)

	December 31, 19x6	December 31, 19x7
Assets		
Cash	$ 450	$ 480
Accounts receivable	380	750
Inventory	400	1,200
Marketable securities	120	120
Total current assets	1,350	2,550
Buildings (net of depreciation)	600	530
Equipment and machinery (net)	2,100	1,810
Other assets	300	180
Total assets	$4,350	$5,070
Liabilities and capital		
Notes payable	$ 630	$1,140
Accounts payable	70	280
Due officers	50	50
Total current liabilities	750	1,470
Debentures (6%)	1,200	600
Total liabilities	1,950	2,070
Common stock	1,800	2,100
Retained earnings	600	900
Total liabilities and capital	$4,350	$5,070

TABLE 3-10.   Banzai Rivet Corporation: Income Statement (in Thousands of Dollars)

	Year Ended December 31, 19x6	Year Ended December 31, 19x7
Net sales	$4,490	$4,860
Cost of sales	3,380	3,900
Gross margin	1,110	960
Expenses	330	360
Net profit before taxes	780	600
Federal income taxes at 50%	390	300
Net profit after taxes	$ 390	$ 300

TABLE 3-11.   Rivet Industry Ratios— 19x7

Current ratio	2.35×
Acid test ratio	1.58×
Cash position ratio	.68×
Inventory—days sales	37.7 days
Average collection period	38.6 days
Profit on sales	7.4%
Profit on net worth	14.8%
Profit on total assets	7.3%
Debt/asset ratio	51.4%

Case Questions:

1. What are the strengths and weaknesses of Banzai Rivet Corporation, based on a ratio analysis of its financial statements?
2. How does the company compare with the other firms in the rivet industry?
3. As an independent financial consultant, what action would you suggest to management to strengthen the company?

Chapter Four

Short-Term Financing of Growth

We live in an expanding dynamic society. The momentum of growth is reflected in the rising output and sale of the firms that make up the business community. The firm that wants to maximize its profits within the framework of an expanding economy becomes a participant in this process of growth. Only by keeping pace with or surging ahead of the industry's rate of expansion can the individual firm preserve or increase, respectively, its share of the market. At times, the firm must also weigh the alternative of shifting in part or completely to a different line of products in order to meet the onrush of new raw materials and products. Constant alertness to changes in the industrial and market environment are essential for successful survival in a dynamic economy.

Ours is also a credit-oriented society. A study by Dun & Bradstreet[1] reported that "About ninety-nine percent of all commercial transactions in the United States and Canada are on credit terms." Under such conditions, the individual firm must at all times assure itself of ready access to the available sources of credit, whether from trade sources, financial institutions, private lenders of funds or a combination of these sources.

However, even the firm that grows only at a moderate pace or "stands still" does not escape dependence on credit and the need to procure short-term financing. Its requirements will be less than those of a rival firm of equal size which pushes aggressively for expansion. The basic problems remain the same for both companies: How much credit is needed, for how long, and from what sources.

[1] "How to Build Profit by Controlling Costs," (Dun & Bradstreet, Inc., New York, 1959), p. 43.

The first two sections of this chapter will examine the major reasons for growth and the effect of growth on the financial structure and needs of the firm. The subsequent sections of this chapter deal with problems that are applicable to all firms, regardless of their rate of growth.

I. THE DIMENSIONS OF GROWTH

The momentum of growth of the individual firm evolves either from external or internal causes, or from a combination of these two basic forces.

A. External Causes

The company that wants to keep up with, or possibly move abreast of, its competitors, must adapt itself to the changes in its economic environment. This analysis will be confined to three external sets of forces: technology, population, and market.

1. Technology Modern industry is constantly searching for new materials and improved equipment. The discovery or development of new materials lessens the dependence on known resources. Frequently, new materials also open the doors to the development of new products. The same is true of the tools of production: machinery and equipment. Thus, raw materials, products, and the tools of production are the three principal facets of technological development. It should also be noted that the evolution of modern industry has been marked by a continuous trend toward capital intensity. That is to say, the ratio of capital to labor has been steadily rising.

2. New Raw Materials The impact of new raw materials is illustrated by the discovery and development of synthetic fibres and plastics. Their introduction has had, and continues to exert, a profound influence on manufacturers and distributors. The individual firm, faced by the introduction of and competition from the new materials, must reappraise its product policy. As an illustration of the financial impact of new raw materials, let us review briefly the position of a manufacturer of textiles. The introduction of nylon, Dacron, and other synthetics makes available to this textile manufacturer—as well as to his customers who are the producers of the finished goods, the so-called "converters"—a wide variety of new synthetic fibers. These can be used either as substitutes for the traditional natural fibers (wool and cotton) or as supplements.

If a manufacturer, or distributor, of textile piece goods decides to confine his firm to the established line of wool or cotton textiles, he will have no need for additional capital investments as a result of the introduction of the new fibres, although he will now have to face competition from the new products.

But suppose that this firm decides to add the new material to its present line. In this case, there arise, immediately, a series of financial problems. If the firm adds the synthetic line to the old line, how much additional money will be required to carry the enlarged inventory? If the firm is able to maintain the present sales volume of the natural fibre textiles and obtains additional, or incremental, orders for the synthetics, by how much will the receivables increase? And how will these additional sales (i.e., accounts receivable) be financed? Will the firm be able to obtain additional loans from the bank? Will it use other financial sources such as finance companies or factors (which will be defined and discussed later in this chapter)? Or can the company get additional credit from its suppliers? Even if the suppliers are prepared to extend liberal credit terms to the firm, it will still need funds to pay for the rise in supplies, wages, salaries, and other expenses which increase as a result of the added volume of output.

Next, suppose that this firm decides to produce, or distribute, only the new (synthetic) line. The questions then arise whether this shift will involve a larger inventory, more receivables, greater expenditures for promotion, advertising, packaging, and so forth, compared with a product line of natural and synthetic fibres. If so, how much more? And, finally, where can it procure the needed additional short-term funds to support the increased requirements?

3. New Products   The same set of financial problems arises with the introduction of a new line of finished goods. Color television, stereo sets for the home, transistors, and a host of other electronic items represent some of the better known of the newer products that have made their appearance in the market in recent years.

Whether the firm is a manufacturer or distributor, it must face up to the challenge of these new products. It may decide to ignore the challenge and confine itself to its traditional line in the expectation that it still has ample room for expansion. Or the decision may be to join the parade either in place of or as a supplement to its current product line. In either of the last two events, the question arises about the magnitude of the added financial needs and the sources of these funds.

4. Tools of Production   Technological progress is reflected in the development of more efficient machinery for production and equipment for distributors. The decision to purchase a better machine or piece of equipment is initially an issue of long-term investment. This problem will be analyzed in Chapter 14 which deals with long-term financing.

Frequently, however, the purchase of a better machine also raises the issue of short-term financing. If, as stated above, the new equipment is capable of turning out more units per day than the present machines, the firm will have to provide, or raise, the funds to finance the increase in output. Suppose a beverage company now uses three semiautomatic bottling machines that require nine workers and have a daily capacity of 60,000 bottles. These machines have reached the end of their usable lifetime. The firm is now considering two alternatives: replacing the present machines with three new machines of the same type or purchasing a fully automated single machine with a daily capacity of 100,000 bottles and requiring only four workers. Ignoring, at this point, the question of the relative cost of three semiautomatic machines versus one fully automated machine, the firm must also face up to the fact that the automated process will yield its maximum benefit at an output level of 100,000 bottles per day. But to operate at, or near, this level would require additional financing for the increased daily requirement of 40,000 bottles, ingredients, labels, electricity, etc., minus the savings of daily wages for five workers.

5. Population   A high rate of population growth—as experienced in many areas of the country since World War II—means a significant increase in the number of potential users of many products and services. A firm that wants to maintain its position in, or share of, the market must, therefore, expand as fast as the market itself. Otherwise, its competitors will obtain a larger slice of the expanding volume of sales.

A rising population in an industrialized society tends to be accompanied by an increase in employment and incomes. The increment or additional income—whether received by an individual or by a nation—is not spent proportionately over the whole range of goods and service. Instead, the demand, in terms of actual spending, will rise faster for some goods than for other commodities. Thus, a firm may find that a relatively small increase in population and national income will expand the market for its products by many times the percentage growth in population and income.

A major characteristic of our American society has been the mobility of population. The rapid rise of the urban centers, the movement of population into suburbia, the rapid transformation of predominantly agricultural states into formidable industrialized regions has been a conspicuous feature of the American scene in the third quarter of this century. As a consequence, new geographic markets have been opened up for numerous products and services.

The penetration of new geographic markets usually requires not only a larger inventory and financing of more receivables but, initially at least, added expenditures for market research, promotions, sales staff, warehousing, and other items of a similar nature. The pressing question then arises as to the financial requirements and sources of funds.

B. Internal Causes

The firm that wants to maximize its profits does not wait for external, or environmental, factors to generate favorable opportunities for growth. Instead, the aggressive firm generates within itself an expansionist momentum.

1. Personal Ambition   When Sir Edward Hillery, the conquerer of Mount Everest, was asked why he had taken the risk, he gave the classic reply: "Because it's there." Many top executives of business firms have a similar urge to capture an increasing share of the market "because it's there." To be sure, these entrepreneurs, whether they own the company or are the hired top executives, do not lack the profit motive. But the profit motive, frequently, is not the overriding force in their decision to expand the business. These men are constantly looking for new worlds (i.e., markets) to conquer in the same way in which the explorer, the scientist, and the mountain climber look for new challenges. The result in terms of financial management is, in most cases, inevitable. The decision of top management to focus on increasing the size of the firm tends to subordinate the objective of the financial officer to maximize the *rate* of return on investment. While the absolute dollar volume of profit may increase in consequence of the larger size, the rate of profit may well go down when measured against the larger total investment.

This analysis is not concerned with the finer shadings of this driving force, i.e., whether and to what extent this type of individual is also motivated by an inner urge to serve the consumer or to create employment opportunities and, thus, to contribute to economic growth, or to amass a personal fortune for himself and his family. What is important is the following fact. If the element of personal ambition plays the dominant, even if not the exclusive, role in the decision-making process, the firm may be pushed ahead at a faster pace than its current and prospective resources justify. The firm swallows more than it can easily digest.

Expansion which is generated primarily by the force of personal ambition produces a corresponding need for financial resources. More importantly, the relative subordination of the profit motive makes it imperative for the financial manager of the firm to estimate, with special care, the short-run fund requirements.

2. Excess Capacity   An enterprise may find that its physical resources—plant and machinery—are not fully utilized throughout the calendar year. This is the usual situation in a business that is subject to seasonal influences. In fact, few lines of business are free from substantial seasonal variations.

In the desire to utilize the excess physical capacity during the off-season, the firm may decide to do one of several things. It may charge less than its regular season price in the hope of attracting a larger volume of sales than would otherwise be the case. Or the firm solicits orders for goods that are different from its regular line but that can be produced with the same equipment and labor force. In either of the two cases, the firm expects to realize, from this action, a price that is above its direct or variable cost. This excess becomes a contribution to those annual overhead costs that remain fixed whether the plant operates at full capacity or only at a fraction.

Excessive manpower is, similarly, the product of seasonal variations. The desire to keep the labor force intact even during the "slow" season is especially strong in the case of firms that employ predominantly highly skilled workers. To lay off these employees during the slack season creates the risk that some or many may look for more permanent jobs with other firms or in other geographic regions.

A firm that expands by means of a merger with another company frequently finds that the combined capacity of either plant and equipment or manpower, managerial and labor force, or both, are in excess of its current volume of sales. This kind of situation is likely to arise because the merger makes possible the continuance of the combined output with less physical capacity and manpower. Although the management of the two merged companies may later require more people than either one of the two firms had prior to the merger, it will probably not utilize fully all members of the two management teams. Thus, some members become underemployed. This partially idle managerial talent presses directly or indirectly for expansion.

In each of the above situations of excess capacity, the financial needs and problems of the firm involve more short-term funds to carry the larger inventory and receivables to pay for the added marketing costs and other expenses incidental to expansion.

3. Research   The firm that has a department for research and product development expects some tangible results at some future date. Suppose the time and money spent on these activities have "paid off." The department comes up with an improved product. Usually, the firm will expect to reap a larger profit not only from the lowered cost or higher price per unit but, more importantly, from a larger volume of sales than could be obtained from the "old" product. If this anticipation proves correct, the rise in output and sales could easily generate a rate of expansion beyond the current short-term resources at the disposal of the firm.

Market research has basically the same objective as product research. The firm wants to determine whether it is taking full advantage of the market in which it is currently operating or whether it has thus far neglected potentially profitable marketing opportunities in other geographic regions, or both. Assume that the marketing study points up a substantial potential of added sales either by means of more intensive sales efforts, a new advertising campaign, or some other device. To take advantage of these expanded opportunities, the firm will need the financial resources to support the anticipated sharp increase in sales.

II. SOURCES OF FUNDS

It must be emphasized that the need for funds is not necessarily the result of expanding operations by the firm. Even an establishment with a prospective constant level of business for the next fiscal year may be confronted by a shortage of funds. For example, a company may consider the desirability of carrying a greater variety of items in its inventory in order to offer its customers better selectivity and, thus, to improve its market position. In other cases, intensified competition in the market may make it necessary to extend to customers more liberal credit terms. As a result, the firm will have more money—in the form of receivables—tied up without any increase in the volume of sales. It is also conceivable that the firm's suppliers have shortened their credit terms and require payment upon receipt of goods. The firm may then find it necessary to procure funds to meet its obligation before it obtains payment from its customers. These few examples suffice to point up the important fact that funds needs can arise even under conditions of a constant volume of business.

In an expanding business, these problems are multiplied. A projected rise in the volume of output or sales usually necessitates additional funds for fixed assets, materials and supplies, payrolls, advertising, and other expenses. In the course of time, the expected rise in the volume of sales, if realized, will generate revenues and profits to support the increased level of activity. Initially, however, the firm must procure the funds that are required for expansion.

The initial responsibility for finding and recommending the potential sources of funds rests upon the shoulders of the financial manager. Basically, he has two courses of action. He can suggest a more effective utilization of the firm's internal sources or he can recommend the use of external funds. Frequently, he will find it advisable, or necessary, to advocate both courses. The factors that influence his selection will be discussed in subsequent chapters. This section will be confined to a description of the general nature of these two sources of funds—internal and external—and their respective financial implications for the firm.

A. Internal Sources

These consist of the initial investment contributed by the stockholders and subsequent earnings retained in the business.

1. Common Stock   For the sake of simplicity, we shall assume that the firm was organized as a corporation and that it sold 10,000 shares at $10 each to the stockholders. The sum of $100,000 represents the capital of the firm and represents the equity of the owners (i.e., stockholders). The $100,000 will be channelled subsequently by management into the several forms of assets: cash, receivables, inventory, machinery, equipment, and so forth.

Subsequently, upon approval of the stockholders, the firm can issue and sell additional stock either to the stockholders on record or to the general public. If it chooses this course of action—an additional stock issue—it will automatically increase the funds at its disposal by the amount obtained from the sale of the additional stock. In this case, the sale of new common stock represents an external source of funds.

2. Retained Earnings Let us next assume that the firm has operated profitably during the first few years of its existence. At the end of each fiscal year, the management, subject to approval by the stockholders, determines whether and how much of the profits, after taxes, will be paid out in dividends. Whatever is not distributed in dividends becomes *retained earnings*. These retained earnings are an addition to the stockholders' equity and also increase the internal source of funds by the amount of the retained earnings. However, the magnitude of the internal funds can increase or decrease as a result of changes in the value of fixed assets. A company may, for instance, own a piece of property that has doubled in value since the date of acquisition. If the firm sells the property, it will realize a capital gain that then becomes a capital surplus on the balance sheet. This surplus is part of the equity and adds to the internal funds of the firm.

The financial manager plays an important role in the dividend policy of the firm. His analysis of the financial needs of the firm in the next fiscal period may induce management to propose to the stockholders the omission of dividends or a reduction in the dividend in order to procure the required funds from retained earnings.

3. Depreciation As a general rule, the firm invests a portion of the capital obtained from stockholders or from retained earnings in fixed assets. At the end of each fiscal year, the firm enters on its books an allowance for the loss in value of these fixed assets. This is known as a capital consumption allowance or, more popularly, as *depreciation* and represents the estimated decrease in the value of a fixed asset as a result of wear and tear. A truck used for one year is worth less than the price originally paid for it. Buildings, machinery, fixtures, and other fixed assets similarly experience a decline in value over a period of time. Loss in value owing to wear and tear is known as *physical* depreciation.

Another frequently important cause of depreciation is *functional* obsolescence. A machine may be only one year old and almost as good as new. However, with the introduction of a new and vastly improved machine, our firm may find it necessary to "scrap" the one year old machine and acquire a new one to maintain its competitive position. Or the plant may become functionally obsolete because it is not suitable for the installation of newly developed equipment or as a result of a geographic shift in markets. These are but a few of many causes of potential functional obsolescence.

The amount included in total costs and therefore in price also includes an allowance for depreciation. Assuming that the price obtained covers at least total costs, the company has received the amount allocated for depreciation, and this amount will then be found either in: cash, accounts receivable, or inventory. Thus, the company has used this amount in its operations.

Another internal source of funds is the sale of one or more fixed assets of the company. This action converts an asset into cash. If the firm should sell an asset (for example, a building) at a price higher than the value at which this asset is carried on the books, the firm not only obtains cash but it also realizes a cash profit on the transaction. Loans from officers represent another internal source of funds.

B. External Sources

Our economy is based, in large part, on credit. Consumers use loans to finance the purchase of durable goods, clothing, or the acquisition of a home. Government—federal, state, and local—borrows funds for a period of months, years, and several decades. And business firms are no exception to this practice. Whether or not to borrow funds, from whom to obtain such loans, and what terms to accept or reject are responsibilities that initially fall upon the shoulders of the financial manager. It is he who weighs the several alternatives and selects the one that he regards as most beneficial to the firm. Top management then accepts, rejects, or modifies his proposed course of action.

1. Suppliers   The most common external source of funds is to be found in suppliers of the firm. In fact, this is a two-way street. The individual company avails itself of credit extended by its suppliers and, in turn, extends credit to its customers. On the liability side of the balance sheet, this dual process generates the item known as accounts payable and, on the asset side, it produces the item accounts receivable.

To the financial manager, two time facets are of crucial significance. First, the interval of time that elapses between the inflow of goods from suppliers and the subsequent outflow to customers. And second, the length of credit extended by the creditors in contrast with the credit interval offered by the firm to its customers.

The time interval between inflow and outflow absorbs a corresponding portion of the credit term obtained from the supplier. For example, if the firm buys on 30 days credit and, on the average, requires 20 days to process and to deliver the goods to its customers, it has only 10 more days in which to make payment. If it has extended 30 days of credit to its customers, the firm must somehow bridge the gap of 20 days between the date when its obligation falls due and the date when its customers will presumably pay their debt. Another fact also needs to be stressed. In the above example, it was stated that the firm requires 20 days in which to process the goods before shipment to the customer. During this interval, the firm incurs additional expenses, most of which have to be paid currently; such as wages, salaries, and rent.

2. Lending Institutions Another external source of funds consists of financial institutions which make loans to business firms. In considering these external sources, the financial manager can choose on the basis of time between (a) short-term loans, (b) intermediate-term loans, or (c) long-term loans. Within each of these three sources, he has the choice among various types of lenders, known as financial institutions and institutional lenders. Commercial banks are classified among financial institutions, while finance companies, factors, and insurance companies are called institutional lenders. In addition, various government agencies are active as lenders of funds to business.

a. Short-Term Loans. The major suppliers of short-term loans are commercial banks, finance companies, and factors. The difference between these types of lenders will be discussed later on in this book. These loans are used by business firms for a period of time equivalent to the length of the production and marketing period of the borrowing firm. Usually, this covers a period ranging from 30 days to 90 days. When the goods are sold and the customer makes payment, the seller obtains the funds to redeem the loan. This is known as a self-liquidating transaction.

A going business is a continuous operation. That is to say, it buys raw materials or finished goods and readies them for sale but, in the meantime, orders a fresh inflow of goods to take the place of those that are expected to be sold. Thus, while the firm receives payment for the sale of the first batch of goods, it has already incurred a liability for the items that will be sold in the second marketing period, and so on.

The loan to finance the first transaction cycle must, therefore, be replaced by a loan to finance the second transaction. And a third loan supports the third cycle; thus, the process tends to continue until the time when one or more of the following conditions arise. In most lines of business, the sales volume follows a seasonal pattern. Thus, sales may move at a fairly high level for six months, for example, and then decline sharply during the next three months as a result of seasonal influences. During this offseason, purchases by the firm will decline while collections on previous (peak-season) sales will flow into the firm. In consequence, the inflow of funds will tend to exceed the outflow and the firm will, thus, be able to "clear up" its obligations to the lenders of funds. Or again, the company's business may be so profitable that its accumulated earnings are sufficient to cover the gap.

Or the suppliers may offer more liberal terms while the customers are willing to accept shorter credit terms; or an increasing number of customers may take advantage of the offered discount and make payment within a few days after receipt of the goods. Again, it will be noted that the financial manager, in estimating the firm's requirements for funds, must consider both the immediate needs and those that are probable in the course of a series of transaction cycles. Therefore, a firm usually negotiates for short-term loans to cover not one but several transaction cycles. Customarily, these loans range for a period of from three months to a year, although some of these loans are for up to three year periods. ~~bank overdraft~~

b. Intermediate-Term Loans. Here the time period involved runs generally between three and ten years. The primary purpose of this type of loan is to finance the purchase of fixed assets with a life expectancy greater than the lifetime of the loan. These loans are sought by firms that anticipate a substantial expansion of business in the immediate future and for some years thereafter. Lacking the funds to acquire the needed assets, the firm attempts to procure a loan that will mature in a number of years.

Repayment of the loan is made out of that portion of the price received for the goods that represents the depreciation of the asset financed by the loan plus profit. The expectation by borrower and lender is that the asset will more than pay for itself (i.e., interest payment plus recovery of the invested funds).

Frequently, a firm may find itself in the reverse position. It has adequate fixed assets to sustain a substantial expansion in output or sales. However, it lacks the funds to support the attendant increase in receivables and inventories. Therefore, it will seek an intermediate-term loan for several years. This will make it unnecessary to negotiate every few months for an extension or a renewal of short-term loans.

The major suppliers of intermediate-term loans are: commercial banks, finance companies, life insurance companies, the Small Business Administration, and Small Business Investment Companies. There exists a wide range of variations in the lending policies, criteria, and terms of the loan among the several types of suppliers (this will be discussed in a subsequent chapter). Each supplier operates under specific laws and is subject to either federal or state regulatory bodies, or both. The exception is the Small Business Administration. This is a federal agency with power to make direct intermediate-term loans subject to the limitation imposed and criteria prescribed by the Act under which this agency was established.

c. Long-Term Loans.   These are loans outstanding for ten or more years. They serve essentially, as a means of acquiring fixed assets with a lifetime of several decades. The instrument often used in these long-term transactions is mortgages. The mortgage may be in the form of a single mortgage indenture, or it may be a mortgage that is divided into a number of bonds with a total face value equalling the debt. The terms of the mortgage and, respectively, of the bonds, are subject to negotiation between borrower and lender. These terms show a wide range of methods of payment of interest, provisions for redemption, restrictions on the distribution of profits in the firm of dividends by the debtor-corporation, and rights of the bondholders-creditors in case of default of interest or principal.

Large private corporations frequently procure long-term funds by issuing debenture bonds. These are certificates of indebtedness that are secured, not by a mortgage against a specific fixed asset of the corporation, but by a prior claim against profit and the unpledged assets of the firm. The debenture holder is in the same basic creditor position as a supplier of goods, except that the debenture matures after a specified number of years rather than days. However, if the debtor fails to meet the interest payments when due, the entire debenture falls due. As in the case of mortgage bonds, the debenture also imposes restrictions on dividend payments and may include other terms limiting some of the prerogatives of the management.

III. FINANCIAL IMPACTS OF GROWTH

Let us now take a closer look at the effects of growth on the specific categories in the current assets of the firm.

A. Receivables

For the sake of illustration, assume that a company anticipates an expansion in its volume of business by 25% in each of the next two years. Does this mean that its receivables will also go up by the same percentage in each of the next two years? The answer depends in large measure on the direction of its growth in terms of customers. Several alternative situations will be considered.

Situation No. 1.   The firm does not contemplate a change either in its product line or in its present customer list as a result of the planned growth. It is hoped that, as a result of population and income rise, the customers of the firm will be able to sell a larger volume and, thus, readily absorb the increased output of the company. In this instance, it is reasonable to assume that the receivables will increase in about the same proportion as sales. As a result, the financial requirements of the firm—i.e., the amount needed to bridge the interval between the due dates of payables and receivables—will increase by 25% of the average accounts receivable currently outstanding.

Situation No. 2.   Here, too, assume no change in the product line of the firm. However, in this case, the firm is projecting a change in the composition of its customers. It expects to sell the increased output to a few large customers. Currently, its customers are made up of relatively small companies. Moreover, the firm anticipates that a portion of the new (large) accounts will take advantage of the cash discount of 1% for payment of the bills within 10 days. The funds which will be received 10 days after the billing date will then flow in a few days before the maturity dates of the incremental payables that represent the increased purchases from suppliers.

The firm's financial requirements for the rise in sales will therefore be substantially less than in situation 1.

Situation No. 3.   Once more assume that there is no change in product line. But this time the firm expects to dispose of the increased output in a new geographic market but to relatively small customers. In this instance, the firm has no past experience record by which to estimate the paying habits of these new accounts. Moreover, it is often necessary to offer more liberal credit terms to new accounts than to old ones. Officially or nominally, the terms may be the same; e.g., 30 days net. However, the salesmen, with the tacit approval of the credit manager, will frequently promise the new prospective account that his firm will not take any action if the 30-day period is exceeded.

In some cases, the firm may authorize the salesmen to sell, if necessary, on consignment. Under such an arrangement, the goods remain the property of the seller until sold by the customer, at which time the customer must pay the invoice price. These goods may be left with the customer for two, three, or more months. In the meantime, the firm has a given amount of its funds tied up in these goods, which are carried on its books not as receivables, since there was no initial sale, but as a part of its inventory, although it does not have physical possession of these goods. If the customer returns the merchandise or the firm recalls it, the goods become, physically, a part of its inventory.

Whether the transaction is a final sale with an implied extended credit or on consignment, the firm's financial requirements will be greater than in situation No. 1. The several situations are illustrated in the following example.

Situation No. 1:

> *Before expansion:* $1,000,000 credit sales; 30 days average collection period; average receivables outstanding: $1,000,000 ÷ 12 = $83,333.
>
> *After expansion:* $1,250,000 sales; 30 days average collection period; average receivables outstanding: $1,250,000 ÷ 12 = $104,166; or 25% greater than prior to expansion. The firm must somehow provide the additional funds ($20,833) to carry the rise in receivables. (Note that the actual need would probably be somewhat higher than indicated because of variation in the pattern of sales.)

Situation No. 2:

> *Before expansion:* same as in Situation No. 1; i.e., average receivables: $83,333
>
> *After expansion:* $1,000,000 credit sales result in the same average receivables of .... $ 83,333
> The incremental sales of $250,000 to a few large customers result in perhaps $200,000 paid within 10 days or $200,000 ÷ 36 = average receivables of .... $ 5,555
> and perhaps $50,000 paid in 30 days or $50,000 ÷ 12 = average receivables of .... $ 4,166
> Total average receivables of .... $ 93,054
> or an increase in average receivables of about 11.3%; i.e., additional funds, internal or external, to the tune of $9,721

Situation No. 3:

> *Before expansion:* $1,000,000 credit sales; 30 days aver-
> age collection period; average receivables:
> $83,000

> *After expansion:* $1,250,000 credit sales; $1,000,000 of
> sales have 30 days average collection period
> and average receivables $ 83,333
> $250,000 of sales have 90 days average collec-
> tion period and average receivables $250,000
> ÷ 4 = $ 62,500
> $145,833

> Average receivables outstanding:
> $83,333 + $62,500 or $145,833; i.e., an in-
> crease of 75 percent; or an incremental finan-
> cial need of $62,500.

Situation No. 4.   Now assume an addition to the product line of the firm and an anticipated increase in sales by 25%; to use the same figures as in the preceding illustration, sales are projected to rise from $1,000,000 in the past year to $1,250,000 in the next year. Furthermore, assume that the new product will account for the increment of $250,000 in sales.

How will the anticipated sales of the new items affect (a) the volume of receivables and (b) the average collection period on the new receivables? The answer depends, in part, on the type of customers who are expected to purchase the new item. On this score, we can again use the same three classifications as before: present customers; a few large customers; or many small customers. It must be emphasized, however, that a given firm may well find it advisable to have four or more classifications in order to reflect more accurately its particular customer mix, both current and prospective.

It is quite conceivable that the customers, old and new, will respond positively to the firm's new line. In this case, the effect will be an increase in accounts receivable by 25% and probably no significant change in the average collection period. On the other hand, it is also possible that the response of the customers to the new line may be an attitude of doubt about its ready saleability. As a result, the customers may be reluctant to purchase the new line. In this instance, most or all of the additional output will remain in the inventory classification; i.e., at least for the time being the funds invested in the additional output are not liquid.

To overcome this reluctance, a firm, not infrequently, takes recourse to one of the following devices. Its salesmen are authorized to assure the customer(s) that the firm will take back any unsold items within a stipulated period of time; e.g., ninety days. On the record, at least, the transaction is entered as a sale and the amount of the invoice becomes a part of the receivables. Or the firm agrees to date the invoice 30 or more days after actual delivery of the merchandise. The net effect is to extend the credit term of 30 days by the interval between delivery and billing date. If either one of these devices is employed, the average amount of receivables will increase proportionately and necessitate additional funds.

The preceding discussion points up an important fact about receivables. Business firms are increasingly using accounts receivable as an effective marketing tool. Instead of adhering rigidly to a single set of credit terms, the sales force is authorized to make adjustments in these terms, usually within a range fixed by management. As a result, the individual salesman is armed with a potent weapon in soliciting orders from old as well as new accounts. By offering more liberal credit terms than competing firms, or being able to match the more liberal terms of competitors, the salesman may be able to obtain orders that otherwise would be lost to his firm.

In projecting the amounts needed to finance receivables, the financial manager must take into account that portion of receivables which will be generated by special concessions. These accounts will automatically become "aged"; i.e., overdue on the books of the firm. This fact in itself does not reflect adversely on the soundness or quality of these receivables. However, the extended credit terms affect the prospective inflow of cash, and in consequence, the financial manager must plan for larger funds to carry these accounts than would be required under the standard terms of the firm.

B. Inventory

As in the case of receivables, the anticipated growth of sales by 25% will also affect the size of the inventory. Much now depends on the answers to the following questions. If there is no change in the product line, will the present level of inventory also suffice for the larger volume of sales?

If the firm contemplates adding a new line, the following question arises. How much inventory does this line require? Does this projected inventory constitute a greater or smaller proportion of the anticipated incremental sales than is the case with the ratio of inventory to sales for the regular line of goods? Suppose the firm contemplates the penetration of a new geographic market. Will it be necessary to set up some inventory of finished goods in a warehouse closer to the new geographic market in order to assure prompt delivery to new customers in that region?

The answers to the above questions can best be provided by the sales and production departments. With the information obtained from these internal sources, the financial manager can then proceed to estimate the prospective future size of the inventory. In turn, this will enable him to calculate the probable size of the funds that will be required to carry this additional inventory and whether the firm has adequate internal sources for this purpose. If the funds are not internally available, he must then determine what external sources are available, as well as the terms and the additional cost of these external funds in relation to the expected incremental profit from the expansion of sales.

C. Growth Elements

An increase in sales—involving either the penetration of a new market or the sale of a new product, or both—is usually predicated on added expenditures for promotions and advertising. At least during the initial period, which may last several weeks or many months, these expenditures will be proportionately greater than the expected rise in sales. For example, the firm may now be spending, on advertising and promotions, an amount equal to 5% of the sales of its regular merchandise in the established market. If it aims to raise this volume by 25%, in a new market or by offering a new product, it will usually have to spend substantially more than 5% of the anticipated increment. These costs, however, are incurred *before* the firm obtains the revenues from the additional sales that are expected to pay for these expenditures. Another, additional, form of promotional expense is the practice often adopted by firms of offering its sales personnel a special incentive commission on sales either in new markets or of a new product. Similarly, a firm will offer a new distributor a premium for carrying the product, for example, in the form of free samples, the proverbial "baker's dozen" (13 units delivered but only 12 invoiced), or an "advertising or display allowance" (which is merely a disguised price concession).

Frequently, the cost of these "special" inducements when added to the variable and fixed overhead costs of producing the additional output may come close to or even exceed the additional sales revenues, assumed to be 25%. This is the price that the firm has to pay to conquer a new market or to introduce a new product. Once the aim has been achieved, these expenses can probably be cut back without loss of sales and a profit becomes feasible. In the meantime, the firm has to provide the funds to execute the promotional program. The financial manager must find the source for these funds, either internally or externally.

IV. MEASURING SHORT-TERM FINANCIAL NEEDS

Five elements enter into the quantitative determination of the funds needed to finance the output and/or sales of the firm in the projected fiscal period. These are (1) the scheduled purchases from various trade sources; (2) the direct out-of-pocket expenses for labor and services during the production cycle—or, in the case of a distributor, during the selling cycle—i.e., during the interval between receipt of the goods from suppliers, their sale to the firm's customers and receipt of payments; (3) promotional and related expenses that are expected to be recovered in the course of the fiscal period rather than in a single production or selling cycle; (4) the average collection period of receivables; and (5) projected profits.

The preceding section has discussed items 3 and 4. We shall now examine items 1, 2, and 5. This will be followed by a presentation of the quantitative determination of the five items in a single schedule. It must be noted that, in addition to the funds needed for the scheduled output and/or sales, the firm must also be prepared to meet other financial requirements; for instance, tax payments, dividends, replacement of assets, or purchase of additional fixed assets. The last two items are clearly of a long-term nature and, thus, become essential parts of the capital budget and long-term financial planning. Dividends and income tax payments should be considered, in the last analysis, as a charge against the income of the past fiscal period, even though paid in the subsequent fiscal period.

A. Purchases

The scheduled purchases generate the liability known as "accounts payable." The purchasing agent, or buyer, of the firm provides the estimated costs of this item, based on the currently quoted or estimated future prices of the suppliers. From the viewpoint of the financial manager, the crucial question centers around the prospective terms of payment.

Basically, there are three possibilities that must be considered by the financial manager. First, will the terms offered by suppliers during the next fiscal year be the same as during the latest fiscal period? In this case, the average, or monthly volume of payables will rise or fall in the same proportion as the projected expansion, or decline, in the firm's sales.

Second, the terms of the suppliers are expected to be either more liberal or more stringent than in the last fiscal period. Let us take the first case; i.e., more liberal terms. In this instance, the (buying) firm gains, initially, a "breathing spell" of, say, 15 days in which to procure the funds for the payment of its bills. The decrease in the outflow (i.e., payment to suppliers) is offset by a corresponding rise in its accounts payable as illustrated in the following examples.

Purchases in last fiscal year	$1,000,000
Monthly purchases (average)	83,333
Terms: 30 days net	
Accounts payable (average)	83,333
Projected purchases in next fiscal year	$1,250,000
Terms: 45 days net	
Monthly purchases (average)	104,000 (in round figures)
Accounts payable (average)	
$\frac{1}{8}$ of $1,250,000 (45 days = $\frac{1}{8}$ yr.)	$ 154,000 (in round figures)

The rise from $83,300 to $154,000 (in round figures) can also be illustrated as shown in Table 4-1. (Assume that the firm receives in the first and third week of each month one-half of the average monthly purchases, or $52,000 every two weeks.)

At the end of January, the payables equal $104,000 which is the amount purchased in that month. But no payment need be made in the first week of February. In the following month, February, the firm purchases $104,000 worth of goods but need only make payment for the $52,000 purchased in the first week of January. In the first week

TABLE 4-1.   Schedule of Payables Under More Liberal Credit Terms[a]

	Purchases (Dollars)	Due (Month)	Payments to Suppliers (Dollars)	Payables (Dollars)
January				
1st week	52,000	2–17	—	52,000
3rd week	52,000	3–5	—	52,000
31st (end of month)				104,000
February				
1st week	52,000	3–17	—	156,000
3rd week	52,000	4–5	52,000	
28th (end of month)				156,000
March				
1st week	52,000	5–17	52,000	
3rd week	52,000	6–5	52,000	
31st (end of month)				156,000
April				
1st week	52,000	6–17	52,000	
3rd week	52,000	7–5	52,000	
30th (end of month)				156,000

[a] To simplify the illustration, it is assumed that the firm "cleaned up" its payables as of December 31 of the preceding year.

of March, it must pay for the purchases in the third week of January and in the third week of March, it must pay for the purchases in the first week of February. Thus, its monthly payments, starting with March, will total $104,000 which equal the monthly purchases.

The advantage of a 45-day credit period lies in the following fact. The longer credit period shortens by 15 days the time interval between the due dates of the account payable to the supplier and the account receivable from its customers. Suppose the firm requires 20 days to process the materials received from the supplier and to deliver the goods to its customers, who agree to pay 30 days after receipt of the merchandise. In this case, the firm will require funds to meet its obligations to the supplier for five days; in contrast with 20 days if the terms had been net 30 days. By the same token, if the firm can process and deliver the goods to its customers within 15 days, the payment received from the latter will automatically provide the funds to take care of the accounts payable to the supplier.

A tightening of the credit terms by the supplier will have the opposite effect. The firm will need a larger amount of available funds to bridge the longer interval between the due dates of the payables and of the receivables.

B. Direct Out-of-Pocket Expenses

After the firm receives the goods, these must either be processed (by the manufacturer) or put on display (by the distributor). During the interval until the goods are sold and payment is received, the firm incurs a variety of cash expenditures, for instance, rent, wages, salaries, commissions, postage, etc. When payment is received from the customers, the excess of these revenues over the payables to the suppliers reimburses the firm for the various out-of-pocket expenses, in addition to the amount included in the selling price for depreciation and anticipated profit.

Until the cycle of purchases-production-sale-collection is completed, a projected increase in sales volume raises the amount which the firm, during the initial production and selling cycle, must have at its disposal for current expenditures (cash outlays).

C. Profits

It is true that the income statement for the latest fiscal period may show a profit. But this does not necessarily mean that this amount is actually available in the form of excess cash which the firm can disburse in dividends and/or retain in the business. In many firms, especially in a period of rapid growth, the actual situation is more likely to resemble the following pattern.

Assume that the firm operated at a profit throughout the last fiscal period. This profit is, however, never set aside in a special cash fund. Instead, it flowed into one or several of the current assets; e.g., receivables, inventory, or a reduction in the firm's short-term indebtedness. The closing date of the fiscal year, when the net earnings for the entire period are recorded, does not always coincide with the firm's off-season when its receivables and payables are likely to be low and the cash item relatively large.

Moreover, if the firm had been, and continues to be, in a process of rapid growth, its earnings are quickly absorbed by the noncash current assets. This process is aptly described in the following statement:[2] "It

---

[2] "Small Business, Tax Rates, and Economic Growth," National Small Businessmen's Association, Washington, D.C., 1961; pp. 1–2.

takes capital to start a business; it takes more capital to make it grow . . . more capital for more growth is needed all across the economic board in America . . . ."

Management must choose between the alternatives of plowing the profits back into the company or borrowing funds to make up for the depletion of the cash position of the firm. Assume that the year-end balance sheet of the firm shows the following picture:

Cash on hand	$ 60,000	Accounts Payable	$200,000
Receivables	200,000	Notes Payable	25,000
Inventory	125,000	Current Liabilities	$225,000
Current Assets	$385,000		

Now, suppose that the firm made a profit of $80,000 during the past year and the management decides on a dividend of $40,000. The disbursement of the dividend will reduce the cash position to $20,000. If the firm requires $60,000 in cash to meet current expenses and to bridge the interval between the due dates of payables and receivables, it will have to borrow about $40,000 from a bank.

V. FINANCIAL SOURCES OF SHORT-TERM FUNDS

In addition to trade sources, the firm can obtain short-term financing from three principal financial sources: (a) commercial banks, (b) factoring companies, and (c) finance companies.

A. Commercial Banks

At the end of 1967, the commercial banks in the United States, as a group, had outstanding close to $90 billion in commercial and industrial loans. This sum compares with roughly $200 billion of receivables on the books of nonfinancial corporations. On the whole, commercial banks provide in the neighborhood of 45% of the total volume of external short-term funds used by business, while trade sources supply close to 45%. Factoring companies account for around 5% and finance companies for another 5%.

A commercial bank provides a variety of services for a business firm, in addition to its function as a lender of funds. It acts as a depository of funds and collector of claims, represented by checks, against other firms. By means of the same instrument (checks), the firm makes payments to its creditors.

Banks also make mortgage loans on real estate for periods of ten years or more and so-called intermediate-term loans ranging between two and five years. These and other types of loans to business will be discussed in subsequent chapters.

A business firm can also utilize the services of a commercial bank for the transfer of funds to or from foreign countries, to buy or sell foreign currencies (i.e., foreign exchange), to purchase or sell securities that are traded in the various securities markets, and to act as a trustee for the firm in the administration of estates, pension funds, or other transactions.

Last, but by no means least, a bank is frequently in a position to provide valuable financial advice and guidance to the management of a firm. This function is of special usefulness when the company desires to raise additional capital through the sale of a new stock issue or bonds.

The extent to which the individual bank can perform all of these services depends on the size of the bank as well as on the skill and aggressiveness of its officers. Smaller banks have neither the manpower nor the experience to act adequately as trustees of pension funds or as advisors on securities issues or dealers in foreign exchange. However, even a small bank can frequently furnish these services indirectly. This is accomplished by means of its correspondent relationship to larger banks in a major urban center. That is to say, the small bank calls upon larger institutions for the service or advice that the customer requires.

1. Short-Term Loans   These business loans run from one month to one year. The borrowing firm gives the bank a promissory note which states the sum of the debt and the due date.

The firm that wants to obtain a loan (assuming that the bank is willing to grant the loan as requested) can use one of two alternative procedures. One course of action involves a single loan for a specified period. For example, in January, the firm borrows $50,000 for a period of three months. After repaying the loan in April, it applies in May for a new loan of $25,000 for two months. In August, it borrows $100,000 for three months. Each of these loans represents a single, complete transaction: application, approval, loan, repayment. Interest will be charged at the rate in effect at the time of the individual loan and is calculated on the amount of this loan.

The second alternative that the firm has is to combine, in advance, the contemplated series of single loans. This purpose is achieved by the device known as the establishment of a *line of credit*. Under this procedure the firm applies, for example, in January for a potential loan maximum of $100,000 for the next twelve months. The firm expects to borrow at various times during the twelve months but does not know definitely at this time (January) the precise amounts it will need or the exact duration of each loan. However, the total at any one time will not exceed $100,000 and the debt, whatever the amount, will be fully paid off by the end of the year. In the case of a line of credit, interest is charged only on the amount actually drawn and for the period of time during which such funds are used by the firm. However, it is customary for the bank to charge a commitment or stand-by fee for the amount not drawn by the firm.

If the bank approves the requested line of credit, the firm need not reapply every time it needs a loan. It simply gives the bank a note for the required amount and for the wanted period; one, two or more months. The loan agreement which fixes the line of credit fixes the maximum amount, the time when all outstanding loans under this agreement must be paid off, the bank's charge for the establishment of the line of credit, the interest rate for the amounts subsequently borrowed, and the minimum balance (called the compensating balance) that the firm agrees to maintain on deposit against any such loans, usually 15 to 20% of the face amount of the loan. Usually, the bank also stipulates that, at some time in the course of the year (usually the off-season of the firm), all outstanding loans be "cleaned up."

The requirement of a minimum balance means, in effect, that the effective rate of interest is higher than the nominal rate. Let us assume that the firm borrows $50,000 in April for three months at an annual rate of 6%, and that it is required to maintain a minimum balance of 20% of the loan. The actual amount that the firm can then draw is $50,000 minus 20% or $40,000. However, the interest of 6% per annum, or 1.5% for 3 months, is calculated on the full amount of $50,000. The firm therefore pays $750 interest on an actual loan of $40,000, which equals 7.5% per annum. The rate of 7.5% is the effective rate, while 6% is the nominal rate. Many firms carry a balance in their checking accounts. To the extent to which the firm ordinarily maintains such deposits, the cost of the compensating balance is reduced and, thus, the effective rate on the loan is decreased.

The Four "C's."   A bank loan can be secured by some specific asset(s) of the firm which is pledged as security for the payment of the debt. However, it must be noted that the value of an asset as security for a loan depends, in large measure, on the prospective liquidation value of the asset if this action should become necessary. Thus, a firm may have two assets—for example, a warehouse and a specialized processing plant—both costing the same amount. From the viewpoint of the lender, the warehouse would justify a higher loan than the plant in terms of prospective liquidation value. In the case of a secured loan, the lender invariably insists on adequate insurance coverage.

Or the loan may be granted on an "unsecured" basis; i.e., the faith of the bank in the borrower's ability to repay the loan on maturity. In evaluating the credit of a potential borrower, the bank considers four basic elements, known as the 4 C's of bank credit: (1) character of the owners or managers, (2) capacity of the firm, (3) capital provided by the owners-stockholders, and (4) collateral. *Character,* the first C, refers to the reputation of the owners or management of the firm in meeting the obligations of the company upon maturity. It is the reputation for honesty and integrity in assuming and meeting debts owed to suppliers, lenders, and others with whom the establishment conducts its business.

Capacity measures the ability of the firm to utilize the loan effectively and profitability. This factor is reflected in the income statements, the projected use of the funds, the cash-flow forecast, and the estimated future income based on these projections. *Capital* represents the stake of the owners in the business. It is measured, in part, by the ratio of capital and surplus (i.e., net worth) to total liabilities, current and fixed. And, in part, it is measured by the ratio of net working capital to current liabilities.

The fourth C, *collateral,* serves as a cushion or shock absorber if one or several of the first three C's are insufficient to give reasonable assurance of repayment of the loan on maturity. Collateral, in the form of a specific pledged asset, serves to compensate for a deficiency in one or several of the first three C's. We shall return to this point after the discussion of secured loans.

2. Collateral Loans   Assume that the bank has fixed a firm's line of credit at $100,000 and that this decision was reached after an evaluation of the firm's character, capacity, and capital. It is conceivable that this amount is not sufficient to meet the firm's requirements for short term funds. In such a situation, the firm can usually obtain an additional loan in excess of $100,000, against a pledge of a specific short-term asset. Most frequently, this asset will consist of the assignment of accounts receivable to the bank. That is to say, the firm obligates itself to turn over to the bank any amount received from its customers in payment of their obligations. A bank will also make a loan secured by a warehouse receipt—which the lender keeps as security—for merchandise that is readily marketable. This method is used by many importers of staple raw materials, by distillers of beverages, wholesalers of eggs (kept in cold storage), and others. A loan may also be secured by promissory notes received from customers.

3. Installment Paper   Many commercial banks have developed a fairly large volume of installment-paper financing. The consumer, for example, can finance the purchase of a new or old car by obtaining a loan, repayable in fixed monthly installments, either by going to the bank directly or by having the dealer procure such a loan. At this point, we are concerned with those transactions in which the firm sells its products to the consumer on the installment plan and, in turn, arranges for the financing of the purchase, minus the downpayment, by a bank.

A firm which offers the customer the choice of a cash or installment purchase usually arranges, in advance, with a bank the terms of this financing; i.e., the downpayment, the lifetime of the contract, interest rate, service charges if any, and so forth. These terms are spelled out in the contract which the customer signs and which is then turned over to the bank. The bank then pays to the firm the face amount of the contract minus the interest and other charges levied by the bank, and the consumer makes the payments to the bank.

4. Conservative versus Liberal Lending   A bank frequently acquires a reputation among local business firms of being "conservative" or "liberal" in its lending policies. While the term "conservative" is supposed to indicate that the institution is reluctant to make unsecured loans, the term "liberal is not meant to convey the opposite attitude. In reality, the distinction should be made between a bank that is thorough in its credit analysis of a prospective borrower and an institution that is superficial in its analysis.

At first glance, it would seem that the firm should seek out the institution that is superficial. In this case, the firm would appear to have a better chance of obtaining the full amount required and with less waste of time. This type of borrowing policy, while attractive on the surface, is short sighted. A bank, like any business firm, has liabilities. Every loan made by a bank becomes automatically a liability, since the amount of the loan is credited to the account of the borrower and, thus, added to his checking account which is a liability of the bank.

But, unlike a business firm, a bank is subject to periodic supervision and examination by the banking authorities. As a consequence of this examination, a bank that pursues a generally superficial policy of credit analysis and lending is not likely to continue on this path for an extended period of time. Business firms which were able to borrow larger amounts than more thorough banks were willing to grant may therefore find that their formerly affluent source of short-term financing has dried up suddenly. Moreover, they may be called upon to reduce their loans substantially and on short notice.

5. "Shopping" for a Bank   Considerable differences exist in the lending policies of banks. Some banks are commercial banks in name only. Their funds are invested largely in real estate mortgages and government securities with only a small portion represented by industrial and commercial loans. Some banks make extensive loans, but the bulk will consist of consumer financing; i.e., installment credit to finance the purchase of appliances, automobiles, and the like.

Most commercial banks channel a substantial portion of their funds into business loans. However, there exists a wide range in the policies of these banks in regard to the length of time for which they will make a loan to a business firm, the amount of these loans to a particular firm, and the collateral required as security. Some institutions, for example, will make loans for several years, while others will not go beyond a one-year loan. Some banks will insist on ample collateral, while others will look primarily at the character and reputation of the owners of the business. In choosing his bank, the financial manager must, therefore, make sure that the institution is willing and ready to make credit available to the firm at reasonable terms and for the required length of time.

The size of the borrowing firm and, thus, the size of the loan for which the firm qualifies have a major effect on the rate of interest charged by the bank. This fact is clearly reflected in Table 4-2.

It must be emphasized, however, that mere size of a bank is no evidence of quality of management. Some of the smaller banks are staffed by officers who are thoroughly competent in analyzing the financial conditions of a business firm, evaluating its future potential, and perform-

TABLE 4-2. Bank Rates on Short-Term Business Loans (Per Cent per Annum)

Area and Period	All Loans	Size of Loan (Thousands of Dollars)				Area and Period	All Loans	Size of Loan (Thousands of Dollars)			
		1–10	10–100	100–200	200 and Over			1–10	10–100	100–200	200 and Over
Year: 19 large cities:						Quarter—cont.:[a] New York City:					
1957	4.6	5.5	5.1	4.8	4.5	1965—December	5.08	5.74	5.59	5.34	4.99
1958	4.3	5.5	5.0	4.6	4.1	1966—March	5.41	5.92	5.78	5.66	5.34
1959	5.0	5.8	5.5	5.2	4.9	June	5.65	6.14	6.11	5.87	5.57
						September	6.13	6.60	6.57	6.39	6.05
1960	5.2	6.0	5.7	5.4	5.0	December	6.16	6.60	6.56	6.38	6.09
1961	5.0	5.9	5.5	5.2	4.8						
1962	5.0	5.9	5.5	5.2	4.8	7 other northern and eastern cities:					
1963	5.0	5.9	5.5	5.2	4.8	1965—December	5.32	5.95	5.80	5.56	5.19
1964	5.0	5.9	5.6	5.3	4.8	1966—March	5.58	6.10	6.05	5.82	5.46
1965	5.1	5.9	5.6	5.4	4.9	June	5.86	6.32	6.35	6.08	5.74
1966	6.0	6.5	6.4	6.2	5.9	September	6.40	6.62	6.75	6.60	6.31
						December	6.38	6.66	6.81	6.60	6.27
Quarter:[a] 19 large cities:						11 southern and western cities:					
1965—December	5.27	5.96	5.74	5.51	5.11	1965—December	5.46	6.07	5.80	5.59	5.23

1966—March	5.55	6.13	5.96	5.76	5.41
June	5.82	6.39	6.25	6.03	5.68
September	6.30	6.73	6.65	6.51	6.18
December	6.31	6.78	6.70	6.51	6.19

1966—March	5.70	6.23	6.01	5.77	5.50
June	6.00	6.52	6.28	6.08	5.82
September	6.42	6.84	6.65	6.51	6.26
December	6.46	6.91	6.73	6.52	6.29

[a] Based on new loans and renewals for first 15 days of month.

Note: Weighted averages. For descriptions see March 1949 BULLETIN, pp. 228–37.

Bank prime rate was 3½% during the period January 1, 1956—April 12, 1956. Changes thereafter to new levels (in percent) occurred on the following dates:

1956—April 13	3¾
August 21	4
1957—August 6	4½
1958—January 22	4
April 21	3½
September 11	4
1959—May 18	4½
September 1	5
1960—August 23	4½
1965—December 6	5
1966—March 10	5½
June 29	5¾
August 16	6
1967—January 26–27	5½–5¾

Source: Federal Reserve Bulletin, February 1967, p. 270.

ing highly useful services as financial advisors. A large institution is not likely to lack competent officers. But, owing to its size, the large bank may be more interested in accommodating the needs of large companies than those of smaller firms.

In summary, the financial manager should exercise, whenever feasible, considerable care in selecting a bank for his firm. While all or most banks in a given community offer the same variety of services, there are often significant differences in the quality of these services. This is especially true of the ability of the individual lending officer of a bank to render valuable services as advisor on types of loans, sources of long term funds, as well as the methods of financing in a particular situation.

B. Finance Companies

These institutions confine themselves to one major function: the direct lending of funds to a prospective borrower. They are customarily divided into three distinct types: (1) consumer finance companies; (2) sales finance companies; and (3) commercial finance companies.

Consumer finance companies are organized under special state laws to grant loans to individuals within specified limits and interest rates. Sales finance companies, as the name indicates, concentrate on the financing of installment purchases by consumers. As a rule, the retailer extends the credit to the customer who signs the installment contract. Subsequently, the sales finance company acquires the contract from the retailer and remits to him the balance of the purchase price.

Commercial finance companies deal with business firms only. Their objective is to make loans secured by accounts receivable, inventories, and other assets of the firms, although their emphasis is usually on the financing of accounts receivable.

1. Scope and Nature of Operations Commercial finance companies have grown at a very rapid pace since World War II. The volume of their loans to business firms in 1940 totalled $400 million. Twenty years later, in 1960, the total was close to $10 billion,[3] a 25-fold increase in a span of only two decades.

In making a loan against a firm's accounts receivable, the commercial finance company enters into an agreement with the firm for a mutually

---

[3] Clyde W. Phelps, "Accounts Receivable Financing, Studies in Commercial Financing No. 2," Commercial Credit Company, Baltimore, 1962, p. 15.

agreed-upon period of time; usually, at least one year. Under the terms of this agreement, the finance company agrees to advance funds to the firm either by making loans secured by pledge of the firm's accounts receivable; or by purchasing these receivables as they are, with recourse to the firm for any losses on these receivables and without notice to the firm's customers whose accounts have been pledged or conditionally sold.

The term "with recourse" means that the borrowing firm assumes financial responsibility for the account. This responsibility becomes effective if an account either becomes excessively delinquent (i.e., past the due date of the invoice) or proves to be uncollectable by the finance company for any reason. In this case, the borrowing firm has two alternatives. It can turn over to the finance company another account receivable of equivalent value or it can pay off in cash the advance obtained from the finance company.

The phrase "without notice" means that the transaction between the finance company and the borrowing firm is not brought to the attention of the account-debtor. The account therefore does not know that the seller has, in a sense, transferred the claim to the finance company and that the latter has become the claimant or creditor, with the seller as a guarantor of payment.

2. Firm-Customer Relationship   Under such an arrangement, the traditional relationship between seller and customer remains unchanged. The seller makes its own credit analysis of the buyer, decides whether to sell on credit and, if so, handles the collection of the account receivable.

At the same time, the firm assumes certain obligations vis-à-vis the finance company. It notifies the finance company of the sale against which it wants to borrow and usually is required to submit documentary evidence of shipment or delivery. Upon receipt of these documents, the finance company then advances to the firm a percentage of the invoice. This percentage is based on the prior financing agreement. Subsequently, when the firm collects the account from the customer, it repays the advance in one or two forms. The agreement may require the firm to turn over to the finance company the check received from the customer. The excess of the check over the advance is refunded by the finance company, or, if the firm desires, applied to a reduction of its indebtedness to the finance company on other loans. Alternatively, another method authorizes the firm to deposit (on its own bank account) the check from the customer and merely requires the transmission of the firm's check for an amount equal to the advance plus interest charges.

3. Finance Company-Firm Relationship The arrangement between finance company and firm contains the following basic provisions. The finance company—after an analysis of the firm's operation, financial conditions, types of customers, collection record, etc.—agrees to advance funds to the firm on the latter's accounts receivable.

The advance is a given percentage of the face value of the invoice, ranging between 70 and 90%. This type of advance is ordinarily more than adequate to cover a manufacturing firm's costs of buying the goods and processing them for sale, as well as all other out-of-pocket expenses for the sale of the goods to the account (for instance, commissions to salesmen, delivery costs, insurance, etc.).

It should be pointed out that commercial banks also extend loans secured by a pledge (i.e., collateral) of accounts receivable. There are, however, two significant differences in the lending policies of banks as compared with finance companies. Banks do not analyze the quality of the accounts that are pledged as collateral; i.e., they do not make a credit analysis of the accounts. By contrast, finance companies do evaluate the accounts and usually reserve the right to reject those accounts which they do not regard as sound. The second difference lies in the ratio of the loan to the face value of the accounts. Since banks do not evaluate the pledged accounts, their ratio tends to be appreciably lower than the ratio extended by finance companies.

There is no obligation on the part of the firm to maintain a given amount of indebtedness to the finance company. The firm decides when and how many of its accounts it wants to finance. Furthermore, the firm does not have to remain a borrower for the lifetime of the account(s) against which it has borrowed. It can pay off its indebtedness at any time.

As compensation, the firm agrees to pay a specified rate of interest to the finance company for the actual cash obtained and for the number of days of indebtedness. That is to say, the interest charged is figured on a per diem basis and is applied to the average daily balance of indebtedness. For example, firm XY obtains an advance of $50,000 on the first of the month, another of $20,000 on the 20th, pays back $30,000 on the 5th of the second month, and clears its debt on the 25th day of the second month. The schedule of advances then is $50,000 for 19 days, $70,000 for 14 days, and $40,000 for 21 days. Assuming that the interest rate is $\frac{1}{40}$ of 1% per diem (which equals $\frac{365}{40}$ for the year, or $9\frac{1}{8}\%$ per annum) the firm then pays in interest $\frac{19}{40}$ of 1% on $50,000, $\frac{14}{40}$ of 1% on $70,000, etc.

Expressed in dollars, the firm would pay the following amounts:

$\frac{19}{40}$ of 1% on $50,000	$237.50
$\frac{14}{40}$ of 1% on 70,000	245.00
$\frac{20}{40}$ of 1% on 40,000	200.00
Total Cost	$682.50

Let us assume that the firm had obtained a line of credit of $70,000 from a bank at a stand-by fee of $\frac{1}{3}$ of 1% and 5% per annum on any amounts actually drawn. The cost would then be:

$\frac{1}{3}$ of 1% on $70,000 (stand-by fee)	$233.35
$\frac{19}{360}$ of 5% on $50,000	131.94
$\frac{14}{360}$ of 5% on $70,000	136.11
$\frac{20}{360}$ of 5% on $40,000	111.10
Total Cost	$612.50

The firm would clearly prefer the bank loan providing (a) it can obtain a line of credit to be secured by accounts of the same maximum amount ($70,000) as the finance company is willing to extend; and (b) the firm derives no benefit from the independent credit rating of the accounts by the finance company. It is, however, quite conceivable that the firm has no adequate credit department of its own. In this case, the rating service performed by the finance company has a monetary value for the firm; i.e., the firm has no need for a credit manager and is able to save his salary plus the other expenses of a credit department (space, secretarial help, etc.).

4. Inventory Loans Finance companies will also make short-term loans against the firm's inventory. This covers both existing inventory as well as additions to inventory. In these cases, the usual requirement is an assignment of the inventory, or a portion of it, to the finance company. The inventory thus assigned becomes legally the property of the finance company during the process of manufacturing. Usually, the agreement provides that, upon the sale of the finished goods, the accounts receivable replace the inventory as collateral, unless the advance has previously been paid off. Generally, a finance company will make inventory loans as an added service, albeit for profit, to the firm that borrows against its accounts receivable.

Here, too, it should be noted that commercial banks make loans secured by inventory. As in the case of loans against accounts, the rate of interest charged by banks is less than the rate charged by finance companies. From the viewpoint of the borrowing firm, it is again a question of the relative size of the loan that the firm needs and the respective maximum that can be obtained from either source.

Other Types of Loans.   As a supplement to accounts receivable financing, but frequently as a separate transaction not tied to short-term financing, finance companies will also make other types of loans. These include intermediate term loans for the purchase of machinery and equipment, and equipment financing on the installment plan for a period ranging from one to several years.

5. Advantages and Disadvantages   The major advantage of borrowing from a finance company lies in the fact that the firm can convert 70, 80, and sometimes even 90% of its accounts into cash as soon as delivery is made or the goods are shipped to the customer. This enables the firm to maintain as high a rate of output as its sales call for. Assuming that its accounts are good, the firm's rate of expansion depends on its sales rather than on either its net working capital or the credit that it obtains from its suppliers. Moreover, the firm is assured of a continuous source of liquid funds, again assuming that the accounts are sound, even though it shows some deterioration in one or more of its operating ratios. For example, the acid-test ratio may have declined from, say, 1.5:1 to 1:1 because the inventory has grown at a faster pace than sales. This fact will have no effect on the firm's ability to borrow as much or more from a finance company as long as its accounts are, on the whole, sound and acceptable to the lender.

The prime disadvantage of this method of financing is the cost of funds. The interest rate is higher than the prevailing bank charges. However, one point must be stressed here, because it is too often overlooked not only by students but, also, by many businessmen. This point involves a comparison of the marginal effect of two different interest rates on two different-size loans available to the firm.

Assume that firm LM can borrow from a bank a maximum of $50,000 at 6%, while a finance company is willing to make the firm a loan of 75,000 at 8%. What is the marginal cost of borrowing $25,000 more from the finance company? The answer is: 2% on $50,000 plus 8% on $25,000 = $1,000 + $2,000 = $3,000 = 12% on $25,000. The calculation can be made more directly as follows: 6% on $50,000 = $3,000; while 8% on $75,000 = $6,000. Thus, the difference is $6,000 — $3,000 or $3,000 additional interest for the additional $25,000 loan or 12%.

C. Factoring Companies

These companies, known as "factors," purchase receivables outright and assume the full risk of "bad debts." Although historically older than commercial banks, factors rank third below finance companies in volume of short-term financing. In 1941, factoring accounted for more than one billion dollars, or over twice the total of loans made by finance companies. Although this type of financing grew at a rapid rate in the postwar period and reached about $4 billion[4] in 1955, it fell far short of the volume attained by finance companies, which was approximately $7 billion.

Historically, factoring is as old as foreign trade. The factor, as he was called, was a combination of agent, sales representative, seller, and collector who acted in behalf of his principal whose business was located in some distant country. Factors played a major role, first, in the commerce of the New England colonies with the mother country and, later, in the trade of the southern colonies with European nations. Their major area of business was in cotton and textiles.

In the nineteenth century, the factoring company emerged in the United States as the financier of textile mills, but was no longer concerned either with the sales function or with the delivery of goods to the customers. Instead, the modern factor deals with and through the selling firm. The selling firm fixes the price and terms of trade, contacts the customers, and solicits the orders. It is after the receipt of the order that the factor enters the scene through the credit function of the seller. Furthermore, factoring companies of today no longer confine their activities to the field of textiles.

1. Scope and Nature of Factoring   Modern factoring involves an agreement between the factor and the firm for a specified period of time. Under this agreement, the factoring company assumes the function of credit analyst for the client. If the factor approves the credit of an account it *purchases* the account *without recourse* to the seller if the customer subsequently becomes delinquent in payment or defaults on the obligation. Instead, the factor assumes the full risk of collection. However, the account (i.e., the customer) is notified that the claim has been factored and is payable to the factoring company.

[4] *Ibid.,* p. 66.

As stated earlier, the factoring company in the 19th century was identified almost entirely with textiles and cotton. In the course of this century, factoring has spread into a wide variety of fields; for instance, chemicals, cosmetics, electrical appliances, furniture, hardware, housewares, paints, paper, and other lines of business. However, the textile industry with its many modern branches—wool, cotton, synthetic fibres; men's, women's and children's apparel; carpets, bedding, etc.—is still by far the largest single industry financed by factoring companies.

2. Effect on Firm's Management Function   The major contribution of the factoring company is its assumption of the functions of credit analysis and collection for the business firm. Viewed from the perspective of managment, the factor offers the following services.

First, the factor assumes the entire responsibility for determining whether or not the customer merits the credit involved in the order. For this purpose, the factoring company maintains its own staff of credit analysts. As a result, the client of the factor need not maintain a separate credit department. To the firm, this represents a saving in salaries and space allocation, plus a corresponding reduction in the management function of evaluating the credit risk of customers.

Second, the factor purchases the account on the date when delivery is made and transfers, to the firm, the face amount of the invoice minus the agreed-upon interest charge. The factoring company also takes on the responsibility for collecting the amounts due from the accounts receivable which it approved. On this score, collection of accounts due, the client-firm saves expenses and management time. It must be noted, however, that the firm may, if it so chooses, extend credit to a customer whom the factor has rejected. In this case, the firm provides the funds to carry the account and assumes responsibility for collection.

3. Costs of Factoring   The charges by the factor consist of two distinct elements. The factor receives a commission for performing the credit and collection functions and for agreeing to purchase the account (for collection) at the expiration of the credit term. The usual charge ranges between 1 and 2% of the net amount due. That is to say, if the customer receives a quantity discount from the sales price or a credit for the return of defective merchandise, or some other concession, these amounts are deducted from the gross amount shown on the invoice and the commission is then calculated on the net sum.

The firm pays interest at the agreed-upon rate on the funds which it draws prior to the due date of the accounts. Conversely, if the firm leaves funds on deposit with the factor after the due date of the factored accounts, the factor pays a stipulated rate of interest to the firm.

Assume that a firm has sold $48,000 worth of goods on March 1 to several accounts. The factor has approved these accounts and the terms of sale call for 1%-10 days net 30 days. The net invoice price is roughly $47,500. Assume, further, that the agreement between factor and firm calls for a commission of 1.5% and interest of 7%. On March 10th, the firm wants to draw $25,000 against the invoices and, on March 20th, another $22,500. The factor's charges will then be as follows:

(a)	Commission 1.5% on $47,500 =	$712.50
(b)	Interest at 7% per annum for 21 days on $25,000 =	99.75
	" at 7% per annum for 11 " on $22,500 =	47.41
	Total charges	$859.66

The sum of $859.66 represents the total cost to the firm in the above example. At the time when the firm confirms the order, the account must be notified that the claim for the net amount of the invoice has been assigned to the factoring company and is payable to the latter. If the customer(s), for any reason whatsoever, is either delinquent in paying the invoice or, in an extreme case, defaults wholly or in part, the factor shoulders the loss.

4. Advantages and Disadvantages   The major advantage to the firm is the fact that it need not maintain its own credit and collection department. The savings in money and managerial time must be weighed against the cost, as expressed in the commission charge. Assume that the firm has monthly net sales averaging $200,000. The factor's commission will amount, if the rate is 1.5%, to $3,000 per month. This cost of $3,000 must then be compared with the following expenses that the firm would incur in the absence of a factor agreement: (a) the cost of operating its own credit and collection department; (b) the average number of days for which accounts receivable are not collected in excess of the credit terms and the cost of borrowing money from another source for this excess of days; and (c) the average losses suffered from default of accounts; i.e., bad debt losses.

If, in the above example, the estimated average of the three elements is close to or exceeds $3,000 per month, the firm would probably be better off in using a factor than operating its own credit and collection department.

The major disadvantages of a factoring arrangement are twofold. First, the firm will find it difficult to obtain accommodations from a commercial bank if it has sold its accounts payable to a factor. The only current asset which the firm could then offer as collateral to a bank would be the inventory. Second, the customers of the firm may look with disfavor upon a transaction in which they will be indebted to a factor. Many customers may feel—rightly or wrongly—that the factor will either not be ready to grant an extension of the due date or will charge an excessive rate of interest.

D. Commercial Paper

In the preceding analysis of short-term financing, the transactions between firm and lender are personal and direct. That is to say, the borrower negotiates directly with the financial institution; and, if the loan is consummated, the firm is the debtor and the institution is the creditor. By contrast, loans based on commercial paper are impersonal and indirect.

The commercial paper is a promissory note of the borrower payable to himself and endorsed by him without qualification. This endorsement makes the paper a bearer instrument. It has a maturity usually between 90 and 180 days. The holder of the paper on the maturity date has a direct and immediate claim against the original endorser; i.e., the borrowing firm. During the interval between date of issue and due date, the paper may pass through many hands by means of sale and purchase without any additional endorsement and, thus, no liability on the part of anyone except the original borrower. The purchaser of commercial paper makes no direct credit analysis of the borrower. Although the dealer, too, assumes no legal liability in selling the firm's paper, he will make good if the borrower defaults in order to protect his own reputation vis-à-vis the purchasers of the paper.

However, only firms with superior financial rating are able to qualify for the ready acceptance of their notes in the commercial-paper market. Their qualifications are determined by specialized dealers in commercial paper to whom the borrower sells the note at face value minus the rate of interest. The dealer in turn sells the paper to banks, business firms, and other financial institutions who desire to invest excess cash funds for a period of a few days or weeks in highly liquid and sound paper.

Borrowing by means of commercial paper offers two advantages to the firm. First, the interest rate is lower than is ordinarily charged by banks on loans of the same quality. Second, the requirements of the firm may be in excess of the amount which the bank is able to lend.

SUMMARY

In our expanding economy, it is necessary for a firm to keep pace with or surge ahead of its industry's rate of expansion if the firm is to preserve or increase its share of the market. Since almost all commercial transactions are on credit terms, it is necessary for the financial manager to ensure that his firm has ready access to the available sources of credit so that it may grow.

There are both external causes of growth, such as technology, population, and market; and internal causes of growth, such as personal ambition, excess capacity, and research. Regardless of the causes of growth, the financial manager must be prepared for the financial impact of growth on the firm.

Growth will cause changes in such asset items as receivables and inventory and will, therefore, often result in short-term needs for funds to finance these changes.

The financial manager must measure the short-term needs for funds by looking at five elements. These are (1) the scheduled purchases from various trade sources, (2) the direct out-of pocket expenses for labor and services during the production or selling cycle, (3) promotional and related expenses, (4) the average collection period of receivables, and (5) projected profits.

Once short-term needs for funds have been measured, the financial manager must obtain the necessary funds to meet these needs. He may be able to obtain these from funds generated through operations or from trade sources. He may also turn to external financial sources for some or all of these needs.

The three principal external financial sources are commercial banks, factoring companies, and finance companies. In seeking a commercial bank loan, the financial manager must be aware of the four C's of bank credit: Character, Capacity, Capital, and Collateral. Finance companies and factors will also be interested in some or all of these four C's.

Questions

1. What financial problems are caused by changes in technology?
2. What factors, internal to the firm, lead to a momentum toward growth?

3. Give some examples of the effect of a firm's growth on receivables. How can the financial manager minimize these problems?

4. What expenses will usually increase when sales increase as a result of penetration of a new market or introduction of a new product?

5. A firm extends its credit terms from 45 days to 60 days. What financial effect will this have on the firm? What effect will a tightening of terms have on the firm?

6. Is it possible for a firm to make a $40,000 profit and still have to borrow $20,000 from the bank to pay its bills? Why?

7. What services does a commercial bank perform for a firm in addition to its function as a lender of funds?

8. What is a line of credit? What are its advantages as compared with a single loan?

9. How does a bank evaluate the credit of a potential borrower?

10. What are the advantages and disadvantages of borrowing from a finance company? From a factor?

Problems

1. Omnicron Company is projecting sales of $3,500,000 in 1967. Purchases of raw materials are approximately 50% of sales. Supplier A is willing to offer 30 days of credit after receipt of invoice by the firm. Supplier B is willing to offer 40 days of credit after receipt of invoice by the firm. Assuming purchases are made monthly in equal amounts throughout the year, calculate Omnicron Company's monthly level of payables if it purchases all its raw materials from supplier A. Calculate Omnicron's level of payables if Omnicron purchases all its raw materials from supplier B.

2. Delta Corporation factors its accounts receivable with Amalgamated Factor Corporation. Amalgamated has approved accounts with a net invoice price of $279,000 on terms of net 30 days beginning December 1. The agreement between Amalgamated and Delta calls for a commission of 1.25% on all accounts approved by Amalgamated plus interest of 6.75% per annum. Delta wishes to draw $100,000 on December 1st against the invoice and $125,000 more on December 15th. What will be the total cost to Delta, as of the close of business on December 30th?

3. The Riklas Company, anticipating an increase in sales, applied to the Central Trust National Bank for an additional loan of $27,000 in October, 1966. Riklas already owes the bank $16,200. Riklas is a wholesaler of home heating equipment. The company leases its physical facilities in order to avoid investing heavily in fixed assets. About 60% of the firm's sales are for repair work. Terms of sale are net 30 days. Estimated annual sales should run from $400,000 to $550,000. Balance sheets and income statements are listed in Tables 4-3 and 4-4.

TABLE 4-3.   Riklas Company Balance Sheets (Dollars)

	June 30, 1966	September 30, 1966
Cash	$ 1,202	$ 452
Accounts receivables	37,050	43,500
Inventory	60,602	87,243
Prepaid expenses	125	232
Equipment (less depreciation)	3,732	4,368
	$102,711	$135,795
Notes payable: bank	0	16,200
Notes payable: trade	200	23,725
Accounts payable	58,535	51,370
Owners equity	43,976	44,500
	$102,711	$135,795

TABLE 4-4.   Riklas Company Income Statements (Dollars)

	Year Ended June 30, 1966	Quarter Ended September 30, 1966
Sales	$398,204	$105,223
Cost of sales	346,927	91,802
Gross margin	51,277	13,421
Expenses	30,317	8,423
Net profit before taxes	20,960	4,998
Taxes	10,480	2,499
Net profit after taxes	$ 10,480	$ 2,499

Mr. John Riklas and his brother Michael together own all the stock. They have been in this business for more than nine years. Should the Central Trust National Bank make the additional loan of $27,000 as requested?

Case: Keen Slot-Car Corporation

Mr. John H. Keen organized the Keen-Slot Car Corporation in 1963 to manufacture and sell slot-cars to hobby centers and individual slot-car enthusiasts. Slot-cars are scale models of racing automobiles. They are raced at special slot-car hobby centers, predominantly by teenage boys. Mr. Keen, who has had over 20 years experience in various phases of the hobby industry, picked a good time to enter the slot-car manufacturing business. Growth in interest in slot-car racing was rapid in the 1960's and demand for Keen's product proved excellent. After nine months of operation, the new venture was operating at a profit. For the fiscal year ending July 1, 1964, a profit of $6700 was earned by the company. Sales and income continued to grow in 1965 and 1966 (see Tables 4-5 and 4-6 for financial

TABLE 4-5.   Keen Slot-Car Corporation: Income Statements (in Thousands of Dollars)

	Year Ending July 1, 1964	Year Ending July 1, 1965	Year Ending July 1, 1966
Net sales	99.3	175.4	252.8
Cost of sales	50.5	92.3	139.8
Gross profit	48.8	83.1	113.0
Expenses	39.2	49.9	62.3
Net profit before taxes	9.6	33.2	50.7
Income taxes	2.9	11.5	20.0
Net profit after taxes	6.7	21.7	30.7
Reconciliation of Retained Earnings			
Retained earnings (beginning of year)	—	6.7	18.4
Net profit after taxes	6.7	21.7	30.7
Total	6.7	28.4	49.1
Less dividends paid	—	10.0	10.0
Retained earnings (end of year)	6.7	18.4	39.1

Table 4-6. Keen Slot-Car Corporation: Balance Sheets (in Thousands of Dollars)

	July 1, 1964	July 1, 1965	July 1, 1966
Assets			
Cash	3.5	3.8	5.2
Accounts receivable	15.2	23.7	30.7
Inventory	17.5	25.8	48.4
Total current assets	36.2	53.3	84.3
Machinery and equipment	16.3	22.8	35.7
Other assets	1.0	1.9	2.7
Total assets	53.5	78.0	122.7
Liabilities			
Accounts payable	15.7	25.3	42.3
Accruals	1.5	5.7	10.0
Notes payable	4.6	3.6	6.3
Total current liabilities	21.8	34.6	58.6
Common stock	25.0	25.0	25.0
Retained earnings	6.7	78.4	39.1
Total liabilities	53.5	78.0	122.7

data). The growth in sales led to increased demand for working capital. With the exception of dividend payments of $10,000 in 1965 and again in 1966, all retained earnings were plowed back for purposes of expansion. Mr. Keen wishes to pay dividends each year to satisfy family stockholders and to build a record for the firm in the event that a public sale of common stock could eventually be made.

Funds were temporarily borrowed from family members to help finance buildups in inventory before the Christmas selling season. Manufacturers of equipment purchased by the corporation helped meet the shortage of working capital by granting short-term loans to the corporation, secured by chattel mortgages on the equipment.

Mr. Keen believes sales will continue to grow at a rapid rate during the fiscal year beginning July 1, 1966. A 50% sales increase would be feasible if sufficient cash is available to finance increases in inventory and accounts receivable levels. Mr. Keen believes that if sales increase 50%, inventory levels will have to increase by about $25,000 to $30,000 over the present levels and receivables will increase $15,000 to $20,000. In addition, equipment purchases of approximately $15,000 will have to be made. Thus, approximately $55,000 to $65,000 will be needed to finance the expected growth in sales.

Mr. Keen does not wish to issue additional common stock at this time. The equipment manufacturer is willing to give the corporation a one-year note for $10,000, to be secured by a chattel mortgage on the $15,000 of new equipment to be purchased. Mr. Keen and his family will lend the firm $25,000 on a subordinated basis.

Thus, if growth is to continue as expected, Mr. Keen must raise $25,000 to $35,000 from some outside source of short-term funds. Mr. Keen believes this loan can easily be repaid out of profits. If sales remain at present levels of $250,000 next year, profits should be enough to repay a $30,000 loan in one year. If sales increase as expected, profits should be between $40,000 and $55,000 in the next year. In addition, funds generated by operations in the form of depreciation should furnish approximately $5000 in the next year.

Mr. Keen is uncertain as to how he should raise the $25,000 to $35,000 needed. One alternative is a short-term loan from the Van Buren State Bank. The bank would be willing to make a loan up to $35,000, effective immediately for up to one year, with interest at 6% per annum on the amount borrowed at any one time. A minimum deposit of $3500 must be kept in the bank during the duration of the loan. The family loans must not be repaid until the bank loan has been repaid. Dividends must not exceed $2500 per quarter. Executive salaries must not be increased during the period of the loan. Current assets must be at least 125% of current liabilities at all times in which the loan is outstanding. Financial statements must be furnished to the bank monthly. In addition, Mr. Keen must personally sign the note and pledge his house (value $50,000) as security for the loan. Finally, the accounts receivable and the inventory could not be pledged to any other lender until the bank loan was repaid.

A second alternative is to sell the present accounts receivable to the Old Line Factoring Corporation. Old Line will purchase all existing receivables for 90% of stated value. The factor will collect these accounts directly from the customers of Keen Slot-Car Corporation. Keen must agree to buy back all accounts not collectible in ninety days.

Old Line also has offered to completely take over the credit function of the corporation. Old Line will investigate all credit requests and will buy all approved future accounts receivable at 92% of stated value. Old

Line would take full responsibility for collecting these accounts and would take any losses owing to bad debts on approved accounts. Keen could still sell on a credit basis to unapproved accounts, but the factor would neither service nor purchase such accounts.

Case Questions:

1. What do you think of Mr. Keen's financial planning?
2. Why has the bank inserted such strict restrictions and conditions in the proposed loan?
3. What are the advantages and disadvantages of selling the receivables to the factor?
4. What should Mr. Keen do to raise the funds needed?

Chapter Five

~~~~~~

The Financial Management of Receivables

As stated in an earlier chapter, most business transactions in the United States are based on credit. Furthermore, these credit sales are in the form of open accounts.[1] That is to say, the receipted invoice of the buyer is the documentary evidence of the transaction and of the terms that the customer accepted. However, unlike the payor on a negotiable instrument (such as a promissory note), the debtor on an open-account transaction can raise a variety of legal arguments in defense of nonpayment; e.g., defective merchandise, failure of the supplier to make repairs or replacements, delays by the seller in fulfilling some provisions of the sales contract. Thus, an open-account transaction always involves some element of risk, other than bankruptcy of the customer, that payment may not be made on the due date and that a considerable expenditure of time and legal costs may be incurred in collecting the debt.

Credit sales in general mean that the seller is financing the customer's purchase for the interval of time that elapses between shipment of the goods and the receipt of the invoice price. Whatever volume is sold on credit automatically becomes a corresponding amount of receivables on the books of the selling firm. This chapter examines the role of the financial manager in the formulation of the firm's policy on credit sales and credit practices.

[1] Domestic transactions in many foreign countries as well as international transactions by foreign and American export firms are, as a general rule, based on negotiable instruments, such as promissory notes, banker's acceptances, and letters of (bank) credit. In these cases, the seller can obtain a quick judgment against the debtor if the latter fails to make payment on the specified maturity date.

I. THE DETERMINANTS OF RECEIVABLES

The objective of the financial manager is to maintain an equilibrium between the customers' demands for credit sales and the firm's supply (resources) of funds at a level of sales that maximizes profits and minimizes risk. We shall first examine the factors that determine the demand for credit sales.

A. Analyzing Demand for Credit Sales

The demand for the firm's goods is influenced to a substantial degree by its credit terms. The customers, whether they are business firms or ultimate consumers, have a given amount of cash on hand. If their purchases exceed the cash funds, they must obtain the difference in credit. This credit can be made available by the seller or by a financial institution that is prepared to advance the necessary amounts.

The business firm that buys on credit expects to meet its obligation (account payable) from the sale of goods. Thus, the willingness of the selling firm to accept payment in, for example, 30 days after its business customer receives the invoice, gives the customer roughly one month in which to sell the goods and obtain the cash for payment of the bill. Now, if this business customer is given 60 days in which to make payment, the probability of resale within two months is obviously greater than in a one-month period. The more liberal the credit terms, the greater the likelihood of increased sales—providing that the customer, in turn, feels reasonably sure that he can sell the goods prior to the expiration of the credit; or, as an alternative, obtain a bank loan to make the payment to the supplier.

1. Cyclical Influences The level of economic activity is characterized by wave-like fluctuations that are known as the business cycle. Its four major phases are: (1) expansion or prosperity, (2) decline, (3) depression, and (4) recovery. Just as the total economy experiences these recurring ups and downs, the individual industry goes through the same four phases. However, the scope of the fluctuation from the peak of prosperity to the low of a recession, or depression, and the duration of either a single phase or of the entire cycle differs among industries and between a particular industry and the economy as a whole.

During the two phases of decline and depression, the rate of business failures, in the form of insolvencies and bankruptcies, rises sharply. The firm that sells on credit assumes, therefore, a greater risk of losses from bad debts. Accounts that were rated as good risks in the preceding prosperity phase may turn out to be poor risks when market conditions turn downward. It then becomes the task of the financial manager to determine whether and to what extent the firm can afford to assume the risk of delinquencies in payment and losses from bad debts.

The first visible symptom of the economic recession is usually an appreciable decline in sales, often accompanied by a drop in prices and profits. If the firm decides to confine its credit sales only to "sound" credit risks, it may automatically lose a substantial portion of its former customers, thus accentuating the drop in sales and profits. The other alternative is to attempt to stem the fall in sales by offering more liberal credit terms to all of its regular customers. However, in this case the bank, or the finance company, may not be willing to provide the necessary credits. Thus, in a period of economic recession, it is the financial manager's responsibility to estimate how far his firm can go in meeting this demand from customers.

But periods of recovery and prosperity also create problems for the financial manager. First, there is the tendency for new enterprises to enter the market when business is on the upswing. A new establishment may conceivably be more progressive and aggressive in its marketing methods. As a consequence, these potential customers may require and want more liberal credit terms in order to sustain their rapidly expanding volume of sales. The financial manager must decide how far the firm can and should go in extending credit to new customers as well as to old customers. Furthermore, even among the older customers, the rate of expansion will vary in a period of recovery and boom. In these cases, too, a determination has to be made as to the extent to which the firm can accommodate the subsequent demand for credit sales.

B. Seasonal Variations

In most lines of business, the volume of sales is affected, favorably or unfavorably, by seasonal influences. While air conditioners sell relatively well in the late spring, few if any are sold in the cold months of the year when oil or gas burners record peak sales. Easter and Christmas exert strong seasonal influences on consumer gift spending.

From the viewpoint of the financial manager, seasonal variations in the sales of the firm's customers have the following implications. In anticipation of a rising seasonal sales volume, the firm's accounts will tend to place correspondingly larger orders with delivery usually required either in advance of or very early in the season. In addition, the whole-saler and, frequently, the retailer, too, wants a full line (i.e., selectivity) and ample inventory of each item in the line in order to maximize his sales potential as the seasonal demand gets into full swing. To the firm, this means that the demand for sales on credit by its customers increases sharply.

The seasonal element operates within the basic frame of the cyclical factor. Thus, if the projection is for a general upswing of the economy or of the particular industry, the seasonal influence will have a corre-spondingly accentuating effect. As a result, the financial manager must anticipate a rise in sales and demand for credit terms due, in part, to cyclical expansion and, in part, to the seasonal element. At the same time, the financial manager must estimate the probable increase in funds for the expanded output—or, in the case of a distributing firm, the expanded inventory—which precedes the subsequent sale.

The next step is a determination of the adequacy of the firm's re-sources (1) to assume the obligations for the expanded purchases and (2) to carry the accounts receivable until they are collected. It is quite conceivable that the firm's projection of sales, collections, and profit are not shared by its traditional source of funds (e.g., the bank or the finance company). In these cases, it would be poor business policy to encourage the sales department to solicit as many orders as can be obtained and then fail to deliver the goods because the firm cannot extend credit to accounts that have a reasonably good credit rating. Conversely, it would be foolish—in terms of lost profit opportunities—for the firm to restrict in advance the volume of orders because the management failed to procure potentially available external sources of short-term funds.

Since seasonal variations are, by their very nature, recurring experi-ences and, within limits, fairly predictable, the financial manager's task is readily defined. How much of an increase in seasonal credit sales can our firm anticipate and what is the maximum which we shall be able to finance from various sources?

C. Competitive Credit Terms

The extension of credit is, in comparison with a cash transaction, an invisible concession in price. Suppose Company ABD receives two offers that involve goods of identical quality and price, but one offer is conditional on payment in cash on receipt of the merchandise while the second offer includes 30 days credit. Other things being equal, there can be little doubt that Company ABD will select the offer that includes the 30 days of credit.

Thus, the extension of credit becomes an important instrument of competition in the market. As a matter of fact, some firms may be willing to pay a slightly higher price in return for more liberal credit terms. This fact is generally recognized in the practice adopted by many firms of quoting literally two prices: the cash price and the credit price. One procedure is to quote, for example, a price of $5 and to specify 1%-10 days, net 30 days.

Although each firm quotes its own terms of sale, the latter are, in large measure, determined by competition in the market. In a competitive market, the basic structure of the terms of sale tend to be fairly uniform throughout the industry. At the same time, however, the individual firm may, and frequently does, depart from its listed terms of sales in an attempt to obtain an edge over its competitors.

Looking at it again from the viewpoint of the financial manager, two questions arise. First, how much of a premium can the firm afford to offer its customers for payment within 10 days? And second, how much will it cost in the form of interest, both real and imputed, as well as possibly other charges if the firm agrees to carry the open account for 30, 45, or more days? These issues are a restatement in financial terms of the economic principle of marginal utility—the addition to net revenues from incremental sales attained through extension of credit—as over the marginal disutility; i.e., the cost of financing these incremental sales.

II. EVALUATION OF RECEIVABLES

For many firms the receivables represent, by a substantial margin, the largest single item among the current assets. The liquidity of these assets—reflected in the rate of inflow of payments compared with the length of credit extended by the firm—determines, in large measure, the ability of the firm to meet its own obligations to suppliers and to the financial lenders of funds. The strategic role of receivables necessitates a periodic evaluation of the firm's credit policy by the financial manager.

A. Classification of Accounts

The relevant data are found in the sales records of the firm. The first step is to divide the accounts into categories by type of accounts.

Depending on the firm's market, its customers usually fall into one or more of the following four major categories: (1) nonbusiness accounts, i.e., governmental bodies (federal, state, county, local) and their departments, agencies, and subdivisions; nonprofit institutions (e.g., colleges and universities, research organizations, charitable organizations, hospitals, religious bodies, and similar organizations); (2) business users, i.e., accounts that buy the products of the firm for direct use in the purchasing company's establishment; (3) distributors, a group made up of wholesalers and retailers who purchase for resale either to other business firms for direct use or to the ultimate consumers; and (4) ultimate consumers.

Each of the above four categories can be further subdivided into specific classifications. Whether and how far such detailed classification is desirable depends on the operations of the firm and its experience record. The objective of the classification of accounts is twofold. It is intended to provide the financial manager with a statistical tool to measure the probable length of time (days) it will take before certain types of accounts make payment for goods received. And second, it also provides a tool with which to measure the quality of some receivables.

It must be emphasized that a customer who is habitually "delinquent" in paying on or before the due date of the invoice is not necessarily a poor credit risk. In fact, some of the best credit risks may be notoriously slow payers of bills. Some of the larger municipalities are known to be habitually late in making payments for goods or services purchased; at times as much as six months or more. To some extent, this may be attributed to excessive red tape within a department before payment is approved and processed. A similar situation is found in some of the departments of the Federal government. Even in some large business firms, it is not unusual for a division to make a purchase and to request the seller to postdate the invoice by 30 days or more because the division has already committed its allocated funds for the next two or three months.

By classifying the sales by types of accounts and by the length of time that elapses between due dates and actual payment, the financial manager obtains a realistic picture of the rate of liquidity of the various types of receivables. This information, in turn, provides the basis for an estimate of the time interval for which these slow accounts have to be financed.

1. Nonbusiness Accounts   Table 5-1 illustrates a breakdown of nonbusiness accounts by the manufacturer of specialized office equipment

TABLE 5-1. Breakdown of Nonbusiness Accounts Covering Fiscal Year 19—

Customer Classification	Total Annual Sales (Dollars)	Percent	Payment Received from Date of Delivery									
			10 Days		30 Days		31–45 Days		46–60 Days		Over 60 Days	
			Dollars	Percent	Dollars	Percent	Dollars	Percent	Dollars	Percent	Dollars	Percent
Federal Government	400,000		100,000	10	100,000	10	75,000	7.5	125,000	12.5		
Department of Agriculture	50,000						50,000					
Department of Labor	75,000						25,000		50,000			
Department of Defense	275,000											
Department of Air Force	100,000		100,000									
Department of Army	25,000								25,000			
Department of Navy	150,000				100,000				50,000			
State Governments	50,000	5			50,000	5						
County Governments	75,000	7.5	50,000	5	75,000	2.5						
Municipalities	300,000	30	100,000	10	50,000	5.0			50,000	5	100,000	10
Institutions	175,000	17.5	100,000	10	25,000	2.5	25,000	2.5	25,000	2.5		
Colleges and Universities	100,000		75,000						25,000			
Organizations	50,000		25,000		25,000							
Hospitals	25,000								25,000			
Totals	1,000,000	100.0	350,000	35	250,000	25	100,000	10	200,000	20	100,000	10

whose customers include all of the previously mentioned categories. This company breaks down its sales by (a) type of account, (b) amount of annual sales, (c) length of time that elapsed before payment was received, and (d) the percentage(s) of all sales for which payment was received within various time intervals.

In analyzing this table, the financial manager first looks at the bottom line. This shows quickly that 35% of all accounts were paid within 10 days. At the other extreme, over 60 days, he finds that 10% of all sales were made to accounts in this category. Looking at this column vertically, he pinpoints municipalities as the slow payors. The same procedure is followed with the other time intervals and percentages of all accounts involved.

The next section will discuss the several alternatives that the financial manager may explore as a means of either cutting down the "waiting period" or, if this is not feasible, of procuring the funds to carry the slow accounts. At this point, it is necessary to merely point out briefly the role that a breakdown like that shown in Table 5-1 plays in considering the several alternatives. All purchase orders from the federal government and its departments or agencies specifically provide that the seller will not assign such claims to a third party. This provision automatically prevents the selling firm from procuring a loan against this claim from a finance company or selling it to a factor who insists that each loan be secured by an assignment of the claim to the lender. However, the contract clause does not prevent the firm from obtaining a bank loan since many commercial banks grant unsecured loans, i.e., without pledge or assignment of specific assets such as accounts receivable. The breakdown of accounts provides one of several guideposts in the planning by the financial manager.

Another advantage lies in the fact that this analysis of the accounts often leads to a reexamination of the sales policy. For example, a revision of the terms of sale to a public authority or to a nonprofit organization from 1%-10 days to 1%-20 days will, at times, work miracles. By stretching the discount period to 20 days, the firm may improve very substantially the chances that the invoice will reach the disbursement officer prior to the expiration of the 1% discount period. Quite often, these invoices are approved for payment while other invoices with expired discount periods are pushed back into the file and payment may be delayed for several weeks, or even months. The major reason for this inequality in the treatment of suppliers is to be found in the complexity of the bureaucratic process. Invoices must pass through several administrative layers before they reach the disbursing officer. While some departments can process invoices fairly rapidly, either because they have adequate staff or relatively few invoices, others may require considerable time for processing the required forms.

2. Business Users Every firm is, in a sense, a "consumer" of durable goods. Machines, tools, furnishings, and many other items constitute the fixed assets of the establishment. These items are purchased either to expand existing capacity or to replace used-up assets. The purchase of these assets, which have a usable lifetime of a few years, is frequently "financed" by the seller by means of either an extended credit of several months or on the basis of an installment-purchase contract for a period of one or more years. In the last case, the seller customarily arranges in advance for the sale of these installment papers to a financial institution; i.e., bank or finance company. The effect is the same as a cash transaction, except that the seller may have to assume liability if the purchaser defaults on payments. In the case of a credit sale, the seller must decide whether to carry the account until the invoice is due or whether to borrow against these receivables from a financial institution and pay the cost; i.e., the interest of the loan.

3. Distributors Wholesalers and retailers are middleman. Their purchases are intended for resale. The rate of turnover and the terms on which they sell determine, in large measure, their ability to take advantage of the cash discount offered by the seller.

Most wholesalers operate in geographic areas that may encompass a portion of a state, several states, or an entire region of the country. Each wholesaler must adapt his selling terms to the retail conditions prevailing in his territory. These will, however, vary from state to state or from region to region. In a predominantly agricultural territory, retailers will, for example, extend credit for considerable periods of time to their farmer-customers. These retailers, in turn, will expect similarly liberal terms from their wholesalers. Most urban retailers, except for larger specialty shops and department stores, sell in a shorter cycle.

A manufacturer who markets his products through wholesalers in different economic regions is, therefore, likely to find that his distributors have a varied pattern of paying their bills. Some distributors will take advantage of the cash discounts. Others will frequently exceed the credit terms as a result of local retail conditions.

The financial records of the company will reveal whether or not the accounts show a distinct and continuous variation in payments as a result of local or regional trade customs. If this type of situation appears to be present, a regional breakdown of wholesaler accounts will enable the financial manager to quickly identify two facets: (1) the relative magnitudes that are involved in the slow-paying regions, and (2) the excess time interval between the firm's normal term—for example, 30 days—and the actual number of days before payment is received. Moreover, the financial manager can prepare a projection of the rate of cash inflow from each of the several territories based on the sales manager's sales forecast for the different regions. Suppose the sales manager of a firm predicts 10% of next year's sales for region D. Assume, that, in the preceding fiscal year, this region showed an average of 50 days from the date of delivery to the date of payment. The financial manager can then estimate that, during the next fiscal year, ten percent of all receivables will be "slow," assuming that the firm has a standard term of 30 days net.

The same would apply to a manufacturer or a wholesaler who sells to retailers. Here, too, a breakdown of retailers by location may reveal the presence of a pattern that deviates from the standard terms of the firm.

4. Ultimate Consumers   Retailers who sell on credit to the ultimate consumer face a more complex problem than wholesalers and manufacturers who make credit sales. The only exceptions are retailers who sell on the installment plan and who have made prior arrangements with a financial institution to finance this installment paper in full. In these cases, the financial manager has no problem. The consumer either pays in cash or he signs the installment contract which is then turned over to the financing institution. The financing institution then pays the retailer the face amount of the bill and assumes the cost of collection and the risk of default. These costs are covered by the excess of the interest charges on the installment loan over the regular bank rate of interest, or by a discount of the face value of the bill. A substantial portion of retail credit to consumers is similar to open-account transactions between business firms. For example, many retailers offer interest-free 3-months credit if one-third of the purchase price is paid each month. Another form of credit is the charge account without interest charge, if payment is made within 30 days after the invoice is received. Many retailers frequently advertise preseason credit sales without downpayment and the purchase price payable in two or three installments at the start of the season, which may be several months away. Retailers of heating equipment frequently offer installation in the spring with the first payment to start in the fall.

Unlike most business firms, the average consumer has few compunctions about being "a little late" in making payment on his credit purchases. This is particularly true in credit transactions between the retailer and customer but is not infrequent in installment contracts as well.

Therefore to the financial manager, it is a matter of major importance to evaluate periodically his firm's experience with consumer credit extended directly by the firm. To be sure, the retailer may, and usually will, obtain a line of credit from a financial institution to enable him to carry the consumer's account. However, the retailer is liable for default of the customer. Moreover, the retailer is expected to pay back the loan at specified periods. If his receipts do not flow in at the anticipated time and volume, he may find himself unable to meet his obligation on time.

By analyzing the record of the various types of credit and the rate of cash inflow from these receivables, the financial manager gains an important insight into the scope and type of short-term funds needed for the financing of credit sales. He can negotiate for loans on terms that will coincide fairly closely with the *actual* rather than the *contractual* credit periods of the firm's customers.

III. IMPROVING THE STRUCTURE OF RECEIVABLES

The procurement of external funds to finance short-term credit sales presents no serious problem to the financial manager of a large company that sells to business firms only. For one thing, a large company can usually count on its customers' compliance with the established credit terms. Large accounts are ordinarily accustomed either to take advantage of the cash discount or to make payment on the due date. Small accounts will not risk their credit standing with the large supplier through delinquency of payment. The large corporation will, therefore, rarely experience any difficulty in obtaining short-term bank loans to carry its receivables.

The small company enjoys few of these advantages. Its large accounts will in this case, too, either take the discount or pay on the due date. However, its smaller accounts will not hesitate to exceed the credit terms. One reason is that the small supplier is frequently under competitive pressure from other suppliers either on price or on terms or both. Moreover, the small supplier, unlike the large corporation, is not inclined to drop an account that is habitually late in payment as long as there is no likelihood of business failure of the debtor. And lastly, the small firm cannot always count on sufficient bank loans to finance the receivables.

As a result, the financial manager of the small firm is constantly striving to find ways and means of reducing the volume of receivables without impeding the firm's sales potential. If successful in this endeavor, he will gain two advantages for his firm. The volume of receivables which has to be financed through short-term loans is reduced. In addition, the ability of the firm to obtain funds at lower costs and for a higher proportion of its receivables is likely to be improved appreciably. There are several alternatives which offer the financial manager the opportunity to attain his dual objective.

1. Changing the Cash Discount   One alternative involves an increase in the discount offered for payment within a stated period. Thus, instead of offering, for example, a discount of 1% the firm may find that an increase to $1\frac{1}{2}\%$ will induce an appreciable number of accounts to take advantage of the higher premium. The financial manager realizes that even a modest increase in the rate of cash discount constitutes a sizeable increase in the firm's cost of extending credit. Thus, if the firm offers its customers terms of 1%-10 days and net 30 days, it is indirectly paying the customer at an *annual* rate of 18% for having the cash 20 days before the due date. If the discount is raised to 1.5% for 10 days, the result is an annual rate of 27%. Clearly, if the firm can borrow the funds from a financial institution at, for instance, 8% per annum, it would be clearly to its advantage not to offer any cash discount but to wait for payment until the due date.

However, the financial manager is cognizant of two factors that compel the firm to offer a cash discount at a rate appreciably above the prevailing rate charged by banks and other financial institutions. One factor is the element of competition among sellers. In most lines of business, it is a well-established tradition for firms to offer a cash discount. Whatever the prevailing industry-wide standard terms happen to be, the individual firm must generally accept this standard as the normal floor of its own terms. Thus, a firm that has ample internal resources to finance the additional 20 days of credit and declines to offer a cash discount is more likely than not to lose many sales to its rivals. Some of many customers anticipate such discounts as an appreciable portion of their profit margin.

The other factor is the ability of the firm to borrow, from external sources, sufficient funds to meet its own obligations to its suppliers and to carry its customers to the due date of the accounts receivable. This factor explains, in large part, the practice of cash discounts and the range of discounts offered in different industries. In an industry dominated by a few large companies, the terms may be ½%-10 days, net 30 days; while, in an industry characterized by a large member of relatively small firms, the terms may be 1½%-days, net 30 days.

Although there is a tendency toward uniformity of credit terms within an industry, at least in a limited geographic area, this does not mean that the individual firm cannot offer more liberal terms to its customers. By raising the cash discount from 1% to 1½%, it is offering, in effect, the equivalent of an additional 9% per annum. The financial manager must determine whether or not this price paid by the firm for the earlier use of the funds—at the end of 10 days instead of 30 days—is greater than the cost of borrowing the funds from an outside source. In addition, he must weigh the sales advantage of the increased discount in terms of the additional sales that may be generated as a direct result of the more liberal rate. He must also be cognizant of the reverse side of the coin. That is to say, it is conceivable that the benefit of increased sales may prove to be a transient gain if competitors meet the new terms. The determination of the probable competitors' response is the primary responsibility of those members of management who are in charge of marketing.

If the tentative decision is reached to liberalize the credit terms, the financial manager must then compare the price paid to the purchaser for the earlier payment with the savings attained by the firm by not borrowing the funds for the full 30 days but rather for 10 days only.

Early payment by customers as a result of a higher discount offer may produce a significant auxiliary benefit for the seller in the nature of improved borrowing leverage. Suppose a firm has current assets and liabilities that make it possible for the firm to obtain a maximum short-term loan of $100,000 from a bank at a charge of 6% per annum.

It would then appear to be profitable for the firm to borrow the full $100,000 and to finance the receivables for as much as 40 days rather than offer its customers a discount of 1%-10 days. The firm's net revenues would be increased by 1% of sales; assuming that the discontinuance of the discount does not have an adverse effect on sales.

Assume that a significant proportion of the accounts do not pay at the end of 30 days, but are "slow" by 10, 20, or more days. This will automatically reduce, by the same amount, the volume of new sales that can be financed in the second month, since the firm has reached its credit limit of $100,000 and cannot support the slow receivables plus another $100,000 of sales. The loss of these potential sales could very easily outweighed the cost of the liberal discount offered for early payment.

2. Extending the Discount Period   Another alternative involves the extension of the discount period. For example, the firm may offer the discount for payment within 30 days and net for 45 days. This type of procedure frequently proves effective in expediting payment by public bodies and private nonprofit organizations. As stated in an earlier section, the disbursement officer may not receive the invoice until the traditional 10-day discount period has elapsed. There is little fear on the part of the disbursement officer that payment beyond the due date will affect adversely the credit rating of the public body or of the organization; or that the supplier will decline future orders. As noted before, invoices that offer a cash discount for a period long enough to overcome the processing lag are more likely to be paid immediately than bills that have approached the due date. The latter will be paid, to be sure, but more often than not at a delay of a few weeks or even months.

Among larger business firm, a different approach to the payment of bills for merchandise has evolved. This is the practice of insisting that invoices and terms be based on EOM., i.e., the last day of the month in which the merchandise was received. For example, the firm delivers the goods to the account early in the month on terms of 1%-10 days, net 30 days, EOM. The 10-day discount period then starts on the first day of the second month and the net 30-day due date is the last day of that month.

By offering EOM terms, the firm may encourage some accounts to make cash payments, at the discount, at an earlier date than would otherwise be the case. EOM billing has basically the same effect as an average increase in the discount period of 15 days. The essential difference lies in the following fact. An extension of the discount period is applied uniformly from the actual date of delivery. For instance, a 1% term of 20 days commences on whatever date of the month the customer receives the goods. On the other hand, a 1% term of 10 days EOM may mean a discount period ranging from 40 days, if the goods are delivered on the first of the month, to a low of 15 days if they are delivered on the 25th day of the month.

The problem confronting the financial manager can be stated in the following terms. If the firm changes to EOM billing, how many of its accounts are likely to pay sooner than otherwise by taking the discount? Conversely, how many customers will take the full 30 days but starting from the end of the month rather than the actual date of delivery? The answer to these two interrelated questions will provide the clue as to whether the average volume of receivables will go up or down, with a given volume of sales, as a result of the extension of the credit terms.

An extension of the cash discount period is usually designed to speed up payments by otherwise slow accounts. At the same time, however, it slows payments by prompt accounts who simply take the added number of days plus the higher discount. It is the task of the financial manager to weigh these two sides of the scale.

3. Purchasing Policy   The problem of financing receivables can be lessened by a change in purchasing policy that will extend the due date of the payables. In the last analysis, the financial manager needs short-term funds to meet the firm's obligations to its suppliers as well as other current expenditures while awaiting payment from its customers. The maturity dates of the payables in relationship to the due dates of the receivables determines the time gap or interval that has to be financed either from internal or external sources or both.

Assume that a given firm has traditionally availed itself of the cash discount offered by its suppliers for payment within 10 days while its own customers have taken full advantage of the 30-day credit term. Further suppose that, on the average, 20 days elapse between the receipt of raw materials and components and their conversion into finished goods and shipment of the finished goods to the firm's customers. In this case, the firm required short-term funds first for the 10-day interval of completing the production cycle (20 days minus 10 days discount) and, second, the 30-day credit extension to its customers.

Assume, for the sake of illustration, that the firm is able to obtain from its suppliers a credit term of 50 days. Although its receivables do not change, the firm would require less financing of its credit sales by a bank or finance company. Its suppliers have, in effect, provided a portion of the necessary short-term funds. The firm would, however, still require the funds to meet the payroll, supplies, and other direct costs, except for the materials or components purchased on the extended credit terms from suppliers. The use of trade credit as a source of funds varies widely among industries as well as between manufacturers, wholesalers, and retailers, as shown in Table 5-2.

TABLE 5-2. Trade Credit as a Percent of Total Liabilities for Selected Industries

Manufacturing:	
Womens dresses	23.38%
Malt liquors	6.68
Caskets and burial supplies	12.53
Drugs and medicines	9.84
Meat packing	10.39
Jewelry	13.52
Farm machinery and equipment	8.49
Metal cans	9.72
Books	9.94
Concrete products	9.40
Wholesale Trade:	
Electrical appliances	28.22
Florists	16.17
Frozen foods	21.71
Furniture	19.49
Steel warehousing	19.61
Retail Trade:	
Aircraft (new and used)	13.21
Books and stationery	14.78
Building materials	12.23
Department stores	11.78
Drugs	16.47

Source: Robert Morris Associates, Annual Statement Studies, 1966.

Next, suppose the firm discontinues its policy of taking the discount and, instead, pays at the end of 30 days. This would reduce the time interval for the financing of material purchases from 40 days to 20 days; i.e., 20 days for production and shipment plus 30 days credit to customers minus 30 days credit from suppliers. The net effect would be twofold. The firm would have to procure short-term funds from a financial lender for an average period of only 20 days. This would result in a saving on interest charges, thus, in part, offsetting the loss of the discount. And, in addition, the firm could support a larger volume of receivables with a given amount of short-term loans, as shown below.

Amount of loan	$ 100,000
(a) Average interval 40 days (= annual turnover of nine times) equals annual sales	900,000
or	
(b) Average interval 20 days (= annual turnover 18 times) equals annual sales	$1,800,000

To be sure, the above illustration is oversimplified since it considers only one source of funds. However, it serves to point up the fact that a change in purchasing policy provides the means to expand the volume of sales with a given amount of funds at the disposal of the firm.

IV. THE COST OF FINANCING RECEIVABLES

The price paid by the firm for the funds with which to carry the receivables constitutes a part of the direct cost of selling the goods. Since the selection of the external source of short-term funds is the responsibility of the financial manager, he faces a twofold task. First, he must keep himself adequately, informed about the prevailing policies and terms of the institutional lenders accessible to his firm. And, second, he must compare and evaluate their respective terms and interest rates in relation to his firm's requirements.

A. Comparing the Costs

In weighing the relative costs of borrowing funds from the several types of lenders, the financial manager must consider several elements that together make up the cost. These elements are: (1) the effective rate of interest as distinct from the nominal rate; (2) charges other than interest; (3) automatic or negotiable renewal of the loan; and (4) the size of the loan actually made available.

3. Effective Rate of Interest   In the case of finance companies and factors, the nominal and effective rates of interest are identical. The borrower pays a specified rate of interest per day for the agreed-upon amount of the advance or of the invoice. This charge is levied for the funds borrowed and for the actual number of days during which they were used by the debtor. If the firm draws, for example, $25,000 on the first of the month, $50,000 on the 10th of the month, reduces its indebtedness to $30,000 on the 15th, draws another $45,000 on the 20th, and pays off the entire loan on the 30th, the firm will be charged:

Interest rate assumed to be $\frac{1}{20}$ of 1% per diem	
$\frac{10}{20}$ of 1% for $25,000 (10 days)	$125
$\frac{5}{20}$ of 1% for $50,000 (5 days)	125
$\frac{5}{20}$ of 1% for $30,000 (5 days)	75
$\frac{10}{20}$ of 1% for $75,000 (10 days)	375
Total interest for this period	$700

The effective rate in the above example remained unchanged at 18% per annum ($\frac{1}{20}$ of 1% per diem = 1.5% per month = 18% per annum).

The situation is different in the case of a short-term bank loan. Commercial banks make two types of business loans. One type consists of a straight loan for a specified sum and period at a fixed rate of interest. The interest is payable on the face amount of the loan irrespective of the amount or the number of days actually used by the borrower. Suppose the rate is 6% per annum and the loan is for $75,000 for 30 days. The cost will then be $375. But what is the effective rate for the money actually used by the firm? We shall assume the same use as in the previous example. To calculate the effective rate, we first calculate the average daily drawing against the loan.

$$\frac{\$25,000\ (10) + \$50,000\ (5) + \$30,000\ (5) + \$75,000\ (10)}{30}$$

$$= \$46,667$$

Interest of $375 for 30 days on an average daily indebtedness of $46,667 equals 0.8%; or an annual rate of 9.6%.

Some banks, particularly smaller institutions, insist that the borrower leave a "compensating balance" of about 20% of the loan on deposit.

Using the same set of figures as above, the firm will have to borrow roughly $95,000 at 6% in order to have available a maximum of $75,000 for the 10-day period at the end of the month. The cost will then be $475 for the month. This sum paid for the use of a daily average of $46,667 for 30 days equals roughly 1%, or a little over 12% on an annual basis. As noted earlier in this chapter, the requirement of a compensating balance is offset to the extent to which the firm customarily maintains cash balances with the bank.

Let us next assume that the firm requires $100,000 for 10 days and $20,000 for 20 days. A loan from the finance company, assuming the same daily rate of $\frac{1}{20}$ of 1% would still have an effective rate of 18% per annum. In the case of the bank loan at the nominal rate of 6% per annum for the full amount of $100,000 for 30 days, the interest of $500 would be the monthly price for the use of a daily average of $46,667; or an effective rate of 1.08% per month or, roughly, about 13% per annum. By the same token, if the firm were to use the $100,000 for the full 30-day period, the nominal rate of 6% per annum would also be the effective rate.

A second type of bank loan is in the form of a line of credit. In our present example, the firm would be authorized to draw, during the month, any amount up to a maximum of $75,000. The interest, at the rate of 6% per annum, would then be charged for the amount(s) actually drawn and for the number of days used. The nominal and effective rate of interest would, therefore, be the same.

2. Charges other than Interest Some banks will, however, levy a flat charge of $\frac{1}{4}$ of 1% for the face amount of the line of credit. Thus, if the line of credit is for one month, the rate would be 6% per annum plus the commission of $\frac{1}{4}$ of 1% which would raise the effective rate to 9% per annum.

Finance companies levy only a single charge, the per diem rate of interest. The latter ranges between 9% and 20%, or more, per annum. Three basic factors determine the rate charged by a finance company: (1) the size of the firm's projected and approved requirements; (2) the percentage of receivables to be made available in advances; and (3) the quality of the accounts to be financed.

The customary arrangement calls for the following procedure. The borrower notifies the finance company of the amount of receivables which it assigns to the lender as the goods are shipped to the account. The firm can then draw cash against the receivables, say, up to 80% of the face value. The rate charged to customers whose monthly average is $400,000 or more of these advances is ordinarily charged at the rate of between 9% and 11% per annum for the cash actually used. Borrowers who use less than $400,000 per month will be charged from 11% to 15%, assuming that their receivables are fairly prompt payers. The charge will, however, go beyond 15% per annum and may even go above 20% if the accounts have a poor record of promptness of payment.

Referring again to the above illustration, the firm will probably have to pay an effective rate of about 12% to 15%. Assume that the receivables are, on the average, reasonably prompt payors, since otherwise the firm would have difficulty in procuring an unsecured bank loan against its receivables. While the bank charges about the same rate to all or most of its business borrowers of comparable risk on unsecured loans, the finance company has a wide range of rates. This means, in effect, that a firm that uses the services of the finance company to a lesser extent than another firm of comparable size and sales pays a premium for borrowing less than the finance company is willing to make available.

Finally, the factor charges an effective rate of 6% per annum on advances and a commission of 1 to 2% on the face value of the receivables which it agrees to purchase on the due dates. This fee or commission is, in part, a premium for the funds turned over to the firm on the due date and, in part, it represents compensation for the functions of credit analysis and collection performed by the factor.

3. Renewal of Loan   Commercial banks are generally prepared to negotiate either single-cycle loans for a period of one to several months or automatically renewable loans for a year. A single-cycle loan has the advantage that the firm pays interest only for the period of time during which it needs the funds. If it subsequently needs funds again, the firm submits a new application for a loan. This may or may not be a handicap, depending on the bank's lending policy at that time.

Finance companies and factors usually insist on a one-year agreement. The borrowing firm is assured of obtaining the funds, subject to the terms of the agreement, for this period of time at least. However, the firm loses its mobility in the short-term market. That is to say, it cannot shift to another lender—bank, finance company, or factor—if it finds that more favorable terms are offered by other suppliers of funds.

4. Size of Loan   Both the finance company and the factor are frequently in a position to offer the firm a larger loan against the same collateral obtained from the bank. The reason is that the finance company and the factor make an independent evaluation of the accounts and are, thus, in a better position to estimate the risk factor—i.e., delinquency and bad debt losses—whereas the bank must rely on the borrowing firm.

In determining the amount of the loans that the bank is prepared to make, the credit officer of the commercial bank looks primarily at the past and present financial condition of the firm. He evaluates the current and quick ratios and the net working capital of the firm. It is the *credit rating of the borrowing firm* that is of decisive importance to the bank.

On the other hand, the finance company and the factor are primarily concerned with the credit quality of the firm's accounts. The firm's net working capital may be tied up in inventory. Or it may represent an insignificant portion of its current assets. What matters to these lenders is whether or not the accounts are good credit risks. As long as they are satisfied on this score, they will make available say, 70 or 80% of the receivables and are not too much concerned over the fact that the profit margin on these sales is small, or that the firm carries too much inventory in relation to sales, or that it is delinquent in meeting its obligations to some suppliers.

B. Evaluating Potential Lenders

The financial manager of the firm is, thus, confronted by a formidable task. If he wants to ascertain the maximum loan and the minimum costs, the financial manager has to literally shop around. Credit officers of banks, even if the institutions are of comparable size, do not always use the same yardsticks in determining the maximum loan to a customer. Also, banks vary significantly in their lending policies and practices. While some institutions make aggressive efforts to attract industrial and commercial borrowers, others prefer to put their funds in real estate mortgages, bonds, and installment loans to consumers. Among those who are prepared to make business loans, there are considerable variations in the analytical skill and financial know-how of the credit officer.

The variations are even greater among finance companies and factors. Whereas banks are subject to regulation, supervision, and examination by national and/or state banking authorities, finance companies and factors are under no such restraints. They set their own standards, use whatever analytical techniques they devise, and may charge "what the traffic will bear."

This lack of uniformity of terms and lending policy makes it imperative for the financial manager to conduct a more or less extensive survey. The lenders of funds are, in this sense, analogous to suppliers of goods and, like the firm's purchasing agent, the financial manager must negotiate with the several suppliers of funds on the terms and size of the loan. Moreover, the individual lenders change their policies and terms in the course of time. A periodic reassessment of the various lenders may therefore reveal the desirability of shifting to another source of funds. This is particularly true of a firm that shows a fast rate of growth. This kind of firm may outgrow the ability of its current lender to provide the expanded short-term needs of the establishment. At the same time, the firm may well reach a level of operations that is attractive to a lender who previously was somewhat indifferent to this account.

Most important, however, is the fact that the broad survey of potential lenders and the periodic reassessment by the financial manager should be undertaken long before the funds are needed. It takes time to contact lenders and to discuss the projected needs of the firm. More time is then consumed by the lender(s) in analyzing the financial records of the firm and in determining the size and the terms of the loan which the lender is prepared to grant. Finally, the financial manager must then make the selection among the several lenders. Too often, a firm limits its inquiries to one or two lenders. This restraint is due, in part, to ignorance on the part of management as to the nature and operating practices of the various types of lenders and, in part, to the fact that the firm begins its inquiries at a time when the pressure for funds becomes irresistible. Time then becomes of the essence. A quick decision must be reached. The results are inescapable. Haste for action leads to waste of opportunities. The firm does not obtain the maximum amount and the best available terms that might have been procured from another type of lender or from an institution with a better appreciation of the firm's potential. In reality, the firm places itself in a position in which the lender holds the advantages of a supplier in a seller's market.

V. MARGINAL ANALYSIS OF FINANCING RECEIVABLES

The analysis in the preceding section was based on the assumption that the amount of the loan made available to the firm by the several types of lenders was the same but that the terms varied. This assumption is seldom true. The financial manager who "shops around" will usually discover that the finance company is more liberal than a factor and that the bank is relatively least liberal in the amount of funds which each is willing to advance. In turn, the "liberal" lender, other things being equal, will usually charge a higher rate of interest and/or special fee than the "conservative" lender.

In determining the relative costs of the funds charged by several lenders, the financial manager should compare the marginal costs rather than the total costs of short-term funds. Moreover, these marginal costs must then be compared with the marginal revenues.

Marginal Cost Analysis   Assume that a given firm has been able to finance its receivables with funds provided by the owners. The management is anticipating an expansion in sales and a rise in receivables by $100,000. The firm lacks the internal resources to carry this additional volume of receivables. It approaches (1) a bank, (2) a finance company, and (3) a factor, and obtains the following offers.

1. The bank is prepared to grant a line of credit, unsecured, for $80,000 at 6% per annum and a "compensating balance" of $10,000.
2. The finance company offers to establish a line of credit for $90,000 at $\frac{1}{40}$ of 1% per day on outstanding balances.
3. The factor is willing to purchase the receivables up to the full amount of $100,000 on the due date for a fee of $\frac{3}{4}$ of 1% and to make advances up to $100,000 prior to the due date at the rate of 6% per annum.

The actual costs of the three offers will then be as follows, assuming that the company is in a position to make full use of the amounts offered.

A. Bank loan: $70,000 (actual use); cost: $400 for 30 days ($\frac{1}{2}$ of 1% per month but based on $80,000 loan).
B. Finance company: $90,000; cost: $900 for 30 days.
C. Factor: $100,000; cost: $750 fee plus $500 interest = $1250.

Table 5-3 summarizes the margins of difference involved in this hypothetical case.

If the marginal costs are translated into a percentage of the accounts receivable figures, we find that the $20,000 additional receivables made possible by the finance company will equal 2.5% of these incremental accounts receivable. To obtain another $10,000 of incremental accounts

TABLE 5-3.

Output (Receivables that can be Financed) ($)		Cost ($)	Incremental Receivables ($)	Marginal Cost ($)	Incremental Cost as Percent of Incremental Receivables
A	70,000	400			
B	90,000	900	20,000	500	2.5%
C	100,000	1,250	10,000	350	3.5%

receivable would cost 3.5% of accounts receivable. The above comparison of incremental sales and cost of funds is predicated on the assumption that the firm has no other sources of funds with which to finance the additional sales.

Thus, the question arises whether the incremental profit at each of these two levels of $90,000 and $100,000, respectively, will exceed these incremental costs. If the incremental profit—i.e., the marginal efficiency of (borrowed short-term) capital—exceeds the incremental costs, the firm will procure a net profit from the expansion of receivables beyond $70,000.

Suppose the firm operates at a profit margin of 5% before interest charges on borrowed funds. If it sells $70,000 worth of goods it will realize $3500. Deducting the cost of the bank loan ($400), it will show a net profit before taxes of $3100. At a sales level of $90,000, the profit will be $4500. After paying $900 in interest, it will retain a profit of $3600. And at a $100,000 level, its earnings will be $5000 minus $1250 (interest) or a net of $3750. On the other hand, if its profit margin is 3% of sales, the corresponding figures will be as follows:

at $ 70,000 sales—$2100 minus $ 400 = $1700
at $ 90,000 sales—$2700 minus $ 900 = $1800
at $100,000 sales—$3000 minus $1250 = $1750

In this instance, the profits will be maximized at a sales level of $90,000.

SUMMARY

Most business transactions in the United States are in the form of open account credit transactions. An open account transaction always involves some risk to the creditor because the debtor has a variety of legal arguments in defense of nonpayment and there is always the risk of bankruptcy. Credit sales generally mean that the seller is financing the customer's purchase for the time between shipment of the goods and the receipt of the invoice price.

The financial manager must maintain an equilibrium between the customer's demand for credit sales and the firm's resources of funds at a level of sales that maximizes profits and minimizes risk. The financial manager must first analyze the demand for credit sales. The level of economic activity (the business cycle) must be examined. Seasonal variations must also be considered. Credit terms of competitors must also be considered since credit terms are an important factor in influencing the demand for a firm's goods.

Receivables must be evaluated carefully by the financial manager since they often represent the largest single item among current assets and since they determine in large measure whether the firm can meet its obligations to suppliers and lenders. Such factors as the structure of receivables and the cost of financing receivables must be carefully analyzed by the financial manager.

The financial manager of every firm, and especially the small firm, must strive to reduce the volume of receivables without impeding the firm's sales potential. Such alternatives as changing the cash discount, extending the cash discount period, and changing the firm's purchasing policy all should be explored.

Costs and suitability of financing receivables can be compared. The effective rate of interest and other charges, possibilities of receiving the loan, the size of loan available and the reputation of the lender all must be considered. Finally, the economist's techniques of marginal cost analysis can be applied to these tasks.

Questions

1. Explain what is meant by an open account transaction.
2. Explain the four major phases of the business cycle. Why are they of importance to the financial manager?
3. What are the financial implications of seasonal variations in sales levels?
4. Why are government agencies often slow payers on account? Does this mean that they are poor credit risks?
5. How can the financial manager encourage customers to pay their bills sooner?
6. What are the financial differences in selling to consumers on open account as compared to selling to other business firms?

7. Why can the finance company offer a firm a larger loan than can be obtained from a bank?

8. If wholesalers have been selling to retailers on terms of 2/10, net 30, and change their terms to 1/10, net 60, how will the levels of any retailers' bank loans be changed? Will the level of wholesalers' bank loans change also? How?

9. How is the current ratio affected by:
   (a) A loan on accounts receivable from a bank?
   (b) Sale of accounts receivable to a factor?

Problems

1. A bank is willing to give the Bradshaw Company a one-year loan of $150,000 at 6% simple interest. The bank will require Bradshaw to keep a compensatory balance equal to 15% of the loan. If Bradshaw normally keeps a balance of $5000 with the bank, what is the effective rate of interest to Bradshaw? What would be the effective rate if Bradshaw normally kept no balance with the bank?

2. Eta Corporation can increase sales by $20,000 if it grants credit on open account to a group of customers. The additional selling and production costs will be 82% of the sales increase. Management estimates that 8% of the sales to this group of customers on open account will be uncollectible. Collection costs on the added sales will probably be about $750. Should Eta grant credit on open account to this group of customers?

3. The bank has offered Brazos Company a $40,000, 120-day loan, discounted at 5.5%. What is the effective rate of interest that Brazos will pay? What are the proceeds that the bank will credit to the company's account?

4. Smithers Corporation plans to purchase $5,000,000 in merchandise in 1967. Thirty percent of this merchandise will be purchased from Alliance Manufacturing Corporation on terms of $\frac{1}{10}$, net 30. The balance of this merchandise will be purchased from Zibrat Company on terms of 2/15, net 60.
   (a) Calculate the effective rate of interest that Zibrat is charging Smithers for using trade credit, assuming Smithers pays Zibrat 60 days after purchase.
   (b) What is the effective interest rate charged by Alliance if Smithers pays at the end of thirty days?

(c) Assume that Smithers takes no discounts on its purchases. Calculate how much Smithers is losing in profits (before taxes) by failure to take its cash discount.

(d) Should Smithers borrow $1,000,000 at 6% simple interest for one year in order to be able to take its cash discounts from Zibrat and Alliance?

Case: Auto Electric Sales Corporation

Auto Electric Sales Corporation is a West Coast distributor of automotive electrical supplies and equipment. Sales in 1966 were $3.6 million. The credit manager of Auto Electric must decide what action to take with respect to the open account of Zoltan Auto Parts. Zoltan has been a customer of Auto Electric for eight years. Prior to 1965, Zoltan had been a good account with payment generally running, at most, a few days late. Auto Electric's stated terms are 2/10, net 30.

Beginning in early 1965, collections from Zoltan became slower than usual. The normal outstanding balance of about $6200 a month had increased to $14,000 by early 1966. In 1966, sales to Zoltan were at normal levels. Zoltan was again somewhat slow in payment and the outstanding balance had reached the credit manager's limit of $15,000 on the account.

At this point, an additional order for $2000 in spark plugs has been received from Zoltan. Auto Electric's sales manager believes the shipment should be made so as to help realize the company sales quota especially since Zoltan has been a good customer for eight years. The sales manager contends that other suppliers have been relaxing their credit terms with regard to Zoltan in view of Zoltan's cash stringencies caused by buying out the widow of Zoltan's late vice-president and through Zoltan's expansion of physical facilities.

The credit manager has available to him a local credit report (Exhibit 5-1) and a balance sheet and income statement for Zoltan for 1965 (Exhibits 5-2 and 5-3).

History

This firm was started by Henry Guerrero, Sr., and William Adams in 1947. The firm was incorporated in 1951 with the following ownership: Henry Guerrero, Sr., 50%; Mrs. Henry (Susan) Guerrero, Sr., 10%; William Adams, 25%; John Wroclaw, 15%. William Adams, formerly vice-president and sales manager, died in May, 1965. By agreement with his

EXHIBIT 5-1:   Auto Electric Sales Corporation, West Coast Credit Agency

November 15, 1966

Report on: Zoltan Auto Parts
567 Main Street
Zoltan, California

Officers: Henry Guerrero, Sr., President
John Wroclaw, Vice President
Henry Guerrero, Jr., Treasurer
Mrs. Henry (Susan) Guerrero, Sr., Secretary

Directors: The officers plus James O'Sheehan, C.P.A.

Payments: Slow, 30 to 90 days

Sales: $875,000 (1965) per year

EXHIBIT 5-2:   Auto Electric Sales Corporation
ZOLTAN AUTO PARTS
BALANCE SHEET, SEPTEMBER 30, 1966
(Unaudited)

Assets		
Cash	$ 4,285	
Receivables	72,528	
Inventory and supplies	460,250	
Current assets		$537,063
Land		30,000
Building, net		150,000
Machinery and equipment, net		42,380
Goodwill		20,000
Total assets		$779,443
Liabilities		
Accounts payable	$ 91,000	
Bank notes (short-term)	85,250	
Accruals and taxes payable	42,378	
Current portion of mortgage	6,250	
Due officers	15,000	
Current liabilities		$239,878
Due Mrs. Adams		100,000
Mortgage		118,750
Due Mr. Guerrero, Sr.		40,000
Total liabilities		$498,628
Common stock		175,000
Retained earnings		105,815
Total liabilities and net worth		$779,443

EXHIBIT 5-3:   Auto Electric Sales
Corporation
ZOLTAN AUTO PARTS
INCOME STATEMENT
January 1, 1966–September 30, 1966
(Unaudited)

Sales	$685,250
Cost of goods sold	517,924
Gross profit	$167,326
Selling expenses	65,212
Administrative expenses	70,580
Operating profit	$ 31,534
Interest expense	24,200
Net profit before taxes	$ 7,334

widow, Heather Adams, the company will buy back the Adams stock over a five-year period—one-fifth each year.

Henry Guerrero, Sr., born 1910, married, employed by Ace Auto Electric 1934 to 1940, United States Army 1940 to 1947.

John Wroclaw, born about 1917, divorced, employed by Central Manufacturing 1941 to 1943, United States Army 1943 to 1946, salesman for G.E. Supply Co. 1946 to 1950, with Zoltan since that date in various capacities (parts manager, sales-promotion manager and, since the death of William Adams, vice-president and sales manager.

Henry Guerrero, Jr., born 1935, married, graduate of West Coast Business College, 1957, employed by Zoltan Auto Parts since graduation.

Mrs. Henry (Susan) Guerrero, Sr., wife of Henry Guerrero, Sr., is not active in the business.

Operation and Location

Subject firm sells auto parts to gas stations, brake and body shops, etc. in the greater Zoltan area. Sales are to over 50 accounts and the territory consists of Zoltan and Pegamug Counties (combined population 1,327,500). Terms are 2/10, net 30. Employees average approximately 25. There are 7 salesmen.

Subject firm occupies a two-story concrete, steel, and glass building built in 1965, of 40,000 square feet. The building replaced smaller adjacent rented quarters. The new building is located on "automotive row" in the industrial area of Main Street. Building is in excellent condition. Plant facilities are somewhat untidily maintained.

Financial Information

The business was successfully operated by management from 1947 to 1963, when a strike followed by a significant wage increase led to unprofitable operations in 1963 and 1964.

The unfavorable operating trend was reversed after the move to the new building in 1965 and operations were slightly above the breakeven point for that year. Mr. Guerrero, Sr., President, stated that operations in 1966 have been profitable except for the months of January and February when slight losses occurred. Full operating details have not been furnished by Mr. Guerrero, Sr.

Mr. Guerrero, Sr., stated that, with the agreement of some larger suppliers, credit terms have been eased, owing to cash stringencies resulting from stock repurchase and down payment and moving costs on the new building.

It is estimated that cash is in the low four figures, receivables in the high five figures, inventory in the middle six figures, short-term bank loan in the middle five figures. Bank relations are satisfactory. There is a twenty-year $125,000 mortgage on the new building. Cash balances are maintained in the local bank in generally low four figure amounts. Short-term bank loans are secured by accounts receivable and personal endorsement by Mr. and Mrs. Henry Guerrero, Sr.

Payments

The latest trade experience, completed on August 1, 1966, is as follows:

HC	Owe	P Due	Terms	August 1, 1966
5,275			1/10/net 30 slow 30	Sold since 1953
1,750	225	225	Net 30 slow 30 to 60	Sold since 1960
300			Regular Ppt	Sold since June 1965
12,000	2,500		Regular Ppt to slow 45	Sold for years
5,200	1,250		2/10/net 30 EOM. Ppt to slow 60	Sold since 1963
500	500		3/10/net 60 discount to Ppt	Sold since 1960

Case Questions:

1. What action should the credit manager of Auto Electric Sales Corporation take with respect to the latest order from Zoltan Auto Parts? Why?
2. What general rules about credit management can be developed from this case?

~~~~~~

Chapter Six

The Financial Management of Inventory

Among the current assets, inventory ranks either above or a close second to receivables in magnitude. This fact in itself would justify major concern over the financial aspects of inventory size and competition. There are, however, several unique facets to this asset item that increase the complexity of the problem and the financial risk of inadequate inventory planning, management, and control.

The potential losses that a firm may suffer from poor inventory management frequently exceed the potential losses from bad debts. For example, in a period of expanding business, a firm may have losses from bad debts amounting to one or two percent of its accounts receivable. This ratio may double or even triple in a period of recession. On the other hand, it is not unusual for a firm to suffer losses of ten or more percent on a portion of its inventory in good times and a still higher percentage in a recession as a result of poor inventory planning or management.

I. INVENTORY DIAGNOSIS AND VALUATION

The volume of inventory carried by a firm is a function of its projected sales. The projection may encompass a month, a quarter, or even a longer span of time depending on the ready availability of the components that make up the inventory, the length of the production cycle, and the buying habits of the firm's customers. Cigarette manufacturers must buy their raw material when the tobacco crop is offered for sale. Distillers carry an inventory for years until it reaches its proper "age." On the other hand, a large bakery may require an inventory of flour and ingredients sufficient for only one week's output. The food department in a department store can operate effectively with an inventory equal to one week's sales while the jewelry department in the same store requires an inventory equal to six months of sales.

Inventory, whether it consists of raw materials or finished goods, ties up funds until such time when it is sold and becomes an account receivable. In addition to the cost of the inventory (purchase price), the inventory may have to be processed, involving additional expenses for wages, supplies, etc. There are also the costs of storage, insurance, and possible losses from spoilage. These costs become cumulatively larger the longer the time interval between purchase and sales. Table 6-1 shows the percentage of inventory in relation to total assets for a number of selected industries. These percentages vary between a low of 11.33% for malt liquors manufacturers to a high of 57.74% for drug retailers.

The firm expects to be able to sell the inventory and to realize a price that will cover all costs and yield a profit. But this expectation contains the element of uncertainty or risk. It is the responsibility of the financial manager to determine the financial magnitude of this risk and to select the course of action that will minimize the cost of this risk. In the performance of these two functions, the financial manager must first diagnose the inventory on hand. This analysis is designed to answer the following type of questions. How much and how soon can the firm expect to generate an inflow of cash from the sale of its inventory? Are these sales likely to yield a profit? Does the firm carry too much of some items in relation to its short-term needs; i.e., one or two marketing cycles? Should the company sell a portion of its inventory at cost or even at loss now rather than store the item(s) until the next selling season which may be several months in the future? What are the actual out-of-pocket costs of this storage and what are the opportunity costs of tying up funds for such a length of time?

In addition to his concern with existing inventory, the financial manager must also measure the cost of financing a proposed inventory; i.e., planned future purchases. It is (financially) more desirable to buy say, every month relatively small lots and pay a higher unit price or to place one large order to meet the anticipated requirements for three months at an appreciable discount from the list price?

The problem of analyzing the inventory on hand will be discussed in this section. The next section will then deal with the financial facets of inventory planning.

TABLE 6-1. Inventory as a Percent of Total Assets for Selected Industries

Manufacturing:

Womens dresses	36.53%
Malt liquors	11.33
Caskets and burial supplies	30.36
Drugs and medicines	29.45
Meat packing	24.20
Jewelry	40.69
Farm machinery and equipment	42.15
Metal cans	31.23
Books	25.87
Concrete products	16.44

Wholesale Trade:

Electrical appliances	41.24
Florists	24.53
Frozen foods	37.93
Furniture	35.99
Steel warehousing	49.44

Retail Trade:

Aircraft (new and used)	40.23
Books and stationery	43.89
Building materials	28.72
Department stores	35.53
Drugs	57.74

Source: Robert Morris Associates, Annual Statement Studies, 1966.

A. Heterogenous Makeup of Inventory

The balance sheet of a manufacturing firm customarily shows a single entry "inventory" but does not indicate its composition. In a manufacturing company, this asset is usually made up of three distinct categories: (1) raw materials; (2) work in process (also known as goods in process); and (3) finished goods.

These differences play an important role if the firm finds it necessary to liquidate a portion of its inventory on short notice. Finished goods are immediately available for sale. If necessary, the company can usually dispose of these goods at a moderate reduction in price. Raw materials must first be processed, which involves expenditures for labor and other items plus the time interval for this processing. Conceivably, the firm may decide that the prospective sales volume for the next few months is too low in proportion to the supply of raw materials originally scheduled for processing into finished goods. In this case, the question arises whether it is feasible to dispose of the excess raw material. The answer depends, in large measure, on the suitability of the raw materials, or components, for other manufacturers. For instance, standard-size parts and components can usually be sold to other manufacturers at a modest reduction in price. On the other hand, components of special size or which bear the imprint of the firm's name are worthless to other producers and, if not needed by the firm, must be literally "junked."

A similar situation is frequently found in the inventory of wholesalers or retailers. Although a distributor does not process the goods in his inventory, the latter may be composed of items, some of which are a staple commodity, while others are subject to changing fashions, seasonal influences, or may be physically perishable. Or the inventory may include staple items of a special size or design for which the demand is sporadic rather than continuous.

Whatever the makeup of the inventory, the financial manager is concerned with its degree of liquidity. How quickly will the stock turn over and how much will it generate in receipts?

B. Valuation of Inventory

Traditional accounting calls for the valuation of inventory either on the basis of invoice price (cost) or (current) market price, whichever is lower. Suppose that a company purchased, in January, a given quantity of cloth at a price of $3 per yard and that it still has this item in stock at the end of the fiscal period. Let us next assume that, at that time, the supplier's list price for this cloth is $2.50. The accountant would then value this portion of the inventory at $2.50 per yard. On the other hand, if the current list price is more than $3 per yard, the accountant would use the purchase price of $3 as the base figure.

This method of inventory valuation is clearly predicated on the proposition that it is preferable to be overcautious rather than optimistic. If the market price is above cost, the assumption is that the firm's selling price is based on the actual cost of inventory. On the other hand, if market price is below cost, the assumption is that competition will force the firm to lower its selling price on the basis of the lowered price at which inventory can be purchased. Both assumptions are arbitrary and, as stated above, are intended to reflect an overcautious evaluation of the inventory.

From the viewpoint of the firm, this method of inventory evaluation is unrealistic in a period of sustained increases in cost and sales price—known as "creeping" inflation—as well as in a period of sustained price decreases. Certainly, the *general* price trend in the past three decades has been in an upward direction. In a few industries, the reverse has been the case as a direct result of technological improvements that have made possible a decrease in total costs. For example, the prices of television sets and various household appliances ("white goods") have shown a downward trend in recent years.

C. FIFO versus LIFO

These real facts of life have led to a modification in the traditional accounting method of inventory valuation. Today, the firm has three accounting alternatives: (1) the lower of cost or market price, (2) FIFO, and (3) LIFO. These latter two terms stand for "First In, First Out" and "Last In, First Out," respectively. As will be shown in the following illustrations, the use of either FIFO or LIFO, respectively, affects the profit of the firm as shown on its books and, therefore, its income tax liability.

D. Tax Advantage Versus Borrowing Capacity

The use of the LIFO method, in a period of rising prices, offers a distinct tax advantage to the firm. If prices of goods purchased in the course of the year go up, the firm will value the closing inventory at the lower prices at which it purchased goods in the beginning of the year. The net effect is that the purchases that have been channeled into production and subsequent sales are valued at the higher prices. The reverse is true in the case of FIFO.

Assume, for example, that the records of a company show the following picture for the last fiscal year:

On hand, at start of fiscal year	500 units @ $5.00 = $ 2,500	
Purchases in the course of the year:	2/1: 500 units @ $6.00 = $ 3,000	
	5/1:1000 units @ $6.50 = $ 6,500	
	2/1:3000 units @ $6.50 = $19,500	
	11/1:2000 units @ $7.00 = $14,000	
On hand, at end of fiscal year	12/31:800 units	

In entering the purchases as part of the Cost of Goods Sold, the results will be as follows:

	FIFO			LIFO
500 units @ $5.00	$2,500			—
500 units @ $6.00	3,000	200 @ $6.00		$1,200
1,000 units @ $6.50	6,500	1,000 @ $6.50		6,500
3,000 units @ $6.50	19,500	3,000 @ $6.50		19,500
1,200 units @ $7.00	8,500	2,000 @ $7.00		14,000
6,200	$39,900	6,200		$41,200

The above figures illustrate the tax advantage of LIFO. It reduces the taxable income by $1300. Under the existing regulations, a business firm is permitted to select either the FIFO or LIFO method. However, once the choice has been made, the firm cannot revert to the other method, except with the permission of the tax authorities. It must also be stressed that, in a subsequent period of declining prices, LIFO magnifies the tax liability. Assume that, in the above illustration, the prices of goods purchased in the second year decline. In calculating the cost of purchases, the firm would value the 800 units at $4300 (500 × $5 plus 300 × $7); whereas under the FIFO method the valuation would be $5600 (800 × $7).

In terms of borrowing capacity, the balance sheet under LIFO would show the inventory at $4300. Actually the inventory has a current value of $5600, unless deflation has set in shortly after the end of the firm's fiscal year. It must be noted that the financial manager can readily prepare a supplementary statement showing the real, that is, current value of the inventory as distinct from the balance sheet figure.

E. The Financial Manager's Approach

The accountant's evaluation of the inventory is focused on a specific date in time, i.e., the terminal date of the fiscal period. On the other hand, the financial manager starts where the accountant's task ends. That is to say, the financial manager's primary concern is with the impact of the inventory on the cash position of the company over a period of time in the immediate future. To him, the crucial questions are: How much will it cost the firm to carry a given volume of inventory into the next production and selling cycles? What are the inherent risks in the inventory? Is it possible to cut down on the size of the inventory without affecting adversely the smooth flow of production and sales?

These questions deal with inventory on hand. In a sense, they involve the same asset that the accountant evaluated in preparing the balance sheet and the profit and loss statement. The financial manager must, however, also deal with the future inventory policy of the firm. This involves, among others, the following questions. What are the economies of a relatively large inventory in terms of lower unit price, special discounts, quick service to customers? The other side of the coin involves the diseconomies of a relatively large inventory. How much will it cost the firm to maintain the proposed level of inventory in terms of interest on borrowed money, storage cost, and insurance premiums? Furthermore, what are the opportunity costs of channelling a given amount of capital into the inventory rather than into advertising or market research or other alternatives that the company would like to undertake but for which the funds will not be available if they are diverted into the proposed inventory.

F. Functional Imbalance

The ideal raw material and supplies situation for a manufacturer is one in which all items are carried in stock in the exact proportion in which they are used in the making of the end product. If the end product calls for 10 units of A, 15 of B, 40 of C, etc., the firm should, ideally and theoretically, order these several items in the required proportions. Such a situation is, however, rarely found in real life. The causes and possible remedies for this imbalance are partly technological and partly financial; they will be discussed in detail in section II of this chapter.

To the financial manager, an imbalanced inventory becomes a matter of major concern when the sale of the end product(s) shows a tendency to fall below the anticipated level(s). As long as sales are at or above the target line, the firm need not worry over the fact that it has, in a given month, more units of, for instance, C, D, and F than are needed for the production quota in that month. The excess will be carried over to the following month and will be reduced as new orders are received. As a matter of fact, these temporary "unbalanced" inventories are usually anticipated, since the purchasing program is based on the projected sales volume of several months and the purchase orders are geared to the month-by-month needs of the firm.

However, when sales in successive months fall short of expectation, an unbalanced inventory becomes a serious financial matter. The items that are in excess of production requirements become, at least for the time being, a frozen investment. Funds are tied up for longer periods than had been anticipated. At the same time, the lower volume of sales reduces the anticipated rate of turnover of the items that appeared to be in balance. The overall result is a strain on the firm's ability to meet current liabilities. The cash flow is slowed down in that receipts are less than anticipated in relation to the required cash outflow. A portion of the firm's funds have been transformed from a revolving self-liquidating asset into a nonrevolving nonliquid asset.

The question therefore arises: To hold or to liquidate? If the excess units are held in stock they will not generate a cash flow of the magnitude and at the time originally scheduled and anticipated. If they are sold now at whatever the market will yield, the company will receive cash, but of a smaller magnitude than anticipated. The financial manager must then weigh the firm's cash position and the price that it is prepared to pay for a greater cash inflow by virtue of liquidating the excess units.

Excessive inventory ties up funds that could be employed profitably in another division of the firm. In this case, the inventory generates "opportunity costs" that must be added to the cash costs of the inventory. If the firm has no immediate alternative use for these funds, it could either cut its cost of borrowing—if the inventory had been financed with a short-term loan—or, if it did not use external financing, the firm could earn interest on the funds by short-term investments (time deposits, commercial paper, etc.). In addition to these opportunity costs, an excessive inventory also gives rise to diverse expenditures for warehousing, insurance, and spoilage.

The financial manager must therefore weigh (1) the firm's current cash position and its need for funds, (2) the opportunity costs of carrying the inventory until it can be sold at the originally anticipated price, (3) the costs of the other direct expenditures. Assuming that the firm can finance, either from internal or external sources, the excess inventory until it is sold at the anticipated price, the problem can be quantified as follows.

Is the difference between future sale at list price (L) and current forced liquidation price (FLP) greater or smaller than opportunity costs (OC) plus other direct expenditure, such as interest on a loan (DE)?

If $LP - FLP \geq OC + DE$, it is to the advantage of the firm to hold the inventory. The reverse is true if $LP - FLP \leq OC + DC$.

However, if the firm finds it difficult to finance the carrying of the inventory--i.e., if it is under pressure from its suppliers and/or financial institutions to make immediate payments on its accounts payable and/or notes—the question of "hold or liquidate" is automatically resolved. The firm has no alternative but to sell the excess inventory at the cash price it can obtain in the current market.

The issue of hold or liquidate is of special significance in the retail field; although the basic principle applies equally to a manufacturer who changes his product line seasonally (e.g., apparel, shoes, furniture, sporting goods).

As the season for a particular line of goods approaches its end, the firm has the alternative of liquidating the inventory at a substantial price reduction or of storing it for next year's season in the expectation of selling these goods at their "regular" price; assuming that there is no likelihood of obsolescense due to changes in fashion or style. In practice, there is no doubt in the mind of top management that it is to the advantage of the firm to sell the seasonal inventory below the list price rather than to hold it for the next year's season. But how far below the list price? What is the minimum or "break-even" price, i.e., the point at which the opportunity cost plus storage and insurance equal the reduction in price necessary to liquidate the merchandise?

The student will readily recall many cases in which retail firms will offer drastic price reductions on staple but seasonal items when the season is just about over; e.g., bicycles, roller skates, tennis rackets, swimming pools late in the summer, and winter sport equipment in February or March. Apparel and furniture are other traditional seasonal clearance items.

G. Impending Model Changes

If the manufacturer, or distributor, schedules the showing and offering of next year's model before he will have had an opportunity to sell the total inventory of the present model at his regular price, the question is: How much of a reduction and how soon? The initial answer is provided by the sales manager. It involves basically an estimate of the price elasticity of demand over a period of time, i.e., the interval before the new model is offered for sale. For example, the sales manager may recommend a 10% reduction now, one month before the new model will be out, and estimates a 25% increase in unit sales; whereas, two weeks later, it may require a 25% price cut to stimulate a 15% rise in unit sales. In both cases, the increase in unit sales is measured from the level that is anticipated on the basis of the current price.

Some firms pursue a policy of initiating a modest price cut—for instance, 10 or 15%—2 or 3 months before the end of the current model year. Others prefer to wait until about one month prior to the new model and then offer a more substantial reduction.

II. CAUSES OF INVENTORY ACCUMULATION

Receivables are the result of sales. Inventory represents the anticipated volume of sales. Therefore, funds tied up in inventory carry a dual risk. First, the anticipated sales may not be realized. And, second, they may not be achieved at the unit sales price in the unit volume that had been projected. The risks of smaller volume and/or lower price than anticipated are inherent in every projection of future market demand. Any excess of inventory that results from a decline in sales is by definition unexpected and therefore "unplanned." The alternatives to resolve these problems have been discussed in the preceding section. In this section, we shall deal with situations in which a firm adopts an inventory policy that, with the advance knowledge of management, will produce an inventory in excess of the requirements for the immediate future. The factors that account for a deliberate "excess" inventory policy can be classified under five headings: (1) internal-technological; (2) internal-financial; (3) external-suppliers; (4) external-cyclical; and (5) other causes.

A. Internal Causes: Technological

The output schedule of the production department is based on but not limited by the projected month-to-month volume of sales. In many cases, the technological nature of the production process is the real determinant of the actual monthly output. Although the annual or semiannual schedule of the production manager will usually correspond closely to the sales projection for the same period, the same is not necessarily true of the monthly output quotas. The basic reason for these discrepancies is to be found in the fact that minimum production cost per unit is a function of production volume and is independent of the monthly *rate* of sales.

Assume that, for the coming fiscal year, the sales manager has projected total sales of 900,000 units. Owing to the seasonal nature of the products, he estimates that monthly sales will vary from a low of 25,000 units to a high of 150,000 units. Top management has accepted these figures and turns them over to the production manager, who is asked to submit his output schedule, inventory needs, and cost estimates.

The production manager's main objective is to produce the annual volume of 900,000 at minimum cost. Ignoring, at this point of the analysis, the details of cost accounting, which are irrelevant to the basic issues, the production manager knows that the *fixed* costs per unit will be the same whether the 900,000 units are scheduled at an even monthly rate of 75,000 over the 12-month period, or at an uneven monthly level as long as the annual total is 900,000 units. This is, however, not true of the *variable* costs for labor. Since labor cost is, in many cases, the largest single element in total manufacturing costs, the production manager is faced with three major alternatives of output scheduling, each of which involves a different month-by-month outflow of funds for wages and materials plus supplies.

1. Level Output   Under this method of production, the monthly output is set at 75,000, irrespective of the actual volume of sales and shipments in any one month. The required labor force is kept fully and evenly employed. Since, by definition, the labor force is just sufficient to produce 75,000 units per month, there will be no overtime costs at the usual one and one-half time the regular hourly wage rate. Moreover, with the labor force kept constant, there will be no expenses for idle labor time—if output is cut back and the full work force kept temporarily on the payroll—or the cost of breaking in new workers whenever output is suddenly raised and more workers are needed.

This concern of the production manager with a constant level of employment is reinforced by recent developments in union negotiations for a guaranteed annual wage, severance pay based on years of service, and the traditional seniority rule both for promotions and layoffs.

However, while labor cost is kept constant and the raw material inventory close to minimum—assuming that purchases can also be scheduled on a level basis—the inventory of finished goods will vary substantially. Whenever seasonal sales fall below 75,000 units per month, the stock of goods on hand will grow cumulatively until sales and deliveries go above the 75,000 mark. This excess of inventory ties up funds that have been expended on materials and labor. In addition, the firm incurs warehousing and insurance costs.

It then becomes a matter of balancing the savings in labor costs against the added expenditures, including the cost of financing the excess stock.

2. Production to Order   At the other extreme is the policy of scheduling output on a month-to-month basis in conformity with the projected sales for a given month. If, for instance, the sales in a particular month fall short of the anticipated volume, the production quota for the next month is adjusted in such a manner as to include the carry-over. Conversely, if sales move above the predicted volume, the output is either stepped up or deliveries are temporarily held up. Either alternative depends on whether the customers insist on immediate delivery or are willing to wait one or two weeks.

But while inventory cost is kept to the minimum, the labor cost is likely to fluctuate widely. If the firm adopts the policy of maintaining a given work force as a minimum, it will either have to pay overtime when output is stepped up, or it must accept the expenses of breaking in the new workers who are hired when output is increased. For the year as a whole, labor unit cost is higher under this method of production scheduling than under the level output policy. Frequently, the latter policy also involves substantial additional capital investments in physical facilities to meet peak needs. On the other hand, as stated above, the inventory cost is apt to be less.

To reduce and, if possible, to eliminate unnecessary carrying costs of excessive inventory, production and inventory-purchase decision must be coordinated. This action will contribute to the minimization of the sales-cost schedule. In practice, the decision to adjust production and purchases frequently involves the resolution of two conflicting objectives: low unit purchase price versus cost of financing. For example, the purchasing agent is anxious to procure the lowest unit price from the supplier(s). He will want to take advantage of special off-season prices or, during the season, of an appreciable discount on quantity purchases. From the viewpoint of the purchasing agent, such a transaction is advantageous to the firm and reflects favorably on his skill in procuring lower-than-usual prices. However, the quantities involved may exceed the requirements as scheduled by the production manager for the next few months. In consequence, the excess will automatically either tie up internal resources of the firm or generate costs for interest, warehousing, and insurance. It is the task of top management to weigh these costs against the savings on purchase price.

3. Cycle Scheduling   This method is a variation of the level-output program. It operates along the following lines. Suppose the firm's product line consists of 6 items. Under the level-output system, the production manager would schedule each month one-twelfth of the annual quota of each item. If he uses the cycle system instead, he will schedule, for instance, item 6 for the last week of January when labor and equipment are no longer needed for items 1 to 5 to meet the February deliveries to customers. The output of item 6 may then be adequuate for the next nine months. In February, he may schedule another item for two full weeks and obtain a stock that will fill requirements for several months; and so forth. The underlying principle of cycle scheduling is to minimize changeover of equipment, down time when machinery has to be adjusted to another product, and loss of labor time because of reassignments of the work force to different jobs. Above all, however, cycle scheduling has the advantage that it makes possible the full utilization of the work force and equipment. Cycle production is also used when sales of some item(s) fall below projection. Instead of cutting back on production, the plant manager raises the output quota for the line(s) that must meet sales goals. Assume that, in March, the output of item 4 equals the projected sales for the period April to May and that the sales of this item in this period are significantly below the anticipated levels while item 5 is selling above its quota. The plant manager would then remove item 4 from the May schedule and put item 5 in its place.

Essentially, therefore, cycle scheduling is designed to achieve a greater economy of labor utilization than can be obtained from the level-output method. By the same token, however, cycle scheduling is likely to increase the average inventory of finished goods, especially if it is accompanied by widespread product diversification.

4. The Dilemma: Profit versus Liquidity   In preparing the output schedule and in selecting the scheduling method, the production manager's objective is to minimize the cost elements under his immediate control. These involve labor, materials used in the production process, physical facilities, supplies, and the possible utilization of by-products. The production manager regards his job as well done if he can devise ways and means of reducing the cost of these elements over which he has direct authority and control.

The financial manager shares this concern over minimum unit production cost—up to a certain point. He parts company with the production manager when minimum production cost threatens liquidity of the firm. That is to say, even if the expense of carrying an excessive inventory is less than the savings obtained from cycle scheduling, for instance, the financial manager may have valid reasons for objecting to this output policy. Conceivably, the procurement of the necessary funds may strain unduly the firm's access to external funds. It may have to go to the limit of its borrowing capacity to obtain the required volume of loans. In this case, the firm runs the risk that any unforseen adverse sales trend will place too heavy a burden on the firm in maintaining a reasonable level of liquidity.

B. External Causes: Suppliers

In scheduling the requirements of the production department for material, components, and supplies, the production manager of a firm often finds himself in a dilemma. He may need X units of a given item (for example, sprockets, gears, stampings, cabinets, etc.) which are not of standard size and are not carried in stock by the suppliers. Instead, they must be produced to the specific requirements of the firm. The required volume of X units may, however, be too small for a regular run by the supplier. The latter's list price is predicated on an order that is, for example, twice the size of the firm's requirements for the next six months.

By ordering only X units, the firm may have to pay a unit price of say, 50 cents, compared with a unit price of 35 cents if the order is for two times X units. This is due to the fact that the bulk of the supplier's costs of making this item consists of labor time in setting up his machinery and equipment to the customer's specifications and the time subsequently required to reset the machines rather than the total number of machine hours actually used on this job.

In cases of this nature, it is usually more profitable to order a larger volume at the substantially lower unit price. The effect is a significant increase in the inventory of this item. In terms of the total funds tied up in inventory, this large order may or may not be significant. Much depends, first, on the number of items that are subject to sizeable price differentials because of the relatively small monthly requirements of the firm; and second, on the dollar amount of these purchases relative to the total purchases of the production department.

C. External Causes: Cyclical

The inventory position of a firm tends to be strongly influenced by the business cycle. This is equally true during the expansion phase as it is during the cyclical downswing when economic activity in the industry and firm decline. However, the pattern and effects are different during these two phases.

1. Expansion In the recovery and prosperity phases of the cycle, the inventory tends to grow at a faster rate than the volume of sales. This is known as the accelerator principle. Its operation is illustrated in the following simplified example involving a retail firm.

This firm had adopted a policy of carrying an inventory equal to two months sales. It anticipates sales of $75,000 for each of the months of March, April, and May. At the end of March, it finds that sales for the month totalled $80,000, reflecting the *cyclical* upswing; for the sake of simplicity, this example assumes the absence of *seasonal* variations. The sale of $80,000 in March reduced the April inventory to $70,000 ($150,000 inventory at the start of March minus $80,000 inventory sold in March). At the start of April, the firm must therefore order $10,000 worth of goods to bring the April inventory up to $80,000, plus $80,000 worth of goods for May since sales for that month are expected to equal the higher March figure. Thus, the total order at the start of April will be for $90,000 instead of for $75,000, which would have been the amount reordered if expansion had not set in during March.

Therefore, the net effect is an increase in inventory purchases in April by 20%—$90,000 rather than $75,000—while sales in April are expected to rise by about 6¾% over the original estimate of $75,000. Now, if the sales in April, too, move above the revised estimate of $80,000, the reorders at the start of May will equal (a) the higher sales in April plus (b) the excess of April sales over the (revised) April estimate. As long as sales go up, the reorders will tend to rise at a higher rate than sales.

Expanding sales also have an auxiliary effect. In response to the favorable market outlook, the retailer is likely to add to his current line of merchandise in one or both of the following directions. He may add goods in a price line that he did not carry previously. That is to say, he will trade up his merchandise in the expectation of a greater demand for goods in the higher price brackets. In addition, he may also expand his stock within the several price lines in order to offer his customers greater selectivity in models, fabrics, colors, or whatever the special feature of the merchandise may be.

Wholesalers and manufacturing firms tend to show the same inventory policy as the retailer in the above illustration. In these cases, too, the volume of inventory is likely to rise at a faster pace than sales.

2. Contraction The opposite policy is followed by business firms in a period of declining sales caused by a cyclical downswing. Inventories are reduced not merely because the stock at the end of the month or quarter is greater than planned originally but, also, because the firm anticipates a further decline in sales. In addition, the firm tends to cut back on assortments and price lines.

The effect, therefore, is twofold. Reorders of inventory are cut back at a higher rate than the actually experienced fall in sales. Furthermore, the firm tends to cut down its stock on hand by means of price cutting. In the economy as a whole, this tendency is reflected in widespread inventory liquidation. This is known as an inventory-induced recession. That is to say, the accelerated inventory accumulation in the prosperity phase turned out to be excessive when sales levelled off. At that point, reorders were cut down sharply by retailers who attempted to liquidate their stock by cutting prices. The drop in reorders by retailers then produced a chain effect on wholesalers, manufacturers of finished goods and supplies, and on the producers of raw materials.[1]

D. Other Causes

Since inventory is accumulated and reordered in anticipation of future sales, the size of the stock is significantly influenced by the interval between purchases and sales. This is known as the lead time. In rare cases, the firm is able to order and receive the goods literally within a day or two. Under these circumstances, there is no or little need for the firm to maintain more than a bare minimum stock for immediate sale.

1. Lead Time   In the typical case, however, the firm cannot obtain daily replacement of stock sold during the previous day. First, because the records do not become available at the close of the day. Second, the filing of orders is in itself a time-consuming process. Third, buying in the relatively small quantities required each day usually involves a higher unit price and disproportionate delivery costs. Finally, the supplier may insist on (a) minimum-size orders and (b) a given number of days of advance notice before he can ship the order. These several factors combined produce what is called the lead time on inventory replacement. This lead time is determined by (1) the supplier's minimum time requirement and (2) the firm's reorder policy.

At times, the suppliers may have so many orders on hand that they are unable to accept new orders for delivery after the customary period.

[1] Jay Forrester, Industrial Dynamics, Massachusetts Institute of Technology, 1961, presents the fullest development of this concept.

The firm that is anxious to have a given volume of goods on hand at a given time must, therefore, place its order earlier than would normally be the case. At the same time, the firm is also likely to increase the size of the order. In this way, it hopes to avoid the risk that a subsequent reorder will be caught in the supplier's backlog of orders. For instance, a manufacturer may ordinarily carry enough raw material for one month's production. If he has reason to believe that his suppliers will not be able, for the reason previously stated, to maintain this flow, he will order a supply adequate for two or three months output. A retailer may ordinarily place an order for one-half of his estimated (future) seasonal needs. Suppose he has reason to believe that the manufacturer will be fully "booked" before the season starts. He is then likely to order more than the customary one-half of expected sales.

2. Impending Strikes   Fear of a strike in a supplier's plant may cause the firm to stockpile a larger inventory than would normally be the case. The immediate effect is an inventory figure which, to the outsider, appears disproportionately large in relation to sales. Even if the stockpiling should involve a heavy drain on the firm's cash funds and an appreciable expense for temporary warehousing, these special costs are basically in the nature of an insurance premium. It is the price which the firm must pay it if wants to assure itself of an adequate supply of materials on hand.

3. Price Increases   Stockpiling of inventory in excess of the normal level is frequently resorted to by a firm that anticipates a substantial advance in the supplier's list price(s) sometime in the near future. The effect on profit is quite different in this situation from the preceding reason of an impending strike. In the latter case, the firm's own selling price may conceivably remain unchanged even if its supplier's plant is closed as a result of the strike. The added costs of stockpiling will, therefore, reduce the profit from sales.

On the other hand, stockpiling in anticipation of price advances by the suppliers is intended to yield an added profit to the firm. It expects to quote future prices on the basis of material prices and labor costs that will prevail at that (future) time. But, since it has purchased inventory at the present lower prices, the firm will reap an additional profit equal to the difference in material prices minus the cost of carrying the inventory for this period of time.

4. A Cost-Yield Model   In estimating the prospective economies and costs, respectively, involved in several alternative inventory policies, the financial manager first establishes the costs of the minimum inventory required by the firm. This is called the rock-bottom inventory (RBI).

Suppose a manufacturing company needs at least one month's stock of materials and finished goods in order to insure the flow of production and deliveries to customers. Anything above this requirement may then be identified as excess inventory (EI). EI generates additional cost for: financing, storage, handling, insurance, and taxes. On the other hand, EI may also provide opportunities for lower unit purchase price, more efficient production, protection against a threatened strike in a supplier's plant, price increases by the suppliers, and so on. Each of these reasons for the carrying of excess inventory involves a cost element as well as a yield element over and above RBI.

Table 6-2 represents a hypothetical schedule of partial cost and yields for three alternative raw material inventory policies. These alternatives, which represent three possible purchasing schedules, are based on the following assumptions.

1. Inventory requirements for the next 6 months: 300,000 units; as per RBI schedule in column 1.
2. Supplier's current list price: $1 per unit:
3. Quantity discounts offered by suppliers:

Under 50,000 units:	none
50,000 to 74,999:	2=
75,000 to 99,999:	3%
100,000 and over:	4%

4. Carrying charges (warehousing, insurance, interest on borrowed money): 3% per month.
5. A price increase of 5% is scheduled by the supplier for the fourth month; orders received for delivery at the start of the third month will be at the present price.

As shown in Table 6-2, a level-purchase schedule—50,000 units per month—will raise inventory costs by $150 (net yield = $150) over a program which corresponds to the scheduled monthly sales. This negative figure of $150 may or may not be more than offset by increased productivity of labor and/or machines by using the level-output schedule.

Similarly, a policy of purchasing 200,000 units in the third month to escape the impending price rise in the fourth month will yield savings of $5750 (discount from list price) plus $7750 (purchase price differen-

TABLE 6-2. Cost-Yield Schedule of Three Inventory Levels

Months	RBI	Order Size (Units)		Excess Inventory at End of Month		Carrying Charges[a] (in Excess of RBI)		Savings (Discount and Price Increase) Compared with RBI		Net Yield (Carrying Charges Minus Savings) Compared with RBI	
		E_1 (Level Output)	E_2 (Impending Price Rise)	EI_1	EI_2	EI_1	EI_2	EI_1	EI_2	EI_1	EI_2
First	35,000	50,000	50,000	15,000	15,000	$ 450	$ 450	$1,000	$1,000	$ 550	$ 550
Second	35,000	50,000	50,000	30,000	30,000	900	900	1,000	1,000	100	100
Third	75,000	50,000	200,000	5,000	155,000	150	4,650	−1,250	5,750 (discount)	−1,400	1,100
Fourth	55,000	50,000	—	—	100,000	none	3,000	none	2,750 (price)	none	−250
Fifth	40,000	50,000	—	10,000	60,000	300	1,800	1,000	2,000 (price)	700	200
Sixth	60,000	50,000	—	—	—	—	none	none	3,000 (price)	none	3,000
Total	300,000	300,000	300,000			$1,800	$10,800	$1,750	$15,500	−$ 150	$4,700

[a] It is assumed that all purchases for the month are received on the first of the month. The carrying charges are calculated for the excess over RBI at 3% per month.

tial). These savings of $13,500 are offset, in part, by the carrying charges which total $9450, leaving a net of $4050. To this sum must be added the corresponding net gain accruing from the discounts in the first two months minus the carrying charges, i.e., $650. Thus, the total net gain will be $4700.

III. MEASUREMENT OF RISK AND COST

The responsibility of defining the risk and cost of carrying a given volume of inventory falls upon the financial manager.

A. Risk: Types and Measurement

The following listing is a recapitulation of the several risks discussed in the preceding sections.

1. Functional imbalance.
2. Seasonal demand.
3. Impending model change.
4. Cyclical influences.
5. Price changes.

In each of the above listed situations, the financial manager deals with events which may or may not occur. The event is feasible and likely to occur but it is not inevitable. Therefore, the basic problem is that of estimating the degree of certainty, i.e., the probability. Once this estimate has been made, the probability becomes quantified and is expressed as a value less than 1.0, this value representing the certainty of occurrence, while 0.0 represents the certainty of no occurrence.

1. Illustration For example, the problem of seasonal demand, which was discussed in section II, can be restated in terms of a hypothetical case. Assume that a retailer finds himself with $60,000 of inventory in the first week of December. He had anticipated a volume of pre-Christmas sales which, if realized, would have produced, at this time, an inventory of only $15,000. The merchandise consists entirely of items especially designed for the Christmas holidays.

An evaluation of the prospects for the remaining sales period leads the store's management to reach the following conclusions. The store can adopt one of three alternative courses of action. First, it can proceed on the assumption that demand will pick up very sharply and that the inventory will be sold at its present prices. This would yield $60,000 in receipts. The second alternative is to take drastic action now and cut the prices by one-fourth. Management is certain that this action would liquidate the inventory and would yield $45,000 within one week. The third alternative is to anticipate a continuation of the recent (slow) rate of sales. In this case, the store will probably be able to sell $15,000 prior to Christmas. The remainder would then have to be sold, after Christmas, at a reduction of 75%, yielding roughly an additional $11,000; or a total of about $26,000.

Reviewing the three alternatives, one thing appears certain, as far as management is concerned. If the store accepts the second alternative, it will realize revenues of $45,000. If the management decides to do nothing now, it will wind up either with $60,000 (first assumption) or with $27,000 (third assumption). Thus, the issue reduces itself to the question: Should the store introduce a price cut now and take a loss of $15,000 in revenues, or should it take a chance of obtaining the full revenues of $60,000 at the risk of winding up with a loss of $33,000 in revenues?

The answer depends on the degree of probability that demand will revive sufficiently to absorb the entire inventory at present prices. The question that the financial manager poses to management can be expressed in the following quantitative terms: Do you believe that the chance of a revived demand is 50–50, 60–40, 75–25, or any other *figure?* To be useful, the answer cannot be qualitative—e.g., "reasonable," "fair," "good"—but must be quantitative. Let us assume that, in management's judgement, the chances are 7:3. This is equivalent to 0.7 acceptance and 0.3 rejection of the proposition that demand will fully revive and absorb the entire inventory at present prices.

With this quantification of expectation as a base, the financial manager can then proceed to set up the following payoff table (Table 6-3).

Under alternative A, the firm is sure—probability 1.0—to realize receipts of $45,000; as shown in the last column. In alternative A_2, the expectation of selling the entire inventory at $60,000 has only a probability of 0.7 and, thus, the value of this expectation is $60,000 × 0.7 or $42,000. The probability of having to sell ¾ of the inventory at a 75% price cut and realizing only $26,000 from this course of action has a value of $26,000 × 0.3 = $7800. By adding these two values, we obtain a combined value of $49,300 for alternative 2 (A_2); as shown in the last column.

TABLE 6-3.

Alternative Action by Firm (A)	Occurrence (Possible Consequences) (OA)	× Probability = (of each Occurrence happening) (POA)	Expected Value (EVO)
A₁ Sell now at ¼ off	O₁A₁ $45,000	1.0	$45,000
A₂ Hold prices	O₂A₂ $60,000	0.7	42,000 }
	O₃A₂ $26,000	0.3	7,800 } $49,300

2. Alternative Action A₂ has an expected value of $50,100, which is greater than the expected value of A₁, which is only $45,000. Thus, A₂ is preferable to A₁. Now, if management had appraised the probability in alternative 2 as 50–50, the expected value of this course of action would be: ($60,000 × 0.5) + ($27,000 × 0.5) = $43,500. This would make the first alternative preferable.

However, before we accept this conclusion, a major note of caution must be injected. The above conclusion rests on the statistical concept of probability which will now be demonstrated in nonmathematical terms.

Assume that this firm will have the same alternative choice (A₂) with the same probability of occurrence (0.7 and 0.3, respectively) in 20 consecutive instances. If the two probabilities remain constant, the result will then be:

in 70% of 20 instances or 14 cases, $60,000 each or $ 840,000
in 30% of 20 instances or 6 cases, $27,000 each or $ 162,000
                                                           $1,002,000

Thus, in 20 instances, it will realize a total return of $1,022,000, which is equivalent to a $50,100 average return in each instance ($1,002,000 ÷ 20). This is the same result that we obtained in Table 6-3.

Let us now return to our firm. Is this confrontation of alternatives a recurring experience? If so, then the odds are in favor of a greater gain in the *long run* by selecting A₂ rather than A₁. However, in any one single "experience," (selection A₂) or even in a consecutive run of two or three such experiences (A₂ decisions), the firm may realize the maximum of $60,000 or the minimum of $26,000. (It is like the proverbial "good luck" or "hard luck" of a series of rolls of the dice.) In the long run, if the probability (or odds) does not change, the ratio of seven good runs ($60,000) to three bad runs ($26,000) will emerge.

The crucial question then is: Can the firm afford a series of bad runs? Can it absorb readily one or more of these losses—$27,000 rather than $45,000 from the immediate sale—until the run of $60,000 starts? Assume that the firm is now in a tight financial situation and that its overriding concern is to survive this Christmas season. The decision may well be to take the $15,000 loss from an immediate sale rather than risk the greater loss of $34,000 in spite of the 7:3 odds that it *may* recover the full $60,000.

IV. OPERATION ALTERNATIVES

The diagnosis of the inventory pattern, current and prospective, and a quantitative evaluation of the several projections by the purchasing, production, and sales department form the framework for an inventory policy. They provide the financial manager with a schedule of the prospective cash outflow in the wake of the proposed inventory requirements. With this information at his command, the financial manager must then face up to the following questions: Does the firm have an adequate cash inflow to carry the inventory? If not, how can the cash outflow for inventory be reduced without impeding the efficiency of production or prompt delivery to customers? And, last, does the inventory picture point up items in company product line which will generate inventory problems—for instance, excessive obsolescence, cost of carrying inventory, violent price fluctuations—out of proportion to the profit on these items?

The answers to these questions involve operational inventory policies. They must be sought before the financial manager attempts to procure outside funds to finance the prospective inventory requirements. It is necessary for the financial manager to look at the major alternatives which may be explored as a means of minimizing the funds committed to inventory for each level of efficiency of the firm's operations.

A. Change in Purchasing Policy

The first area to be explored is the purchasing policy of the firm. This involves three facets: (1) lead time; (2) credit terms by suppliers; and (3) method of payment.

3. Lead Time Any downward revision in the time interval between the receipt of material and components and their actual use in the production process can be utilized to reduce the volume of stocks and, thus, the amount of money tied up in inventory. Any one or several of the following reasons may be the cause of too much lead time. Some suppliers will quote a given price on orders with a delivery schedule of, for instance, three weeks. They quote a slightly higher price on urgent orders to be delivered in one week. To take advantage of this price differential, the production manager will place his orders three weeks prior to needs. In this case, it might well be more profitable, from the viewpoint of the firm rather than of the production department, to pay the small premium for the shorter delivery schedule than to tie up funds for two weeks extra in every production cycle.

A reexamination of the production schedule of the firm may also reveal the feasibility of cutting down the interval between finishing the goods and their shipment to customers. For example, the production department may have a schedule of cycle production, i.e., concentration on one product at a time in order to maximize productivity of labor. However, the effect may be to turn out finished goods too soon for delivery. Conceivably, a change in the cycle schedule could cut down appreciably on the inventory of items that represent a relatively large tie-up of funds.

The emergence of air-freight accompanied by a cut in the ton-mile rate has opened another avenue for reducing the time interval between producing the goods and their receipt by the customer. Suppose a firm located in Massachusetts has customers in California and that these customers expect delivery of goods within seven days after placing the orders. If the goods are shipped overland—either by freight train or truck—it may take seven days for delivery. The manufacturer must, therefore, have a given amount of finished goods on hand in order to make immediate shipment on receipt of the order. This may no longer be necessary with air express available. It may be quite possible to execute an order from California in, say, four or five days, and then ship the goods by air to California where they will arrive in less than 24 hours. In the case of transatlantic shipments, the time saving of air freight over sea freight may be as much as three weeks.

2. Credit Terms By Suppliers An extension of the credit terms by the suppliers has a positive effect on the cash position of the firm, i.e., it tends to close the time gap between inflow and outflow. Suppose the firm had been buying its goods on 30 days credit and the interval between the receipt of goods and their subsequent sale and receipt of payment from customers ranges between 50 and 60 days. Under these conditions, the firm had to finance its sales for a period of 20 to 30 days. With an extended (60 day) credit from the suppliers, the firm can expect to obtain the proceeds from sales on or before the dates when its payables fall due. Next, assume that the firm had, in the past, found it necessary to finance the time gap of 20 to 30 days by loans obtained from external sources. The extended credit of 60 days will then enable the firm either (1) to save the cost of external financing or (2) to use the proceeds of such available loans for alternative profitable opportunities.

Suppose the firm maintains, as a matter of liquidity policy, a cash balance in the bank of $5000. It asks for, and obtains, a loan of $50,000 at 7% per annum without the requirements to maintain a compensatory balance. The proceeds from this loan are being used for the financing of accounts receivable and expanded inventory. Let us next assume that the management of the firm is considering the advisibility of borrowing an additional $35,000 at 7% and taking advantage of a 1% discount offered by suppliers for payment on delivery. The bank is willing to increase the present loan and to make available an additional $35,000 but it requires a 20% compensating balance. Thus, a total loan of $100,000 is necessary to yield an additional $35,000: ($100,000 loan *plus* $5000 cash balance) *minus* ($20,000 compensating balance plus $50,000 already lent) = $35,000. The monthly cost of the additional loan of $50,000 is $350 ($\frac{1}{12}$ of 7% per annum). But this will also be the cost of the actually available proceeds from the loan, i.e., $35,000. The effective rate on the $35,000 is 1% or the same as the discount offered by the supplier. Thus, the marginal cost of the loan equals the marginal gain from the discount and the firm will be better off in paying net 30 days rather than in taking the discount of 1%.

3. Hedging Operations   A distinct type of purchasing activity is known as hedging. It is widely used by business firms that require substantial quantities of raw materials or agricultural products that are traded in the so-called commodities markets and are subject to price fluctuations. Basically, a hedging operation involves the simultaneous sale and purchase of the "future" contract for the same commodity, as illustrated in the following case.

Suppose a company is engaged in the manufacture of leather goods. Its production schedule calls for the use of 500 calfskin hides per week for the next 26 weeks or a total of 13,000 skins, based on orders from its customers for the next six months. The present price per skin is assumed to be $5. In the skin market, there is also quoted a "future" price of $5.15 in 30 days, $5.30 in 60 days, $5.45 in 90 days, etc.

The firm has three alternatives. Each week, it can buy 500 skins and take a chance that the price will either remain constant at $5 or go up or go down. In the first case, it will realize as a profit the difference between the sales price and its total costs, including the cost of skins calculated at present market prices. If the skins should go down in price, the firm will realize an additional (windfall) profit. The contrary will be true if the skins should go up in price.

The second alternative is to purchase 13,000 skins today, add to the purchase price the cost of storage, handling, insurance, etc. calculate the average cost per skin and use this figure in calculating the firm's prospective profit.

The third alternative is to purchase 3000 skins today and a series of (five) future contracts for 2000 skins each, the first of these contracts being due one month from now with the other four contracts staggered at intervals of one month each. The price which the firm must pay for the future contracts is generally higher than the present price, called the "spot" or "cash" price for immediate delivery. The difference, or excess, between future and spot prices is usually equal to the seller's cost of carrying and financing the inventory for one, two, or more months, plus a small profit. In fact, some sellers of future contracts do not intend to buy the skins and hold them for future delivery. Instead, they speculate on the possibility that they may be able to cover their commitment later on in the spot market at a lower price than the price that the firm agreed to pay for the future contract. At times, speculators may be of the firm opinion that the subsequent spot market will be appreciably lower than the current market price. In this case, the excess of the future price over the present spot price could conceivably be less than the customary markup over the spot or cash price.

The firm that can assure itself of the required raw materials at the time when needed by purchasing a series of futures reduces, proportionately, its investment in stock. At the same time, it knows the precise (future) costs of its raw materials. Therefore, it assures itself of whatever profit margin it has calculated into its selling price. In essence, the firm has built a "hedge" around its materials costs and prospective profit.

An auxiliary advantage of hedging is that the firm's credit rating is often improved. Since it has fixed the costs of the future inventory, it has eliminated the risk of a subsequent rise in raw material prices which may wipe out most or all of the profit embodied in the acceptance of future orders from its customers.

By means of hedging, the firm can specialize in the manufacturing of leather goods and shift the speculative risk of price fluctuations in hides to those who specialize in trading in futures.

4. Changes in Sales Policy   The financial manager can also attempt to cut down the inventory by initiating a reexamination of the firm's sales policy along the following lines.

a. Preseason Sales.   Frequently, an excessive inventory is a result of the fact that the firm is accumulating a substantial stock of finished goods in anticipation of its customers' seasonal demand. This practice is quite common among manufacturers and, also, among distributors. Manufacturers who pursue a policy of level production are particularly apt to build up sizeable excess inventories prior to the customers' peak season.

A price-reduction on preseason purchases offers the firm's customers an opportunity to realize an additional profit. Although it decreases the firm's gross margin by the amount of the price cut, it also reduces the firm's costs of carrying the stock. These cost savings will usually offset only a portion of the price reduction. However, the advantage of greater liquidity, while not measurable in dollars and cents, may not be inconsequential. It relieves top management of the necessity to preserve a precarious balance between the relatively small inflow of funds preparatory to the selling season compared with the substantial obligations to suppliers that is a function of output. More specifically, the firm cuts back on its loan requirements. This factor plays an important role in the small firm, in contrast to the large firm with ready access to bank funds.

b. Improvement in Inventory Control.   A fruitful area of exploration is the firm's method of inventory control. This term refers to the method employed in determining whether the estimated needs of stock on hand conforms to the actual withdrawal from the stock either for production, sales, or both. Two cases will illustrate the role and importance of inventory control.

c. Warehousing.   For a number of years, firm A had maintained a single central warehouse from which all orders were filled. Goods were shipped to customers either by rail or truck, depending on the distance of the customer from the warehouse. Stock on hand in the warehouse averaged about $300,000. This arrangement proved satisfactory until the firm's market began to expand geographically. As a result, deliveries to distant customers took one week or longer. Delays in shipments were especially pronounced on small orders involving less than one thousand dollars. Customers located at some distance from the warehouse increasingly complained about these delays. Cancellations were not infrequent. Salesmen also reported many instances in which customers did not place orders because no assurance could be given of early delivery.

To meet these complaints the firm set up two smaller warehouses in two additional geographic centers. Its inventory in the main warehouse was reduced to $200,000, but each of the new warehouses was stocked with $100,000 of finished goods, raising its total warehouse inventories to $400,000. Although the inventory costs went up, the firm found this arrangement profitable because of the added orders and greater customer satisfaction.

With expanding sales volume, the warehoused inventory rose to over $500,000. At that point, the financial manager proposed a reexamination of the policy. Following his recommendations, a study was made of the cost of air freight from the main warehouse to the customers serviced by the two subsidiary warehouses, taking into consideration the size and frequency of orders and comparing the cost of air freight with the present cost of shipment. The results of this study, omitting the details, showed that the main warehouse with an inventory of $250,000 could service all customers, by means of air shipment to the distant customers, as effectively as the existing setup, at a lower overall cost. The savings in warehouse rent, handling, insurance, etc. more than offset the higher freight rate by air compared to rail or truck freight rates. In addition, the capital requirements for inventory were reduced by one-half, yielding additional savings in finance charges.

d. Coordination of Inventory Flow.   In the second case, the financial manager initiated an analysis of the orders for replacement parts from customers with the inventory carried for this purpose. The study showed that about one-half of the inventory accounted for 90% of the orders. In other words, the turnover of one-half of the inventory was nine times as great as the turnover of the other one-half of the stock. The slow-moving items could, and were, cut back to less than one-fourth their former volume, without any undue delays in servicing the orders for these items.

As in the preceding case, the cost of carrying the inventory was reduced appreciably, funds were released for other operational purposes, and the overall liquidity of the firm was improved.

SUMMARY

Along with receivables, inventory is a balance sheet item of major concern to the financial manager. The financial risks of inadequate inventory planning, management, and control may lead to greater financial losses than from bad debts. As a result of poor inventory planning, a firm could easily suffer losses of 10% or more on a portion of its inventory, even in good times. The volume of inventory is a function of anticipated sales. Hence, the adequacy of inventory levels is often based on the accuracy of sales forecasts. Other factors, including the dilemma of profit versus liquidity, influence inventory levels.

In order to perform a meaningful analysis, the single balance sheet item "inventory" must be broken down into its component parts, such as raw material inventory, work in process inventory, and finished goods inventory. Knowledge of the accountant's method of valuing this inventory is necessary to the financial manager. Should the firm use lower of cost or market or FIFO or LIFO?

Funds tied up in inventory carry the dual risk of failure to realize anticipated sales or failure to sell the goods at the forecasted price. Thus, the financial manager must carefully plan an inventory policy. A policy of maintaining inventory levels in excess of the requirements for the immediate future may be desirable for several reasons, for instance, economic size of production runs, fear of shortages, anticipated price rises of raw materials, lead time, or impending strikes. The use of various quantitative techniques can aid the financial manager in planning levels of inventory. Other methods of inventory control such as examination of warehousing and transportation policies can reduce the levels of inventory needed by the firm.

Questions

1. Why is the risk element generally greater in a firm's investment in inventory than in its investment in receivables?

2. How can the risks of investment in inventory be minimized?

3. In periods of falling prices, is it better for a firm to value its inventory by FIFO or by LIFO? Why?

4. Why might a firm adopt a policy of maintaining an inventory in excess of the requirements for the immediate future?

5. How does the business cycle influence inventory levels?

6. What are the advantages of a hedging operation?

7. As a lender, what percentage of value would you loan on each of the following:

   (a) Assembled plastic hula hoops in a toy manufacturer's warehouse.

   (b) Refrigerators for sale in a department store.

   (c) Bananas in the hold of a refrigerated ship.

   (d) Large quantities of miscellaneous transistors in an electronics plant.

   (e) Silver and gold at a dental supply house.

   (f) Ladies' slips at a clothing factory.

   (g) Paper-bound books at a distributor.

Problems

1. Refer back to the cash budget you prepared for Ajax Corporation (Chapter Two, Problem Four). Under the borrowing schedule shown, what is the cost of financing the bank borrowings in dollars for the period if the bank charges an effective rate of 6%? As the banker, what type of collateral would you prefer? As the financial manager of Ajax, would you agree?

2. The Consolidated Widget Sales Corporation had 450 widgets on hand on January 1, 1966, which were purchased at a cost of $12 each. In March, 1966, the corporation purchased 300 widgets at a cost of $11.25 each. In June, 1966, the corporation purchased 400 widgets at a cost of $10.50 each. In August, the corporation purchased 2000 widgets at a cost of $8.50 each. In November, 1500 widgets were purchased at a cost of $7.50 each. At the end of the fiscal year, on December 31, 1966, the corporation had 1100 widgets on hand.

   (a) Calculate the value of the ending inventory of widgets under both FIFO and LIFO.

   (b) If net sales for the firm totaled $74,000 and other expenses amounted to $14,200, calculate the firm's profit before taxes under both IIFO and LIFO.

3. The Cromar Company of Newark, New Jersey, has $100,000 of air conditioners in stock, valued at market value, on August 1, 1966. If a heatwave occurs during August, at least $80,000 of this inventory will be sold during the month at list market prices. If sales continue at the present rate, only $25,000 of this inventory will be sold in August. If prices are slashed by 25% now, management is certain that the entire inventory will be moved this month. Any inventory remaining after September 1st can be liquidated at 50% of the market price.

   (a) Calculate net sales under each alternative.
   (b) If management is 65% certain that a heatwave will occur in August, which alternative appears to be most desirable? What other factors, if any, should management consider before it makes a decision?

4. Owing to increased sales, the Dashbank Manufacturing Corporation must expand its inventory by $150,000. The financial manager can finance this expansion through any of several sources. Assume that the full amount of inventory will be needed for 60 days. Calculate the effective financing cost in dollars and as an annual percentage (assume a 360 day year) for each of the following alternatives:

   (a) Purchase on terms of 1/10, net 30; do not pay until the 60th day.
   (b) Purchase on terms of 1/10, net 30; pay on 30th day; borrow from a finance company for 30 days on the value of inventory at the rate of 8% per year.
   (c) Purchase on term of 1/10, net 30; pay on 10th day; borrow from a finance company for 50 days on the value of inventory at the rate of 8% per year.

Case: AIRPORT LUMBER, INC.

Airport Lumber, Inc. operates a large lumber yard and home-improvement center located adjacent to the airport in a growing suburb of a large city in Minnesota. The company began operations in 1947 and grew rapidly along with the suburb. Management expanded from selling lumber to selling hardware and everything for the do-it-yourself hobbyist and, in 1953, added a complete home-improvement center. Beginning in 1959, Airport Lumber began to stock aluminum combination storm and screen windows.

In April 1966, Subajian Extrusion Company, the supplier of aluminum windows to Airport Lumber, offered a 10% discount to Airport Lumber if they would purchase 5000 windows and accept delivery and make payment by June 15, 1966.

The sales manager from Subajian explained to the purchasing agent of Airport Lumber that the seasonality of its aluminum window sales was causing production problems. Most aluminum combination windows are sold in the fall and in the early part of the winter. Because of working capital problems, Subajian could not afford year-around level production

TABLE 6-4.   Airport Lumber
Company; Monthly Sales of
Combination Windows

Month	Sales
January, 1965	70
February, 1965	47
March, 1965	228
April, 1965	425
May, 1965	437
June, 1965	319
July, 1965	233
August, 1965	385
September, 1965	1097
October, 1965	1215
November, 1965	805
December, 1965	135
Year 1965	5396
January, 1966	85
February, 1966	63

of the windows—which constituted over 90% of its business. On the other hand, if the windows were produced completely on a seasonal basis, Subajian would not have enough capacity on its extrusion machines to meet the total demand for windows. Consequently, Subajian would be willing to grant the special 10% discount to Airport Lumber if it would purchase and pay for the windows at a time (up to June 15th) when excess capacity was available on Subajian's extrusion machines.

The purchasing agent promised the sales manager of the extrusion company that he would carefully consider this offer and would give the sales manager an answer by the end of the week. The normal average wholesale price, in season, for combination storm and screen windows was $3.75

per window. Average prices are used if the purchaser buys a standard assortment of sizes and models. Thus, Airport Lumber would save 37½ cents per window if it made the special purchase. At present, Airport Lumber has approximately 500 windows in stock. If it makes the special purchase, Airport Lumber can store the windows in its wholly owned warehouse. The storage of 5000 windows would take up approximately 3000 cubic feet of space in the warehouse. Ample space is currently available in the warehouse since it is only filled to 80% of its capacity of 75,000 cubic feet.

The purchasing agent is not certain that sales of combination storm and screen windows in 1966 will repeat the history of the preceding year. However, these figures might be of some help to him in reaching a decision. They are reproduced in Table 6-4.

Case Questions:

1. What alternatives are open to the purchasing agent?
2. What decision should he make on the Subajian Extrusion Company offer? Why?

~~~~~~

Chapter Seven

New Techniques in Managerial Finance

In recent years, financial managers have made increasing use of the "new approaches" to theoretical analysis and to managerial decision making. These new approaches are known as game theory, linear programming, and operations research. In the more advanced phases of each of these approaches, mathematical techniques play an important part. However, the basic concepts and their application to business situations can be understood without the use of mathematical tools. In fact, many problems of financial management lend themselves to a nonmathematical application of operations research techniques.

A. The Evolution of Operations Research

This technique, commonly abbreviated as OR, evolved in World War II as a valuable tool of military planning. Problems of military strategy—which, under the traditional approaches, would have been tackled on the basis of intuition or experience—were turned over to teams of scientists. These teams were made up of mathematicians, physicists, psychologists, economists, and members of other disciplines. Their task was to evolve scientific methods that would provide more effective solutions to military problems than could be expected from intuitive or empirical decisions. For example, these scientists were asked to determine mathematically the optimum size of ocean convoys that would incur the least losses from enemy submarine attacks; the setting of depth charges to be dropped by submarine-hunting planes that would produce the optimum number of successes; the type of defensive tactics that would minimize the damage caused by Japanese suicide pilots, etc.

The success of this new technique of finding solutions by scientific methods that proved to have advantages over the intuitive or experimental answers of the past, led business firms to adapt the same approach to the solution of a variety of management problems. Experts in this technique developed a lucrative practice as management consultants. Economists applied the technique to economic analysis and found it a useful tool in developing so-called economic models. Financial managers also found OR useful in developing financial models and for other financial purposes.

B. The Nature of OR

In operations research, the aim is to find the one combination of elements that will produce the optimal combination of benefits and costs. This objective is familiar to every student of elementary economics who recalls the principles of diminishing returns, optimum output per input unit, maximizing profits, etc. But while economic theory deals with concepts and examines one or at most two variables—keeping, for example, land and labor constant while varying the input of labor per acre—OR analyzes, simultaneously, all variable factors that are involved in a given situation.

The central feature of OR is the quantitative treatment of all relevant factors or elements that enter into a problem. All assumptions by management about future events must, therefore, be first transformed into specific quantities. For example, the assumption that next year's sales will be "better" or "worse" than those of the past year are of no use in OR. However, when management translates "better" to mean, e.g., 10% higher, this assumption can then be treated as a quantity by multiplying last year's sales volume by 110%. Or, if management is only 50% sure of its forecast of a 10% rise, the OR technician can then calculate the results, first on the quantitative assumption that the forecast is 100% correct and, then, on the basis of a 50% probability. He can then tell management what cost (i.e., risk) and what profit (i.e., premium) will be obtained from each of the two assumptions about next year's sales.

It must be emphasized that it is management which must define quantitatively its assumptions and the quantitative value that it places upon certain objectives and elements. For example, how much is it worth to the company, in dollars, to have available financial advice from its bank where it carries a large cash balance on a noninterest-bearing checking account rather than to deposit a sizeable portion with a savings institution and obtain a return of say, 4% per annum?

1. A Big Case A leading food processor, with sales running into several hundred millions of dollars, was confronted by the problem of determining the most efficient warehousing system to serve both its factories located in various parts of the country and its retail customers spread across the nation. Specifically, the company wanted to know (1) how many warehouses it should operate, (2) where to locate them, (3) which customers should be served from any one of the warehouses, (4) how much volume each warehouse should handle, and (5) how the entire distribution system should be set up.

The company had the needed statistical facts and records to make a thorough and complete cost analysis of every feasible layout and operational structure. However, the analysis of one single alternative national distribution system would have required 75 million calculations! This would have taken two full-time clerks close to two years. On the other hand, it was found that an electronic computer could do the same job for the company in less than one hour. But there were at least twenty alternative systems that had to be considered. It would have taken 2000 clerks one full year to make the calculations of only 20 alternatives.

The OR experts developed a so-called program that was "fed" to the electronic computer. Every element that entered into the company's distribution system was expressed as a quantity. Each minute piece of quantitative information was then stored on the computer's magnetic tape. The computer was then programmed to digest (i.e., calculate) a series of alternatives. As the computer completed the calculations for a given configuration (i.e., combination) of elements, the results were evaluated and a different configuration was put into process which showed the effects of shifting elements or items. Each successive configuration represented an improvement over the preceding one until finally the most efficient configuration emerged. At the end of this chain, the management of the company had available a picture of the relative costs and operational structure of each configuration.

2. A Simple Situation The following illustration is intended to demonstrate on a simple level the applicability of OR concepts by the financial manager.

Assume that Mr. Adams has $10,000 that he wants to invest for an indefinite period of months or years. His objective is to obtain maximum returns on his investment and safety of principal. The choice has narrowed down to three alternatives: a savings institution that offers interest at the rate of $4\frac{1}{4}\%$, commercial bank that pays $3\frac{1}{2}\%$ on savings deposits, and a 10-year mortgage that yields $5\frac{1}{2}\%$ per annum and has two more years to run until it is due. On the basis of returns, the mortgage will yield the most, followed by the savings institution, with the commercial bank ranking last. But Mr. Adams also wants maximum safety of principal. Now, suppose that the two financial institutions are insured by the Federal Deposit Insurance Company, while the mortgaged property has an appraised value of about $15,000 but lacks such insurance. Furthermore, Mr. Adams does not know whether he will keep the money invested for a few months or several years. What happens if he should find it necessary to convert his investment into cash on short notice? Finally, Mr. Adams believes that he may have occasion in the near future to ask the bank for a temporary loan to buy a new car for cash rather than on the installment plan.

Using this information, a simple job of OR can be performed by setting up a schedule of the several alternatives and criteria in nontechnical language (Table 7-1).

TABLE 7-1.   A Simple Investment Matrix

	Contractual Yield ($)		Special Features	Estimated Yield
Commercial bank	$3\frac{1}{2}\%$ per annum	350	A_1 B_1 C_1 D_1	
Savings bank	$4\frac{1}{4}\%$ per annum	425	A_2 B_2	
Mortgage	$5\frac{1}{2}\%$ per annum	550	A_3 B_3	

In the above schedule (i.e., matrix), A represents safety of investment; B stands for the method of calculating interest; C connotes a temporary loan; and D represents financial advice.

Assuming that both financial institutions are insured by the Federal Deposit Insurance Corporation, A_1 and A_2 are identical. However, the mortgage does not have such insurance. If Mr. Adams should want to convert the mortgage into cash he will, as is customary, have "to give points," i.e., to take a loss of $100 on principal. Therefore, A_3 represents the potential risk of a loss of 1%. Thus, A_3 is less than A_1. In consequence, the interest rate on the mortgage is really worth less than $5\frac{1}{2}\%$ per annum to Mr. Adams.

TABLE 7-2.   Estimated Yield of Three Investment Alternatives (Dollars)

	Contractual Yield	Risk	Interest	Loan	Advice	Estimated Actual Yield
Commercial bank	350	0	0	+50	+75	475.00
Savings bank	425	0	−50	0	0	375.00
Mortgage	550	−100	0	0	0	450.00

As for B_1, assume that the commercial bank calculates the interest from day of deposit to day of withdrawal (B_1). On the other hand, the savings institution is assumed to calculate the interest from the first day of the month following the deposit to the last day of the month preceding the withdrawal (B_2). Thus, B_1 is worth a little more than B_2. Interest on the mortgage is paid for the full period and, thus, B_3 is equal to B_1.

C represents the opportunity to obtain a temporary loan at the prevailing minimum rate. This is only available at the commercial bank. C is, therefore, worth something to Mr. Adams.

Finally, D_1 represents financial service. Mr. Adams must determine the monetary value to him of such services by the bank.

In each instance, Mr. Adams, or his financial advisor, must translate the label in each square of the table into his estimated dollar value. These are then added to or subtracted from the first figure in the same row ($350, $425, and $550, respectively). The result is then entered in the column "estimated yield."

In Table 7-2, hypothetical dollar values have been entered in the respective squares or cells.

Based on the assumed relative monetary value of the several features, the commercial bank emerges as the most desirable alternative, followed by the investment in a mortgage and the savings bank, in this order.

If Mr. Adams should make a different assumption on a given item—for example, that the financial institutions will raise the interest rate in the next few weeks, or that the discount on the sale of the mortgage may go up to 2 points—this will automatically change the results in the last column. The next question then is: Which of the several assumptions is more likely to become a reality? OR techniques provide a method that makes it possible to express in quantities the several assumptions; i.e., their relative likelihood of occurrence.

Chapter six gave an example of applying probability techniques to the measurement of risk and cost in the area of inventory policy (section III). These same techniques can be applied to other financial problems, e.g., the problem discussed above. Further, the use of the computer makes it possible for the financial manager to simulate what would occur under varying probabilities. This gives him knowledge of the consequences of various risks and alternatives.

Operations research techniques can also be used to solve problems under conditions of certainty. The appendix to this chapter demonstrates how operations research techniques under certainty can be applied to the problem of inventory levels.

C. Choosing the Source of Funds—an OR Approach

An OR model can be constructed as an aid in selecting the best external source of short-term financing. The first phase in constructing this model consists of a precise definition of objectives, criteria, and alternative courses of action. Each of these components of the model is initially expressed in quantitative terms or in qualitative (literate) form if the quantitative values have not yet been estimated by management.

1. First Phase   Assume, for example, that the management of Company X has established the fact that the projected sales volume for the next year will require short-term financing. The financial manager has prepared the following estimates:

1. External short-term financing is necessary.
2. Assuming that the sales forecast is accepted as definitive, the requirement will be:
   (a) $50,000 starting in month 2 through month 4;
   (b) $100,000 in months 5 and 6;
   (c) $75,000 in month 7;
   (d) no external funds are needed for the balance of the year.
3. The company is presently preparing plans for a substantial expansion of physical facilities in the subsequent fiscal year.
4. No decision has yet been reached as to whether the contemplated expansion should be financed by means of (a) an intermediate term loan, (b) the public sale of a stock issue, or (c) the procurement of a mortgage on the plants, old and new.

The problem then presents itself: What are the relative advantages and disadvantages of the three sources of short-term financing (commercial banks, finance companies, and factoring companies)? In order to provide an analytical frame of reference, a matrix of all relevant factors can be set up. This type of matrix is presented in Table 7-3.

2. Second Phase   Having prepared this schedule, the second phase involves the substitution of actual or estimated dollar figures in every element (box) of the matrix marked by a question mark. Also, the present figures in several elements must be translated into the appropriate dollar figures. After these entries have been made, a second schedule is prepared which is confined to rows 4, 6, 7, 8, 12, and 13. These are the "payoff" data; i.e., the financial manager now has a series of quantitative data for each of the three sources. Row 13 shows the relative

TABLE 7-3.   Relevant Factors in Three Alternative Sources of Funds

	Alternative Sources		
	Commercial Bank	Finance Company	Factoring Company
1. Maximum loan required	Yes	Yes	Yes
2. Interest rate	6% per annum	$\frac{1}{30}$% per diem	$\frac{1}{25}$% per diem
3. Requirement of compensating balance (percent of loan)	20%	None	None
4. Calculation of interest charges	On face amount of loan	For amount actually used	For amount actually used
5. Assumption of credit and collection	No	No	Yes
6. Charge for credit and collection	—	1.5%	—
7. Firm's savings on credit and collection	—	—	1.5%
8. Firm's estimated cost of delinquent accounts and losses	2%	2%	None
9. Assignment of accounts receivable	No	Yes	Yes
10. Notification of accounts	No	No	Yes
11. Probable reaction of accounts	—	—	Partly unfavorable
12. Probable loss of profit because of points 10 and 11	—	—	—
13. Actual cost of anticipated loans	?	?	?
14. Potential source of unsecured intermediate term loan	Yes	No	No

TABLE 7-4.   Quantitative Schedule of Relative Factors in Three Alternative Sources of Funds (Dollars)

Row (see Table 7-3)	Commercial Bank	Finance Company	Factor
4. Cost of loan	2575	4250	5100
6. Charge for credit and collection	—	1000	—
7. Firm's savings on credit and collection department			−1500[a]
8. Firm's estimated bad debt losses	2000	2000	—
12. Probable loss of sales			+1000[a]
13. Actual cost of anticipated loan	4750	7250	4600
14. Potential source of unsecured term loan	Yes	No	No

[a] Savings by the firm reduce the cost of the loan by an amount equal to the savings ($1500). By the same token, the loss of profit from the anticipated decrease in sales is an added cost of the loan.

"payoff" that the firm obtains from each of the three lenders. Table 7-4 shows the entries for the relevant rows and elements.

Under the assumed conditions, row 13 in Table 7-4 indicates the best payoff favors the factor with the bank in second position. But the financial manager must turn now to row 14, which is assumed to play a role in the final decision. Only the commercial bank is presumed to be available as a future source of an unsecured intermediate-term loan. How much is this potential availability worth to the firm today? Is the value sufficient to compensate for the lower payoff of the bank (row 13)? It should be mentioned at this point, that the past lending experiences of a bank vis-à-vis a given firm plays a major role in the granting of inter-mediate-term loans.

D. OR and Product-Mix Problems

Accountants generally divide costs into variable costs and nonvariable or fixed costs. Variable costs are those costs that vary directly with or roughly proportional to changes in the volume of output. Thus, variable costs will increase about 25% when output increases 25%. For example, if you drive a compact car 100 miles it will use perhaps 5 gallons of gasoline. If you drive the car 200 miles it will use approximately 10 gallons of gasoline. As output (transportation) increases, the cost of gasoline increases proportionately; it is variable with output.

Fixed costs, on the other hand, remain constant regardless of the level of output. For example, the cost of the license plate for a car remains constant whether you drive one mile in a year or 100,000 miles. (The cost of the license plate is a fixed cost unless you decide not to license the car at all.) The accountant's concept of costs presents few problems to the financial manager when only one product is being produced and sold by the firm.

Typically, however, several products are usually being produced or considered for production by the firm. This leads to several problems. First, there is a problem of allocating costs to the different products being produced. OR techniques can do little to improve the proper allocation of costs among products. Second, there is a problem of the real nature of some costs once a firm manufactures more than one product that is not adequately covered by the accountant's definition of costs as either fixed costs or variable costs. In this problem area, OR specialists have defined a third type of costs, which they call programmed costs. Programmed costs consist of such costs as setup time for machinery, time lost by workers who are shifted between two jobs, the advertising material for two products instead of for one, and other marketing costs (two kinds of customers, shipping expense, etc.) which arise from the decision to produce two (or more) products instead of one product.

The use of the concept of programmed costs may cause a firm to switch from producing two products to making a single product or to some other product mix. For example, a small pharmaceutical firm was making two products (A and B) in its factory, which was operating at capacity. Before OR techniques were applied, the firm showed the situation depicted in Table 7-5.

TABLE 7-5. Profit in a Pharmaceutical Firm Before Application of OR Techniques (Dollars)

	A	B	Total
Sales	$50,000	$50,000	$100,000
Fixed costs	10,000	10,000	20,000
Variable costs	20,000	20,000	40,000
Profit before programmed costs	20,000	20,000	40,000
Programmed costs	15,000	15,000	30,000
Profit	$ 5,000	$ 5,000	$ 10,000

Assuming that total sales volume would remain at $100,000 with a different product mix, the OR specialist calculates what would happen if more of product B were produced and less of product A. The results would be as shown in Table 7-6.

TABLE 7-6.   Profit in a Pharmaceutical Firm if More of Product B is Produced (Dollars)

	A	B	Total
Sales	$25,000	$75,000	$100,000
Fixed costs	10,000	10,000	20,000
Variable costs	10,000	30,000	40,000
	5,000	35,000	40,000
Programmed costs	10,000	15,000	25,000
Profit	$ (5,000)	$20,000	$ 15,000

It will be noted that an increase in the output of product B with a corresponding reduction in product A will cut the total programmed costs. Although product A would now be produced at a loss, the total profit of the firm would be increased by the new product mix. Thus, it would be advantageous for the firm to produce A at a loss rather than at a profit, since the incremental profit on B more than compensates for the loss on A.

In the same case, the OR specialist decided to see what would happen if product A were completely eliminated and only B were produced. Again, it was assumed that sales volume would remain at $100,000. Table 7-7 shows the results of this change.

In this case, all of the programmed costs associated with product A could be eliminated. By making only one product, more profit could be made than by making two products. Of course, this would only be true provided the firm could increase its sales of B to $100,000 per year. The firm may, in fact, wish to accept a lower profit now by producing both products so that when plant capacity is expanded, it will have a place in both markets. More sophisticated OR techniques, including sampling and probability analysis, can also be applied in the product-mix area by the OR specialist. It is often sufficient for the financial manager to know in what type of product-mix problem OR techniques may prove

TABLE 7-7.   Profit in a Pharmaceutical Firm if only Product B is
Produced (Dollars)

	Product B Only
Total sales	$100,000
Fixed costs	20,000
Variable costs	40,000
	40,000
Programmed costs	15,000
Profit	$ 25,000

helpful. The actual application of these techniques can often best be made by the OR specialist or statistician.

E. Decision Making

The area of OR that is perhaps of greatest use to the financial manager is that of *decision theory*. This term refers to a formal approach to decision making under *uncertainty*. The last word in the definition must be stressed. The approach is one whose merit is most significant when management is uncertain as to the "shape of the ball park," but is willing to quantify its best guess. The case that follows is an illustration of its working.

> Mr. Baker, the treasurer of Y. G., Inc., is faced with a short-term need for $200,000. He can borrow this amount from a finance company at a charge of ¼₀ of 1% per day, paying only for the number of days during which the firm needs the money; or he can turn to the bank and borrow the funds at an effective interest rate of 6% with the minimum interest payment on the loan fixed at one month. Mr. Baker is sure that the company will not need the loan for more than one month. But the precise number of days of need (depending on when a major customer pays his outstanding bill) is unclear. Which lender should Mr. Baker turn to?

Table 7-8 consists of a payoff chart that shows all the possible results of Mr. Baker's choice. As can be seen from the table, there is a greater *probability* of saving money if Y. G., Inc. uses the finance company than if it uses the bank. For 19 out of the 30 days this holds true.

TABLE 7-8.   Y. G., Inc.: Payoff Chart (Dollars)

Day	Finance Company Charge	Bank Charge	Value of Decision to Choose Bank as Lender	Value of Decision to Use Finance Company as Lender
1	50	1000	− 950.00	950.00
2	100	1000	− 900.00	900.00
3	150		− 850.00	850.00
4	200		− 800.00	800.00
5	250		− 750.00	750.00
6	300		− 700.00	700.00
7	350		− 650.00	650.00
8	400		− 600.00	600.00
9	450		− 550.00	550.00
10	500		− 500.00	500.00
11	550		− 450.00	450.00
12	600		− 400.00	400.00
13	650		− 350.00	350.00
14	700		− 300.00	300.00
15	750		− 250.00	250.00
16	800		− 200.00	200.00
17	850		− 150.00	150.00
18	900		− 100.00	100.00
19	950		− 50.00	50.00
20	1000		0.00	0.00
21	1050		50.00	− 50.00
22	1100		100.00	− 100.00
23	1150		150.00	− 150.00
24	1200		200.00	− 200.00
25	1250		250.00	− 250.00
26	1300		300.00	− 300.00
27	1350		350.00	− 350.00
28	1400		400.00	− 400.00
29	1450		450.00	− 450.00
30	1500		500.00	− 500.00
	Sum of value		−6750.00	+6750.00
	Divided by the number of days		− 225.00	+ 225.00

The bank as a lender is preferable for only 9 days, while the 20th day would be a toss-up.

Even the novice at finance can quickly compute the break-even point in this example. The bank loan will cost a minimum of one month's payment or $\frac{1}{12}$ of 6% $\times$ $200,000 ($1000). The finance company loan on a per diem basis would cost $\frac{1}{40}$ of 1% $\times$ 200,000 ($50 per day). On this basis, if Mr. Baker has more faith in the use of the money being limited to less than 20 days than for a longer period, he will probably choose the finance company. On the other hand, if, in his judgment, it is more probable that the loan will be needed for more than 20 days, the bank will probably be his choice as a lender.

With a little more analysis, however, it can be seen from the table that the absolute level of maximum saving for the choice of the bank over the finance company is $500. If Y. G., Inc. only needs the money for one day, however, the choice of the finance company would produce a benefit of $950 and, similarly, the finance company shows more plus days as a concomitant of its choice over the bank. Indeed, if all the possible benefits for each of the days are added up (notice that the financial manager has assumed, in this table, that each of the days is equally likely, equally probable) the selection of the finance company would seem to far outweigh that of the bank.

The initial determination that there was a "break-even point" at 20 days did not take into consideration the comparative probability offered by the choice of the finance company. The financial manager of Y. G., Inc. would have to estimate the probabilities of the company needing its loan for more than 20 days being considerably *more* than 50–50 in order to warrant the choice of the bank financing. Just how much greater the probabilities would have to be will become clearer in later chapters. But, at this point, a brief summary of decision theory is in order.

The elements of decision making under uncertainty are relatively simple. A decision maker must choose among several choices, which can be denoted as choice 1, 2, and so on (in the example of Y. G., Inc., choice 1 would be to use the bank, choice 2, to use the finance company). Insofar as possible, the set of choices should include all reasonable possibilities in the situation.

Choosing among the various possible acts requires analysis of the results following upon the choice. In the example just cited, if the financial manager knew the exact length of time the loan would be needed, his choice would be relatively simple. Since he is unsure as to which state of nature (each of the 30 different periods that conceivably would be the "right" period to base his decision on) will be the appropriate one, he must list them all with financial results that, in his judgment, they will entail.

Since the financial manager of Y. G., Inc. is not sure which of the states of nature will turn out to be the actual shape of the future, he must assign probabilities to each of them. Where statistical evidence is available, this can be most useful. If Y. G., Inc. anticipated repaying its loan upon payment of an outstanding bill by a customer who, 90% of the time, had made payments on the 10th of the month, this experience factor could be incorporated into the probabilities of the various states of nature. Regardless, however, of the lack of past history, probabilistic projections of the shape of the future must be made. In this regard, decision theory does not differ from "seat of the pants" decision making. It merely requires the explicit quantification and analysis of the factors that go into this decision making.

In considering alternative acts, neither the payoffs nor the probabilities attached to them are easily determined. Experience and judgment play a major role in their projection. One of the values of decision theory is the requirement that all the factors involved must be made explicit, together with the probabilities ascribed to each of them. It must be kept in mind that even the crudest approximations of probabilities for the several states affecting a decision are better than none at all. It is not easy to assign odds or probabilities to events. But the decision maker *must* continually do this. At present, in many companies, the judgment going into the continual decision making of financial executives' managerial decisions is often largely intuitive. Decision theory calls for the formalization of this process; for making explicit what is frequently merely visceral. In itself it may not improve personal judgement, but it exposes this judgment to analysis by others and, with experience, tends to improve systematic thinking.

Once the several acts and the various possibilities that evolve from each of the acts (with the cash values involved, and the probabilities of their occurring) have been listed, the financial manager can then examine the alternatives in terms of their *expected* payout.

The method of doing this for each act is to multiply the dollar results of each of the occurrences by its probability. The sum of these gives the financial manager the expected value of the act. By comparing the expected values of the acts, he can determine the optimum choice for the company.

In the chapters that follow, it will be seen that expected value is only the starting point rather than the end of decision making in financial management. Questions of strategy and policy often intercede. In addition, the degree of risk that the company should take is often open to question. An investment by a small company of $20,000 may have a 50% chance of yielding a $100,000 return and a 50% possibility of complete loss of the investment and bankruptcy. The expected value of the act is:

$$
\begin{array}{ll}
50\% \text{ of } \$100,000 = \$50,000 \\
\underline{50\% \text{ of } \quad 0 \qquad = \quad 0} \\
\text{Expected Value} \qquad \$50,000
\end{array}
$$

While the investment from an expected value point of view makes sense in this example, it may well be questioned whether, regardless of the payoff, the risk of going out of business is worthwhile.

By using operations research techniques, the financial manager can therefore do much to systematize his decision making. This may well lead to better decisions being made than if he relied only on intuitive processes.

Appendix A   THE GENERAL INVENTORY PROBLEM UNDER CERTAINTY

The general inventory problem under certainty may be formulated into a simple question. Given a fixed and known demand with a constant rate of usage and no shortages allowed, how many units of an item will be ordered on every order so as to minimize the sum of ordering cost and inventory carrying cost?

The solution to this general inventory problem can be arrived at by answering another question: How many units of a product should be ordered on a given order so as to minimize the opposing costs of ordering goods for inventory and carrying goods in inventory? Therefore, the solution must answer two questions:

(a) How many units must be ordered?

(b) How long a time should there be between orders, given the criteria of minimum cost?

Notation and Example

Let

R = the number of units to be supplied during a fixed period T.

T = the planning period; that period of time during which the ordering rule will be in effect. (e.g., 24,000 units of product will be demanded annually.)

t = an interval of time T; specifically, the interval of time between placing orders; e.g.,

$$\underline{\mid t \mid t \mid t \mid t \mid}$$
$$T$$

The actual length of time t will be determined in the solution.

q = the number of units to be ordered on any order. The actual number will be determined on the solution.

C_1 = the cost of holding one unit in inventory for a unit of time. (e.g., the cost of placing an order; \$350/order.)

The Mathematical Formulation of the General Problems

A typical inventory cycle beginning with the reception of the ordered quantity into inventory and ending with the complete depletion of inventory would appear as triangle ABC in Figure 7-1.

The line AB represents the quantity q ordered into inventory.

The line BC represents the constant rate of usage of the inventory over time t.

The line AC represents the time period t between placing orders.

The next and subsequent triangles represent the exact same cycle occurring until the end of time period T.

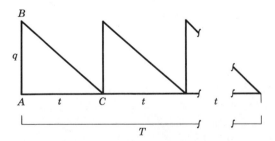

Figure 7-1.

The number of times the cycle will repeat itself depends on the amount of product demanded and the number of units ordered on each order.

$$\frac{R}{q}$$

Therefore
$$t = \frac{T}{R/q} = \frac{Tq}{R}$$

For example, suppose that $R = 3000$ annually and $q = 1000$, then there will be 3 inventory cycles. The length of t will be $\frac{1}{3}$ of a year or 4 months.

If we assume that the internal t begins with q units in stock and ends with 0, then the average amount carried in inventory during the interval will be $q/2$.

The inventory carrying cost during the interval t will be the amount of inventory carried times the time covered times the cost of carrying; or $q/2\ tC_1$.

Then the total cost of the time period t will be the sum of the inventory carry cost and the order cost.

$$TC \text{ for time } t = \frac{q}{2} C_1 t + C_2$$

Now if we know the TC for time t (one cycle) and we know how many cycles there are (R/q), then we can multiply the cost of one cycle by the number of cycles. Therefore

$$TC \text{ for time } T = \left(\frac{q}{2} C_1 t + C_2 \right) \frac{R}{q}$$

Furthermore, we have shown that $t = Tq/R$. Therefore, in place of t, its equal may be substituted. Then

$$TC \text{ for time } T = \left(\frac{q}{2} C_1 \frac{Tq}{R} + C_2 \right) \frac{R}{q}$$

which simplifies to

$$TC = \frac{C_1 Tq}{2} + \frac{C_2 R}{q}$$

It is helpful at this point to draw a diagram (Figure 7-2) of the cost curves.

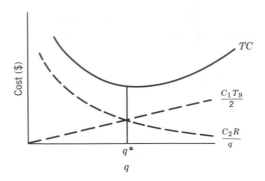

Figure 7-2.

The curve $(C_1 T q)/2$ is the cost of carrying inventory. Notice that it rises for increasing values of q.

The curve $(C_2 R)/q$ is the cost of ordering inventory. It falls for increasing values of q.

Notice that the two cost curves are opposing in the sense that, for increasing values of q, they are moving in opposite directions.

The TC curve is the sum of the two elements for every value of q. It falls; reaches a minimum; and rises. The solution to the problem then is that value of q (call it q^*) which minimizes the sum of the opposing costs. For this case, q^* occurs (the TC curve is minimized) at the intersections of the 2 cost elements $(C_1 T q)/2$ and $(C_2 R)/q$; that point where the opposing costs are in equilibrium.

To find q^* then, the two elements can be equated and solved for q.

Thus

$$\frac{C_1 T q}{2} = \frac{C_2 R}{q}$$

$$C_1 T q^2 = 2 C_2 R$$

$$q^2 = \frac{2 C_2 R}{C_1 T}$$

$$q^* = \sqrt{\frac{2 C_2 R}{C_1 T}}$$

The formula for q^* then supplies the answer to how many units to order so as to minimize total cost.

The answer to the question (how often to order) comes from R/q^*.

The Solution to the Proposed Problem

$$R = 24,000 \text{ units annually}$$
$$T = 1 \text{ year, or } 12 \text{ months}$$
$$C_1 = 0.10/\text{unit/month}$$
$$C_2 = \$350 \text{ per order}$$

If we take the TC equation and supply values for q, the following result occurs:

q	$\dfrac{C_2 R}{q}$	$+$	$\dfrac{C_1 T q}{2}$	$=$	TC
3000	\$2800		\$1800		\$4600
3250	2585		1950		4535
$q^* \rightarrow 3500$	2400		2100		4500
3740	2246		2240		4486
3750	2240		2250		4490
4000	2100		2400		4500

Notice that the costs move in the opposite direction and that the TC falls to a minimum and then rises.

By our formulation for q^*:

$$q^* = \sqrt{\frac{2C_2 R}{C_1 T}}$$

$$q^* = \sqrt{\frac{2(350)(24,000)}{(0.10)(12)}}$$

$$q^* = 3740 \text{ (approximate)}$$

SUMMARY

Such new approaches as game theory, linear programming, and operations research have proved helpful to the financial manager both in theoretical analysis and as aids in managerial decision making. Many financial problems lend themselves to a nonmathematical application of operations research and other new techniques. Operations research techniques have the aim of finding the one combination of elements that will produce the optimal combination of benefits and costs. All relevant factors that enter into an OR problem must be treated quantitatively.

The area of OR that is perhaps of greatest use to the financial manager is decision theory. Decision theory refers to a forward approach to decision making under uncertainty. The use of probability and payoff charts can help the financial manager to quantify his best guess. Simple probability techniques are helpful to the financial manager, especially in such areas as product mix problems and optimum levels of inventory.

Questions

1. What is the aim of operations research? How can this aim be achieved?
2. Give examples of how the computer may be helpful to the financial manager in operations research problems.
3. Explain how a matrix can be used to quantify the relative advantages and disadvantages of different methods of short-term financing.
4. What is meant by decision theory? How is it useful to the financial manager?
5. Why is it helpful to the financial manager to assign probabilities to events?
6. How does the financial manager arrive at the expected payment or the expected value of an act?

Problems

1. Mr. George Drake has recently devided to build a home in a housing development that lacked a city water supply. As a consequence, he was faced with the expense of and certain decisions concerning the drilling of a well.

   To be *certain* of hitting an ample supply of water in the area of this development, it was necessary to drill to a depth of 200 feet. However, because of irregularities in the water table, some residents have struck fully adequate water supplies at depths ranging from 50 to 90 feet.

   Upon questioning the developer, Mr. Drake learned that some of the residents had employed a water witch[1] (or dowser) in deciding where to drill. These residents had had a measurably greater success in striking water at shallow levels than had those drilling without the guidance of the witch. Seven of ten residents who employed the witch had struck ade-

---

[1] A person allegedly having the ability to detect underground water by manipulation of a forked willow wand.

quate water supplies at levels averaging 80 feet, (the other three were required to drill to about 200 feet before finding adequate water). Among 16 residents who did not employ the witch only four hit water at shallower depths (averaging 80 feet), and the other twelve were required to drill to depths averaging about 200 feet.

Since drilling costs had been quoted to Mr. Drake at $5 per foot for depths between 0 and 250 feet he was anxious to take any measure that might minimize the drilling depth required to hit water. On the other hand, Mr. Drake was sceptical of water witches and thought that the $100 fee demanded by this particular one (payable whether or not water was struck at a shallow level) seemed extremely steep.

Advise Mr. Drake on the course he should follow in drilling his well. The decision tree (Figure 7-3) and partially completed table of expected values (Table 7-9) help sort out the alternatives and possible consequences facing Mr. Drake. (Completing the table for alternatives BEH, ACF, and ACGI, and summing and comparing the expected costs should indicate a possible course of action for Mr. Drake.)

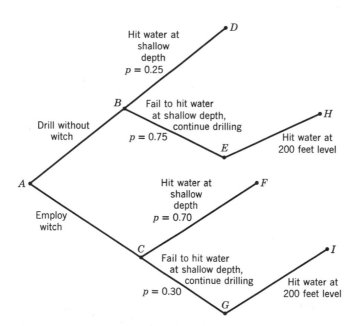

Figure 7-3. The term p stands for the probability that an event will happen. Thus, the probability of hitting water at a shallow depth is 25%, or 25 times, out of 100 times, based upon the 4 of 16 residents (25%) who hit water at shallow levels.

TABLE 7-9.

Act	Possible Consequences	Probability of Consequences	×	Drilling Cost of Consequences ($)	=	Expected Cost of Consequences ($)
	BD	0.25		400		100
AB	BEH	___		___		___
	Total expected cost of consequences					
	AC	1.00		100		100
AC	ACF	0.70		___		___
	ACGI	___		___		___
	Total expected cost of consequences					

2. Given the following information, how would you change the decision tree of Figure 7-3, and how, if at all, would you alter your evaluation of alternatives and your advice to Mr. Drake?

A second water witch is available who charges a flat fee of only $25. This witch, however, is given to seizures that affect his witching ability. His certified lifetime success record for finding water at shallow levels is 90% on days when he is unaffected by seizures. This record, however, drops to 30% on days when he is affected by seizures. Unfortunately, his seizures occur randomly and are unpredictable. But on any given day there is a 40% chance of his having a seizure.

Case: ROMAC APPLIANCE CO.

"If you hadn't played around with our reorder points, Pete," said Mr. Ian Ward to his assistant, Mr. Peter Samuels, "we wouldn't be in a stockout position on our number 842 gears, and we wouldn't have experienced all the expense of the expediting and production schedule changes we've had to resort to." (Mr. Ward was Manager of Production and Inventory Control for Romac Appliance Company, and Peter Samuels was his assistant.) Mr. Ward continued, "Pete, I'll have to ask you to call off your experiments with our inventory control system. I just don't think we can afford to tamper with a system that has worked well for a long period of time."

When Pete Samuels left his boss' office he wondered what, if anything, he could do or say to convince Mr. Ward that some of his ideas concerning inventory control had merit and could save Romac money. Also, the thought crossed his mind that he should look for work elsewhere, since Mr. Ward seemed so reluctant to try new ideas and to accept the risks that they sometimes implied. If the latitude for experimentation were taken from his job, then the job would lose much of its interest and challenge.

After completing his education in business administration, Mr. Samuels was offered employment as an inventory planner by Romac. His work in this position over a two-year period showed sufficient promise that Mr. Ward offered him a position as his assistant. In this new position, Mr. Samuels' main duties were to compile statistical information concerning such things as stock turnover, value of goods in inventory, past usage rates, stock shortages, etc.

The new position was especially welcome to Mr. Samuels because in addition to these primary duties, the position gave him the opportunity to experiment with some ideas concerning inventory control that he had gained from various college courses he had taken. One of Romac's practices that Mr. Samuels was interested in improving concerned the company's present system for determining reorder points for purchased parts (that is, determining at what level of stock on hand an item should be reordered so that stock would not be depleted by the time an order was received).

The company's present reorder practice was to place an order for an item when the amount of stock on hand was sufficient to provide for maximum experienced usage over the maximum experienced lead time. For example, the 842 gear mentioned above, which the company used on a regular basis in several of its products, had experienced a usage rate as high as 52 units per day. And the lead time (or delivery time) for the same part had been as long as 25 days in the past two years. Therefore, the company ordered this part when its stock-on-hand figure fell below 1300 units (25 days $\times$ 52 units/day). Thus, if usage over the lead time period were to rise as high as 1300 units, Romac would still be protected against a stockout.

The company's present practice in determining reorder points provided ample protection against running out of stock. But, at the same time, Mr. Samuels believed that it added unnecessarily and excessively to the costs associated with carrying inventory (including such things as interest and opportunity costs on capital invested in inventory, the costs of space and utilities applied to inventories, insurance and taxes levied upon the value of inventories, and deterioration and the risk of obsolescence of items carried in inventory).

In investigating the stock history of the 842 gear over the past year and a half, Mr. Samuels determined that the maximum part usage over 15 past lead time periods had been 700 parts. In other words, it appeared that Romac's present reorder-point determination practices caused it to carry 600 more units (1300 — 700) than would normally be needed to protect against stockouts, except in the unlikely event that an extremely long lead time would coincide with an extremely high usage rate.

TABLE 7-10.   Romac Appliance Co.: Usage Rate and Lead Time Information for 842 Gear

Stocking Period	Average Daily Usage (Units)	Leadtime (Days)	Usage during Leadtime
1	40	12	480
2	36	14	505
3	32	19	608
4	33	17	561
5	36	14	504
6	28	25	700
7	38	14	532
8	52	12	624
9	39	14	546
10	36	15	540
11	33	14	462
12	36	15	540
13	38	13	494
14	37	16	592
15	37	14	518

Information that Mr. Samuels developed in studying the stock history of the 842 gear is shown in Table 7-10. This information concerning stock usage over the last 15 lead time periods, Mr. Samuels arrayed in a cumulative probability distribution as shown in Table 7-11 and in Figure 7-4. Observation of the cumulative probability distribution of Figure 7-4 indicated that a reorder point of 700 units would have given adequate protection against stockouts during the past year and a half. And, according to the distribution, a reorder point of 640 units would have provided protection against stockouts 95% of the time. Or, in other words, over 100 similar stocking periods (about 8.3 years), the company might expect to run out of stock only 5 times.[2]

Carrying his analysis further, Mr. Samuels reasoned that, if the average inventory of this gear were reduced by 760 units (1300 — 640), the savings would be quite significant. Since the cost of the gear was $1.50, the value of the inventory reduction would amount to $1140 ($1.50 × 760). At the

TABLE 7-11.   Romac Appliance Co.: Usage of 842 Gear during Cumulative Leadtime Periods

Column 1: Cumulative Percent of Leadtime Periods where Usage Rates ≤ Usage Rates of Column 2	Column 2: Usage during Leadtime Periods
100.0	700
93.3	624
86.6	608
80.0	592
73.3	561
66.7	546
60.0	540
53.3	540
46.7	532
40.0	518
33.3	505
26.7	504
20.0	494
13.3	480
6.7	462

20% carrying charge that the company applied to its inventory, the $1140 reduction in the value of average annual inventory would amount to $228. The $228 was a very small consideration against the $15 million annual sales volume that the company had experienced in recent years. But if savings in anywhere near this proportion could be applied to Romac's

---

[2] One hundred stocking periods of about a month each would amount to about 8.3 years (100 months/12 months per year = 8.3 years; during 5% of these periods (100% — 95%) the company might expect to run out of stock if it used a reorder point of 640 units.

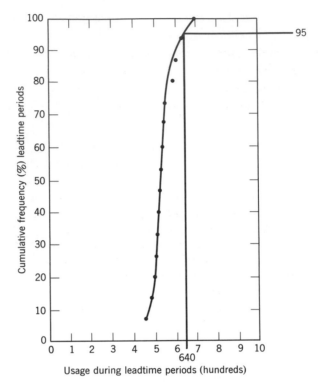

Figure 7-4. Romac Appliance Company Graphic portrayal of usage of 842 gear during cumulative leadtime periods.

average annual inventories of about $6 million, the savings would be very substantial.

When Mr. Samuels presented his analysis to Mr. Ward, Mr. Ward was wary of so drastically reducing reorder points and safety reserves. At the same time, he was so strongly attracted by the potential savings offered by Mr. Samuels' plan that he granted Mr. Samuels permission to experiment with reorder points on fifteen different parts that were representative of the variety of items Romac carried.

In less than a week, Mr. Samuels had converted reorder points on the 15 selected parts to lower levels in accordance with his analysis of stockout probabilities. For about six months all went well with the new reorder-point quantities and Mr. Samuels was considering asking Mr. Ward's permission to extend his reorder-point determination system to several other parts. But at that time, trouble occurred concerning the 842 gear.

The vendor of the gear experienced an unanticipated wildcat strike lasting four weeks. The strike occurred two weeks[3] after Romac had placed an order for gears. The 800 gears included in the order lacked only a day or two of work to complete them. But, because of the strike, shipment of the parts did not take place until 30 days after they had been ordered. The order had been placed when Romac's stock on hand of the gear stood at 660 units, and subsequent usage of the gear, which averaged 37 units per day, had exhausted this inventory in 18 days.

A rush order was placed with an alternate vendor immediately after the strike had been called. But this order was not delivered until 14 days after its placement, or 24 (working) days after the placement of the original order. As a consequence of the delays, shortage of the 842 gear lasted for 6 days. During these days, it was necessary to alter production schedules and shift assembly workers to other operations. Although the cost of these schedule changes and employee reassignments could not be estimated accurately, the production manager thought they probably amounted to between $300 and $400.

When Mr. Ward learned of the shortages and the resultant schedule alterations, he called Mr. Samuels to his office. Mr. Ward acknowledged his responsibility in letting Mr. Samuels experiment with reorder levels, but noted that had the old reorder points been in effect, the shortage would not have occurred. Terming the new system for determining reorder points a "failure," Mr. Ward directed Mr. Samuels to discontinue, immediately, his analysis and experimentation with the reorder points for the other 15 parts, and to return their reorder points to their previous higher levels.

Case Questions:

1. What were the weaknesses in Mr. Samuels' techniques?
2. As financial manager of Romac, would you agree with Mr. Ward's action?
3. What should be done by Romac to improve the system for determining reorder points?

[3] Two weeks or ten working days. Weeks and days mentioned assume a five-day "working week."

~~~~~~

Chapter Eight

Short-Term Financial Planning Techniques

The preceding chapters have examined the various components of current assets and liabilities that play a major role in the short-term financial operations of the firm. We have also analyzed the several tools that are available to the financial manager in the analysis of the current operations of the enterprise. Each component was treated as a variable while the other components were kept constant. This "compartmentalized" approach represents the first phase in the preparation of the financial program of the firm for the next fiscal year. It provides the basic building blocks for the construction of the proposed financial model that is to serve as the strategic blueprint for the financing of the planned volume of sales.

In the second phase, the preparation of the short-term financial plan, the several components of current assets and liabilities are treated as *interdependent* variables. In this type of situation, a proposed change in one component affects, to a greater or lesser degree, the other components in the program. The task of the financial manager consists in determining the most advantageous combination of the several components.

Therefore, this chapter deals with the step-by-step procedure of preparing the short-term financial plan or model. For the purposes of this analysis, we shall assume that the short-term period covers the fiscal year of the firm. The same principles, and procedure, applies to a firm that is engaged in a highly seasonal business that operates only for, say, six months every year; e. g., an establishment in a summer resort.

The elements that go into the preparation of the short-term financial plan can be summarized as follows:

    I. Goals
        A. Liquidity
        B. Minimizing the cost of short-term funds
    II. Constraints
        A. The element of uncertainty in the sales forecast
        B. Seasonal fluctuations
        C. The long-range plans of management
        D. Explicit and implicit costs
    III. The Planning Schedules
        A. Cash budget
        B. Funds-flow schedule
    IV. Management of Temporary Excess Cash
        A. The money market
        B. Treasury bills
        C. Certificates of deposit
        D. Finance company paper
        E. Other outlets

I. GOALS

In a sense, production and purchasing, research and development, promotion and selling are distinct and autonomous functions within the complex of the firm. The head of each of these divisions is an expert in his respective field. At the same time, they are interdependent in terms of the magnitude of their respective operations. The effectiveness of the sales force provides the output target of the production department, while the capacity of the production department sets the limit to sales volume. In turn, the ability of the purchasing agent to buy the required materials and supplies at prices acceptable to management affects output and sales. Yet, all activities of the firm are predicated on the availability of liquid capital to finance the stream of input of labor, materials, supplies, etc.

Liquidity The input operations of the firm create short-term liabilities. On the other hand, the sale of the output generates claims. The claims usually do not mature—i.e., are not collected in the form of cash received—prior to or at the same time when payment is due on the liabilities. To bridge the time gap between the two sets of maturities, the firm must have at its disposal liquid funds at least equal to the excess of maturing liabilities (payables) over collected claims (receivables). If the firm possesses these funds, it is liquid and the circular flow of input-output-sales-input can continue.

The funds needed to ensure liquidity are not of a constant magnitude. The differential between maturing payables and collected receivables fluctuates—and, in many cases, very substantially—in the course of the fiscal year.

The first goal of financial planning is, therefore, to make as good an estimate as possible of the amount of liquid funds that will have to be available at, for instance, monthly intervals, to provide the necessary liquidity of operations. Table 8-1 shows the aggregate of current

TABLE 8-1.   Current Assets and Liabilities of Corporations[a] (In Billions of Dollars)

	At End of Period		
	1964	1965	1966 Third Quarter
Current Assets			
Cash	45.0	49.2	46.9
United States government securities	19.1	16.7	14.6
Notes and accounts receivable	175.4	193.5	207.0
Inventories	114.3	126.3	139.4
Other	15.5	22.1	23.5
Total	371.0	407.9	431.4
Current Liabilities			
Notes and accounts payable	142.7	160.3	171.5
Accrued federal income taxes	17.0	19.2	17.9
Other	50.2	45.0	50.4
Total	209.9	224.5	239.9
Net working capital	161.1	183.4	191.5

[a] The figures in this table are exclusive of banks, savings and loan associations, and insurance companies.
Source: Federal Reserve Bulletin, No. 1, January 1967, p. 126.

assets and liabilities of all United States corporations, exclusive of financial institutions.

At the end of 1965, all nonfinancial corporations had in cash and its equivalent (marketable United States government securities) an aggregate of $65.9 billion. This sum represented over 40% of their aggregate payables. To be sure, a substantial portion of the cash was earmarked for dividends, interest payments, taxes, and liabilities other than those due to current suppliers of labor, material, and services. Nevertheless, it is evident that business firms maintain a substantial amount of funds in liquid form.

Usually, the "cash" is in the form of demand deposits in banks. These demand deposits serve several purposes. First and foremost, they provide the liquid funds to meet time gaps between payables and collections. Second, they allow for various contingencies. For example, the firm's estimate of the time gap and, thus, the excess of payables over collections, may turn out to be greater than projected. The firm may also want to have ready cash available if a special opportunity presents itself to make a highly attractive purchase of materials or supplies. A third reason for a cash balance in the bank is to have a fund that can be used as a compensating balance for a bank loan. And, last but not least, a cash balance also serves as a basis for a favorable credit rating by banks and trade creditors.

Minimizing Net Working Capital The figures in Table 8-1 showed, for all nonfinancial corporations, total current assets of $407.9 billion and total current liabilities of $224.5 billion. The difference of $183.4 billion represented net working capital. It reflects the allocation of long-term funds to the financing of current operations. A part of these funds supports the maintenance of inventory. And a portion of the net working capital serves as a liquidity cushion.

The firm obtains its long-term funds, first, from the contributions of the owners. In a corporation, these contributions assume the form of a purchase of common stock (and sometimes preferred stock also) issued by the corporation. These long-term funds are called the *equity capital* of the firm. Usually, the bulk of the equity capital is channeled into fixed assets (buildings, machinery, equipment, fixtures, and the like).

A second source of long-term funds is in the nature of *debt capital*. The corporation obtains the money for a period of time, usually more than ten years, by giving the supplier of this capital one of several types of debt instruments, which will be described in detail in later chapters. The best known of these debt instruments is the corporate bond.

As a general rule, short-term lenders insist that the borrower show net working capital, i.e., the allocation of long-term funds to current operations. By the same token, if the long-term funds in the form of net working capital were adequate to meet the liquidity requirements of the firm, the latter would have no need for short-term loans.

Minimizing Cost of Short-Term Borrowing The firm often has available several sources of short-term loans (such as banks, finance companies, and factors) for the purpose of helping meet liquidity requirements. Given the size of the firm and its financial condition, the amount and the terms of the loan that it can obtain from any one source depends on whether it is a secured loan—e.g., receivables and/or inventory—or an unsecured loan. The financial manager must therefore compare the relative costs of alternative sources of short-term funds. The least-cost alternative—whether in the form of a single loan or a package deal involving two or more lenders—minimizes the cost of funds and, thus, contributes to the profit of the firm. However, other factors, as described in previous chapters, may lead a firm to choose a higher cost lender.

II. CONSTRAINTS

The financial manager operates within a frame of reference which result from (a) policy decisions by top management; (b) specific operational features within the firm; and (c) the competitive climate in the market. The frame of reference produces the constraints to which the financial model must be adapted.

Sales Forecast The projection of sales targets is, initially, the function of the sales manager and, ultimately, the responsibility of top management. But every forecast of sales for an individual firm over the next fiscal year contains an element of uncertainty. This is true of the month-to-month projections and of the forecast for the year as a whole. The financial model is an estimate of the monthly inflows and outflows of funds. Thus, the reliability of these financial estimates is dependent on the reliability of the sales forecast.

Usually, a sales forecast allows for a plus or minus deviation from the projected monthly volume. The deviations, plus and minus, constitute the range within which actual sales are expected to fall. To the sales manager, the plus figure, or upper limit of the range, if reached, means the attainment of a perfect goal; i.e., his sales force has realized the most optimistic projection. To the financial manager, the plus figures, while highly desirable from the viewpoint of the firm, indicate the possibility of increased cash-flow deficits. Since neither he nor the sales manager can be certain about the actual future sales performance, the financial manager must at least prepare for this eventuality. In other words, he must negotiate for a contingent line of credit or loan equal to the maximum needs.

Thus, the financial manager will negotiate for loans on the basis of his estimated minimum needs, the lower limit of the range, and for contingent loans or commitments if the upper limit of the range should be reached. The cost or fee of this commitment by the prospective lender is only a fraction of the regular interest charges on a short-term loan. As a result, the actual cost of funds will be reduced if the forecast should prove to have been overly optimistic.

Cyclical Trend versus Seasonal Pattern   In most lines of business, the volume of sales is subject to seasonal fluctuations. These oscillations tend to repeat themselves every year. For instance, December usually marks the peak month of sales for toys while June sets the low point. New-car sales, on the other hand, reach their high point in June with December as the low month.

From the viewpoint of the financial manager, the month (or months) of peak sales also represent the "season" in which the firm experiences a sharp rise in its receivables. On the other hand, the corresponding accounts payable that precede the peak sales and receivables usually fall due before the firm obtains payment from its customers. By the same token, when sales drop off as a result of the seasonal influence, the firm obtains payment on the sales in the preceding peak period while its purchases and, thus, the volume of its accounts payable declines. At such times, the firm will have more cash coming in from its customers than it has to pay out to its suppliers.

The cyclical trend, either up or down, extends over years rather than months. In a sense, therefore, the cyclical trend pulls the seasonal pattern up or pushes it down, respectively, depending on whether the industry of which the firm is a part is in a cyclical upswing or decline. The net effect of the cyclical trend is to magnify, or to reduce, the magnitude of receivables as well as of payables. Of greater relevance to the financial manager is the impact of the cyclical trend on the pace of the collection of receivables. In a period of upswing, the firm's customers will sell their goods relatively fast and at a profit. This, in turn, will enable them to pay their bills either at the end of the credit term (e.g., 30 days) or to take advantage of the discount offered for payment, e.g., within 10 days after receipt of the goods.

The reverse is likely to take place in a cyclical downturn. First, the sales decline. Second, the customers of the firm, experiencing a slow-down in their sales and accumulation of inventory, will forego the discount for early payment. And, in addition, they frequently will also exceed the credit terms. As a result, the firm will find its inflow of cash from receivables slowing down in relation to the maturing obligations to its suppliers.

If the sales forecast adopted by top management anticipates a cyclical upswing, the financial manager will be justified in projecting a relatively optimistic projection of cash inflows from receivables. That is to say, he will project a higher percentage of collections within 10 days after delivery and a smaller percentage of "delinquent" accounts; i.e., collection after the expiration of the credit term. The opposite projection will have to be made if top management's sales forecast is predicated on a prospective cyclical downswing.

Long-Range Plans   The long-range plans of the firm, in as far as they involve the next fiscal year, may involve one or more of the following programs.

1. *Expansion of Capacity.* (a) Additional long-term funds are to be procured in the first part of the fiscal year either through the sale of additional stock, debt securities, or a combination of both. The proceeds are then to be expended on a new plant, machinery, and equipment in the second part of the fiscal year. In this situation, the financial manager can anticipate the temporary availability of funds from the proposed sale of securities and, thus, a corresponding reduction in the need for short-term borrowing during this period.

b. Existing old machines are to be replaced by new machines with superior productivity; e.g., fully automated equipment to replace partly automated machinery. The new acquisition is to be purchased with cash generated through operations. Theoretically, this step will require no new funds from external sources. The original cost of the present equipment, now old and presumably obsolete, has been fully recovered through allocations for depreciation, during its lifetime. Realistically, however, this depreciation reserve has been set up on the books only. The funds themselves have been and are presently used in the current operations of the firm. They may have been channeled into inventory, receivables, or cash (as the liquidity cushion). Let us assume that the firm, in the next fiscal year, diverts cash into the replacement of the old machinery. On the books, cash will be reduced by X dollars, the cost of the new equipment, while the value of the fixed assets will be increased by X dollars.

Since the current asset item "cash" will be reduced by X dollars, net working capital will also decrease by the same amount. The net effect is to reduce the liquidity of the firm. It is the responsibility of the financial manager to determine whether or not the projected action will have an adverse effect on the ability of the firm to remain liquid. If such adverse effect is probable, he must then determine the feasibility of procuring external funds to assure liquidity in the next fiscal year.

c. Top management has decided to dispose of one of its divisions, which has suffered a decline in sales, and to concentrate on the remaining product lines whose sales can be expanded without additions to existing capacity, at least in the next fiscal year.

In this situation, the proposed sale of capital assets will convert a fixed asset into a highly liquid cash asset. This will automatically reduce, by a corresponding amount, the need to procure external short-term financing.

In recent years, quite a few companies that had purchased extensive tracts of land for their new plants in the 1930's and 1940's, made substantial capital gains on the sale of some of their excess land and, thus, were able to finance internally an expansion of sales.

2. *Contraction of Capacity.* The top management of a company may reach the conclusion that it has over-extended its operation. Therefore, it may decide to dispose of some of its branches. In these instances, the proceeds from the sale of these properties will initially flow into the cash account of the firm. Conceivably, the company may find it necessary to liquidate some of its assets in order to meet long-term obligations that are approaching maturity in the course of the next fiscal year. In the meantime, however, the funds are available to the firm for short-term use.

INSTRUMENTS OF PLANNING

One of the major developments in the post-World War II period has been in the area of cash management. In theory and practice, the problem of effective financial planning, both short term and long range, has generated a growing interest in the development of new tools and techniques of cash management. One reason for this increased concern of corporate financial officers has been the strain on working capital flowing from rapid growth. Many companies have been under pressure to make their internal funds "work harder." The development of improved techniques for projecting cash flows, increasing the speed of collections, and better inventory control provide sophisticated tools for the financial manager in maximizing the efficiency of capital and, thus, minimizing its costs.

The two basic tools for the forecasting of the short-term financial requirements of the firm are (1) the cash budget and (2) the funds-flow projection.

Cash Budget

The nature and basic features of the cash budget were discussed in Chapter Two. Table 8-2 is the same work sheet that was used

TABLE 8-2.   Cash-Flow Budget: Work Sheet (Dollars)

	Month 1	Month 2	Month 3	Month 4
Sales	50,000	50,000	50,000	50,000
Collections		24,750	24,750	24,750
			25,000	25,000
Total receipts	0	24,750	49,750	49,750
Disbursements:				
Payments on accounts payable	0	20,000	20,000	20,000
Wages	10,000	10,000	10,000	10,000
Payments on direct factory expenses	3,000	3,000	3,000	3,000
Payments on administrative expenses	800	800	800	800
Payments on selling expenses	1,200	1,200	1,200	1,200
Payments for equipment	0	0	0	500
Total disbursements	15,000	35,000	35,000	35,500
Net monthly cash gain (loss)[a]	(15,000)	(10,250)	14,750	14,250
Cumulative cash gain (loss)	(15,000)	(25,250)	(10,500)	3,750

[a] Total receipts less total disbursements.

in Chapter Two to illustrate the cumulative cash position of the firm over a 4-month period.

As indicated in the subheading "work sheet," such a schedule is the first step rather than the end product; i.e., the financial model for the projected time period. To make the cash budget an effective tool for financial planning, several structural refinements must be added. These refinements are necessary whether the financial program covers only a few months (as illustrated in Table 8-3) or encompasses an entire fiscal year.

The first refinement applies to the use of time intervals. For external reporting purposes, particularly in conjunction with tax liabilities, operating data are aggregated by the accountant monthly, quarterly, semi-annually, and annually. This well-established procedure has the distinctive merit of consistency and comparability over time as well as between companies. However, for internal short-term managerial decision making, this methodology has three major defects. First, it does not take cognizance of the firm's *operating cycles* within the 12-month time period. Second, a single budget schedule implies certainty whereas the financial plan should make allowance for uncertainty and therefore, project several *alternative schedules*. And third, the cash budget is often confined to cash flows from current operations. However, in the course of the year, the business firm generates noncurrent income and expenditures. To encompass both current and noncurrent items, the financial plan must be in terms of a *funds flow*. We shall next discuss the treatment of these three elements: operating cycles, alternative schedules, funds flow.

Operating Cycle   At the outset, it must be stressed that the time intervals of the operating cycles within the fiscal year period will differ among industries and frequently even among firms in the same line of business. Briefly defined, an operating cycle is that period of time in which the operations of the firm remain relatively unchanged and in which the *operating* investment of the firm is disinvested. An operating cycle consists of four phases in a manufacturing company and of three phases in a firm engaged in distribution.

The four phases of a manufacturing company are:

1. The *opening phase* which starts with investible short-term funds in the form of cash and immediately available credit. These funds are invested in the purchase of material and supplies.

2. The *production phase* in which materials and supplies are processed into the firm's products.

3. The *selling phase* in which the products are stored as inventory and sold to the customers of the firm.

4. The *disinvestment phase* in which receivables are normally collected—i.e., within the firm's terms of credit to its customers and new funds become once more available for reinvestment in another cycle.

In the case of a firm engaged in the distribution of goods, wholesale or retail, the three phases are:

1. The *opening phase* which has the same characteristics as the first phase of the manufacturing company.

2. The *storage phase* which represents the period during which the goods are customarily held in stock before they are sold.

3. The *disinvestment phase* starting with the shipment of the goods to the customers and terminating with the normal collection of the receivables.

The determination of the actual time interval of the operating cycle involves two sets of calculations. The first set calls for the calculation of the average number of days of each phase, as illustrated in the example of a manufacturing company (Table 8-3).

TABLE 8-3.   Length of Operating Cycle

Phase	Transaction	Source of Information	Days	
1. (a)	Receipt of materials and storage prior to processing	Production manager	20	
(b)	Purchase terms are 1%–10 days, net 30 days. Firm customarily takes discount	Comptroller	10	10
2.	Actual production (assembly and finishing)	Production manager	8	
3.	Storage of finished goods—receipt and processing of shipping order—actual shipment	Shipping department	4	
4. (a)	Receipt of shipping documents—processing of invoices—mailing of invoices to customer	Billing department	4	
(b)	25% of customers take discount and pay 10 days after billing		10	26
(c)	75% of customers take full 30 days		20	36

The above schedule shows that the firm "invests" funds for 36 days or roughly 7 work-weeks before the firm is able to "disinvest" one-fourth of the funds plus its indirect costs and its profit before taxes, assuming that its sales price exceeded its *total* cost of production. Another 20 days elapse before the balance of the receivables become "disinvested" and are once more available for reinvestment in another cycle.

Let us assume that the firm projects, and plans, an output of 100,000 units for each of the first three months of the fiscal year. The relevant sales and cost figures are assumed to be as shown in Table 8-4.

TABLE 8-4.   (Dollars)

Sales	450,000	
Discounts (1% on 25% of sales)	1,125	448,875
Gross operating profit		198,875
Monthly purchases of materials, supplies, services		75,000
Wages and salaries		105,000
Direct factory expenses		180,000
Administrative costs		50,000
Selling costs		20,000
Cost of goods		250,000

Applying the figures in Table 8-4 to the operating cycle will give the results shown in Table 8-5.

TABLE 8-5.   Summary Cash Budget Based on Operating Cycle (Dollars)

	First Month	Second Month	Third Month
Funds "invested"	250,000	250,000	250,000
Funds "disinvested"			
25% collected in 10 days	0	111,375[a]	111,375
75% collected in 30 days	0	0	337,500
Investment	(250,000)	(250,000)	(250,000)
Disinvestment	0	111,375	448,875
Cumulative change	(250,000)	(388,625)	(189,750)

[a] ($450,000 × 0.25) = $112,500 − (0.01 × 112,500) = $111,375.

The summary schedule in Table 8-5 differs from the accountant's cash budget in substance rather than in form or structure. One difference lies in the fact that the operating cycle highlights the time lag between production and sales; or, in other words, the interval between the time when the firm assumes a definitive current liability (payables, wages, etc.) and the time when it has the counterpart in receivables. Goods in process or in storage represent values on the books of the company. But they are not cash "in sight" as is the case with receivables. Even in the ideal case of straight cash sales, the financial manager in the present case would have to plan for an investment of about $300,000 before the firm would receive any cash income; i.e., the 26-day or 5-work-week period from receipt of raw material to delivery of the goods to the customers.

A cash budget that ignores the length of the operating cycle as illustrated in the table and uses instead the terms of trade as a basis for projecting revenues would project receipts of $74,250 in the first month (10 days after delivery) and the balance of $225,000 in the second month. As a result, a cash budget that does not take account of the operating cycle shows an earlier inflow of funds and, thus, less need for external funds than the firm actually requires.

Another fact needs to be stressed here. Most firms select a fiscal year for reporting and tax purposes that terminates at the seasonal "low" of the company's activities. At this point of time, the firm's receivables will be relatively at a minimum and its cash position at the maximum. Moreover, in the last month of the fiscal year—when production or distribution, respectively, are at the seasonal low of the 12-month period—payables are also at a relatively low level and the firm usually "cleans up" its bank loans.

The second difference is to be found in the variation of the length of the operating cycle in the course of the fiscal year. In the schedule in Table 8-3, the time interval for receipt of raw materials and storage prior to processing was 20 days. However, this period is likely to be substantially less in the "low" season of the firm. The same is probably true of the time interval used by the shipping and billing departments, respectively, in a period of full production compared with the months when the firm operates at a relatively low level of capacity. The operating cycle provides, therefore, a more realistic basis for projecting the cash flow than monthly averages based on annual totals.

Alternative Schedules   The operating cycle contains several components over which the firm has some degree of control and which can therefore be readjusted if the financial manager finds it difficult to procure the required external funds. For example, in Table 8-3, it was assumed that the firm will, in the next fiscal year, take advantage of the discount offered by the suppliers. Now if the company should decide to take full advantage of the 30-day credit offered by the suppliers the interval on this investment would be reduced from 30 days to 16 days or about 3 work weeks. This would automatically cut the number of days and the amount of required external financing. Other areas of time savings are the intervals for receipt of materials and their storage, shipping time, and billing. The firm may have to pay a premium to suppliers for deliveries on shorter notice, overtime to employees in shipping and billing.

Table 8-6 illustrates two alternate cash budgets based on different sets of assumptions regarding (a) use of the full 30 days credit from suppliers, (b) reduction in shipping and billing time, and (c) shorter interval between receipt of materials and their use in production.

If the firm finds it feasible to make the changes postulated in schedule B, the cash position would change drastically. The firm's needs for external borrowing would be cut from three months (Schedule A) to one month. Furthermore, it would have to borrow only $76,500 compared with a maximum loan of $287,125 under the assumption in Schedule A.

Funds Flow.   The preceding discussion was confined to projected inflows and outflows of funds which are the result of *current* operations. Frequently, however, the firm has temporarily at its disposal internally generated funds which do not flow from current sales and collections. Conversely, the firm either periodically or at irregular intervals makes disbursements that are not directly tied in with current operations. In order to maximize the total financial resources of the company—and conversely to prepare for special disbursements—the short-term financial plan must include these items. The latter will be designated as *noncurrent* expenditures. We shall first discuss those noncurrent inflows which add temporarily to the available funds and subsequently those noncurrent disbursements which increase the outflow.

Sale of Securities.   An expanding company decides to sell either additional stock or debt securities in order to finance in whole or in

TABLE 8-6.   Cash Budget under Varying Assumptions (Dollars)

	Month 1	Month 2	Month 3
A. Firm pays for purchases in 10 days; storage prior to processing, 20 days; production, 8 days; shipping, 4 days; billing, 4 days;[a] receivables collected: 25% in 10 days, 75% in 30 days.			
Outflow of cash:			
Purchases	75,000	75,000	75,000
Payment to suppliers	74,250	74,250	74,250
Factory wages and salaries	105,000	105,000	105,000
Selling and administrative	70,000	70,000	70,000
Total outflow of cash	249,250	249,250	249,250
Inflow of cash:			
Cash on hand	100,000		
Sales (receivables)		450,000	450,000
25% in 10 days	0	111,375	111,375
75% in 30 days	0	0	337,500
Total inflow	100,000	111,375	448,875
Net changes in cash	(149,250)	(137,875)	199,625
Cumulative change in cash	(149,250)	(287,125)	(87,500)
B. Firm pays for purchases in 30 days; storage prior to processing, 10 days; production, 8 days; billing and shipping, 4 days (total: 4 work weeks).			
Outflow of cash:			
Purchases	75,000	75,000	75,000
Payment to suppliers	0	75,000	75,000
Factory wages and salaries	106,500	106,500	106,500
Selling and administrative	70,000	70,000	70,000
Total outflow of cash	176,500	251,500	251,500
Inflow of cash:			
Cash on hand	100,000		
Sales (receivables)		450,000	450,000
25% in 10 days	0	111,375	111,375
75% in 30 days	0	337,500	337,500
Total inflow	100,000	448,875	448,875
Net changes in cash	(76,500)	197,375	197,375
Cumulative change in cash	(76,500)	120,875	318,250

[a] It is assumed that overtime in shipping and billing departments will increase costs by $1500 each month.

part a program of plant expansion. Suppose this sale is scheduled for the second quarter of the next fiscal year for which the financial plan is being prepared. It is unlikely that the proceeds from the sale of the securities will be disbursed in the month in which the company receives those funds. It is more likely that the money will be expended over a period of several months. During this interval the funds are "idle" and therefore can be employed in current operations and, thus, reduce the need to borrow from a financial institution.

Disposal of Excess Property. Top management may decide to sell a branch plant, land, or machinery that will no longer be required, either because the company desires to discontinue a portion of its product line or to concentrate its operations in fewer plants or, in the case of land, because it had originally acquired more property than needed for purely speculative reasons. Whatever the specific motivation, the sale of a long-term asset causes an inflow of funds. Until management decides to reinvest the money in some other asset it is available for short-term financing of the firm's current operations.

Tax Refunds. Under existing federal tax laws, a corporation can "carry back" its losses in any one fiscal year up to three years into the past and five years forward. Suppose the corporation had a profit of $1,000,000 in the year 19X1. We are now close to the end of 19X4 and the financial manager is preparing the cash budget for 19X5. The comptroller estimates that the corporation will end the current fiscal year, 19X4, with a loss of $300,000. Under the carry-back provision, the firm can recalculate the taxable profit for 19X1 and show a tax liability of $700,000 for that year, assuming for the sake of simplicity a tax rate of 50%. It actually had paid $500,000 in income taxes. The refund in 19X5 will, therefore, bring in $150,000 in tax refunds. This refund will add to the cash inflow in 19X5 and thus reduce the need for external funds.

Interest on Debt Capital. The normal selling price (and thus current revenues) includes interest on long-term debt securities among the fixed costs. These interest payments are due on dates fixed in the debt instrument. They therefore represent a disbursement and reduction in current funds. Usually, this interest is paid quarterly or semiannually, although it is included in the price calculation and, thus, the monthly portion is received in the revenues recorded each month. Thus, while "collected" currently it is payable say, quarterly, and two months out of every three the firm has this money available for temporary use.

Dividends. The distribution of all or a portion of the earnings is optional with the board of directors. Assuming that the board decides to declare a dividend, the dividend is usually paid two or three months after the close of the period for which it is declared. Unlike a debt security on which interest must be paid at previously fixed intervals, the board of directors can declare a dividend at the end of each quarter, semiannually or annually as the board deems it desirable; or the board may omit the payment of a dividend even at the end of a profitable year. Until the board of directors votes to distribute a dividend and until the month in which it is actually disbursed, the total after-tax profit can be used for short-term financing.

Taxes. Federal, state, and local taxes are due on certain dates. In the interval, the amount that is "earmarked" for taxes is part of the firm's current funds and, thus, available for use in its current operations. By the same token, this amount must be entered as a projected disbursement in the month(s) in which these taxes are due.

Table 8-7 illustrates a funds-flow schedule "superimposed" on the cash budget in Table 8-6, Schedule A.

TABLE 8-7.   Projected Funds Flow for First Quarter (Dollars)

	Month 1	Month 2	Month 3
Cash inflow			
Current operations	100,000	111,375	448,875
Noncurrent items			
Sale of asset	50,000		
Tax refund		150,000	
Sale of securities			250,000
Total inflow	150,000	261,375	698,875
Cash outflow			
Current operations	249,250	249,250	249,250
Noncurrent items			
Purchase of asset			100,000
Dividends			
Interest on bonds	75,000		
Total outflow	324,250	249,250	349,250
Net change	(174,250)	12,125	349,625
Cumulative change	(174,250)	(162,125)	187,500

The firm's requirement for external borrowing is for a maximum loan of $174,250 (in the first month) and a "clean-up" of its indebtedness to short-term lenders in the third month. The funds-flow schedule shows a greater cash deficit in the first and second month than Schedule A in the cash budget of Table 8-6. This is due to the fact that the cash budget did not include $75,000 interest payment due on bonds in the first month. Similarly, Schedule B of Table 8-6 if adjusted for noncurrent cash inflow and outflow would show the following funds flow.

	Month 1	Month 2	Month 3
Net change from current operations	($ 76,500)	$197,375	$197,375
Net change from noncurrent items	(25,000)	150,000	(100,000)
Cumulative change in cash	($101,650)	$245,725	$343,100

Thus the funds-flow schedule points up the need to borrow $101,650 in the first month and an excess of cash in each of the next two months. Under Schedule B of Table 8-6, the firm would need a loan of $76,500 for the first month and it would have excess cash in the next two months.

Improving Cash Inflows   A company may need to accelerate the inflow of cash from its receivables; either because it cannot obtain sufficient short-term loans or because it is reluctant to commit its total credit to the financing of receivables. If possible, management likes to have some surplus cash funds as a liquidity reserve for contingencies in the collection of receivables.

One solution would be for the firm to adjust the credit terms that it extends to its customers. However, this alternative has one serious drawback. If the firm offers credit terms less favorable to the customers than those granted by competitors of the firm, it is likely to experience a decline in sales. A more effective approach has been discussed in the preceding section; i.e., shortening the time interval for shipment to and billing of the customer.

There are, in addition, several other avenues available that can expedite the actual receipt of the funds from customers. In the normal course, the firm deposits the checks received from its customers. As a general rule, the bank does not treat these deposits as subject to withdrawal by the depositing firm until the bank has received notice that the checks have been paid. Suppose the firm is located in Boston and receives a check in payment from a customer in San Francisco. The

Boston bank will then forward the check to the Federal Reserve Bank in Boston which forwards the check to the San Francisco Federal Reserve Bank for collection. After the latter "clears" the check with the San Francisco bank, it credits the Boston Reserve bank which, in turn, credits the Boston bank. During this interval the check is a "float." Depending on the geographic distance between the two banks, the time lag may be two days or as much as one week until final clearance has been made.

This time lag can be cut substantially if the firm's bank agrees to release the deposit for withdrawal as soon as it receives credit from the Reserve Bank of its district; this usually takes about two days. A company can further expedite collections by requesting its customers to forward the check by air mail.

Larger firms which have branch offices in different parts of the country use these branch offices as collection centers. As soon as the branch office obtains the release of the funds it transmits the proceeds to the home office. This technique cuts the two-way travel of the check to a one-way route. Another method is to arrange with the customers to have them forward the check to a post office lock-box in a central city; e.g., New Orleans or Cleveland. By prearrangement, a bank in the particular central city picks up the checks every day, collects the funds, and transmits them directly to the firm's local bank. The lock-box technique can also be used in a different manner if the customer is a large account and generates a fairly steady stream of orders. In this case, the firm may arrange with a bank close to the customer to pick up the checks, collect the funds, and forward them by wire, air mail, or regular mail to the firm's own bank.

MANAGEMENT OF EXCESS CASH

At various times during the year, the firm will find its cash funds to be substantially in excess of its immediate requirements. Furthermore, a company periodically finds it necessary to accumulate relatively sizeable cash funds in anticipation of due dates for the payment of dividends, interest, repayment of loans, income and other taxes. In Table 8-1, it was shown that all nonfinancial corporations had over $46 billion in cash at the end of the third quarter of 1966. This figure is an aggregate amount. At any one time, some corporations will have sizeable surplus cash while other corporations are seeking short-term loans.

The magnitude of excess funds, particularly in the case of large corporations, accounts for a growing interest of top management in the profitable utilization of temporary excess funds. The importance of this function by the financial officer can be readily visualized by assuming that a corporation has, at various periods of the year, an average of $10 million in excess funds and that, in the course of the year, this average is available for a total of 73 days. If this amount is invested in risk-free securities at a rate of 5% per annum, the investment will yield $100,000 in revenues. In the case of a giant corporation, the volume of excess funds may at times run into $100 million or more.

The four major outlets for excess funds are:

1. United States Treasury bills and notes
2. Short-term obligations of other public bodies
3. Commercial paper
4. Certificates of deposits

Treasury Bills and Notes   The United States Treasury sells periodically, customarily each week, its own obligations (Treasury bills) with a maturity of 91 days. The Treasury also sells periodically bills and notes with longer maturities. Treasury bills are sold at a discount from their face value and are redeemed at par. The difference between issue and redemption prices constitutes the interest paid by the Treasury. There is a constant market for Treasury bills and the price goes up each day by a fraction which generally equals the annual rate of interest divided by 365. Suppose a corporation buys a bill maturing in 1 month for $10,000,000 at an interest rate of 5%. It will pay, in round figures, $9,958,330. Assuming that the interest rate does not change, the bill will appreciate every day, and be saleable at this increment, by $1388. At the end of, say, 20 days, the corporation will then receive $27,760 more than it paid. If the purchaser holds the bill to its maturity, 10 days later, he will obtain the full face value of $10 million; that is, the purchaser will earn an additional $13,900 in interest.

Other Public Issues   Beginning in the 1950's, five federal credit agencies—Federal Land Banks, Banks for Cooperatives, Federal Intermediate Credit Banks, Federal National Mortgage Association, and Federal Home Loan Banks—have issued short-term notes as a means of raising additional funds for their operations. At the end of 1966, these five agencies had outstanding about two billion of short-term obligations with a maturity of less than one year.

States and municipalities also sell, at irregular intervals, short-term notes. The interest on these obligations is exempt from the Federal income tax. This feature increases the relative attractiveness of these obligations. For this reason, the interest yield is generally below that of Treasury bills.

Certificates of Deposit (CD's)   These are negotiable certificates of time deposits with interest rates higher than those paid by the issuing bank on ordinary time deposits. But, unlike the latter, CD's have a fixed maturity date, ranging from six months to one year. The yield on CD's generally ranges between $\frac{1}{4}$ and 1% above the Treasury rate, depending on the size and location of the bank.

The CD as an important instrument in attracting time deposits was introduced in 1961 into the financial market when a major New York City bank offered to sell interest-bearing negotiable time certificates of deposit. This step marked a radical departure from the policy of the leading commercial banks which had not paid interest on *corporate* time deposits (as distinct from individual savings deposits) since the early 1930's. Other banks quickly followed suit and in recent years, many banks in all parts of the country have sold CD's to corporations and individuals.

Commercial Paper   This instrument represents unsecured promissory notes issued and sold by corporations that enjoy an excellent credit rating. The typical paper has a maturity of 120 to 180 days, although notes with a maturity of as little as 30 days or as much as 18 months are not rare.

Finance Company Paper   Large national finance companies sell their own promissory notes directly to holders of liquid funds. The denomination and maturity are usually tailored to suit the specific requirements of the purchaser. In the absence of an unforeseen emergency, the corporation will hold the note to maturity. For this reason, there has not developed a continuous market as is the case with treasury bills, notes of other public bodies, and commercial paper. In fact, a corporation that is uncertain as to the length of time for which it can safely invest its funds in finance company paper obtains from the issuer the right to a "put." Under such an arrangement, the holder can ask the issuer to redeem the paper prior to maturity but subject to a proportionate adjustment in the amount of interest. Smaller regional finance companies usually avail themselves of the services of a dealer who will dispose of their paper.

Risk in Cash Management

The three basic risks of a short-term cash investment are: (1) the issuer becomes insolvent; (2) the investment cannot be readily liquidated; and (3) if liquidated prior to maturity, the holder may suffer a loss.

In the case of the United States Treasury, the several federal credit agencies, the states, and many municipalities, the risk of insolvency is, for practical purposes, nonexistent. This is certainly true of investments for a few weeks, months, or even a few years. Some quasi-governmental agencies (e.g., sewer districts and turnpike authorities), where the agency is not backed by the full faith and credit of the state or municipality, have presented greater risks. An issuer of commercial paper or a finance company could, conceivably, suddenly become insolvent. However, the probability is generally very small since the issuers of such paper are analyzed by dealers at frequent intervals.

Liquidity also presents little risk to the investor in Treasury bills and notes and in other paper. There exists a constant market in which these short-term bills and notes are bought and sold. Therefore, the holder need not generally worry about the possibility of liquidating his holding in a matter of minutes. A number of financial houses that specialize as dealers provide a means for buyers and sellers to "meet" via these dealers who also maintain their own portfolio from which they sell and to which they add depending on the relative demand and supply. Moreover, the Federal Reserve System, through its open-market committee, assures the presence of a reservoir for support of marketability. However, this protection does not apply to finance company paper and CD's.

Basically, certificates of deposits (CD's) also generally present no liquidity problems to the financial manager in sudden need of cash. Despite the fixed maturity dates of CD's, the firm usually can borrow up to the face amount of the CD from the bank (with the CD as security for the loan), provided, of course, that the bank has available funds.

There does exist one risk. The holder of commercial paper or Treasury bills may lose, or gain, if he decides to sell the paper prior to maturity. This potential risk can best be illustrated by an example. Suppose the financial manager purchases paper with a face value of $1 million maturing in 90 days and it is purchased at a discount of 4.5% per annum. The firm will then pay $988,750 and the paper will go up in value $125 every day. Next, assume that the firm wants to liquidate the paper 5 days later and that the market rate of interest on this type of paper has risen in the intervening week to 4.75%. In this instance, the market price of the paper will be: $1,000,000 (face value) — $11,875 (interest at 4.75% per annum for 90 days) + 5 × $131.90 (daily appreciation at 4.75% per annum = $988,652. The firm bought the paper for $988,750 and is, thus, losing $98. On the other hand, if the market rate should decline to 4.25%, the firm will realize a total return of $1215, since the value of this paper, discounted at 4.25% per annum for the remaining 85 days, will be $989,965 instead of $989,375; or an additional gain of $590.

It is clear from the above example that the financial manager has, actually, two investment functions. One task is to place the excess funds into that short-term paper which has the desired maturity and which is relatively most attractive to the financial manager in terms of denomination, effective yield (after taxes), days to maturity, etc. The second task is to decide whether to hold or to liquidate in the light of probable changes in interest rates. If the financial manager makes the right decision before the rate goes up, he will realize the full earnings for the period during which his firm held the paper. After the rate goes up, he can then reinvest the funds and pay less for the new purchase than he received from the sale. The need to "trade" in paper arises only in a period when the market rate appears to lose its usual stability. The year 1966 was such a period in which the market rates moved relatively rapidly in an upward direction (as shown in Table 8-8).

Between March and November, 1965, the yield rate of prime commercial paper remained constant at 4.37% per annum. Finance company paper started a modest climb in October of that year. United States Treasury 3-month bills fluctuated between 3.83% and 4.08%, although the month-to-month changes moved within a range of less than $\frac{1}{10}$ of 1%. In December, 1965, the picture changed drastically. Starting in that month and continuing in the first 3 quarters of 1966, the rates showed an uninterrupted rise in each month. Let us assume that a firm purchased a 3-month finance company paper in March, 1966, at a yield of 5.02% per annum and had to sell this paper one month later

TABLE 8-8.   Money Market Rates 1965 to 1966 (Percent Per Annum)

Month	Prime Commercial Paper		Finance Company Paper 3 to 6 months		United States Government Securities 3 months (Market Yield)	
	1965	1966	1965	1966	1965	1966
January	4.25	4.82	4.05	4.82	3.81	4.75
February	4.27	4.88	4.12	4.88	3.93	4.86
March	4.38	5.21	4.25	5.02	3.93	4.96
April	4.38	5.38	4.25	5.25	3.93	5.00
May	4.38	5.39	4.25	5.38	3.89	5.18
June	4.38	5.51	4.25	5.39	3.80	5.39
July	4.38	5.63	4.25	5.51	3.83	5.58
August	4.38	5.85	4.25	5.63	3.84	5.67
September	4.38	5.89	4.25	5.67	3.92	5.75
October	4.38	6.00	4.32	5.82	4.02	5.72
November	4.38	6.00	4.38	5.88	4.08	5.67
December	4.65	6.00	4.60	5.88	4.37	5.60

Source: Federal Reserve Bulletin, February 1966, p. 234 and February 1967, p. 271.

at a yield of 5.25%. The company earned only 4.46% instead of the anticipated 5.02% annual rate.[1]

SUMMARY

The financial manager must prepare a short-term financial plan or model to integrate the several components of current assets and liabilities as these components are interdependent variables. The goals of the short-term plan are liquidity and minimizing the cost of short-term funds.

The input operations of the firm create short-term liabilities. The sale of the firm's output generates claims. The firm must have at its disposal liquid funds at least equal to the excess of maturing liabilities

---

[1] Assume that the firm purchased a paper with a face value of $1,000,000. At a discount of 5.02%, it paid $987,451. Subsequently, it received one month later $991,250, or a gain of $3799 for one month, which equals 4.46% per annum.

(payables) over collected claims (receivables). The problem is compounded since the funds needed to ensure liquidity are not of a constant magnitude. The financial manager must make a good estimate of the amount of liquid funds that will have to be available to provide the necessary liquidity.

Such constraints as the element of uncertainty in the sales forecast, seasonal fluctuations, the long-range goals of management, and explicit and implicit costs must be considered in this planning process.

The two basic tools for the forecasting of short-term financial requirements of the firm are the cash budget and the funds flow forecast. These tools help the financial manager in the planning process to ensure an adequate amount of liquidity.

The financial manager must also plan for the management of any temporary excess cash revealed by the plan. These excess funds may be profitably invested in such outlets as United States Treasury bills and notes, commercial paper, and certificates of deposit.

Finally, if the financial planning reveals any periods of cash shortage the financial manager must plan to secure additional funds, or he must revise his plans to avoid liquidity problems.

Appendix   THE FINANCIAL PACKAGE

The final phase in the short-term financial plan calls for a program of financing the projected monthly cash needs. If the firm can procure the required funds from any one of the several sources of lenders—i.e., commercial banks, finance companies, factors, or money market—the program resolves itself into a simple case of arithmetic: which lender is asking for the lowest effective rate of interest? Given the maximum monthly amount required, the relative cost of financing is easily calculated and the best alternative method quickly established.

Many, if not most, firms are not always in such a position. Although the firm may have access to the several suppliers of short-term funds the individual lenders not only ask for different rates but they will usually also impose constraints and limits on the loanable funds which vary among the lenders. The problem therefore arises as to whether a combination of lenders, called the financial package does not offer a better alternative than a single source of funds.

Let us assume that the funds flow of the firm for the next fiscal year

TABLE 8-9. Selected Components in Projected Funds Flow Schedule (Millions of Dollars)

	Month in Fiscal Year											
	1	2	3	4	5	6	7	8	9	10	11	12
Receipts												
Accounts receivable (end)	3.0	4.5	4.25	4.25	2.0	3.5	4.5	4.5	4.25	3.5	2.5	3.5
Collections on accounts receivable	2.0	1.5	2.75	2.5	4.0	1.5	2.0	3.0	2.5	3.0	3.0	1.5
Other receipts	1.5	1.0	1.25	2.0	1.0	4.8	1.0	1.0	1.0	1.6	1.9	1.7
Total receipts	3.5	2.5	4.0	4.5	5.0	6.3	3.0	4.0	3.5	4.6	4.9	3.2
Disbursements												
Accounts payable (end)	2.0	2.5	2.5	2.5	1.0	1.0	2.0	2.5	2.5	1.5	1.0	2.0
Payments for purchases	2.0	2.0	2.5	2.5	2.5	1.0	1.0	2.0	2.5	2.5	1.5	1.0
Other disbursements	2.0	2.0	3.4	1.5	1.9	1.4	2.5	3.5	3.6	1.5	1.5	1.5
Total disbursements	4.0	4.0	5.9	4.0	4.4	2.4	3.5	5.5	6.1	4.0	3.0	2.5
Receipts—disbursements	(0.5)	(1.5)	(1.9)	0.5	0.6	3.9	(0.5)	(1.5)	(2.6)	0.6	1.9	0.7

shows the cash requirements indicated in Table 8-9.[2] To focus on the problem at hand, all categories of expenditures and receipts have been omitted in the table except for receivables and payables which are relevant to the solution.

After conferring with several potential lenders, the financial manager is confronted by the following proposals.

1. *Unsecured Line of Credit.* The bank is willing to establish an unsecured line of credit which would permit the firm to borrow a maximum of $1,500,000. The firm must maintain a compensating balance of not less than 20% of the money actually borrowed. The interest rate on the line of credit is 0.9% per month.

2. *Pledging of Accounts Receivable.* The firm can pledge its accounts receivable as security for a bank loan. The amount outstanding under this alternative is limited to a maximum of $3,750,000. The bank will lend up to 80% of the face value of pledged accounts receivable. The cost of borrowing under this alternative is 1.4% per month. This cost includes the interest charged by the lender plus the out-of-pocket costs associated with the additional work required under this alternative.

The bank will not allow the firm to have an unsecured line of credit

[2] Table 8-9 and the subsequence analysis in this section make extensive use of *Optimal Short Term Financing Decisions* by A. A. Robichek, D. Teichroew, and J. M. Jones, *Management Science,* vol. 12 no. 1, pp. 1–36, 1965.

TABLE 8-10.   Minimum Total Relevant Costs under Various Alternatives

Case	Term Loan ($)	Line of Credit	Pledging	Interest Cost ($)	Implicit Costs			Total Relevant Costs ($)
					Stretching ($)	Term Loan ($)	End Conditions ($)	
1	1,111,111	Yes	No	281,741	23,121	37,997	2,727	345,586
2	1,176,642	No	Yes	270,150	204	40,242	2,750	313,346
3	0	Yes	No	366,710	50,033	0	3,503	420,246
4		No	Yes	342,299	13,378	0	4,471	360,148

and at the same time pledge its accounts receivable on an additional loan.

3. *Stretching of Accounts Payable.* The firm may stretch up to 80% of the payments due for purchases in the period in which they first became due. The discount loss, on the average, amounts to $3\frac{1}{2}\%$ if the payments are stretched one period. Once the accounts payable are stretched, the firm may stretch them for one additional period at no loss of discount

TABLE 8-11.   Detailed Statement of the Optimum Solution

Period	1	2	3	4
Requirement	(500,000)	(1,500,000)	(2,000,000)	500,000
Interest				
Pledging of receivables	—	—	(11,521)	(39,548)
Stretched payables	—	—	—	(919)
Term loan	—	(9,413)	(9,413)	(9,413)
Less: income	—	2,707	—	—
Total interest	—	(6,706)	(21,034)	49,880
Adjusted requirement for period	500,000	(1,506,706)	(2,021,034)	450,120
New borrowing				
Pledging	—	830,064	2,243,809	403,208
Stretching	—	—	26,244	—
Term loan	1,176,642	—	—	—
Total new borrowing	1,176,642	830,064	2,270,053	403,208
Repayments				
Pledging	—	—	(249,019)	(847,456)
Stretching	—	—	—	(5,872)
Term loan	—	—	—	—
Total repayment	—	—	(249,019)	(853,328)
Net new borrowing	1,176,642	830,064	2,021,034	(450,120)
Change in excess cash	(676,642)	676,642	—	—
Requirement financed	500,000	1,506,706	2,021,034	(450,120)

(but with a loss of goodwill on the part of the creditors) but the amount which it can stretch one additional period is limited to 75% of the amount already stretched for one period.

4. *Term Loan*. The bank will offer the firm a term loan to be taken out at the beginning of the initial period. The loan is limited to $2,000,000 and it cannot be taken out in an amount of less than $500,000. Repayment is to be made in ten equal installments; with the first installment due six periods after the loan is initially taken out; and with the subsequent installment due at six-period intervals.

Under this alternative, the bank insists on further constraints on the combined borrowing under the term loan and either the line of credit or the pledging of accounts receivable. The maximum borrowing under the term loan, plus a line of credit is $2,500,000. The maximum borrowing under the term loan and the pledging of receivables is $4,500,000. The interest rate on the term loan is 0.8% per month.

5. *Investment of Excess Cash*. The firm may invest any excess cash in short term securities which yield a return of 0.4% per month.

5	6	7	8	9	10	11	12
600,000	4,000,000	(500,000)	(1,500,000)	(2,700,000)	600,000	2,000,000	700,000
(33,328)	(25,812)	—	—	—	(37,919)	(30,168)	(2,709)
—	—	—	—	—	—	—	—
(9,413)	(9,413)	(9,413)	(8,472)	(8,472)	(8,472)	(8,472)	(8,472)
—	—	8,484	6,010	—	—	—	—
(42,741)	(35,225)	(929)	(2,462)	(8,472)	(46,391)	(38,640)	(11,181)
557,259	3,964,775	(500,929)	(1,502,462)	(2,708,472)	553,609	1,961,360	688,819
177,295	—	—	—	2,708,472	258,932	—	—
—	—	—	—	—	—	—	—
—	—	—	—	—	—	—	—
177,295	—	—	—	2,708,472	258,932	—	—
(714,182)	(1,843,720)	—	—	—	—	(1,961,360)	(193,503)
(20,372)	—	—	—	—	—	—	—
—	—	(117,664)	—	—	—	—	—
(734,554)	(1,843,720)	(117,664)	—	—	(553,609)	(1,961,360)	(193,503)
(557,259)	(1,843,720)	(117,664)	—	2,708,472	(553,609)	(1,961,360)	(193,503)
—	(2,121,055)	618,593	1,502,462	—	—	—	(495,316)
(557,259)	(3,964,775)	500,929	1,502,462	2,708,472	(553,609)	(1,961,360)	(688,819)

Decisions To Be Made

Initial Decision

1. Should the firm take out a term loan and, if so, for how much?
2. Should the firm arrange for a line of credit or for pledging of accounts receivable, or neither?

Decisions at the Beginning of Each Period

1. Should any money be borrowed? If so, how and how much?
2. Should any borrowing be voluntarily repaid? If so, which and how much?

In arriving at its optimum strategy, the firm may use any combination of the alternatives, except that the bank will not permit the use of the line of credit in combination with the pledging of accounts receivable, or a switch from one alternative to the other during the periods under consideration.

Solution

The problem may be formulated as a linear programming problem.[3] Since there are only four different combinations, each one can be considered a separate linear programming problem. The optimum solution out of these four is the optimum for the problem.[4]

Table 8-10 gives the minimum values of the objective function for the various alternatives. Case 2, with the lowest Total Relevant Costs of all four alternatives, represents the optimum solution.

Table 8-11 represents a detailed statement of the optimum solution.

Questions

1. What happens to a firm's accounts receivable during a cyclical downturn? Why?
2. How can the financial manager use the firm's operating cycle to help him forecast cash flow?
3. Give examples of noncurrent cash inflows and outflows. How do they affect the cash budget?
4. What can a company do to accelerate its cash inflows when it faces a problem of liquidity?
5. What are the major outlets for excess corporate cash funds?
6. What are the major risks in investing in short-term paper?

[3] *Ibid.,* p. 15.
[4] *Ibid.,* pp. 15–21 and p. 21.

Problem

1. Epsilon Corporation purchases $5,000,000 in face value of commercial paper of Sigma Finance Corporation maturing in 60 days at a discount of 5% per annum.

   (a) How much did Epsilon pay for the commercial paper?

   (b) If Epsilon decides to sell the paper in ten days and interest rates have increased to 5.25% per annum, how much cash will Epsilon receive for the commercial paper? What return or loss (in dollars and percent) will Epsilon receive on its investment?

   (c) If Epsilon decides to sell the paper in ten days and interest rates have declined to 4.5% per annum, how much cash will Epsilon receive for the commercial paper? What return or loss (in dollars and percent) will Epsilon receive on its investment?

Case: SKINNER AIR BRAKE CORPORATION

Sales for the Skinner Air Brake Corporation were as follows in the last four months of 19X6:

September 19X6	$260,000
October 19X6	$300,000
November 19X6	$380,000
December 19X6	$500,000

The sales manager has made the following sales estimates for the first four months of 19X7:

January 19X7	$ 530,000
February 19X7	$ 670,000
March 19X7	$ 840,000
April 19X7	$1,000,000

All sales of the Skinner Air Brake Corporation are made for credit. 75% of accounts receivable are collected in the month of sale; 20% the month after the sale, and the remainder in the third month.

All purchases are paid for within the month of purchase. It can be assumed that all goods are manufactured in the month of purchase and that factory wages and direct factory expenses are paid in the month in which the goods are manufactured.

Cost of goods sold are forecast to be about 75% of sales.

Selling and administrative expenses are forecast as follows:

January 19X7	$125,000
February 19X7	$140,000
March 19X7	$150,000
April 19X7	$160,000

The company expects to make a tax payment in March 19X7 of $165,000. As of December 31, 19X6, Skinner Air Brake had $87,000 in cash, and an inventory of finished goods of $115,000. The company wishes to maintain a minimum cash balance of $85,000 at its bank and a minimum inventory of finished goods of $115,000.

Case Questions:

1. Prepare a cash flow budget for Skinner for the next four months.
2. How much will Skinner have to borrow on its line of credit to maintain its minimum cash balance at the bank?
3. What actions could Skinner's Treasurer take to reduce its needs to borrow?

Part II

Intermediate-Term Financing

~~~~~~

Chapter Nine

Capital Budgeting

One of the tasks of the financial manager is to plan for a properly balanced group of investments in assets on the one hand, and a properly balanced capital structure on the other. Capital budgeting is the matching of funds uses (investment in assets) and sources (capital structure) in line with the overall objectives of the firm.

I. IMPORTANCE OF CAPITAL BUDGETING

Capital budgeting is probably the most important single area of decision making for the financial manager. Actions taken by management in this area can affect the operations of the firm for many years to come. For example, the decision made by the management of Sears-Roebuck after World War II to budget substantial sums for the construction of new stores and other facilities enabled Sears to greatly increase its sales compared to Montgomery Ward, whose management decided to invest much of its available funds in United States Government securities. By the time management at Montgomery Ward decided to budget substantial sums to initiate the construction of new stores, material and labor costs had risen substantially. Furthermore, many desirable store sites were no longer available. Thus, the opportunity cost of investing substantial funds in government securities in preference to the other available opportunity was very high.

The selection of the most profitable assortment of capital investments can, therefore, be considered a key function of financial management. One of the main issues in making these decisions is the risk factor. If it were possible to reduce all elements of capital-budgeting decisions to highly reliable quantities, the process of capital budgeting could be reduced to a simple mathematical calculation. Unfortunately, capital budgeting is not yet an exact science; approximations and best guesses must be used and there are always risks of human error. In addition, there are differing human concepts of risk. One businessman is optimistic, another is pessimistic; one is daring, another is conservative. Furthermore, business is dynamic, not static. The financial manager must plan capital budgets often years in advance. Some of the large automobile companies, for example, have ten-year capital-budgeting programs. Gas, water, telephone, transportation companies, i.e., public utilities, large mining and manufacturing companies which are either monopolies or play a dominant role in their respective industries can and must plan in terms of years and even, in some cases, of decades. In contrast, it is difficult for many firms, especially small firms, to look ahead more than a year or two with much confidence; management often commits funds to those opportunities that look best now. Given a limited amount of funds, management may regret its present decision when better opportunities come about in a few years. It may be possible to alter present decisions in the future but only at great cost. Table 9-1 shows the long-term investments by business firms during the period 1958 to 1966.

Conceptually, there is no difference between the operating expenditures made day by day and capital expenditures made as a result of capital budgeting. Management buys raw materials and adds labor with the hope of making a product which will be sold in order to realize a return on investment (profit). Management also invests in buildings, new equipment, etc. for the same expected goal of profit.

1. Time Factor

Capital expenditures usually take a longer period of time to yield profits than do operating expenditures. Moreover, the recovery of the initial investment by means of funds generated by operations and allocated to depreciation usually extends over a substantial portion of the lifetime of the asset. Consequently, some demarcation in terms of time is necessary for purposes of effective financial planning. Generally, therefore, capital expenditures are those whose benefits (return on investment) are realized in periods longer than one year; operating expenditures are those whose benefits are realized in less than one year. Obviously, even this distinction breaks down in practice. In a large company, expenditures of less than $1000 (in some companies the figure would be even higher) are not considered in the capital budget. For example,

TABLE 9-1. Business Expenditures on New Plant and Equipment (In Billions of Dollars)

Period	Total	Manufacturing		Mining	Transportation		Public Utilities	Communications	Other[a]	Total (S.A. Annual Rate)
		Durable	Non-durable		Railroad	Other				
1958	30.53	5.47	5.96	0.94	0.75	1.50	6.09	2.62	7.20	
1959	32.54	5.77	6.29	0.99	0.92	2.02	5.67	2.67	8.21	
1960	35.68	7.18	7.30	0.99	1.03	1.94	5.68	3.13	8.44	
1961	34.37	6.27	7.40	0.98	0.67	1.85	5.52	3.22	8.46	
1962	37.31	7.03	7.65	1.08	0.85	2.07	5.48	3.63	9.52	
1963	39.22	7.85	7.84	1.04	1.10	1.92	5.65	3.79	10.03	
1964	44.90	9.43	9.16	1.19	1.41	2.38	6.22	4.30	10.83	
1965	51.96	11.40	11.05	1.30	1.73	2.81	6.94	4.94	11.79	
1966[b]	60.86	13.96	13.11	1.46	1.96	3.62	8.16	18.60		
1964										
IV	12.84	2.83	2.76	0.33	0.35	0.64	1.76	1.17	3.01	47.75
1965										
I	10.79	2.25	2.28	0.29	0.39	0.58	1.32	1.08	2.59	49.00
II	12.81	2.76	2.70	0.33	0.44	0.77	1.71	1.24	2.85	50.35
III	13.41	2.91	2.82	0.32	0.44	0.72	1.88	1.22	3.10	52.75
IV	14.95	3.48	3.24	0.35	0.46	0.73	2.04	1.41	3.25	55.35
1966										
I	12.77	2.87	2.74	0.33	0.40	0.75	1.60	1.26	2.83	58.00
II	15.29	3.51	3.27	0.40	0.55	1.00	2.09	1.42	3.06	60.10
III	15.64	3.54	3.30	0.36	0.47	0.90	2.22	4.84		61.60
IV	17.16	4.04	3.80	0.37	0.54	0.97	2.25	5.19		63.55

[a] Includes trade, service, finance, and construction.
[b] Anticipated by business.
Note. Dept. of Commerce and Securities and Exchange Commission estimates for corporate and noncorporate business, excluding agriculture.
Source: Federal Reserve Bulletin, September, 1966.

the purchase of an electric typewriter costing $650 with a usable lifetime of many years would not be treated as a capital expenditure. Other expenditures that may produce returns over many years (e.g., company-paid tuition to an executive's attendance at a university executive development program, or advertising and promotion expenditures) are usually not considered in capital budgeting.

2. Dimensions of Capital Budgeting

Investment decisions are subject to two basic constraints. One constraint is the availability of funds for the individual firm. The top management of the company may "see" many profitable opportunities for new investments. If these projects call for external funds, the prospective investors may be reluctant to share the optimism of the management, or the cost of the funds may be greater than anticipated. The second constraint is to be found in the fact that the several investment opportunities differ in risk and prospective profits. In consequence, some rational ranking of long-term investment opportunities must be made on the basis of their desirability (i.e., economic return or vital necessity for the continuation of the enterprise). Some items, for instance, a statue of the founder of the firm or an employee recreation room may, of course, be difficult or impossible to rank according to economic return or vital necessity.

II. PROCEDURES IN CAPITAL BUDGETING

Assume a firm is preparing a capital budget for next year. How does the firm go about it? Capital-budgeting decisions are usually broken down into two levels: the departmental level and the top management or company-wide level. Some firms break it down in other ways, e.g., geographically (United States and international); or they add intermediate levels between the department and the top management level. For simplicity, let us assume a two-level capital-budgeting process in a firm.

Generally, each department head will determine the various possible capital expenditures that may be economically desirable for his department. There are often many conflicting proposals. For example, the office manager may submit a proposal for the establishment of an employees' lounge. On the other hand, the production manager wants this space to be converted into a cafeteria. At the same time, the sales department asks that this space be converted into a meeting room for the sales force. Each department head submits sound arguments—in terms of improved employee morale and efficiency—for his particular project. It is obvious that the three projects cannot be effectively reconciled in the available space. Top management must choose, and decide, which request is to have priority. Conflicting proposals are mutually exclusive. If one is adopted, the others must be rejected. For example, the management of a department store has decided to discontinue the operation of its restaurant and to allocate the space to an expansion of its women's wear lines. At this point, the manager of the higher priced women's wear requests the additional space for his line while the manager of the low priced line also asks for the same space. A decision in favor of either request involves a basic issue: the image of the store in the mind of the woman shopper. Does the store stress low price and bargain or high price and quality? In this instance, we have a conflict between two possible images.

Competing proposals are not mutually exclusive as are conflicting proposals. However, they may not be equally desirable. Hence, the department head must rank the various competing proposals in some order of priority before he submits his proposals to top management.

For instance, the factory manager asks for the installation of some automated equipment. The head of the warehouse and shipping department requests an additional elevator shaft. And the accounting department wants a computer for bookkeeping operations. Each proposal is supported by projected cost savings. Taken by itself, each project appears promising; i.e., it will reduce the present labor cost of the respective department. At this point, the financial manager picks up the loose threads. He examines not only the prospective profit but also the feasibility and desirability of making the proposed investments in terms of the cost of funds. He attempts to answer such questions as: What are the present terms of borrowing funds; i.e., interest and repayment? Are these costs constant; i.e., whether the firm wants the money for one, two, or the three projects? Is it likely that the conditions in the capital market will tighten or loosen up in the next year or two? Which, if any, of the proposed expenditures can be postponed; and, if so, for how long?

The answers to these questions are vital to a determination of the financial feasibility and advisability to undertake one or more capital expenditures. The final decision then rests with top management which must evaluate the proposals and allocate funds for those that are most desirable for the company as a whole. Proposals are generally ranked in accordance with economic gain at both the departmental and company-wide levels, although exceptions are often made for such morale-building expenditures as a parking lot and landscaping of the plant site.

Economic Ranking of Projects

The basic process of capital-expenditure analysis consists of matching the economic gains provided by a capital expenditure with the cost of the funds used for the expenditure. Before the relative desirability of projects can be assigned, it is necessary to establish the nature of the components of capital-expenditure analysis. These components are expressed in terms of cash flows.

1. Net Investment (NI)   The concept of net investment refers to the amount of funds committed to the investment in any one project. Net investment is thus equivalent to marginal or incremental capital investment. Such a project might be the purchase of a new machine, permanent increase in working capital to support larger operations, construction of a new parking lot, or purchase of a new factory. In these cases, the net investment is equal to the funds committed to the new assets (including freight in, installation, start-up costs, and increased funds needed for working capital).

When a project replaces an existing asset (for example, a new type of milling machine replacing an old milling machine), the remaining accounting value or book value of the old asset is disregarded for purposes of computing the net investment since this book loss is a sunk cost as a result of a previous decision. Perhaps management had originally overestimated the economic life of the old asset and did not depreciate it at a sufficient rate. In any event, the errors of the past should not be blamed on the new decision. The loss on the old machine (except for tax purposes and the effect it has on taxable profits) is only a bookkeeping entry. It involves no outflow of cash.

However, any salvage value received from the sale of the old asset is a relevant cash flow. This cash inflow is deducted from the amount of investment required, since the funds tied up in the old asset have been released by sale (salvage) of the old asset. If the old asset were sold at a profit (above its accounting or book value), there generally would be a capital-gains tax payable on the profit. This cash outflow should be added to the net investment. Similarly, if the old asset had been sold at a loss, the resulting tax savings (a decreased cash outflow equals a cash inflow) should be deducted from the net investment. Many financial managers also deduct the estimated salvage value of the new asset (discounted to present value, as will be explained later) from the net investment.

2. Net Cash Benefit (NCB) after Taxes   Once the net investment has been determined, it is necessary to calculate the net cash benefit after taxes of the project. If the company keeps the old asset, there will be no change in cash flows. If it purchases a new asset, either cash outflows will be reduced—as a result of cost savings in production—or additional cash will flow into the firm if the same input generates a larger output. Reductions in cash outflows are frequently as beneficial to the firm as increases in cash inflows. Thus, the differential costs saved by buying the new asset are a net cash benefit to the firm.

Other capital expenditures are made in order to provide additional profits or increased cash flows to the firm. It is important in all types of capital expenditure to make sure that all relevant cash flows are fully considered by including all changes in cash flows as a result of purchase of the new asset. Management must ask such questions as: Will the purchase of the new asset (net investment) result in eliminating expense items? What items of expense will increase as a result of adding the new asset? For example, will the purchase of the new asset decrease the amount of scrap materials? How will it affect labor costs?

It must be stressed, again, that accounting allocations are ignored in capital budgeting unless they affect cash flows. For example, if an investment releases some floor space in the plant, the accountant will probably now charge the department rent only on that floor space still used. However, if there is no other productive use for this floor space, then the investment has not realized any operating savings or changed the cash flows. The process can be succinctly summarized in the question: Will this investment increase the amount of cash inflows (decrease the amount of cash outflows) into the business? That is, what will be the net cash benefits as a result of this investment?

Hopefully, the purchase of new assets or other capital expenditures will increase profits. Increased profits generally result in increased income taxes. These additional taxes must be considered as a relevant cash flow. Thus, the financial manager must calculate net cash benefits *after* taxes. This causes a complication since taxes are paid on the basis of accounting profits. The difference between accounting profits and cash flows are caused by accounting allocations for such items as depreciation. As mentioned earlier in the text, depreciation is an allocation of a past expenditure—it is not a cash outlay. Depreciation must be considered, however, in capital budgeting insofar as it affects taxes on income (and, consequently, cash flows).

The process of considering additional taxes can best be explained by a simple example. Assume a firm is considering buying a new machine for $20,000. Assume, further, that the machine is to be depreciated for tax purposes on the straight-line basis over five years and that it will have no salvage value at the end of that time. Assume that the machine to be replaced could also be used for five more years and is being depreciated at the rate of $2000 per year. Suppose that the savings (net cash benefits before taxes) in labor, materials, and repairs will be $10,000 per year as a result of buying the new machine. Given the above information, a simple table will enable determination of the net cash benefits after taxes, as illustrated in Table 9-2.

TABLE 9-2.   (Dollars)

		On Accountant's Books	Cash Flow
Net cash benefits before taxes (savings)		10,000	10,000
Depreciation on new machine	4,000		
Less depreciation on old machine	2,000		
Additional depreciation expense		2,000	
Additional taxable income		8,000	
Increase in income tax (@ 50%)		4,000	4,000
Additional net profit after tax		4,000	
Net cash benefits after taxes			6,000

In the example, once taxes have been calculated according to the laws and the rules of accounting conventions, it is possible to show the cash-flow effect of the additional income taxes.

3. Complications   Use of accelerated depreciation methods would complicate the calculation of net cash benefits after taxes, since annual depreciation charges under these methods are not uniform. Nevertheless, the principle would remain the same: the financial manager, for purposes of capital budgeting, is interested in the cash flow in net cash benefits after taxes rather than in accounting profits per se.

A further complication is the fact that capital budgeting expenditure decisions deal with future events. Estimates often have to be used as to the amount of the net cash benefits that will be realized as a result of the addition of new assets. Once the asset has been purchased, the actual net cash benefits may prove to be different. Some financial managers calculate ranges of net cash benefits—e.g., the highest expectation, the most likely expectation, and the lowest expectation. Probability techniques can then be applied to these expectations. Additional complexities are introduced when the new assets (net investment) are added in several stages over a period of years. As mentioned previously, the further away from the present, the more problematical it is for the financial manager to plan actual investments with precision, as the uncertainty factor increases.

4. The Time Value of Money   In economic theory, interest is the price paid to the owner of funds for exchanging present consumption for future consumption. If the owner of funds invests his funds in a business as a part owner rather than lender he expects to maximize the return on the investment by, hopefully, obtaining a profit greater than the rate of interest paid to the lender.

The business firm which has at its disposal internal funds in excess of current operating requirements has three basic choices. It can disburse this excess to the stockholders. Or it can keep the cash-funds for the purpose of maintaining a higher degree of liquidity; i.e., it attaches a value to "liquidity preference." Finally, the firm can invest the funds in fixed assets. If the firm selects the third alternative, this choice is predicated on management's conclusion that such action will yield a greater return or benefit to the stockholders than either of the first two alternatives. In other words, the investment in fixed assets will maximize profits. The same basic reasoning applies to the borrowing of funds (debt capital) which the firm wants to invest in fixed assets. The prospective profit-before-interest must be appreciably in excess of the interest payment. Otherwise it does not pay to assume a fixed interest obligation based on the prospect of only a moderate residual profit *if* management's expectations are fully realized. The latter contain an element of uncertainty while the interest obligation is fixed and therefore certain.

In determining the present value of say, $1000 a year from now, the financial manager must first get the minimum rate of return (profit) that the firm will accept if it is to borrow and invest $1000 today. If the firm must pay 6% interest the maximum present value of the $1000 can be calculated by simple arithmetic using the formula $P = An/(1 + r)^n$ where A = dollar amount realized at the end of a period of time, n = the number of periods of time, r = the rate of interest, and P = the present value of the stream of income. Applied to the example, the calculation is: $P = \$1000(1)/(1 + 0.06) = \$943.40$.

Obviously, it will not pay to invest the $943.40 for one year, take managerial responsibility for the employment of the money, and just earn enough to pay the interest. Now let us assume that the management decides that it must earn at least 10% above interest to compensate for the risk of uncertainty. In this case the present value of $1000 a year from now is: $P = \$1000 \ (1)/(1 + 0.16) = \$862$. To put it differently, an investment today of $862 "pays off" if management can expect to realize at least $1000 one year from now.

Actually, it is not necessary for the financial manager to make these calculations, since tables have been prepared for this purpose. Table A (Present Value of One Dollar) is an example of these tables. Using Table A, the financial manager will quickly find that the present value of $1 received in one year at 12% is $0.893. In other words, if the financial manager invests $0.893 now at 12%, at the end of one year he will have $1.

If the present value of $1 received a year from now is $0.893, and the present value of $1 received two years from now is $0.797, and the present value of $1 received three years from now is $0.712 (see Table A), the financial manager can easily calculate the present value of a stream of net cash benefits of $1 per year for the next three years, discounted at 12%. Obviously, it is the sum of $0.893 + 0.797 + 0.712$ or $2.402. Again, it is unnecessary for the financial manager to go through even this simple arithmetic because Table B (Present Value of One Dollar Received Annually for N Years) shows the present value of $1 received annually for a certain specified period of years. (Tables A, B, C, and D are located at the end of the book.)

Tables A and B both assume that the net cash benefits are received at the end of each year. Actually, it is more likely that benefits will be received monthly or continuously. Tables C and D have been prepared on the basis of monthly receipts of benefits. The tables also assume that the original investment will be recovered in computing the rate of return.

III. RATE OF RETURN METHOD OF ECONOMIC RANKING OF PROJECTS

A. True Rate of Return

Once the financial manager has calculated the net investment and net cash benefits after taxes of a proposed capital expenditure, he may proceed to compute the expected annual rate of return to be gained from this capital expenditure. The financial manager knows the firm will make a net investment of a certain amount now and will receive a return in the form of net cash benefits of a certain amount (assuming his estimates are accurate) each year for a certain period of years. The financial manager would like to know the rate of return on this investment so that he may compare the investment with others and with his cost of capital or other cutoff points.

For example, assume that a firm is considering the purchase of a new machine, at a net investment of $18,000. Net cash benefits after taxes are estimated at $6000 per year for five years, and they will be received monthly. At the end of this period, the machine will have no economic or salvage value. The financial manager can estimate the rate of return by making guesses as to its value, with the help of Table D. For example, he might try a rate of 24%. Table D shows that the present value of $1, received monthly for 5 years and discounted at 24%, is $3.036. If this factor is multiplied by the $6000 the firm will actually receive, the present value of $6000 per year for 5 years discounted at 24% = 3.036 × $6000 = $18,216. This tells the financial manager that, if he invested $18,216 in return for $6000 net cash benefits per year, the rate of return would be 24% per annum. Actually, however, the financial manager is investing only $18,000. Hence, the true rate of return is more than 24%. Suppose he now tries 25%. The present value of $6000 per year for 5 years discounted at 25% (using Table D) = 2.985 × $6000 = $17,910. Since the financial manager is investing more than $17,910, the rate of return is somewhat less than 25%. The true rate of return can be arrived at by interpolation between the two figures as follows:

	Rate	Present values	Difference in Present Value and required investment
	24%	$18,216	$18,216
	25%	17,910	18,000
Difference:	1%	$ 306	$ 216

$$\frac{\$216}{\$306} \times 1\% = 0.706\%$$

The true rate of return is, therefore, 24% + 0.706% or 24.706%.

Much of this calculation, by trial and error, can in fact be avoided when the net cash benefits after taxes are the same each year. This can be done simply by dividing:

$$\frac{\text{Net Investment}}{\text{Annual Net Cash Benefits after Taxes}} = \text{Present Value Factor}$$

The resulting factor can then be discovered on Table D (or Table B) on the line with the economic life of the investment. For example, using the figures given above:

$$\frac{18,000}{6,000} = 3,000$$

Look on the 5-year line of Table D for the factors closest to 3.000 and the return is revealed at between 24% and 25%. It is still necessary to interpolate for a more exact rate of return, provided the financial manager has several projects to consider.

When the net cash benefits after taxes vary from year to year, it is necessary to find the rate of return by trial and error. For example, a firm is considering a net investment of $25,000 in a machine. Net cash benefits will be $7500 per year in years 1, 2, and 3 and $5000 per year in years 4, 5, and 6. The financial manager can turn to Table C and calculate the present value of this stream of net cash benefits by trial and error. He might begin by assuming a rate of return of 118%, as shown in Table 9-3.

TABLE 9-3.

Period (Year)	Net Cash Benefits after Taxes ($)	Table C Present Value Factor @ 18%	Net Present Value @ 18% ($)
1	7500	0.915	6,862
2	7500	0.776	5,820
3	7500	0.657	4,928
4	5000	0.557	2,785
5	5000	0.472	2,370
6	5000	0.400	2,000
			24,765

Clearly, the rate of return is going to be somewhat less than 18% since the net investment is $25,000, not $24,765. If the financial manager tries a rate of return of 16% he will get the results shown in Table 9-4.

In this instance, the rate is more than 16%. By interpolation, the financial manager finds that the true rate of return is about as follows:

$$\left(2\% \times \frac{25755-25000}{25755-24765} = 1.44\% + 16\%\right) = 17.44\%.$$

TABLE 9-4.

Period (Year)	Net Cash Benefits after Taxes ($)	Table C Present Value Factor @ 16%	Net Present Value @ 16% ($)
1	7500	0.924	6,930
2	7500	0.796	5,970
3	7500	0.686	5,145
4	5000	0.592	2,960
5	5000	0.510	2,550
6	5000	0.440	2,200
			25,755

B. Present-Value Method

Another method of computing expected rates of return is the present-value method. This method involves calculating the present value of the net cash benefits discounted at a rate equal to the firm's cost of capital (for example, the rate of interest at which funds may be lent or borrowed). In other words, "the *present value* of an investment . . . [is] the maximum amount a firm could pay for the opportunity of making the investment without being financially worse off."[2] The financial manager compares this present value to the cost of the proposal. If the present value is greater than the net investment, the return is obviously greater than the cost of capital and there are financial benefits in making the investment. Conversely, if the present value is smaller than the net investment, the return is less than the cost of capital. Making the investment in this case will cause a financial loss to the firm.

Assume that the cost of capital after taxes of a firm is 6%. Assume that the net cash benefits after taxes on a $5000 investment are forecasted as being $2800 per year for two years. The present value of this stream of net cash benefits discounted at 6 percent can be found in Table D as follows:

$$1.883 \times \$2800 = \$5272$$

Therefore, the present value of the net cash benefits = $5272
less the present value of the net investment   =   5000
Net present value   = $ 272

[2] Harold Bierman, Jr. and Seymour Smidt, *The Capital Budgeting Decision* (New York: Macmillan, 1960), p. 28.

The present-value method can tell the financial manager in one step whether it pays to go ahead with a project. If the present value of the net cash benefits exceeds the present value of the net investment, the investment will be profitable to the firm.

One disadvantage of the present-value method is that it is not easy to rank projects on the basis of net present value. This drawback can be eliminated by the use of a profitability index. The present value of net cash benefits after taxes divided by the present value of the net investment of any project will result in a profitability index for that project. For example, the profitability index of the $5000 investment discussed above would be:

$$\frac{\text{Present value of net cash benefits}}{\text{Present value of net investment}} = \frac{\$5272}{\$5000} = 1.05$$

The higher the profitability index, the more desirable the investment. By computing profitability indices for various projects, the financial manager can rank them in the order of their respective rates of profitability.

A more serious disadvantage to the present-value method is its assumption that the cost of capital will be fixed. In actuality, the supply of funds available to a firm at a given cost is limited. As the firm raises more capital (either debt or equity), the cost of capital will generally increase. The true rate-of-return method, on the other hand, does not depend upon the calculated cost of capital. Since, as will be discussed later, it is extremely difficult to develop a calculated cost of capital, it is generally preferable to use the true rate-of-return method and, thus, avoid dependence on what may be only a guess as to the cost of capital in ranking projects. Furthermore, it is often easier for the businessman to think in terms of percentages (e.g., a 14% return) than in terms of a profitability index such as 1.23.

C. Simplified Rates of Return

The true rate-of-return method and the present-value method have the disadvantage of requiring relatively more calculations than many businessmen are willing to make, either because of a lack of comprehension of present value or because of a need for rapid calculation. Therefore, two other approaches are often used. Both of these approaches have the weakness of ignoring the time value of money.

The simplest approach is *payback*. The payback period is the length of time necessary for the net cash benefits after taxes to equal the net investment. For example, if a firm is considering a net investment of $18,000 in a machine, which has a net cash benefit after taxes of $6000 per year, it will have a payback period of 3 years.

$$\left(\text{Payback}^3 = \frac{NI}{NCB \text{ after Taxes}} = \frac{18,000}{6,000} = 3.000\right)$$

The payback figure tells the financial manager that, if the net cash benefits after taxes continue for at least three years, the firm will get its net investment back. Payback gives the financial manager no information on net cash benefits after the payback period. If it is assumed that all projects must have a payback of three years, the financial manager might go ahead with the above project instead of buying an $18,000 machine that returned $4000 per year in net cash benefits after taxes for seven years. This decision would not maximize profits if the net cash benefits from the first machine lasted only for three years, as the firm would only get its money back and would receive no return (in interest or profit) on its investment.

Payback has a second disadvantage. Two different $18,000 machines might have net cash benefits after taxes as follows:

Year	Machine No. 1	Machine No. 2
1	$7000	$5000
2	6000	6000
3	5000	7000

Each machine will have the same payback period: three years. Obviously, machine 1 would be a better investment since more cash would be returned sooner and this cash could be put to work in other investments.

Despite its disadvantages, payback is useful to the financial manager. When the firm is having extreme liquidity problems (i.e., it is very short of cash), the financial manager may accept only those investments that have an extremely short payback period.

Another simplified device often used by financial managers is the simple rate of return. This is the reciprocal of the payback (Simple rate of return = NCB after Taxes/NI). All of the disadvantages of the payback apply equally to the simple rate of return which is the reciprocal

---

[3] Although the payback factor is the same as the factor used in present value for projects with level cash inflow, it is used for a different purpose.

of payback when cash inflows are level or constant. At best, the simple rate of return is an approximation of the true rate of return derived from present value. In investments with extremely long lives, the simple rate of return will be fairly close to the true rate of return. Simple rate of return is often used by financial analysts to measure current performance (efficiency) of a firm.

A variation of the simple rate of return is to divide accounting profits less depreciation by net investment or, in some cases, by average investment. As with simple rate of return, this accounting or average rate of return is distorted by its failure to take into consideration the time value of money. Use of payback or simple rate of return may well cause serious distortions in the selection of capital expenditures.

D. Deficiencies of All Techniques

Even if the more sophisticated true rate-of-return technique is used for capital expenditure proposals, there are many inadequacies in capital budgeting. Estimates of net cash benefits are based on potential future savings (and/or increased profits). These savings might not materialize. Expected labor savings through automation may not materialize as planned in the calculations. For example, the railroads found it extremely difficult to discontinue the use of firemen when they switched from steam to diesel locomotives because of union resistance. The economic life of a new asset might prove to be much shorter than anticipated as a result of further research and development or rapid obsolescence due to modern technology.

Two capital-expenditure proposals may project the same rate of return; e.g., 8%. However, one proposal involves an investment for five years while the other involves a period of ten years. Evaluating the respective prospects, it is quite conceivable that the financial manager will attach a greater degree of certainty to the realization of the projected profits to the first proposal. To reflect the smaller degree of certainty the financial manager will therefore show a range for the rate of return on the second project (i.e., 5–8%) rather than a single rate.

One approach sometimes used by the financial manager to reduce uncertainty is to apply probability techniques to his estimated net cash benefits. No businessman is ever fully certain of the validity of his forecasts—be they sales forecasts, price forecasts, or cost forecasts. A probability distribution may be used to help the financial manager make a better forecast of net cash benefits.

Let us assume that the financial manager is planning to purchase a new machine that will yield the following forecasted net cash benefits:

There are 5 chances in 100 that net cash benefits will be $0
There are 20 chances in 100 that net cash benefits will be $100
There are 40 chances in 100 that net cash benefits will be $200
There are 30 chances in 100 that net cash benefits will be $300
There are 5 chances in 100 that net cash benefits will be $400

The most probable net cash benefit will be $200 as there are more chances of this occurring than any other net cash benefit. However, there are 60 chances out of 100 that $200 will not be received. In this example it is more likely that more than $200 will be received (35 chances out of 100) than less than $200 will be received (25 chances out of 100). In this case, the financial manager would most likely use $200 as his forecast of expected net cash benefits. He might wish to discount his net cash benefit somewhat, however, as there is still one chance in four that net cash benefits will be $100 or less.

Suppose, however, the situation is the reverse of the above, as follows:

There are 5 chances in 100 that net cash benefits will be $400
There are 20 chances in 100 that net cash benefits will be $300
There are 40 chances in 100 that net cash benefits will be $200
There are 30 chances in 100 that net cash benefits will be $100
There are 5 chances in 100 that net cash benefits will be $0

Again, the most probable net cash benefit will be $200 as there are more chances of this occurring than any other net cash benefit. Again, there are 60 chances out of 100 that $200 will not be received. In the last example it is more likely that less than $200 will be received (35 chances out of 100) than more than $200 will be received (25 chances out of 100). To allow for this uncertainty, the financial manager should adjust his expected net cash benefits downward. The financial manager can easily find the mean expected net cash benefit by simple calculation as follows:

$$
\begin{aligned}
0.05 \times \$400 &= \$\ 20 \\
0.20 \times\ \ \ 300 &= \ \ \ \ 60 \\
0.40 \times\ \ \ 200 &= \ \ \ \ 80 \\
0.30 \times\ \ \ 100 &= \ \ \ \ 30 \\
0.50 \times\ \ \ \ \ \ 0 &= \underline{\ \ \ \ \ \ 0} \\
& \ \ \ \ \ \ \$190
\end{aligned}
$$

Thus, the financial manager would adjust his expected net cash benefits down to at least $190. He might adjust them downward still further as there is more than one chance in three that the expected net cash benefits will be $100 or less. The greater the variance in probable outcomes in a downward direction, the more the expected net cash benefits should be adjusted downward to achieve a more certain forecast of minimum expected net cash benefits.

Even when the frequency distribution of forecasted net cash benefits is perfectly symmetrical above and below an average level, the forecasted net cash benefit figure should be reduced or discounted. This is because the financial manager has more to lose (possible bankruptcy) than to gain (high net cash benefits) when the chances are equally probable for him to make high profits or suffer high losses from an investment in new equipment.

There is one major weakness in the probability approach to reduce uncertainty in forecasting estimated net cash benefits. The financial manager must somehow decide how many chances out of 100 there are for an expected net cash benefit figure of, say, $200 to occur. Often, it is difficult to quantify this on the basis of past experience in the firm or elsewhere. Thus, the value of the probability forecast is based on the accuracy of the financial manager's judgment in assigning chances of an expected net cash benefit being achieved. It is very difficult, then, to fully quantify expected returns since, almost always, the estimates are based on some kind of judgment. Nevertheless, the financial manager finds it necessary to make some judgment. Quantitative techniques like probability may help him to lessen his margin of error. In any event, the financial manager often will find it fruitful to discount expected net cash benefits for both futurity (by true rate-of-return techniques) and for riskiness (by probability techniques).

Some capital expenditure proposals may be almost impossible to quantify in terms of a true rate of return. Ethical drug companies often make substantial allocations to basic research with little knowledge as to what return, if any, will be realized. A soap company may launch an expensive advertising campaign for a new product with little knowledge as to what return will be achieved. From past experience, drug companies have found that research expenditures pay off in the long run and soap companies have found that advertising generally pays off. But it is almost impossible to be sure that the results will be the same for the particular capital expenditure proposed in the capital budget. If the financial manager is aware of the deficiencies of his quantitative techniques, he will be able to caution top management so that it does not place sole reliance on them. On the other hand, these techniques can do much to rationalize decision making in the area of capital expenditures. They are a decided improvement over mere intuition and intestinal wisdom.

SUMMARY

Capital budgeting is the matching of fund uses (investment in assets) and sources (capital structure) in line with the overall objective of the firm. Capital budgeting is probably the most important single area of decision making for the financial manager, since decisions in this area affect the firm's operations for many years in the future. The goal in capital budgeting is to select the most profitable assortment of investments, consistent with the risk factor. Capital budgeting decisions are subject to two basic constraints: the availability of funds to the individual firm and the difference in risk and prospective profits of each investment opportunity.

Capital budgeting decisions are generally broken down into several levels such as the departmental level and the top management level. Department heads must rank proposals as to desirability within the department. Top management must evaluate the proposals of all departments and allocate funds to those proposals which are most desirable for the company as a whole.

The basic process of capital expenditure analysis consists of matching the economic gains provided by a capital expenditure with the cost of funds used for the expenditure. Components of capital expenditure analysis can best be expressed in cash flows.

The financial manager, or whoever is making the capital budgeting decision, can rank investment opportunities according to their true rate of return (based on the cash flows) or by some other method of economic ranking, e.g., as a profitability index or by some simplified matter of return like payback.

There are many inadequacies of capital budgeting even when the most sophisticated techniques are used. However, the use of quantitative techniques, including probability, is a decided improvement over mere intuition in helping the financial manager reach his decisions on capital budgeting.

Appendix A HOW TO EVALUATE NEW CAPITAL INVESTMENTS[4]

• In evaluating new investment projects, why are return-on-investment figures preferable to years-to-pay-out figures?

• Of various possible methods for calculating return on investment, why is the discounted-cash-flow procedure likely to yield the best results?

• What techniques and assumptions will help executives who want to make practical use of the discounted-cash-flow methods?

Obviously, I cannot answer these questions satisfactorily for all companies. I shall attempt only to describe some of the answers developed by the Continental Oil Company. Faced with a need for better methods of evaluating investment proposals, management decided in 1955 to adopt the discounted-cash-flow method. The procedures adopted, the reasons for choosing them, and the results obtained during the past three years may serve as a useful "case example" for other companies to study.

Of course, the techniques that I shall describe were not invented by Continental. They have been used for centuries in the field of finance and banking and have been fully described in many textbooks and articles in the field of industrial management and business economics during the past 25 years. It is only recently, however, that they have been applied in the industrial field, and their usage is still limited to a fairly small number of companies.

MANAGEMENT CONCERN

Prior to 1955, we had relied heavily—as many oil companies do—on years-to-pay-out figures as the primary means of judging the desirability of investments and as a yardstick for measuring one investment opportunity against another. We had also made use of return-on-investment figures computed in a variety of different ways, which I shall describe later.

In the latter part of 1954 our financial group, consisting of the controller, the financial vice president, and myself, undertook a comprehensive review of the techniques we were then using in making capital investment decisions. We were concerned about this matter because of the large

[4] By John G. McLean, reprinted from the *Harvard Business Review*, **36**, (6), November-December, 1958.

amounts of new money we found it necessary to channel back into the oil business each year. Characteristically, oil companies have a very high rate of capital turnover because they operate assets which deplete at high rates, and large amounts of new funds must be reinvested each year if earnings are to be maintained and increased.

The capital expenditures of Continental Oil, for example, normally run in the neighborhood of $100 million per year, or about $385,000 each working day—roughly twice our net income, which is about $50 million per year. To the best of my knowledge, there are few, if any, other major industries with such a high ratio of capital expenditures to current net income.

In the oil business, therefore, the making of capital investment decisions assumes considerably more significance as a part of top management's job than is usually the case. In our own situation, it was apparent that the management judgment exercised in directing the flow of new funds into our business had a very significant bearing upon current and future earnings per share and a profound influence on the long-term growth and development of our company. We decided, therefore, that we should make a maximum effort to develop the best possible yardstick for comparing one investment opportunity against another and for evaluating the returns that particular projects would earn on the stockholder's dollar.

NEW TECHNIQUES

As a background for outlining the new techniques which our financial group recommended as a result of its study and which were later implemented throughout the company, let me first outline the steps which are normally involved in the appraisal of new capital investments:

1. Estimate the volume of sales, prices, costs of materials, operating expenses, transportation costs, capital investment requirements, strength and nature of competition, rates of obsolescence or depletion, and other economic and business factors.
2. Summarize basic estimates of annual income, life of project, and capital investment in convenient form for appraisal purposes. (Commonly used yardsticks include years to pay out and return on investment.)
3. Exercise managerial judgment in determining whether or not:
   (a) The anticipated return is large enough to warrant the business risks involved;

(b) The investment opportunity is attractive in view of the various alternative opportunities for capital spending;

(c) The timing of the investment is right relative to anticipated developments in the near future.

The discounted-cash-flow techniques which we introduced in 1955 had to do only with step 2; that is, with the way we did our arithmetic in adding up the basic estimates of annual incomes, life of project, and capital investments to arrive at payout and return on investment.

It was clearly recognized that there was nothing in the discounted-cash-flow method which would make it any easier to estimate the items listed in step 1 or which would improve the accuracy of those estimates. It was likewise recognized that there was nothing in the discounted-cash-flow techniques which would relieve management at any level of the responsibility for exercising judgment on the various matters, listed under step 3. We were concerned fundamentally, at this time, with improving the mechanics of our capital-investment analyses in order that management might render better judgments on the three points under step 3.

Payout versus Return

Our first recommendation as that we use the return-on-investment figures as the primary yardstick for evaluating new capital investments and pay much less attention to years-to-pay-out figures than had been our custom in the past.

Our reason for deemphasizing payout figures was simply that they do not provide an adequate means of discriminating among new investment opportunities. They merely indicate how long it will take to recover the original capital outlay and do not tell us anything about the earning power of an investment. There is, of course, no point in making investments which just give us our money back. The true worth of an investment depends on how much income it will generate *after* the original outlay has been recovered, and there is no way that can be determined from a payout figure. Generally speaking, payout figures are reliable measures of the relative worth of alternative investments only when the income-producing life of all projects under consideration is about the same—which is far from the case in our particular situation.

To illustrate how misleading payout figures can be, I have prepared an example consisting of three different projects, each involving an investment of $125,000 (see Exhibit 9-1).

EXHIBIT 9-1.   DIFFERENCES IN RATES OF RETURN WHEN PAYOUT PERIODS ARE EQUAL

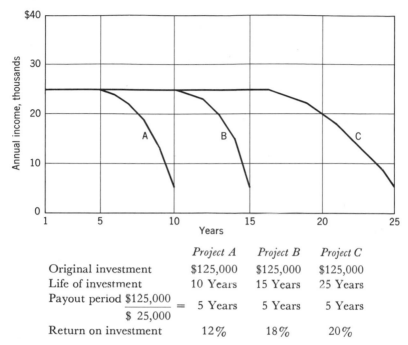

	Project A	Project B	Project C
Original investment	$125,000	$125,000	$125,000
Life of investment	10 Years	15 Years	25 Years
Payout period $\frac{\$125,000}{\$\ 25,000} =$	5 Years	5 Years	5 Years
Return on investment	12%	18%	20%

The annual income generated by the investments begins at $25,000 and then declines in later years in each case as shown on the graph. Since the annual incomes are identical in the early years, each project has the same payout period; namely, five years. By this standard of measurement, therefore, the projects would be equal from an investment standpoint. But actually the returns on investment range from 12% per year for Project A, which has the shortest life, to 20% per year for Project B, which has the longest life.

At first glance, you might be inclined to say that this is all pretty simple—all you have to do is look at both the payout period and the total estimated life to reach a correct decision. And it *is* relatively easy if the payout periods are all the same, as they are in this example, or even if the payout periods are different but the total economic lives are the same.

Unfortunately, however, we are usually looking at projects where there is a difference in both the payout period and the project life. Under such circumstances, it becomes very difficult to appraise the relative worth of two or more projects on the basis of payout periods alone. For example, consider the three projects shown in Exhibit 9-2.

The payout periods here range from 8 years in the case of Project A, which has a high initial income and a short life, to 11.5 years in the case of Project C, which has a low initial income and a long life. On the basis of payout periods, therefore, Project A would appear to be the best of the three. Actually, however, the true rates of return on investment range from 5% for Project A to 8.5% for Project C. The order of desirability indicated by payout periods is thus exactly the reverse of that indicated by return-on-investment figures.

It was for these reasons that our financial group recommended that in the future we make use of return-on-investment figures as our primary

EXHIBIT 9-2.   Failure of Payout Periods to Rank Investments in Order of Desirability

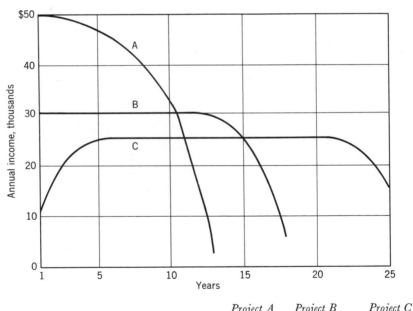

	Project A	Project B	Project C
Original investment	$372,000	$267,000	$230,000
Life of investment	13 Years	18 Years	25 Years
Average annual income, after taxes before depreciation	$ 37,200	$ 26,700	$ 23,000
Payout based on average income	10 Years	10 Years	10 Years
Payout based on actual income	8 Years	8.7 Years	11.5 Years
Return on investment	5%	8%	8.5%

guide in evaluating new projects rather than the payout figures which had customarily been our main guide in the past.

Alternative Calculation

Our second recommendation had to do with the procedures used in calculating the return-on-investment figures. There are at least three general ways to make the calculation:

(1) In the first method, the return is calculated on the *original investment;* that is, the average annual income from a project is divided by the total original capital outlay. This is the procedure we had been using in our producing, refining, petrochemical, and pipeline departments.

(2) In the second method, the return is calculated on the *average investment.* In other words, the average annual income is divided by half the original investment or by whatever figure represents the mid-point between the original cost and the salvage or residual land value in the investment. This is the procedure which was used in our marketing department for calculating returns on new service station investments.

(3) The third procedure—the *discounted-cash-flow* technique—bases the calculation on the investment actually outstanding from time to time over the life of the project. This was the procedure used in our financial department in computing the cost of funds obtained from various sources or in estimating the yields we might obtain by investing reserve working capital in various types of government or commercial securities.

These three methods will produce very different results, and the figures obtained by one method may be as much as twice as great as those obtained by another—i.e., a project that showed a return of 10% under the procedures used in our refining department could show as much as 20% under the procedures used by our marketing department, and might show 15% or 18% under those used by our financial department.

It was clear, therefore, that we must settle on one of these three methods and use it uniformly throughout all departments of the company. Otherwise, we would be measuring some investments with long yardsticks, others with short yardsticks, and we would never be sure exactly what we were doing.

Relative Advantages

Our selection of discounted cash flow was based on three primary considerations:

1. It gives the true rate of return offered by a new project. Both of the other methods merely give an appoximation of the return. The original-investment method usually understates the return, while the average-investment method usually overstates the return. By contrast, the discounted-cash-flow method is a compromise and usually gives figures lying in between those that would be obtained by the other two methods.

2. It gives figures which are meaningful in relation to those used throughout the financial world in quoting interest rates on borrowed funds, yields on bonds, and for various other purposes. It thus permits direct comparison of the projected returns on investments with the cost of borrowing money—which is not possible with the other procedures.

3. It makes allowance for *differences in the time* at which investments generate their income. That is, it discriminates among investments that have (a) a low initial income which gradually increases, (b) a high initial income which gradually declines, and (c) a uniform income throughout their lives.

The last point was particularly important to us, because the investment projects which we normally have before us frequently have widely divergent income patterns. Refining projects usually have a relatively uniform annual income, because they must be operated at 75% to 100% of capacity from the time they go on stream in order to keep unit costs at reasonable levels. On the other hand, producing wells yield a high initial income, which declines as the oil reservoir is depleted; while new service station investments have a still different pattern in that they frequently increase their income as they gain market acceptance and build up their volume of business.

As an illustration of the usefulness of the discounted-cash-flow method in discriminating among investments with different income patterns, consider the three examples presented in Exhibit 9-3.

These three projects all require the same original outlay, have the same economic life, and generate exactly the same total income after taxes and depreciation. The return on the original investment would be 12%, and the return on average investment 24% in each case. By these standards, therefore, the projects would appear to be of equal merit. Actually, however, Project A is by far the best of the three because it generates a larger share of its total income in the early years of its life. The investor thus has his money in hand sooner and available for investment in other income-producing projects. This highly important difference is clearly reflected

EXHIBIT 9-3. Comparison of Return-on-Investment Calculations

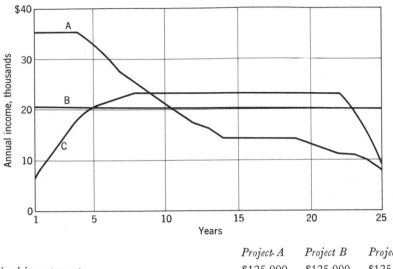

	Project A	Project B	Project C
Original investment	$125,000	$125,000	$125,000
Life of investment	25 Years	25 Years	25 Years
Total income, after taxes, before depreciation	$500,000	$500,000	$500,000
Average annual income, after taxes before depreciation	$ 20,000	$ 20,000	$ 20,000
Deduct depreciation ($125,000 + 25 years)	$ 5,000	$ 5,000	$ 5,000
Annual income after taxes and depreciation	$ 15,000	$ 15,000	$ 15,000
Return on Original Investment $\dfrac{\$\ 15,000}{\$125,000}$	12%	12%	12%
Return on Average Investment $\dfrac{\$\ 15,000}{\$\ 62,500}$	24%	24%	24%
Return by Discounted Cash Flow Method	24%	15.5%	13%

in the discounted-cash-flow figures, which show 24% for Project A, 15.5% for project B, and 13% for Project C.

SIMPLE APPLICATION

To facilitate the adoption of the new system on a company-wide basis, we recommended a very simple application. Assumptions were made at many points in order to reduce the complexity of the calculations involved. In most instances, we found the range of possible error introduced by these simplifying assumptions to be negligible relative to that involved in the basic estimates of income, costs, and economic life of a project. As a further means of facilitating the computations, we prepared a number of special arrangements of the discount tables.

Uniform Income

The procedures that we developed for investments with a uniform annual income are illustrated in Exhibit 9-4.

The payout period is computed in the usual manner by dividing the cash flow after taxes into the original investment. Then, since the life of the project is estimated at 15 years, the payout period is carried into the 15-year line of a cumulative discount table, and the column in which a matching number is found indicates the discounted-cash-flow rate of return. The numbers in this table are simply sums of the discount factors for the time periods and rates indicated. Thus, $4.675 is the present worth of $1.00 received annually for 15 years, discounted at a 20% rate.

It is apparent, therefore, that the discounted-cash-flow procedure involves nothing more than finding the discount rate which will make the present worth of the anticipated stream of cash income from the project equal to the original outlay. In this case, the anticipated cash flow of $20,000 per annum for 15 years has a present worth equal to the original outlay—$93,400—when discounted at 20%. Alternatively, it can be said that the discounted-cash-flow procedure simply computes the rate of return on the balance of the investment actually outstanding from time to time over the life of the project, as illustrated in Exhibit 9-5.

The cash flow of $20,000 per annum, continuing over 15 years, is shown in column 1. Some part of this must be set aside to return the original outlay over the 15-year period, as shown in column 2. The remainder, tabulated in column 3, represents the true earnings.

On this basis, the balance of the original capital outlay outstanding (not yet returned to the investor) at the beginning of each year is shown in column 4. The ratio of the earnings to this outstanding investment is 20% year by year throughout the life of the project, as shown in column 5. The graph at the top of the form shows the declining balance of the investment and the division of the annual cash flow between repayment of principal and earnings.

It will immediately be recognized that the mechanism of the discounted-cash-flow procedure here is precisely the same as that involved in a house-

EXHIBIT 9-4. Application of Discounted-Cash-Flow Method in a Situation with Uniform Income

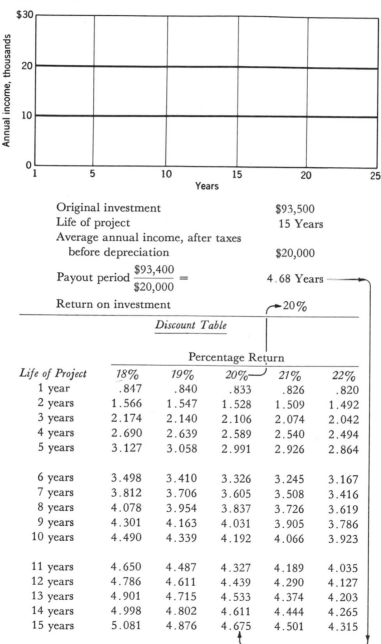

Original investment $93,500
Life of project   15 Years
Average annual income, after taxes
    before depreciation $20,000

Payout period $\dfrac{\$93,400}{\$20,000} =$ 4.68 Years

Return on investment   20%

Discount Table

Percentage Return

Life of Project	18%	19%	20%	21%	22%
1 year	.847	.840	.833	.826	.820
2 years	1.566	1.547	1.528	1.509	1.492
3 years	2.174	2.140	2.106	2.074	2.042
4 years	2.690	2.639	2.589	2.540	2.494
5 years	3.127	3.058	2.991	2.926	2.864
6 years	3.498	3.410	3.326	3.245	3.167
7 years	3.812	3.706	3.605	3.508	3.416
8 years	4.078	3.954	3.837	3.726	3.619
9 years	4.301	4.163	4.031	3.905	3.786
10 years	4.490	4.339	4.192	4.066	3.923
11 years	4.650	4.487	4.327	4.189	4.035
12 years	4.786	4.611	4.439	4.290	4.127
13 years	4.901	4.715	4.533	4.374	4.203
14 years	4.998	4.802	4.611	4.444	4.265
15 years	5.081	4.876	4.675	4.501	4.315

EXHIBIT 9-5.   Return Calculated by Discounted-Cash-Flow Method

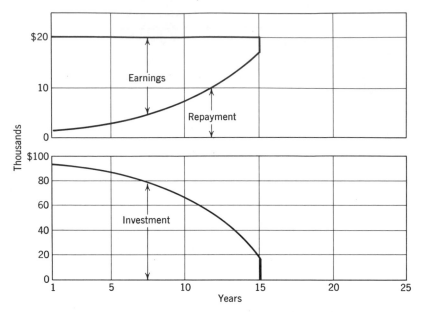

Year	Annual Income	Repayment of Investment	Available for Earnings	Investment Outstanding	Return on Investment
1	$ 20,000	$ 1,298	$ 18,702	$93,510	20%
2	20,000	1,558	18,442	92,212	20
3	20,000	1,869	18,131	90,654	20
4	20,000	2,243	17,757	88,785	20
5	20,000	2,692	17,308	86,542	20
6	20,000	3,230	16,770	83,850	20
7	20,000	3,876	16,124	80,620	20
8	20,000	4,651	15,349	76,744	20
9	20,000	5,581	14,419	72,093	20
10	20,000	6,698	13,302	66,512	20
11	20,000	8,037	11,963	59,814	20
12	20,000	9,645	10,355	51,777	20
13	20,000	11,574	8,426	42,132	20
14	20,000	13,888	6,112	30,558	20
15	20,000	16,670	3,330	16,670	20
	$300,000	$93,510	$206,490	0	

hold mortgage where one makes annual cash payments to the bank of a fixed amount to cover interest and payments on the principal. This is the reason for my earlier statement; i.e., that the discounted-cash-flow procedure gives rates of return directly comparable to the interest rates generally quoted for all financial purposes. It is worth noting that in this particular case the conventional procedure of computing a return on the original investment would have given a figure of 15%. Had the calculation been based on the average investment, a figure of 30% would have been obtained (assuming straight-line depreciation in both cases and zero salvage value).

Increasing Income

Our application of the discounted-cash-flow procedure in a situation with increasing income—e.g., investment in new service stations—is illustrated in Exhibit 9-6. In this case, we assume a build-up of income during the first 5 years, a 20-year period of relatively stable income, and a 5-year period of declining income at the end of the station's life (assumptions now undergoing modification in the light of recent statistical studies of volume preference).

To simplify the calculations and to avoid discounting the income on a year-by-year basis, however, we break the calculations into three parts. We assume that the income in the first to the fifth years is roughly comparable to a uniform series of payments of 60% of the normal level. We also ignore the decline in income at the end of the life, since it would have little effect on the results, and assume that the normal level of income will continue for the sixth to twenty-fifth years. And, finally, we assume that the land would, or could, be sold at the end of the twenty-fifth year at its original cost.

We have, thus, been able to make use of a special, and much simplified, discount table like the one shown at the bottom of Exhibit 9-6. The first column contains the sum of the discount factors for the first five years, and the second column shows the sum of the factors for the sixth to twenty-fifth years. The last column shows the present worth of $1.00 received 25 years from now. These factors may then be applied directly to the three segments of the anticipated cash flow from the project in the manner shown. The calculation proceeds by trial and error until a series of factors, and a corresponding discount rate, are found which will make the present value of the future cash flow equal to the original outlay.

EXHIBIT 9-6.   Application of Discounted-Cash-Flow Method in a Situation with Increasing Income

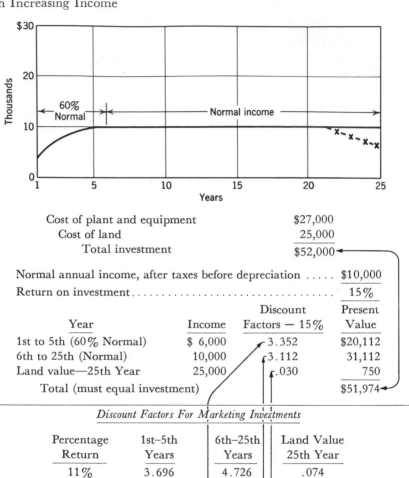

Cost of plant and equipment	$27,000
Cost of land	25,000
Total investment	$52,000

Normal annual income, after taxes before depreciation $10,000

Return on investment. 15%

Year	Income	Discount Factors — 15%	Present Value
1st to 5th (60% Normal)	$ 6,000	3.352	$20,112
6th to 25th (Normal)	10,000	3.112	31,112
Land value—25th Year	25,000	.030	750
Total (must equal investment)			$51,974

Discount Factors For Marketing Investments

Percentage Return	1st–5th Years	6th–25th Years	Land Value 25th Year
11%	3.696	4.726	.074
12	3.602	4.238	.059
13	3.517	3.813	.047
14	3.433	3.440	.038
15	3.352	3.112	.030
16	3.274	2.823	.024
17	3.199	2.567	.020
18	3.127	2.325	.016
19	3.058	2.138	.013
20	2.991	1.957	.010

Declining Income

Our application of the discounted-cash-flow procedure in a situation of declining income is shown in Exhibit 9-7. In this case—e.g., an investment in producing wells with a gradually depleting oil reservoir—we have found, again, that the cash flow can usually be divided into three pieces, with a uniform annual income assumed for each. The first year must be treated separately, since the cash flow is usually high as a result of the tax credits for intangible drilling costs. We then select a middle and end period of varying lengths, depending on the characteristics of the particular well, and simply assume an average annual income throughout each period.

These assumptions make it possible to use a simplified arrangement of the discount tables. The first line contains the discount factors for the first year alone, while the remainder of the table consists of cumulative factors beginning in the second year.

The factors for the first year and the middle period may then be read directly from the table, and the factor for the end period is obtained by deduction, as shown. The calculation proceeds by trial and error until discount factors are found which will make the present value of the cash flow equal to the original outlay—in this case 22%.

Irregular Cash Flow

Somewhat more complicated applications of the discounted-cash-flow procedure occur whenever the cash flow is more irregular. To illustrate, here are two special situations:

A. Oil Payment Deals Exhibit 9-8 shows the application when the problem is to analyze the profitability of acquiring a producing property under an oil payment arrangement.

The total cost of the property is $35 million, of which $30 million is supplied by an investor purchasing an oil payment. The terms of sale provide that he shall receive a specified percentage of the oil produced until he has recovered his principal and interest at 6%. The remaining $5 million is supplied by the new operator, who purchases the working and remaining interest and who agrees to do certain additional development drilling as shown in column 1.

The cash flow after expenses accruing to the operator from the properties is shown in column 2. Column 3 shows the operator's net cash flow after deduction of the development expenses in column 1. It is negative

EXHIBIT 9-7.   Application of Discounted-Cash-Flow Method in a Situation with Declining Income (Annual Income, After Taxes, Before Depreciation and Depletion)

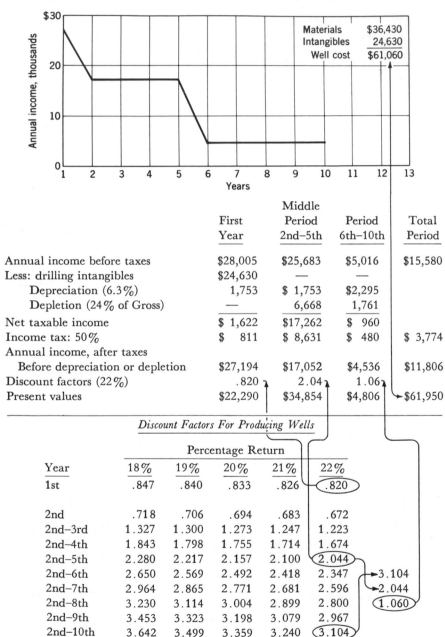

	First Year	Middle Period 2nd–5th	Period 6th–10th	Total Period
Annual income before taxes	$28,005	$25,683	$5,016	$15,580
Less: drilling intangibles	$24,630	—	—	
Depreciation (6.3%)	1,753	$ 1,753	$2,295	
Depletion (24% of Gross)	—	6,668	1,761	
Net taxable income	$ 1,622	$17,262	$ 960	
Income tax: 50%	$ 811	$ 8,631	$ 480	$ 3,774
Annual income, after taxes				
Before depreciation or depletion	$27,194	$17,052	$4,536	$11,806
Discount factors (22%)	.820	2.04	1.06	
Present values	$22,290	$34,854	$4,806	$61,950

Discount Factors For Producing Wells

Year	Percentage Return				
	18%	19%	20%	21%	22%
1st	.847	.840	.833	.826	.820
2nd	.718	.706	.694	.683	.672
2nd–3rd	1.327	1.300	1.273	1.247	1.223
2nd–4th	1.843	1.798	1.755	1.714	1.674
2nd–5th	2.280	2.217	2.157	2.100	2.044
2nd–6th	2.650	2.569	2.492	2.418	2.347	3.104
2nd–7th	2.964	2.865	2.771	2.681	2.596	2.044
2nd–8th	3.230	3.114	3.004	2.899	2.800	1.060
2nd–9th	3.453	3.323	3.198	3.079	2.967	
2nd–10th	3.642	3.499	3.359	3.240	3.104	

EXHIBIT 9-8. Application of Discounted-Cash-Flow Method in a Situation with Irregular Cash Flow (A)

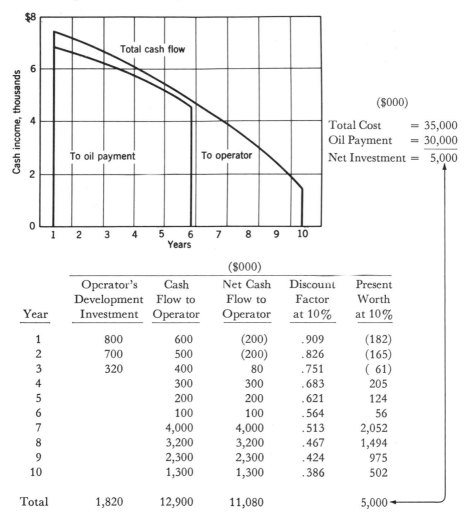

($000)

Total Cost   = 35,000
Oil Payment   = 30,000
Net Investment = 5,000

($000)

Year	Operator's Development Investment	Cash Flow to Operator	Net Cash Flow to Operator	Discount Factor at 10%	Present Worth at 10%
1	800	600	(200)	.909	(182)
2	700	500	(200)	.826	(165)
3	320	400	80	.751	(61)
4		300	300	.683	205
5		200	200	.621	124
6		100	100	.564	56
7		4,000	4,000	.513	2,052
8		3,200	3,200	.467	1,494
9		2,300	2,300	.424	975
10		1,300	1,300	.386	502
Total	1,820	12,900	11,080		5,000

in the first two years, and remains small until the oil payment obligation is liquidated. Thereafter, it increases sharply and ultimately amounts to more than twice the original investment of $5 million. The discounted-cash-flow method recognizes that most of this income does not become available until late in the life of the project, and the resulting return on investment is 10% per annum. (If the same total income had been received in equal annual installments, the return would have been 15%.)

In situations of this kind, it is difficult to see how the analysis could be handled without resorting to the discounted-cash-flow approach. The conventional methods of calculating rates of return would give wholly misleading results.

B. Water Flood Project   Exhibit 9–9 contains a second application of the discounted-cash-flow approach to situations in which the income generated by an investment is irregular. Normally, the free flow of oil from a reservoir (primary recovery) diminishes with the passage of time. In some cases, however, secondary recovery measures, such as injection of water into the reservoir, may result in a substantial increase in the total amount of oil produced.

The problem is to determine the profitability of acquiring a small producing property. The primary reserves have been nearly exhausted, and an investment of $2.5 million will be needed at the appropriate time for a water flood to accomplish recovery of the secondary reserves. No immediate payment will be made to the selling party, but he will receive a $12\frac{1}{2}\%$ royalty on all oil produced from the property, whether from primary or secondary reserves.

The calculations in Exhibit 9-9 are made under the assumption that the water flood investment will be made in the fourth year. During the first three years all the primary reserves will be recovered, and income in the fourth to the tenth years will be attributable solely to the water flood project.

As shown by the table, the discounted-cash-flow analysis gives *two solutions* to this problem. At both 28% and 49%, the net present worth of the cash flow is zero; i.e., the present worth of the cash income is equal to the present worth of the $2.5 million investment. The correct solution is 28%, because the net present worth is declining as we move from the lower to the higher discount rates. The reverse is true at the 49% level.

In general, two solutions may arise whenever the net cash flow switches from positive to negative at some stage in the life of the project, possibly as a result of additional capital outlays required at that time, as in the case of secondary recovery projects. It is important, therefore, to recognize the possibility of two solutions and not to settle for the first one found. A false solution can easily be identified by noting the direction of change in the present worths as higher discount rates are introduced in the trial-and-error calculations.

EXHIBIT 9-9. Application of Discounted-Cash-Flow Method in a Situation with Irregular Cash Flow (B)

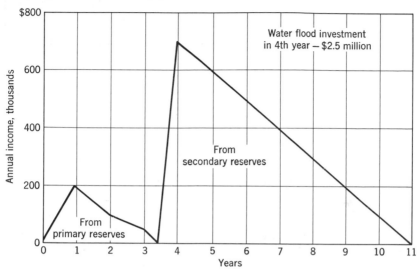

Water Flood in 4th Year   (Figures in Thousands)

	Cash	Present Worth of Cash Flow At:						
Year	Flow	10%	20%	28%	30%	40%	49%	50%
1	$ 200	$ 182	$167	$156	$154	$143	$134	$133
2	100	83	69	61	59	51	45	44
3	50	38	29	24	23	18	15	15
4	−1,800	−1,229	−868	−671	−630	−469	−365	−356
5	600	373	241	175	162	112	82	79
6	500	282	167	114	104	66	46	44
7	400	205	112	71	64	38	24	23
8	300	140	70	41	37	20	12	12
9	200	85	39	21	19	10	5	5
10	100	39	16	8	7	3	2	2
Total	+650	+198	+42	0	−2	−8	0	+1

Bench Marks

As a final step in applying the discounted-cash-flow procedure to our business, it was necessary to develop some bench marks that could be used in appraising the figures resulting from the calculations.

As a starting point, we recommended that approximately 10% after taxes be regarded as the minimum amount we should seek to earn on investments involving a minimum of risk, such as those in new service stations and other marketing facilities. We further recommended that the minimum acceptable level of returns should be increased as the risks involved in the investment projects increased. Accordingly, we set substantially higher standards for investments in manufacturing, petrochemical, and exploration and production ventures.

We arrived at these bench-mark figures by considering:

- Our long-term borrowing costs.
- The returns which Continental and other oil companies have customarily earned on their borrowed and invested capital (substantially more than 10%).
- The returns which must be earned to make our business attractive to equity investors.
- The returns which must be earned to satisfy our present shareholders that the earnings retained in the business each year are put to good use.

In this latter connection, it may be noted that whenever we retain earnings instead of paying them out as dividends, we in effect force our stockholders to make a new investment in the Continental Oil Company. And clearly, we have little justification for doing that unless we can arrange to earn as much on the funds as the stockholders could earn by investing in comparable securities elsewhere.

CONCLUSION

The discounted-cash-flow method rests on the time-honored maxim that "money begets money." Funds on hand today can be invested in profitable projects and thereby yield additional funds to the investing company. Funds to be received at some future date cannot be profitably invested until that time, and so have no earning power in the interim. For this reason, a business concern must place a *time value* on its money—a dollar in hand today is much more valuable than one to be received in the distant future. The discounted-cash-flow method simply applies this general concept to the analysis of new capital investments.

The procedures which I have been describing in regard to the discounted-cash-flow method of analyzing new capital investments were adopted by Continental's top management in the fall of 1955 and were implemented throughout the company. Our subsequent experience in using the discounted-cash-flow approach may be summarized as follows.

1. We have found it to be a very powerful management tool. It is an extremely effective device for analyzing routine investments with fairly regular patterns of cash flow, and also for analyzing very complicated problems like those involved in mergers, acquisitions of producing properties under oil payment arrangements, and other ventures that require a series of capital outlays over a period of many years and generate highly irregular cash flows.

2. We have also found that the discounted-cash-flow techniques are far easier to introduce and apply than is commonly supposed. We had anticipated considerable difficulty in gaining acceptance of the new methods and in teaching people throughout the organization to use them; however, this turned out to be a very minor problem. Once the new methods were properly explained, they were quickly adopted throughout our operating and field organizations, and the mechanics of the calculations presented no problems of any importance.

3. There is one major theoretical and practical problem in using the discounted-cash-flow procedure for which we have not yet found a fully satisfactory solution. This problem is that of developing a return-on-investment figure for whole departments or groups of departments which may be computed year by year and compared with the returns calculated under the discounted-cash-flow procedures at the time individual investment projects were undertaken. Clearly, division of the cash income or the net income after taxes and depreciation by either the cost investment or the depreciated investment for the department as a whole will not produce statistics comparable to the discounted-cash-flow figures.

On the whole, our experience with the discounted-cash-flow techniques has been very satisfactory. To my mind, these techniques represent part of the oncoming improvements in the field of finance and accounting. Just as new technological discoveries continually bring us new opportunities in the fields of exploration, production, manufacturing, transportation, and marketing, so too there are occasionally new techniques in finance and accounting that offer opportunities to improve operations. The discounted-cash-flow method of investment analysis falls in that category, and I would expect that steadily increasing application will be made of it by industrial companies in the years ahead.

Questions

1. What is meant by the term "capital budgeting?"
2. Why is capital budgeting so important to management?
3. What is the difference between conflicting and competing capital expenditure proposals?
4. Should the financial manager disregard the book value of an old asset being replaced, when he computes the net investment for capital budgeting purposes?
5. Explain why reductions in cash outflows are just as beneficial to the firm as increases in cash inflows.
6. Why is it more advantageous for the financial manager to receive a dollar now rather than one year from now?
7. What are the advantages and disadvantages of each of the following to the firm in ranking capital expenditure proposals?
   (a) Payback.
   (b) Simple rate of return.
   (c) True rate of return.
   (d) Present value profitability index.
8. Why does the financial manager rank capital expenditure proposals according to rate of return?

Problems

1. Calculate each of the following using (1) the yearly present value tables and (2) the monthly present value tables:
   (a) The present value of $5,000 for 16 years, discounted at 10%.
   (b) The present value of $5,000 to be received at the end of 16 years, discounted at 10%.
2. Calculate each of the following, using the yearly present value tables:
   (a) The present value of $10,000 for 7 years, discounted at 12%.
   (b) The present value of $8,000 for 3 years, followed by $12,000 for 4 more years; both discounted at 12%.
3. Purple Corporation is considering two conflicting proposals for the purchase of new drilling machines for its machine shop.

	Proposal No. 1	*Proposal No. 2*
Net investment	$15,000	$20,000
Estimated life in years	4	6
Salvage value	0	0
Net cash benefits after taxes		
Year:		
1	$ 4,400	$ 7,600
2	4,400	4,300
3	4,400	7,500
4	4,400	4,000
5		3,000
6		1,200

(a) What is the payback for each proposal?
(b) What is the simple rate of return for each proposal?
(c) What is the true rate of return for each proposal?

Case: Urban Press Company

Urban Press Company is considering the purchase of a new press to replace two old presses. The purchase of the new press will enable the Press Company to produce the same volume of printed material as with the two old machines, but with one less worker. Urban Press pays each pressman $7000 a year. In addition, substitution of the new press will free 700 square feet of floor space in the press room. The rent on the press room is allocated at the rate of 18¢ per square foot. No alternative use of the space is foreseeable at this time. The purchase price of the new press is $16,000. Delivery costs amount to $500. Installation of the new press will cost $2500, including $500 to dismantle the old presses. The old presses have a combined book value of $4000. If the new press is installed, the old presses will be sold as scrap for $1000. The manager of the press room estimates that the new press will last four years and that it will have no salvage value at the end of that time. Urban Press Company pays Federal income taxes of about 50% of its net income.

Case Questions:

1. Calculate the payback and the true rate of return on the proposed investment.
2. What other information would you need to know before making a decision on whether or not to purchase the new press?

~~~~~~

Chapter Ten

The Cost of Capital

When the financial manager has calculated the rate of return on the various capital-expenditure alternatives for the department or the company at large, his job is not complete. Before he can decide to go ahead with capital expenditures, the financial manager must know what it will cost to procure the necessary capital to finance these expenditures. Obviously, if it will cost the company more to raise the capital than the rate of return on the proposed expenditures, it will be unprofitable (i.e., the company and its stockholders will be worse off financially) for the company to commit funds to these proposed expenditures.

DETERMINATION OF COST OF CAPITAL FUNDS

Once the financial manager has calculated the projected rates of return for the various proposed capital expenditures, he can rank them according to return. The next step calls for a similar ranking of the amounts that can be procured from the several sources of funds on the basis of their relative costs. Basically, the capital-budgeting process is the matching of uses of funds (capital expenditures) with the sources of funds (sale of capital stock, profits, and debt financing). Such ranking of uses and cost will enable the financial manager to find the break-even point in capital expenditures. The break-even point is reached at that level at which the rate of return from a given project equals the cost of procuring funds for the proposed capital expenditure. Thus, as long as the cost of financing projects (cost of capital) is lower than the expected rate of return, capital expenditures should continue to be made. The difficulty is in determining the cost of capital.

There is much controversy among financial managers, economists, and other business experts as to the proper way to determine the cost of capital. Every source of funds has or involves some cost to the firm. This seems obvious in the case, for example, of debenture bonds on which interest must be paid. Also, if funds are used for one purpose, they are unavailable for other purposes. No funds are, therefore, free to the firm.

1. Inadequacy of Economic Theory   Economic theory of the investment of the firm assumes that the relevant rate of cost of capital is some given interest rate on money that is borrowed. However, this theory is inadequate since firms use other sources of funds in addition to debt. Moreover, as the firm borrows more money, the interest rate (cost of borrowing) tends to increase because of the added risk. Some theorists, such as Modigliani and Miller, believe that the cost of capital is independent of the firm's capital structure and that it is the same for all sources of capital, if taxes and costs of flotation are disregarded.[1] However, this would only be true of a firm that has achieved an optimal capital structure and where financial markets were completely rational. The Modigliani-Miller theorem is of little use in helping the financial manager develop a cost of capital for his firm, given imperfect security markets as well as the existence of taxes and flotation costs.

The financial manager can attempt to quantify the cost of capital for his firm. He begins this task by determining the cost of each type of funds needed in the capital structure of his firm. Each firm will have some ideal "mix" of various sources of funds—debt, capital stock of various kinds, and retained earnings or profits. The cost of capital is shown in terms of a rate rather than a dollar amount. It is best to show this rate after taxes so that cost of capital may be compared with rates of return on capital expenditures that are based on net cash benefits after taxes (as described in the last chapter). Once the cost of each type of capital (debt, common stock, etc.) has been arrived at by the financial manager, he can compute a weighted cost of capital, based on its expected future proportion of total capital in the company.

2. The Cost of Debt Capital   Generally, in capital-budgeting techniques, short-term sources of capital (e.g., trade credit or short-term bank loans) are disregarded, just as the short-term uses of capital (tem-

---

[1] F. Modigliani and M. H. Miller, "The Cost of Capital, Corporation Finance, and the Theory of Investment," *American Economic Review*, pp. 268–270, (June, 1958).

porary increases in working capital) are disregarded in capital-expenditure analysis. However, when bank loans are in fact a permanent part of capital (i.e., the short-term bank loan is renewed every year by the bank) the financial manager should consider it in his analysis. Furthermore, he must also include in each project the required addition to working capital. The interest rate on these bank loans must be adjusted to an after-tax basis, as is true for longer-term bank loans and bond interest.

The calculation of interest on bonds is complicated by the fact that bonds are generally sold at a premium (higher price) or discount (lower price) on face value and the fluctuations in market price of bonds. For example, Beta Company issues a bond with a face and maturity value of $1000 which will mature in 20 years and pays a coupon rate of interest of 5%. The bond is sold to the public for $960. What is the true interest rate? Beta Company must pay $50 per year in interest on this bond and, at the end of twenty years, must pay the bondholder $1000. It would be incorrect to state that the true interest rate is 5%. It is obviously more since Beta Company has only received the use of $960. It is not 5% of $960 since Beta must pay the bondholder not $960 but $1000 at the end of the twenty years. In effect, the difference between the $1000 and the $960 is additional interest that Beta must pay at the end of the 20-year period. Comprehensive bond tables have been prepared, based on the time value of money, to calculate the true cost. When a bond table is not available, an approximate figure can be arrived at which is reasonably satisfactory. Since Beta must pay $40 more in twenty years than it received at the time the bond was sold, the company owes about $2 per year ($40/20 years) more in interest than it is actually paying each year. (The figure is not exactly $2 because of the time value of money.) Similarly, the actual principal amount is an average of the beginning principal ($960) and the amount to be paid at maturity ($1000) or $(960 + 1000)/2 = \$980$. With this adjustment, it is possible to figure the approximate annual interest rate as follows:

$$\frac{\$50 \text{ coupon rate} + \$2 \text{ imputed interest}}{\dfrac{\$960 + \$1000}{2}} = 5.3\%$$

It is now necessary for Beta, if it wishes to compute the cost of its long-term debt, to adjust the approximate pretax interest rate of

5.3% for federal income taxes. Assuming a 48% income tax rate, for every dollar paid in interest, payments on income tax are reduced 48 cents, since interest is a tax deductible expense. Consequently, only 52% of the interest paid by Beta to the bondholders is a net cash outlay. Thus, it is possible to compute the after-tax cost of interest for Beta as follows: $0.52 \times 5.3\% = 2.76\%$. If Beta has outstanding any other long-term debt besides these bonds, similar computations would be made. The tax exemption of interest payment is known as a tax shield. The advantage of this tax exemption can be readily seen by comparing the interest payment on debt capital with dividends on preferred stock. Assume that the company decides to sell 5.3% cumulative preferred stock. If this investment should earn 5.3% the firm would have to pay an income tax of 52%, thus earning 2.76% after tax but before dividends. Putting it differently, in order to pay the agreed upon dividend of 5.3% the firm would have to earn before taxes almost 11%.

3. Invisible Cost of Debt Capital   The financial manager may wish to look further than this at the cost of debt capital. Borrowing may have additional costs to the firm besides the actual interest paid. For example, if a firm increases its debt-equity ratio, common-stock investors may view the enterprise as more risky and not be willing to pay as much for the common stock of the firm. Thus, excess use of debt may reduce the price of the common stock in the market. The financial manager may wish to consider this effect as part of the cost of the debt. As the debt-equity ratio of a firm increases through the flotation of more debt, the absolute amount of the interest payments increase even when the interest rate remains constant. Since interest payments are fixed, risk increases. In addition to the increase in risk, earnings per share may tend to become more unstable with a higher debt-equity ratio, since in a poor year, owing to unfavorable leverage, there may be little left over for the common shareholder after payment of the large fixed interest. This greater instability of earnings may cause the common-stock investor in the market to value the shares of the company at a lower rate.

In short, as the amount of debt increases, the cost of the debt capital will rise explicitly since purchasers of the debt will demand a higher interest rate because of the increased risk. The hidden cost of the debt capital will also rise in the form of a decline in the market price of the firm's common stock. A relatively high debt-equity ratio has an adverse effect on the price at which the firm can sell additional stock.

The lowered market price of the outstanding stock will automatically set the upper limit at which new stock can subsequently be issued notwithstanding the fact that the new stock issue will reduce the debt-equity ratio.

In computing the cost of debt capital, the financial manager may wish to adjust the after-tax cost of interest to include the hidden cost of debt capital (decline in the firm's common-stock price). The problem arises of how this is to be done. Some analysts try to calculate in dollars the loss in market value to the common-stock investors. They then add this amount to the cost of the interest and adjust the interest rate upwards to include this hidden cost. Perhaps the majority of financial managers ignore this hidden cost of debt in their calculations, either because of the complexity in determining exactly how much this cost amounts to or because of a belief that every firm seeks some sort of an ideal mix of capital—debt and equity—over the long run and that, as it approaches this mix, this hidden cost of debt would be minimized or would not exist.

4. Cost of Equity Capital   The cost of capital of preferred stock is ordinarily simple to calculate. If Beta Company has sold preferred stock for $50 per share and must pay $3 per share per annum in dividends, the preferred stock has an after-tax cost of 6% ($3/$50), since otherwise no payments could be made regularly by the company on the common stock. Even if no actual preferred dividends payments are made, it is the cost of this form of capital as the preferred shareholders would have a claim on future earnings for the amount of dividends due.

The cost of common-stock capital is more complex or involved to formulate. The common stockholders are generally most interested in having the highest possible earnings per share, provided that there is no decrease in the rate at which these earnings are capitalized in the market (due to risk or other factors). Thus, any capital-budgeting decision that increases the market price of the common stock in the long run is in the interest of the common shareholder.

The cost of issuing new common stock would seem to be the current earnings per share compared to the current market price per share. This is the earnings/price ratio. Thus, if a common stock is earning $15 per share and it sells for $100 per share, it would seem that the cost of common-stock capital is 15%. Actually, use of the current earnings/price ratio as the cost of common stock capital is misleading for several reasons. Investors generally purchase common stock on the basis of expected future earnings rather than on present earnings.

This is particularly true for growth stocks such as Xerox or Litton which often sell for as much as fifty times present earnings or even more. If present earnings are used for such a growth stock, at a rate of fifty times earnings, a rate of return of 2% would be arrived at. Clearly, no investor would buy a growth stock with the hope of earning a return of only 2%. The investor obviously expects higher earnings in the future.

The problem is complicated still further by price fluctuations in common stocks. What price should be used? Today's? The year's high price? Some average? What about an unlisted stock, whose price may be even harder to determine? One approach that the financial manager can take in the area of estimating cost of common-stock capital is to estimate some kind of expected earnings for the company and match this with the expected net receipts to the company of a new issue of common stock that would be available through an underwriter or investment banker. If more common stock is to be issued, the company must pay flotation costs and generally must sell the stock at some discount from the current market price if a large issue is being made. Thus, the cost of capital of new common stock must be computed on the basis of expected earnings divided by the market price of the stock less the discount and flotation costs. Thus, if the financial manager of Beta Company believes common stock can be sold for $50 per share (net to the company) and anticipates earnings to be about $5 per share, the cost of common-stock capital for Beta will be ($5/$50 =) 10%.

The dividends/earnings ratio is not a useful measure of the cost of common stock for capital for two reasons. First of all, use of dividends/earnings assumes that cost is equivalent to cash outlay. In actuality, all the earnings of the company, after payment of fixed charges, legally belong to the common shareholders whether they are paid out in dividends or retained for use in the company. More importantly, earnings, whether paid out or retained, are the main factor in determining the market prices of common stock—not dividends. Stockholders tend to hold those stocks whose dividend rate fits their desires and tax position for a certain payout ratio. Earnings statistics generally have a much greater impact on stock market prices than do dividend statistics in the long run.

The cost of retained earnings or earned surplus also presents difficulties to the financial manager. Some analysts mistakenly disregard the cost of retained earnings, arguing that they are "free." However, retained earnings (in theory at least) belong to the common stockholder. If retained earnings were paid out, the stockholder could invest them elsewhere and earn a return. If the corporation were required to pay out all profits to the common shareholder and issue new common stock every time the corporation wanted to increase its equity capital, the cost of common-stock capital would be calculated as described above. In real life, corporations, as a rule, do not distribute their entire earnings in dividends. The major reason is that the corporation does not want to depend on the securities market every time it needs some additional capital for expansion. Another reason is that the retention of a portion of the earnings by the corporation lessens the impact of double taxation on the holder of common stock. Under the existing tax laws, the corporation pays an income tax on its total earnings. Subsequently, the shareholder must pay income taxes on common-stock dividends. Thus, if he wants to reinvest the dividends in the corporation, he will have less money to invest as a result of taxes. By retaining the earnings in the corporation and reinvesting them for the shareholder, these income taxes are avoided. Thus, the cost of capital for retained earnings will equal the cost of common-stock capital less the cost of flotation of new shares and discount and less the stockholder's income tax rate. Of course, all stockholders will not have the same tax rate. Thus, the financial manager will have to estimate some average tax rate for the corporation's stockholders. If for Beta Company, an average stockholder tax rate of 30% is assumed, the cost of retained earnings will be arrived at by multiplying the expected earnings per share by one minus the average stockholder tax rate and dividing the product by the market price of the common stock. The cost of retained earnings capital of Beta Company will be: $[\$5(1 - 0.30)/\$50] = 7\%$. Stockholders with a tax rate of less than the average stockholder rate of 30% will be unhappy that the company is costing retained earnings at 7%.

Even disregarding the tax advantages (from the point of view of the common shareholder) of using retained earnings instead of selling new common shares, the cost of capital of retained earnings must be lower than the cost of new common shares. When new shares are sold, as mentioned earlier in this chapter, the company will have flotation costs (underwriting, SEC fees, etc.) to pay out of the proceeds and probably will have to sell the shares at some discount from current market price to sell them in a reasonable period of time. Thus, the cost of capital of retained earnings is always lower than the cost of capital of new common shares. Normally, therefore, a firm will use retained earnings to finance capital expenditures before it will issue new common shares. Since the amount of retained earnings are limited in any company, it is obvious that the company should issue new common shares to finance profitable capital expenditures when the amount of retained earnings is inadequate.

5. Weighted Average Cost of Capital   Once the costs of debt capital and the various forms of equity capital have been computed,[2] the financial manager can construct a weighted average cost of capital. In order to do this, however, he must know the "mix" or proportion of the various types of capital. Few companies will want a capital structure of 100% common stock and retained earnings. The cost of capital for debt seems to be much lower than the cost of equity capital. Why does not the firm use as much debt as possible? The reason is fairly simple. The more a firm borrows, the higher an interest rate it will have to pay for the debt capital. Too much debt will quickly push the cost of debt capital so high (if it is available to the firm at all) that the firm will have to turn to another source (preferred stock, common stock) for additional capital. Even more important, the cost of equity capital increases with the degree of financial leverage owing to the hidden cost of debt, as described earlier in this chapter. Over a period of time, the financial manager will develop what he will consider to be an ideal mix or proportion of the sources of capital for his firm, i.e., the combination that will minimize the overall cost of capital. From time to time, as conditions for selling various types of securities alter due to changes in the funds market, he may deviate to some extent from his ideal mix. Over the long run, the capital structure of a firm tends toward a certain pattern or mix.

Assume that the financial manager of Beta Company discovers, over a period of time, that the "ideal" proportion of capital for his company is 10% long-term loan, 15% bonds, 10% preferred stock, 40% common stock, and 25% retained earnings. Having computed the after-tax cost

---

[2] The cost of capital generated through the sale of fixed assets is generally not computed in most companies. It is usually assumed that such funds can be profitably invested in the business. Generally, they are too small, comparatively, to worry about. Furthermore, the cost of funds generated as a result of noncash charges against income is also usually ignored.

330   INTERMEDIATE-TERM FINANCING

of capital of each item and knowing the proportion, he can compute a weighted average cost of capital for Beta, as shown in Table 10-1.

As mentioned earlier in this chapter, each firm will evolve some ideal mix of the major sources of funds-debt, common and preferred stock, and retained earnings. A calculation of a weighted average cost of capital will enable the financial manager to arrive at a figure that will serve as a cutoff point on capital expenditure projects.

Thus, the financial manager of Beta Company would look very closely at those capital expenditure projects whose rates of return were not much greater than the firm's weighted average cost of capital of 7.08%. It is likely that the financial manager would set a cutoff point for approval of projects somewhere above the weighted average cost of capital, perhaps at 10%, for several reasons. First, the estimate of the projected average cost of capital contains an element of uncertainty. The final weighted figure represents an educated guess and therefore calls for a safety margin. Second, the estimate of the future rate of return on the capital expenditure project itself has also a built-in element of uncertainty. Third, the firm is not likely to undertake a new project that will just pay for itself without making an appreciable contribution to the aggregate profit of the enterprise. Risks, organizational manning problems, and the problem of possible loss of control through issuance of too much common stock may also lead the financial manager to set a cutoff rate somewhat above the weighted average cost of capital.

It is very important for the financial manager to look at the overall weighted cost of capital to set a cutoff rate rather than to do this on a year by year basis. If the financial manager considered capital budget-

TABLE 10-1.

Type of Capital	Amount Provided ($)	Proportion of Total (%)		After-Tax Cost of Capital		Weighted Cost (%)
Long-term bank debt	2,000,000	10	×	3.00	=	0.30
Bonds	3,000,000	15		2.86		0.43
Preferred stock	2,000,000	10		6.00		0.60
Common stock	8,000,000	40		10.00		4.00
Retained earnings	5,000,000	25		7.00		1.75
	20,000,000	100				7.08

ing only on the basis of the sources that are available this year and matched them with this year's projects for capital expenditures, profits might not be maximized over the long run. For example, in year one, the company might be in a position to borrow $1,000,000 at an after-tax cost of capital of 2.53%. The financial manager might approve, for example, capital expenditures with rates of return of 5% for the $1,000,000 if the weighted cost of capital were ignored. In year two, the firm may have to raise capital by a sale of common stock at a cost of 12%. Capital-expenditure projects earning returns of 9% might be available and have to be rejected because of the high cost of equity capital. If this firm used a weighted average cost of capital, such short-sighted capital-budgeting policies (accepting a 5% investment one year, rejecting a 9% project the next) would be avoided.

It is important to point out the influence of external factors on the mix of capital structure. The federal income tax laws generally make debt more favorable to the firm than equity capital. The income tax laws (together with flotation costs) again make use of retained earnings more attractive than issuance of new common shares. In fact, companies would probably use all debt to finance new capital expenditures were it not for the riskiness of too much debt, from the point of view of purchasers of bonds, and for the hidden costs of debt to the common stockholder, through the effect of excess leverage on the price of the common stock.

Financial managers are sometimes influenced by other factors than cost of capital compared with expected rate of return in their capital-budgeting policies. Managers do not always act in the best interests of their common shareholders. Desire for managerial prestige may influence building and expansion plans and may thus favor some projects over others with a better return. Fear of potential loss of control by management may lead to failure to sell more common stock when this would be necessary to go ahead with desirable capital-expenditure proposals. Timing factors in the securities markets (such as a temporary slump in stock prices) may also lead to postponement of otherwise attractive capital-expenditure proposals.

The problems of measuring the cost of capital in a small company are essentially similar to the problems in a large company with the exception that there is generally no public market for the shares of a small company. What one is really trying to do here is to increase the net wealth of the owner or owners of the firm in the long run. Hence, when considering whether an additional capital expenditure should be made in the small company, it is often enough to ask whether the return to the owners (shareholders) will be greater than alternative investments which are available to him outside the firm. What the owners can earn elsewhere on these funds can be used as the cutoff point for further investment in the firm. The tax effects should be considered in any calculations. For example, if the owners could earn 6% on money invested outside the firm, the firm would have to earn 12% before taxes in order to produce an equal return to the owner, assuming that the firm is in a 50% corporate income tax bracket.

DIMENSIONS OF CAPITAL BUDGETING

The financial manager must keep in mind the three dimensions of capital budgeting: policy, plan, and program. These three "P's" of capital budgeting must be applied to back up the quantitative analysis described above.

1. Policy   Overall capital-budgeting policy raises several questions for the financial manager. How likely is it that the proposed capital expenditure will be successful? Does our current management have the talent and time to take on the additional responsibility that the project will require? Many firms have started on projects with highly favorable projected rates of return and sufficient capital only to find that management was not capable of carrying the project to a successful conclusion. The difficulties of Kaiser in the automobile business and of Olin Mathieson and Revere when they first entered the aluminum industry are examples of this problem.

Top management must also decide, before setting capital-budgeting policies, whether the company is to be capital oriented or labor oriented. That is, should the company try to automate as much as possible or should it automate more slowly so that labor will not be unduly upset? The expected rate of return from automation may not be realized if a strike is provoked.

Another area of policy is whether the company should be a pioneer in terms of new materials, new technologies, new end products, or should it allow others to take the lead. Companies have succeeded (and companies have gotten into trouble) following either one of these roads without adequate evaluation of the resources in relation to the project.

2. Plan Once overall capital-budgeting policies have been decided upon, the company must set up a capital-budgeting plan or procedure. Such a plan might consist of each department evaluating projects according to their merits. Small projects under a certain dollar amount (such as $250) could be approved by the department head. Larger projects beneficial to the department would then be ranked according to their rate of return and then forwarded to the financial manager. When he receives the requests, a system of priorities will have to be set up, if projects above the cut-off rate exceed the amount of funds available. Other projects, even some below the cut-off rate, may receive priority (for example, a parking lot for employee morale or an unprofitable product needed to maintain the company's image or to provide a full product line).

3. Program Once the financial manager has reviewed the projects, he will recommend a detailed program, both of capital expenditures and of sources of capital to meet them, to top management. Possibly, the financial manager will present several alternative capital-expenditure budgets to top management, based on differing amounts of funds to be raised. Top management will finally approve a capital budget for the firm.

An important part of the capital-budgeting process is an evaluation of the program after the fact. Was the net investment greater than anticipated? Were the expected net cash benefits after taxes realized? Hopefully, management will improve its capital-budgeting technique for the future as a result of an evaluation of past performance. Such an evaluation also has the advantage of forcing department heads to be more realistic, since their performance will be followed up by top management.

SUMMARY

Once the financial manager has calculated a rate of return for the various capital expenditure alternatives, he must learn what it will cost to procure the capital to finance these expenditures. As long as the cost of financing projects (cost of capital) is lower than the expected rate of return, capital expenditures should continue to be made. There is much difference of opinion as to how best figure the cost of capital. Every source of funds has some cost to the company. The financial manager must somehow quantify these costs in order to establish a cutoff point for new investments. The authors of this book suggest a weighted cost of capital approach as a solution to this problem. Finally, the financial manager should keep in mind the three P's of capital budgeting: Policy, Plan, and Program.

Appendix A   RISK ANALYSIS IN CAPITAL INVESTMENT*

Of all the decisions that business executives must make, none is more challenging—and none has received more attention—than choosing among alternative capital investment opportunities. What makes this kind of decision so demanding, of course, is not the problem of projecting return on investment under any given set of assumptions. The difficulty is in the assumptions and in their impact. Each assumption involves its own degree—often a high degree—of uncertainty; and, taken together, these combined uncertainties can multiply into a total uncertainty of critical proportions. This is where the element of risk enters, and it is in the evaluation of risk that the executive has been able to get little help from currently available tools and techniques.

There is a way to help the executive sharpen his key capital investment decisions by providing him with a realistic measurement of the risks involved. Armed with this measurement, which evaluates for him the risk at each possible level of return, he is then in a position to measure more knowledgeably alternative courses of action against corporate objectives.

Need for New Concept

The evaluation of a capital investment project starts with the principle that the productivity of capital is measured by the rate of return we expect to receive over some future period. A dollar received next year is worth less to us than a dollar in hand today. Expenditures three years hence are less costly than expenditures of equal magnitude two years from now. For this reason we cannot calculate the rate of return realistically unless

---

* By David B. Hertz, reprinted from the *Harvard Business Review,* **42** (1), January–February 1964.

we take into account (a) when the sums involved in an investment are spent and (b) when the returns are received.

Comparing alternative investments is thus complicated by the fact that they usually differ not only in size but also in the length of time over which expenditures will have to be made and benefits returned.

It is these facts of investment life that long ago made apparent the shortcomings of approaches that simply averaged expenditures and benefits, or lumped them, as in the number-of-years-to-pay-out method. These short-comings stimulated students of decision making to explore more precise methods for determining whether one investment would leave a company better off in the long run than would another course of action.

It is not surprising, then, that much effort has been applied to the development of ways to improve our ability to discriminate among invest-ment alternatives. The focus of all these investigations has been to sharpen the definition of the value of capital investments to the company. The controversy and furor that once came out in the business press over the most appropriate way of calculating these values has largely been re-solved in favor of the discounted cash flow method as a reasonable means of measuring the rate of return that can be expected in the future from an investment made today.

Thus we have methods which, in general, are more or less elaborate mathematical formulas for comparing the outcomes of various investments and the combinations of the variables that will affect the investments.[1] As these techniques have progressed, the mathematics involved has become more and more precise, so that we can now calculate discounted returns to a fraction of a percent.

SUMMARY OF NEW APPROACH

After examining present methods of comparing alternative investments, Mr. Hertz reports on his firm's experience in applying a new approach to the problem. Using this approach, management takes the various levels of possible cash flows, return on investment, and other results of a proposed outlay and gets an estimate of the odds for each potential outcome.

[1] See for example, Joel Dean, *Capital Budgeting* (New York, Columbia Uni-versity Press, 1951); "Return on Capital as a Guide to Managerial Decisions," *National Association of Account Research Report No. 35,* December 1, 1959; and Bruce F. Young, "Overcoming Obstacles to Use of Discounted Cash Flow for Investment Shares," *NAA Bulletin,* March 1963, p. 15.

Currently, many facilities decisions are based on discounted cash flow calculations. Management is told, for example, that Investment X has an expected internal rate of return of 9.2%, while for investment Y a 10.3% return can be expected.

By contrast, the new approach would put in front of the executive a schedule which gives him the most likely return from X, but also tells him that X has 1 chance in 20 of being a total loss, 1 in 10 of earning from 4% to 5%, 2 in 10 of paying from 8% to 10%, and 1 chance in 50 of attaining a 30% rate of return. From another schedule he learns what the most likely rate of return is from Y, but also that Y has 1 chance in 10 of resulting in a total loss, 1 in 10 of earning from 3% to 5% return, 2 in 10 of paying between 9% and 11%, and 1 chance in 100 of 30%. Or portrayed graphically:

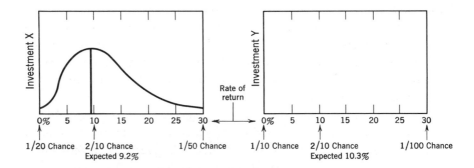

In this instance, the estimates of the rates of return provided by the two approaches would not be substantially different. However, to the decision-maker with the added information, Investment Y no longer looks like the clearly better choice, since with X the chances of substantial gain are higher and the risks of loss lower.

Two things have made this approach appealing to managers who have used it:

1. Certainly in every case it is a more descriptive statement of the two opportunities. And in some cases it might well reverse the decision, in line with particular corporate objectives.

2. This is not a difficult technique to use, since much of the information needed is already available—or readily accessible—and the validity of the principles involved has, for the most part, already been proved in other applications.

The enthusiasm with which managements exposed to this approach have received it suggests that it may have wide application. It has particular relevance, for example, in such knotty problems as investments relating to acquisitions or new products, and in decisions that might involve excess capacity.

But the sophisticated businessman knows that behind these precise calculations are data which are not that precise. At best, the rate-of-return information he is provided with is based on an average of different opinions with varying reliabilities and different ranges of probability. When the expected returns on two investments are close, he is likely to be influenced by "intangibles"—a precarious pursuit at best. Even when the figures for two investments are quite far apart, and the choice seems clear, there lurks in the back of the businessman's mind memories of the Edsel and other ill-fated ventures.

In short, the decision-maker realizes that there is something more he ought to know, something in addition to the expected rate of return. He suspects that what is missing has to do with the nature of the data on which the expected rate of return is calculated, and with the way those data are processed. It has something to do with uncertainty, with possibilities and probabilities extending across a wide range of rewards and risks.

The Achilles Heel   The fatal weakness of past approaches thus has nothing to do with the mathematics of rate-of-return calculation. We have pushed along this path so far that the precision of our calculation is, if anything, somewhat illusory. The fact is that, no matter what mathematics is used, each of the variables entering into the calculation of rate of return is subject to a high level of uncertainty. For example:

The useful life of a new piece of capital equipment is rarely known in advance with any degree of certainty. It may be affected by variations in obsolescence or deterioration, and relatively small changes in use life can lead to large changes in return. Yet an expected value for the life of the equipment—based on a great deal of data from which a single best possible forecast has been developed—is entered into the rate-of-return calculation. The same is done for the other factors that have a significant bearing on the decision at hand.

Let us look at how this works out in a simple case—one in which the odds appear to be all in favor of a particular decision:

The executives of a food company must decide whether to launch a new packaged cereal. They have come to the conclusion that five factors are the determining variables: *advertising and promotion expense, total cereal market, share of market for this product, operating costs,* and *new capital investment.* On the basis of the "most likely" estimate for each of these variables the picture looks very bright—a healthy 30% return. This future, however, depends on each of the "most likely" estimates coming true in the actual case. If each of these "educated guesses" has, for example, a 60% chance of being correct, there is only an 8% chance that *all five* will be correct (.60 × .60 × .60 × .60 × .60). So the "expected" return is actually dependent on a rather unlikely coincidence. The decision-maker needs to know a great deal more about the *other* values used to make each of the five estimates and about what he stands to gain or lose from various combinations of these values.

This simple example illustrates that the rate of return actually depends on a specific combination of values of a great many different variables. But only the expected levels of ranges (e.g., worst, average, best; or pessimistic, most likely, optimistic) of these variables are used in formal mathematical ways to provide the figures given to management. Thus, predicting a single most likely rate of return gives precise numbers that do not tell the whole story.

The "expected" rate of return represents only a few points on a continuous curve of possible combinations of future happenings. It is a bit like trying to predict the outcome in a dice game by saying that the most likely outcome is a "7." The description is incomplete because it does not tell us about all the other things that could happen. In Exhibit 10-1, for instance, we see the odds on throws of only two dice having six sides. Now suppose that each die has 100 sides and there are eight of them! This is a situation more comparable to business investment, where the company's market share might become any one of 100 different sizes and

EXHIBIT 10-1.   Describing Uncertainty—A Throw of the Dice

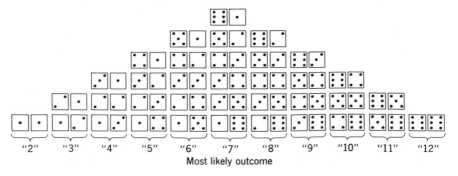

where there are eight different factors (pricing, promotion, and so on) that can affect the outcome.

Nor is this the only trouble. Our willingness to bet on a role of the dice depends not only on the odds but also on the stakes. Since the probability of rolling a "7" is 1 in 6, we might be quite willing to risk a few dollars on that outcome at suitable odds. But would we be equally willing to wager $10,000 or $100,000 at those same odds, or even at better odds? In short, risk is influenced both by the odds on various events occurring and by the magnitude of the rewards or penalties which are involved when they do occur. To illustrate again:

Suppose that a company is considering an investment of $1 million. The "best estimate" of the probable return is $200,000 a year. It could well be that this estimate is the average of three possible returns—a 1-in-3 chance of getting no return at all, a 1-in-3 chance of getting $200,000 per year, a 1-in-3 chance of getting $400,000 per year. Suppose that getting no return at all would put the company out of business. Then, by accepting this proposal, management is taking a 1-in-3 chance of going bankrupt.

If only the "best estimate" analysis is used, management might go ahead, however, unaware that it is taking a big chance. If all of the available information were examined, management might prefer an alternative proposal with a smaller, but more certain (i.e., less variable), expectation.

Such considerations have led almost all advocates of the use of modern capital-investment-index calculations to plead for a recognition of the elements of uncertainty. Perhaps Ross G. Walker sums up current thinking when he speaks of "the almost impenetrable mists of any forecast."[2]

How can the executive penetrate the mists of uncertainty that surround the choices among alternatives?

Limited Improvements

A number of efforts to cope with uncertainty have been successful up to a point, but all seem to fall short of the mark in one way or another:

1. More Accurate Forecasts. Reducing the error in estimates is a worthy objective. But no matter how many estimates of the future go into a capital investment decision, when all is said and done, the future is still the future. Therefore, however well we forecast, we are still left with the certain knowledge that we cannot eliminate all uncertainty.

[2] "The Judgment Factor in Investment Decisions," HBR March–April 1961, p. 99.

2. Empirical Adjustments.   Adjusting the factors influencing the outcome of a decision is subject to serious difficulties. We would like to adjust them so as to cut down the likelihood that we will make a "bad" investment, but how can we do that without at the same time spoiling our chances to make a "good" one? And in any case, what is the basis for adjustment? We adjust, not for uncertainty, but for bias.

For example, construction estimates are often exceeded. If a company's history of construction costs is that 90% of its estimates have been exceeded by 15%, then in a capital estimate there is every justification for increasing the value of this factor by 15%. This is a matter of improving the accuracy of the estimate.

But suppose that new-product sales estimates have been exceeded by more than 75% in one-fourth of all historical cases, and have not reached 50% of the estimate in one-sixth of all such cases? Penalties for overestimating are very tangible, and so management is apt to reduce the sales estimate to "cover" the one case in six—thereby reducing the calculated rate of return. In doing so, it is possibly missing some of its best opportunities.

3. Revising cutoff rates.   Selecting higher cutoff rates for protecting against uncertainty is attempting much the same thing. Management would like to have a possibility of return in proportion to the risk it takes. Where there is much uncertainty involved in the various estimates of sales, costs, prices, and so on, a high calculated return from the investment provides some incentive for taking the risk. This is, in fact, a perfectly sound position. The trouble is that the decision-maker still needs to know explicitly what risks he is taking—and what the odds are on achieving the expected return.

4. Three-level Estimates.   A start at spelling out risks is sometimes made by taking the high, medium, and low values of the estimated factors and calculating rates of return based on various combinations of the pessimistic, average, and optimistic estimates. These calculations give a picture of the range of possible results, but do not tell the executive whether the pessimistic result is more likely than the optimistic one—or, in fact, whether the average result is much more likely to occur than either of the extremes. So, although this is a step in the right direction, it still does not give a clear enough picture for comparing alternatives.

5. Selected Probabilities.   Various methods have been used to include the probabilities of specific factors in the return calculation. L. C. Grant discusses a program for forecasting discounted cash flow rates of return where the service life is subject to obsolescence and deterioration.

He calculates the odds that the investment will terminate at any time after it is made depending on the probability distribution of the service-life factor. After calculating these factors for each year through maximum service life, he then determines an overall expected rate of return.[3]

Edward G. Bennion suggests the use of game theory to take into account alternative market growth rates as they would determine rate of return for various alternatives. He uses the estimated probabilities that specific growth rates will occur to develop optimum strategies. Bennion points out:

"Forecasting can result in a negative contribution to capital budget decisions unless it goes further than merely providing a single most probable prediction. . . . [With] an estimated probability coefficient for the forecast, plus knowledge of the payoff for the company's alternative investments and calculation of indifference probabilities . . . the margin of error may be substantially reduced, and the businessman can tell just how far off his forecast may be before it leads him to a wrong decision."[4]

Note that both of these methods yield an expected return, each based on only one uncertain input factor—service life in the first case, market growth in the second. Both are helpful, and both tend to improve the clarity with which the executive can view investment alternatives. But neither sharpens up the range of "risk taken" or "return hoped for" sufficiently to help very much in the complex decisions of capital planning.

Sharpening the Picture

Since every one of the many factors that enter into the evaluation of a specific decision is subject to some uncertainty, the executive needs a helpful portrayal of the effects that the uncertainty surrounding each of the significant factors has on the returns he is likely to achieve. Therefore, the method we have developed at McKinsey & Company, Inc., combines the variabilities inherent in all the relevant factors. Our objective is to give a clear picture of the relative risk and the probable odds of coming out ahead or behind in the light of uncertain foreknowledge.

A simulation of the way these factors may combine as the future unfolds is the key to extracting the maximum information from the available forecasts. In fact, the approach is very simple, using a computer to do the

[3] "Monitoring Capital Investments," *Financial Executive*, April 1963, p. 19.
[4] "Capital Budgeting and Game Theory," HBR November–December 1956, p. 123.

necessary arithmetic. (Recently, a computer program to do this was suggested by S. W. Hess and H. A. Quigley for chemical process investments.)[5]

To carry out the analysis, a company must follow three steps:

(1) Estimate the range of values for each of the factors (e.g., range of selling price, sales growth rate, and so on) and within that range the likelihood of occurrence of each value.

(2) Select at random from the distribution of values for each factor one particular value. Then combine the values for all of the factors and compute the rate of return (or present value) from that combination. For instance, the lowest in the range of prices might be combined with the highest in the range of growth rate and other factors. (The fact that the factors are dependent should be taken into account, as we shall see later.)

(3) Do this over and over again to define and evaluate the odds of the occurrence of each possible rate of return. Since there are literally millions of possible combinations of values, we need to test the likelihood that various specific returns on the investment will occur. This is like finding out by recording the results of a great many throws what per cent of "7"s or other combinations we may expect in tossing dice. The result will be a listing of the rates of return we might achieve, ranging from a loss (if the factors go against us) to whatever maximum gain is possible with the estimates that have been made.

For each of these rates the chances that it may occur are determined. (Note that a specific return can usually be achieved through more than one combination of events. The more combinations for a given rate, the higher the chances of achieving it—as with "7"s in tossing dice.) The average expectation is the average of the values of all outcomes weighted by the chances of each occurring.

The variability of outcome values from the average is also determined. This is important since, all other factors being equal, management would presumably prefer lower variability for the same return if given the choice. This concept has already been applied to investment portfolios.[6]

[5] "Analysis of Risk in Investments Using Monte Carlo Techniques," *Chemical Engineering Symposium Series 42: Statistics and Numerical Methods in Chemical Engineering* (New York, American Institute of Chemical Engineering, 1963), p. 55.

[6] See Harry Markowitz, *Portfolio Selection, Efficient Diversification of Investments* (New York, John Wiley and Sons, 1959); Donald E. Fararr, *The Investment Decision Under Uncertainty* (Englewood Cliffs, New Jersey, Prentice-Hall, Inc., 1962); William F. Sharpe, "A Simplified Model for Portfolio Analysis," *Management Science*, January 1963, p. 277.

When the expected return and variability of each of a series of invest-ments have been determined, the same techniques may be used to examine the effectiveness of various combinations of them in meeting management objectives.

Practical Test

To see how this new approach works in practice, let us take the experi-ence of a management that has already analyzed a specific investment proposal by conventional techniques. Taking the same investment schedule and the same expected values actually used, we can find what results the new method would produce and compare them with the results obtained when conventional methods were applied. As we shall see, the new picture of risks and returns is different from the old one. Yet the differences are attributable in no way to changes in the basic data—*only to the increased sensitivity of the method to management's uncertainties about the key factors.*

Investment Proposal   In this case a medium-size industrial chemi-cal producer is considering a $10-million extension to its processing plant. The estimated service life of the facility is 10 years; the engineers expect to be able to utilize 250,000 tons of processed material worth $510 per ton at an average processing cost of $435 per ton. Is this investment a good bet? In fact, what is the return that the company may expect? What are the risks? We need to make the best and fullest use we can of all the markets research and financial analyses that have been devel-oped, so as to give management a clear picture of this project in an uncertain world.

The key input factors management has decided to use are:

1. Market size.
2. Selling prices.
3. Market growth rate.
4. Share of market (which results in physical sales volume).
5. Investment required.
6. Residual value of investment.
7. Operating costs.
8. Fixed costs.
9. Useful life of facilities.

These factors are typical of those in many company projects that must be analyzed and combined to obtain a measure of the attractiveness of a proposed capital facilities investment.

Obtaining Estimate How do we make the recommended type of analysis of this proposal?

Our aim is to develop for each of the nine factors listed a frequency distribution or probability curve. The information we need includes the possible range of values for each factor, the average, and some ideas as to the likelihood that the various possible values will be reached. It has been our experience that for major capital proposals managements usually make a significant investment in time and funds to pinpoint information about each of the relevant factors. An objective analysis of the values to be assigned to each can, with little additional effort, yield a subjective probability distribution.

Specifically, it is necessary to probe and question each of the experts involved—to find out, for example, whether the estimated cost of production really can be said to be exactly a certain value or whether, as is more likely, it should be estimated to lie within a certain range of values. It is that range which is ignored in the analysis management usually makes. The range is relatively easy to determine; if a guess has to be made—as it often does—it is easier to guess with some accuracy a range rather than a specific single value. We have found from past experience at McKinsey & Company, Inc., that a series of meetings with management personnel to discuss such distributions is most helpful in getting at realistic answers to the a priori questions. (The term "realistic answers" implies all the information management does *not* have as well as all that it does have.)

The ranges are directly related to the degree of confidence that the estimator has in his estimate. Thus, certain estimates may be known to be quite accurate. They would be represented by probability distributions stating, for instance, that there is only 1 chance in 10 that the actual value will be different from the best estimate by more than 10%. Others may have as much as 100% ranges above and below the best estimate.

Thus, we treat the factor of selling price for the finished product by asking executives who are responsible for the original estimates these questions:

1. Given that $510 is the expected sales price, what is the probability that the price will exceed $550?

2. Is there any chance that the price will exceed $650?

3. How likely is it that the price will drop below $475?

Managements must ask similar questions for each of the other factors, until they can construct a curve for each. Experience shows that this is not as difficult as it might sound. Often information on the degree of variation in factors is readily available. For instance, historical information on variations in the price of a commodity is readily available. Similarly, management can estimate the variability of sales from industry sales records. Even for factors that have no history, such as operating costs for a new product, the person who makes the "average" estimate must have some idea of the degree of confidence he has in his prediction, and therefore he is usually only too glad to express his feelings. Likewise, the less confidence he has in his estimate, the greater will be the range of possible values that the variable will assume.

This last point is likely to trouble businessmen. Does it really make sense to seek estimates of variations? It cannot be emphasized too strongly that the less certainty there is in an "average" estimate, *the more important it is to consider the possible variation in that estimate.*

Further, an estimate of the variation possible in a factor, no matter how judgmental it may be, is always better than a simple "average" estimate, since it includes more information about what is known and what is not known. It is, in fact, this very *lack* of knowledge which may distinguish one investment possibility from another, so that for rational decision making it *must* be taken into account.

This lack of knowledge is in itself important information about the proposed investment. To throw any information away simply because it is highly uncertain is a serious error in analysis which the new approach is designed to correct.

Computer Runs   The next step in the proposed approach is to determine the returns that will result from random combinations of the factors involved. This requires realistic restrictions, such as not allowing the total market to vary more than some reasonable amount from year to year. Of course, any method of rating the return which is suitable to the company may be used at this point; in the actual case management preferred discounted cash flow for the reasons cited earlier, so that method is followed here.

A computer can be used to carry out the trials for the simulation method in very little time and at very little expense. Thus, for one trial actually made in this case, 3,600 discounted cash flow calculations, each based on a selection of the nine input factors, were run in two minutes at a cost of $15 for computer time. The resulting rate-of-return probabilities were read out immediately and graphed. The process is shown schematically in Exhibit 10-2.

Data Comparisons   The nine input factors described earlier fall into three categories:

1. *Market analyses.* Included are market size, market growth rate, the firm's share of the market, and selling prices. For a given combination of these factors sales revenue may be determined.

2. *Investment cost analyses.* Being tied to the kinds of service-life and operating-cost characteristics expected, these are subject to various kinds of error and uncertainty; for instance, automation progress makes service life uncertain.

3. *Operating and fixed costs.* These also are subject to uncertainty, but are perhaps the easiest to estimate.

These categories are not independent, and for realistic results our approach allows the various factors to be tied together. Thus, if price determines the total market, we first select from a probability distribution the price for the specific computer run and then use for the total market a probability distribution that is logically related to the price selected.

We are now ready to compare the values obtained under the new approach with the values obtained under the old. This comparison is shown in Exhibit 10-3.

Valuable Results

How do the results under the new and old approaches compare?

In this case, management had been informed, on the basis of the "one best estimate" approach, that the expected return was 25.2% before taxes. When we ran the new set of data through the computer program, however, we got an expected return of only 14.6% before taxes. This surprising difference not only is due to the fact that under the new approach we use a range of values; it also reflects the fact that we have weighted each value in the range by the chances of its occurrence.

Our new analysis thus may help management to avoid an unwise investment. In fact, the general result of carefully weighing the information and lack of information in the manner I have suggested is to indicate the true nature of otherwise seemingly satisfactory investment proposals.

EXHIBIT 10-2.   Simulation for Investment Planning

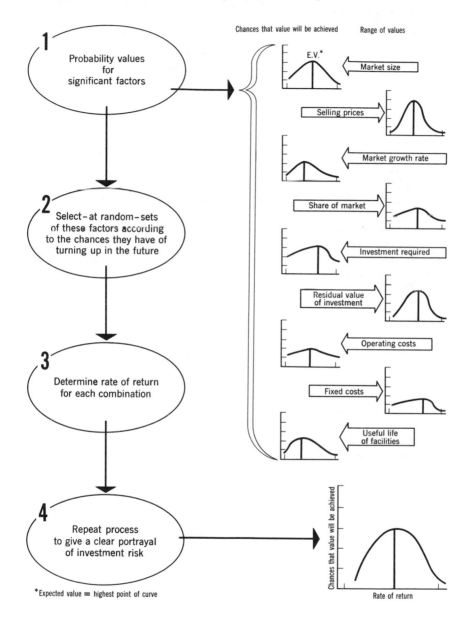

*Expected value = highest point of curve

Exhibit 10-3. Comparison of Expected Values Under Old and New Approaches

	Conventional "best estimate" approach	New approach
MARKET ANALYSES		
1. *Market size*		
Expected value (in tons)	250,000	250,000
Range	—	100,000–340,000
2. *Selling prices*		
Expected value (in dollars/ton)	$510	$510
Range	—	$385–$575
3. *Market growth rate*		
Expected value	3%	3%
Range	—	0–6%
4. *Eventual share of market*		
Expected value	12%	12%
Range	—	3%–17%
INVESTMENT COST ANALYSES		
5. *Total investment required*		
Expected value (in millions)	$9.5	$9.5
Range	—	$7.0–$10.5
6. *Useful life of facilities*		
Expected value (in years)	10	10
Range	—	5–15
7. *Residual value (at 10 years)*		
Expected value (in millions)	$4.5	$4.5
Range	—	$3.5–$5.0
OTHER COSTS		
8. *Operating costs*		
Expected value (in dollars/ton)	$435	$435
Range	—	$370–$545
9. *Fixed costs*		
Expected value (in thousands)	$300	$300
Range	—	$250–$375

Note: Range figures in right-hand column represent approximately 1% to 99% probabilities. That is, there is only a 1 in a 100 chance that the value actually achieved will be respectively greater or less than the range.

If this practice were followed by managements, much regretted overcapacity might be avoided.

The computer program developed to carry out the simulation allows for easy insertion of new variables. In fact, some programs have previously been suggested that take variability into account.[7] But most programs do not allow for dependence relationships between the various input factors. Further, the program used here permits the choice of a value for price from one distribution, which value determines a particular probability distribution from among several that will be used to determine the value for sales volume. To show how this important technique works:

Suppose we have a wheel, as in roulette, with the numbers from 0 to 15 representing one price for the product or material, the numbers 16 to 30 representing a second price, the numbers 31 to 45 a third price, and so on. For each of these segments we would have a different range of expected market volumes; e.g., $150,000–$200,000 for the first, $100,000–$150,000 for the second, $75,000–$100,000 for the third, and so forth. Now suppose that we spin the wheel and the ball falls in 37. This would mean that we pick a sales volume in the $75,000–$100,000 range. If the ball goes in 11, we have a different price and we turn to the $150,000–$200,000 range for a price.

Most significant, perhaps, is the fact that the program allows management to ascertain the sensitivity of the results to each or all of the input factors. Simply by running the program with changes in the distribution of an input factor, it is possible to determine the effect of added or changed information (or of the lack of information). It may turn out that fairly large changes in some factors do not significantly affect the outcomes. In this case, as a matter of fact, management was particularly concerned about the difficulty in estimating market growth. Running the program with variations in this factor quickly demonstrated to us that for average annual growths from 3% and 5% there was no significant difference in the expected outcome.

In addition, let us see what the implications are of the detailed knowledge the simulation method gives us. Under the method using single expected values, management arrives only at a hoped-for expectation of 25.2% after taxes (which, as we have seen, is wrong unless there is no variability

[7] See Frederick S. Hillier, "The Derivation of Probabilistic Information for the Evaluation of Risky Investments," *Management Science,* April 1963, p. 443.

in the various input factors—a highly unlikely event). On the other hand, with the method we propose, the uncertainties are clearly portrayed:

Per cent return	*Probability of achieving at least the return shown*
0%	96.5%
5	80.6
10	75.2
15	53.8
20	43.0
25	12.6
30	0

This profile is shown in Exhibit 10-4. Note the contrast with the profile obtained under the conventional approach. This concept has been used also for evaluation of new product introductions, acquisitions of new businesses, and plant modernization.

Comparing Opportunities

From a decision-making point of view one of the most significant advantages of the new method of determining rate of return is that it allows top management to discriminate between measures of (1) expected return based on weighted probabilities of all possible returns, (2) variability of return, and (3) risks.

EXHIBIT 10-4.   Anticipated Rates of Return under Old and New Approaches

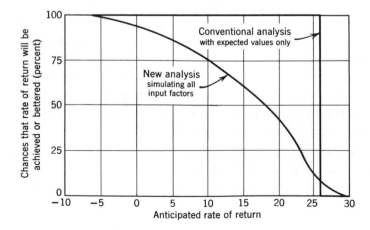

To visualize this advantage, let us take an example which is based on another actual case but simplified for purposes of explanation. The example involves two investments under consideration, A and B.

When the investments are analyzed, the data tabulated and plotted in Exhibit 10-5 are obtained. We see that:

• Investment B has a higher expected return than Investment A.

• Investment B also has substantially more variability than Investment A. There is a good chance that Investment B will earn a return which is quite different from the expected return of 6.8%, possibly as high as 15% or as low as a loss of 5%. Investment A is not likely to vary greatly from the expected 5% return.

EXHIBIT 10-5.   Comparison of Two Investment Opportunities

SELECTED STATISTICS	INVESTMENT A	INVESTMENT B
AMOUNT OF INVESTMENT	$10,000,000	$10,000,000
LIFE OF INVESTMENT (IN YEARS)	10	10
EXPECTED ANNUAL NET CASH INFLOW	$ 1,300,000	$ 1,400,000
VARIABILITY OF CASH INFLOW		
1 CHANCE IN 50 OF BEING *GREATER* THAN	$ 1,700,000	$ 3,400,000
1 CHANCE IN 50 OF BEING *LESS** THAN	$ 00,000	($600,000)
EXPECTED RETURN ON INVESTMENT	5.0%	6.8%
VARIABILITY OF RETURN ON INVESTMENT		
1 CHANCE IN 50 OF BEING *GREATER* THAN	7.0%	15.5%
1 CHANCE IN 50 OF BEING *LESS** THAN	3.0%	(4.0%)
RISK OF INVESTMENT		
CHANCES OF A LOSS	NEGLIGIBLE	1 IN 10
EXPECTED SIZE OF LOSS		$ 200,000

* In the case of negative figures (indicated by parentheses) "less than" means "worse than."

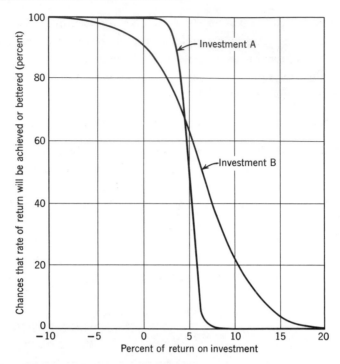

• Investment B involves far more risk than does Investment A. There is virtually no chance of incurring a loss on Investment A. However, there is 1 chance in 10 of losing money on Investment B. If such a loss occurs, its expected size is approximately $200,000.

Clearly, the new method of evaluating investments provides management with far more information on which to base a decision. Investment decisions made only on the basis of maximum expected return are not unequivocally the best decisions.

Conclusion

The question management faces in selecting capital investments is first and foremost: What information is needed to clarify the key differences among various alternatives? There is agreement as to the basic factors that should be considered—markets, prices, costs, and so on. And the way the future return on the investment should be calculated, if not agreed on, is at least limited to a few methods, any of which can be consistently used in a given company. If the input variables turn out as estimated, any of the methods customarily used to rate investments should provide satisfactory (if not necessarily maximum) returns.

In actual practice, however, the conventional methods do *not* work out satisfactorily. Why? The reason, as we have seen earlier in this article, and as every executive and economist knows, is that the estimates used in making the advance calculations are just that—estimates. More accurate estimates would be helpful, but at best the residual uncertainty can easily make a mockery of corporate hopes. Nevertheless, there is a solution. To collect realistic estimates for the key factors means to find out a great deal about them. Hence the kind of uncertainty that is involved in each estimate can be evaluated ahead of time. Using this knowledge of uncertainty, executives can maximize the value of the information for decision making.

The value of computer programs in developing clear portrayals of the uncertainty and risk surrounding alternative investments has been proved. Such programs can produce valuable information about the sensitivity of the possible outcomes to the variability of input factors and to the likelihood of achieving various possible rates of return. This information can be extremely important as a backup to management judgment. To have calculations of the odds on all possible outcomes lends some assurance to the decision-makers that the available information has been used with maximum efficiency.

This simulation approach has the inherent advantage of simplicity. It requires only an extension of the input estimates (to the best of our ability) in terms of probabilities. No projection should be pinpointed unless we are *certain* of it.

The discipline of thinking through the uncertainties of the problem will in itself help to ensure improvement in making investment choices. For to understand uncertainty and risk is to understand the key business problem—and the key business opportunity. Since the new approach can be applied on a continuing basis to each capital alternative as it comes up for consideration and progresses toward fruition, gradual progress may be expected in improving the estimation of the probabilities of variation.

Lastly, the courage to act boldly in the face of apparent uncertainty can be greatly bolstered by the clarity of portrayal of the risks and possible rewards. To achieve these lasting results requires only a slight effort beyond what most companies already exert in studying capital investments.

Questions

1. Explain what is meant by the hidden cost of debt capital. Why is it important to the financial manager?

2. It is sometimes stated that retained earnings are "free" to the company. Why is this statement incorrect?

3. Why is the cost of capital of retained earnings always lower than the cost of capital of new common stock?

4. Should you be willing to borrow money at an effective rate of interest of 10% per annum if you could earn 15% on the investment of those funds?

5. Why should not the financial manager make capital-budgeting decisions on the basis of comparing this year's sources of funds with this year's projects for capital expenditures?

6. Is the dividends/earnings ratio a useful measure of the cost of common stock capital? Why or why not?

7. What is the effect of the federal income tax laws on a firm's capital-budgeting policies?

Problems

1. Calculate the weighted cost of capital for the Upsilon Company. Assume the optimum mix of capital is represented in the amounts as follows:

Term Loan:
   $5,000,000, 6% interest on face amount.
   Company receives entire proceeds of the term loan.
Debenture Bonds:
   $5,000,000, 20-year debenture bonds.
   Interest on face amount, 5%. Company receives $990 per bond.
Preferred Stock:
   $7,000,000, 6% preferred stock. Net proceeds to company from sales, $100 per share.
Common Stock:
   $10,000,000 common stock. Present earnings per share $6.25. Best estimate of next year's earnings per share $8.00. Latest market price of common is $95 per share. Present common dividend is $3.00 per share per annum.
Retained Earnings:
   $8,000,000 retained earnings.

The company is in a 50% income tax bracket. The stockholders have an average marginal tax rate of 25%.

2. Calculate the weighted cost of capital for a large American corporation. Disregard short-term debt. Assume a federal income tax rate of 50% and an average stockholder marginal rate of 30%. To simplify calcula-

tions, use the coupon rate for all bond issues and disregard sinking funds.

Case: SASNAK OIL COMPANY

The Sasnak Oil Company is an integrated petroleum company with headquarters in Oz, Kansas. Sales were $34.4 million in 1966 and net profit after taxes in 1966 was $10.3 million. The company had a net worth of $57,625,000 as of January 1, 1967. Total assets were $64,279,128 on that date. The company has no long-term debt at present.

Sasnak is organized into five major divisions, each headed by a vice-president. The Exploration and Production division has the responsibility to find crude oil and bring it to the surface. The Transportation and Storage division has the responsibility to transport the crude oil to the refineries and to transport and store refined products. The Refining division has the task of converting crude oil (both produced by Sasnak and purchased from other producing companies) to the various products required. The Marketing division has the responsibility of selling the products through bulk dealers and distributors, company-owned service stations, and franchised dealer service stations. Sasnak also has an autonomous Research division with the responsibility of doing basic and applied research relating to energy sources and the improvement of company products.

Capital-budgeting procedures have long been handled at Sasnak in four basic categories. Expenditures of less than $10,000 can be made on the authority of the divisional vice-president. Expenditures of between $10,000 and $100,000 are approved by the president upon the recommendation of the divisional vice-president after review by the treasurer. Expenditures of more than $100,000 must be approved by the capital-expenditures committee. This committee consists of the president, the treasurer, and the five divisional vice-presidents. In addition, all expenditures over $1,000,000 must be approved by the board of directors of the corporation, as well as by the capital-expenditures committee.

In general, the capital-expenditures committee has used a return after taxes of 15% on assets as the cutoff point for capital expenditures above $10,000. Exceptions have been made for "necessary expenditures" such as repairs to keep facilities operating or to meet competitor's moves. For "risky" expenditures, the committee has often insisted on higher rates of return than 15%.

The new treasurer of Sasnak has received copies of five proposals from the divisional vice-presidents for discussion and vote by the capital-expenditures committee at its next meeting at the end of this month.

Proposal No. 1. Submitted by Vice-President for Exploration and Production

It is proposed that we buy the Greenforest Oil Company for $10,000,000. Sasnak now must purchase over 40% of its crude oil from outside sources because of our limited success in finding good domestic producing wells. At current crude prices, Sasnak could save over $1,300,000 after taxes per year by using Greenforest's crude instead of purchasing in the open market. If crude prices continue to increase, as they have in the last few years, the savings could be much larger. In addition, purchase of Greenforest will give us a greater assured supply of crude for our refinery, preventing costly shutdowns in the event of inability to purchase crude from outside producers at reasonable prices.

Proposal No. 2. Submitted by Vice-President for Refining

It is proposed to spend $270,000 to replace cracking unit D at the Oz Refinery. The present cracking unit was built in 1947 and does not yield as much gasoline per barrel as is now desirable. There is no salvage value to the old unit. Installation of the new cracking unit will increase profits (after taxes) by approximately $60,000 per year as a result of technological improvements and higher profits from sale of more gasoline per barrel. If cracking unit D is not replaced, it must be repaired by the installation of new parts at a cost of $18,000 within the next six months if it is to continue operating. Closing unit D down will cause a loss of $10,000 per year after taxes.

Proposal No. 3. Submitted by Vice-President for Marketing

It is proposed to spend $3,000,000 to recast the image of the company before the public as follows:

$2,000,000 to repaint our owned and franchised service stations in green and white, to refurbish old stations, and to install new modern plexigas signs featuring a new shortened trademark at all stations: "SASNAK" in green letters on a white oval sign.

$1,000,000 for a special advertising campaign to call attention to the new **SASNAK** trademark and our new image. Many of our competitors have modernized their stations and streamlined their trademark. Our image is of generally older stations and our trademark and signs are not up-to-date. If we do not modernize, we will have increased difficulty in attracting new and younger motorists in the future.

Proposal No. 4. Submitted by Vice-President for Research

It is proposed to spend $250,000 to set up a pilot plant to extract oil from shale in Colorado. Sasnak owns extensive shale oil reserves in Colorado that have not been exploited. With the increasing costs of exploration and production of crude oil, it is evident that the company that can first develop a feasible method of extracting oil from shale will gain a great advantage in the industry. Additional matching funds of $250,000 can be obtained from the United States Government to support this research.

Proposal No. 5. Submitted by Vice-President for Transportation and Storage

It is proposed to spend $2,000,000 to participate in a five-company venture to build a crude oil pipeline from South Texas to our western bulk-storage facilities. This new pipeline should save us approximately $400,000 per year after taxes in transportation costs to our western bulk-storage facilities.

Having examined the five proposals, the treasurer is wondering whether the present capital-expenditure policies of Sasnak are adequate. With the growth in sales and income in recent years, raising the funds by sale of stock or by a debt issue to cover these expenditures and others presently planned should be no problem for Sasnak. However, the treasurer is uncertain as to what additional information, if any, the vice-presidents should submit with their proposals.

Case Questions:

1. What additional information (if any) should the vice-presidents submit with their proposals?
2. What changes would you recommend be made in the capital-expenditure policies of Sasnak Oil Co.?
3. Establish a range of priorities for the five proposals that have been submitted. Which would you approve at this time? Why?

~~~~~~

Chapter Eleven

Intermediate-Term Loans

Part II of this volume discussed the needs of the firm for short-term funds. This involves essentially the temporary financing of receivables and/or inventories for a period of one or several months. The lender advances to the firm funds that are expected to be repaid from the proceeds of sales already consummated or projected for the near future. In either case, the transaction between firm and lender is designed to enable the former to meet its current liabilities to suppliers.

By contrast, intermediate-term financing calls for the procurement of funds that will be at the disposal of the firm for a period of years rather than months. Whereas the typical short-term loan serves the seasonal needs of the firm, the intermediate-term loan is intended to broaden the financial base of the firm for a considerable span of time.

It has become customary for the suppliers of these funds to refer to these transactions as "term loans" rather than as intermediate-term loans. For the sake of simplicity, we shall use this abbreviated nomenclature in the discussion of such transactions.

I. CHARACTERISTICS OF TERM LOANS

The three major features of a term loan are: (1) the lifetime of the loan; (2) method of repayment; (3) the underlying security.

A. Lifetime

Term loans range between three and fifteen years. The most impor-. tant single factor determining the lifetime of the transaction is the lender. Legal restrictions and/or basic policy decisions by the supplier of funds play a major role in the minimum or maximum lifetime of the loan.

For example, Small Business Investment Companies are required by law to make loans with a lifetime of not less than five years and not more than twenty years. Many commercial banks, particularly the medium-sized and smaller institutions—to the extent to which they make term loans—frequently select a range of three to five years. A detailed analysis of the lending policies of these and other suppliers of term loans will be given is the next chapter. At this point, it is sufficient to point out that there exists a fairly wide range of time for term loans.

Another element that plays a role in the lifetime of the loan is the size of the firm.[1] A company which needs, and asks for, a term loan of say, $100,000, may, in the opinion of the lender, qualify for this amount but only with a maturity of five years. On the other hand, the same lender may be perfectly willing to make a 10-year term loan to a firm that needs one million dollars. In this phase of life, as in many others, bigness or sheer size in itself seems to generate confidence in the future capacity of the firm to meet its obligations.

The reverse is equally true: the size and resources of the lender are also significant. Suppose the institution has available (for term loans) a maximum of two million dollars. Such a supplier would be reluctant to put all of his eggs (i.e., lending capacity) in just a few baskets (i.e., firms). A single bad loan could easily wipe out the interest earned on the other few loans plus a portion of the lender's capital. This supplier would, therefore, look essentially at proposals that involve transactions ranging between say, $10,000 and $50,000, with perhaps one or two very promising looking deals of say, $150,000. Since the size of the firm and loan, as previously pointed out, affect the lifetime of the loan, may suppliers with relatively small funds at their disposal tend to make term loans in the lower range of the time spectrum.

The age and past performance record of the firm also play a role in the lifetime of the loan. This fact is of special concern to the lender. A good record of growth and profit extending over the last several years prior to the loan provides a better basis to judge and evaluate the pro-

[1] A giant company may be able to negotiate and obtain a term loan for 25, 50, or more years. IBM, for instance, in 1952 procured a 100-year term loan from the Prudential Life Insurance Company. Under the terms of the loan agreement, IBM has options for accelerated repayments. Chrysler and Union Carbide are other notable cases of term loans extending over a period of several decades. Similarly, railroad companies have, at times, obtained such loans for 25 or more years. To be sure, these are exceptional cases. Moreover, although the firm and the lender apply the label "term loan" to transactions with such extended lifetime, it would be more correct to identify them as long-term loans.

spective borrower's future outlook than the same or somewhat higher rate of profit in the last year or two. The lifetime of the loan is also affected by such factors as the nature of the firm's product, the extent of its product diversification, cyclical sensitivity, and intensity of market competition.

B. Method of Repayment

As a general rule, term loans call for repayment at stated intervals; monthly, quarterly, or semiannually. Suppose that a firm obtains a 4-year term loan of $96,000 at 6% interest per annum repayable quarterly. It will then pay every three months $\frac{1}{16}$ or $6000 against the principal plus $1\frac{1}{2}\%$ interest on the outstanding balance of the loan at the start of the quarter. By the same token, a monthly repayment schedule would call for installments of $\frac{1}{48}$ of the original loan plus interest on outstanding balance of the loan at the start of the month. The payment of interest only on the outstanding balance of the term loan is another major advantage of the term loan as compared with an installment loan under a leasing arrangement. In the last case, the interest is frequently calculated against the face amount of the loan added to the principal. Thus, in a 5-year, 7% lease-installment loan of say, $100,000, the firm would make 60 equal monthly payments on a debt of $135,000 or $2250 per month. Under a term loan of the same original amount, interest and lifetime, the firm would make 60 equal monthly payments of $1981; i.e., a savings of $16,140.

Frequently, the lender agrees that the first payment will start several months after the close of the transaction. The purpose of this arrangement is to enable the borrower to put the funds into their intended profitable use. This will ordinarily involve a period of several months before these funds generate profits. The waiver of payments for say, the first six months, therefore places no strain on the current liquid assets of the firm, assuming that the projection of the firm is realized. A waiver of payment for the first six months (again assuming a four-year term loan) reduces the denominator from 48 to 42 and the monthly installments become $\frac{1}{42}$ instead of $\frac{1}{48}$.

Some financial institutions, particularly Small Business Investment Companies (SBIC's) will make term loans that do not call for periodic installments. Instead, the full amount matures at a specified date. During the lifetime, the firm pays the stipulated rate of interest at specified intervals; i.e., quarterly or semiannually.

Commercial banks usually stipulate that the term loan may be fully paid off by the borrower prior to its maturity date, at the firm's option. Some lenders—insurance companies and many finance companies—stipulate that such prepayment is subject to a penalty. That is, the borrowing firm agrees to pay a penalty of, for example, 2% of the face amount of the loan if it pays off a 10-year loan 4 years prior to maturity, $1\frac{1}{2}\%$ if it is paid off 3 years prior to maturity, etc. At first glance, it may seem strange that the lender penalizes the borrower for repaying the loan sooner than the loan agreement calls for. Upon closer examination, it will be seen that there are sound reasons on the part of the lender for the inclusion of such a penalty clause.

From the viewpoint of the lender only that portion of interest is pure profit that is left after an allowance for the cost of capital to the lender—i.e., the interest which he pays to those whose capital he invests—and the cost of operating the business of a lender (rent, salaries, taxes, etc.) Thus, the residue or pure profit retained from 6% interest may range between 1 and $1\frac{1}{2}\%$. Now the investigation of the prospective borrower, the time and talent (legal and technical) in negotiating and closing (i.e., consummating) the loan agreement are rather substantial. If the loan of, e.g., $250,000, is repaid at the end of two or three years, the lender's initial costs of investigation, etc. may easily exceed the pure profit retained during these two or three years. In other words, the loan has not run long enough to yield a pure profit in excess of these costs.

Another reason for this prepayment penalty is the lender's desire to offset, at least in part, the risk of a decline in the interest rate during the lifetime of the term loan. Suppose a 12-year loan is made at 6%. Subsequently, in the sixth year the going market interest rate for comparable loans is $5\frac{1}{2}\%$. In the absence of a penalty clause, the firm would find it profitable to pay off the balance of the loan by borrowing the funds at $5\frac{1}{2}\%$. The lender, in turn, would have to reinvest the funds at $5\frac{1}{2}\%$ and, in addition, incur the costs of investigating and closing the new transaction.

Some finance companies will make a term loan for say, four or five years, which calls for installments totalling less than the amount of the loan but with a "balloon" note due at the maturity. This balloon note is equal to the unpaid balance of the loan.

Another method of repayment—employed by some SBICs and other institutions on some smaller loans calls for installments on a declining

TABLE 11-1.   (Original Loan: 100%)

	Straight Line		Declining Payments	
	(1) Payment (%)	(2) Balance (%)	(3) Payment (%)	(4) Balance (%)
At the end of year 1	20	80	40	60
At the end of year 2	20	60	24	36
At the end of year 3	20	40	14.6	21.6
At the end of year 4	20	20	8.64	12.76
At the end of year 5	20	—	12.76	—
	100		100.0	

scale. Thus, the firm will pay in the first year (of a 5-year loan) 40% of the loan; in the second, third, and fourth year again 40% of the outstanding balance; and in the fifth year the remainder of the loan. The difference between the straight line and the declining payments is illustrated in Table 11-1.

Under the declining balance, the lender's risk (i.e., unpaid balance) is substantially less at the end of each of the first three years. However, from the viewpoint of the debtor-firm, the payment in the first year may easily prove too burdensome. One year is usually too short a time in which to digest profitably the expanded capacity and to generate sufficient profit to pay off 40% of the loan. Whether this type of program of installments is *mutually* desirable and profitable depends upon the facts in a specific case; i.e., the prospective ability of the firm to meet readily the heavy debt burden in the first year.

II. UNDERLYING SECURITY

A term loan can be either (1) secured; or (2) unsecured.

A. Secured Term Loans

In the case of a secured term loan, the lender is primarily concerned with the quality of the "security" rather than the calibre of the management and the prospects of the firm to earn profits in the future. This is particularly true if the term loan is secured by a mortgage on the real property of the firm.

1. Real Property   The security for the term loan is in the form of a mortgage on the land and building owned by the firm. The amount of these mortgage-secured loans will very rarely exceed the appraised value of the property. Banks are subject to regulations imposed by federal or state banking authorities which limit these mortgages to 70% of the appraised value of the property. Other suppliers, not subject to regulatory limitations, may go beyond this limit, although such action is rare. In fact, many lenders will not go beyond 50% of the appraised value of the property.

The lender who makes a secured loan amounting to say, 70% of the property value proceeds on the following assumption. In case of default by the firm in making the stipulated periodic payments on principal and interest, the property will be foreclosed and yield a sufficient amount to meet the lender's claim. Furthermore, the property is presumed to be indispensable to the continued operation of the firm. As a result, the firm will make every effort to meet the stipulated payments, even if the firm does not operate at a profit.

Before proceeding with foreclosure, the lender will frequently attempt to work out an arrangement with the debtor firm for a recasting of the loan, assuming that there is a reasonable chance that this measure will enable the firm to get back on its feet. Recasting of the agreement implies a new schedule of payments and perhaps a higher rate of interest than the original loan.

Mortgage-secured term loans therefore generally raise few serious problems in obtaining such funds. This is especially true if the amount wanted is not in excess of 70% of the value of the property. Insurance companies and banks provide a ready source of these loans. If the firm wants a mortgage loan in excess of 70%, it will have to seek accommodation from one of the other types of term lenders; these will be discussed in the next chapter.

2. Personal Property This group of assets includes items like machinery and equipment, fixtures, furniture and furnishings, trucks and automobiles.

The security for the term loan is a *lien* on one or more pieces of personal property of the type listed above. Here, too, it is customary for the lender to insist that the firm retain some "equity" in the item; i.e., the loan will be for an amount less than the value of the asset pledged as security. However, it should be pointed out that loans equaling the full value of this kind of asset are not uncommon.

Term loans against personal property usually evolve in one of three ways. First, the firm needs a term loan and has unencumbered personal property with a value in excess of the amount sought. It can then use the lease-back method of borrowing. To illustrate this alternative, let us assume that these assets have a value on the books of the firm of $100,000 and a usable lifetime of eight more years, and that this value represents the fair current market value of the assets. The firm wants to borrow $75,000 for five years. It may then "sell" these assets to a lender—usually a leasing or finance company—for the sum of $75,000 and, at the same time, enter into a leasing agreement. The leasing agreement would then call for periodic installments; e.g., 20 quarterly installments of $3750 plus the agreed-upon rate of interest. Upon payment of the last installment, the "lessor" would turn over to the firm a clear title to these assets. During the intervening years, however, these items would be the "property" of the lessor.

The second alternative is to borrow the $75,000 and give the lender a lien of $75,000 on the specified assets. In this case, the firm is liable for any unpaid balance if it is in default and the sale of the pledged asset(s) is insufficient to meet the claim of the lender.

The third alternative arises in those situations in which the firm needs a term loan for additional machinery or equipment but does not have assets that are acceptable to the lender as satisfactory security. The firm may then be able to acquire the needed new assets by means of an installment purchase financed by a leasing company, a finance company, or by the seller of the items in question. Either one of these may ask, or waive, a partial downpayment of the purchase price by the firm.

3. Common Features of Secured Loans   Whether secured by real or personal property, the appraised current value of the asset(s) represents the maximum amount of a secured term loan which the firm can expect to obtain. In both instances, real or personal property, the lender's analysis is focused on the asset offered as security as well as on the future prospects of the firm. To be sure, if tht firm's performance record is poor the lender may either cut down the amount of the loan or ask for additional security; e.g., a personal note from the owner(s), life insurance policies, "blue chip" common stock, or some other asset belonging to the owner(s) of the firm rather than to the firm itself.

B. Unsecured Loans

An unsecured term loan is one in which no specific tangible asset is pledged as collateral. Instead, the lender's recourse, in case of default, is to the "net worth" of the business; i.e., the excess of the liquidation value of the firm's assets over its liabilities, exclusive of the loan. Furthermore, the term lender has no prior claim to the net worth against other creditors of the establishment.

In essence, therefore, the lender relies on the capacity of the firm's management to achieve its future goals—which form the basis for the term loan—and, thus, to generate increased revenues and profits. This heavy reliance on the competence of management has a significant bearing on the relationship between lender and borrower. It changes, to a substantial degree, the position of the lender from an impersonal creditor to the role of an "outside partner" whose claim is limited to the principal and interest. As will be demonstrated in the next chapter, some suppliers of term loans become, in effect, also part-owners of the firm as part of the term-loan agreement.

By their very nature, unsecured term loans involve a substantially greater risk than a secured loan to the same firm; yet the fact remains that most unsecured loans, if and when granted, exceed by a considerable margin the funds that the firm could obtain on a secured loan. The explanation for this seemingly paradoxical situation is rather simple: "if and when granted." That is to say, the unsecured term loan calls for a determination by the lender of the soundness of the firm's projections for the future. Assuming that the lender's analysis is in substantial agreement with the facts and prognosis submitted by the borrower, the lender is ready to accept the risk of the transaction. Basically, the making of an unsecured term loan depends on the credit rating of the prospective borrower as determined by the lender. In turn, this credit rating is a function of the size of the firm and the quality of its management, with book value of equity and physical assets playing a supporting rather than a central role.

Furthermore, as stated previously, the term lender assumes the role of an "outside partner." As such, he will insist on the inclusion of a variety of covenants, restrictive and otherwise, that are designed to minimize the risks inherent in an unsecured term loan. These covenants will be discussed in detail in the last section of this chapter.

1. Role of Planning   The procurement of an unsecured term loan places a special responsibility upon the financial officer of the firm. It becomes his task to prepare the material for submission to the potential supplier of the funds. The basic "raw materials" are the accountant's financial statements—profit and loss and balance sheets—for the last five years; or less if the firm has not been in existence for this length of time.

These financial statements are year-end results. It is the task of the financial officer to relate these summary data to specific events that may have occurred in the course of a given fiscal year. For example, the profit and loss statement of a firm's operations for the last year shows an appreciable decline in the rate and amount of profit compared with the preceding year. Conceivably, in the last year the firm may have initiated an expansion of its product line by adding several new products. This program may have necessitated considerable expenditures for advertising, literature, displays at business shows, etc. Also, the changeover to new products is likely to have resulted, at least initially, in a rather low level of productivity per worker. The total effect of these and other related factors had the effect of cutting down the profit for the last year.

Or let us assume that the profits in the last fiscal year showed a modest increase over the preceding year. This may have been owing to abnormally heavy write offs of losses incurred in that period; or innovations in the product line had just started to show results; or the firm initiated a research and development program at substantial costs with the results now ready to be put into production and necessitating the addition of the funds sought in the term loan.

In brief, the financial officer must translate the financial snapshots supplied by the accountant into the motion picture that will demonstrate the living anatomy of the firm. He must also project past and present activities into future prospects in terms of anticipated sales and profits.

Next, the financial officer must reexamine the balance sheet(s) of the firm with a view to any understatement of assets or liabilities. An understatement of assets by the accountant is frequently found in the firm's land and building account. If the company has been in existence for 10 or more years, it is quite conceivable that, as a result of inflation, the current value of land and buildings may exceed the original cost. In this instance, the balance sheet has in a real sense a "hidden" or invisible capital surplus.

A long-term lease may similarly have a substantive value not shown in the statement. Suppose the firm entered 10 years ago into a 30-year lease and that in this particular location comparable rentals today are, say, 50% higher. This differential in the contract rent of the firm gives the latter a corresponding cost advantage and thus a source of greater profit. Furthermore, if the firm can readily transfer its operations into another location at about the same rental as it is now paying, the firm adds to its profit by subleasing the present space.

Many companies place in the balance sheet a nominal value of $1 on patents, franchises, and goodwill. These may, however, have a substantial current market value. In this case too the asset is understated.

An understatement of liabilities occurs whenever a firm does not reflect in its financial statement impending losses with a fair degree of certainty. An experienced lender is likely to ask questions regarding law suits, investments in other companies, endorsements or guarantees of loans by other than the firm, or contractual commitments extending for more than 3 years. The answers to such questions will quickly reveal whether or not the balance sheet understates liabilities. While the end picture will be the same, whether revealed voluntarily or in response to probing questions, the result is not the same. An involuntary admission of understated liabilities casts doubt on the integrity of management and at best it weakens the firm's bargaining power for favorable terms. At worst, the potential lender may regard the risk as too great and turn down the deal.

2. Budget Program   The projection for the future calls for a budgetary program of capital expenditures—for which the term loan is intended—as well as their anticipated impact on costs, revenues, and earnings. In preparing this forecast, the financial officer must obtain the market outlook prepared by the sales manager and the cost estimates submitted by the production manager and personnel officer. After these data and projections have been carefully evaluated by the financial officer, they are submitted to the prospective term lender. The lender will usually also request detailed data and facts about the background of the members of management, current and prospective competition, extent and nature of obligations (current and fixed) of the firm.

Subsequently, the term lender will initiate his own investigation and analysis of the firm, using the financial officer's report as an indicator of the firm's future plans and expectations. The approval or rejection of the firm's request for the term loan then depends on whether the lender's evaluation of the prospects meets certain minimum standards set by the lender. In this case, the lender not only shares the borrower's outlook for the future, but he is also prepared to take an economic risk. The magnitude and probability of this risk then become the decisive factors in the determination of the amount of the term loan rather than the net worth of the firm as shown in the accounant's balance sheet.

III. OBJECTIVES OF TERM LOANS

In the case of short-term loans, the firm uses the funds to finance accounts receivable, inventory, or both. On the other hand, the proceeds from an intermediate-term loan may be channeled into one or more of several alternative uses. These may be classified under two broad categories: (1) economic objectives, and (2) financial objectives.

A. Economic Objectives

In examining the several alternative economic uses to which the term loan may be applied, we shall start with two basic assumptions. First, the firm is contemplating a major program of expansion in the immediate future. And second, management expects the proposed expansion to generate an incremental rate of profit per dollar of investment that will exceed its current rate of profit.

1. Added Capacity If a firm is operating close to or at its existing capacity, a term loan may be used if management believes that the firm can expand its sales substantially, providing the funds can be procured to increase the capacity of the business. Or the firm desires to penetrate new geographic markets that hold out the promise of substantial sales. Another rather frequent situation is one in which the company desires to set up its own branch offices in order to serve its existing market more effectively rather than to sell through independent distributors who are carrying a variety of competing items.

Any one of these objectives involves the acquisition of additional capital assets. These may consist of machinery and equipment and, in addition, building space. After these assets have been purchased and put to use—with the proceeds of the term loan—the firm will automatically incur a series of current obligations. That is, the periodic payments of principal and interest become a current obligation for that particular year in which they are due. It is the task of the financial officer to estimate how soon and at what rate of return these added assets will generate incremental profits.

This estimated annual yield—profit plus depreciation allowance—divided into the cost of the assets constitutes the payback period. Let us assume that the purchase price of the assets is $100,000 and that the usable lifetime of the assets is 10 years. The financial officer estimates that the incremental sales minus variable costs will yield a residue of $20,000 in each of the ten years. Suppose the term lender charges 7% interest on the unpaid balance. For the sake of simplicity, we shall assume that the installments for principal and interest will be payable annually. The payback schedule will then be as shown in Table 11-2.

TABLE 11-2

	Interest (7% on Outstanding Balance)	Residue (Available for Repayment of Principal)	Outstanding Balance
Year 1	$7000	$13,000	$87,000
Year 2	6090	13,930	73,070
Year 3	5114	14,886	58,184
Year 4	4073	15,927	42,157
Year 5	2951	17,049	25,108
Year 6	1757	18,243	6,865
Year 7	481	6,865	
		$12,654 = Net residue	

At the end of the seventh year, the firm will have repaid the term loan of $100,000, including the interest, and will have a cash residual of $12,654. The pay-back period is roughly 6⅓ years. The projected yield of $20,000 in each of the last 3 years will add another $60,000, bringing the total cash residual to $72,654 for the 10-year period, ignoring the returns on these reinvested earnings.

If the term lender is willing to grant a 10-year 7% loan, the annual interest payments will be higher (starting with the end of the second year) but each year the firm will retain a gradually increasing portion of the $20,000. Its total cash residual over the 10-year period will, however, be less than $72,654, again ignoring the income from reinvestments.

2. Research and Development   To keep abreast, and if possible ahead, of competition is the goal of every expanding firm. More often than not, the achievement of this goal requires expenditures over a period of time for research and (product) development. Usually, these costs are defrayed out of current revenues and charged to current expenditures.

The following situation is, however, not rare. The firm has spent time and money in research on a particular product. The results are satisfactory and management has every reason to believe that it has achieved a significant breakthrough—in the laboratory or in small test samples. To be reasonably sure of the success, it now becomes necessary to test the item in question either in the market or in quantity production or both. The funds required for this task may well be far in excess of the sums previously spent every year on research. Management does not want to divert the required funds from its current assets in order not to endanger its current liquidity. Realistically, the firm needs capital for two purposes. First, it requires X dollars to defray the cost of the additional equipment in order to produce the scheduled output. And second, the firm needs some back-up funds to insure against the possibility that some further research may be necessary to remove the "bugs" that usually show up in large-scale production as distinct from small-scale laboratory tests. Suppose the firm estimates that this may involve as much as two years, although management hopes that it may take no more than one year. If these expectations come true either at the end of one or of two years, the firm will then need Y dollars to finance the projected expansion of output.

In effect, the firm's total requirements are $X + Y$. However, the firm expects definitely to spend X dollars now and, possibly, Y dollars if there should be some temporary delays in the production schedule as a result of unforeseen "bugs." The required term loan therefore consists of X dollars as a definite advance of funds at the present and a commitment by the term lender to make Y dollars available if and when production delays should occur.

3. Discontinuing Subcontractors   There are several advantages in "farming out" one or more production jobs to subcontractors. Essentially, these advantages are (1) no need to invest capital in the assets required to produce the subcontracted item(s); (2) avoidance of the risk that sales may fall off and hence the item(s) may not be required in the same quantities; (3) management may not yet have the know-how to supervise effectively the production of the item(s); and (4) the firm finds it too expensive to install equipment that has a far greater capacity than the relatively small quantities required by the firm.

As the firm grows and expands its sales significantly, it may reach the point at which the above cited advantages are more than offset by the price paid to the subcontractor. In other words, management reaches the conclusion that it can cut the cost substantially by producing the items rather than buying them. But to do so calls for funds not currently available to the firm. The term loan is intended to fill the gap.

The major difference between this situation and the two preceding cases lies in the following fact. Although the firm proposes to increase its assets, this does not of itself require a corresponding growth in sales. Instead, the firm will increase its internal costs—for labor, material, and depreciation—by a smaller amount than it is currently paying to the subcontractors. Thus, its profit will be increased even if its sales remain at about the present level.

4. Temporary Expansion Suppose a firm is offered a substantial contract by a public authority—federal, state, or local government—or a large private company. The acceptance of this offer calls for sizeable additions to the machinery and labor force of the firm for the duration of the contract, which may run for several years. This situation is frequently encountered by companies that are qualified and anxious to obtain contracts from the Department of Defense, NASA, or other governmental agencies. Usually, the contract provides for a unit price and volume that will, in effect, amortize the investment in machinery during the lifetime of the contract.

Conceivably, the firm may not have the funds to finance the execution of the order. A term loan then becomes the most effective means of procuring the needed capital. The absence of a market risk—intensified competition, obsolescence of the product, and the like—makes it generally fairly easy to obtain a term loan at a relatively low rate of interest.

5. Correcting An Imbalance in Assets Many firms, and at times even very large companies, are caught in a financial squeeze because their net working capital—i.e., current assets minus current liabilities—is insufficient to support their volume of sales. This situation arises frequently in a period of rapid expansion. The firm needs additional capital assets to keep up with the demand for its products. It directs what appear to be ample cash funds into investments in machinery, equipment, etc. In doing so, it overlooks two important facts. Expanding sales usually call for a sizeable increase in inventory, thus tying up a portion of the net working capital. And second, the expansion in sales may also lead to a lengthening of the collection period. This automatically reduces the firm's ability to meet its current liabilities to the suppliers as they fall due. As a result, the reduction in the net working capital of the firm—in spite of an increase in its net worth—tends to have an adverse effect on its ability to procure short-term loans.

Quite frequently, a firm will try to "muddle through"; i.e., it will attempt to offset this imbalance by a series of short-term loans. However, sooner or later the financial manager is forced to the realization that these stopgap measures offer no solution. This is especially the case if the firm continues to expand and, thus, is confronted by a gap in the flow of funds which places a strain on working capital. In fact, its short-term lenders will probably suggest the procurement of additional capital in order to overcome the inadequacy of the working capital. A term loan will frequently prove the most desirable avenue of closing the financial gap.

B. Financial Objectives

There are several reasons, other than internal economies of production, that induce a firm to seek a term loan. It must be pointed out that these considerations are not necessarily incompatible with one or more of the economic reasons previously discussed.

1. Going Public Most business firms, even if incorporated, begin operations as "closed" corporations; i.e., the stock is held by a few individuals who are the owners, management, and directors. Assume that a firm of this type has a fairly rapid growth rate. Its owners are considering, for reasons of their own, "going public"; i.e., selling stock in the corporation to the general investment public in order to obtain additional capital. However, they are reluctant to take this step at the present. This reluctance may be due to a belief on the part of the owners that the corporation's profit performance will show a substantial further improvement in the next few years. If this expectation should come true, they will be able to obtain a significantly higher price per share than they would currently receive on the basis of present earnings.

The term loan then serves a dual purpose. The firm obtains the funds to finance the further expansion of the firm. At the same time, the planned sale of the stock to the public can be postponed to a future date when a more favorable price per share can be obtained.

2. Unfavorable Capital Market This situation represents a variation from the preceding objective. Here we are dealing with a case in which the firm is prepared to sell stock in the corporation to the general public. For one reason or another, the current investment climate is unfavorable to the flotation of a stock issue by the corporation. The management of the firm is therefore advised by the broker or the underwriter, who has been asked to sell the proposed stock issue to the public, to postpone the offer to a future date.

The company is prepared to accept this advice. However, it needs the capital to finance the planned expansion. In this instance, too, a term loan provides the answer.

3. Tax Advantages Suppose a firm is considering the sale of 100,000 shares to the public at a net yield to the company of $400,000 after payment of commission and other costs incidental to the stock sale. Its present stockholders hold 200,000 shares. The projection for the next year is that the firm can earn a profit of $150,000, before taxes, with its present financial resources. If it obtains an additional $400,000, it is anticipated that the firm's profit before taxes will be doubled; i.e., $300,000.

In terms of earnings per share of the present stockholders, the two alternatives are:

1. No new stock issue
   Prospective earnings $150,000
   Corporate income taxes (federal and state)
       assumed to be 50%   75,000
   Profit after taxes $ 75,000
   Earnings per share (200,000 outstanding) $ .37½
2. Sale of additional 100,000 shares
   Prospective earnings $300,000
   Corporate income taxes (50%)   150,000
   Profit after taxes $150,000
   Earnings per share (300,000 outstanding) $ .50

Thus, looking only at profit after taxes, the old stockholders will gain 12.5¢ per share or one-third more than without the sale of the 100,000 shares.

Now, suppose that instead of procuring the $400,000 through the sale of stock, the firm can obtain a term loan of $400,000 at 6% interest per annum. Interest payments are a tax deductible expense. The picture then will be:

Prospective earnings	$300,000
Interest on term loan	24,000
Profit before tax	276,000
Corporate income taxes (50%)	138,000
Profit after taxes	$138,000
Earnings per share (200,000 outstanding)	$ .69

In this case, the present stockholder's earnings per share will be almost 40% greater than under the second alternative, which involved the sale of 100,000 shares; and 84% greater than would be earned without either a new stock issue or a term loan.

The decision to raise the needed funds through a stock issue or by means of a term loan hinges on the degree of probability that the projected profits will be earned. To be sure, while the tax angle is an important factor, there are other elements that enter into the decision whether to raise the funds through equity capital (stock issue) or debt capital (a loan). One of these elements is the desire not to dilute ownership; this will be discussed next.

4. Retention of Control   The sale of stock to the public reduces automatically the ownership of the original stockholders in the ratio of the new stock issue to the former number of shares outstanding.

This dispersion of ownership does not necessarily mean loss of control. If the original owners retain more than one-half of the total stock outstanding, old and new, they will have a majority and, thus, be "in control." Nevertheless, the owners-managers of small corporations are reluctant to share ownership with "outsiders" for a number of reasons. One reason is simply emotional. The owners-managers feel strongly attached to "their" firm and resent outside owners to whom they must give periodic reports and to whom they must account for policies and decisions.

Another reason is the fear that these outsiders may insist, as a prerequisite for the purchase of stock, that they be given one or more places on the board of directors. For their part, the owners-managers may be reluctant to share the decision-making process with directors over whom they have no control. Also, many owner-managers wish to avoid the disclosure requirements of a public stock offering. Finally, there are institutional factors—e.g., the Small Business Administration, a positive attitude on the part of banks, the development and growth of leasing companies, the willingness of larger finance companies to enter this field—that have stimulated a growing interest in term loans as an alternative to a stock issue.

III. THE TERM LOAN AGREEMENT

An unsecured short-term loan customarily involves a single instrument: a promissory note. This note is legally a negotiable instrument and constitutes a promise on the part of the debtor to pay a specified sum—either in a single payment or in specified installments—on a certain date, or dates, to the creditor. The note may be signed by one or more persons. In the case of a corporation, it is usually the president and treasurer who sign the note as officers of the corporation.

By contrast, the unsecured term loan is customarily based on a rather elaborate instrument, known as the term loan agreement, which supplements the promissory note; both the agreement and note are signed by the authorized officers of the corporation. While the note, or notes, merely specifies the amounts payable on certain dates, the agreement contains a series of provisions, known as covenants, which spell out in detail various actions that the firm agrees to take as well as actions that the management of the firm agrees not to take.

A. Restrictions on Management

Both the positive and negative covenants involve future financial decisions of the firm. Their effect is to circumscribe and, in some areas, to restrict the financial decision-making powers of management. They are designed to inhibit actions by the debtor-firm which are likely to endanger its liquidity and engender the risk of failure and bankruptcy. These covenants set up a series of benchmarks that a sophisticated financial officer would and should observe. In a real sense, therefore, the term lender superimposes on top management the obligation to observe and comply with financial criteria that experience has demonstrated to be sound.

B. Agreement Is Tailor-Made

The scope and nature of the covenants differ among lenders. Furthermore, a given lender will usually adapt the details of a particular covenant to the specific situation of the individual borrower. In other words, the lender may widen or narrow the decision-making powers of management in a particular financial area depending on the age and size of the firm, the amount of the loan in relation to net worth, the financial know-how of top management, etc. Although each agreement is tailored to a specific borrower, the differences are a matter of degree rather than of kind.

The following discussion of the major covenants, positive and negative, must therefore be looked upon as a "norm" with deviations in degree the rule rather than the exception.

C. Positive Covenants

In this portion of the loan agreement, the firm obligates itself to make available to the lender specific financial and operational information.

1. Financial Statements   Operating statement for each fiscal quarter must be supplied within 30 to 45 days after the close of the quarter. These statements are prepared by the controller of the firm. The lender usually reserves the right, at his discretion, to assign his own accountant to inspect the records and verify the statement.

At the end of the fiscal year, the firm must provide the lender, within a stipulated period after the close of the fiscal year, with an income statement for the year as well as with a balance sheet. Both must be audited and prepared by a firm of certified public accountants that is acceptable to the lender.

In addition to financial statements, the term lender will frequently require the submission of a cash-flow forecast (cash budget) for the fiscal year. This requirement serves a dual purpose. It provides the lender with a translation into financial terms of the firm's production and/or marketing program for the next fiscal year. An analysis of this cash forecast enables both lender and borrower to determine whether and to what extent the firm will require short-term credits from financial institutions, suppliers, or both. This advance knowledge makes it possible for the lender to point out to the management of the firm any undue risks of excessive short-term indebtedness that the cash-flow forecast may generate. Conceivably, the lender may, after discussions with the firm, decide to permit the borrower to incur such excessive short-term debts for a limited time and waive, for this period, the restrictive clause on such debts.

The second objective in requiring a cash-flow forecast is more "subtle." It furnishes the lender with a yardstick to measure the ability of management to plan with a fair degree of probability. In the last analysis, the cash forecast reflects the firm's evaluation of its market prospects for the coming fiscal year. By comparing the cash forecast submitted prior to the fiscal year with the quarterly statements in the course of the fiscal year the lender can measure anticipation against realization. Thus, he can determine the degree of reliability that he can attach to the firm's capacity to plan for the future. We must bear in mind that the term lender expects the firm to expand appreciably with the aid of the term loan and perhaps to come back for more money well before the loan is repaid in order to maintain its pace of growth.

2. Inspection   Every unsecured term loan involves an element of risk for the lender. The right to inspect the property and records of the firm enables the lender, if and when he deems it desirable or necessary, to make sure that the company actually has the assets shown in the statements and that these assets are in good physical condition. This inspection may be essential in the course of the fiscal year since, as a general rule, audited statements are required only for the end of the fiscal year. During the 12-month interval, the lender depends entirely on the borrower's quarterly statements.

3. Insurance and Maintenance   Adequate insurance coverage is imperative as protection against losses from fire, flood, and a variety of other external causes as well as lawsuits involving liability for personal injuries and property damages. The aggregate of insurance premiums can be fairly substantial. Failure to maintain sufficient coverage may, in the case of an actual incident, involve the firm in heavy losses or liability and, in extreme cases, force it into bankruptcy.

To eliminate these risks the loan agreement usually stipulates the types and extent of insurance coverage and requires the firm to maintain this insurance during the lifetime of the loan.

Replacement of worn-out equipment and furniture, sufficient repairs on fixed assets and their proper maintenance are essential for the preservation of the productive capacity of the firm. These expenses are likely to be fairly small in the case of new or recently acquired new assets. However, they tend to go up rather sharply in the course of time since these assets are "used up" in the operations of the firm.

If the firm makes insufficient provision for replacement, repairs, and maintenance, it will magnify its profits by the amount of these omitted expenditures. At the same time, it is likely that the failure to make these expenditures at the proper time will accelerate the rate of actual wear and tear. Thus, the financial costs in the future, and their adverse effect on profits, will also be magnified.

Therefore, the term lender has a direct interest in the proper preservation of the firm's assets over the whole lifetime of the loan.

4. Representation on Board   The board of directors is usually the ultimate body within the firm to make major policy decisions. Therefore, many term lenders regard it as important to be represented at directors' meetings. This affords them a better insight into the problems, performance, and policies of the debtor firm than can be obtained from an analysis of financial statements.

The form of this representation on the board differs among term lenders. Some demand, as part of the loan agreement, that one or more representatives of the lender be elected as board members. Others will reserve the right to ask for such election if and when they deem it desirable. And finally, some lenders merely insist on the right to delegate a representative who sits in as an observer rather than as a voting board member.

D. Negative Covenants

This portion of the loan agreement sets forth those actions that management may not take. Failure to comply with any one of these restraints gives the lender the right to call for immediate payment of the unpaid balance.

1. Working Capital Requirement   The borrower is required to maintain at all times a specified minimum working capital; i.e., cash, receivables, and inventory. This minimum is usually expressed in terms of dollars. The usual procedure in fixing the minimum dollar amount is illustrated in the following example.

At the time of the loan agreement, the firm has a working capital of $400,000. The term loan is for $500,000. Of this amount, the firm, according to the projection submitted to the lender, expects to spend $300,000 for fixed assets and to channel the balance of $200,000 into working capital. Its total working capital will then be $600,000. The typical agreement will then provide that the working capital shall at no time be less than 80% or, roughly, $500,000.

By providing a "floor" of $500,000, the lender wants to reduce the risk of future nonliquidity. At the same time, the borrowing firm is given an "elbow room" of $100,000. This is intended to provide a cushion or reserve for addtional fixed investments that may prove necessary at some future time.

2. Outside Borrowings   As a general rule, the firm is restrained from borrowing long-term funds, either secured or unsecured, during the lifetime of the agreement. This prohibition also applies to the acquisition of buildings, machinery, and equipment either on the installment plan, on lease-purchase, or other similar plans. The reason behind this provision is simple. The term lender does not want the firm to incur financial obligations for interest and principal that may become a heavy drain on its working capital. Also, an unsecured lender does not want to run the risk that some of the fixed assets of the firm may be foreclosed by a secured creditor if the firm defaults in payments to other creditors.

Restrictions are much less severe on short-term borrowing from banks. Usually, the agreement provides that the firm shall be free of short-term bank debts for a period of at least 30 days in every fiscal year. In this way, the term lender can be reasonably sure that these bank loans are used by the firm only to meet seasonal requirements; i.e., when the cash inflow from receivables temporarily lags behind the cash outflow on payables.

Frequently, the loan agreement prohibits the firm from selling or discounting its receivables except for the face value of these receivables.

3. Loans and Investments   Here the restriction applies to loans or investments by the firm. The firm is prohibited from making loans to its officers or investments in other corporations. A similar restriction applies to long-term investments in other firms. These actions reduce the funds at the disposal of the firm. Thus, their effect is to lower the firm's liquidity and to create the risk of a severe financial squeeze.

4. Dividends   The firm is usually limited to a distribution of dividends out of earnings to one-half of these earnings. The remainder must be retained as part of the earned surplus. In this way, the net worth, and thus the safety of the term loan, rises as the firm operates profitably. At the same time, the firm has this retained portion of the profits available for additional investments in fixed assets or for increased working capital.

5. Managerial Compensation   Loan agreements frequently limit increases in the salaries of the officers to a percentage of the profits after taxes but before dividends. This restriction is designed to inhibit the management of a closely held corporation from circumventing the limitation on dividends by granting substantial salary increases to the officers. Here, too, the objective is to assure an expanding financial base for the firm rather than permit an excessive disbursement of earnings.

6. Long-Term Leases   Rentals for building and office space constitute fixed expenses and, thus, a regular drain on the cash funds of the firm. Loan agreements therefore often prohibit the conclusion of leases with a lifetime in excess of 3 years. The 3-year limit is based on the assumption that management can anticipate, with a fair degree of certainty, its actual space needs for 2 or 3 years ahead. Thus, a rental agreement for a limited period engenders no unreasonable risk of miscalculating space needs and paying a rental for space that is substantially in excess of requirements.

7. Mergers   A merger of the borrowing firm with another company may or may not be advantageous to the firm. The answer depends on a variety of factors; e.g., financial structure, competence of management, nature of the business of the second company in relation to the borrowing firm. A "bad deal" clearly endangers the term loan. The prohibition against mergers is intended to eliminate this risk.

An Overall View.   Divorced from their objectives and underlying reasons, and covenants, singly or in the aggregate, clearly represent severe restrictions on the decision-making powers of the firm. But when viewed from the perspective of sound financial management, the opposite conclusion emerges.

Each of the covenants discussed above reflects sound principles derived from experience. Many term lenders had to learn the hard way that the art of financial management is not a by-product of rapid growth and substantial profits. If the top management of a firm has mastered this art, it will accept these covenants as guideposts that this management would observe of its own volition with or without a term loan. On the other hand, a firm that lacks competency in the art of financial management requires the imposition of these covenants to protect the mangement against its own deficiencies.

It must also be pointed out that term lenders generally are flexible during the lifetime of the agreement. With the passage of time, they have an opportunity to evaluate management in its actual operations. In consequence, the term lender is in a position to appraise the soundness of the firm's subsequent request to modify or waive one or more of the covenants in the light of new developments.

Although the following point is not spelled out in the loan agreement, it is usually stressed by the term lender in the course of the negotiations. Most term lenders look upon the transaction as a prelude to larger loans long before the particular loan reaches maturity. They anticipate a substantial growth of the firm as a direct result of the loan. They also expect that, in many cases, this expansion will generate a need for additional term financing.

SUMMARY

Intermediate term financing calls for the procurement of funds which will be at the disposal of the firm for a period of years rather than months. The intermediate term loan is intended to broaden the financial base of the firm for a considerable span of time. The three major features of a term loan are: the lifetime of the loan, the method of repayment, and the underlying security.

A term loan can be either secured or insecured. In the case of a secured term loan, the lender is primarily concerned with the quality of the "security" rather than with the calibre of the management and the prospects of the firm to earn profits in the future, especially if the term loan is secured by a real estate mortgage. Thus, the lender's analysis is focused on the asset offered as security as well as on the future prospects of the firm. In the case of an unsecured term loan, no specific tangible asset is pledged as collateral. Instead, the lender's recourse is to the "net worth" of the business. Thus, the lender relies more on the capacity of the firm's management to achieve its future goals than the lender of a secured loan does.

The objectives of the term loan may be economic (for example, adding capacity, providing for research and development, or temporary expansion) or financial (for instance, preparing to go public, tax advantages, or retaining control).

The financial manager, together with the banker, must carefully tailor a term loan agreement to meet the needs of the company while protecting the lender. The agreement contains covenants spelling out in detail various actions that the firm agrees to take as well as actions that management agrees not to take. These covenants are designed to restrict the financial decision-making powers of management in some areas so as to protect the banker from actions that might lead to a lack of liquidity or even bankruptcy. Lenders generally require covenants covering the furnishing of quality financial statements and cash flow forecasts, the right of inspection, insurance, working capital requirements, the limit on outside borrowing, and the limit on dividends and salaries. The purpose of covenants is not to hamper management—most covenants have been found to be consistent with normal good financial management. Generally also, the lender will be flexible if conditions change so as to enhance the possibilities of repayment or to encourage future business with the borrower. The financial manager, at the time the loan is negotiated, can often prevent undue restrictions from being inserted in the loan agreement, as the agreement is tailor-made by the lender for the specific loan and company.

Questions

1. How does an intermediate-term loan differ from a short-term loan?
2. Why do some lenders charge a penalty for prepayment of term-loan principal before the date stipulated in the loan agreement?
3. What types of security are used for term loans? What are the advantages and disadvantages of each type?
4. Why are some lenders willing to make unsecured term loans?
5. How does a firm use the proceeds of a term loan?
6. What is the difference between a note for a term loan and the term-loan agreement?
7. Why does a lender require covenants as a condition for granting a term loan?
8. What are the advantages of requiring a borrower to prepare a cash-flow forecast (cash budget) before granting a term loan?
9. Why do lenders wish to be represented on boards of directors of borrowing firms? Is this desirable from the point of view of the borrower?
10. Discuss the working capital requirements usually found in term-loan covenants.
11. If a firm plans eventually to issue more common stock to replace an intermediate-term loan, why should the firm enter into a term loan at all?

Problems

1. State National Bank is willing to make the Alpha Company a term loan of $8000, repayable in 18 monthly installments of $475 each. What is the approximate effective rate of interest that Alpha will have to pay? What is the dollar cost of interest charged?
2. Sigma Corporation, a small distributor of automotive electrical products, has applied to the Third State Bank for a two-year term loan of $50,000 beginning July 1, 1967, in order to finance an expected continued increase of sales. Sigma already has an outstanding loan of $25,000 from the Third State Bank. The company owns no real estate.

TABLE 11-3.   Sigma Corporation: Balance Sheet June 1, 1967 (Dollars)

Assets		Liabilities	
Cash	900	Bank loan	25,000
Net accounts receivable	67,258	Notes payable to trade	41,275
Inventory	141,975	Accounts payable	81,520
Equipment (after depreciation)	8,920	Other liabilities	728
		Stockholder's equity	70,530
	219,053		219,053

Estimated sales for the fiscal year beginning June 1, 1967 are between $775,000 and $1,150,000. Approximately 75% of sales are made between April 1 and October 30. It is estimated that cost of sales and other expenses will increase in the same relative proportion as sales increase. The 1967 balance sheet and income statement for Sigma Corporation are shown in Tables 11-3 and 11-4.

TABLE 11-4.   Sigma Corporation: Income Statement for Year Ended June 1, 1967 (Dollars)

Sales	742,883
Cost of Sales	643,792
Gross margin	99,091
Other expenses	56,279
Net profit before taxes	42,812
Federal and State taxes	21,406
Net income after taxes	21,406

(a) Should the bank make the term loan on the basis of the information presented?

(b) What additional information should the bank ask for?

(c) Assuming the bank makes the loan, what covenants should the bank insert in the loan agreement? What collateral should be required? What repayment schedule would you suggest?

Case: GENERAL BURIAL VAULT COMPANY

General Burial Vault Company is in the business of making concrete burial vaults in a medium-sized city in the Midwest. Most orders are for concrete vaults known in the trade as casket liners in which the casket is placed at the time of earth burial. Cemeteries sometimes encourage or require use of casket liners in order to reduce cemetery maintenance costs arising from the substance of the soil after burial. Undertakers, who receive a good margin on the sale of casket liners, often promote their use on psychological grounds (casket liners prevent moisture from reaching the casket). Health groups sometimes advocate use of casket liners for sanitary reasons.

The city council has recently passed an ordinance requiring use of casket liners in the municipal cemetery in the city in which General Burial Vault Company is located. The owners of the company believe sales will increase at least 30% as a result of the new ordinance. In order to meet the expected demand, it will be necessary to install new machinery at a cost of $30,000. This machinery can be paid for out of the expected future profits in about 3½ years.

One partner favors a four-year term loan to finance the machinery. A term loan would probably call for a 6% interest rate. The bank would also require the firm to maintain current assets greater than 125% of the long-term debt outstanding, and maintain a 2 to 1 current ratio. Other long-term liabilities would be subordinated until the term loan was repaid. Principal would have to be repaid quarterly in equal amounts beginning after one year.

A second partner favors use of short-term bank credit to finance the machinery. The firm maintains accounts at two local banks. Both banks would be willing to increase the firm's line of credit or make the term loan. Interest rates on short-term financing (less than one year) are currently at a rate of 5¾%. Since, on short-term financing, it is generally necessary for the firm to completely pay off all loans to a bank during at least one month out of the year, the second partner recommends alternating the borrowing between the two banks on a series of six or nine-month loans.

The first partner argues that use of short-term credit for long-term assets is unsound financial policy, even though the cost may be lower. He wonders whether the risks of such a policy might not be too great. In addition, the short-term interest rate may increase in future years. The six percent interest rate in the term loan is guaranteed for the period of the loan.

The second partner points out that use of a term loan might result in the company holding more cash than it needs, especially if sales increase faster than forecasted. Furthermore, the financial restrictions imposed upon the firm by the term-loan agreement might reduce the firm's financial flexibility in the future.

The third partner must decide which method of financing he should favor for the machinery. Since all decisions are taken by majority vote of the three partners, his vote will make the decision.

Table 11-5 shows the balance sheet of the General Burial Vault Company for the year ending December 31, 1966.

TABLE 11-5. General Burial Vault Company: Balance Sheet, December 31, 1966 (Dollars)

Assets		
Cash	3,278	
Accounts receivable	18,503	
Inventory: raw materials	7,219	
Inventory: work in process	3,251	
Inventory: finished goods	8,982	
Total current assets		41,233
Land and buildings, net		15,750
Equipment, net		27,520
Other assets		1,231
Total assets		85,734
Liabilities and Equity		
Accounts payable	12,529	
Bank loans	3,158	
Federal income taxes payable	4,789	
Total current liabilities		20,476
Loan: N. Elkins		15,000
Loan: T. Davies		5,000
Total liabilities		40,476
Equity: partner 1		15,086
partner 2		15,086
partner 3		15,086
Total liabilities and equity		85,734

Case Questions:

1. Compare the conditions and restrictions required by the term loan with those implicit in the short-term credit.
2. List the risks to General Burial Vault Company of the two alternatives. Which method of financing is likely to be riskier to the Company?
3. What decision would you make if you were the third partner? Why?

~~~~~~

Chapter Twelve

Suppliers of Term Loans

As in the case of short-term funds, there are a number of distinct groups of term lenders seeking and competing for this business. The major sources, or suppliers, are (1) commercial banks; (2) life insurance companies; (3) finance companies; (4) the Small Business Administration (a governmental agency); (5) investment companies; and (6) government licensed but privately operated Small Business Investment Companies. Each of these sources of term funds has its own unique objectives, criteria, and policies in making loans. To be sure, within each of these groups there are differences among the individual lenders. However, these are differences in degree rather than in basic principles.

A. Commercial Banks

The majority of banks do not make term loans. Two reasons account for their absence from this market. First, and most important, the management of a term-loan portfolio calls for special training and skill quite different from those required in the making of short-term loans. A competent term-loan officer commands a salary substantially greater than a credit officer. And second, the majority of banks do not have the capital to set up a separate department for term loans. Many banks also find that the demand for these loans is insufficient in their respective communities to justify the expenses of a separate department and the allocation of funds for its operations.

Banks that engage in term lending are usually fairly large with adequate resources in capital and manpower to set up such a specialized department.

1. Bank's Objective From the viewpoint of the commercial bank, its major and primary area of operations involves short-term services;

i.e., checking accounts and short-term credit. Term lending, like other services of the bank, holds a secondary rank. The basic purpose of these services is best described in the slogan "a one-stop bank;" i.e., the customer will find available under one roof all the services that a commercial bank can legally and effectively perform.

The term-loan department, although set up usually as a separate unit, is designed to serve the regular bank customer. That is, it serves the firm that maintains its checking account with the institution, procures short-term loans whenever needed, and then finds it necessary to seek a loan with a lifetime of years rather than months. Frequently, it is the short-term loan officer who suggests to the firm the desirability of procuring a term loan. He subsequently acts as liaison between the firm and the term-loan department in the early stages of negotiations.

2. Tie-in with Credit Department   Although the term-loan officer makes his own independent determination on the loan application of the firm, there are several important functions that the credit officer performs for the term-loan department. One of these has already been noted: the preliminary screening of the firm, especially its past record of borrowing and repayment of loans. Next, the files of the credit department often contain valuable information about the firm's plans in the past, which were submitted in conjunction with its requests for bank credit, and the department's subsequent observations on the firm's actual performance. A good record as a short-term borrower, while not decisive, plays an important role in the evaluation of the risk of the term loan.

It is taken for granted that the firm will continue to ask, and obtain, short-term loans to meet its seasonal cash needs. These requirements may actually increase in magnitude, especially if the proceeds of the term loans are used largely for expansion of productive capacity rather than for broadening of the working capital base of the firm. In either event, the continued credit relationship between the bank and the firm places the credit officer in a strategic position to supply the term-loan department with current information about the firm. This flow of intelligence facilitates significantly the task of the term-loan department to "police" the debtor firm. In fact, the credit officer performs this task in conjunction with his own subsequent decisions to extend short-term loans to the firm.

3. Attracting New Accounts   By means of the term loan, the bank expects to gain new customers for its regular banking business: checking accounts, extension of credit, trust department, etc. That is, the term-loan department will entertain applications from firms who are not customers of the bank. In these instances, it will clearly indicate to the firm that the opening of an account in the bank is expected if the loan is approved. That does not mean that the firm must break off its existing relationship to one or more other banks. Instead, what the potential term lender desires, and expects, is to obtain a fair share of the firm's banking business.

4. Lending Policies   It is customary to express a term loan in relation to the firm's net worth. There exists no uniform cut-off point on term loans, as in the case of real estate mortgages for which the regulatory authorities have fixed the maximum percentage of the mortgage in relation to the value of the property.[1]

However, most banks appear to follow an unwritten rule not to make term loans in excess of seventy percent of the firm's net worth.[2] One reason is that banks are reluctant, as a matter of policy, to become involved in loan transactions that carry an appreciable risk. Term loans with a lifetime of years have a built-in element of uncertainty and risk that becomes significant when the amount of the loan approaches the net worth of the borrower.

Another reason is the attitude of the regulatory authorities. All banks are subject to supervision and periodic examination by the national and/or state banking authorities. Bank examiners, acting for these agencies, rarely possess the competence to evaluate the soundness, or lack of it, of loans with a lifetime of several years. Their experience is usually confined to short-term credit transactions. In consequence, these examiners have an almost professional bias against transactions that they regard as long term. Rather than face adverse reports by examiners and prolonged subsequent explanations to their superiors, most banks simply follow a self-imposed rule of thumb that appears acceptable to bank examiners.

The same two basic reasons—reluctance to take an appreciable risk and the attitude of the examining authorities—account for the fact that banks rarely make unsecured term loans for more than four or five years. In each case, the institution insists on periodic installment pay-

[1] National banks, for example, are not permitted to make mortgage loans on undeveloped land in excess of 50 percent of the value of such land; and not in excess of 70 percent on commercial property; i.e., land and building.

[2] This figure is based on the author's interviews with about 60 banks in various parts of the country. See *The Role of Commercial Banks in the SBIC Industry* by S. J. Flink, American Bankers Association, 1965.

ments. This procedure may be changed if the term loan is for, say, three years and the borrowing firm demonstrates the need for more liberal terms. The bank may then agree that one-half of the loan be repaid in six semiannual installments. The balance, or one-half of the loan, becomes due at the end of the three-year period. At that time, the bank may agree to make a new term loan for the balance, increase the amount of the new loan, or insist on payment. Its decision at that juncture depends on the firm's performance during the three years.

The interest rate charged by the bank for a term loan is generally 1 to $1\frac{1}{2}\%$ above the rate for short-term loans. This excess is often more apparent than real. Many banks insist that the short-term borrower mantain a "compensating balance" equal to about 20% of the loan. Thus, if the short-term loan amounts to $100,000, the borrower is expected to keep at least $20,000 in his checking account during the life of this loan. Suppose the bank charges the firm at the rate of 6% interest and the loan is for six months. The borrower then pays $3000 interest on $80,000, the amount that is actually made available to him, or an annual rate of 7.5%. The impact of the compensating balance depends upon the balance that the firm customarily maintained prior to the loan and its cash-flow balance after it obtains the loan. Conceivably, this balance may equal or even exceed the compensating balance requirement. In this case, the effective rate is the same as the nominal rate; i.e., 6%.

On term loans, no compensating balance is stipulated. Hence, an interest rate of, say, 1% above what is nominally the short-term rate may actually represent a lower effective rate on the term loan. In addition, short-term rates will fluctuate over time as the discount rate or the prime rate changes. The rate on a term loan generally is frozen, regardless of what happens to short-term interest rates. This will be to the firm's advantage in a period of rising interest rates.

B. Finance Companies

Most finance companies limit their term loans to secured loans. This security consists either of equipment, machinery, furniture, or the like, which is purchased by the firm with the proceeds of the term loan. Transactions of this type are analogous to the installment purchase of automobiles, appliances, or furniture by consumers. Since this chapter deals with unsecured term loans, we need not discuss the installment type of secured term loan provided by these finance companies.

Some finance companies do, however, also make unsecured term loans. This applies primarily to sales finance companies. A sales finance company specializes in making installment loans to the customers of a dealer; for example, automobiles sold to consumers as well as trucks bought by business firms. At times, a dealer may lack the resources for an expansion of his physical facilities, or he requires additional working capital to carry a larger inventory. In these cases, the sales finance company will consider the extension of an unsecured term loan for several years. The past sales record of the dealer and his prospects for future growth then becomes the real security for the term loan.

The motivation of the sales finance company is similar to that of the commercial bank. It will derive its major source of profit from the sales made by the dealer and financed by the term lender rather than from the interest on the loan.

C. Life Insurance Companies

To the larger life insurance companies, the term-loan market offers an additional outlet into which they can channel a portion of their investible funds. Traditionally, these companies have invested the bulk of their funds in bonds of the federal, state, county and local governments as well as those of private corporations, especially public utilities.

Since the 1950's, life insurance companies have entered the term-loan market in increasing numbers. Three major reasons account for this move. First, the interest rate on this type of loan is generally between 1 and 2% higher than on bonds. A second reason is the evolution of a positive policy on the part of these companies to make a portion of their funds available for the expansion of sound business firms in need of capital. Finally, the term-loan market offers an additional investment alternative to insurance companies. Prior to their entry into this field, insurance companies channelled their investible funds into mortgages and into the bond market.

1. Industrial Loan Departments Insurance companies recognized from the outset that the management of a term-loan department calls for unique skills and an experience background unlike those required of the securities investment department. Proceeding from this premise, these companies have set up a separate division, commonly called the Industrial Loan Department, which reports and is responsible to a special Finance Committee made up of one or more senior officers and several board members with a considerable industrial and commercial background.

Although no precise figures are yet available, it would appear that the total volume of term loans granted by life insurance companies by the end of 1967 amounted to several billion dollars.

2. Lending Policies   Unlike a commercial bank, the life insurance company derives no secondary benefits from a term loan. Whereas the bank expects the firm to carry its business checking account with the institution and to avail itself of the credit facilities and other services, the insurance company does not ask the term borrower to take any life insurance, individual or group, in return for a loan.

The sole benefit to the lender consists, therefore, of the interest earned on the loan. But to make a loan necessitates analysis, negotiations, and the custom-made preparation of the loan agreement. Each of these phases involves an expenditure of manpower and, therefore, of money. For these reasons, the bulk of the insurance company term loans, both in the number of transactions and in dollar volume, range from one million dollars up. A few insurance company term loans are made of less than $500,000 and, very rarely, a loan is made of as little as $100,000.

To be eligible for a term loan, the borrowing companies must have been is existence for at least five years and present a good record of profits for at least the last three years. That is, the profit after taxes should be at least equal to the industry's average ratio of profit expressed as a percentage of net worth.

On the other hand, the insurance company, unlike a bank, is reluctant to make term loans for less than ten years. The reason is again the relatively low interest on the loan. Although the lender obtains a rate that is 1 or 2% above the interest rate on bonds, the costs of analysis and investigation may be fairly substantial on a term loan. For example, on a term loan of half a million dollars, these costs often absorb the interest differential for the first year or two of the term loan. On a term loan running into millions of dollars, the rate of interest may be no more than $\frac{1}{2}$ of 1% above the market rate of prime corporate bonds.

Insurance companies usually insist on a "penalty" for prepayment of the loan. If the borrower desires to pay off the balance of the loan, e.g., at the end of the sixth year, he may be required to pay a "penalty" of 2% of the face value of the loan. This penalty *rate* goes down as the loan approaches its maturity.

The objective of this penalty is intended to compensate the lender in part for the loss of the interest differential. Furthermore, the firm, for obvious reasons, will like to pay off a term loan whenever the going rate in the term-loan market declines. This makes it possible to recast the debt by borrowing from another lender at the lower rate. By the same token, the first lender had, at the time of the original loan, foregone the opportunity to place the funds in securities with a fixed rate of interest and with a lifetime at least as long as that of the term loan. It must also be remembered that a decline in the market rate for term loans is, as a rule, the sequence of a fall in the interest rate in the capital market. Thus, if the rate for, e.g., government bonds should drop from 4 to $3\frac{1}{2}\%$, the market price of an earlier issue of 4% bonds will automatically go above 100% of the face value of these bonds. In accepting prepayment of the term loan without a penalty, the lender would have to invest the funds either in another term loan or in securities with a lower effective rate of interest.

In relation to the net worth of the firm, insurance companies may go as high as 100%; although 80 to 85% appears to be the general ceiling for the first term loan to a firm. The term lender anticipates that the effective (i.e., profitable) utilization of the loan will not only lead to an expansion of the firm's volume of business, but that this expansion will also generate a need for additional term funds. If this eventuality develops, the insurance company will be ready to recast the original loan for a higher amount and greater percentage of the net worth, since the net worth itself will also have increased as a result of the retained earnings.

3. Package Deals On term loans of less than one million dollars, insurance companies like, if possible, to obtain the participation of a bank; preferably, the bank with which the firm has its regular business account. If this can be arranged, the bank acts as a "watchdog" for the insurance company. In these deals, known as "package deals," the customary arrangement calls for the periodic payments—for example, $\frac{1}{20}$th of a 10-year loan repayable in semiannual installments—to be applied to the bank's portion of the loan until this has been paid off. Subsequent periodic payments are made to the insurance company.

In package deals that involve more than two participating lenders, it is customary for the lenders to agree among themselves whether one or more of the lenders shall be subordinate in regard to the periodic installment. As far as the principal or the outstanding balance of the loan is concerned, all participating lenders have the same rank; i.e., none is subordinated.

4. Syndication   Some term loans will run into tens of millions of dollars; at times, a single large corporation may seek a term loan of well over 100 million dollars. Few financial institutions are both able and willing to tie up such large sums in a single transaction. In these instances, it is customary for a group of banks and/or insurance companies to participate in the loan. This is known as a "syndicate."

Syndicated term loans are particularly favored by banks. Under existing regulations, a bank is limited in the amount of an unsecured loan to a single borrower to 10% of the bank's capital and surplus. A 75-million dollar term loan to Schenley Industries was made by a syndicate of 15 banks. Pan American World Airways,Inc., obtained a term loan of $130 million from a syndicate of 39 banks.

C. Other Sources of Term Loans

Private investment companies are incorporated under state laws. They represent a hybrid type of financial institution. That is to say, these companies are at the same time term lenders and equity investors. They provide capital either in the form of debt capital (debentures) convertible into common stock or they make direct equity investments. In either case, the private investment company is primarily interested in business firms that have a technical-scientific orientation and which appear to have a strong growth potential in a relatively short time; i.e., in a span of a few years. Among leading private investment companies are the American Research and Development Corporation (Boston), the Whitney Fund and the Rockefeller Fund (New York), and the Electronics Corporation of California.

Unlike other term lenders, the private investment company does not confine its financial operations to already established and proven enterprises. The investment is ready to provide most or all of the capital that is required to finance a new enterprise. Obviously, the investment company will in every case make a thorough investigation of the management of the enterprise, existing or proposed, the products(s), and the market potential. As a rule, the investment company, if it is favorably disposed to the proposal, will also insist on close supervision of the enterprise by its representatives either on the board of directors or as members of management, or both.

The amount of the convertible loan or equity purchase by the investment company will range from $100,000 to a million or more. In addition to providing the "seed money" for an enterprise, the investment company will usually arrange for short-term financing by a bank. If and when the enterprise attains the projected rapid growth, the investment company will also act as the liaison between the enterprise and an underwriter for a public offering of common stock, partly to raise additional capital and, more important, to establish a market for the shares held by the investment company. It is at this stage in the life of the enterprise that the investment company can either cash in on the substantial increase in the value of the stock or hold the shares for further capital gains.

It must be noted that the investment company as a state chartered private corporation is not subject to any restriction or supervision in its investment policy other than those that apply to any other corporation chartered under the general corporation laws of the state.

Pension trusts have, in the course of the post-World War II years, become the administrators of many billions of dollars. Their investment policies are determined largely by the terms of their charters and bylaws. Larger pension trusts are reported to have made sizable investments in term loans to medium-size and large business firms. Some pension funds have also ventured into transactions with firms that meet the SBA criteria of "small."[3]

Questions

1. What institutions are the major sources (suppliers) of term loans?
2. Why do many banks follow a policy of not making term loans?
3. In view of your answer to question 2, why do some banks make term loans?
4. Why do sales finance companies make term loans? Who are their customers for term loans?
5. What are the reasons for the increased activity of insurance companies in the term loan market in recent years?
6. Compare and contrast insurance company term loans with commercial bank term loans.

[3] This statement is based on the authors' personal observations. These are naturally limited in scope. For this reason, no generalization is intended.

Case: MAGNOLIA NATIONAL BANK

Magnolia National Bank, located in a large and rapidly growing city in the South, has a reputation as an aggressive lender and pioneer in the area of term loans. Magnolia was one of the first banks in the United States to devise a term-loan arrangement to finance the acquisition of jet aircraft by a major airline. Term loans have been made by Magnolia to such diverse industries as construction and television broadcasting. The bank is equally interested in smaller term loans as well as in the type of loans mentioned above.

In July, 1966, Mr. Jerrold Rogers, President of Hush Puppies Restaurants, Inc., requested a four-year $25,000 term loan for the purpose of buying completely new equipment for three of the four restaurants operated by Hush Puppies. Hush Puppies holds ten-year leases (as of June 30, 1966) on four restaurants located on Route 301, one of the major north-south tourist routes between the Northeast and Florida. The restaurants serve fried chicken with hush puppies, as well as sandwiches, hamburgers, etc. All service is at counters or on a take-out basis. Some novelties and souvenirs are sold to the tourists. The restaurants also sell pocket books and magazines. Most of the customers are tourists, although there is some local trade.

Mr. Rogers and several other friends formed Hush Puppies Restaurants, Inc., in 1963, for the express purpose of taking over the leases and purchasing the existing equipment of the four restaurants from the former owner, who desired to retire. Mr. Rogers, age 47, has spent his entire working life in the food service business, working with several major restaurant firms before forming Hush Puppies. As President, Mr. Rogers is paid $15,000 for his full-time services to Hush Puppies. Mr. Rogers and his immediate family own two-thirds of the common stock. The other two investors are not active in the business although they serve on the board of directors along with Rogers, his wife, and the company attorney.

During the past fiscal year, ending June 30, 1966, Rogers explained to the bank loan officer that over $10,000 has been spent on new equipment to completely refurbish one of the restaurants. As a result of the new equipment and a new paint job, profitability has increased markedly at the refurbished restaurant owing to greater patronage as well as to lower labor costs, less spoilage, and decreased pilferage from the new arrangement of facilities. The funds for the new equipment installed were raised by an increase in notes due officers of $5000 and from retained earnings generated by operations.

According to Rogers, the firm intends to refurbish the other three restaurants in a similar manner to the first. A term loan will enable the firm to refurbish all three restaurants this year and will bring cost savings through quantity purchase of new equipment.

The loan officer asked Mr. Rogers for balance sheets and a profit and loss statement. They are shown in Tables 12-1 and 12-2. The loan officer

TABLE 12-1.   Hush Puppies Restaurants, Inc., Balance Sheets (Dollars)

	June 30, 1966	June 30, 1965
Assets:		
Cash	5,732	2,149
Accounts receivable	528	354
Inventory	17,987	13,656
Prepaid expenses	1,182	923
Total current assets	25,429	17,082
Equipment, net	38,507	34,797
Loans to stockholders	250	—
Total assets	64,186	51,879
Liabilities:		
Accounts payable	7,699	8,904
Bank loans	1,275	3,500
Taxes payable	5,837	4,628
Total current liabilities	14,811	17,032
Note due officers	10,000	5,000
Common stock	25,000	25,000
Retained earnings	14,375	4,847
Total liabilities	64,186	51,879

stated that the bank is pretty well loaned up at present but would like to accommodate a good customer, if possible. Mr. Rogers was promised a decision by the end of the week.

The loan officer must decide whether or not to grant the term loan to Hush Puppies Restaurants, Inc. If he decides to grant the loan, he must also decide what covenants and restrictions should be inserted in the loan agreement, including the interest rate and repayment schedule.

TABLE 12-2. Hush Puppies Restaurants, Inc., Profit and Loss Statement and Reconciliation of Surplus for Year Ending June 30, 1966 (Dollars)

Sales		247,525
Cost of sales		86,583
Gross profit		160,942
Less expenses:		
Selling expenses	62,412	
Administrative expenses	27,400	
Depreciation	6,570	
Rent	42,750	
Other expenses	3,185	
Total expenses		142,317
Operating profit		18,625
Interest expense (net)		728
Net profit before taxes		17,897
Taxes		5,369
Net profit		12,528
Retained earnings, June 30, 1965		4,847
Plus net profit year ending June 30, 1966		12,528
		17,375
Less dividends paid, year ending June 30, 1966		3,000
Retained earnings, June 30, 1966		14,375

Case Questions:

1. As loan officer of the Magnolia National Bank, list the pros and cons of granting the term loan to Hush Puppies Restaurants, Inc. Would you grant the loan?
2. Assuming that the bank decides to grant the term loan requested by Mr. Rogers, what restrictions and provisions should be inserted in the loan agreement?
3. As Mr. Rogers, would you agree to these restrictions? What alternatives do you have?

~~~~~~

Chapter Thirteen

Term Loans for Small Business

Two sources of term funds, specifically designed to provide such capital to small firms, were created by the Small Business Investment Act of 1958. There are (1) The Small Business Administration; (SBA); and (2) Small Business Investment Companies (SBIC's).

The Act of 1958 marked the deliberate entry of the Federal Government into the field of term financing for small companies. The SBA, which had been established as a temporary agency in 1953, became the permanent instrument for the execution of this policy. At the same time, the 1958 legislation created an Investment Division within the SBA. This division became the administrative and regulatory branch of the SBA in the licensing and supervision of SBICs.

A thumbnail sketch of the background of the 1958 Act highlights the problems of small firms who seek term capital. Studies by the staffs of the Senate and House Committees on Small Business, a major survey by the Federal Reserve System,[1] and several independent studies had arrived at the same basic conclusion: small business firms were seriously impeded in their growth by the absence of a capital market for these firms. Although none of these studies found it possible to measure the magnitude of the demand, the experts had little doubt that the demand was significantly in excess of the supply. The legislation was designed to narrow and, hopefully, in the course of time, to bridge this gap between demand and supply.

---

[1] *Financing Small Business,* Report to the Committee on Banking and Currency and the Select Committee on Small Business, United States Congress; Washington, GPO, 1958.

I. THE SMALL ADMINISTRATION (SBA)

This agency is charged with a variety of tasks, each of which is designed to aid the small business firm.[2] In this section, we are concerned with its term-lending policies. The record of the SBA is rather significant both in terms of the total volume as well as in number of loans.

By the end of 1965, the SBA had made a total of over 58,000 loans with an aggregate dollar value in excess of 2.5 billion dollars. This figure represents the cumulative record for the period 1953 to 1965, although the results of the first five years of its existence were rather modest in terms of number of loans and their dollar volume. Loans for the 5-year period 1953–1957 totalled 8597 and involved less than $400 millions. By contrast, in the next eight years the SBA made close to 50,000 loans totalling over $2 billion dollars. This represents an increase of over six times the number of loans and over five times the amount of loans.

At the end of 1965, the SBA had 15,559 loans outstanding with a value of over $250 million. In addition, another $541 million dollars of loans to 18,563 firms involved transactions in which the SBA was either the participant in or the guarantor of, term loans made by banks to business firms.

SBA loans range from $350,000, the legal maximum, down to $1000, or even less in a few cases. We shall deal only with term loans ranging from $15,000 up to $350,000, since the basic terms differ for loans in this range from those below $15,000, which are intended for "very small business."

1. Lending Policies   Loans between $15,000 and $350,000 can be for a period of up to ten years. In order to be eligible aside from sound financial conditions and reasonable prospects of future earnings—the applicant must submit evidence that his request for this loan has been turned down by his local bank; or by two banks if his business is in a community with a population in excess of 200,000. This turndown by a bank should indicate that the financial institution either does not make term loans for a period of five to ten years or that its resources do not permit it to make loans of the size requested by the firm. The SBA may also require the prospective borrower to substantiate his claim

---

[2] The major divisions are (1) Direct Financing; (2) Investment Division (SBIC's); (3) Management Research and Counseling; (4) Government procurements and contracts for small business.

that adequate funds are not available to the firm at reasonable rates from other financial institutions. The purpose of these prerequisites is to remove the SBA from direct competition against local institutions which are willing and able to accommodate the term loan needs of expanding sound firms.[3] In other words, the SBA is designed to fill local gaps between the demand for and the supply of debt capital.

2. Terms   SBA loans range up to 10 years at an interest rate not to exceed 5½%. Loans that are designed to supply working capital are limited to a maximum of 6 years. These terms can be liberalized for "pool loans." Assume that a group of small firms organize a corporation that is to act as the central purchaser of supplies or equipment for the use of the group members, or to carry on research and development for the benefit of the group members. In a situation of this type, the SBA may make a loan of as much as $250,000 multiplied by the number of members. Interest is generally at the rate of 5% and the loan may run for as long as 20 years.

As a government agency, the SBA must attempt to keep the risk of its loan to a minimum. Its interest rate is usually about 1% above the rate that the government pays on its borrowing. Such a small "spread" compels the agency to stress secured loans. Collateral acceptable to the SBA may consist of one or more of the following: a mortgage on land and building or equipment, assignment of warehouse receipts, personal endorsements or guarantees, and in some instances, assignment of current receivables.

3. Bank Participation   Under this phase of its lending program, the SBA offers a bank two alternatives. The bank can take a portion of the loan with the SBA taking as much as 90%. On these transactions, the bank may charge the borrower, on its portion of the loan, a higher rate than the SBA charges for its portion. However, the bank's rate cannot exceed 8%.

The second alternative is for the bank to make the entire loan—after approval of the loan by the SBA—with the agency guaranteeing up to 90% of the loan. In return for this guarantee, the SBA receives from the bank ½ of 1% "interest" as a sort of insurance premium. Under this arrangement, the bank is permitted to carry the SBA portion of the loan as a nonrisk asset. Furthermore, these loans are not subject to the legal lending limitations of national banking laws.

---

[3] As stated by the SBA in its brochures, "By law, the agency may not make a loan if a business can obtain funds from a bank or other private source."

II. SMALL BUSINESS INVESTMENT COMPANIES (SBICs)

These private companies are incorporated under state laws and licensed by the Investment Division of the SBA. To qualify for a license, the company must have at least $300,000 capital.[4] It may then request the SBA to purchase from the SBIC an equivalent amount in subordinated debentures. This is known as a Section 302 (investment) purchase by the SBA. The total—the capital raised by the SBIC from private sources plus the Section 302 purchase by the SBA—constitutes the capital and surplus of the SBIC. However, the maximum "matching" purchase by the SBA in an SBIC is limited to $700,000. In addition to such matching capital funds, the SBIC may also apply to the SBA for a Section 303 loan up to one-half of its total capital but not in excess of $4,000,000.

About 700 of the licensed SBICs obtained their capital—exclusive of the 302 funds—through a private placement of the stock, i.e., 20 or fewer shareholders. Forty-five SBICs procured their capital through a public offering of their common stock. These SBICs range in capitalization between one million and twenty million dollars.

By the end of 1965, the SBA had licensed almost 750 SBICs. Of this number, about 640 were active in varying degrees as suppliers of capital to small firms. About 100 had either turned in their license or were still totally "dormant." The active companies had total assets with a book value of 700 million dollars. Of this sum, over 125 million dollars represented SBA purchases of subordinated debentures (Section 302 funds) and 85 million dollars were Section 303 loans from SBA. In effect, therefore, the Federal government had provided, through the SBA, one-third of the funds that the SBICs had available for loans to and investments in small business firms.

In 1965, the Administrator of the SBA issued, among others, three regulations that represent a major change in the agency's policy on the issuance of new licenses. An applicant for a license must agree to have a full-time manager. And second, this manager must possess reasonable background and experience in the field of financial analysis and management. At first glance, it would seem that an SBIC would of its volition and in its own economic interest encompass both features

---

[4] In 1965, the Administrator of the SBA raised the minimum capital requirements to $500,000. In 1967, the SBA proposed to Congress that the legal minimum be raised to $1,000,000 by the year 1975.

in its organization plans. In reality, a substantial number of SBICs are deficient on one or both counts. Many SBICs are still managed by lawyers, accountants, or businessmen who organized an SBIC as a "sideline" to their full-time occupation. Moreover, the competency of many of these part-time SBIC managers in the field of financial analysis and management is open to serious doubt.

The third major change applies to the investment policies of new licensees. Under the new regulation, these SBICs cannot make real estate loans aggregating more than twenty percent of their capital and surplus. The significance of this regulation lies in the fact that too many of the SBICs channelled their capital plus Section 303 loans into straight real estate (mortgage) secured loans.

A. Types of SBICs

These companies can be classified either by size (capital and surplus), primary field of operations, or affiliation with commercial banks.

1. Classification by size   At the end of 1965, the breakdown was as follows:

Small (capital $300,000 to $324,000)	220 active SBICs
Medium ($325,000 to $1,000,000)	150 active SBICs
Large ($1,000,000 to $5,000,000)	43 active SBICs
Largest ($5,000,000 and over)	21 active SBICs

Even if each of the 220 small SBICs would avail itself of the right to borrow from the SBA as much as one-half of its capital, the total resources of each would still fall short of half a million dollars. Small investment companies therefore look for firms whose needs are for loans between $10,000 and $50,000. Moreover, most of the small SBICs tend to make only secured loans; i.e., loans secured by mortgages on real estate or pledges of capital assets; e.g., equipment and machinery.

2. Classification by Type of Loans   Table 13-1 shows the composition of the portfolios of SBICs as of March 31, 1965.

It must be emphasized that the figures in the last column (equity) do not include stock options held but not yet executed by SBICs. As will be pointed out later in this chapter, these options play an important role in the transactions of many SBICs. Basically, stock option is a contingent equity ownership. The holder may or may not exercise his right. This decision to convert the option into stock ownership depends on the success of the company and, in the last analysis, on the value of its equity shares at the time when the option can be exercised.

Publicly held SBICs are required, under the rulings of the Securities and Exchange Commission, to make full disclosure of stock rights, options, and warrants. It is of some interest to note the variance in the experience record of these SBICs.

Debentures represent unsecured loans; i.e., they are claims against the net income of the firm and, in case of default, against the assets of the debtor after all secured claims have been paid off. Since we are concerned in this chapter with unsecured term loans, the figures on debentures are relevant. It will be noted from Table 13-1 that, for

TABLE 13-1. Portfolio of SBICs, March 31, 1965 (Percent)

Size of SBICs	Loans	Debentures	Equity (Stock)
Small	51.7	16.4	8.0
Medium	48.3	25.2	7.3
Large	29.5	47.4	10.1
Largest	24.1	30.1	16.1

the small SBICs, secured loans constitute over three times the amounts channeled into unsecured loans (debentures). This ratio drops sharply as the SBICs grow in size. Among the large and largest SBICs, unsecured loans exceed secured loans. In fact, the large SBICs have a ratio of better than $1.50 of unsecured loans for every dollar of secured loans.

In the case of the large and largest SBICs, the secured loan frequently assumes the character of a quasi-equity investment. As will be shown later in some detail in this chapter, the secured loans made by these companies give the companies options to purchase a specified number of common stock at a predetermined price. In effect, therefore, the SBIC is a creditor at the time when the loan is made and a potential future shareholder in the borrowing firm.

3. Classification by Bank Affiliation   The Act of 1958, as amended in 1960, expressly authorized banks and bank holding companies to invest up to 2% of their capital and surplus in an SBIC. About 80 investment companies have been organized with banks or bank holding companies as stockholders. Of this number, 23 are wholly bank-owned investment companies. In the other 60 SBICs, banks hold a minority position ranging from about 5% to about 25% of the SBIC stock.

Although these 80 SBICs constitute less than 15% of all investment companies, they account for approximately 40% of the aggregate capital and surplus of this industry and for about one-third of all investments.

4. Classification by Transactions SBICs basically fall into two categories. One category, which embraces a substantial majority of the small and medium-sized SBICs, is almost entirely security oriented. That is, the loans by these companies are secured by mortgages or real estate or prior liens on equipment or other capital assets of the borrowing firms. In fact, many of those SBICs confine their operations to the financing of real estate ventures; e.g., loans on newly constructed apartments, houses, office buildings, and the like that have not yet reached the occupancy level required by institutional mortgage lenders, e.g., insurance companies and banks.

The second category includes those SBICs that are "venture minded." That is, these companies are oriented toward loans that take the form of equity investments (common stock) on which the SBIC hopes to convert at some future date into an equity investment. In this volume, we are dealing with SBICs which fall into the second category.

B. Lending Policies

SBICs that are prepared to make unsecured loans to small business firms, as defined by the SBA, perform this task in a rather unique manner. Although they are legally creditors of the firm, they almost invariably act as "partners" of the management. That is to say, the SBIC deliberately maintains close contacts with the firm during the lifetime of the loan. This takes the form of frequent meetings with the officers of the firm, an analysis of its performance in the preceding period—usually monthly—and a discussion of management's plans for the immediate future. In brief, the SBIC keeps itself informed about all operational activities of the firm. Many investment companies, in fact, act either as a voluntary management consultant to the firm; or they require, as part of the loan agreement, that they be retained on a fee basis as consultants.

There are several reasons for this close relationship between lender and borrower. SBICs have no specific cutoff point for a term loan in relation to the net worth of the firm. It is not unusual for an SBIC to make a loan that is twice the net worth of the firm. Quite often the firm is relatively young; i.e., less than five years old. The term loan is intended to launch the firm on a major phase of expansion relative to its size. The firm, due to its relatively small size, too often lacks adequate internal financial controls and financial planning. These several factors create an appreciable risk that reasonably good prospects may yield poor results because of poor management in the execution of these plans. By "policing" and advising the firm in this phase of rapid expansion, the SBIC hopes to reduce the risk to a minimum.

1. Syndication   Under the provisions of the 1958 Act, an SBIC cannot loan to, or invest in, any one firm in excess of twenty percent of the SBIC's capital and surplus. In turn, the typical investment company is not inclined to put its loanable funds in only five or six firms. It wants to have diversification as an additional means of reducing the risk that a single poor loan may jeopardize its solvency. On the other hand, an SBIC may receive a proposal from a firm that appears highly attractive but involves an amount in excess of the twenty percent limitation.

To solve this dilemma—to act affirmatively on very promising deals and yet not commit too much of its own funds in a single firm—SBICs resort to *syndications*. Two or more investment companies participate in a single transaction. This makes it possible to obtain diversification of investments and also to accommodate borrowers whose financial requirements exceed the legal limit for the individual SBIC.

The law requires that an SBIC loan be for a minimum of five years. In practice, the typical loan runs between five and seven years. If the firm succeeds in achieving its goals—as spelled out in the proposal to the SBIC which rarely projects for more than three years in the future— the firm will very likely find it necessary to recast its financial structure well before the loan agreement matures.

Interest rates show a wide range. The large SBICs charge 1 to 2% above the going rate for term loans by banks and insurance companies. This differential is explained by the higher ratio of loan to net worth in the case of these SBICs. However, the interest rate is generally only the visible price paid for the loan. In the typical situation the SBIC will only make an unsecured loan if the borrowing firm is prepared to give the SBIC a "sweetener." This will be discussed in detail in the next section.

2. "Sweeteners"   Investment companies that make unsecured loans are cognizant of the risk inherent in these transactions. They are also aware of the fact that this risk is enhanced if the amount of the loan exceeds the net worth of the firm. Another factor that contributes to the risk element is the uncertainty about whether the firm will actually be able to attain its objectives—substantial expansion of sales and profits—as a result of the loan. From the viewpoint of the SBIC, the higher interest rate that it charges is not an adequate compensation for this risk.

These SBICs therefore insist on a "sweetener"; i.e., a premium for the fact that the investment company is asked to assume a sizeable portion of the risk. One type of premium or "sweetener" takes the form of an option to purchase a specified number of shares of common stock at a fixed price at any time during the lifetime of the term loan. The investment company thus becomes a potential shareholder of the firm. It will exercise the option if the business succeeds in realizing the anticipated growth and profits. In this case, the value of the shares purchased by the SBIC under its option will have a value significantly in excess of the purchase price. As a matter of fact, a few investment companies have "struck it rich" in some cases.

For example, the Greater Washington Investment Co., a licensed SBIC, made a $900,000 term loan to the C-E-I-R Corporation against 6-year 8% debentures that were convertible, at the SBIC's choice, into common stock at $8 per share; or a total of 112,500 shares. Less than two years later (1961), the market price of C-E-I-R shares sky-rocketed to over $50 a share. The SBIC thus had made a paper profit that was greater than the total of its own capital and surplus. Another SBIC, the Franklin Corporation, had made a $350,000 term loan to Astrex, Inc., convertible into common stock, which had a book value of $75,000 at the time when the loan was made. At the height of the stock market boom in 1961 these shares were worth over $1,000,000. If the SBIC had converted the debentures into common stock and sold the stock at that market price, it would have realized a capital gain of $650,000. To be sure, these and similar examples are exceptions rather than the rule. Quite a few SBICs, regardless of size, have suffered sizeable losses on their deals without reaping compensating large profits or spectacular successes.

The size of the stock option, or sweetener, depends on the size of the loan relative to the net worth of the firm, the past growth record of the firm and, above all, on the bargaining skill of the management of the business. Options therefore will range from 10% of the firm's stock to as much as 50% and more. It is not uncommon for an SBIC to insist on a majority of common stock, in addition to debentures, if the requested loan is several times as large as the owners' equity in the firm. The SBIC would then become a major creditor as well as majority stockholder.

3. Package Deals   Large SBICs—and this is true of bank-affiliated investment companies of all sizes—favor "package deals" involving commercial banks. In this type of transaction, the SBIC agrees to subordinate its debentures to an agreed-upon short-term line of credit by a bank. This arrangement, generally initiated by the SBIC, has a twofold objective. First, the line of credit provides the firm with a given amount of working capital and correspondingly reduces the funds that the SBIC need furnish. And second, the bank functions as a "part-time policeman" for the investment company.

It must be emphasized, however, that term loans to small firms always involve an appreciable degree of risk. Very few of the SBICs, including the largest ones, have escaped losses from deals that turned "sour." Even many of the bank-affiliated companies have made serious mistakes of judgment in evaluating the potentials of firms; or have failed to police their debtor-firms adequately.[5]

4. Relationship to Firm   As previously pointed out, the venture-minded SBIC regards itself as a "partner" of the borrowing firm. This figurative partnership assumes concrete form in one or two ways. Most SBICs insist either that they be given a place on the board of directors, or they reserve the right to ask for a directorship at any time during the life of the loan. This demand is based on the argument that the SBIC must be in a position to assure itself that the firm does not adopt policies that are likely to endanger the SBIC's investment.

Many SBICs insist, as a prerequisite for the loan, that they be retained as management consultants for the duration of the investment. The supporting argument is the same as for a position on the board. However, there are significant differences in the charges for management consultation: some SBICs ask for a nominal charge of about $50 per day plus travel expenses. Others ask for an annual retainer of several thousand dollars.

---

[5] See S. J. Flink, *The Role of Commercial Banks in the SBIC Industry,* American Bankers Association, 1965; especially pages 111–122, "An Anthology of Investment Errors."

5. Ratio of Man to Net Worth   A venture-minded SBIC looks to the growth potential of the firm as the primary source of security of the loan and also as the major source of gain for the investment company. That is, the expected profit from an appreciation in the value of the common stock plays a greater role in the investment decision of the SBIC than does the interest on the loan. A thumb rule of many SBICs is the expectation that the firm will double its net worth or equity in five years or less. The investment company thus hopes to have a capital gain on its stockholding of at least 100% plus the interest received on the debentures.

TABLE 13-2.   Maximum Ratio of Loan to Net Worth

Maximum Investment as Percentage of Net Worth	Public SBICs (11)[a]	Bank-Owned SBICs (15)[a]	Partly Bank-Owned SBICs (15)[a]
Less than 100%	3	3	3
100% to 124%	—	2	—
125% to 149%	1	—	1
150% to 199%	—	—	1
No fixed cutoff point	7	10	10

[a] These figures represent the number of SBICs interviewed by the author.
Source: Flink *supra* p. 91.

Rapid growth, in turn, is in large part a function of adequate capital to finance the projected breakthrough by the business firm. Quite often, the capital needs of the firm exceed its net worth by a substantial margin. It is not a rare case for an SBIC to make a loan amounting to five or more times the net worth of the firm. Even bank-affiliated investment companies, which usually pursue a more conservative policy, do not hesitate to make loans that are two or three times the net worth of the firm. This fact emerged from interviews with 41 SBICs who represent a cross section of venture-minded investment companies. Table 13-2 shows the distribution of the responses to the question whether the SBIC had a fixed maximum ratio of loan to net worth of the borrowing firm.

The significance of the figures in Table 13-2 lies in the following fact. Commercial banks and insurance companies usually have an unwritten rule that the amount of a term loan cannot exceed a predetermined percentage of the borrower's net worth. This maximum percentage ranges between 70 and 80% of net worth. The figures in Table 11-2 indicate that the majority of SBICs, in contrast, have no fixed cut-off point.

C. A Note of Caution

Measured in terms of time as well as performance, the SBIC is still in its infancy. During the first six years after the adoption of the Act the SBA was eager to license newly formed SBICs with no regard to the competency of the organizers or managers. A total of more than 800 licenses were issued between 1959 and the end of 1966. Almost one-fifth of the licensees never started operations. Of about 650 SBICs who became active, probably no more than 350 made any serious attempt to engage in the type of investment program that had been anticipated by the legislature; i.e., making venture capital available to small business firms. Instead, too many SBICs preferred to make term loans secured by mortgages on real estate at fairly high interest rates. In many instances the SBICs were unconcerned about the management and prospects of the debtor-firm as long as the real estate offered an adequate margin of safety for the loan.

But even those SBICs which attempted to make genuine equity investments in small business firms had a spotty performance record. Too often the management of these SBICs lacked competency in evaluating the economic prospects of the borrowing firm. More importantly, many SBICs were only moderately less illiterate in the science and art of financial planning, management, and control than their debtors. In consequence, the gains from profitable equity deals did not in many cases compensate for the losses suffered from poor investments. The larger publicly owned SBICs were not immune to reverses in their investments. This fact is clearly reflected in the lack of confidence of the investment market in the asset value of many SBICs. Table 13-3 shows the price at which the shares of the 10 largest SBICs were traded in May 1967.

The rather poor overall performance record of the first nine years does not mean either that the SBIC industry has been a failure or that SBICs in the years ahead will not play an important role in providing a source of capital funds to small firms. Both within the industry itself and on the part of the SBA reforms were initiated in 1966 and 1967 that promise to cure most of the past ills of the industry. Mergers of and voluntary abandonment of licenses are increasing the financial resources of the surviving investment companies. Moreover, the managers of many SBICs have acquired experience and know-how in evaluating prospects and in the art of financial management.

In turn, the SBA has initiated steps, both administrative and legislative, to encourage more equity investments by SBICs. To achieve this end, the SBA asked Congress to authorize the SBA to raise the maximum which the larger SBICs can borrow from the SBA to $10 million (compared with the $4.7 million limit under the existing law), providing

Table 13-3. Asset Value and Market Price of the Ten Largest SBICs

SBIC	Asset Value per Share ($)	Stock Market Price ($)	Percent Discount
Boston Capital	17.20	10.25	−40.4
Capital Southwest	19.67	12.37	−37.1
Central Investment	4.60	2.50	−45.7
Electronics Capital	20.77	11.25	−45.8
Franklin Corp.	12.06	6.87	−43.0
Midland Capital	17.80	9.25	−48.0
Narragansett Capital	21.26	10.25	−51.8
SBIC of New York	22.35	20.62	− 7.7
Southeastern Capital	13.43	7.62	−43.2
Texas Capital	8.31	6.25	−24.8

that such SBIC has at least 65% of its funds in equity investments. The SBA is exercising more rigorous administrative supervision over the lending practices of SBICs. Furthermore, the SBA has adopted a rather stringent policy in the issuing of new licenses both in regard to capital and competent management.

D. The Task of the Financial Manager

The transition of the SBIC industry from infancy to adolescence poses a problem for the financial manager of the firm who is considering the SBIC as one of the potential sources of capital funds, either in the form of term debt capital or equity capital. The problem arises from the fact that SBICs show a great diversity in their investment, or loan, objectives and criteria, and in their relationship to the firm during the lifetime of the loan. Moreover, the individual SBIC usually has no fixed rules or policy in regard to the lifetime of the loan, the type of instrument (straight debentures, convertible debentures, outright stock purchases, stock options), rate of interest, participation in policy decisions (through representation on the board of directors), etc. Instead, it is open to negotiation on each major facet of the loan agreement.

This absence of standards is both an advantage as well as a drawback from the viewpoint of the financial manager. The advantage lies in the fact that it affords the borrowing firm an opportunity to negotiate for terms that are tailored to its specific needs and prospects. In fact, most SBICs in the category of venture-minded investment companies stress the fact that they are prepared to negotiate for an agreement tailored to the distinct requirements of the individual borrowers.

On the other hand, negotiations are time consuming. If the SBIC and the firm reach a deadlock, the latter must then seek out another SBIC that may be willing to negotiate an agreement acceptable to the firm. The loss of time as a result of fruitless negotiations can become a serious handicap to the firm. Conditions in the economy, and particularly in the capital market, are in a constant state of flux. Thus, while the firm suspends the project in an effort to procure the needed funds on acceptable terms, the change in the economic environment may have an adverse, or favorable, effect on the firm's bargaining position.

This uncertainty injects an additional risk factor. It can be reduced or eliminated by first screening SBICs who are most likely to be receptive to the firm's projection and capital needs. And second, the firm's projection of output, sales, and profit must be supported by adequate financial analysis, capital budget, cash-flow projections, and financial controls. These are tasks that fall in the province of the financial manager. If top management has these data, it can quickly determine whether or not it is in the same ball park as the SBIC. One or, at most, two conferences with the SBIC will reveal whether or not there is a reasonable chance of reaching an agreement.

SUMMARY

The major suppliers of term loans are commercial banks, life insurance companies, finance companies, the Small Business Administration, investment companies, and Small Business Investment Companies. When looking for a term loan, the financial manager should compare the unique objectives, criteria and policies of each type of supplier, as well as the differences among individual lenders in each category.

A majority of banks do not make term loans since they do not have the specialized personnel or the capital to enter this business. Large commercial banks with adequate resources in capital and manpower have often gone into the term loan business to serve their regular customers and the customers of smaller correspondent banks.

The Small Business Investment Act of 1958 created two sources of term funds specifically designed to provide capital to small firms—the Small Business Administration and Small Business Investment Companies. Government action was necessary since the absence of a capital market for small firms impeded their growth. The Small Business Administration has made a significant number of term loans to small business. Loans between $15,000 and $350,000 are made with terms up to ten years. Licensed SBICs also make loans and other investments in small business. Although SBICs are legally lenders, they often provide many services to aid management that are not ordinarily undertaken by lenders. Financial managers of small business firms should be familiar with both direct SBA loans and SBICs as well as with the traditional lenders to business.

Questions

1. What are the requirements imposed on a prospective borrower for eligibility for an SBA loan? What are the purposes of these restrictions?
2. How can a commercial bank participate in an SBA loan? Why are banks willing to participate in these loans?
3. How do SBICs raise their capital? What portion can they raise from the Federal Government?
4. How do SBIC loans differ from commercial bank loans? In what ways are they similar?
5. What "sweeteners" are available to SBICs to encourage them to make unsecured loans? Are these "sweeteners" fair to the borrower?

Case: REYNOLDS EQUIPMENT COMPANY

The Reynolds Equipment Company was organized in 1950. Its initial capital was $20,000. The company manufactured semiautomatic collators. These came in three sizes: 6, 8, and 10 racks. Each rack could hold up to 150 sheets. An operator—who required no special training or skill—would place sheets in each rack and press a button that would electrically activate precision rollers. Each roller would push forward exactly 1 sheet from each rack and the sheets would fall in proper sequence into a bin at the bottom of the machine. The operator would lift each set from the bin and then staple them manually. The average capacity of these collators was between 1500 and 2000 sheets per hour. These machines offered substantial savings in time and space. Sales were to small printing establishments, schools, business firms, and organizations that ordinarily would collate by hand multiple sets of 6 to 10 sheets.

The company was capitalized at $50,000 and issued 250,000 shares of no par value stock all of which was held by four individuals: the President (General Sales Manager); the Executive Vice-President (in charge of production); the plant Supervisor (in charge of manufacturing operations); and the Vice-President in charge of research and development who was responsible for product improvement.

The company did not have its own manufacturing facilities but subcontracted for the manufacturing of these collators. Its annual sales increased at a modest pace from $50,000 in the first year of operation to approximately half a million at the end of 1960. Its annual net profits ranged between $15,000 and $20,000. No dividends were paid.

In 1961, the company brought out a fully automatic collator that could assemble 6000 sheets per hour in sets ranging from 6 sheets to 16 sheets each. The only function performed by a clerk-operator was to insert the sheets in the individual racks, each of which could hold up to 200 sheets. Once the sheets were inserted, the machine would perform the rest of the job and work without supervision or "feeding" for approximately one-half hour. At the completion of each run, the sets that were assembled by the machine in staggered fashion could be removed and subsequently be either stapled or bound in individual folders. The semiautomatic collators were retailed at $250 for the small unit and $650 for the large unit. The price of the fully automatic collator was $3500.

With the introduction of the fully automatic 16-station collator, the volume of business doubled in the course of a year. Customers for this large unit consisted of printing establishments, chain stores, banks, insurance companies, and branches of the Federal Government as well as municipalities. At the end of 1962, the company brought out a highly sophisticated automatic collator with 50 stations and a capacity of 30,000 sheets per hour. Furthermore, this unit could be adjusted to handle sheets either

$8\frac{1}{2} \times 11$ or 17×11. A special attachment would fold sheets of 11×17 in half, thus producing a set of 100 sheets $8\frac{1}{2} \times 11$ or the equivalent of 200 pages. Another attachment that could be used for either size sheets would staple each set. The retail price of this unit was $10,500; and the price of the stapler and folder was $1500 each. Total sales in 1963 were approximately $2,300,000.

In 1962, the company obtained a bank loan of $100,000. In 1963, it also established its own manufacturing facilities in a new plant leased at an annual rental of $40,000.

With the introduction of the large 50-station collator, the company needed to finance the purchase of additional equipment, a larger inventory, and receivables. It obtained from its bank a 3-year term loan at $5\frac{1}{2}\%$, repayable in 12 equal quarterly installments of $16,333, plus interest on the unpaid balance.

In the fall of 1963, the company entered into an exclusive distributor contract with a small midwestern manufacturer of plastic bindings. The president of the company believed that the addition of this line would provide an additional service to the purchasers of the collators since plastic ring binders appeared to have a strong appeal. The treasurer of the company had made a market study and concluded that the company should generate sales of $500,000 at the end of the first year and reach one million dollars at the end of the second year. The estimated inventory needs called for $100,000 and promotional expenses were estimated at $25,000 per year.

The company had also experienced a rapid growth of sales of semiautomatic and fully automatic collators in Europe. By the end of 1962, sales in Europe exceeded the quarter million mark. In 1963, the directors decided to set up a branch plant in Belgium for the dual purpose of cutting the costs of manufacturing for the European market and also servicing European purchasers more effectively. Also, the company wanted to be in the Common Market and eliminate both shipping costs and tariffs. It was estimated that this branch plant would require an investment of about $40,000 in machinery, about $20,000 in organizational expenses, and approximately $20,000 in operating expenses before the branch plant would reach the level at which it would have a properly trained labor force and supply the European market. It was estimated that the breakeven point would be reached at the end of about one year after the establishment of the branch plant.

In 1964, the controller reported that sales of the plastic binders were far short of expectations. Monthly sales ranged between $10,000 and

$15,000. The unsatisfactory level of sales had led to an accumulation of unsold inventory that was approaching the $150,000 mark. At this rate, the company was losing money on plastic binders. The European branch plant was still running at a deficit. The sales of the collators in the American market were rising. The company was in a financial squeeze. The quarterly repayments on the term loan represented a serious drain on the cash flow. European sales by the branch plant could no longer be financed by Ameri-

TABLE 13-4. Reynolds Equipment Company: Consolidated Income Statement, Fiscal Years Ended August 31 (Dollars)

	1959	1960	1961
Sales	501,486.17	510,420.24	775,080.34
Cost of sales	265,372.98	268,709.33	440,147.36
Gross profit	236,113.19	241,710.91	334,932.98
Selling expense	37,663.97	49,728.36	53,733.32
Advertising expense	44,259.36	43,394.41	91,461.83
Administrative expense	124,279.21	127,471.42	183,141.85
Total expense[a]	206,202.54	220,594.19	328,337.00
Profit before taxes	29,910.65	21,116.72	6,595.98
Taxes on income	9,210.39	7,023.57	16,427.68
Addition to surplus	20,700.26	14,093.15	(856.90)[b]
[a] Includes depreciation and amortization of	13,163.23	15,745.77	16,476.25
[b] Loss by a subsidiary of			26,921.90

can banks as a result of the policy of the Federal Government to discourage banks and other financial institutions from financing new foreign operations by American companies.

The controller recommended that the board of directors raise between $400,000 and $500,000 of outside funds for a term of at least 6 to 8 years.

He also reported that he had negotiated and received a proposal from an SBIC and another proposal from the Industrial Loan Department of a large insurance company. The respective proposals were as follows:

1. The SBIC was prepared to make a loan for 8 years of $500,000 in 5½% debentures. 20% of these debentures were to be convertible into 80,000 no par value common stock to be issued by the corporation in addition to its already outstanding 240,000 shares whenever the SBIC

TABLE 13-5. Income Statements for Fiscal Years Ending August 31, for Years 1962, 1963, 1964; Consolidated Statement of the Reynolds Equipment Company

	1962		1963		1964		Percent Change 1963/62	Percent Change 1964/63
	Dollars	Percent Distribution	Dollars	Percent Distribution	Dollars	Percent Distribution		
Total sales	2,302,007	100	2,485,326	100	2,808,928	100	+ 8.0	+ 13.0
Total cost of sales	1,182,422		1,414,065	56.9	1,548,453	55.1	+ 19.6	+ 9.5
(cost of goods sold, royalties and depreciation)								
Gross margin	1,119,585	48.6	1,071,261	43.1	1,260,475	44.9	− 4.3	+ 17.7
Total selling expense								
Total advertising expense								
Total selling and advertising expense								
Total administrative expense								
Total selling, administrative and advertising expense	823,305	35.8	948,344	38.2	1,001,891	35.7	+15.2	+ 5.6
Net income before taxes	289,510	12.6	97,147	3.9	239,562	8.5	−66.4	+146.6
Taxes based on income	145,000	6.3	35,000	1.4	135,000	4.8	−75.9	+285.7
Net income after taxes	144,510	6.3	62,147	2.5	104,562	3.7	−57.0	+ 68.2

TABLE 13-6.   Balance Sheets for Fiscal Years Ending August 31, for Years 1962, 1963, 1964; Consolidated Statement for the Reynolds Equipment Company

	1962 ($)	1963 ($)	1964 ($)	Percent Change 1963/62	Percent Change 1964/63
Current assets	976,691	1,090,853	1,419,083	+11.7	+30.1
Fixed assets	87,751	99,871	133,263	+13.8	+33.4
Other assets	38,166	27,855	43,116	−27.0	+54.8
Total assets	1,102,608	1,218,579	1,595,462	+10.5	+30.9
Current liabilities	337,260	470,809	823,005	+39.6	+74.8
Noncurrent liabilities	262,500	187,500	112,500	−28.6	−40.0
Total liabilities	599,760	658,309	935,505	+ 9.8	+42.1
Capital stocks	322,260	322,260	322,260	0	0
Retained earnings	180,588	238,010	337,697	+31.8	+41.9
Total net worth	502,848	560,270	659,957	+11.4	+17.8
Total liabilities and net worth	1,102,608	1,218,579	1,595,462	+10.5	+30.9

wanted to convert. The purchase price of these 80,000 shares was to be $1.25 per share. The SBIC also insisted on the right to elect 2 out of 6 members of the board of directors. $96,000 of the $500,000 term loan was to be used to repay the balance of the 3-year bank term loan.

2. The insurance company offered to make a term loan of $400,000 repayable over a 13-year period in semiannual installments of $16,000 plus interest at $6\frac{1}{4}\%$ on the unpaid balance. Also, the insurance company was willing to have the bank participate in the $400,000 to the extent of the $96,000 outstanding balance. Under this package proposal, the bank's portion would have a seniority position; i.e., the first 6 semiannual installments of $16,000 each would be paid to the bank. At the end of 3 years, the subsequent installments would be paid toward the $304,000 balance held by the insurance company.

Tables 13-4 to 13-6 show the income statements and balance sheets for the Reynolds Equipment Company.

Case Question:

Which proposal should the company accept? Why?

Part III

Long-Term Financing

Chapter Fourteen

Long-Term Debt Financing

The importance of long-term debt financing to American business is illustrated in Table 14-1. In each of the eight years 1959–1966, the sale of new debt securities ranged between 71 and 88.1% of the total volume of new corporate securities. The annual dollar figures ranged between a low of $8081 million and a high of $15,561 million. These data clearly indicate the dominant role played by debt securities as a means of obtaining long-term funds from external sources.

Borrower's Problems In deciding whether or not to sell debt securities, the financial officer must consider four basic issues. First, he must weigh the relative advantages—i.e., the cost and uncertainty—of a long-term bond issue versus a series of term loans. Suppose that a firm needs $1 million for a 15-year investment in new machinery and major physical improvements in its building. A bank is willing to make a five-year term loan at a lower interest rate than the current rate for a 15-year bond issue. But what will the situation be five years from now? Conceivably, the firm may have suffered some reverses in the months or year prior to the maturity of the term loan. Will the firm then be able to procure another term loan to repay the present one? Will the going interest rate then be as favorable as the current rate? And how about the economy as a whole? If there should be an economic recession, what is the likelihood of obtaining a replacement loan? Even if this should prove to be feasible, it is very likely that the lender will insist on more restrictive covenants and, probably, also a higher rate of interest. These uncertainties must be weighed against the advantage of a lower rate on a term loan.

Second, if the financial officer and top management decide on a 15-year bond issue, who should sell the debt securities? Should the firm

TABLE 14-1. Total New Issues (in Millions of Dollars)

Gross Proceeds, All Issues

| Period | Corporate | | | | | | Grand Total | Bonds as Percent of Total |
| | Bonds | | | Stock | | | | |
	Total	Publically offered	Privately placed	Total	Preferred	Common		
1959........	7,190	3,557	3,632	2,558	531	2,027	9,748	73.8%
1960........	8,081	4,806	3,275	2,073	409	1,664	10,154	79.6
1961........	9,420	4,700	4,720	3,844	450	3,294	13,164	71.0
1962........	8,969	4,440	4,529	1,736	422	1,314	10,705	83.8
1963........	10,856	4,713	6,143	1,454	343	1,011	12,319	88.1
1964........	10,865	3,623	7,243	3,091	412	2,679	13,956	77.6
1965........	13,720	5,570	8,150	2,272	725	1,547	15,992	85.8
1966........	15,561	8,018	7,542	2,513	574	1,939	18,074	86.1
1967........	21,954	14,990	6,964	2,844	885	1,959	24,798	88.5

Source: Federal Reserve Bulletin, July 1968, p. A-44.

attempt to find a buyer (e.g., a pension fund, an insurance company) or should it make a direct offer to sell to the public? Or is it more advantageous to employ the services of an underwriter or investment banker to act as an intermediary?

Third, if an intermediary is to be used, should the firm invite competitive bids from several brokers or investment bankers? Or should it confine itself to one investment banker and negotiate for the best terms attainable from this investment house?

Last, but by no means least, how does one measure the monetary value of "invisible" costs (e.g., options, warrants, conversion rights) that may be asked by the underwriter or the direct buyer of the debt securities?

The answers to each of these questions depends on experience and judgment. The capital market, over a period of many decades, has evolved a wide variety of covenants and terms of purchase. A basic familiarity with these features is indispensable if the firm is to strike a bargain that is fair to the borrower and reasonable to the lender(s).

The analysis in this chapter will deal with four major areas:

1. Types of debt securities.
2. Investors.
3. The management perspective.
4. The market.

I. TYPES OF DEBT SECURITIES

The two most frequent types of long-term debt instruments are (1) mortgage bonds, and (2) debentures or debenture bonds.

In addition, there have evolved over the years a variety of debt securities that are designed to meet special stituations. The major forms of these hybrid instruments will be discussed at the end of this section.

Common Features The agreement between the corporation (debtor) and the purchasers of the security (creditors) is called the *indenture*. This instrument sets forth in detail the type of the security pledged by the corporation, the precise obligations assumed by the debtor, special rights or privileges granted to the holders, and other provisions agreed to by the debtor. Quite frequently, the indenture runs into a score or more of printed pages.

The bond itself is usually a single-page document. It is clearly identified as a "bond" and bears a face value (as a rule, $1000) which represents a fraction of the total debt specified in the indenture. Whereas the indenture constitutes the agreement between the corporation and the bondholders as a group, the bond sets forth the basic claims of the individual holder; e.g., rate of interest, date of payment, due date of principal, and other major provisions regarding the financial relationships.

As a practical matter, it would be impossible for each single bond-holder to assure himself of full compliance by the corporation with all the covenants of the indenture. To provide adequate protection for the multitude of bondholders that their interests are safeguarded within the terms of the indenture, the indenture provides for the appointment of a *trustee* in behalf of the bondholders.

The trustee, acting in behalf of the bondholders, is obligated to make certain that the debtor complies with the terms of the indenture. This involves the periodic examination of the financial and other records that the debtor has agreed to supply at stated intervals. In case of violations of the indenture, the trustee is automatically authorized, and obligated, to take the appropriate measures.

The trustee also receives, from the corporation, the funds that are to be distributed to the bondholders as interest and principal. If the indenture calls for the establishment of a sinking fund, the trustee acts as its administrator.

It is customary for the corporation to pay the trustee's fees, although the trustee acts only in the interest of the bondholder. To minimize the risk of a conflict of interest, the Trust Indenture Act of 1939 imposes a series of specific responsibilities on the trustee and makes violators both civilly and criminally liable. Furthermore, the trustee named in the indenture must be an incorporated entity and have a capital and surplus of at least $150,000. The administration of this act was placed in the hands of the Securities and Exchange Commission. However, it must be noted that the act applies only to bond issues in excess of one million dollars.

A. Mortgage Bonds

As the name already indicates, this type of bond is secured by a mortgage on specified fixed assets of the corporation. In form, the corporate mortgage is similar to the mortgage on a piece of residential property. There are, however, important differences in substance. These differences merit an analysis in some detail.

The holder of a mortgage on a residential property looks to the property as the real security for his loan. He is reasonably sure that he can foreclose and sell the property for at least the amount of the mortgage. If he holds a first mortgage, he is not concerned with the placement of a second or even a third mortgage on the same property. As far as he is concerned, he has a prior claim to the proceeds from a forced sale of the property. The holder of the first mortgage expects that, even in a distress sale of the property, the proceeds will be sufficient to cover the cost of the foreclosure and commission on the forced sale and the full claim of the first mortgage. If the debtor cannot meet the interest payments on the second and third mortgages, the holders of the mortgages may foreclose if they so desire. But their respective claims will go unsatisfied until the holder of the first mortgage receives his claim in full.

The situation is quite different in the case of a corporate mortgage. In this instance, the bondholder looks at the earning capacity of the corporation as his primary security. The value of the property pledged as security in the mortgage may shrink substantially if the corporation is forced to liquidate the asset. This is particularly true of industrial properties that are designed to fit the specific needs of firms; e.g., size, layout, construction, location, etc.

The holder of a corporate mortgage bond has, therefore, a vital interest in protecting himself against an excessive pledge of the corporation's income to subsequent secured creditors. Thus, the indenture of a first mortgage bond may provide that the total amount of bonds to be issued under the first mortgage will not exceed, for instance, $3 million on the property that has an appraised value of e.g., $5 million. This is known as a *closed-end* mortgage.

Conceivably, the corporation in this hypothetical case may not want to raise, at the present, more than $2 million through the sale of bonds. However, it wants to keep the door open to a subsequent issue of another million dollars of bonds. Furthermore, the corporation's present plans may call for the acquisition of additional property in the not too distant future. In either one of these two cases, an offering of second mortgage bonds would involve less favorable terms for the corporation. The device employed in situations of this type is the *open-end* mortgage. To continue our illustration, the corporation would offer first-mortgage bonds with a limit of 60% of the value of the property pledged as security. Thus, if it does not acquire additional property, it could later issue another million dollars of bonds. And if it subsequently acquired a piece of property assessed at $2 million, it could issue another $1.2 million of first-mortgage bonds winding up with a total first mortgage of $2 million plus $1 million plus $1.2 million, or $4.2 million secured by property with an appraised value of $7 million.

Another provision found frequently in corporate indentures is the *after-acquired* clause. Under this clause, any property subsequently acquired by the corporation becomes automatically an added security for the bonds already issued. The after-acquired clause may create a serious financing problem in the case of a closed-end mortgage. Suppose that, in our illustration, the corporation has sold $3 million of first-mortgage bonds against property valued at $5 million. It wants to acquire another piece of property costing $2 million and needs $1.2 million of debt capital to finance the transaction. Under the after-acquired clause, this new property would be included in the pledge for the first-mortgage bonds. The corporation could, therefore, only sell *junior* bonds that would involve a higher rate of interest than first-mortgage bonds.

In general, prospective investors may insist on a closed-end mortgage while corporations would rather have an open-end mortgage. However, there are exceptions to this rule. A water company, for example, encounters no difficulty in selling bonds secured by an open-end mortgage. A subsequent acquisition of additional facilities—i.e., expansion of the reservoir, more pumps, etc.—usually means a corresponding expansion of output, revenues, and profit. If these facilities can be financed under an open-end mortgage, the interest rate is likely to be lower than on a second-mortgage bonds. This, in turn, means a larger profit. Unlike a public utility company which enjoys a franchise monopoly, a manufacturing or distributing firm is neither limited in its field of operations to a specific product nor does it enjoy the absence of direct competition from other firms offering the same product. In these cases, therefore, the investor is generally reluctant to invest in bonds secured by an open-end mortgage.

However, it should be noted that corporations have evolved various devices to circumvent the after-acquired clause. It is sufficient to mention only two. One involves a lease arrangement on the new property and the other calls for the creation of a subsidiary corporation which acquires the new property subject to a purchase money mortgage of $1.2 million on the property.

B. Debenture Bonds

Two major reasons may inhibit a corporation from using mortgage bonds as a means of raising debt capital. Finance companies, for example, have no real property on which to place a mortgage bond. Firms engaged in distribution or service trades generally operate with a relatively low rate of real estate to other assets. Large department stores are heavily oriented toward inventory, fixtures, and furnishings compared with real property. In these cases, the amounts that could be raised on a mortgage-bond issue may be insufficient for the needs of the establishment.

A second reason is that the corporation enjoys a high credit rating in the capital market which makes it possible to procure the desired funds without the security of a mortgage. In other words, the firm does not have to pledge some or all of its property in order to obtain the required debt capital. Its past earning record and future prospects offer adequate security to the prospective investors.

The debenture then becomes the debt instrument. Since the debenture is tied directly to the prospective income of the corporation, the protective provisions of the indenture are focused primarily on the disposition of future earnings by the firm, just as the bond indenture is oriented toward property.

The scope and details of the indenture depends on a great number of factors; e.g., type of industry, size of company, rate of earnings, plans for future expansion, dividend policy, conditions in the capital market, and last but not least, the bargaining power of the corporation. Basically, the indenture will include provisions covering the following areas. It usually restricts the corporation in its *dividend policy;* i.e., a specified portion of the after-tax profit must be retained in the company. Next, the corporation will be limited in issuing additional debentures unless these subsequent debentures will be *subordinate* or junior debentures. Frequently, the indenture will also have an *after-created mortgage* provision. This clause provides that any mortgage subsequently placed on property owned by the corporation will not have priority over the debenture in case of default or liquidation. The debenture will thus have parity with any future mortgage bond. It is also customary to place restrictions on the *sale of assets* by the corporation.

Each of the above restrictive covenants may conceivably interfere with future management decisions that would strengthen the corporation and actually improve the quality of the debenture. For example, the corporation may be offered, at some future date, a highly attractive price for a piece of property. The funds realized from this sale could then be used by the corporation for more profitable operations. In order not to bind the corporation inflexibly for the lifetime of the debenture, the indenture may include a provision permitting a modification of the restriction upon approval by a fixed proportion of the bondholders.

C. Hybrid Instruments

The financial manager of a company desiring to secure long-term financing frequently finds that the optimum form of borrowing agreement in terms either of cost or of long-term strategy involves giving the lender some direct claim on the company's future growth and earnings.

There is an infinite variety of these arrangements. Frequently, new companies are financed by *package deals*. For example, the investor must purchase the company's bonds or debentures in a tie-in with the purchase of common stock. When Belco Petroleum, then a relatively unknown gas and oil producer, went public in 1959, the first offering was of units of $36 in debentures and two common shares of stock for $54.30 per unit.

Even more common is the use of *warrants* or *options* to "sweeten" a long-term debt issue, or a refinancing. The warrants, usually given in proportion to the number of bonds secured, allow the holder to purchase the common stock of the company at a set price for a given period of years.[1]

When Mack Trucks, Inc., in 1961 issued $20,000,000 in subordinated debentures, each $1000 bond carried with it five warrants, each of which entitled the holder to buy for $46 one share of Mack's common stock at any time until April 1, 1971. These warrants, as is commonly the case, are detachable from the bond whose sale they make easier, and are separately traded. In the Mack case, the warrants were worth approximately $10 each shortly after the issue. At that rate the purchaser of a Mack bond, instead of paying $1000, actually acquired the bond, assuming he sold the warrants, at a net cost of $950. Mack, on the other hand, secured a more favorable reception for its debt issues than would otherwise have been the case. In return, however, the value of the company's future growth to its stockholders was diluted to the degree that there would be more potential equity holders to enjoy it.

---

[1] There are a few warrants around such as those of the Alleghany Corporation which have no expiration date. As in the case noted, these usually are the result of the bargaining associated with a corporate refinancing after serious difficulties.

In addition to their use in "sweetening" bond issues and refinancings, warrants are frequently given to underwriters as part of their fee.

From management's point of view the immediate effect of this action on the company's financial structure may be relatively slight. Indeed, as was noted, these "sweeteners" may minimize the immediate costs of borrowing. In the long run, however, they may depress the value of the company's common stock since they serve to increase the number of shares with a corresponding dilution of earnings that would otherwise have been available to the stockholders.

1. Convertible Bonds The most commonly used form of hybrid instrument is the convertible bond. Convertible bonds are issued in the same form as ordinary debenture bonds, with all of the restrictions on managerial conduct previously discussed. In addition, however, the holder of a convertible bond has the right to convert his debt holding into the common stock of the debtor on some prearranged basis.

In this case, the company's debt may have all of the elements of a regular bond or debenture: fixed rate of interest, redemption provisions, ultimate maturity of the debt and repayment by the borrower, sinking fund and so on, plus the privilege at the lender's option of converting the bond into common stock. Almost 10% of the nearly 5000 companies listed in *Moody's* 1963 *Industrial Manual* had floated issues of convertible bonds.

An example of the use of this form of financing is the $7,500,000 issue of 4⅜% Convertible Subordinated Debentures Sold by the American Greetings Corporation in July of 1963. As a pure loan, the debentures, judging from the *Ba* rating given them, would have had to bear an interest charge of approximately 5⅜%. The difference in the interest charge (which is a not inconsiderable $75,000 per year) is a tribute to the conversion privilege extended the lenders. The lenders may, at their option, through the life of the loan, convert it into shares of the company at $41.64 worth of loan for a share of common stock.[2]

The question may well be asked why the financial manager of the company did not turn directly to an issue of common stock. The reasons for this strategy are complex.

---

[2] The period during which conversion may take place varies considerably. The most usual provision is for conversion to be possible for the first several years at one price, and at increased prices in the future. For example, Economics Laboratory Inc. Convertible Debentures, issued in 1961, have the following conversion provision: until April 1, 1964: 30.48; from then until April 1, 1967: 33.33; and from then until their maturity in 1971, at 38.10.

a. Cost.   At the time of the issue, the common stock of American Greetings was selling for $37.25 per share. By essentially floating the stock through the initial medium of a convertible bond issue, the company is able to get at least a 12% premium ($41.64 versus $37.25) on the offering price of the common stock. In all probability, this understates the differential since a direct offering of additional common stock would probably have to be at a price significantly under the market in order to attract new buyers. It should be noted, however, that the news of a new offer of a company's convertible bonds tends to depress the common-stock price. The effect generally is smaller, however, than an equivalent direct offer of common stock.

The company was paying a dividend of $0.67 per share, or approximately 1.8% of its market price. The 4⅜% yield of the convertible debenture therefore appeals to potential investors in the company desirous of a high yield on their funds. At the same time, however, the cost to American Greetings of servicing its bonded debt is not as radically different as would appear on the surface. In order to pay $18 on $1000 worth of common stock, the company must earn roughly $36 before taxes. Since the interest on bonds, even convertible ones, is legally a cost of doing business, it is deductible as an expense and therefore amounts to $43.75 of pretax earnings.[3] The actual cost differential, after consideration of the impact of the income tax, is $7.75 per $1000 ($43.75 versus $36), or 0.775%. From the viewpoint of the company, this difference is relatively insignificant.

In addition, the underwriting costs of the convertible issue tend to be much lower than those associated with an equivalent issue of common stock. American Greetings, for example, paid $150,000 to its underwriters for their services in marketing the bonds. A stock issue of $7,500,000, on the other hand, would probably have cost the company in the neighborhood of $250,000 in underwriting fees.[4]

The use of convertible bonds, however, is far from a one-way street. In return for the privilege of using the instrument, management has accepted, at least initially, a creditor with many rights and privileges that must be honored. Unlike the dividend of the common stockholder, the interest charges on the convertible bonds must be met and, ulti-

---

[3] Assuming a 50% income tax rate.

[4] It should be added that these bonds were considered so desirable as to be offered to the public at $1020 per $1000 bond. Within a day after their issue, they were selling at $1100.

mately, the face value of the bonds must be repaid if the holder does not convert them to common stock.

b. Forced Conversion. If the price of the common stock moves past the conversion price—if, for example, the common stock of American Greetings should in the future sell for $62 a share—the bonds would be worth over $1500 each ($62/41.64 × 1000/1). Another factor must be stressed. If the market price of the common stock goes above the conversion point, the market price of the convertible bond will also move proportionally above the face value of the bond. The holder of this security therefore has a twofold advantage. He receives the stipulated rate of interest and has an opportunity to realize a capital gain. If management should then call the bonds for redemption (as is its privilege under the bond indenture) at little more than $1000, in order to protect their investment, the holders would have to convert their holdings into common stock. In this fashion, the company could avoid repaying its loan by converting a debt obligation into an equity claim.

On the other hand, if the common stock remains under the conversion point, there is no way to get the bondholders to forsake their loans in return for common stock and the company must live with all the restrictions usually embodied in the indenture as far as investment and operating policies are concerned. In addition, the rigid requirements of interest rates, sinking funds, and ultimately of redemption will have to be met.

As long as the price of the common stock is below the conversion price, the debenture holder is locked in or "frozen" in his position as creditor.

One of the dangers of "frozen" convertibles (i.e., those where the prices of stock are such that the company cannot force conversion) is that they restrict the issue of more common stock. Investors are often reluctant to purchase new issues of common stock in companies with "frozen" convertibles outstanding, since the threat of ultimate conversion once earnings increase will lead to a dilution in earnings per share and in voting power in the new issue of common stock once the conversion takes place. Since the investors are uncertain about when the "frozen" convertible will become "unfrozen," they tend to shy away from other equity securities of the firm. The existence of a "frozen" convertible may also limit the firm's ability to issue more debt, because, essentially, a "frozen" convertible may be considered as part of the regular debt outstanding as the likelihood of conversion in the near future is scant.

The decision to sell convertible debentures rather than common stock frequently hinges on factors other than a comparison of relative costs; i.e., dividends after tax vs. interest before tax plus respective expenses of underwriting. One factor involves the matter of dilution of ownership and thus control. Until the convertible debentures are at some future date exchanged for common stock, the controlling interest of the corporation remain unaffected.

Another factor is the climate in the securities market. In a declining or "soft" market for common stock, a new stock offering by the corporation is not readily saleable except at a price that is appreciably below the current market price of the company's outstanding stock. Furthermore, the underwriters may be reluctant to underwrite the new stock issue even at the relatively low price; i.e., buy the stock from the company and assume the risk of holding a large block of shares that is not purchased by investors at the issue price. Parenthetically, if a new issue is offered at a price below the current market price the price of the "old" stock quickly drops to the lower level.

Convertible debentures also have a strong appeal to some investors in a rising stock market. Since the conversion is at the discretion of the debenture holder, the latter can play both sides of the table. He is a creditor and as such has a claim to a fixed rate of interest. At the same time, the investor can gamble on a long-run upward movement of the stock. If this happens he converts the debenture into common stock. He thus escapes the risks of a sudden reversal in the stock market. However, the investor pays a price for this option to be creditor or equity owner. The price is the difference between the price of the debenture and the current price of the common stock. It will be recalled that, in the case of American Greeting, this price equalled 12% of the current price of the common stock.

2. Income Bonds   Income bonds, also known as preference bonds or adjustment bonds, are usually issued to security holders in reorganizations to readjust fixed interest debt downward.[5] Income bonds provide for payment of interest only to the extent that net earnings are available. However, the principal of income bonds is payable in exactly the same manner as other bonds. Income bonds may be secured by mortgages or may be debentures.

---

[5] This practice has been frequently used in the reorganization of railroads.

Generally, income bonds provide that interest must be paid by the corporation to the extent it has been earned in each year, sometimes after specified deductions. The interest on income bonds, like preferred dividends, may be made cumulative or noncumulative. When cumulative, unpaid interest must generally be paid for all periods owed before shareholders can receive dividends. In some cases, unpaid interest must be paid upon maturity of the bonds. Noncumulative income bonds lose all claims on interest not paid in any period. Like other bonds, the exact features of the interest bond will vary depending upon the debenture.

In recent years, income bonds have been used in lieu of preferred stock in some instances, since interest paid on income bonds is generally tax deductible for federal income tax purposes and preferred dividends are not tax deductible. However, since most income bonds are issued as a result of financial weakness in corporate reorganizations, many firms are reluctant to issue these securities for fear that the financial community will think the firm to be in financial difficulty.

Impact of Debt Capital

Debt capital is by far the major external source of borrowed funds employed by American corporations. The time interval for which the funds are sought, the size of the company, and the nature of the fixed assets that are offered as security for the debt determine, in large measure, the debt instrument and the terms of the indenture. In each instance, however, the debtor firm is required to make substantial policy commitments—defined in the restrictive covenants of the indenture—in order to induce the investor or lender to place the capital at the disposal of the firm.

In negotiating the terms of the bond indenture, management must weigh the advantage of having long-term funds at a fixed rate of interest but subject to restrictive covenants versus the advantage of fewer restrictions on an intermediate-term loan but uncertainty of future interest rates when the loan must be renewed and the larger amounts required for periodic installments on the loan. Short-term loans for a year or two, in the very limitation of their life, are relatively more relaxed than are intermediate-term loans.

Attractive though the leverage and tax attributes of borrowed money are, they must be examined and weighed against the dangers of taking on fixed obligations that must be met. The securing of equity funds means that present stockholders must share future growth with the new equity holders. In times of poor profits, however, dividends may be eliminated; debt service cannot be.

The firm must also consider the probable impact of debt capital on the cash flow of the firm. Fixed interest payments are a drain on the cash assets. In a period of declining sales, this may become a serious threat to the liquidity of the company. This adverse effect is magnified if the indenture calls for fixed periodic payments on the principal, either by calling a specified portion of the debt securities or by specified payments into a sinking fund.

II. INVESTORS

The owner of capital who desires to make an investment in a corporation has the choice between equity securities or debt securities. What are the attractions of debt securities and the specific reasons that prompt an individual or an institution to put the funds in debt securities? The answers lie partly in the objectives of the investors and partly in existing legal restraints imposed upon the holder of investible funds.

1. Safety of Principal Unlike an equity security—common stock—a debt security represents a definitive obligation on the part of the debtor to pay a specific sum of money on a given (maturity) date. Assuming that the debtor-firm is solvent and liquid on the maturity date the creditor—i.e., the holder of the claim—will be paid the specified amount. If the claim is secured by a lien on an asset of the firm, the creditor will be paid in full if the firm is in default providing the asset yields a sufficient amount in liquidation to pay off the debt.

The investor in debt securities thus starts from the premise that his primary objective is safety of principal and that, in his judgment, the firm will be able to meet this obligation. He is willing to forego the chance of a capital gain which he may obtain from an equity investment in order to avoid the risk of a capital loss if the firm fails to generate an adequate profit.

There are, however, occasions when debt securities, too, offer an opportunity for a potential capital gain. This is true, for example, in a period of high interest rates. At such times, a new issue of bonds must offer the going high rate of interest if the securities are to be sold at or close to their face value. Conversely, the market price of previously issued bonds with a lower interest rate declines; e.g., if the going rate is 6% a $1000 bond paying 4½% may sell for $850. If the going rate subsequently declines to 5%, the market price 6% bond will go above face value while the 4½% bonds, which had dropped to $850, may go to $950 for instance. Thus, the investor who purchased either bond in a period of high interest rate procures a capital gain when interest rates decline and the market price of the acquired bonds rises.[6]

2. Constant Returns   Safety of principal is one side of the coin. The other side of the coin calls for a fixed rate of interest payable at specified intervals to the holder of the debt security. This obligation to pay interest is not contingent on the firm's volume of profit. Even if the firm operates at a loss, it is obliged to pay the agreed-upon interest on the debt. Failure to make this payment is tantamount to a default on the total debt. The holders of these securities may then proceed to take legal action for a receivership or any other course of action spelled out in the indenture. A corporation that fails to earn a profit need not automatically default on interest payments. It can "tap" excess cash built up through retained earnings from previous years. This will reduce the net worth of the corporation and may have an adverse effect on its liquidity. But it preserves the solvency of the firm. Or the corporation may sell some of its unpledged fixed assets in order to meet its interest payments. The effect will also be a decline in its net worth, unless the assets are sold at a higher price (i.e., capital gain) than the value at which they are carried on the books. Finally, in order to preserve its liquidity, the corporation may be able to obtain a loan and use the proceeds to pay the interest on the bonds.

By accepting a constant return on the debt, the investor foregoes any participation in a future rise in the firm's earnings. Conversely, he is not subject to a cutback in the rate of return if the corporation fails to make a profit.

3. Legal Directives   The individual owner of capital has the choice of investing his funds in equity stock or in debt securities. This choice is not open to life insurance companies, administrators of trusts and trust funds, except where the settlor—i.e., the creator of the trust— specifically authorizes the trustee to invest the funds in equity securities.

---

[6] Bonds of American Tobacco with a coupon rate of 4⅝% and maturing in 1990 sold in September 1966 at $850. The high early in 1966 was $960. Similarly, the price of United States Steel 4⅝% bonds maturing in 1966 were $857 and $957.50, respectively.

In most states, insurance companies and trustees are required by law to invest the funds in specified investments; e.g., mortgages, government bonds, corporate bonds, etc. In the case of corporate bonds, these laws also frequently prescribe the "ratings" that corporate bonds must have in order to qualify for this investment. Some states now permit life insurance companies to invest up to a fixed percentage of their funds in equity securities.

a. Risk Elements.　The investor in a debt security faces two basic risks. One risk involves the possible loss of purchasing power as a result of *inflation*. Even if the investment itself is repaid in full upon maturity, the real value of the principal, measured in buying power, may be significantly less than the same sum of money at the time the investor acquired the security.

The other risk is the possibility that the firm may be in *default* and thus unable to meet its obligation. The fact that the debt is secured by a lien, or mortgage, on a fixed asset (e.g., land and building(s) or equipment and machinery) does not automatically assure full recovery of the debt in a foreclosure sale of these assets. Much depends on the saleability of the asset. If the latter consists of a highly specialized building, designed for a specific use, there may be few firms who have an interest in purchasing the property, unless it is offered at a fraction of its reproduction costs. Or local tax rates and labor conditions may be such that few companies care to pay more than a give-away price.

Thus, the real security of the debt rests not so much in the possible future liquidation value of the pledged asset but rather in the debtor-firm continuing as a going concern. If the debtor remains in business and operates at a fair profit, its ability to meet its obligation out of accumulated reserves or by means of refinancing offers the best security for the debt. It is for this reason that knowledgeable investors look primarily to current and prospective future earnings and, if satisfied on this score, are willing to purchase debt securities that are not backed by the pledge of specific assets.

An upward change in the *market rate of interest* has an adverse effect on the market value of outstanding debt securities. Suppose an investor purchased a 20-year bond paying 5% interest (i.e., $50 per annum) and that this bond will mature in 2½ years. Next assume that, 6 months after the purchase, the interest rate on newly issued bonds of comparable quality goes up to 6%. Our investor will still receive $50 interest for each of the next 2 years and the principal sum of $1000 on the maturity date. If, for some reason, he has to sell the bond today, he will receive only $980 dollars. Since the newly issued bonds of comparable quality will pay an investor $60 per annum, the older bond will be discounted by about $10 per year, i.e., the difference between the yields of $50 and $60, respectively.

The opposite also holds true. If the market rate of interest declines, the value or price of bonds with a higher rate of interest will go up. In the previous case, the bond sells at a "discount," whereas, in the latter case, it is sold at a "premium." In either case, if the investor holds the bond to maturity, he will receive the face amount (i.e., $1000).

b. Bond Rating. In order to aid the investor in bonds, a system of formalized ratings has been used for a number of years. Although generated by private companies, the ratings of Standard and Poor's or Moody's Financial Service have achieved an essentially official position in determining the investment caliber of new and extent issues. For the country bank without an investment analyst, for the lawyer serving as the guardian of an estate—or for the private investor—these services provide a simple means of evaluating the *risk* element behind all the major public issues. Moody's, for example, rates bond issues on the following scale:

Aaa	*Baa*	*Caa*
Aa	*Ba*	*Ca*
A	*B*	*C*

The *Aaa* category is reserved for the very few major companies whose ability to service and repay their debt is beyond any question short of a major industrial upheaval. *C* grade bonds on the other hand are usually in default with little hope of revitalization. The full definition given by Moody's for *Baa* bonds is representative of the factors taken into account:

"Bonds which are rated *Baa* are considered as lower medium grade obligations, i.e., they are neither highly protected nor poorly secured. Interest payments and principal security appear adequate for the present, but certain protective elements may be lacking or may be characteristically unreliable over any great length of time. Such bonds lack outstanding investment characteristics and in fact have speculative characteristics as well."

The investor's willingness to trade present money for future interest payments and the promise of ultimate return of capital is usually a function of his belief in the future of his debtor. The rating services provide professional insight into the latter. When these prospects are uncertain, higher interest rates are required as an inducement to overcome risk. In mid-1963, for example, *Aaa* bonds bore a typical interest rate of 4.21%. *Aa* bonds sold at a yield of 4.35% while *A* ratings were at 4.46%. The treasurer of a company contemplating a new bond issue with an anticipated rating of *Baa* at that time would have found that comparable securities were available at a 4.8% yield, while companies that could anticipate only a *Ba* rating would probably have to give the creditor anywhere from 5 to 6%. The costs of long-term debt in even more speculative situations obviously was much higher.

III. THE MANAGEMENT PERSPECTIVE

When and why should the financial manager of a company recommend long-term debt instead of other forms of financing? This is not a simple problem. A number of basic questions must be resolved as way stations on the road to effective decision making.

1. Can the firm's financial needs be pinpointed reasonably clearly into the future?

2. What are the immediate out-of-pocket costs of selling long-term debt securities as contrasted with other forms of financing?

3. Since long-term debt implies a fixed obligation over a period of years without renegotiation of carrying charges, is this the right time in terms of current interest rates for committing the firm or should the corporation wait for a more propitious market?

4. What operational strictures will be imposed on the firm by prospective lenders as a condition of investing their funds in this firm for a period of years?

5. How does the financial officer evaluate the overall impact of the proposed debt in terms of the financial balance of the firm—its flexibility in the face of future exigencies?

6. What effect will the new debt have on the equity value of the firm? Will it increase earnings per share? Will the additional risk lower the price earnings ratio and, hence, the market price of the common stock?

TABLE 14-2.   Total Debt to Total Assets in 1961 for Selected Industries (Billions of Dollars; Zeros Omitted)

	Total Assets	Long-Term Debt	Long-Term Debt as a Percent of Total Assets
All industrial divisions	1,289,516,071	165,520,929	12.8
Mining	17,943,960	2,977,333	16.6
Construction	17,745,002	1,961,593	10.5
Manufacturing	275,963,520	35,133,299	12.7
Transportation, communications, electric, gas, and sanitary services	155,534,789	60,955,175	39.2
Wholesale and retail trade	94,590,990	10,389,767	11.0
Finance, insurance, and real estate	699,887,834	46,794,899	6.7
Services	22,829,046	6,353,433	27.8

Source: U.S. Treasury Department, Internal Revenue Service, Statistics of Income . . . 1962, Corporation Income Tax Returns, pp. 334–335.

These questions by no means exhaust the considerations required of astute management. The short-term loan by its very nature usually has only a transient effect on the company. In a matter of months, its existence is automatically terminated, and therefore alternative strategies can be employed if the initial approach proves unsatisfactory. Long-term debt, on the other hand, will affect the company's future for many years and therefore requires understanding of the instrument, its virtues, and its limitations. Table 14-2 shows the percentages of long-term debt to total assets for a number of selected industries in 1961. Notice that the ratios range from a low of 6.7% to a high of 39.2%.

The Financial Leverage Principal

The virtues of long-term debt financing are simply stated. It permits the equity owners in a company to secure additional funds without taking in additional "partners." If the borrowed funds yield greater returns to the company than their cost, the increment will fully accrue to the equity holders. Furthermore, the interest costs of borrowing are tax deductible while the dividends or increases in equity (by plowing back earnings) which attract stock purchasers are available only after taxes are paid.

A simple example illustrates the operation of the financial leverage principle in debt financing as compared with equity financing. Company A has an earnings before taxes of $200,000 with 100,000 shares of common stock outstanding. Its operating statement (assuming a 50% tax rate) would be as shown in Table 14-3.

TABLE 14-3.

Company A earnings before taxes (pretax profit)	$200,000
— taxes @ 50%	100,000
Earnings after taxes	$100,000
Earnings per share (EPS)[a]	$1.00

$$^a EPS = \frac{\text{Earnings after taxes and preferred dividends (if any)}}{\text{Number of common shares}}$$

The management of the company has the alternative of borrowing $1 million at 6% interest or selling 100,000 new shares at $10 each. What will happen if earnings before interest and taxes (EBIT) should increase 50%? The profit statement would then look like the one shown in Table 14-4.

TABLE 14-4.

	Alternative A	Alternative B
	$1,000,000 bonds	100,000 Additional shares issued
Earnings before interest and taxes	$300,000	$300,000
— interest	60,000	
Earnings before tax	$240,000	$300,000
— taxes @ 50%	120,000	150,000
Earnings after taxes	$120,000	$150,000
Number of shares of common stock	100,000	200,000
Earnings per share	$1.20	$0.75

Under Alternative A the earnings per share have increased 20%. The stockholders find that each of their shares now represents $1.20 in earnings without any increase in their investment. Under Alternative B the earnings per share would be $0.75.

But financial leverage works both ways. What would happen if, instead of earnings increasing by $100,000, they should slump by the same amount? Fresh injections of funds may have little effect in the face of a business recession, or of product obsolescence, or any of the many inhibitors of business profits. The new profit statement would look like the one shown in Table 14-5.

TABLE 14-5.

	Alternative A	Alternative B
Earnings before income and taxes	$100,000	$100,000
— interest	60,000	
Earnings before tax	$ 40,000	$100,000
— taxes @ 50%	20,000	50,000
Earnings after taxes	$ 20,000	$ 50,000
Earnings per share	$0.20	$0.25

Under Alternative A, the after-tax earnings per share have declined by 80%, compared with a decrease of 75% under Alternative B. Next, let us assume that the corporation has suffered an operating loss of $100,000 before interest and taxes. Its income statement would be as shown in Table 14-6. Very simply stated, the financial leverage principle merely indicates that earnings per share can be increased very rapidly by the use of borrowed funds. However, the incremental gross profits generated by the latter must first pay the cost of the borrowing. If they cannot do this, the borrowed funds decrease the company's profits after interest payments. The basic principle of the priority of debt service before profits means that, in a highly leveraged company, slight decreases in gross profit can be reflected by great declines in net profit available to stockholders.

Conversely, highly leveraged companies can, on relatively slight increases in gross income, generate very considerable increases in net income per common share. The use of minimal amounts of equity supported by a high ratio of debt capital is frequently attempted despite the catastrophe that frequently has been the result of such financial policies. Real estate holding companies are perhaps the prime example; since they are highly leveraged with mortgages frequently representing more than 85% of the cost of their properties, not infrequently a 10% change in gross revenue can either double profits—or completely obliterate them. Similarly, companies whose output is subject to substantial fluctuations in the course of the business cycle experience sharp swings from sizeable profits in good years to heavy losses in a period of economic recession. This fact explains the traditional reluctance of companies in the mining and construction industries to incur more than a modest proportion of debt capital; see Table 14-2.

Table 14-6.

	Alternative A	Alternative B
Deficit before interest and taxes	($100,000)	($100,000)
— interest	60,000	
Deficit after taxes[a]	($160,000)	($100,000)
Loss per share	($1.60)	($0.50)

[a] In this case there would be no taxes since the company operated at a loss. Under the carry-back provision of the tax laws, the corporation could "carry back" the loss of $100,000 to the previous year in which (it is assumed) the firm had a taxable profit of more than $100,000; i.e., a refund of $50,000 at an assumed tax rate of 50%. The net result would then be:

	Alternative A	Alternative B
Operating loss	$100,000	$100,000
Carry-back refund	50,000	50,000
Net loss	50,000	50,000
Interest	60,000	—
Deficit after interest and taxes	$110,000	$ 50,000
Loss per share	$1.10	$0.50

Other Considerations   It is the function of the financial manager to balance the profit increments available from long-term debt financing against the risks that are generated by its use. In this appraisal, the influence of present tax laws cannot be disregarded. If we assume that Company A of the previous illustration would have to pay a 5% dividend in order to attract new equity investors, then the prospective pretax earnings on new funds from this source would have to be at least 10% (assuming a 50% tax rate). Actually the pretax profit would have to be in excess of 10% since it is common practice not to distribute the entire after-tax earnings in dividends. Many corporations have a payout ratio of 50 to 60%. At a pay-out ratio of 50% the corporation would have to earn 20% before taxes. On the other hand, a 5% interest burden can be readily met if prospective earnings are below 10% but above 5%.

The appeal of tax deductibility of interest is obviously strong, especially in conjunction with the fact that equity is not diluted and that equity holders reap the benefit of profits in excess of interest payment after payment of the tax on such excess earnings. But, as pointed out earlier, this advantage of debt financing must be balanced by the financial officer against the comparative rigidity of debt financing. Interest and sinking fund obligations must be met, and repayment of the debt is obligatory. Management's responsibility to equity holders, on the other hand, is less rigid. Dividends can be omitted—at a price. Failure to declare a dividend depresses the market value of the common stock. Although this affects the stockholder directly—a decline in the value of his investment—it also lowers the credit rating of the corporation.

In a period of expanding sales and profits, the management may tend to prefer debt capital because the prospective use of the funds promises to enhance the earning power per share of the equity of the company and, thus, make a subsequent sale of common stock easier and more remunerative.

However, too high a ratio of debt capital generates a series of side effects that are not immediately apparent. One consequence is the rising cost of additional debt capital. In order to sell successive issues of debt securities, the corporation must pay progressively higher interest rates. At some point, the market may actually refuse to absorb another offering. Furthermore, the growth of debt capital has an inhibiting effect on the ability of the corporation to sell equity securities as an alternative to its failure to sell debt securities. In essence, a rising ratio of debt capital to equity capital has the tendency to lower the rating of the corporation's securities.

Voting Control   Long-term debt is frequently preferred by management over the issue of new common stock in order to maintain voting control over the company. As long as the requirements of the loan agreement are met, the holders of debt do not vote in company elections. Common stockholders usually do. Management, particularly in closely held family companies, may be sensitive on this point and, therefore, turn to debt financing rather than to the equity equivalent even though this may be the more appropriate.[7]

---

[7] Many companies faced with this problem have two classes of stock, one of which may have voting privileges far in excess of the other. Original stockholders will own the first and use the second to secure additional equity. This approach, however, is not permitted by Stock Exchange rules to listed companies.

In a small company that is engaged in product research and development, the owners-managers are reluctant to give up a portion of the anticipated future profits by selling a portion of their ownership at the current value of the company. In other words, the present owners believe that the value per share will be substantially greater after the research has been successfully completed. At that time, the company may be able to sell stock at a price several times the price it can obtain while product research and development are not yet completed.

IV. FACTORS AFFECTING THE ISSUING OF DEBT

The ability of a corporation to obtain debt capital and the willingness of the investor to purchase these securities involves several major elements other than rate of interest and the pledge of specified assets. These elements are:

1. Sinking fund.
2. Earnings coverage.
3. Restrictive covenants.
4. Conversion privileges, options, warrants.

Each of these factors must be considered initially by the financial officer and ultimately by the top management of the corporation.

Sinking Fund   In a few industries, it is possible to make the reasonable assumption that the demand for the product or service of a certain corporation will continue to grow over the next 10, 20, or more years. Water companies, electricity, gas, and telephone services are well-known examples of this market demand. Moreover, the individual corporation represents a franchise monopoly and is therefore protected against competition in its specified market. By contrast, most industries operate under conditions of interfirm competition and, frequently, interindustry competition, i.e., rival products or services that are available as substitutes.

For most companies, the long-term future contains a strong element of uncertainty about its position and earning capacity in the years ahead. In order to reduce the risk of this uncertainty, most indentures call for the setting up of a sinking fund. The money paid into this sinking fund is either invested in government bonds or the securities of other corporations; or it is used to repurchase part of the bonds. In the last case, the indenture will usually have a provision making these bonds "callable" at certain dates. The decision to call or not to call is at the discretion of the corporation. In some cases, the indenture provides that instead of repurchase by the corporation, the corporation may use the contribution to the sinking fund for the purpose of acquiring additional assets. These additional assets then become automatically added security for the bonds.

Two cases illustrate some of the variations that will be found in sinking-fund provisions. In 1962, the Container Corporation sold $25 million of 4.40% debenture bonds maturing in 1967. The indenture provided:

> Annually, 1968–86, the company must retire on June 1, $1,000,000 in debentures at par (i.e., $1,000,000 face value of bonds). The company may, at the same time, at its own option, retire a similar additional amount. Debentures redeemed from optional payments and other than pursuant to the sinking fund may be credited against future mandatory payments.

Furthermore, the corporation reserved the right to "call in"—i.e., pay off—either a part of or the whole bond issue prior to 1987 providing that it gave at least 30 days notice and paid the security holders the following prices (issue price equals 100%):

1963: 104.40*	1964: 104.20	1965: 104.00
1966: 103.80*	1967: 103.60	1968: 103.40
1969: 103.20*	1970: 103.00	1971: 102.80
1972: 102.60*	1073: 102.40	1994: 102.20
1975: 102.00	1976: 101.80	1977: 101.60
1978: 101.40	1979: 101.20	1980: 101.00
1981: 100.80	1982: 100.60	1983: 100.40
1984: 100.20		1987: 100.00

(The asterisk indicates: not callable prior to June 1, 1967 from funds borrowed at less than 4.40%.)

In the same year, 1962, the Missouri Power and Light Company issued first mortgage bonds with the following sinking-fund provision:

> Bonds of any series may be issued from time to time on the basis of (1) 60% of Property Additions after adjustments to offset requirements; (2) retirement of Bonds or qualified lien bonds otherwise than

with Funded Cash; and (3) deposit of cash. With certain exceptions in the case of (2) above, the issuance of Bonds is subject to adjusted net earnings for 12 out of the preceding 15 months before income taxes being at least twice the annual interest requirements on all Bonds at the time outstanding and on all indebtedness of prior rank, including the additional issue. Such adjusted net earnings are computed after expenses for maintenance and provision for retirement and depreciation of property; provided that in lieu of the actual provision for retirement and depreciation of certain mortgaged utility property and automotive equipment, there shall be used an amount equal to the currently existing replacement fund requirement for such period.[8] Furthermore, if the corporation has an earnings coverage ratio, the investor can expect the corporation to recoup a deficit in one or two years by a subsequent sharp rise in sales and profits.

The interest coverage ratio, often referred to as times interest earned, may be computed by dividing the annual interest charges into earnings before interest and taxes (EBIT). When more than one issue of bonds is outstanding, the interest charges of each issue considered must be combined with all issues of senior or equal standing to compute the coverage ratio. For example, let us look at part of the income statement of the Toonerville Railroad for the year ending December 31, 1967:

Earnings before interest and taxes	$5,000,000
Interest on first mortgage bonds	2,000,000
Interest on subordinated debentures	1,000,000
Earnings before taxes	2,000,000
Federal Income Taxes (at 50%)	1,000,000
Earnings after taxes (to common shareholders)	1,000,000
Sinking fund on first mortgage bonds	500,000
Earnings available to common shareholders	$ 500,000

Interest charges on the first mortgage bonds were covered 2½ times in 1967 ($5,000,000/$2,000,000). If coverage on the junior debt security was computed separately, it would appear that the interest on the subordinated debentures was covered 3 times in 1967 [(5,000,000 − $2,000,000)/$1,000,000]. Obviously, this would be misleading since a subordinated security cannot have better protection than

---

[8] Prospectus, dated April 11, 1962.

a senior issue. The only proper method of computing the coverage ratio for a junior issue is to combine the interest charges of the junior issue with all senior interest charges and compare this with the earnings before income and taxes (EBIT). In the case of the Toonerville Railroad, the interest on the subordinated debentures was covered 1.67 times in 1967 [$5,000,000/($2,000,000 + 1,000,000)].

The same methodology is employed if a corporation, in addition to debt securities, had issued preferred stock. Let us assume that the Toonerville Railroad had outstanding $5,000,000 of 6% cumulative preferred stock. Since the dividend claim is subordinated to the income tax and sinking-fund payments, the coverage ratio would be: 1.11 times.

$$\frac{\$5,000,000}{\$2.000,000 + \$1,000,000 + \$1,000,000 + \$500,000}$$

If the senior claims had been ignored the ratio would be 1.66 times ($500,000 after-tax earnings ÷ $300,000 dividends).

Some analysts of debt securities add the funds generated by depreciation to earnings before interest and taxes in computing the interest coverage ratio. This approach is justified on the ground that the reserve for depreciation does not constitute an immediate claim on the corporation's funds and therefore is a "postponable" charge against future earnings. The contrary view, shared by the authors, is that this "postponement" is tantamount to the payment of interest, etc. out of capital rather than income. Furthermore, this postponement would in a subsequent period reduce the actual earnings of that period by the accumulated deferred charges for depreciation.

The potential investor in debt securities is also interested in the coverage of all fixed charges. However, since sinking-fund payments are made after corporate taxes and interest payments are tax deductible, the analyst must convert all figures to either a pretax or a post-tax basis before computing coverage ratios for all fixed charges (times fixed charges earned). Generally, it is easiest and most useful to compute the coverage ratio for all fixed charges on a before-tax basis. This is done by computing the number of pretax dollars needed to meet the sinking-fund payment and adding this to all interest charges to arrive at total fixed charges before taxes. This sum (total fixed charges before taxes) is then divided into earnings before interest and taxes to arrive at times fixed charges earned. In the case of the Toonerville Railroad, there is a sinking-fund requirement of $500,000 after taxes in 1967. Since Toonerville is in a 50% federal income tax bracket, Toonerville requires $1,000,000 in earnings before taxes (after interest payments) to cover the sinking fund payment. Total fixed charges for Toonerville were covered 1.25 times in 1967 [$5,000,000/($2,000,000 + 1,000,000 + 1,000,000)].

Adverse developments in the economy as a whole or in the railroad business may cut Toonerville's EBIT to $3,000,000 or even less. With an earnings before interest and taxes of $3,000,000, Toonerville could still meet its interest requirement.

Most business firms are subject to cyclical fluctuations of sales and earnings. Moreover, many industries are characterized by varying degrees of intraindustry competition. Thus, a given corporation may have, in one year, a rate of profit above its industry average and in the next year fall far below the industry average, or even show a loss while its competitors enjoy a satisfactory rate of profit. A high ratio of debt capital to equity capital may, thus, prove too heavy a burden when earnings drop sharply and are insufficient to meet the fixed contractual payments. A situation of this type may lead to reorganization or bankruptcy proceedings. In general, the more subject a firm is to the vagaries of substantial fluctuations in sales and earnings, the greater is the necessity for caution in the use of debt securities as a source of capital.

The investor, for his part, is aware of the fact that in many lines of business a drop in sales by 20 or 25% will quickly convert a substantial profit into a deficit. A high earnings coverage ratio therefore offers some assurance that a decline in sales and profit will not endanger the payment of interest and sinking fund. Furthermore, if the corporation has generally favorable earnings-coverage ratios, the investor can expect the corporation to recoup a deficit in one or two years by a subsequent sharp rise in sales and profits.

To help protect the public from excessive corporate use of debt securities, the Securities and Exchange Commission has required public utilities to institute sinking funds to amortize corporate debt. These requirements have not been instituted for industrial or manufacturing firms. In general, since industrial firms are more competitive than utilities and, thus, more likely to suffer earnings declines due to competition or the vagaries of the business cycle, investors generally expect industrial debt securities to have greater coverage ratios than utilities debt securities. By the same token, the investor will generally accept a higher ratio of debt capital to equity capital in a public utility than in other corporations of comparable size and earnings.

SUMMARY

Debt securities have played a dominant role in recent years as an external source for long-term funds to American business. The financial manager should be aware of the major types of debt securities (mortgage bonds, debenture bonds, convertibles, and other hybrid instruments). He must know who the potential investors are for his debt securities and how he can reach them (i.e., by direct placement, through underwriters or some other means).

The virtues of debt are simply stated. Long-term debt permits the equity owners in a company to secure additional funds without taking in equity partners. If financial leverage is favorable, the incremental profits will fully accrue to the equity holders. In addition, the interest costs of borrowing are tax deductible.

The financial manager must also consider other means of financing to determine whether long-term debt is the appropriate method of financing at this time in view of the needs of the firm, the risks of debt, and the expected state of the capital market at the time he plans to float his bonds.

In deciding whether or not to sell debt securities the financial manager must consider four basic issues. First, he must weigh the relative advantages of a long-term bond issue versus a series of term loans. Second, he must decide whether direct placement should be made or whether the firm should use an intermediary. Third, if an intermediary is used should the firm seek bids or should it negotiate with one investment banker. Fourth, the monetary value of such costs as options, warrants, and conversion rights must be measured.

However, leverage works both ways. If the incremental profits generated by borrowed funds do not earn enough to pay the interest cost of the debt, the common stockholders will be worse off. Failure to pay interest and sinking fund requirements could cause bankruptcy or other reorganization. Thus, the financial manager should seek to avoid a high ratio of debt capital to equity capital.

Questions

1. What are the difference between a mortgage bond and a mortgage on residential property? What are the similarities?
2. Why do firms sometimes issue debentures instead of mortgage bonds?

3. What are the advantages and disadvantages of convertible bonds from the point of view of the financial manager? The investor?

4. In what respects do income bonds differ from other bonds?

5. Discuss the pros and the cons of debt securities as an investment.

6. What is meant by financial leverage? How can it be helpful to the equity owners of a firm? What are a firm's risks in using financial leverage?

7. Do the present income tax laws encourage firms to use debt capital? Should they?

8. What is the purpose of sinking funds?

9. How do financial managers and investors use coverage ratios?

Problems

1. Lambda Corporation has recently issued (at par) $2,000,000 of 6% convertible debenture bonds. The debentures are convertible into common stock at a rate of 50 shares of stock for each $100 (at par) of debentures converted.

A portion of the balance sheet of Lambda Corporation for December 31, 1966 follows;

Convertible debenture bonds, 6%, due 1991	$2,000,000
Common stock, $1 par	1,500,000
Retained earnings	2,500,000

(a) If all the debenture bonds are converted by the bondholders into common stock, what changes would be made in the balance sheet?

(b) Calculate the book value (per share) of (1) the present common stock before conversion of the debentures; (2) the common stock after conversion of the debentures.

2. The Hardluck Company is to be liquidated. How much will each class of investors and creditors receive?

Hardluck Company
Liabilities January 1, 1967

Accounts payable	$ 20,000
First-mortgage bonds	40,000
Second-mortgage bonds	27,000
Debentures	28,000
Preferred stock	30,000
Common stock	60,000
Retained earnings	(5,000)
Total liabilities	$200,000

First- and second-mortgage bonds are secured by plant, property, and equipment. After liquidation costs, the following amounts were realized from sale of the assets:

Cash (on hand)	$ 2,000
Plant, property, and equipment	63,000
Accounts receivable	32,500
Inventory	24,000
Other assets	1,500

3. On October 15, 1966, Omega Telephone Company announced that it would call its 4% convertible second-mortgage bonds for redemption on January 1, 1967 at 102. Holders of each $1000 of convertible second-mortgage bonds would receive $16\frac{2}{3}$ shares of common stock. The common stock of Omega Telephone Company was selling at $78\frac{3}{8}$ at the close of trading on October 15, 1966.

   (a) Calculate the approximate market price of the 5% convertible mortage bonds on October 15, 1966.

   (b) At what price would the bondholders be willing to accept the call rather than convert their bonds to common stock?

4. The Iroquois Electric Corporation has $12,000,000 in 6% mortgage bonds outstanding which mature in 12 years. These bonds, which are currently selling at 103, are callable at 103. Federal Reserve policies of easier money plus improvements in the company's growth prospects make it possible for the company to issue new mortgage bonds to net 100 (after refunding costs) with an interest rate of $4\frac{3}{4}\%$ to refund the presently outstanding bonds. Assume Iroquois is in a 50% tax bracket. Disregard interest on any interest saved.

   (a) How much in new bonds would have to be issued if the bonds are refunded?

   (b) Calculate the annual savings in interest paid out to the bondholders if the bonds are refunded.

   (c) Should Iroquois refund its bonds at this time?

Case: SOUTHERN AMALGAMATED TELEPHONE COMPANY

Southern Amalgamated Telephone Company is an independently owned telephone company that serves part of the southern United States. Population growth in Amalgamated's service area has been at a rate much faster than the national average in recent years. Consequently, Amalgamated has had to open several new exchanges and has had to install much equipment to keep up with the growing demand for telephone service. Tables 14-7 and 14-8 present financial data on the company.

TABLE 14-7. Southern Amalgamated Telephone Co., Balance Sheet, December 31, 1965 (in Millions of Dollars)

Assets:

Cash	20	
Marketable securities	87	
Accounts receivable, net	67	
Supplies and materials	29	
Prepaid rent	9	
Total current assets		212
Plant, property and equipment		2064
Other assets		26
Total assets		2302

Liabilities:

Accounts payable	65	
Customer advances	14	
Accrued taxes	41	
Accrued interest	5	
Other current liabilities	20	
Total current liabilities		145
First-mortgage bonds, 1987		250
Second-mortgage bonds, 1992		141
Debentures, 1979		305
Reserve for depreciation and amortization		581
Deferred liabilities		7
Common stock, par $1		500
Capital surplus		171
Retained earnings		182
Total liabilities		2302

The company plans to raise $50,000,000 of new capital in 1966 for purposes of new construction of facilities and modernization of existing equipment. In view of recent uncertainties in the stock market, management does not believe it will be feasible to sell an issue of common stock in 1966 except at an excessive discount in market price. Furthermore, the recent trading range of the stock has been between $41 and $45 per share in early 1966. This is down somewhat from the all time high price of $51, reached before the confrontation between President Kennedy and the steel industry in 1962. If growth continues to increase at the present rate in the next few years, management believes the stock should sell at a considerably better price than at present.

One alternative being considered by management is to issue $50,000,000 in 20-year debenture bonds. Because of the large amount of long-term debt now outstanding, it is unlikely that these bonds could be issued unless a top interest rate of 5¾% were paid.

TABLE 14-8.   Southern Amalgamated Telephone Co., Total Revenue and Net Profits 1956 to 1965 (in Millions of Dollars)

Year	Total Revenue	Net Profit
1956	255	44
1957	269	49
1958	301	46
1959	337	47
1960	380	49
1961	407	47
1962	444	49
1963	480	48
1964	512	44
1965	598	51

The other alternative being considered is to issue $50,000,000 in 20-year convertible debenture bonds ($100 par). Present corporate stockholders would be given the rights to purchase these bonds on the basis of $100 worth of bonds for each share of stock owned (there are 500,000 shares of stock outstanding). The bonds would be convertible into common stock, at any time during the twenty years, on the basis of two shares of stock for each $100 worth of bonds. Management believes that such an issue of convertible debenture bonds can be marketed at an interest rate of 5¼%.

Case Questions:

1. What are the risks to Southern Amalgamated under each alternative?
2. Which alternative would you recommend to management? Why?

~~~~~~

Chapter Fifteen

Equity Financing

EQUITY CAPITAL

The stockholders of a corporation are the residual owners of the net worth or equity of the firm. This ownership gives the stockholders certain legal rights. The scope of these rights may be, and frequently is, subject to limitations either set forth in the charter or bylaws of the corporation or in the laws of the state or nation from which the corporate charter has been obtained. The presence or absence of such limitations on the full exercise of ownership has a direct bearing on the selection of the source of long-term funds.

I. COMMON STOCK

Basically, the stockholder, within the limits set in the charter or state law, has proprietary rights to the following:

1. To vote on all major decisions affecting his position as owner of the corporation.
2. To share in the earnings or losses of the firm.
3. To preserve his pro rata ownership.
4. To receive the net worth or residue if the corporation is liquidated.

Voting Rights   The stockholder exercises his voting rights essentially in the election of the board of directors. This board is charged with the responsibility of appointing the officers, determining the broad policies of the corporation, and declaring the dividends, if any, that are to be paid to the stockholders out of earnings. In addition, board actions of a major nature which affect the stockholders' financial interests in the corporation must be submitted for the approval of the stockholders;

e.g., sale or merger of the company, a change in the capital structure through a new stock issue, or the issuing of debt securities.

Under the rules of common law, each share is entitled to one vote. A majority of the shares voted at the annual meeting elects the directors and approves the report and recommendations of the board on those matters that require stockholders' approval. A stockholder who cannot be present at the meeting may appoint a *proxy* who acts in behalf of the shareholder.

However, the "one share one vote" rule may be modified by an appropriate provision in the charter or bylaws of the corporation. For instance, in the 1920's a number of large corporations issued *nonvoting Class A stock;* the voting stock was designated as Class B stock. This practice was discontinued in the 1930's. The Securities and Exchange Commission and the leading national stock exchanges were in large part responsible for the cessation of this practice by larger corporations. The stock exchanges generally refuse to list firms that have issued non-voting common stock.

Smaller corporations occasionally still resort to this device, but for reasons that are peculiar to small firms. In the typical small firm the common stock is held by the owners-officers. Suppose that such a firm needs additional capital which the owners are unable to supply. They do not want to dilute their voting control over the corporation by selling common stock to outsiders. They are able to obtain the needed funds from personal friends, business acquaintances, and suppliers in return for adequate compensation and security. The corporation may then sell preferred stock to these investors and, for each share of preferred stock, give one share of nonvoting stock, usually called either Class A or capital stock. This capital stock is often made callable at a fixed price. This price is the potential "sweetener" offered to the investor, on top of the fixed dividend on the preferred stock.

Another device occasionally resorted to by corporations is to issue a class of common stock which has *multiple* voting rights; i.e., each share has more than one vote. This stock usually does not participate in the earnings of the corporation. Its objective is to assure the retention of control in the hands of the owners of multiple voting stock even if the number of single-vote shares is increased substantially by a new issue of such stock. For example, the Class B stock of the Ford Motor Company, held by members of the Ford family, has multiple voting rights.

The principle of majority vote may work a hardship on the minority. Theoretically, at least 49% of the eligible votes at the annual meeting may be totally ineffective if outvoted by the 51% on all matters calling for majority approval. By means of *cumulative* voting, the corporation affords the minority a means of electing some members of the board and, thus, assure themselves of representation in the deliberations of the directors. In fact, twenty-one states explicitly require that all corporations chartered in these states provide for cumulative voting in their charter.

Under cumulative voting each share has as many votes as the number of directors to be elected. The stockholder may cast these votes in any manner he chooses; e.g., all votes for one director. Suppose there are 10,000 shares and five directors are to be elected. In order to be assured of electing one director the formula is:

$$\frac{\text{Total number of shares} \times \text{number of directors sought}}{\text{Total directors to be elected} + 1} + 1$$

or substituting, if one directorship is sought,

$$\frac{10,000 \times 1}{5 + 1} + 1 = 1667 \text{ shares}$$

and, if a majority of three directors is sought,

$$\frac{10,000 \times 3}{5 + 1} + 1 = 6001 \text{ shares}$$

To be able to obtain minority representation on the board does not necessarily mean that those who elect the majority are prevented from exercising control. The majority of the board is able to make all decisions in matters that the charter and bylaws delegate to the board. Nevertheless, an articulate, and knowledgeable, minority of directors can inhibit actions by the majority which may be challenged in the courts as not in the best interests of the corporation. On the other hand, the minority may use their position to create disharmony in the board for the purpose of preparing for a proxy fight. Thus, cumulative voting may possibly result in hindering the effectiveness of management. Although 1001 shares would be enough (using the previous example) to elect one director in nine, more shares would be needed to elect a director if the number of directors were reduced, for example, to seven. Laws of some states would make such management devices of dubious legality.

Maturity   Unlike debt securities (and some preferred stocks) common stock has no maturity date. Except in the case of reorganization or bankruptcy, common shareholders cannot be forced to sacrifice their claims to the income and assets of the corporation, without their consent.

Corporate Terminology   At this point, it may be well to define the several terms that appear in the corporate balance sheet under the heading of Capital. These items will be found on the liability side since they represent the liability of the corporation to its owners-stockholders.

Capital stock consists of the total number of shares that the corporation is *authorized* to issue and sell. The next item indicates the actual number of *issued* shares. Customarily, a corporation provides in its charter for authorization in excess of the number of shares that it expects to sell in the foreseeable future. This makes it unnecessary to amend the charter every time the directors find it necessary to sell additional stock.

The stock may be either par-value or no-par stock. *Par-value* means that each stock certificate bears a given dollar figure—say, $50—which represents the cash value or its equivalent in assets received by the corporation at the time of sale. By contrast, a no-par stock certificate bears no such identifying dollar figure. The price at which no-par stock is sold by the corporation then represents the dollar figure for this item in the balance sheet. The directors enter a "stated value" per no-par value stock. This stated value may at their discretion be less than the actual price received. The difference would then be entered in the item "capital surplus" or "paid-in surplus." The same procedure is followed if the par-value shares are sold at a premium; i.e., above the face value of the certificate.

Treasury stock represents shares which had been sold but have subsequently been donated back to the corporation or have been repurchased by the corporation from some stockholders. A gift of stock to the issuing corporation is occasionally made by one or more shareholders in a closely held corporation with a few owners-stockholders. One objective is to improve the balance-sheet value of the remaining outstanding shares. At the same time, the directors can sell treasury stock without regard to the par value or the stated value of no-par stock. On the other hand, the directors of a corporation may decide to repurchase some of the outstanding shares when the market price declines substantially below the original issue price.

Preemptive Rights   The stockholder is a pro rata owner of the corporation. His share in the fortunes, or misfortune, of the firm is in proportion to his percentage holdings of the total number of shares issued and outstanding. Under common law, the stockholder has the right to acquire the same proportion of any new stock issued by the corporation. The only exceptions, under common law, are treasury stock, stock not sold in the initial offer by the corporation, and stock for which officers and employees have been given options.

There is, however, no uniformity on this preemptive right in state laws. A few states will issue charters which either limit or abrogate the preemptive right of stockholders.[1] Some states expressly provide for such rights and will not issue charters excluding the preemptive feature. Other states negate the right unless the charter expressly provides for such rights.

The preemptive right has considerable value to a stockholder who wants to retain his position of influence in the corporation although he owns only a minority of the stock. If the corporation has cumulative voting, his holdings may be sufficient to assure him of one or more places on the board. An additional issue of stock may, however, reduce his vote below the minimum required for the election of "his" directors.

The right to subscribe to new securities is very important to the common shareholder, regardless of whether he gets this right as a result of the law or terms of the corporate charter or whether it is given at the discretion of management, since the right to subscribe to new shares is often made at a price below the current market price. This gives an advantage to the holder of rights, as compared to those who have to buy the security in the open market. Rights may be given to any class of equity or debt security for the purchase of the same or another security, although they are mainly used to enable present common shareholders of a corporation to purchase additional common shares.

Once a company has announced a rights issue, trading in the stock is on a *cum* rights or "rights on" basis. This means that the seller of the stock agrees that the buyer will receive the rights to buy new shares to be issued by the company as well as the shares of stock he has purchased from the seller. After a designated date, rights are traded separately from the shares of stock, which are now referred to as being sold *exrights* or "rights off." Rights may be issued which may be exer-

---

[1] The laws of Illinois provide that "the preemptive right of a stockholder to acquire additional shares of a corporation may be limited or denied to the extent provided in the articles of incorporation.

cised over an indefinite period or which become valueless after a certain period. For example, suppose that on January 2, 1967, Alpha Corporation announced it would issue rights to its common shareholders on the following basis. On January 10, 1967, each stockholder would receive one right for each share of stock held. For every five rights, plus $50, the stockholder would receive one new share of Alpha Corporation common stock. The stock would be traded cum rights until January 6, 1967. The rights would expire on January 23, 1967, unless exercised.

If the Alpha Corporation stockholder did not care to exercise his rights he could sell them in the market. Once Alpha was selling on an exrights basis, the stockholder could easily calculate the value of a right. The value of one right is the difference between the exrights market price of one share and the subscription price, divided by the number of rights needed to purchase one share. A formula incorporating this is generally used to perform this calculation where:

P = Theoretical value of one share exrights
S = Subscription price
N = Number of old shares that entitle the stockholder to purchase one new share
M = Market value of one share cum rights
$\dfrac{P - S}{N}$ = Theoretical value of one right, exrights

The theoretical value of one right can also be predicted when the stock is selling *cum* rights by using the formula:

$$\frac{M - S}{N + 1} = \text{Theoretical value of one right, } cum \text{ rights}$$

Using the example of Alpha Corporation, with a *cum* rights market closing price of, say, $85 on January 5, 1967, it is simple to calculate the theoretical value of one right *cum* rights as follows:

M = $85
S = $50
N = 5

$\dfrac{M - S}{N + 1} = \dfrac{85 - 50}{5 + 1}$ = $5.83 = theoretical value of one right of Alpha Corporation, *cum* rights.

If we assume no other influence on the price of Alpha shares, one share exrights should sell for about $79⅛ since the exrights theoretical market price of one share plus the value of one right should theoretically be equal to the *cum* rights market price of one share ($85 - 5.83 = \$79.17$). Of course, there will be other influences on the market price of Alpha stock besides the fact of the rights offering. Assume that the exrights market price goes to $82 by January 20. The shareholder can now use the formula $(P - S)/N$ to calculate the value of a right on that date. For Alpha, $(P - S)/N$ or $(82 - 50)/5 = \$6.40$, which equals the theoretical value of one right, exrights on January 20, 1967. The actual market value of the right may be different as a result of speculation by investors in the rights. Note that where the exrights market price went from $79\frac{1}{8}$ to 82 (or an increase of less than 4%) the value of one right went from $5.83 to $6.40 in the same period of time (or an increase of almost 10%). Since market price changes tend to be magnified in rights, speculators are often more interested in purchasing rights than the stock itself. However, when rights are issued with an expiration date (as Alpha) a day of reckoning must come. Either the rights must be exercised before the expiration date or they become worthless.

In theory, the value of one right will equal the anticipated dilution of the market value of one old share. Hence, if the stockholder sells his rights, he will sustain no loss in the total market value of his holdings, if income tax questions are disregarded.

The exrights formula $(P - S)/N$ may also be used in all instances where the right to subscribe to issues of preferred stock or bonds is given, since dilution is not involved.

Stock Splits   The stock split is a device to increase the number of shares outstanding without any change in the capital funds, or equity, of the corporation. Thus, while the number of shares is increased, the total dollar value of the capital stock of the retained earnings remains unchanged. If the corporation has issued any outstanding par value shares the number of shares is increased in the inverse proportion to the reduction in the par value. For example, if the corporation decides to have a stock split of 2 new shares for 1 old share and the old share has a par value of $50, each of the 2 new shares will have a par value of $25. In the case of no par value stock, no such adjustment is necessary.

Table 15-1 shows a partial list of 106 stock splits in 1965 by corporations listed on the New York Stock Exchange. One or more of the following reasons usually account for a stock split. First, and the most frequent cause, a stock split tends to stimulate greater marketability

TABLE 15-1.   Stock Splits in 1965 for Corporations listed on the New York Stock Exchange. (During 1965 there were 106 stock splits or stock distributions amounting to 50% or more. A list of these issues is shown in the following table.)

10 for 1	Superior Oil Co.	
5 for 1	Pittsburgh & West Virginia Ry. Co.	
4 for 1	Polaroid Corp.	U.S. Smelting, Refining & Mining Co.
3 for 1	Carolina Tel. and Tel. Co.	Lukens Steel Co.
2½ for 1	Arlan's Dept. Stores, Inc.	Great Northern Paper Co.
	Glidden Co.	
2 for 1	ACF Industries, Inc.	National Acme Co.
	American Chain & Cable Co., Inc.	National Airlines, Inc.
	American Enka Corp.	Niagara Mohawk Power Corp.
	American Water Works Co., Inc.	Ohio Edison Co.
	Beckman Instruments, Inc.	Outlet Co.
	Borden Co.	Owens-Illinois, Inc.
	Brown Shoe Co., Inc.	Pan American Sulphur Co.
	Burlington Industries, Inc.	Panhandle Eastern Pipe Line Co.
	Cenco Instruments Corp.	Peoples Drug Stores, Inc.
	Central Illinois Light Co.	Pet Milk Co.
	Cities Service Co.	Pillsbury Co.
	Coca-Cola Co.	Pittston Co.
	Consolidated Edison Co. of N.Y., Inc.	Reliable Stores Corp.
	Copperweld Steel Co.	Rexall Drug and Chemical Co.
	Crane Co.	Riegal Paper Corp.
	Cutler-Hammer, Inc.	Rochester Telephone Corp.
	De Vilbiss Co.	Ryan Aeronautical Co.
	Delta Air Lines, Inc.	Sears, Roebuck & Co.
	Diamond Alkali Co.	Simmons Co.
	Diebold, Incorporated	South Carolina Electric Co.
	Dresser Industries, Inc.	Southern Natural Gas Co.
	Eastman Kodak Co.	Starrett U.S. Co.
	Edison Brothers Stores, Inc.	Storer Broadcasting Co.
	Emhart Corporation	Stouffer Foods Corp.
	Falstaff Brewing Corp.	Taft Broadcasting Co.
	Ferro Corp.	Thatcher Glass Manufacturing Co., Inc.
	General Amer. Transportation Corp.	Thompson Ramo Wooldridge, Inc.
	General Bronze Corp.	Timken Roller Bearing Co.
	Grumman Aircraft Engineering Corp.	Torrington Co.
	Gulf States Utilities Co.	Tri-Continental Corp.
	Hamilton Watch Co.	Unarco Industries, Inc.
	Harsco Corp.	Union Carbide Corp.
	Hart, Schaffner & Marx	United Utilities, Inc.
	Honeywell Inc.	Universal Leaf Tobacco Co.
	International Harvester Co.	UTD Corporation
	Kansas Power & Light Co.	Valley Mould & Iron Corp.
	McGraw Edison Co.	Vasco Metals Corp.
	Minnesota Power & Light Co.	Whirlpool Corp.
	Mississippi River Corp.	Worthington Corp.
	Monon Railroad, Class B	
3 for 2	Associated Dry Goods Corp.	Kendall Co.
	Carrier Corp.	Lane Bryant, Inc.
	Colgate-Palmolive Co.	Link-Belt Co.
	Dover Corp.	Motorola, Inc.
	Foxboro Co.	National Starch & Chemical Corp.
	Gardner-Denver Co.	SuCrest Corp.
	Globe-Wernicka Industries, Inc.	United Aircraft Corp.
	Interchemical Corp.	Van Raalte Co., Inc.
	Jewel Tea Co., Inc.	Wayne Knitting Mills

Source: New York Stock Exchange Fact Book, 1966.

of the shares held by stockholders. The reduction in the price of the new shares puts the latter in a correspondingly lower price range and thus within reach of a larger spectrum of potential investors. Individual investors are more likely to purchase 100 (new) shares in a given company at $20 per share than 10 (old) shares at $200.

Second, the increase in the number of shares outstanding provides a correspondingly larger supply of shares available for sale. Transactions are likely to be more frequent and involve a smaller percentage of the total number of shares outstanding. As a result, the market price at any given time is less likely to be as volatile as would be the case with a relatively small supply of shares.

Finally, a stock split camouflages large earnings per share. Instead of declaring a dividend of say, $20 per (old) share the corporation declares a dividend of $2 per (new) share, assuming a stock split of 10:1. Although, in the last analysis, the "reduced" dividend per share is apparent rather than real, some corporations believe that their public image may suffer from a dividend of more than $10 but will escape adverse public opinion if the dividend is only $2 or $3. The management may also feel that a modest dividend per share is less likely to generate excessive demands of labor unions.

Dividends and the Stockholder   The stockholder values his holding partially in terms of the dividends paid by the corporation. This involves both current and prospective dividends. The same approach characterizes the potential investor. The market price of a stock reflects the monetary value placed on the dividends by the present owner-seller and the prospective investor-purchaser. In each case, the expected future dividends are, at least in part, capitalized. By *capitalization* of the dividend is meant the determination of the amount of money on which the dividend yields the desired return. Suppose a corporation, paying out its total earnings, has a constant dividend record of $5 per share with a reasonable probability that it will be able to continue the same dividend for many years to come. How much of an investment is a return of $5 worth? If the investor is satisfied with a return of 5% the stock would be worth $100 to him.

This illustration is an oversimplification of the problem of capitalization. Both the holder and the investor know that the directors are under no contractual or legal obligation to declare a dividend. They are also aware of the fact that future earnings of the corporation (and, therefore, dividends) are uncertain. Although earnings may be substantial, the board may decide not to declare a dividend but to reinvest the entire profit in the business. In this case, the stockholder receives no current return on his investment in spite of the profitability of the corporation. Furthermore, the acceptable rate of return depends also on other variables, such as the prevailing rate of interest on other forms of investment, the prospects of inflation or deflation, the absence or presence of a substantial earned surplus. The stockholder is also cognizant of the fact that the corporation cannot declare any dividends until fixed claims of creditors—bondholders, term lenders, etc.—are first satisfied. If the corporation has obtained debt capital or a term loan, the contractual repayments of principal and interest must be paid first out of the earnings; and, if required by the loan agreement, a portion of the remaining earnings must be allocated to the surplus account before the stockholders can receive a dividend. Thus, dividends are paid out of earnings after all fixed contractual debt payments have been met.

Stock Dividend   As a rule, a corporation pays the dividend in cash. However, the board may decide to declare a *stock dividend* in place of, or in addition to, the cash dividend. A stock dividend reduces the drain on the cash of the corporation. It also leaves the pro rata position of the individual stockholder unchanged. However, if the stockholder wants the cash and sells the stock dividend, he reduces his share in the total stock outstanding. Assume that an investor holds 100 shares out of 10,000, and that the corporation declares a stock dividend of one share for each ten shares held; the investor's holding, after selling the stock dividend, declines from 1% to about %10 of 1%.

The stock dividend is often a source of confusion. Stock dividends are really recapitalizations, as can be shown by the following example of a 25% stock dividend on the equity section of the corporate balance sheet:

Before:

Common stock (100,000 shares at $1 par)	$100,000
Retained earnings	$150,000

After:

Common stock (125,000 shares at $1 par)	$125,000
Retained earnings	$125,000

All that has happened is that $25,000 has been transferred from retained earnings (earned surplus) to the common stock account. From the stockholder's point of view, he now has more shares of stock. For example, the holder of 100 shares now has 125. Is he actually any better off? In fact, he still has the same proportionate share of the corporation as he had before the stock dividend. Furthermore, a stock dividend creates no additional earnings for the company. Consequently, the stockholder has no more earnings to claim than previously. Earnings per share necessarily decline as a result of a stock dividend. If earnings were $50,000 before the 25% stock dividend, earnings per share were $0.50 ($50,000/100,000 shares). As a result of the stock dividend, earnings per share are now $0.40 ($50,000/125,000 shares).

However, these changes have no effect upon the owner's claim on earnings (provided he does not sell shares received in the stock dividend). This can be shown as follows:

	Number of shares owned	×	Earnings per share	=	Total claim on earnings
Before 25% stock split	100	×	$0.50	=	$50.00
After 25% stock split	125	×	$0.40	=	$50.00

Reasons for Stock Dividend   Why then do companies issue stock dividends? One reason is to provide some recognition to the stockholder that a portion of the earnings is retained. Another reason is to conserve cash in the corporation and still give the stockholder "something." Those stockholders who need a current return can sell the stock dividend. However, they will suffer dilution (both of earnings and control) in future years if they do. Since, in fact, stock dividends just give the shareholder more pieces of paper, many financial managers have argued against giving stock dividends.

One justifiable reason for stock dividends is to reduce the market price of the stock to a more favorable trading range where it will be attractive to a broader group of potential investors. The market price can be lowered for this purpose also by means of a stock split. Rapidly expanding "growth" companies find it necessary to issue stock splits periodically to keep the market price within reason. For example, IBM split its stock in 1966, issuing one new share for every two shares outstanding to widen the market. Even though such a stock dividend or stock split just gives the present shareholder more pieces of paper representing the same claim on earnings and ownership as before the dividend or split, the lower market price may stimulate demand for the stock in the stock market and may result in a higher market price, which will benefit the present shareholder if he wishes to sell his shares in the future. Sometimes corporations apply a reverse stock split, in which one new share is issued in exchange for several old shares if the stock is selling at too low a price to attract buyers. Reverse stock splits are unlikely to help the market price of a stock unless earnings and/or dividends improve.

Capital Gain   The investor in common stock assumes the risk that is inherent in the ownership of a business. He also is the beneficiary of a rise in profits. The market price of a stock depends both on the present and prospective magnitude of the profit or earnings per share and the dividend paid by the corporation. A rise in the dividend of, say, 10% may cause the market value of the stock to go up by more than 10%, assuming that the profits after taxes but before dividends have also increased by at least 10% and that the corporation has, in the opinion of a prospective investor, a reasonable prospect of further growth in earnings.

The purchaser of common stock may thus look to income in the form of dividends as a means to an end. His ultimate objective usually is the prospect of a capital gain. This is true whether he is actively identified with the management of the corporation or is an absentee-owner. The only difference is that the former thinks in terms of accumulating his capital gain over a period of many years, while the typical absentee-owner thinks in terms of a few months or a few years.

Simple Common Stock Structure   Most corporations start with common stock and without any long-term debt. An exception to this rule is a newly organized corporation which obtains a franchise for a water company or gas and electric utility. In cases such as these—which represent franchise monopolies—it is not difficult for a new company to procure a portion of the needed capital through the sale of long-term debt securities.

A newly organized corporation that has to make its mark in a competitive environment faces the uncertainties of the market place. It will therefore generally procure its capital through the sale of common stock. The magnitude of its equity capital—measured by the ratio of net worth to liabilities—will determine its ability to obtain short-term credit from suppliers and banks. These creditors need not worry about prior claims to the income of the firm by long-term creditors. Furthermore, the absence of long-term debt also means that there are no restrictions on managerial decisions. It will be recalled from the analysis of term loans in Chapter Eleven that such loans are usually attended by restrictive covenants. In the case of long-term debt, which was discussed in Chapter Fourteen, these covenants may be even more restrictive.

Table 15-2.   Total Assets, Common Stock, Retained Earnings of Selected
Companies in 1967 (Millions of Dollars)

	Total Assets	Common Stock	Retained Earnings
Great Atlantic and Pacific Tea Company	884	25	386
International Nickel Co. of Canada, Ltd.	1,116	90	714
Phelps Dodge Corp.	591	126	386
Ohio Oil Company	977	155	444
United Fruit Company	398	193	154
North American Aviation, Inc.	573*	8	280
Pullman, Inc.	411	91	93
Libbey-Owens-Ford Glass Company	291	53	185
Freeport Sulphur Co.	274	77	122
Otis Elevator Co.	340	26	185

* Balance Sheet as of end of 1966.

It should be noted that a simple common stock structure is not confined to new corporations. Some of the leading corporations have grown to their present size by relying solely on reinvested profits and the sale of additional common stock. Moody's Investors Service lists, among others, the corporations shown in Table 15-2 which have only common stock outstanding.

Each of these corporations preferred to obtain a portion of its growth capital from the sale of stock either to its stockholders or to the public. Smaller corporations frequently have little choice in the selection of their source of long-term capital for the financing of growth. They either lack sufficient fixed assets or their prospective future profits have too large an element of uncertainty to offer adequate security to long-term creditors. In these instances, the corporation has no other alternative except to retain a simple common stock structure.

But what prompts a corporation that has access to long-term debt capital to bypass this source of capital? The answer will vary among different corporations. One or several of the following reasons will account for the decision to use common stock as the sole source of additional capital, aside from retained earnings.

Advantages of Common Stock Structure   Two reasons have already been briefly referred to and need no further elaboration: insufficient fixed assets and sizeable fluctuations in the annual rate of profit.

An important reason is the desire of management to retain complete flexibility of decision making. With only common stock outstanding, the management can act freely and quickly in acquiring another company through an exchange of stock. It can dispose of assets that are no longer needed for the effective operation of the company. The board can freely enter into lease agreements. The corporation can borrow on short term as much as it needs and is able to obtain. It can borrow from finance companies or factor its receivables. And, last but not least, the board has complete discretion to distribute as much of the earnings in dividends as it may deem advisable. With an all common-stock structure, each of these matters rests solely with the board.

Another reason is the desire of management to take full advantage of a favorable market for new stock issues. There are periods of time when the owners of investible capital are literally anxious to buy common stock and to pay a price per share that may be twenty or more times the earnings per share. In the parlance of the market, the market is "bullish" on common stock. This bullish climate offers a strong temptation to management that needs capital for expansion—or anticipates this need in the not too distant future—to take advantage of the easily available capital.

It must also be borne in mind that the decision to issue and sell more stock is made at a point of time. Assume that, in choosing between more equity capital or debt capital, the corporation decides upon the equity capital. This does not prevent the corporation, at some future date when the same choice is present, from selling debt securities as a source of additional capital. As a matter of fact, if the corporation has over a period of time sold two or three successive issues of common stock, for instance, its net worth or equity capital has automatically increased, unless it suffered some severe losses. A broadened base of equity makes it easier to obtain dept capital at some future date when the equity market is "bearish" and the corporation needs additional capital.

II. PREFERRED STOCK

Preferred stock is a hybrid corporate instrument. It combines some features of common stock with some characteristics of a debt security. How much or how little it shares with the holders of the equity stock and with the creditors who have acquired debt capital is determined by the provisions in the certificate. The scope of "preference" is defined in the contract between the corporation and the purchasers of this security. The actual preference will therefore range between two extremes.

At one end of the range is a preferred stock that enjoys almost all privileges of the equity holders—sharing in profits, vote, and control—as well as the priorities of a creditor in regard to receipt of a fixed rate of return, redemption at a predetermined maturity date, and priority over common stock in case of liquidation. At the other extreme is a preferred stock that has only a limited claim to priority in dividends. Whatever the features of the preferred stock may be in a given case, the tax authorities treat this security as part of the corporation's equity captial. The dividend payable and paid to preferred stockholders is therefore not a tax deductible item. Dividends on this stock are therefore paid out of income after taxes.

Specific Denomination   Common stock is issued either as par value or no-par value. Preferred stock generally has a fixed face value. This may be as little as $5 or as much as $100. The amount stated on the certificate represents an obligation of the corporation to the holder to redeem the security at some future date at or above this face value.

Maturity   The obligation to redeem the preferred stock at a fixed date sets a time limit to the risk assumed by the holder of preferred stock. Failure to pay off this obligation is tantamount to default in a debt. The creditor, in this case the holder of preferred stock, can take legal action against the corporation. Generally, preferred stocks do not have a fixed maturity date since equity investment is generally considered to be permanent. However, since preferred holders are in a sense a special class of owners, provision is often made for voluntary repayment and sometimes for compulsory redemption by means of a maturity date or a sinking fund.

Redemption of preferred stock is either at face value or at a premium. This premium, fixed in the contract, is a "sweetener." It is designed to make these shares more saleable by the corporation since the owner is promised this premium in addition to the dividend during the lifetime of the stock. The willingness of the corporation to pay such a premium upon redemption has a bearing on the rate of dividend promised to the holder of preferred stock. In consideration for the premium, the purchaser can be induced to accept a lower rate of (promised) dividend. Thus, a 10-year 5% preferred stock redeemable at about 115% of face value will yield about the same annual rate as a 6% preferred stock with the same lifetime. From the viewpoint of the corporation, its image is better if it has outstanding 5% preferred stock rather than 6% preferred.

The contract frequently also provides for a *call* date. Under this clause the corporation has the right to "call in" the preferred prior to its maturity date (if any). Usually the right to call is accompanied by a provision for the payment of a premium above face value.

Dividend It is customary for preferred stock to bear a fixed percentage of its face value as the promised annual dividend. This does not mean that the corporation *must* pay this dividend every year. The decision to pay or to omit dividend payments rests with the board of directors. They may decide to omit the declaration of a dividend even though the corporation has an after-tax profit in excess of the dividend requirement. Conceivably, the board may decide that the corporation should retain its earnings to meet its financial needs for expansion.

Failure to pay the stipulated dividend on the preferred stock automatically forecloses the payment of any dividend on common stock. This is one of the basic features of preferred stock. It has preference or priority over common stock. But this preference has little meaning if the corporation decides to omit dividend payments for one or more years. The retention of these earnings would simply increase the surplus and, thus, the book value of the common stock, at the expense of the dividendless preferred stock.

To assure the preferred stockholder that he will receive the promised rate of dividend, if at all feasible, it is customary to make the dividend *cumulative*. By this term is meant that the omission of dividends in one or more successive years creates an accumulated claim. Until the accumulated and current dividend claims are paid, no dividends can be paid to the common stockholders. For example, if a $5 preferred has not been paid its dividend for three years and the corporation decides to declare a dividend on the common stock at the end of the fourth year, it must first pay the preferred stockholder $20 dollars before it can distribute a dividend to the holders of common stock. Furthermore, any unpaid dividends at the time of maturity become a claim added to the face value of the stock, plus the premium, if this has been provided in the contract.

Noncumulative preferred stock is usually issued in cases of reorganization as a result of insolvency and bankruptcy proceedings. At such times, the holders of junior securities—for example, third-mortgage bonds or income bonds—who see little chance of recovering more than a fraction of their claims may be willing to accept noncumulative preferred stock in exchange for their debt securities. By means of this exchange, they hope that the corporation may be able to get back on its feet. They accept the noncumulative preferred as the lesser of two evils.

Occasionally, a corporation desperately in need of additional capital may agree to sell cumulative *participating* preferred stock. In addition to the preferred position and accumulation of claims, this type of preferred also participates in the dividends paid to common stock. Suppose it is a 5% preferred stock with par value of $10. After receiving the 5% dividend, the participation feature entitles the preferred stock to the same dollar-for-dollar dividend paid to common stock on a per share basis. If there are 16,000 preferred and 100,000 common and the common receives $2 per share each preferred stock receives $2 in addition to the 50¢ representing the 5% dividend on $10 par value. Participation can be *unlimited* as in the preceding example or *limited* as spelled out in the contract.

Convertibility   A corporation may also give the holder of preferred stock the right to convert his shares into common stock. This right of conversion is usually expressed in terms of shares; e.g., one preferred for two common. Suppose the preferred stock has a face value of $25 and the conversion right is 1 for 2. If the price of the common stock should go to $13, it would seem to pay to convert the preferred stock into two common shares with a combined market value of $26. In this case, the market value of the preferred would increase also to about $26. The preferred holder may wish to wait for a further rise or until management calls the preferred stock before availing himself of the option. He would then avoid the risk of holding the common and taking the risk of a loss if the common declines below $12.50.

The right to conversion could, however, be nullified by the corporation by splitting the common as it approaches a market price of $12.50. A stock split of 2 for 1 would tend to make the price of the new common stock one-half or, for instance, $6.00 per share. To eliminate this risk of a meaningless conversion privilege, the contract usually contains an antidilution covenant. Under this provision, the stipulated conversion ratio is automatically adjusted for subsequent stock splits. In our illustration, each preferred could be exchanged for four common shares.

Voting Rights   Here again the right of the preferred-stock holder is what the contract says it is to be. Preferred stock can be nonvoting, simple voting, or even multiple voting. Bethlehem Steel and Consolidated Edison, among others, have issued simple-voting preferred; i.e., one vote per share. On the other hand, Eastman Kodak has floated preferred which has 25 votes per share. United States Steel preferred has 6 votes per share. In these cases of multiple voting rights, the number of preferred issued is small compared with common. Otherwise, the preferred would easily control the corporation. Multiple voting is intended to give the preferred a minority position of some weight in the nomination and election of directors.

Veto Powers It is customary for the corporation to give the preferred some veto powers in matters that have a direct vital bearing on the security of these shares. For example, a two-thirds or three-fourths affirmative vote of the preferred may be stipulated for a proposed merger and consolidation with another corporation. A specified majority approval may also be required for the issue of additional preferred with "superior" or the same standing. The General Motors contract calls for a three-fourth affirmative vote if the corporation wants to issue a "prior preferred" stock that would have some preference over the outstanding issue. But no approval is required for the issuance of more preferred stock with the same rights as the outstanding preferred. However, International Paper must obtain a two-thirds approval for the sale of more preferred in the same class as that outstanding.

SUMMARY

Since the stockholders of a corporation are the residual owners of the net worth of the firm, they have certain legal rights. These legal rights of ownership have a direct bearing on the selection of the sources of long-term funds. An all-common stock structure of long-term funds has several advantages particularly to the firm with limited fixed assets and sizable fluctuations in the annual rate of profits.

Preferred stock is a hybrid corporate instrument. It has features of both common stock and debt securities, varying according to the specific provisions of the certificate. The financial manager should be aware of the major features of both common and preferred stock.

Most corporations (except franchised utilities) generally start out with an all common stock structure. Insufficient fixed assets and sizable fluctuations in the annual rate of profit leads many corporations to avoid use of debt. An important reason for an all common stock structure is that it enables management to retain complete flexibility of decision making in such areas as disposing of assets, acquiring another company through an exchange of shares, and short-term borrowing. The board in an all common stock structure also has complete discretion in distributing as much of the earnings in dividends as it wishes.

Questions

1. Discuss the major advantages and disadvantages of cumulative voting. Should cumulative voting be mandatory for all corporations?
2. What is meant by preemptive rights? What value do preemptive rights have to the common stockholder?
3. How does a stock dividend differ from a cash dividend?
4. What are the advantages of an all common-stock capital structure to a corporation?
5. It is sometimes said that a preferred stock is, in effect, a bond with a tax disadvantage, from the point of view of the corporation. Do you agree?
6. Why would a company agree to pay a premium upon redemption of shares of preferred stock?
7. What are the similarities of preferred stock and common stock? What are the differences?

Problems

1. Iota Corporation has 3000 shares of voting stock outstanding but only a total of 2600 shares are represented at a meeting called to elect a board of directors of 9 members. Each share has 1 vote. How many shares would you have to own or hold proxies for to elect 1 member of the board if:
   (a) Cumulative voting is used?
   (b) Straight voting is used?
   (c) One-third of the directors are elected each year and cumulative voting is used?
2. Kappa Corporation has the following items (among others) on its balance sheet:

   Cash $250,000   Common stock ($1 par),
                            225,000 shares issued $225,000
                            Retained earnings $500,000

   What changes would be made in these items as a result of the following actions (consider each action separately; do not cumulate results):
   (a) A cash dividend of 25¢ per share.
   (b) A 10% stock dividend.
   (c) A 3 for 1 stock split.

3. On December 31, 1967, the capital structure of Beta Corporation was as follows:

> 7%, cumulative preferred, par $100,
>> 50,000 shares issued and outstanding $5,000,000
>
> Common stock, par $1,
>> 4,000,000 shares issued and outstanding $4,000,000

What will be the dividends per share on each kind of stock in 1968, 1969, and 1970 if Beta earns and distributes total dividends of:

> 1968: $250,000
> 1969: $500,000
> 1970: $350,000

Case: INTERNATIONAL BUSINESS MACHINES

Exhibits 15-1 and 15-2 of this case are portions of letters from the Chairman of the Board of International Business Machines Corporation to the stockholders. Exhibit 15-3 is made up of the first page and part of the second page of the Prospectus sent to the stockholders of IBM. Exhibit 15-4 is a list of price ranges of the capital stock of IBM for the last few years.

Case Questions:

1. What are the likely reasons for the 50% IBM stock split in May, 1966?

2. What is the theoretical value of one Right on May 31st if the closing price of IBM stock was $370 per share on that date?

3. If a stockholder has 7 shares of IBM stock on May 31, 1966, what will he have to pay for one additional share, if he exercises his Rights?

4. Why did IBM have an underwriter in connection with its subscription offer?

5. The IBM Rights expired on June 21, 1966. What would have probably occurred if the Rights were perpetual? Should they have been?

6. Based solely on the past performance of IBM stock, should an investor exercise his IBM Rights or should he sell them if he can invest his funds in another security that will grow in market value at a rate of 10% a year? Disregard dividends in your calculations.

EXHIBIT 15-1.   IBM International Business Machines Corporation

---

Armonk, New York 10504
April 25, 1966

To the Stockholders of
International Business Machines Corporation:

At today's Annual Meeting, the stockholders of IBM:

Elected the directors for a one-year term;
Voted to carry out the 50% stock split;
Approved the new 1966 IBM Employees Stock Purchase Plan
and the new 1966 IBM Stock Option Plan for officers
and key employees; and
Defeated the stockholder proposal relating to cumulative voting.

At the Meeting, the IBM Board of Directors also announced a plan to offer additional shares of IBM capital stock to IBM stockholders for purchase at a discount from the market price, the offer to be made during a twenty-one day period, June 1–21, 1966. The purpose is to raise approximately $350 million of additional equity capital in order to finance increased production required to meet our orders for IBM System/360, which, to date, have been larger than originally anticipated.

You will be receiving in the mails in the near future some very valuable documents from IBM, namely:

1. On May 17th, the 50% stock split will be mailed. You will receive an IBM stock certificate for the full shares of IBM stock to which your holdings at the close of business on May 3rd, the split record date, entitle you (on the basis of one new share for each two held) and an IBM Order Form (good for 12 months time) for any odd one-half share to which you may be entitled.

2. On June 3rd, the new stock offering will be mailed. You will receive a Warrant (good only until June 21, 1966) entitling you to purchase IBM stock at the special subscription price, together with a Prospectus making the offer and describing its terms. The subscription offer will have a record date of the close of business on May 27th and will expire at 3:30 P.M. New York time on Tuesday, June 21, 1966.

3. On June 10th, the second quarter cash dividend will be mailed, payable on shares of record at the close of business on May 27th. This cash dividend was declared at the rate of $1.10 per share and, since it will be paid on the shares outstanding after the stock split, will represent a 10% increase in the cash dividend rate.

EXHIBIT 15-1.   (*Continued*)

About the Subscription Offer:

The entire issue of new stock will be offered to IBM stockholders in proportion to their holdings on the record date, May 27th. The offering period will be June 1–21, 1966. As is customary in matters of this kind, the exact number of shares to be offered and the subscription price per share cannot be finally determined until just before the offering is made, because they depend upon stock market conditions existing at that time. Present indications are, however, that the offering will be made on the basis of one new share of stock for every forty shares held. Thus, on June 3rd a stockholder would be sent a Warrant stating that he had one Right to subscribe for each outstanding share held by him on May 27th (which would include shares issued in the stock split) and that forty Rights would be required to subscribe for one new share. A New York City bank will act as the subscription agent and will buy or sell Rights for IBM stockholders. The subscription price to stockholders will be set below the market price of IBM stock at the commencement of the offering. As required by law, the offer to stockholders will be made only after the Securities and Exchange Commission declares effective IBM's Registration Statement (still to be filed) covering the new shares. The exact number of shares and the subscription price and the details of how to exercise or how to sell your Rights or how to buy more Rights will be fully explained in the Prospectus which will be mailed to stockholders together with the Warrants evidencing their Rights to subscribe.

A group of investment bankers under the management of Morgan Stanley & Co. will underwrite the offering and will distribute to the public any shares not subscribed for by IBM stockholders.

Warrants and the Rights to subscribe will expire at 3:30 P.M. New York time on Tuesday, June 21st, and the subscription offer will then terminate.

If you plan to be away during the proposed subscription period (June 1–21, 1966) you may wish to make arrangements so that someone in whom you have confidence will be fully authorized to act for you with respect to your Rights.

This letter is not an offer of any shares of stock or of any Rights to subscribe. The subscription offer will be made only by the Prospectus mentioned above.

The contemplated stock offer is, of course, dependent upon favorable conditions existing at the time the offering is to be made, and the Board reserves discretion to postpone the subscription offer until a later time, or to refrain from making it, if in its judgment such a course of action seems advisable. In addition, it is contingent upon the Registration Statement with the Securities and Exchange Commission becoming effective.

Very truly yours,

Thomas J. Watson, Jr.
Chairman of the Board

EXHIBIT 15-2.   International Business Machines Corporation

Armonk, New York 10504
May 31, 1966

To the Stockholders of
International Business Machines Corporation:

We are now issuing to stockholders the Rights to buy additional shares of IBM capital stock during a special subscription period beginning June 1 and ending June 21, 1966.

Stockholders will be able to buy at $285.00 per share, one new share for each 40 shares held on May 27th. IBM stock opened on the New York Stock Exchange today (May 31st) at $370.00 per share. (Additional information on the price of IBM stock over the past 10 years is shown in the enclosed Prospectus.)

With this letter is a Warrant card which shows the number of Rights to which you are entitled. One Right is granted for each share held, with 40 Rights needed to buy one share of stock at the subscription price. Also enclosed is a Prospectus by which the new shares of IBM stock are offered.

Bankers Trust Company, of New York City, is acting as the subscription agent, and you may send them your Warrant in the enclosed, pre-addressed envelope to do any of the following with your Rights:

1. Buy one share of IBM for each 40 Rights;
2. Buy the additional Rights needed to round out to a total of 40 so that you may buy a share of IBM stock;
3. Sell all your Rights or part of them;
4. Have a new Warrant issued in the name of someone else;
5. Split up your Warrant in accordance with your instructions for disposing of the new Warrants.

The Rights will be traded on the New York, Midwest, and Pacific Coast Stock Exchanges. Price quotations for Rights will be reported in the newspapers.

The Rights expire at 3:30 P.M., New York time, on June 21, 1966, and will have no value thereafter. You should, therefore, act upon your Rights before that time.

Very truly yours,
Chairman of the Board

. . . .

According to counsel, Warrants and Rights have the following principal Federal income tax consequences:

(a) the receipt by you of the Warrants and Rights is tax free;
(b) the exercise of Rights to purchase additional IBM stock is tax free;
(c) the sale of Rights gives you a capital gain or loss; and
(d) you can elect either to transfer a part of your cost base of your original IBM shares to the Rights, or take a zero tax base for the Rights.

Counsel also has informed us that, subject to certain limitations, the Federal margin requirement on a loan to purchase additional IBM stock on the exercise of Rights is 25% compared to the 70% normally required.

Exhibit 15-3.   Prospectus

1,324,136 Shares
International Business Machines Corporation
CAPITAL STOCK
($5.00 Par Value)

As more fully set forth herein, the Corporation is offering to the holders of its Capital Stock the right to subscribe for additional shares of Capital Stock at the rate of one share for each forty shares held of record at the close of business on May 27, 1966. The Subscription Offer will expire at 3:30 P. M., New York Time, on June 21, 1966.

THESE SECURITIES HAVE NOT BEEN APPROVED OR DISAPPROVED BY THE SECURITIES AND EXCHANGE COMMISSION NOR HAS THE COMMISSION PASSED UPON THE ACCURACY OR ADEQUACY OF THIS PROSPECTUS. ANY REPRESENTATION TO THE CONTRARY IS A CRIMINAL OFFENSE.

SUBSCRIPTION PRICE $285 A SHARE

	Subscription Price		Underwriting Discounts and Commissions(1)		Proceeds to Corporation(1)(2)
Per Share.....	$285.00	Minimum	$3.55	Maximum	$281.45
		Maximum	$10.00	Minimum	$275.00
Total........	$377,378,760.00	Minimum	$4,700,682.80	Maximum	$372,678,077.20
		Maximum	$13,241,360.00	Minimum	$364,137,400.00

(1) The Corporation has agreed to pay the Underwriters $3.55 a share in respect of all the shares offered hereby plus an additional $6.45 a share in respect of each share of Capital Stock acquired by them through the exercise of Rights purchased for their account and each share of Unsubscribed Stock. The minimum and maximum underwriting commissions are based on the assumptions that (a) all the shares offered hereby and (b) none of such shares, respectively, will be subscribed for by persons other than the Underwriters. Reference is made to the caption "Underwriters" herein concerning a contingent payment to the Corporation.

(2) Before deducting estimated expenses of $1,160,000 payable by the Corporation.

During and after the subscription period, the several Underwriters may offer shares of Capital Stock to the public at prices which it is intended shall not be increased more frequently than once in any calendar day and which will be not less than the Subscription Price set forth above (less, in the case of sales to dealers, the concession allowed to dealers) and not more than the greater of the last sale or current offering price on the New York Stock Exchange, plus an amount equal to the applicable New York Stock Exchange commission. As a result, the Underwriters may realize profits or losses independent of the underwriting compensation stated above.

The acceptance of the Unsubscribed Stock and the offering thereof by the Underwriters are subject to the approval of certain legal matters by Davis Polk Wardwell Sunderland & Kiendl, counsel for the Underwriters.

Exhibit 15-3.   (*Continued*)

MORGAN STANLEY & CO.
May 31, 1966

    No person is authorized to give any information or to make any representations not contained in this Prospectus; and any information or representation not contained herein must not be relied upon as having been authorized by the Corporation or by an Underwriter.

    Until July 12, 1966, all dealers effecting transactions in the registered securities, whether or not participating in this distribution, may be required to deliver a Prospectus. This is in addition to the obligation of dealers to deliver a Prospectus when acting as Underwriters an with respect to their unsold allotments or subscriptions.

· ·

    IN CONNECTION WITH THIS OFFERING, THE UNDERWRITERS MAY OVER-ALLOT OR EFFECT TRANSACTIONS WHICH STABILIZE OR MAINTAIN THE MARKET PRICES OF THE CAPITAL STOCK AND RIGHTS AT LEVELS ABOVE THOSE WHICH MIGHT OTHERWISE PREVAIL IN THE OPEN MARKET. SUCH TRANSACTIONS MAY BE EFFECTED ON THE NEW YORK, BOSTON, MIDWEST, PACIFIC COAST AND PHILADELPHIA-BALTIMORE-WASHINGTON STOCK EXCHANGES OR IN THE OVER-THE-COUNTER MARKET. SUCH STABILIZING, IF COMMENCED, MAY BE DISCONTINUED AT ANY TIME.

Exhibit 15-4.   Price Range of IBM Capital Stock

    The following table indicates the high and low sales prices for IBM Capital Stock on the New York Stock Exchange from 1956 through May 27, 1966 as reported by *The Commercial and Financial Chronicle,* adjusted for stock dividends and splits including the 50% split effected May 3, 1966. The closing price of the Capital Stock on the New York Stock Exchange on May 27, 1966 was $371 per share.

Year	High	Low
1956	62	33⅝
1957	85	56⅛
1958	127⅝	69⅜
1959	173½	117⅛
1960	213⅜	144¾
1961	323¾	206¼
1962	308½	160
1963	271¾	204⅞
1964	329⅜	270⅝
1965	366	269⅜
1966 (through May 27)	375	314⅝

Chapter Sixteen

Small Companies: The Problem of Going Public

The differences in equity financing between the medium-sized and large corporation as against the small company are of such scope as to justify a separate analysis. To use a colloquial analogy, the small firm not only operates in a ballpark with different dimensions, but it must also play the game of equity financing under a different set of ground rules.

The personal savings of the owners is the prime source of equity capital in the small company, particularly in the new enterprise. Generally, impersonal sources are unwilling to contribute equity capital to new firms unless the owners have committed extensive funds. With outside equity capital not readily available, the small enterprise generally relies on earnings, which represents another form of savings by the owners, as its main source of equity capital.

As the firm grows, the owners may wish to consider a public offering of stock as a further source of equity capital. Compared with owners savings and retained earnings, public offerings of stock for small companies is of relatively small importance, particularly for new enterprises. For new businesses with sales under $100,000, the possibilities of a successful public issue of stock are practically nil. There are two reasons for this. First, the owners of a new firm are generally reluctant to share the expected profits and control of the firm with outsiders. Second, public offerings of stock involve substantial risks to the investment banker or the underwriter as well as considerable overhead costs with the result that costs of new and small issues may be prohibitive. Since institutional investors are generally reluctant to make equity investments in new firms without some kind of "track" record of performance, the market for these issues is apt to be very thin. Therefore, the investment banker may have higher selling costs for such issues and may be unable to sell the entire issue. As the firm grows in size and builds a record of performance in earnings, the company may gradually reach a level of operations and profits that make a public stock offering feasible.

I. OBJECTIVES

Suppose a small company has attained a plateau of sales and profit that appears adequate as a basis for a public stock offering. What considerations prompt the management of such small concerns to go public? In contrast with the purely financial motivations in the case of large corporations, the decision of the small firm to make a public offering of stock is frequently prompted by personal motivations rather than by the financial needs of the firm as such.

A. Personal Motivations

The personal elements fall into three major categories: (1) estate taxes; (2) dissension among officers-owners; and (3) diversification of personal investments.

1. Estate Taxes The owners of a successful small corporation are seriously concerned about the estate tax in case of death. This is of particular importance in those instances in which the company has been able to earn a high rate of profit on a relatively low net worth. The tax authorities generally adopt the rule of capitalizing the earnings in arriving at the value of the business rather than accepting the net worth of the business as a basis for the inheritance tax. As a result, the amount of the tax is likely to absorb a substantial portion of the price at which the estate can sell either the business, if the deceased was the sole owner, or sell the deceased owner's share to his surviving partners. If, as is frequently the case, the widow or children decide to continue the business, the tax may seriously drain the net working capital of the firm.

By floating a stock issue, some of these problems of the inheritance tax are expected to be resolved in favor of the estate. Thus, if the stock of the company is traded in the over-the-counter market, the market price at the time of death becomes the basis for the computation of the value of the stock held by the estate and, thus, of the inheritance tax. Suppose the market price is $4 per share and the net profits, after taxes, are 68¢ per share. In the absence of a market price, the tax authorities may capitalize the earnings at, for instance, ten times and thus value each share at $6.80. With a market price of $4, however, the value would be placed at $4. Thus, the capitalized value of earnings would yield a tax base 70% higher than the market price. Since the tax rate is on a graduated scale, the actual tax bill in the first case would exceed, by more than 70%, a tax based on market value of the stock. However, it is possible for the market price to be higher than the price that might be set by the tax authorities. Thus, it is possible that estate tax problems will be magnified by public trading of the stock.

Another advantage is found in the fact that an established market for the company's stock makes it possible to dispose of a block of shares, if necessary, to pay the tax. If subsequent to the death of the owner, or part-owner, the market price goes up a smaller portion of the holding need be liquidated. The reverse is true if the stock price declines between the date of death and the due date of the tax.

2. Personality Conflicts   In a small firm with a few owner-managers, personal frictions are not rare occurrences. This type of situation is likely to develop when the business grows at a fast rate. These frictions may arise either because one of the owners believes that the other(s) is not "pulling his weight" in the expanded scope of operations, or because the partners are divided by some basic divergence of opinion on the wisdom of changing the product line, dividend withdrawal policy, or some other major facet of operations.

When these conflicts cannot be resolved amicably, the owners face three alternatives: (1) to dissolve the firm, the least desirable course of action; (2) to "buy out" one or more stockholders, usually not feasible because of lack of money; or (3) to go public.

3. Diversification   The owners of a successful small firm usually have few income-earning assets other than those of the business itself. They plough back most of the earnings in order to finance the continued growth of the company. As a result, their current and future income—in the form of salaries and dividends—depends entirely upon the earnings of this single firm. It is, therefore, not difficult to appreciate the desire of the owners of some small firms to diversify their income-producing wealth. This objective can be attained by divesting themselves of a portion of their stockholdings in the small firm and investing the proceeds in a variety of other assets. The latter may consist of real estate, "blue chip" securities, and even minority interests in other lines of business.

By going public, the owners hope to establish a ready market for the gradual liquidation of a portion of their stockholdings. If they desire to make these outside investments in the immediate future, they will offer some of their holdings as part of the total stock issue. The proceeds from the issue thus transfer a portion of the original owners' equity to outside stockholders and partly supplies additional funds to the firm.

The presence of a "bull market" for "growth stock" adds a powerful stimulant to a latent desire to go public. This is particularly true of small firms in "glamour industries" which capture the investing public's imagination as the potential giants of the near future. In the 1950's and 1960's this group included: electronics, synthetics, computers, automated office equipment, discount chains, motels, shopping centers, and many others.

The possibility of raising a relatively large sum of money quickly and, apparently, painlessly becomes an irresistible lure to many small firms. The management pays little or no attention to the obligation assumed by the company. It is true, as pointed out in Chapter 15, that the owner of common stock does not have a specific claim to dividends. At the same time, however, the inability of the corporation to generate sufficient earnings to pay a dividend commensurate with the price at which the stock was purchased by the investing public has an adverse effect on the future of the small corporation.

If subsequent earnings are inadequate in relation to the price paid by the stockholder, the market price tends to drop sharply. This development also reduces the (market) value of the stock retained by the owners. And, more significantly, it substantially weakens the firm's chances for another future issue of stock.

B. Financial Objectives

The three major financial reasons for a public stock offering by a small business are: (1) to remedy an unbalanced capital structure; (2) to procure funds for the acquisition of another company; and (3) to prepare for a merger.

1. Unbalanced Capital Structure The lack of sound financial management—notwithstanding the fact that the firm yields a satisfactory profit—frequently induces the management to plough profits back into additional fixed assets at the expense of net working capital. As a result, the company depends heavily on sources of short-term funds to support the larger output of the expanded facilities. Furthermore, the decision to reinvest profits in additional fixed assets is generally reached without prior consultation with institutional lenders of short-term funds. As a result, firms that pursue these policies are severely shocked to learn that they have sufficient net worth but inadequate net working capital to insure a reasonable liquidity as required by the supplier of short-term funds. Notwithstanding their rate of expansion, they fail to obtain adequate bank loans.

A study made in 1962 and 1963 indicated that the need of small business to sell stock to raise working capital was four times as frequent as the need for fixed capital.[1] In its semiannual report of 1960, the SBA stated that 58% of the term loans approved by the agency were intended either for additions to working capital or for the consolidation of short-term obligations, in contrast with 29% of the loans for the purchase of fixed assets.

2. Acquisitions   In this instance, the major objective of the stock issue is to obtain ready cash to be used if and when the issuing company finds another firm in the same line of business which is "for sale." Instead of purchasing new machinery, equipment, etc. for expansion, the management prefers, if possible, to acquire such assets in the liquidation of a competitor. This purchase would yield two advantages. The assets could be bought at substantially less than their replacement value. And, in addition, the purchasing company would also acquire direct access to the customers of the other firm.

3. Mergers   While most small growth firms expand by virtue of successful penetration of the market, others decide to accelerate this process by means of a merger with another company. In these cases, a stock issue may be regarded by the owners of a firm as an important bargaining weapon in the contemplated merger negotiations. The flotation of an issue is expected to yield a twofold advantage in the negotiations. First, the additional funds improve materially the net working capital position of the firm. And, more important, the establishment of a market value for the stock of the company is likely to enhance the exchange ratio of its shares relative to those of the other company.

[1] Salomon J. Flink, *Equity Financing of Small Manufacturing Companies in New Jersey*, New Jersey Dept. of Conservation and Economic Development, Trenton, N.J., 1962.

One of the major issues in merger negotiations centers around the determination of the ratio in which the stock of Company A is to be exchanged for shares in Company B. If the stock of B is quoted in the market at, e.g., $7.50, while the stock of A—assuming it has not yet gone public—has a book value of $3.75, the management of B will argue for an exchange ratio of one share of B for two shares of A. The owners of A will argue—again assuming that the earnings per share are about the same in both companies—for a ratio of 1:1 based on earnings. To be sure, this argument carries some weight. But it is admittedly less effective than if reinforced by a market price of $7.50 for A's shares, or even higher. By going public, Company A therefore hopes to establish a high market price for its shares as the basis for the determination of the exchange ratio. An additional reason is that the stockholders of B are more likely to approve a merger with an exchange ratio based on the relative market prices of the two issues than to accept a ratio based on earnings per share.

II. FEDERAL REGULATIONS (SEC)

The Act of 1933 provides for special treatment of stock issues which involve an amount not in excess of $300,000. Some small firms are capable of floating an issue well in excess of $300,000. However, since only a small company is likely to make a public sale of less than $300,000, the analysis in this section deals with problems that are peculiar only to small firms.

Regulation A Issues

A public offering not in excess of $300,000 is subject to SEC Regulations knows as Regulations A; thus, the term "Reg. A" issues.

The philosophy behind the rather liberal treatment of Regulation A issues was the desire of the Congress to aid small business in attracting external funds; i.e., equity capital. It was felt that small firms could not afford the expenses involved in obtaining audited and certified financial statements, technical evaluations of products and markets, and highly specialized legal talent. Thus, the information that the Federal Government requires small companies to file is rather elementary. Most important, the balance sheet, profit and loss statement, and other financial data need not be audited by a Certified Public Accountant. It is sufficient that these financial data are the same as those that had customarily been prepared by the firm for its management and stockholders.

For the same reason, the seller of a Regulation A issue need not file the rather complex, and costly, registration statement that is required on issues above $300,000. Instead, the firm files a *statement of notification* which contains basic information about the company, specified exhibits, and a copy of the offering circular (prospectus) which is to be used in the sale of the stock.

In the case of issues in excess of $300,000, the SEC has twenty days in which to raise objections to one or more items in the registration statement. On Regulation A issues, the waiting period is limited to ten days, exclusive of Saturdays, Sundays, and holidays.

Under SEC regulations, each person who is solicited for the purchase of shares in a stock offering must be furnished with a prospectus. In the case of Regulation A issues, the legend on the front page of the prospectus must read as follows:

> THESE SECURITIES ARE OFFERED PURSUANT TO AN EXEMPTION FROM REGISTRATION WITH THE SECURITIES AND EXCHANGE COMMISSION. THE COMMISSION DOES NOT PASS UPON THE MERITS OF ANY SECURITIES NOR DOES IT PASS UPON THE ACCURACY OR COMPLETENESS OF ANY OFFERING CIRCULAR OR OTHER SELLING LITERATURE.

III. THE OVER-THE-COUNTER MARKET

Trading in the securities issued by small firms takes place in the "over-the-counter" market since listing requirements of the stock exchanges (e.g., number of shareholders, total capitalization, etc.) clearly preclude the listing of securities of small firms on the stock exchanges. The over-the-counter market consists of individual dealers who are specialists in a number of securities. These dealers are, in a sense, securities merchants rather than brokers. They buy and sell for their own account as well as for customers who consist of other dealers, brokers, financial institutions, corporations, and individuals. Organized stock exchanges have trading floors and a variety of physical facilities for efficient transactions in the listed securities. By contrast, the over-the-counter market for small issues is not an identifiable physical trading area. Instead, transactions are consummated either in the office of a broker or between brokers via telephone, teletype, or personal contact.

Customarily, *all* transactions outside the organized exchanges are treated as over-the-counter operations. This term is therefore also applied to the sale and purchase of government bonds—which total tens of billions of dollars in the course of a year—and the securities of large private corporations, as well as to the transactions in the stocks of small firms. Realistically, however, the market for small issues is significantly different from the over-the-counter market for government securities and those of large corporations, as will be shown subsequently.

The first distinctive feature of the market for small issues is the narrow range of supply and demand in individual securities. The shares sold by a small firm are rarely held by more than a few hundred stockholders. Only in rare cases are these shares bought by financial institutions, trusts, or private corporations. Each small issue thus appeals only to a very limited number of investors. This is particularly true on the offering date and for some time after the initial sale.

The second distinctive feature of the market for small issues is the absence of a continuous flow of orders to buy and to sell, respectively. Orders to buy or to sell flow in sporadically rather than continuously. Furthermore, there is always a strong probability that, for a particular security, the total wanted in the course of a day is either substantially above or below the total offered for sale. For this reason, the dealer in small issues assumes the function of a merchant. That is, he usually has an "inventory" of the issues in which he specializes. He therefore sells from his inventory and adds to it as he buys from those who wish to dispose of their holdings. This function is known as "taking a position."

Prior to the effective date of the new offering, the underwriter and affiliated dealers agree as to who shall be designated as dealer(s) in the issue. It must be emphasized that the daily "bid" and "ask" quotations represent the dealer's bids to buy and to sell. In effect, therefore, the bid and ask quotations represent *negotiated* prices first between the designated dealers and then between these dealers and their customers.

IV. THE ROLE OF THE UNDERWRITER

Small firms, as a rule, have little or no contacts or experience with investment bankers or securities underwriters. For this reason, they frequently employ the services of a "finder."

A. The Finder

The essential task of the finder is to act as intermediary between the firm and one or more underwriters. Customarily, the finder receives a fee for his services. The amount ranges between 1 and 3% of the gross amount of the new issue. In some cases, the fee may be greater depending on the scope of services that the finder expects and offers to perform.

As in every area of services, the specific services performed by finders cover a wide range of quality and scope. Within this range, it is possible to distinguish three types of finders: (1) the professional finder, (2) the incidental finder, and (3) the one-time finder.

1. The Professional Finder   This group is composed primarily of individuals who are either attorneys or certified public accountants by training and professional background. The sizable earnings potential as a finder may induce an accountant or attorney to devote an increasing proportion of his time, although not necessarily his entire activities, to the role of finder. His services in this capacity are available to any firm that plans a public issue.

2. The Incidental Finder   This individual does not specialize either in SEC work or as a finder. He usually is a CPA, attorney, or financial consultant for a number of firms. Since he is active as a consultant to or auditor for a number of firms, he may also acquire some familiarity with the market for unlisted securities and have some contacts with underwriters or brokers.

3. The One-Time Finder   This individual has neither a special knowledge of the investment market nor contacts with underwriters. He is usually the accountant of the firm or its attorney. When the owners decide to go public, they ask him to locate a suitable dealer who will act as underwriter or will sell the issue on a "best efforts" basis. Thus, he becomes, involuntarily, a finder.

B. Underwriters and Dealers

The small firm often sells its equity securities directly without benefit of the services of any middleman. This is often true for new companies where the number of buyers for the stock is so limited that it can be usually best reached through a direct selling effort by company officials.

As a firm becomes larger, it may seek the services of an underwriter or broker. Basically, the underwriter is a distributor. He acts as a middleman between the issuing firm and the ultimate buyers of the new securities.

The underwriter offers his services under a variety of arrangements. In underwritten issues, one or a group of underwriters assure the firm a guaranteed amount of funds at a guaranteed time. The underwriter agrees to purchase the entire issue at an agreed price and assumes the risk that he will be unable to sell the entire issue to the public. In other words, when an issue is underwritten, the underwriter adds the function of risk taking to his selling function. In return for underwriting an issue, the underwriter will charge a larger commission for his services than if he did not guarantee to sell the entire issue at a stated price and time.

Underwriters also offer their services to firms issuing securities on a "best effort" basis. Under these arrangements, the underwriter assists the firm in designing the various details of the security (time of issue, price, preferred-dividend rate, etc.) and in organizing dealers to sell the securities. The underwriter receives a fee for his services and the dealers receive commissions according to the sales of the issue. Particularly in small equity offerings, the underwriter may act as a dealer as well as advisor on terms of issue, etc.

Dealers in small issues can be divided into two major categories.

1. Brokers-Underwriters This group is composed of security dealers who are members of the national exchanges; e.g., New York Stock Exchange, American Stock Exchange. In addition to their activities as brokers on these exchanges, these firms are also active as originators of participants in the flotation of new issues. However, this group of dealers will only rarely handle primary issues of less than $750,000. They are strongly disinclined to float Regulation A issues of $300,000 or less.

2. Promotional Dealer-Underwriters This type of dealer is either a dealer in unlisted securities or confines his activities solely to underwriting small issues or selling them on a "best efforts" basis. Compared with the broker-underwriter previously discussed, he has usually a small organization. This consists largely of salesmen who sell the securities to their own individual lists of customers or who utilize the lists of the dealer-underwriter. Unlike the investment banker or the large broker, the promotional underwriter rarely has a research and securities analysis department. Frequently, his is a one-man operation in the sense that one individual is the sole owner of the underwriting firm. While he engages the services of accountants and attorneys, as needed, he relies extensively on his own judgment. His background is that of a securities analyst and dealer in securities with a number of years of experience in the sale and distribution of stock.

The promotional dealer-underwriter plays a prominent role in the underwriting of Regulation A issues. This may be attributed to two factors. First, the SEC requirements are far less rigorous on small issues than on those exceeding $300,000. This makes it possible for the promotional dealer-underwriter to be equally "liberal" in evaluating the financial conditions and prospects of the company. Moreover, the less rigorous registration requirements facilitate compliance with less documentation and without a certification by a public accountant (CPA). And second, the commission earned on Regulation A issues quite often is as great or even greater than on issues two or three times as large, as will be shown later.

C. Dealers' Terms

The basic compensation of the dealer is the commission, which is a percentage of the issue price. The range of the commission rate on primary small issues is extremely wide.

1. Commission In Regulation A (primary) issues, a rate of 10 to 15% is rare. Commissions of 18 to 25% represent typical rates. Occasionally, they run as high as 30% and up. These rates generally apply to issues with a gross yield between $250,000 and $300,000. Dealers will very rarely undertake the flotation of issues below $250,000 except on a "best efforts" basis. Commissions are usually smaller on a "best efforts" issue than on an underwritten issue.

On issues between $300,000 and $1,000,000, the rates generally range between 10 and 20%. The lower figures—10 to 13%—apply to issues between $750,000 and $1 million while the higher rates are more frequent in issues of less than $500,000.

The commission does not constitute the total compensation of the dealer on an underwritten issue. It represents the basic and immediate earnings of the underwriter. An additional potential source of income consists of options granted to the underwriter. Their nature and effects on the company will be discussed under a separate heading.

2. Expenses, Fees   While these costs are greater in a large issue of $5 million than in an issue of $500,000, the expense in the first case is more likely to be perhaps only three times as great as in the second instance. As a percentage of the gross yield, therefore, these expenses constitute a significantly higher proportion in a small issue than in large issues. On a $300,000 issue these costs may run between $15,000 and $25,000. Expressed as a percentage of the issue, they will generally range between 5 and 8%.

3. Options, Warrants   An option gives the underwriter the right to purchase a fixed number of shares at a predetermined price within a specified period of time. For example, the company gives the underwriter an option to buy 10,000 shares at $1 each with the provision that the option cannot be exercised earlier than 30 days after the sale of the stock to the public, and not later than 1 year after the offering date of the issue.

Options may be classified on the basis of the price per share to be paid by the underwriter as compared with the issue price paid by the public.

Warrants are similar to options, except for two features. First, warrants are in terms of individual shares. That is, each warrant entitles the holder to acquire one share at a predetermined price within a specified period of time. And second, the warrant itself has a price tag. In the typical case of small issues, the underwriter pays a nominal price for the warrants which ranges between 1¢ and 10¢ per warrant.

4. Representation on Board   Frequently, the underwriting agreement also provides that one or more individuals, to be designated by the underwriter, are to be elected to the company's board of directors. The owners of the company, who will still control a majority of the stock after the issue, agree to include the specified number of individuals in the new slate of directors and to cast their ballots for election of the underwriter's nominees. This provision has a twofold objective. First, it gives the underwriter an insider's view of the operations of the company, subsequent to the stock issue. This insight becomes of considerable importance in those cases in which the underwriter has an option. Second, it is intended to give the purchasers of the new issue some assurance that their interests will be safeguarded by the directors nominated by the underwriter.

5. First Refusal   Another provision, which is practically a standard clause, gives the underwriter the right of "first refusal" on a secondary issue. Suppose the company decides to float a second issue and, for reasons of its own, prefers to negotiate with one or more other underwriters and obtains terms that it regards as desirable. If profits increase, as anticipated, the result will be reflected in a corresponding rise in the market price of its shares. This fact does not escape trade creditors and banks, just as a decline in the market price will be duly noted by the several types of creditors. And, as pointed out earlier in this volume, a sustained favorable after-market provides a desirable basis for an eventual second issue.

F. "Blue Sky" Laws

A majority of the states have adopted legislation which, similar to the Federal Securities Act of 1933, is designed to prevent fraud in the issue and sale of new securities. These laws are known as "blue sky legislation."

Forty-three states require that specific information be filed with a state agency prior to the sale of new securities within these states. An underwriter, who has customers in these states, must file the required information and pay the registration fee. The underwriting agreement provides that the costs are to be paid by the issuing company. In the typical case, these expenses will run between $1500 and $2500, depending on the number of states in which the underwriter and affiliated dealers propose to offer the new securities.

V. THE AFTER-MARKET

Assume that the entire offering of a small issue has been purchased by the public at or moderately above the issue price. The company receives the net yield, the underwriters and dealers have earned their commissions plus expenses, and the second phase of going public has come to an end. Now begins the next and final phase: the maintenance of an after-market for the small issue.

Both management of the company and its shareholders, old and new, have an immediate stake in the maintenance of an after-market. Management desires a continued interest of the small investors in the stock of the company.

Shareholders in the firm have an immediate financial stake in the after-market. It provides a means of liquidating an asset, i.e., the stock in the firm, if and when the need for cash funds arises.

The underwriters, too, have a stake in the after-market. For one thing, a sustained investors' interest in issues floated by an underwriter is a valuable asset in attracting new clients, both potential issuers and investors. And, additionally, the underwriter may have obtained options or warrants. These rights have value to the underwriters only if they can profit by exercising these options and selling the shares at an appreciably higher price in the market.

1. Free Market Play   Some underwriters make it a deliberate policy to leave the after-market to the free interplay of demand and supply. Having successfully floated the issue, they take the attitude that their task is finished. This does not mean that these underwriters will remove themselves completely from the market. They or the syndicate members originally selected for this function continue to act as the merchant-dealers in the issue. However, these dealers carry only a small inventory of the stock. They will buy small blocks of shares if they have reason to believe that they can dispose of the shares within a few days at a profit. Similarly, they sell small blocks to bridge a short-time gap until private investors put up their shares for sale. Thus, these dealers take a position in the market as a temporary stopgap. Otherwise, their activity in a given stock is that of a broker rather than a dealer-merchant.

2. Support of the After-Market   A second group of underwriters prefer to maintain close contact with the after-market. This is particularly true of those who have obtained options at less than issue price. They have a direct, and frequently substantial, financial interest in the price trend. Every rise in the market value of the shares means a proportionate profit on the shares which they can purchase under the options and warrants. Moreover, under the income tax laws, a profit realized on stock held for more than six months is subject to the capital gains tax of 25%, whereas the personal income tax rate is applicable to profits from the sale of stock held for less than six months.

SUMMARY

The personal savings of the owners are the prime source of equity capital in the small company. As the firm grows and builds up retained earnings, the owners may consider "going public" for either personal motivations or to meet financial needs, or both.

Personal elements fall into three major categories: estate taxes, dissension among owners, and the desire to diversify personal investments.

The major financial reasons for a public stock offering by a small business are to remedy an unbalanced capital structure, to procure funds for the acquisition of another company, or to prepare for a merger.

Federal regulations of the SEC provide for special treatment of stock issues of less than $300,000. Trading in most small issues takes place in the over-the-counter market. The services of a finder are often helpful to the small business seeking help in finding an underwriter or investment banker to help the firm go public.

The after-market, once the firm has gone public, is important to the firm, to the shareholders, and to the underwriter. Management desires a continued interest by the small investors in the stock of the company. Shareholders also have an immediate financial stake in the after-market. This market provides a means of liquidating an asset if and when the need for cash arises. The underwriter hopes that the after-market will stay active since a sustained investors interest in issues floated by an underwriter is a valuable asset in attracting new clients and the underwriter may have optional warrants or options which will only be valuable if the market price of the stock rises.

The financial manager of the small company should be aware of the possibilities of a Reg. A issue as his firm grows and builds up retained earnings.

Questions

1. What personal motivations lead small businessmen to make a public offering of stock?
2. What are the major financial reasons for a small company to go public?
3. Discuss the advantages and disadvantages of a small firm going public prior to a merger.
4. What are the SEC requirements for a Regulation A issue? Why are they more lenient than for other public offerings?
5. What is meant by the over-the-counter market?
6. What are the differences in the over-the-counter market between securities of large corporations and small firms?
7. Why do small firms use a finder? How is he compensated?
8. How is the underwriter compensated for flotation of a small issue? Do you think this compensation is reasonable? Why (not)?

9. Why do underwriters ask for a representative on the board of a company?

10. What is the importance of the after-market for an issue to a small firm that has gone public?

Case: N & G COMPANY

John Newman, President of the N & G Company, had just about completed his negotiations with an underwriter for the flotation of 100,000 shares in his company when he was approached by the investment officer of the Brunswick Business Development Corporation with an offer to purchase 100,000 shares in the company.

The N & G Company had been organized in 1962 by John Newman and Percival Goodfine. Newman and Goodfine had been employed for a number of years as assistant general sales manager and engineer, respectively, in the photographic equipment division of a national company. Both were still in their early 30's and decided to set up their own business for the manufacture and sale of cameras and plate-making equipment for commercial photographers and printing establishments.

Their initial investment was $50,000, one-half of which was contributed by Newman and Goodfine with the balance obtained in the form of a 5-year loan from several friends. The company was organized as a corporation and issued 200,000 no par value shares with each of the two organizers receiving 100,000 shares.

In 1953, Newman and Goodfine concentrated on the manufacturing of semiautomatic daylight processing systems. This equipment dispensed roll film in sizes up to 14 inches wide, processed and delivered finished negatives in daylight, and cut the negatives to preset sizes. A specially designed prismatic head provided photo copies in positive or negative form, or direct electrostatic plates.

In order to maximize efficient use of their limited financial resources, the company obtained most components for the semiautomatic equipment from subcontractors. The company itself only manufactured the precision units and assembled the components in these units into the final product. By the end of 1963, the company employed 15 semiskilled workers. Sales for the year totalled about $250,000, with more than one-half of the sales in the last quarter of the year. Profits after taxes and owners salaries amounted to $25,750. Newman and Goodfine drew salaries of $10,000 each. The entire profit was reinvested in the business.

Early in 1964 the company introduced a fully automatic daylight processing system and added a line of specially designed cameras. It continued
the practice of using subcontractors owing to a lack of capital to set up
its own manufacturing facilities. Its payroll increased in the course of the
year to a peak of 30 skilled and semiskilled workers by the end of the
summer of 1964. Sales for the year exceeded $600,000 with a net profit
after taxes and owners' salaries of $75,000. Newman and Goodfine were
drawing $17,500 each.

Early in 1965, the two owners of the company decided to sell stock
in the company. In their opinion, $150,000 of capital was needed as a
downpayment on machinery and equipment for the manufacture of the
total line by the company itself. The cost of the machinery and equipment
plus installation ran to $350,000. The suppliers was willing to accept a
downpayment of $150,000 with the balance payable in five annual install-
ments of $40,000 each and interest charges of 6% on the unpaid balance,
payment to be made in semiannual installments of $20,000.

TABLE 16-1. N & G Company; Statement of Income, Profit and Loss
for Year Ending December 31, 1964 (Dollars)

		1964		1963
Sales				
Sales		641,000		254,500
Less discounts and allowances		9,000		3,750
Net sales		632,000		250,750
Cost of Goods Sold				
Inventory—January 1	39,250		8,550	
Purchases	155,900		135,200	
Wages	178,500		49,200	
Total	373,650		192,950	
Less Inventory, December 31	30,900		39,250	
Cost of goods sold		342,750		153,700
Gross Profit on Sales		289,250		97,050
Selling and Administrative				
Selling expenses	94,750		37,600	
Administrative expenses	53,750		32,400	
Total selling and administrative expenses		148,500		60,000
Net Profit before Taxes		140,750		37,050
Federal and State Income Taxes		65,450		11,300
Net Profit after Taxes		75,300		25,750

The two owners were also anxious to obtain some "cash" for their own personal use. It was their intention to sell 15,000 shares each from their own holdings and 70,000 shares to be newly issued. The proceeds from the sale of the 70,000 shares was to go to the company.

Goodfine estimated that by establishing their own manufacturing facilities, N & G Company could easily increase its profit by 50%.

An underwriting firm to whom they submitted the financial statements, as shown in Tables 16-1 and 16-2, after examining the company's sales,

TABLE 16-2. N & G Company; Balance Sheet as at December 31, 1964 (Dollars)

Assets		
Current Assets		
Cash in bank	62,850	
Accounts receivable	166,700	
Inventory	39,250	
Prepaid expenses	14,300	
Total current assets		283,100
Fixed Assts		
Machinery and equipment	28,000	
Less depreciation	5,600	
Leasehold improvements	4,500	
Total fixed assets		26,900
		310,000
Liabilities and Net Worth		
Current Liabilities		
Accounts payable		38,500
Banknotes payable		55,000
Estimated income taxes payable		65,450
Long-term debt notes due April 1, 1967		25,000
Capital Stock		
Common no-par value:		
Authorized: 400,000 Shares		
Issued: 200,000 Shares	25,000	
Retained earnings	101,050	
Total Net Worth		126,050
Total Liabilities and Net Worth		310,000

operations, and financial records offered to sell 100,000 shares at an issue price of $3. The underwriter's commission was to be 15% plus an additional $10,000 for printing, legal, and other expenses. In addition, the underwriter asked for an option to purchase an additional 50,000 shares at the following prices: $3 per share if excerised at the end of one year; $4 at the end of two years; and $1 additionally for the third, fourth, and fifth years.

In the course of subsequent negotiations, the underwriter agreed to raise his option price to $4 for the first year and one additional dollar per share for each of the next four years.

Newman and Goodfine were giving serious thought to the acceptance of this offer when they received the following offer from the Brunswick Business Development Corporation. Brunswick offered to purchase 100,000 shares at $2.70 per share with a 2-year option to buy an additional 50,000 shares at $5. The Brunswick Business Development Corporation also insisted on the right to elect two out of five directors.

Brunswick is a venture capital company that specializes in buying shares in small companies that have possibilities of rapid growth and development. It has been quite successful in the last twelve years and Brunswick shares have recently been listed on a national stock exchange.

Case Questions:

1. Evaluate the advantages and disadvantages of each offer.
2. What additional information should Messrs. Newman and Goodfine seek from the underwriter? From the business development company?
3. On the basis of the information presented in the case, which offer should N & G Company accept? Why?

~~~~~~

Chapter Seventeen

Planning the Choice of Securities

The three preceding chapters have analyzed the features of equity and long-term debt securities in general. This chapter will look at these basic security types from the viewpoint of the financial manager of a corporation that needs to raise long-term capital through an issue of bonds, preferred stock, or common stock. Which of the three shall the corporation issue? Obviously, the answer to this question will depend upon a variety of factors based upon the needs of the individual corporation at a point in time with a given capital structure and given objectives of the firm.

The corporation will be faced with this problem at different times in its life cycle. When the corporation is first organized, this decision will have to be made, although, as was pointed out in Chapter Fourteen, a corporation will generally begin with an all common-stock capital structure. Depending upon the corporation's rate of growth and the amount of earnings the firm is able to retain, the company may return to the long-term securities market often or perhaps not at all. Many firms will issue new long-term securities only four or five times in a 25-year period. Other corporations must issue securities as often as once a year. The issuance of long-term securities is one of the key financial analyses that the financial manager must make.

How, then, can the financial manager best make this important analysis? It is assumed that the financial manager, in approaching this problem, will take the point of view of doing what is best for the owners of the corporation—the present common shareholders. These shareholders have accepted the risks of ownership. They also have the power to name the board of directors, who legally represent the common shareholder. The financial manager must consider the probable reaction of the present stockholders since their interest may well be different from that of potential new shareholders who may desire features in a new stock offering which would be at the expense of the present stockholders. For example, marketing a new issue of common stock, without giving the present shareholders an opportunity to purchase the stock, at a price below the book value of the shares outstanding would probably not be in the interest of the present common stockholder (who would thereby suffer dilution of equity and earnings, in addition to the dilution of control) unless such dilution should lead to higher earnings in the long run for the present common shareholders than any other alternative. Management's point of view should be to maximize the earnings of the present common shareholders in the long run.

In fact, financial managers sometimes are swayed by other interests and points of view than that of what is best for the present common shareholder. Bondholders, for example, may influence management to issue preferred stock rather than more bonds since the issuance of equity securities would strengthen the security of the bondholder because of their prior claim on assets. Management itself sometimes has an inclination to do what is most likely to promote the continuation of the present management, or what will most enhance the value of managerial stock options regardless of what is truly best for the present common shareholder. Despite these caveats, this chapter will assume that the financial manager will adopt a point of view, for the purposes of deciding upon alternative choices of long-term securities, of doing what is in the long-run interest of the present common shareholders.

To compare bonds with common stock and preferred stock, it is necessary to look at what effect each security would have on a variety of factors of importance to the present common stockholders of a particular corporation at one point in time. The financial manager should be most concerned with three main factors: income, risk, and control. In addition, he is also concerned with several other factors; e.g., marketability and timing, and maintenance of flexibility in regard to future financing.

I. PRIMARY CONSIDERATIONS

A. Income

By the use of financial leverage, the financial manager may be able to raise the "income" or the rate of return on the present shareholder's investment. Whenever funds are obtained in return for a limited payment (e.g., preferred dividends or bond interest) favorable financial leverage will be employed if the firm can earn more on the use of these funds than the limited payment that must be made for them. From the point of view of the present common stockholders, favorable financial leverage will also result from the issue of new common shares, if the incremental income to the present shareholder is greater than the cost of the new shares (earnings per share to the new shareholders). Financial leverage can also be unfavorable to the present common shareholder. Dilution in the earnings per share of the present common shareholders will occur when the payments (in the form of preferred dividends, bond interest, or earnings per share to new common shareholders) are greater than what the firm can earn on the new capital provided to the corporation. The following example will demonstrate the concept of the effect of financial leverage (from the point of view of the present common stock-holder) in the case of an additional stock issue.

X Corporation shows the following capital structure in its balance sheet:

Capital:
  authorized 250,000 no-par value shares;
  outstanding 100,000 shares $1,000,000
Retained earnings   750,000
Net worth $1,750,000

The corporation needs $875,000 of new capital to finance a major program of expansion. Its earnings before interest and taxes (henceforth referred to as EBIT) amounted to roughly $400,000 in each of the preceding three years. Earnings after taxes averaged about $200,000 and this level is projected for the future if the proposed expansion is executed. We shall assume that the corporation is able to sell 50,000 shares at $17.50 each without the services of an underwriter or broker.

How will the new issue of 50,000 shares affect the earnings per share of the old shares if (A) the corporation realizes an incremental profit from the investment of the new capital projected at $350,000 before interest and taxes; (B) the expansion does not pay off; instead, the earnings before interest and taxes (EBIT) decline to $100,000?

Table 17-1 shows the results for A and B.

In case A, the old stockholders have gained from the issue of new stock. Their earnings per share have increased from $2 to $2.50. The

TABLE 17-1.   X Corporation—Expected Earnings per Share (Dollars)

A. Projected Increase in Earnings is Realized

	Without New Issue	With New Issue
Earnings before interest and taxes (EBIT)	400,000	750,000
Interest	0	0
Earnings before taxes	400,000	750,000
Federal income taxes @ 50%	200,000	375,000
Earnings after taxes	200,000	375,000
Earnings per share	2.00[a]	2.50[b]

B. Projected Increase in Earnings is not Realized

	Without New Issue	With New Issue
Earnings before interest and taxes	400,000[c]	100,000
Interest	0	0
Earnings before taxes	400,000	100,000
Federal income taxes @ 50%	200,000	50,000
Earnings after taxes	200,000	50,000
Earnings per share	2.00[a]	0.33[b]

[a] Before new issue, 100,000 shares outstanding.
[b] After new issue, 150,000 shares outstanding.
[c] There is no expansion because of decision not to issue new stock.

financial leverage as a result of the new issue of common stock has been favorable to the old common stockholders.

The picture is reversed in case B. The financial leverage on the existing common shareholders has been unfavorable as a result of the issue of the new common shares. In consequence, the old stockholders must share a portion of their reduced earnings with the new investors in the corporation. Earnings per share are lower than they would have been if no new shares had been issued.

Instead of procuring the additional $875,000 of new capital through an issue of common stock, the financial manager of X Corporation has two other alternatives. He could sell debt securities or he could issue preferred stock. Assume that he could issue nonparticipating cumulative preferred stock with a 6% dividend or that he could issue twenty-year debenture bonds with an interest rate of 6%. Assume again (as in case A) that, if the expansion is successful, EBIT will be $750,000. If the expansion is unsuccessful (as in case B) EBIT will be $100,000. With these facts, it is simple to calculate the effect on earnings per share of each proposal. Table 17-2 shows this effect. To give a complete comparison, the figures for the issue of new common stock are also included in this table as well as the figures if no expansion takes place.

From the point of view of the present common shareholder, it is clear that if the expansion is a success and EBIT rises to $750,000, earnings per share will be greatest (financial leverage will be the most favorable) if bonds are issued. EPS will be higher if preferred stock is issued than if new common shares are issued.

On the other hand, if the expansion is a failure and EBIT falls to $100,000, the old common shareholders will be worse off from the point of view of income (i.e., EPS) if preferred stock is issued. Earnings will not be at a high enough level in that case to cover the preferred

TABLE 17-2.   X Corporation: EPS as a Result of Issuing New Securities (Dollars)

	No Expansion	New Common Stock	New Preferred Stock	New Bonds
A. Projected Expansion is Successful and Projected Increase in Earnings is Realized:
EBIT	400,000	750,000	750,000	750,000
Interest	—	—	—	52,500
Earnings before taxes	400,000	750,000	750,000	697,500
Federal income taxes @ 50%	200,000	375,000	375,000	348,750
Earnings after taxes	200,000	375,000	375,000	348,750
Less preferred dividends	—	—	52,500	—
Earnings to common	200,000	375,000	322,500	348,750
Earnings per share	2.00[a]	2.50[b]	3.22[a]	3.49[a]
B. Earnings Fall as a Result of Unsuccessful Expansion:
EBIT	400,000	100,000	100,000	100,000
Interest	—	—	—	52,500
Earnings before taxes	400,000	100,000	100,000	47,500
Federal income taxes @ 50%	200,000	50,000	50,000	23,750
Earnings after taxes	200,000	50,000	50,000	23,750
Less preferred dividends	—	—	52,500	—
Earnings (deficit) to common	200,000	50,000	(2,500)	23,750
Earnings (deficit) per share	2.00[a]	0.33[b]	(0.02½)[a]	0.24[a]

[a] 100,000 shares of common stock outstanding.
[b] 150,000 shares of common stock outstanding.

dividend. If the preferred dividend is paid, the common stockholder will incur a deficit of 2½ cents per share. The old common stockholder will be best off if expansion has not occurred at all. If it had occurred, the common stockholder would be better off (i.e., will suffer less unfavorable financial leverage) if the corporation had issued new common stock rather than bonds or preferred stock.

There is one further complication that must be mentioned at this stage. Bonds, unlike preferred or common stock, do not represent permanent capital. They must either be refunded or retired at maturity. Some financial managers, therefore, refine their calculations concerning earnings per share to include the concept of uncommitted earnings per share (UEPS) so as to allow for the payment of a sinking fund to retire the bonds. If X Corporation applied a 5% sinking fund to the retirement of its bonds each year so that the bonds would be retired after twenty years, UEPS at levels of $750,000 of EBIT and $100,000 of EBIT would be as shown in Table 17-3.

TABLE 17-3. X Corporation: UEPS at EBIT Levels of $750,000 and $100,000 if New Bonds Are Issued (Dollars)

	750,000	100,000
EBIT	750,000	100,000
Interest	52,500	52,500
Earnings before taxes	697,500	47,500
Federal income taxes @ 50%	348,750	23,750
Earnings after taxes	348,750	23,750
Less preferred dividends	—	—
Earnings after preferred dividends	348,750	23,750
Less bond sinking fund (5% × 875,000)	43,750	43,750
Uncommitted earnings to common	305,000	(20,000)
UEPS	3,05[a]	(0.20)[a]

[a] 100,000 shares of common stock outstanding.

In the case of X Corporation, on the basis of the UEPS concept, the preferred stock would not appear the most attractive alternative, from the point of view of income to the old common shareholders, at an EBIT level of $750,000. At an EBIT level of $100,000, the common shareholders would have to pay 20¢ per share which would be charged against the retained earnings account to fully cover the bond sinking fund.

Many financial analysts and managers believe the UEPS concept is not appropriate in comparing alternatives of bonds versus equity capital on the factor of income for several reasons. They state that the only fair way to compare alternatives is on the basis of using the same amount of capital. If a sinking fund is used for bonds, after the first year the amounts of capital remaining in the firm will be unequal since equity capital is generally permanent and is not usually paid back to the suppliers of the capital by means of a sinking fund. Second, if the sinking fund is used, the amount of bond interest will decline each year as bonds are retired. Again, these analysts believe it would be unfair to use the first year's interest in this case for comparative purposes with common and preferred if the sinking fund is also taken into consideration. In larger firms (which refund bonds when they mature so that bonds are, in effect, a permanent part of long-term capital) it would seem appropriate to ignore the effect of the sinking fund on the factor of income, when comparing alternative choices of securities.

Financial managers may wish to make further refinements in their comparison of securities under the factor of income. For example, the costs of issuing various securities will vary depending on the type security issued, the size of the corporation, and the state of the capital market. These costs could be prorated over the life of the securities and deducted from EBIT by the financial manager so as to arrive at a more accurate EPS. Table 17-4 shows the costs of selling common stock in the early 1950s for various sized issues.

TABLE 17-4.   Cost of Selling Common Stock; By Size of Issue; As Percentage of Gross Proceeds

Size of Issue	Underwriting	Other Expenses	Total
Under $500,000	21.0	6.2	27.2
500,000 to 990,000	17.1	4.7	21.8
1,000,000 to 1,900,000	11.3	2.3	13.6
2,000,000 to 4,900,000	8.5	1.5	10.0
5,000,000 to 9,900,000	5.3	0.9	6.2
10,000,000 to 19,900,000	4.2	0.5	4.7
20,000,000 to 49,900,000	5.0	0.4	5.4

Source: Securities and Exchange Commission, Cost of Flotation of Corporate Securities, 1951–1955; U.S. Government Printing Office, 1957; pp. 37ff.

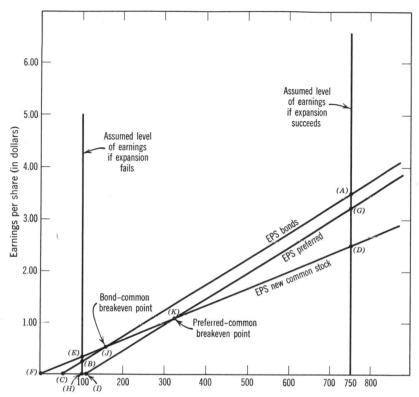

Figure 17-1. X Corporation; range of earnings chart showing comparison of bond, common stock, and preferred stock alternatives at different levels of EBIT in terms of EPS.

Once the financial manager has calculated EPS based on two different levels of EBIT, he can make use of a helpful tool of analysis which was developed at the Harvard Business School in his comparison of debt with common stock and preferred stock. There is a simple mathematical relationship between EBIT and EPS for each security type. This relationship can be represented in linear form on a graph that is usually known as a range of earnings chart or more simply as an EBIT chart. Figure 17-1 shows a comparison among bonds, common stock, and preferred stock for X Corporation, using the data derived above.

Figure 17-1 shows what the EPS will be at any likely level of EBIT on the common stock for each alternative: $875,000 of additional common stock, $875,000 of bonds, or $875,000 of preferred stock.

The three lines can be drawn by determining any two points on each line as the relationship between EPS and EBIT is always linear. For example, point A on the bond line is taken from Table 17-2, which shows an EPS of $3.49 for the bond alternative at an EBIT of $750,000. Point B on the bond line is taken from the EPS of $0.24 at an EBIT of $100,000. In a similar manner, points D and E were derived for the common stock line and points G and H for the preferred stock line. Actually, it is unnecessary to calculate EPS for more than one EBIT level to develop the range of earnings chart. The second point on each line can be derived more simply by calculating the level of EBIT which is required to achieve an EPS of exactly zero. In the case of an all common-stock capital structure (such as the present structure of X Corporation) EPS will always be zero at zero EBIT. That is, the common-stock line will always intersect the x and y axes of the graph at zero for an all common-stock capital structure. In the case of X Corporation, this can be seen at point F on the chart. If some senior securities are already outstanding, the common stock line will cross the x axis at a point where there is enough EBIT to cover existing bond interest plus existing preferred dividends (tax related).

The bond line will intersect the x axis at the level of EBIT required to just cover the bond interest. In the case of X Corporation, this would be $52,500 (point C). The preferred line will intersect the x axis at the level of EBIT required to cover the preferred dividend, tax related. In the case of X Corporation, this would be at $105,000 (point I). Again, if some senior securities are already outstanding, the x axis will be crossed by the bond and preferred lines further to the right at EBIT points where all prior senior security bond interest and preferred dividends (tax related) are covered plus the new bond interest or preferred dividends, tax related.

When preparing a range of earnings chart, it is often helpful to plot a third point to insure that no error has been made in the calculations. The relationship between EPS and EBIT is always a straight line.

Note the difference in slope between the bond line (or the preferred-stock line) and the common-stock line. At some level of EBIT, the bond line will intersect the common-stock line. At this point, referred to as the bond-common breakeven point or the point of indifference, the EPS will be the same for both bonds and common stock. For levels of earnings below this point, the common-stock alternative will produce the more favorable income; at levels above this point, the bonds will produce the more favorable income to the existing common shareholders. This difference in slope between the bond and the common-stock lines is due to the differing number of common shares outstanding under the respective alternatives.

Because of the tax factor, preferred dividends are paid after income taxes, and because bond interest is a deductible expense for tax purposes, the preferred stock line will parallel the bond line and will always provide a lower income (in EPS) than the bonds, provided the before-tax counterpart of the dividend rate (12%) is greater than the bond interest rate (e.g., 6%). Consequently, normal EBIT levels would have to be at a higher level for the financial manager to prefer preferred stock to new common stock, with regard to the factor of income.

B. Risk

Because of the tax laws, analysis of choice of securities with respect to income will generally reveal an advantage to the use of bonds by most corporations. However, the financial manager must consider other factors besides income. Suppose, in a certain firm, EBIT levels are generally such as to give appreciably more income as a result of using bonds. However, perhaps once in every five years EBIT declines to such low levels that bond interest and sinking-fund requirements cannot be met out of current income. In these circumstances, it may be highly risky for the firm to issue bonds since if the interest (and sinking fund) is not paid, the bondholders may foreclose, with the result that the common stockholders may lose part or all of their investment. Similarly, if too much preferred stock is outstanding to pay dividends in a year of low earnings, there will be no dividends to the common shareholders in that year or in succeeding years until the preferred dividend arrearages have been paid.

The range of earnings chart is helpful in demonstrating the magnitude of risk. In the case of X Corporation, an EBIT level of $52,500 is needed to cover bond interest (point C). If an UEPS line were drawn on the chart, it would show a necessary EBIT of $130,000 to cover both interest and sinking fund. An EBIT of $105,000 is needed to cover the preferred dividend of X Corporation (point I).

How can the financial manager resolve the problem of how much risk can the company stand to get as much income as possible? One thing is certain: it is seldom possible to both eat well and sleep well.

Some financial managers believe that any debt is too risky for the corporation. Perhaps a majority, however, find it necessary to borrow at some time in the history of their firm. Many financial managers follow a policy of letting the creditors decide. They will borrow as much as the creditors will lend on a reasonable interest basis—perhaps at the "prime" rate. Another common approach is to use about as much debt and preferred as other firms in the industry are using.

Another approach to resolve the problem of risk is to use operations research techniques. The financial manger can simulate earnings levels under varying conditions in the business cycle (perhaps with the aid of a computer). Other factors such as the effect of a strike, for example, can be simulated. Different levels of debt can be plugged into the simulation to determine at what levels cash will run out. In any event, the problem of risk is still difficult to solve on any generalized basis as shareholders, businessmen, and their firms differ in their willingness to bear risk.

Before any financial leverage is used, the financial manager must weigh the possible risks involved in the financial leverage against the expected income as a result of the new capital. In this sense, there can be risks in the issuance of new common stock. Although these risks are of lower magnitude (i.e., new common stockholders cannot force liquidation as can bondholders on default of interest payments) they are real in that earnings per share of the old common stockholders might decline as a result of unfavorable financial leverage owing to dilution of earnings.

C. Control

Neither bond issues nor preferred-stock issues can affect the voting control of the corporation by the common shareholders provided bond indentures and preferred-stock covenants are complied with. The various loan covenants and the preferred position of the preferred stock do create indirect controls. Bondholders can force reorganization (and a possible change of control) as a result of corporate failure to pay bond interest and principal as required by the indenture. Similarly, preferred stockholders are sometimes given several seats on the board of directors if preferred dividends are in arrears.

The issue of new common stock does, however, involve a question of control, assuming the new common shareholders are to receive voting shares of common. Generally, for each new share of common stock issued there will be one new vote. When the new common stock is purchased by new shareholders, the control of the old shareholders is diluted. The amount of dilution can be measured by dividing the former number of shares outstanding by the new total of shares outstanding. In the case of X Corporation, as described above, there were 100,000 shares outstanding. If 50,000 shares will be sold if new common is issued then 100,000/150,000 = 67% of the voting power will remain with the old shareholders (assuming there is no rights offering). Thus, if someone held 60% of the old shares of X Corporation, he would now hold only 40% of the shares, i.e., he would no longer hold majority control of X Corporation.

If the present majority common stockholder of X Corporation desires to maintain his control, it is clear that X Corporation must issue preferred or bonds if addtional long-term funds are required by the corporation. However, as mentioned above, too much debt (or preferred stock) may cause the corporation to face reorganization or bankruptcy. It may be more desirable to give up some control to avoid risk of losing complete control. Or, it may be wiser to postpone expansion until expansion can be financed by retained earnings.

II. SECONDARY CONSIDERATIONS

A. Marketability and Timing

In addition to considerations of risk, income, and control, the financial manager must ask several questions in planning which alternative of long-term funds should be chosen. One key question is: "At what price can the issue be sold?" In addition to the terms of the proposed issue, such factors as size, earnings history, and general reputation of the company (and perhaps the investment banker's reputation as well) are crucial in answering this question.

The factor of timing is important here also. During the depths of the depression even major corporations could not successfully sell common stock. Few corporations were willing to issue common stock after the sharp market break in the spring of 1962. In prosperous times, the successful firm can usually sell an issue when it chooses provided it meets the terms of the market. Even in prosperous times, stock market prices and interest rates can fluctuate rapidly. A ½% increase in the interest rate will cost a firm $50,000 per year on a $10,000,000 bond issue. Over the twenty-year life of a bond issue (with no sinking fund) this would mean $1,000,000 in additional interest. In periods of declining interest rates, the corporation may prefer to borrow on a short-term basis in order to prevent getting locked in on a relatively high rate. Timing may favor debt at times and common or preferred at other times. For a rapidly expanding firm, the timing question often may be expressed as debt now and common stock later or common stock now and debt later. However, timing is not the only factor to be considered. Even "cheap" debt should not be added if it causes too much risk. Similarly, control considerations may lead a company to avoid issuing common even when the stock market is at a peak. A delay in the use of bonds, for example, because of hopes for lower interest rates, means that some alternative source of financing must be used in the meantime. The costs and the potential risks of the temporary alternative must be fully considered by the financial manager.

B. Future Financing

As explained in the chapter on capital budgeting, every firm will strive toward some ideal mix of long-term funds. Every time the corporation goes to the market with one particular alternative, it influences future financing possibilities. For example, if a firm has more debt than others in the industry, it may be unable to get more debt from lenders, no matter how "easy" the capital funds market in debt is. The firm may be forced, therefore, to raise equity capital at a time when equity money is expensive (i.e., it is scarce) or it may be forced to postpone expansion until equity capital is cheaper.

Financial flexibility for future financing may also be impaired by commitments made to get prior financing. For example, if a railroad has mortgaged all its real estate and equipment to secure presently outstanding bond issues, it will have difficulty in securing further long-term debt. For this reason, many financial managers do not use the maximum of senior securities (bonds and preferred) that they can raise in the market. They like to "keep the top open" on senior securities in the event that a change in plans or other unforeseen contingencies make more senior securities financing desirable in the future. Similarly, to preserve future maneuverability in the capital funds market, financial managers try to bargain to insert call features in both debt and preferred issues. Whether prospective long-term lenders and investors will agree to such features will depend upon the respective bargaining powers of the lenders and/or investors vis-à-vis the corporation.

SUMMARY

The financial manager of a corporation that needs to raise long-term capital must make a choice among common stock, preferred stock, or bonds; or some combination of securities must be planned. In order best to make this important decision, the financial manager must look at a variety of considerations, based on the goal of maximizing profits to the present common shareholder, in the long run. Major considerations will generally include income, risk, and control.

By the use of financial leverage, the financial manager may be able to raise the income or the rate of return on the present shareholders' investment. The use of an EBIT chart can graphically depict the income under various alternative choices of securities. However, financial leverage may be unfavorable. The financial manager must measure the magnitude of risk under each alternative. The question of control, particularly when common stock is being considered, is important, because when new common stock is purchased by new shareholders the control of the old shareholders is diluted.

Such secondary considerations as marketability, timing, and future financing should also be analyzed by the financial manager. One key question is: At what price can the issue be sold?

When the financial manager has analyzed all these considerations, he can proceed to prepare a financial plan to raise the funds needed.

Questions

1. Why should the financial manager take the point of view of the present common stockholders in deciding which long-term security the corporation should issue?
2. Give examples of both favorable and unfavorable financial leverage. Should a firm use financial leverage at all, in view of its risks?
3. Discuss the uncommitted earnings per share (UEPS) concept with respect to the income factor for bonds. Can the financial manager use UEPS to help him make a better decision on choice of a long-term security?
4. What is the significance of the bond-common breakeven point on the range of earnings chart (Figure 17-1)?

5. How can the financial manager resolve the problem of how much risk the company can stand and still get as much income as possible?
6. Why does the financial manager try to "keep the top open" with respect to long-term debt?

Problems

1. The board of directors of Delta Corporation are considering two methods of financing their new corporation. The firm will need $1,000,000 to begin operations. One method of financing the corporation would be to issue 100,000 shares of common stock. The other alternative is to issue 50,000 shares of common stock and $500,000 worth of 7% cumulative nonparticipating preferred stock. The corporation expects to pay income taxes at a rate of about 50%.
   (a) Compare earnings per share (EPS) under each alternative assuming EBIT levels of $50,000 and $150,000.
   (b) Prepare a range of earnings chart for Delta Corporation. At what level of EBIT will the two alternatives break even in terms of earnings per share?
2. Beta Corporation intends to raise $25,000,000 to finance its expansion program. Funds may be secured from one of three alternative sources. One source is a $25,000,000 issue of 5% debentures. The debentures will be retired through annual sinking-fund payments of $1,000,000 per year. A second source is a $25,000,000 issue of 6% cumulative nonparticipating preferred stock. A third alternative is to issue $25,000,000 of common stock, sold at $100 per share. Disregard underwriting and other issue expenses.
   Beta now has outstanding a 3% debenture issue of $11,000,000 with an annual sinking fund of $1,000,000, and 1,000,000 shares of common stock. The company currently has an EBIT of $220,000,000 and its earnings are taxed at 50%. The Treasurer of Beta Corporation believes that the new expansion will increase EBIT by $3,000,000.
   (a) Calculate the EPS for each alternative after issuance of the $25,-000,000 in new securities, assuming the expansion is a success.
   (b) Calculate the EPS for each alternative, assuming that no new income results from the expansion.
   (c) Which alternative should Beta employ if it believes the expansion will succeed?

3. A group of investors control 54% of the 525,000 shares of Zeta Corporation.

   (a) If Zeta issues 60,000 new shares, how many shares will the investors have to buy to retain 50% control of Zeta?

   (b) If the investors do not buy any new shares, what percentage of the shares will they control?

Case: HOOPER STOVE COMPANY

In February, 1966, management of the Hooper Stove Company decided to refund its 8% income bonds. $10,000,000 of the 8% income bonds were outstanding at that time and they were callable at face value.

The Hooper Stove Company manufactured stoves and kitchen cabinets. The great majority of the company's sales were made on a contract basis to large United States retail and mail-order chains who private-branded the merchandise. Sales were also made to similar Canadian firms through a wholly owned subsidiary.

The company generally did not produce for inventory, except for a relatively small stock of replacement parts. As a means of compensating for the disruption in the appliance business due to the Korean War, the company in 1951 and 1952 undertook several production contracts for the United States Air Force. The cost and difficulty of conversion of production facilities to Air Force contracts was much greater than anticipated. In addition, the company underestimated the costs of producing for the government and bid too low on several large contracts. This, together with a shortage of materials for civilian production, led to large losses in 1951 through 1953. A protracted strike due to union organization of the company caused further losses in 1954 and 1955. The company began to recover from these losses only to be hit by new labor troubles in 1958. However, sales and earnings began to increase substantially beginning in late 1959. The company's earnings during this period are shown in Table 17-5.

The company's difficulties of the early 1950's coupled with a tight money market led to the issuance of the 8% income bonds in 1954. Management desired to refund these bonds in view of their high interest rate and because many financial men (including the company's new treasurer) felt that income bonds tend to give a company a poor image in the financial community.

TABLE 17-5. Hooper Stove Company; Consolidated Financial Data (Figures in thousands of United States Dollars)

Year	Net Profit or (Deficit) Before Taxes
1947	3353
1948	2159
1949	2037
1950	1835
1951	(792)
1952	(1829)
1953	(1183)
1954	(438)
1955	(522)
1956	527
1957	2750
1958	(512)
1959	(220)
1960	3028
1961	4375
1962	5420
1963	6128
1964	6234
1965	5375

All but the three following alternative methods of financing the proposed refunding have been eliminated by management:

1. The issue of $10,000,000 (net to the company after underwriting and issue expenses of about $450,000) of 6% cumulative preferred stock. The new preferred would be callable at 108% of face value. In the event of nonpayment of a total of six quarters dividends the preferred stockholders would elect 3 of Hooper's 15 directors. The preferred would have no sinking-fund provisions.

2. The issue of $10,000,000 par value 5% 20-year first mortgage bonds. The investment bankers believed that these debentures could be sold to the public (as of February 15, 1966) at a price of about $103.75. Underwriters' fees and other expenses would total about 3¾% of par so that Hooper would net the face value of the bonds. Proposed sinking-fund

provisions called for retirement of 4% of the par value of the issue each year. Bonds would be called by lot at a price of $105. A baloon amount of $2,000,000 would be outstanding at maturity after all sinking-fund payments ($400,000 of face value per year plus call premium) had been made.

3. The sale of additional common stock to the public. The price range of the present common stock on the American Stock Exchange in the past four years had been as follows:

	High	Low
1962	9	$7\frac{3}{4}$
1963	10	7
1964	$10\frac{1}{2}$	$7\frac{1}{2}$
1965	$8\frac{3}{4}$	7

The present common shareholders do not have preemptive rights to the purchase of new shares of common stock issued by the corporation.

A group of three investment banking firms, all located in New York, believed that each of the three alternatives was feasible in terms of present market conditions. The three firms would agree to jointly underwrite any of the three alternatives, unless there was an unusual change in the market. The investment bankers recommended that the new common stock be sold to the public at a price of about $7 if Hooper decided to issue common. Expenses of issue and underwriting fees would amount to approximately $570,000. Therefore, the company would have to issue approximately 1,510,000 new shares of common to net $10,000,000.

Currently, Hooper has 4,490,000 shares of common outstanding. No single individual or group controlled a majority of the shares, as shares were well distributed around the United States and Canada.

The company planned to use its United States and Canadian government securities plus excess cash to meet anticipated increased working capital and fixed capital needs arising from company plans to manufacture a new line of electric stoves to serve customers in Canada plus some rebuilding of United States facilities. The treasurer expected depreciation to be at the rate of about $1,150,000 per year for the foreseeable future.

The treasurer regarded the short-term outlook for earnings as very favorable. Earnings before interest and taxes in the last half of 1965 amounted to approximately $2,720,000 ($1,360,000 after United States and Canadian taxes of approximately 50%). The current backlog of unfilled orders from large United States retail and mail-order firms was equal to about 14 month's normal production. Canadian sales prospects were also favorable

Table 17-6. Hooper Stove Company; Consolidated Balance Sheet, January 1, 1966 (Figures in thousands of United States Dollars)

Assets		
Cash		5,279
United States and Canadian government securities, at cost (United States dollars)		4,596
Accounts and notes receivable		7,076
Inventories:		
Raw materials	3,689	
Work in process	8,734	
Finished goods	918	13,341
Fixed assets, net		11,875
Deferred charges		189
Other assets		117
Total assets		42,473
Liabilities		
Accounts and notes payable		4,912
Accrued liabilities		2,237
Customer advances		5,078
Reserve for United States and Canadian income taxes		3,216
Contingency reserves		3,852
8% income bonds		10,000
Common stock (par value $1)		4,490
Retained earnings		8,688
Total liabilities		42,473

for 1966. The treasurer anticipated that earnings before taxes would be about $6,000,000 in 1966. United States and Canadian income tax rates would probably be about 50% of earnings in 1966. Table 17-6 shows the balance sheet for January 1, 1966.

Case Questions:

1. Prepare a range of earnings (EBIT) chart for Hooper Stove Company.
2. Which alternative method of financing the proposed refunding would you recommend? Why?

~~~~~~

Chapter Eighteen

Sources of Long-Term Funds

Basically, the corporation has available two main sources of long-term capital: (1) funds generated internally by the firm, and (2) funds procured externally from investors. These two sources are not mutually exclusive. Furthermore, each has its own peculiar advantages and drawbacks. The relative extent of their respective favorable and unfavorable features is a function of time and conditions in the capital market. These factors will be examined in this chapter.

Long-term capital is needed by the firm either to replace existing capital assets or to add to its existing capacity, or both. The portion of after-tax profits which is not disbursed in dividends and funds allocated to depreciation may become available for the acquisition of additional capital assets, such as plant and equipment.

Table 18-1 shows the sources and partial uses of new corporate securities in recent years. Changes in the annual total reflect, in large measure, the influence of the business cycle. In periods of economic expansion (the prosperity phase of the cycle), the profits and retained earnings of business firms tend to increase. At such times, investments by companies also rise.

Expansion of plant and equipment has generally been accompanied by increases in inventories, receivables, cash, and cash equivalents financed with long-term funds. That is, firms that made capital investments in additional physical assets also found it necessary to expand their investments in the current assets. In recent years, the aggregate requirements for physical assets and current assets has exceeded the total of the depreciation reserves and retained earnings. In consequence, the balance of the funds needed has been raised from external sources.

Exhibit 18-1   Securities Offerings; New Corporate Securities Offered for Cash in the United States by Type of Issuer and Type of Security (Estimated Gross Proceeds in Thousands of Dollars)

	1964	1965	1965 Jan.–July	1966 Jan.–July
Total corporate	13,956,774	15,992,343	9,493,916	11,301,653
Bonds	10,865,394	13,720,349	8,023,075	9,367,187
Publicly offered	3,622,699	5,569,912	3,311,357	4,154,882
Privately offered	7,242,695	8,150,438	4,711,718	5,212,305
Preferred stock	412,050	725,238	431,241	400,500
Common stock	2,679,329	1,546,756	1,039,599	1,533,966
Manufacturing	3,046,227	5,416,839	3,413,810	4,623,549
Bonds	2,818,858	4,712,079	2,853,347	3,580,759
Preferred stock	41,728	112,154	93,654	42,594
Common stock	185,641	592,606	466,808	1,000,197
Extractive	420,946	342,074	184,200	213,236
Bonds	289,078	242,883	135,848	132,243
Preferred stock	5,250	0	0	11,758
Common stock	126,618	99,190	48,352	69,236
Electric, gas and water	2,759,885	2,936,022	1,548,254	2,257,509
Bonds	2,139,665	2,332,279	1,181,629	1,908,028
Preferred stock	320,122	466,044	297,113	268,994
Common stock	300,098	137,699	69,512	80,486
Railroad	333,088	283,743	200,650	246,401
Bonds	333,088	280,467	198,602	246,401
Preferred stock	0	0	0	0
Common stock	0	3,276	2,048	0
Other transportation	649,023	729,053	410,831	874,099
Bonds	611,275	672,686	389,027	784,526
Preferred stock	0	0	0	0
Common stock	37,749	56,368	21,804	89,572
Communication	2,189,219	947,137	512,251	1,058,855
Bonds	668,756	808,489	442,494	916,121
Preferred stock	6,150	46,900	11,500	43,600
Common stock	1,514,314	91,748	58,256	99,134

Exhibit 18-1   (*Continued*)

	1964	1965	1965 Jan.–July	1966 Jan.–July
Financial and real estate (excluding investment companies)	3,856,407	4,275,779	2,533,854	1,285,622
Bonds	3,391,208	3,762,173	2,218,192	1,159,315
Preferred stock	25,650	78,989	12,900	18,927
Common stock	439,549	434,617	302,762	107,379
Commercial and other	701,977	1,061,697	690,066	742,382
Bonds	613,467	909,294	603,935	639,793
Preferred stock	13,150	21,151	16,075	14,627
Common stock	75,361	131,252	70,056	87,962

I. INTERNAL SOURCES

From the viewpoint of the economy as a whole—known as national income accounting—the aggregate depreciation reserve is treated as an offset of the decreased usability of the capital assets in the private sector of the economy. It is presumed that the private sector is spending an amount equivalent to the depreciation reserve on the acquisition of new capital assets to replace those that have outlived their usefulness. Thus, the spending of the depreciation reserve does not add to the economy's productive capacity. It merely keeps the capacity constant. If, in a given year, the expenditures on physical plant fall below the aggregate depreciation reserve, the capacity of the product factor capital is presumed to be below that of the preceding year. Conversely, if expenditures for capital assets exceed the depreciation reserve, the economy's capacity is increased.

The situation is different in the case of the individual firm. In the individual case, the depreciation reserve set up by the business in any one year is not necessarily equal to the actual loss of usefulness of the asset. When measured against the actual wear and tear of a given asset, the amount allocated to depreciation may be equal to, greater, or less than the loss of usability. It is in the long run, i.e., the estimated lifetime of the asset, that the depreciation reserve is expected to equal the initial cost of the fixed asset.

Table 18-1. Securities Offerings; Proposed Uses of Estimated Net Proceeds from Corporate Offerings (Amounts in Thousands of Dollars)[a]

	1964	1965	1965 January–July	1966 January–July
All corporate offerings	13,792,256	15,800,629	9,376,146	11,161,282
New money	11,232,997	13,063,471	7,758,747	9,932,965
Plant and equipment	7,003,241	7,711,741	4,579,384	7,573,162
Working capital	4,229,756	5,351,730	3,179,364	2,359,803
Retirements of securities	754,089	995,846	559,072	155,613
Other purposes	1,805,170	1,741,312	1,058,326	1,072,703
Manufacturing	3,015,822	5,352,949	3,371,933	4,564,312
New money	2,273,288	4,347,653	2,807,514	4,064,309
Plant and equipment	1,261,247	3,014,569	2,026,626	2,997,062
Working capital	1,012,041	1,333,083	780,888	1,067,247
Retirements of securities	243,498	337,825	222,749	57,516
Other purposes	499,036	667,471	341,671	442,487
Extractive	415,452	337,277	181,194	210,016
New money	283,042	248,819	126,993	167,922
Plant and equipment	171,505	155,661	84,465	75,982
Working capital	111,537	93,158	42,528	91,940
Retirements of securities	8,928	5,319	5,319	25,465
Other purposes	123,483	83,138	48,882	16,628
Electric, gas and water	2,725,237	2,903,430	1,531,834	2,227,697
New money	2,405,670	2,448,840	1,316,284	2,129,016
Plant and equipment	2,401,872	2,440,178	1,308,393	2,104,429
Working capital	3,798	8,661	7,891	24,586
Retirements of securities	280,179	357,422	179,611	34,923
Other purposes	39,387	97,168	35,939	63,759
Railroad	330,547	281,400	198,956	244,538
New money	330,547	263,326	180,882	244,538
Plant and equipment	317,983	248,804	170,053	244,538
Working capital	12,564	14,522	10,829	0
Retirements of securities	0	18,074	18,074	0
Other purposes	0	0	0	0

Table 18-1.   (*Continued*)

	1964	1965	1965 January–July	1966 January–July
Other transportation	642,348	721,769	406,269	866,426
New money	499,815	613,484	328,475	641,896
Plant and equipment	450,087	582,611	307,443	628,053
Working capital	49,728	30,872	21,032	13,843
Retirements of securities	32,023	18,090	4,125	2,943
Other purposes	110,510	90,195	73,669	221,587
Communication	2,169,381	939,127	507,867	1,047,542
New money	1,966,227	822,977	430,651	1,006,479
Plant and equipment	1,846,902	799,047	423,033	991,851
Working capital	119,325	23,930	7,618	14,628
Retirements of securities	36,315	92,412	59,473	3,692
Other purposes	166,840	23,738	17,743	37,372
Financial and real estate (excluding investment companies)	3,802,529	4,220,851	2,499,343	1,270,123
New money	2,984,428	3,454,022	1,984,672	1,125,930
Plant and equipment	367,049	245,565	151,889	260,353
Working capital	2,617,379	3,208,456	1,832,784	865,577
Retirements of securities	79,887	92,572	35,744	12,822
Other purposes	738,214	674,258	478,926	131,371
Commercial and other	690,940	1,043,827	678,750	730,628
New money	489,980	864,352	583,276	552,876
Plant and equipment	186,597	225,305	107,482	270,895
Working capital	303,384	639,047	475,794	281,981
Retirements of securities	73,261	74,131	33,977	18,252
Other purposes	127,699	105,344	61,497	159,500

[a]*Source:* Securities and Exchange Commission.

At first glance, it will appear that it is a contradiction to regard the depreciation reserve as a source of capital for the *expansion* of capital assets of the individual firm. This contradiction is more apparent than real. It arises out of the accounting concept of depreciation, which is not necessarily the same as actual financial management.

A. Depreciation as a Source of Capital

To resolve the seeming paradox, it is necessary to view the depreciation reserve not as a book entry but as a function of the going concern. A simple illustration will clarify this point.

Suppose a firm constructs a new plant costing one million dollars and that this building has an estimate usable lifetime of 50 years. If the firm uses straight-line depreciation, it could set up a cash reserve of $20,000 annually to match the decreased book value of its building. At the end of, e.g., five years, it will have a cash reserve of $100,000. In other words, it will be assumed that the firm's volume of business has remained fairly constant over this period of time and that its current asset "cash and cash equivalent" has increased by $100,000.

Theoretically, the building has been "used up" or depreciated to the extent of $100,000 in the course of the first five years. Actually, the physical condition of the structure may still be "as good as new." Parenthetically, the reader need only think of a 1-year-old automobile that has been driven only 10,000 miles and, thus, is just "broken in" but has "depreciated" by 25% of its purchase price. To return to our firm and the plant, assume that during the five years the funds generated by operations equal to depreciation of the building have been kept in the form of cash. At the end of five years, the company has $100,000 in cash and needs a new machine in order to expand its output in the sixth year. If it purchases the machine, the accountant will reduce the cash account by $100,000 and raise the entry for machinery and equipment by $100,000. Thus, on the books, the depreciation reserve has been cancelled.

However, functionally, in the sixth year the firm has the full use of the plant *plus* one more machine. Its productive capacity has been increased by the contribution of the new machine to total output. To be sure, at some subsequent point of time the firm will require the full sum of $1,000,000 to replace the plant, which has reached the end of its usable lifetime. In the interval, however, the firm has put to productive use the cash generated through operations. Conceivably, this use may generate incomes that, over the lifetime of the plant, are sufficient to (a) amortize the investment in the machine and thus "restore" the depreciation reserve of the plant which had been diverted into the machine, and (b) yield an additional profit derived from the machine itself. This additional profit, in turn, increases the value of the equity of the owners and thus adds to the credit standing of the firm.

But suppose the $100,000 depreciation reserve has been channelled by the firm into inventories? From the viewpoint of the economy as well as from that of the firm, its total operating capital—fixed assets and inventory—has been increased by $100,000. Thus, whenever the sum set aside by the firm (on the books) for depreciation is employed in the operations of the firm—while still enjoying the full use of the assets that are being depreciated—the firm's productive capacity has been increased.

Decision Making   The problem for the financial manager is to determine, first the length of time during which the depreciation reserve will be "hibernating" in the firm unless it is productively employed; i.e., generates a profit. If the asset being depreciated has an estimated remaining usable lifetime of say, five years, it would be foolish to invest the reserve in an asset that has a lifetime of 20 years. In this instance, the new asset could not ordinarily generate in five years a depreciation reserve equal to the cost of replacing the first asset.

The second factor to be determined involves the probable after-tax profit that the new asset may be expected to yield in the next 5 years. If this prospective profit added to the depreciation reserve should equal the cost of replacing the first asset, it will be profitable to divert the depreciation reserve into the second asset. At the end of the 5-year period, the firm would then have a new replacement for the fully depreciated asset plus 15 more years of usable lifetime in the second asset. The equity is larger by the cost of the second asset minus its depreciation reserve of 5 years.

The one major uncertainty is the actual operating income that the second asset will generate in the next 5 years. If the expected profit does not materialize, the firm will not have the internal funds to replace the first asset. In this case, assuming that the first asset is indispensable for the continued operations of the business, the firm may find itself in a financial squeeze. It will be compelled to seek external sources of funds in order to remain in business. What are the chances that the firm will be able to procure the capital externally on terms that are not oppressive? The answer to this question calls for an estimate, or determination of the rate of interest (on debt capital), dividend rate (on preferred stock), prospective price at which a common stock offering can be sold, whether or not the corporation will have to concede special features in order to sell the proposed securities (e.g., a price below par, convertibility, a premium upon maturity in the case of debt capital or preferred stock, options to the underwriter in the case of a common stock offering).

B. Retained Earnings

This is often a desirable source of long-term capital, from the point of view of the financial manager. Its use does not dilute ownership and control. It imposes no obligation on the firm to pay interest or dividends. It does not involve the corporation in expenses for underwriters, legal fees, etc. Table 18-2 shows the extent to which large corporations tend to retain a significant portion of their after-tax profits.

On the other hand, the retention of profit or earnings means a corresponding reduction in the dividend on the outstanding common stock. The probable reaction of the owners of the common stock to a low pay-out ratio—i.e., the proportion of earnings disbursed in dividends—must be taken into consideration first by the financial manager and, ultimately, by top management and the board of directors. In deciding on the pay-out ratio, several factors must be evaluated and determined.

1. Prospective Incremental Profit   Suppose the firm has earned an after-tax profit of 500,000 which equals 15% of the equity value of the common stock. Will the firm be able to earn an incremental profit of more than 15% on retained and reinvested profit? If the answer is in the affirmative, the management has a strong argument in favor of ploughing back a sizable portion of the earnings. A negative answer—i.e., a prospective incremental profit of say, 10%—would in effect mean that next year the earnings per dollar of equity value would be less than 15%, although the dollar earnings would be larger. In this case, the stockholders may not be willing to approve a low pay-out ratio.

2. Tax Position of Shareholders   Assume that the common stock of the firm is held by a few individuals whose income, aside from any dividends from this corporation, places them in the upper tax bracket. These stockholders may prefer a reinvestment of the entire profit by the corporation, even if the prospective rate of incremental profit is only 10%. The corporate income tax of 48% on earnings is substantially less than the tax rate applicable to the stockholders' personal incomes. Thus, the corporation provides a tax shield; i.e., the difference between the tax paid by the corporation and the tax applicable to the stock-

Table 18-2.   Sales, Profits, and Dividends of Large Corporations
(In Millions of Dollars)

Industry	1961	1962	1963	1964	1965
Manufacturing					
Total (177 corps.):					
Sales	123,669	136,545	147,380	158,253	176,676
Profits before taxes	13,268	15,330	17,337	18,734	22,043
Profits after taxes	7,167	8,215	9,138	10,462	12,482
Dividends	4,730	5,048	5,444	5,933	6,541
Nondurable goods industries (78 corps):[a]					
Sales	49,362	52,245	55,372	59,770	64,635
Profits before taxes	5,602	5,896	6,333	6,881	7,818
Profits after taxes	3,225	3,403	3,646	4,121	4,798
Dividends	2,031	2,150	2,265	2,408	2,541
Durable goods industries (99 corps.):[b]					
Sales	74,307	84,300	92,008	98,482	112,041
Profits before taxes	7,666	9,434	11,004	11,853	14,225
Profits after taxes	3,942	4,812	5,492	6,341	7,684
Dividends	2,699	2,898	3,179	3,525	4,000
Selected industries:					
Foods and kindred products (25 corps.):					
Sales	12,951	13,457	14,301	15,284	16,345
Profits before taxes	1,280	1,460	1,546	1,579	1,710
Profits after taxes	682	698	747	802	896
Dividends	397	425	448	481	508
Chemical and allied products (20 corps.):					
Sales	12,506	13,759	14,623	16,469	17,938
Profits before taxes	1,579	2,162	2,286	2,597	2,878
Profits after taxes	1,034	1,126	1,182	1,400	1,627
Dividends	833	868	904	924	926
Petroleum refining (16 corps.):					
Sales	14,483	15,106	16,043	16,589	17,878
Profit before taxes	1,237	1,319	1,487	1,560	1,946
Profit after taxes	1,025	1,099	1,204	1,309	1,555
Dividends	528	566	608	672	752

Table 18-2.   (Continued)

Industry	1961	1962	1963	1964	1965
Primary metals and products (34 corps.):					
Sales	20,234	21,260	22,116	24,195	26,530
Profits before taxes	1,999	1,838	2,178	2,556	2,951
Profits after taxes	1,067	1,013	1,183	1,475	1,704
Dividends	843	820	734	763	818
Machinery (24 corps.):					
Sales	17,446	19,057	21,144	22,558	25,148
Profits before taxes	1,701	1,924	2,394	2,704	3,116
Profits after taxes	859	966	1,177	1,372	1,621
Dividends	508	531	577	673	775
Automobiles and equipment (14 corps):					
Sales	23,314	29,156	32,927	35,338	42,662
Profits before taxes	2,786	4,337	5,004	4,989	6,263
Profits after taxes	1,404	2,143	2,387	2,626	3,298
Dividends	973	1,151	2,447	1,629	1,890
Public utility					
Railroad:					
Operating revenue	9,189	9,440	9,560	9,778	10,208
Profits before taxes	625	729	816	829	980
Profits after taxes	382	572	651	694	816
Dividends	359	367	356	438	468
Electric power:					
Operating revenue	12,478	13,489	14,294	15,156	15,961
Profits before taxes	3,349	3,583	3,735	3,926	4,116
Profits after taxes	1,883	2,062	2,187	2,375	2,568
Dividends	1,374	1,462	1,567	1,682	1,833
Telephone:					
Operating revenue	8,615	9,196	9,796	10,550	11,320
Profits before taxes	2,473	2,639	2,815	3,069	3,185
Profits after taxes	1,438	1,327	1,417	1,590	1,718
Dividends	867	935	988	1,065	1,153

[a] Includes 17 corps. in groups not shown separately.
[b] Includes 27 corps. in groups not shown separately.
Source: Federal Reserve Bulletin, Sept., 1966.

holders. This tax shield would tend to disappear if the corporation had many shareholders with none or only a few in the upper income bracket.

3. Effect on Market Price   Last, but by no means least, the financial manager must weigh the probable effect of a low pay-out ratio on the market price of the stock. As will be explained in the next section of this chapter, the market price of its stock does not affect the corporation directly. If the price declines, the value of the stockholder's shares goes down and he takes the loss if he decides to sell. A decline in the market price of the corporation's stock, however, will have an adverse effect on the firm if it should decide to issue and sell additional stock.

The ultimate decision on the pay-out ratio is thus contingent on the evaluation of the above factors. In addition, the management must also decide whether it is in the best interest of the firm to maintain a policy of a constant dollar dividends over a period of years even if profits rise sharply, or decline, in any one year. If the management decides to retain most or all of the earnings, it may try to soften the adverse effect on stockholders and market price by declaring a *stock dividend*. Suppose the earnings of the corporation equal 15% of the equity value, and that the management would like to maintain its previous pay-out ratio of two-thirds of profit. By declaring a stock dividend of $\frac{1}{10}$ share for each share outstanding, it gives each shareholder a dividend in kind, rather than cash, equal to 10%. An owner of 100 shares would receive 10 additional shares. He could either keep these 10 shares or sell them in the market and, thus, obtain a cash income. However, his ownership in the corporation would be reduced by the (dividend) shares that he sold.

II. EXTERNAL SOURCES: THE CAPITAL MARKET

A decision to procure some or all of the long-term funds from external sources means that the corporation will seek the funds in the capital market.

A. Capital Market Defined

At the outset, it must be stresser that the capital market is not synonymous with the securities market; i.e., the organized securities exchanges or the over-the-counter market.

The capital market refers to the aggregate of savings by individuals, business firms, and nonprofit institutions who desire to channel these savings into direct investments in securities; either in the form of debt capital or equity capital. In the financial community, the capital market is called the *primary* market. By this term is meant that there is a direct flow of funds from the holder of capital into the corporation seeking these funds. Through the instrumentality of the capital market, social savings become social investments. The capital market forms the link between the two well-known macroeconomic factors S and I (savings and investments). Table 18-3 shows the total of new corporate securities sold by corporations in the years 1964 to 1966.

Secondary Markets   In contrast with the capital market, the securities market constitutes a *secondary* market. Transactions in this market involve the sale and purchase of already issued and outstanding securities. Once the securities have been sold by the corporation and purchased by the investor, all subsequent transactions in these securities take place in the secondary market. Whatever price the owner of these securities obtains from the sale accrues to him, not to the corporation. If he purchases, e.g., 100 common shares from the corporation at $5 per share and subsequently sells them at a price of $10, the gain of $500 belongs to the seller. The corporation has no share in this profit. The reverse is equally true. If the holder disposes of these shares at $3 each, he alone suffers the loss. The corporation is not involved in this transaction.

Furthermore, the transactions in the secondary market do not in themselves add to or deduct from net investment. Instead, they represent transfer of funds from the buyer to the seller of the securities. Unless the seller purchases new issues, there will be no addition to capital in the macroeconomic sense.

III. SELLING A NEW ISSUE

We shall first analyze the process of selling a new issue of common stock or preferred stock.

1. Sale to Old Stockholders   It is customary to refer to the shareholders of a corporation as "old" as distinguished from "new" investors to whom the corporation proposes to sell a part or an entire new issue of stock.

The sale of a new issue to old stockholders has several important advantages. First, it cuts down substantially the cost of floating the issue. There is no need to employ the services of a middleman to undertake the task of selling the issue to the general public. These costs can be rather substantial on smaller issues, as will be pointed out later in this chapter. But recourse to this source—old stockholders—is based on an important premise. It assumes that the officers and directors of the corporation can be reasonably sure that such an offer will find a favorable response on the part of the old stockholders. This is not likely to be the case in smaller corporations with only a few shareholders and probably limited resources for additional investments in the corporation, particularly if the proposed issue is fairly large in proportion to the current capital of the firm.

Another advantage of a sale to old stockholders is the time factor. Negotiations with one or more underwriters is a time-consuming process. A large corporation will have little difficulty in selecting its underwriters, negotiating the terms of the proposed issue of stock, and consummating the transaction in a fairly short time. Medium-sized and, particularly, small corporations do not enjoy this advantage. Investigation by the prospective underwriter and prolonged bargaining over the terms may extend over a period of several months. During this interval, the climate in the capital market may change in an adverse direction. This risk of poor timing is eliminated if the issue can be sold directly to the old stockholders.

A third advantage is the retention of their pro rata ownership by the old stockholders. The old shareholder who is willing to purchase shares in the same proportion as his old holdings retains his voting power and his portion in the equity of the firm. Thus, if all old stockholders absorb the new offering, there will be no dilution of voting power or ownership. This advantage assumes significance if the old shareholders desire to retain control and ownership.

Stand-by Agreements   The success of a new flotation among the old stockholders is uncertain if the number of these holders is fairly large. The directors may feel reasonably sure of a favorable response but they cannot be sure whether the entire offer will be absorbed. To avoid the risk of only a partial success, the corporation can negotiate a stand-by agreement with an investment banker.

Under this agreement, the investment banker obligates himself to purchase the unsold portion of the new issue. In return, the corporation agrees to pay the investment banker a negotiated "commitment fee" plus a discount from the price at which the stock is offered to the old shareholders. This discount or "spread" constitutes the compensation of the investment banker for (a) the cost of selling the unsold portion to the public, (b) the risk that he assumes if the market should subsequently turn "weak," and (c) the anticipated profit. If the market turns weak, the underwriter has the alternative of holding the stock or taking a loss.

TABLE 18-3. Securities Offerings; New Corporate Securities Offered for Cash in the United States by Type of Issuer and Type of Security (Estimated Gross Proceeds in Thousands of Dollars)

	1964	1965	1965 January–July	1966 January–July	1966 May	1966 June	1966 July
Total corporate	13,956,774	15,992,343	9,493,916	11,301,653	1,105,995	2,427,009	1,093,231
Bonds	10,865,394	13,720,349	8,023,075	9,367,187	1,037,275	1,615,831	983,233
Publicly offered	3,622,699	5,569,912	3,311,357	4,154,882	481,163	831,799	439,834
Privately offered	7,242,695	8,150,438	4,711,718	5,212,305	556,112	784,032	543,398
Preferred stock	412,050	725,238	431,241	400,500	13,169	73,869	70,328
Common stock	2,679,329	1,546,756	1,039,599	1,533,966	55,550	737,309	39,670
Manufacturing	3,046,227	5,416,839	3,413,810	4,623,549	392,097	1,168,374	449,178
Bonds	2,818,858	4,712,079	2,853,347	3,580,759	371,823	591,790	428,331
Preferred stock	41,728	112,154	93,654	42,594	4,180	11,400	11,854
Common stock	185,641	592,606	466,808	1,000,197	16,094	565,185	8,993
Extractive	420,946	342,074	184,200	213,236	49,793	52,695	12,420
Bonds	289,078	242,883	135,848	132,243	32,280	41,698	7,500
Preferred stock	5,250	0	0	11,758	0	9,300	0
Common stock	126,618	99,190	48,352	69,236	17,513	1,698	4,920
Electric, gas and water	2,759,885	2,936,022	1,548,254	2,257,509	277,343	330,381	288,356
Bonds	2,139,665	2,332,279	1,181,629	1,908,028	272,154	287,712	230,259
Preferred stock	320,122	466,044	297,113	268,994	5,189	42,669	55,974
Common stock	300,098	137,699	69,512	80,486	0	0	2,123
Railroad	333,088	283,743	200,650	246,401	47,084	15,571	20,604
Bonds	333,088	280,467	198,602	246,401	47,084	15,571	20,604
Preferred stock	0	0	0	0	0	0	0
Common stock	0	3,276	2,048	0	0	0	0

Other transportation	649,023	729,053	410,831	874,099	28,365	196,901	35,266
Bonds	611,275	672,686	389,027	784,526	28,365	122,875	35,266
Preferred stock	0	0	0	0	0	0	0
Common stock	37,749	56,368	21,804	89,572	0	74,026	0
Communication	2,189,219	947,137	512,251	1,058,855	43,643	279,154	50,668
Bonds	668,756	808,489	442,494	916,121	37,435	218,557	45,855
Preferred stock	6,150	46,900	11,500	43,600	2,300	0	0
Common stock	1,514,314	91,748	58,256	99,134	3,908	60,597	4,812
Financial and real estate (excluding investment companies)	3,856,407	4,275,779	2,533,854	1,285,622	156,913	282,865	159,015
Bonds	3,391,208	3,762,173	2,218,192	1,159,315	148,184	249,314	143,648
Preferred stock	25,650	78,989	12,900	18,927	1,000	10,500	2,500
Common stock	439,549	434,617	302,762	107,379	7,729	23,051	12,867
Commercial and other	701,977	1,061,697	690,066	742,382	110,757	101,067	77,724
Bonds	613,467	909,294	603,935	639,793	99,951	88,315	71,770
Preferred stock	13,150	21,151	16,075	14,627	500	0	0
Common stock	75,361	131,252	70,056	87,962	10,306	12,753	5,954

Source: Securities and Exchange Commission.

In addition, the investment banker will make his own determination on the probable success of an offer to the old stockholders. This independent analysis may indicate a low probability of success. In this case, the investment banker must be prepared to purchase the bulk of the new issue. If this should be the prospect, the spread may well be almost as large as an outright purchase of the entire issue. The corporation would then save little, if anything, in costs by attempting a direct sale to the old stockholders.

2. Sale Through Rights   Unless the charter of the corporation or the laws of the state in which the firm is incorporated expressly waive the preemptive rights of the stockholders, the corporation must first offer the new issue to its old shareowners. To make the purchase attractive, it is customary to price the new shares at less than the prevailing market price for already issued and outstanding shares. This privilege of buying the new stock at less than the market price of the old is known as a "right." The use of rights has been discussed in Chapter Twelve.

3. Private Placement   Life insurance companies, banks, pension funds, foundations, mutual funds, and large personal trusts are known as institutional investors. The accumulation of funds at their disposal for investment in securities has grown at a rapid pace in the post-World War II period. In consequence, these institutional investors are literally constantly on the lookout for good new issues, partly to invest the new funds flowing into their resources and partly to reinvest the funds obtained either from the redemption of securities that have reached maturity or from the sale of securities that they desire to replace with other securities.

These institutional investors are "bulk" purchasers. They have the resources to make a purchase of several million dollars' worth of securities offered by a single corporation. A few large institutional investors can readily absorb a new offering totalling tens of millions of dollars. By the same token, a single investor in this category will readily take an entire issue involving less than one million dollars, provided that the issuer meets the investor's standard of performance and the price is attractive.

1. Importance   Private placement plays an important role in the sale of new debt securities. In the 1950's, the annual percentage of private placements of debt securities ranged between a low of 35% in 1958 and a high of about 52% in 1959. In 1964, it reached a peak of over 67%.[1]

---

[1] Annual Reports of Securities and Exchange Commission.

In the case of equity capital, private placement of new issues constitutes a much smaller proportion of the total new offerings. The reason is rather simple. Most institutional investors, especially insurance companies and banks, are subject to restrictions by legislation and the supervisory authorities in their investments in equity capital. This does not apply to the other institutional investors; e.g., mutual funds, private pension funds, foundations.

2. Advantages Lower cost and speed of negotiation and sale are the two major advantages of a private placement. The issuing corporation can negotiate directly with the prospective purchaser(s) of the issue. If there is a basic meeting of minds, the terms and price can usually be arrived at with little difficulty. The institutional investor determines his maximum price and minimum terms which he regards as cut-off points. The reverse is true for the issuing corporation, which sets its minimum price and maximum terms. Bargaining can then take place if the two parties believe that there exists an area within which they can meet and compromise. In a public offering, the middleman must try to estimate what the market will be ready to pay if and when an agreement is reached.

A private placement also obviates the cost of the middleman for commissions to salesmen, printing of literature, registration with the SEC, and a premium for the risk that he may not be able to sell the entire issue at the agreed-upon subscription price and in a fairly short time after the offer is made public.

However, it should be pointed out that many medium-size and particularly smaller corporations may find it necessary to employ a "finder." The finder acts as an agent for the issuer in trying to interest an institutional investor in the proposed offering. The fee for the successful finder ranges between 1 and 4% of the total issue.

3. Disadvantages A private placement has, however, several serious drawbacks, especially in the case of equity capital. For one thing, the management of the corporation may not cherish the prospect that one or a few investors will hold and control a substantial block of shares. A determined and articulate substantial minority may attract enough votes from a widely dispersed majority to gain a controlling vote on the board of directors. Even if they have no such intentions, institutional investors may not appear desirable to the management of the corporation for another reason. Institutional investors are far more sophisticated than most individual shareholders. The knowledgeable institutional investor, therefore, evaluates performance more rationally and is not inclined to accept at face value the decisions of the board or the actions of the officers as the best of available alternatives.

Another drawback is the absence of a broad secondary market. Since the institutional investor purchases the securities for his portfolio as an investment, there may be insufficient or no trading of the stock in the secondary market. As a result, another subsequent issue would lack an established market and price since the privately placed issue is, by its nature, kept out of the market. Furthermore, the corporation has no control over the institutional investor as to when he should or should not dispose of his holdings. Therefore, it is quite conceivable that the institutional investor may decide to register his stock with the Securities and Exchange Commission and unload its holdings at a time when the market is generally high. But this decision may come at a time when the corporation is also planning to make a public offering of an additional issue to take advantage of the favorable climate in the market. The institutional investor can always move more quickly than the corporation in such a situation. All it need do is comply with the registration requirements of the SEC before selling the stock to the public. On the other hand, the corporation must first find and negotiate with an underwriter before it can proceed with the registration of the stock.

A. Public Offering

This alternative calls for the sale of the new issue to the "general investing public." It appeals to those investors who, for reasons of their own, are presumed to be willing to purchase the offered stock at the subscription price. Unlike the other two alternatives—old stockholders and private placement—a public offer is not predicated on a direct relationship between the issuer and the buyer. Naturally, the corporation hopes for a response sufficient to absorb the entire offering. But since the appeal is to the investing public at large, the corporation has no way of estimating the probable response. Nor has it the know-how or mechanism for the actual sale of securities to prospective investors. This important role is performed by the investment banker.

1. Investment Banker   This term covers a wide range of firms that specialize in the distribution of new issues. At the top of this group of specialists are about 15 firms that enjoy a national as well as an international reputation. Among them are firms such as Morgan Stanley; Lehman Brothers; Halsey Stuart; Harriman, Ripley and Company; and the firm of Merrill Lynch, Pierce, Fenner and Smith. At the other end of the spectrum are found a large number of small firms that specialize in small issues or act as local distributors for issues which the larger firms have undertaken to distribute.

a. Functions. The investment banker, whether large or small, is basically a merchant who deals in securities. He purchases the entire issue from the corporation and subsequently sells the securities to the ultimate investor. In performing this task, he may invite other investment bankers or brokers to share with him in this phase of the business. Whether or not he will handle the entire issue himself depends in part on the size of the issue and, in part, on his resources at a given time. If the issue is too large for him to handle it alone, or if he has committed too much of his funds to other issuers, he will invite other firms to join him in the purchase and sale of one or more issues.

The investment banker, large or small, has a list of regular customers as well as of prospective investors. He maintains a staff of salesmen, each of whom, in turn, cultivates his own group of regular buyers and endeavors to develop new clients. It is through this mechanism that new issues are channelled from the issuer to the investment banker and through his distribution channels to the ultimate investor.

b. Structure. The investment bank that negotiates with the corporation is known as the originating house. It investigates the issuer, prospective reception of the offer by the public, and the subscription price which, in his opinion, will insure ready acceptance by the investing public. On the basis of this determination, the investment banker negotiates the agreement with the corporation on the issue price—i.e., the price at which the security is to be offered to the public—and the commission and other compensation for the originating house.

A small number of investment banks specialize in the function of originating house. They handle, as a matter of policy, only issues floated by nationally known large corporations. These houses have lists of special customers, individuals and institutions, who are in a position to purchase large blocks of new issues floated by these houses.

Once rung below these leading houses are the larger brokerage firms and smaller investment bankers. This group functions occasionally as originators and primarily as distributors of new issues. Many of these firms maintain offices in all major cities of the United States and have an extensive "customer list." In addition, they sell new issues to the public at large.

Finally, there are several thousand brokers and dealers who act as originators and distributors of smaller issues ranging to as little as a few hundred thousand dollars. The great majority of these firms confine their activities to the over-the-counter market rather than to the organized securities exchanges.

2. The Investment Banker as Financial Expert   Although the ultimate task of the investment banker involves the sale of the proposed securities issue, he is far more than a mere intermediary between the issuing corporation and the capital market. As a matter of fact, he wears three hats. First, he functions as a financial entrepreneur. In this capacity, he makes his own independent evaluation of the corporation's past performance record, its future prospects and, above all, the marketability of the proposed issue in terms of price, prospective yield, and special features; e.g., convertibility and callability (bonds and preferred stock). As an entrepreneur, he must also estimate his own costs of marketing the issue. On this score, the reputation of the issuing corporation and the size of the issue play a decisive role. A large issue by a well-known public utility or by a large established manufacturing company may be easily saleable, literally within a day or two after the securities are offered to the public. In this instance, the investment banker may accept a commission or *spread*—the difference between the price paid by the purchasers and the net price to the issuing corporation—of a point or even less. On the other hand, an issue may be such that the investment banker finds it necessary to dispose of a portion by selling it to other dealers who, in turn, have to dispose of their respective shares through salesmen, as does the investment banker himself. In this case, the costs of distribution are likely to be rather substantial and the spread correspondingly larger.

Second, the success of the investment banker is closely linked to the reputation that he enjoys among prospective investors as a competent evaluator of new issues. This fact plays no important part in an issue offered by a well-established nationally known large corporation. The corporation speaks for the issue. But this reputation does play an important role in an offering by a corporation that is relatively young or not yet well known. Here the investment banker, in effect (although not legally), puts his own reputation on the line. Although the investor is presumed to evaluate the information supplied in the prospectus and to make up his own mind, the fact is that the average investor relies more on the judgment of the investment banker than on his own.

And third, the investment banker also makes available to the issuing corporation his expertise in the final determination of the type of security to be issued, the size of the issue, special features that need be added to assure ready acceptance of the issue by the market, the issue price, and, last but not least, the timing of the offer.

3. Timing of Issue   The capital market is comparable to a large reservoir that feeds many small lakes. That is, the savings that flow into the capital market for investments do not flow at a constant rate into the many outlets; e.g., bonds, debentures, preferred stock, common stock. Furthermore, each of these broad categories divides itself into numerous subcategories; e.g., utilities, manufacturing, distribution, mining, etc. Finally, investors have special preferences within these categories. At one time, sentiment may be strong for electronics, while a few months later it swings to plastics or chemicals.

The investment banker thus faces a dual task. First, he must keep himself informed about the *current* sentiments in the investment market. And second, he must also attempt to estimate the prospective sentiments, or preferences, by the time the proposed issue will be ready for sale. In many cases, there is a lag of several months between the first contact of the issuing corporation and the investment banker and the issue date. The length of this interval depends on the time needed by the investment banker to analyze and evaluate the corporation, the negotiations leading to the agreement on the terms of the issue, the printing and filing of the necessary forms and documents with the Securities and Exchange Commission, and the lapse of the required waiting period before the issue may be offered for sale.

In an underwritten issue, the investment banker thus assumes the risk that the price at which he will be able to dispose of the securities may be less than the price that he agrees to pay the issuing corporation. For example, the investment banker (underwriter) agrees to bring out a common-stock issue at $10 per share and that his commission is to be $1 per share. Conceivably, by the time the actual offer is made to the investors, the market has turned sluggish and the investment banker realizes only $8.75 per share. He will still have to pay the corporation $9 per share and absorb the expenditures of marketing the issue. Or the investment banker agrees to buy the bonds from the corporation at $98\frac{1}{2}$ and has to sell them not at 100, as he anticipated, but at say, 98. Conceivably, the opposite development may occur during the interval between the consummation of the underwriting agreement and the actual sale of the securities. In this case, the investment banker retains the excess as his profits. Whether or not this risk is to be assumed by the investment banker depends on the terms of the agreement. Basically, the agreement may provide for any one of three alternatives.

a. Outright Purchase.   In this instance, the investment banker assumes the risk as previously described. He agrees to pay the corporation the stipulated price per share, usually on the day when the proposed issue has reached the final day of the waiting period required by the SEC and may, therefore, be offered for sale. In short, he underwrites the issue.

b. Best Effort.   Under this form of agreement, the investment banker assumes no risk. He will offer the securities at the issue price fixed in the agreement. At the end of the period fixed in the agreement—usually 30 days—he will report to the issuing corporation the number of securities sold at the fixed price and turn over to the corporation the agreed-upon net price per share. The spread on these shares then constitutes his compensation. Naturally, he also returns to the corporation the unsold portion of the issue.

c. All or Nothing.   Here the investment banker agrees to return the total issue to the corporation at the end of say, 30 days, if he did not dispose of the entire issue at the fixed price. In this case, all expenses incurred by him are also borne by him. During this selling period of 30 days, the investment banker does not sell the issue but, instead, he accepts buying offers from the investing public. At the end of the period, the investment banker has two alternatives. If the aggregate of these buying offers falls appreciably short of the total issue, he notifies the prospective investors and the corporation that the issue is being withdrawn from the market. Or, if the aggregate of the offers falls a few percent short of the total issue, he may decide to buy the unsold portion himself in order to hedge his commission. Suppose that his commission is 10% and 95% of the issue has been subscribed to by investors. If he calls off the issue he will receive nothing in compensation for his expenditure of time and money. By acquiring the unsold 5%, he can report the sale of the total issue and turn over to the corporation 90% of the issue price of $^9\!\%_{95}$ths of the price obtained from the subscribers. Thus, he will retain $\frac{5}{95}$ths of the gross proceeds plus 5% of the issue, or whatever price he can subsequently obtain for these securities.

4. The Bargaining Process   Each agreement between investment banker and issuer is tailor-made to fit the requirements of the corporation, the conditions in the capital market relative to the proposed issue, and the investment banker's evaluation of his prospective risk and expenditures. As a result, the specific terms of the issue, price, and obligations as well as compensation for the investment banker are "negotiable." The outcome of these negotiations depends on the relative bargaining skill of the corporation's management. In this phase, the financial manager plays a pivotal role, although the actual negotiations are carried on by the top officers of the corporation and the investment banker. It is the task of the financial officer to advise top management of the probable effects on the corporation of the terms offered by the investment banker.

For example, the investment banker may suggest, in the case of a 15-year $5,000,000 bond issue, a 5.38% interest rate and a price of 102 of which 2 points are to be deducted as the investment banker's commission. As an alternative, he suggests a 5.50% rate, a price of 97.55 and a commission of 2 points. The relative cost to the corporation is as follows:

Alternative A:

5% bond to be sold at	100
Minus commission	2
Net proceeds to corporation	100 or $1000

Alternative B:

5.2% bond to be sold at	97.50
Minus commission	2.00
Net proceed to corporation	95.50 or $955

Plus $45 which the corporation will have to repay at the end of 15 years in addition to the $955 actually received.[2]

On the surface, it would appear that the cost is the same in both cases:

$$\$55 \text{ interest per annum on } \$1000 = 5.5\%$$
$$\$52 + \$3 \text{ per annum on } \quad \$ 955 = 5.5\%$$

Yet from the viewpoint of the financial manager, there is one significant difference between the two alternatives. Under Alternative A, the corporation would receive $5 million dollars in cash while Alternative B would provide only $4,775,000. Thus, by selecting the first alternative, the corporation would have $225,000 more available for investment in productive, and hopefully profitable, capital assets.

Or, take another feature: suppose the investment banker proposes a straight 15-year bond issue. However, the financial manager is of the opinion that the current interest rate in the capital market, say 5.5%, likely to decline in a few years to 5% or less. He therefore

---

[2] To simplify the illustration, it is assumed that the corporation will set aside each year $3 per bond and that these sums will not earn anything in the intervening years.

advocates that the bonds be made callable starting with the sixth year. This provision would make this 5.5% bond less attractive to prospective investors than bonds of comparable quality offering 5.5% interest and maturing in 15 years, thus assuring the investor of a constant rate even if the market rate should subsequently decline. Therefore, to make the callable bond saleable in the present market, the corporation must be prepared to offer some compensating "sweetener." Usually, this will take the form of a premium if the bond should be called prior to maturity. The question then arises as to the size of this premium; e.g., if called in the 6th to 8th year the bond will be redeemed at 102, if called in the 9th to 11th year at 101, etc. The financial manager must, in this case, estimate the probability of a decline in rates, the probable dimension of this decline, the probable cost of refunding the original issue, and the monetary value of this option to call the bond for the corporation.

III. THE SECONDARY MARKET

As previously pointed out, the secondary market performs an important economic function. It provides a mechanism for the quick sale and purchase of securities. It thus creates a liquidity for the holder of securities which, by their nature, represent long-term capital investments of a nonliquid character. Through the mechanism of the secondary market, otherwise nonliquid investments are converted into liquid assets.

The secondary market also acts as an index of investors' preferences. The holder of capital-to-be-invested can make quick comparisons of prices, earnings, and yield (dividends or interest) of a great variety of securities. In channeling his funds into the securities that he regards as most attractive, he registers his preference through the price and volume record of the market. The aggregates of these individual preferences is then reflected in the price movements of the several components of the secondary market; i.e., debt capital versus equity capital and their respective subdivision (e.g., government, municipal, and corporate bonds, common stock of say, steel, electronic, auto manufacturers, etc.). A shift in investors' preference is therefore quickly reflected in a price decline in those securities for which demand relative to supply is decreasing while prices tend to go up for those securities for which buying sentiment is on an upsurge. By watching the behavior of the secondary market, the financial manager can assess, first, the general climate in the capital market and, second, the relative attractiveness of debt capital or equity capital securities to investors and, thus, their probable receptiveness to a new offering.

A corporation whose securities are, subsequent to the initial sale, accepted for trading on the secondary market provides also a valuable means of public relations. The price at which its securities are traded in the secondary market has a bearing on the corporation's credit rating by banks, term lenders, and even suppliers. Furthermore, this price has a major bearing on the corporation's ability to sell a subsequent security issue and the price as well as the cost of underwriting this issue. These effects of the secondary market are magnified if the corporation's securities have been accepted for trading on the organized exchanges, as will be shown later in this section.

A. Organized Exchanges

There are 18 organized stock exchanges[3] in the United States. Of these, the New York Stock Exchange (NYSE) is by far the most prominent and important market. This exchange accounts for about 90% of the dollar volume and roughly 75% of all transactions in the 18 organized exchanges. Furthermore, the NYSE is the market for securities issued by nationally and internationally known American corporations. The American Stock Exchange (ASE), also located in New York City, ranks second in importance. It accounts for about 5% of the dollar volume and 15% of transactions on the organized exchanges. The relative importance and growth of the New York Stock Exchange, the American Stock Exchange, and the other exchanges during the period 1936 to 1964 is shown in Table 18-4.

1. NYSE The New York Stock Exchange has the most rigorous requirements for the listing of a security; i.e., permitting its sale on the floor of the exchange. In order to qualify, the corporation must have tangible assets of at least $8 million; its earnings must be at least $1 million; the aggregate market value of its common stock must be no less than $8 million; and it must have outstanding at least 400,000 common shares with no fewer than 1500 holders. In addition, the corporation itself must qualify in terms of ". . . the degree of national interest

---

[3] In addition to New York City, the following cities have stock exchanges which are largely local or regional in character: Boston, Cincinnati, Detroit, New Orleans, Pittsburgh, Salt Lake City, Spokane, Colorado Springs, Honolulu, Richmond, Wheeling. There are also larger regional exchanges, such as the Midwest Stock Exchange (Chicago), the Philadelphia–Baltimore–Washington Stock Exchange, the Pacific Coast Stock Exchange, and the recently formed National Stock Exchange (New York City).

in the company, its standing in its particular field, the character of the market for its products, its relative stability and position in the industry, and whether or not it is engaged in an expanding industry with prospects of maintaining its position."[4]

2. Other Exchanges   The American Stock Exchange has no specific minimum requirements relative to size of assets or earnings. It evaluates each applicant-corporation on its own merits. However, it requires at least 100,000 shares and no fewer than 500 holders, exclusive of officers and directors. Requirements on the other exchanges are similarly adapted to the size and geographic location of the individual exchange.

3. Registered Exchanges   The Securities and Exchange Act of 1933 authorized the Securities Exchange Commission (SEC)—which was set up in 1934—to regulate the secondary market. The SEC also was empowered to regulate and supervise the sale of new securities issues.

Under the rules issued subsequently by the SEC, all national securities exchanges are required to register with the commission. Of the 18 organized exchanges, 14 meet the requirements and have been approved by the SEC for trading. Colorado Springs, Honolulu, Richmond, and Wheeling have been exempted from the registration requirements.

Registered exchanges must submit their rules of membership, annual financial statements, and their respective rules for expulsion, suspension, and disciplinary action of members whose conduct on the exchanges is "inconsistent with just and equitable principles of trade." Specifically, exchange members are prohibited from manipulating securities prices through "matched orders" or "wash sales" which create the fictitious picture of active trading in a given security. Also, they are restricted in "short sales"; i.e., the sale of stock which they do not hold at the time of the sale but expect to purchase at a later date when they expect the price to be lower. Other requirements impose limits on borrowing by brokers-dealers to finance their own purchases to 20% of their net capital; call for adequate disclosure to customers; and impose safeguards for customers' funds and securities held by brokers, and periodic inspection of their books.

4. Corporate Reports   The SEC also requires all corporations whose securities are listed on the organized exchanges to file with the commission detailed reports on a great many organizational and financial facets. Among others, the corporation must supply detailed information on terms, position, and rights of the different classes of securities that it has issued; the names and number of shares held by officers, directors,

[4] NYSE, *Listing Procedure,* page 1.

TABLE 18-4.   Value of Stocks on Exchanges (in Billions of Dollars)

December 31	New York Stock Exchange	American Stock Exchange	Exclusively on Other Exchanges	Total[a]
1936	59.9	14.8		74.7
1937	38.9	10.2		49.1
1938	47.5	10.8		58.3
1939	46.5	10.1		56.6
1940	41.9	8.6		50.5
1941	35.8	7.4		43.2
1942	38.8	7.8		46.6
1943	47.6	9.9		57.5
1944	55.5	11.2		66.7
1945	73.8	14.4		88.2
1946	68.6	13.2		81.8
1947	68.3	12.1		80.4
1948	67.0	11.9	3.0	81.9
1949	76.3	12.2	3.1	91.6
1950	93.8	13.9	3.3	111.0
1951	109.5	16.5	3.2	129.2
1952	120.5	16.9	3.1	140.5
1953	117.3	15.3	2.8	135.4
1954	169.1	22.1	3.6	194.8
1955	207.7	27.1	4.0	238.8
1956	219.2	31.0	3.8	254.0
1957	195.6	25.5	3.1	224.2
1958	276.7	31.7	4.3	312.7
1959	307.7	26.4	4.2	338.4
1960	307.0	24.2	4.1	335.3
1961	387.8	33.0	5.3	426.2
1962	345.8	24.4	4.0	374.2
1963	411.3	26.1	4.3	441.7
1964	474.3	28.2	4.3	506.8

[a] Total values 1936–47 inclusive are for the New York Stock Exchange and the American Stock Exchange only.
Source: Securities and Exchange Commission, Thirty-First Annual Report, 1965, p. 167.

underwriters, and individual stockholders who own more than 10% of any class of equity stock (common or preferred); bonus and profit sharing agreements; management and service contracts; options granted to officers and others; and annual certified financial statements.

In 1964, the Act was amended and the powers of the SEC were broadened. Under this and subsequent amendments, a corporation with more than $1 million in assets and 500 or more stockholders must register the security with the SEC and furnish annual financial reports.

B. Over-the-Counter Market

Measured by volume of securities traded and aggregate dollar transactions, this portion of the secondary market exceeds by a substantial margin the organized exchanges. The explanation lies in the fact that almost all federal, state, and municipal bonds, as well as many corporate bond issues, are traded over-the-counter. Furthermore, this is also the market for the shares of many banks and insurance companies. Finally, it serves as the trading mechanism for the issues of small corporations that, due to size, are not eligible for listing on the organized exchanges. It should also be noted that the over-the-counter market serves as a direct outlet for new issues, large and small.

This market differs from the organized exchanges in two major features. First, as the name implies, the over-the-counter "market" is not a physically centralized and identifiable organization. Instead, trading takes place through the offices of individual dealers and brokers who specialize in specific securities. For example, a few large firms are known as dealers in "municipals." Others are known to be the "dealers" in certain corporate issues, or insurance companies, banks, etc.

Second, each of these dealers maintains a portfolio of such securities from which he sells and to which he adds its purchases. These firms, in turn, receive from investors inquiries and/or orders by telephone, telegraph, or teletype to buy or sell. The individual firm is in fairly constant touch with the other firms in its specialty. They exchange information about their respective "bid" (buy) and "offer" (sell) prices. These quotations will change in response to the orders from customers who want to buy at the offer price or sell at the bid price. Thus, the actual price at which the individual dealer sells or buys the security is the result of *negotiation,* in contrast with the organized exchanges in which the price is the result of "auction."

Each specialist dealer takes a "position" by quoting his bid and ask prices. He adjusts his position by calling the other specialists and adjusting his quotations to the relative predominance of buy or sell orders. The spread of the dealer's bid and ask price constitutes in part his commission and, in part, it provides his compensation for the risk that he assumes in carrying a portfolio of securities. This portfolio is, in a sense, his trading inventory.

C. Registration of New Issues

The fundamental principle that led to the passage of the Securities and Exchange Act and which is central to the regulatory philosophy of the commission can be summed up in two words: *full disclosure*. All relevant facts are to be made available to the "reasonable investor" who requires this information in arriving at his decision whether or not to purchase the offered security. Furthermore, the form and substance of the data and other relevant facts must be presented in such a manner that they are intelligible to the reasonable investor. Table 18-5 shows the total of new issues and the type of issuer during the fiscal year ending June 1965.

1. Prospectus   SEC regulations spell out, in detail, the specific types of information that the issuing corporation must provide. The regulations also require that all essential and relevant facts must be incorporated in the prospectus. A copy of this booklet must be furnished to every investor prior to the sale of the security to this investor. Upon receipt by the SEC of the data, documents, and prospectus, the staff of the commission examines the "registration statement" and the prospectus. This examination is focused solely on the question of full disclosure. It does not involve any judgment about the quality of the issuing corporation, the soundness, or lack of it, of the corporation's plans and programs. This determination is left to the prospective investor. The SEC explicitly assumes no responsibility for the quality of the proposed security issue.

To indicate in unmistakable language the absence of any value judgment by the SEC, each prospectus must bear on its front page in prescribed type size the following legend:

THESE SECURITIES HAVE NOT BEEN APPROVED OR DISAPPROVED BY THE SECURITIES AND EXCHANGE COMMISSION NOR HAS THE COMMISSION PASSED UPON THE ACCURACY OR ADEQUACY OF THIS PROSPECTUS. ANY REPRESENTATION TO THE CONTRARY IS A CRIMINAL OFFENSE.

To visualize the importance of full and meaningful disclosure to a prospective investor, we need only review some of the "legitimate" practices indulged in by corporations prior to the SEC legislation. Suppose the corporation fails to mention that the proposed sale of common stock is for the benefit of some large shareholders who wish to dispose of some or all of their holdings? Clearly, the investor is likely to give second thought to the purchase of stock whose proceeds will not add capital to the corporation. Moreover, he may also wonder why the large shareholders are anxious "to get out." Conceivably, the investor may not be concerned over these matters. But this determination should be made by him rather than by the corporation. Or to take a more serious point, assume that the corporation has given the underwriter an option on a substantial block of shares at a price that is only a fraction of the price paid by the investor. The investor should have an opportunity to decide whether this potential dilution of equity has an effect on the attractiveness of the security to him. Ambiguities in financial statements, omission of unfavorable factors, or withholding of information about impending adverse developments in the corporation's operations obviously place the investor at a great disadvantage in evaluating the proposed offering.

The above are but a few of the practices in which many corporations and underwriters indulged prior to 1934. True, the investor could theoretically bring suit against the officers of the corporations. But lawsuits cost money and if successful, after years of litigation, recovery may no longer be feasible. Recourse to the courts was beyond the means of the small investor who had purchased a few thousand dollars worth of an issue.

The SEC legislation was therefore designed to inhibit practices that made it difficult or impossible for the average investor to arrive at a decision based on true facts. On the other hand, the Act was not designed to relieve the investor of the consequences of his action as long as he had the relevant facts and chooses to take his chances. Thus, the investor may purchase a highly speculative security and lose his entire investment without recourse to anyone, as long as the information provided by the sellers of the security stated clearly the speculative character of the project.

2. Exemptions   As stated previously, full disclosure is the objective of the SEC Act. Certain classes of securities have been exempted from the registration requirement because there is little or no risk of misleading or inadequate information being made available to the investor. All government issues clearly fall into this category. Common carriers are generally exempted since they are subject to regulations and supervision by the Interstate Commerce Commission. Similarly, banks, savings and loan associations, and insurance companies are under the jurisdiction of federal and/or state authorities and, therefore, generally pose no problem of selling equity capital under misleading statements. Also exempted

TABLE 18-5. Registrations Effective under the Securities Act of 1933, Fiscal Year Ended June 30, 1965; Purpose of Registration and Industry of Registrant (Amounts in Thousands of Dollars)

Purpose of Registration	All Registrations	Type of issuer								
		Manufacturing	Extractive	Electric, Gas and Water	Communication	Financial and Real Estate	Commercial and Other	Foreign Governments	Investment Companies	Other Types
Number of statements	1,266	222	49	79	20	198	125	15	218	340
Number of issues	1,463	275	52	88	20	221	163	15	238	391
All registrations (estimated value)	$19,436,768	$4,895,314	$224,504	$1,784,865	$784,748	$1,417,007	$1,018,125	$306,112	$6,355,388	$2,650,705
For account of issuer	16,645,942	2,502,234	219,322	1,774,567	769,291	1,279,355	792,076	303,352	6,355,039	2,650,705
For cash sale	14,655,896	1,450,816	140,808	1,719,109	718,877	921,801	395,388	303,352	6,355,039	2,650,705
For immediate offering	5,650,151	1,450,816	140,808	1,719,109	718,877	921,801	395,388	303,352		
Corporate	5,346,799	1,450,816	140,808	1,719,109	718,877	921,801	395,388			
Foreign governments	303,352							303,352		
For extended sale	9,005,744								6,355,039	2,650,705
Investment companies	6,355,039								6,355,039	
Employee saving plan certificates	797,334									797,334
Securities for employee stock option plans	1,583,635									1,583,635
Other	269,766									269,736
For other than cash sale	1,990,046	1,051,418	78,514	55,458	50,414	357,554	396,688			
Exchange transactions	876,466	374,437	50,036	19,850	50,414	256,776	124,954			
Reserved for conversion	1,022,781	627,768	20,983	34,044	0	94,805	245,180			
Other	90,799	49,214	7,495	1,564	0	5,973	26,553			
For account of other than issuer	2,790,826	2,393,080	5,183	10,298	15,456	137,652	226,042	2,760	349	
For cash sale	1,836,539	1,518,146	3,916	6,494	10,418	78,616	215,840	2,760	349	
Other	954,288	874,934	1,267	3,804	5,038	59,036	10,209			

Source: Securities and Exchange Commission, Thirty-First Annual Report, 1965, p. 163.

547

are most securities issued by nonprofit organizations that operate in religious, educational, fraternal, or charitable areas.

Private placements of corporations in all other fields are exempted, providing the offer is made without the use of mail and to a "small" group of investors. Although the commission has never laid down a hard and fast rule as to what constitutes a private placement, the thumb rule has been that 25 or fewer investors constitute a private placement.

Issues of less than $300,000 are subject to less stringent regulations than those in excess of $300,000. The former are known as Regulation A issues. The SEC requirements covering such issues have already been discussed in Chapter Sixteen.

3. Registration Requirements   The list of documents and financial data which must be filed with the registration statement is rather extensive and detailed. Their nature and scope can be visualized from the following summary of the more important items.

The corporation must file a certified balance sheet not older than 90 days as of the date of filing plus profit and loss statements for the last fiscal year and each of the preceding two years. The reserve, surplus, and other accounts must be supported by schedules showing clearly the underlying criteria used by the corporation in arriving at the figures.

A detailed description of the capital structure, both debt and equity capital, showing their respective terms, rights, and other pertinent facts must be filed.

The corporation's program for the use of the funds from the sale of the proposed issue must be stated. A detailed account must also be given of the disbursements in conjunction with the sale of the securities. This includes such items as commission and other expenses to be paid to the underwriters, options and warrants given to the underwriters and their respective terms, finder's fees, if any, and all other fees.

The prospectus must also list the names of all stockholders who own more than 10% of the shares and state their respective holdings. Similarly, the listing of the officers and directors must identify the number of shares held by each. If the company has given options to officers, directors, or individual stockholders the terms of these options must be stated.

Profit-sharing and bonus agreements, as well as salaries in excess of $25,000, must be spelled out in some detail.

After filing the registration application, the supporting documents, and a copy of the prospectus, the corporation must wait 20 days before the issue can be offered for sale. However, the 20-day "running time" comes to an automatic stop if the commission requests additional data or some change in the prospectus. In practice, the actual lapse of time is substantially more than 20 days. In 1962, the average interval for 1646 issues was 78 days. In 1964, when the number of issues was less than 1000, the average was 36 days.

However, the termination of the 20-day waiting period does not relieve the officers, directors, underwriters, and other parties who are involved in the preparation of the documents and sale of the issue of responsibility for misleading statements. This liability encompasses both civil and criminal action. If the registration statement, and therefore the prospectus, contains misstatements of facts or omits relevant facts the holder of such security has a civil claim against the seller even if the plaintiff was not a direct purchaser from the underwriter or the corporation. This liability extends to all those who are named in the prospectus as directors. It also includes accountants, engineers, and members of other professions who provided statements or reports that were included, with their consent, in the registration statement and which were misleading or omitted essential facts.

SUMMARY

The two main sources of funds available to the firm are funds generated internally by the firm and funds procured externally from investors. Funds generated from operations equivalent to depreciation are a major internal source. The other major internal source is funds generated by profits and retained in the firm as retained earnings.

A decision to procure funds from external sources generally means that the corporation will seek funds in the capital market. The capital market is not synonymous with the securities market. The capital market refers to the aggregate of savings by individuals, business firms, and institutions who desire to channel these savings into direct investment in securities—whether debt or equity capital. The capital market is the primary market for external funds for the corporation. The financial manager must be familiar with the role of the investment banker in facilitating access to the primary capital market either through a public offering or by private placement. The investment banker basically specializes in the distribution of new issues. He often purchases the entire issue from the corporation and subsequently sells the securities to the ultimate investor. His role is much broader than that of an intermediary—the investment banker is a financial expert who provides services to both the issuing firm and the investor.

The financial manager must also be familiar with the function of the securities market. The securities market is a secondary market since transactions in this market involve the sale and purchase of already issued and outstanding securities. The securities market provides liquidity for the holders of securities which, by their nature, represent long-term capital investments of a nonliquid nature. The price movements in the secondary market serve as an indication of investors' preferences. By watching the behavior of this market, the financial manager can assess the general climate of the market and the relative attractiveness of debt capital or equity capital securities to investors.

Questions

1. In what way may it be said that depreciation is a source of capital?
2. How does the capital market differ from the securities market? How does the difference affect the economy as a whole? The individual investor?
3. What are the advantages of selling a new issue directly to the present shareholders of the corporation?
4. Discuss the advantages and disadvantages of private placement when compared with a public offering.
5. What is the main function of the investment banker?
6. What is the difference between an underwritten issue and an issue sold on a best efforts basis?
7. Why do corporations often wish to list their securities on a stock exchange?
8. What is the main purpose of the SEC regulations?

Case: MAMMOTH NATIONAL BANK

In late August, 1964, the executive committee of the board of directors of Mammoth National Bank met to consider the advisability of listing the common stock of the bank on the New York Stock Exchange. The question came up at this time as a result of new security legislation signed by President Johnson on August 20, 1964. In effect, the legislation removed one of the main advantages of a bank's staying unlisted. As a result of passage of the legislation, unlisted securities of major banks and other large corporations now had to meet the strict reporting of financial data and other disclosure requirements that the SEC had long required only for securities listed on major stock exchanges. New rules proposed as a result of this legislation by the Federal Reserve Board and the Federal Deposit

Insurance Corporation for unlisted bank securities followed closely the SEC rules for listed securities.

Because of its size, number of shares outstanding, and number of stockholders, Mammoth National would have no trouble in listing its shares on the New York Stock Exchange. Conversations with exchange officials indicated that the exchange would warmly welcome a listing application from the bank. Mammoth National is one of the 20 largest banks in the nation with assets of more than four billion dollars. Mammoth has 72,479 stockholders and over 10,000,000 shares outstanding.

One member of the executive committee argued strongly at the meeting in favor of listing the bank's shares on the stock exchange. He stated that the main advantage of listing to Mammoth National would be a broader market for its shares. Member firms (brokers, dealers, etc.) of the stock exchange have largely ignored depth research in bank stocks because bank stocks have not generally been listed. Listing of Mammoth National should lead to more interest by these firms in the bank. In turn, this greater interest will lead the member firms to gradually interest the public customer in buying bank shares as an investment. Thus, the market for Mammoth National's shares truly would be broadened.

A second member of the executive committee pointed out that Mammoth National's shares were not as popular with the investment companies as those of such larger banks as Chase Manhattan and First National City. Investment companies held 4.8% of all the stock of Mammoth National in June, 1964, as compared with 5.6% of all Chase stock. This member of the executive committee stated that the prestige of listing would lead to greater interest by investment companies in Mammoth National. He also pointed out that certain institutions are forbidden to buy stocks that are not listed on the New York Stock Exchange. The wide publication of listed stock prices would also benefit the bank, in his opinion.

Another member of the executive committee stated that he opposed listing of the shares on the stock exchange. He stated that many banks formerly were listed on the stock exchange in the 1920's. During the 1920's there were wide swings in the price of listed bank shares owing to speculation. To lessen anxieties of depositors about the safety of the bank, the large banks gradually moved over to the less obtrusive unlisted market. In this member's opinion, it was wise that they did so in view of what happened to the stock exchange's reputation in the early 1930's.

One of the members of the executive committee favoring listing pointed out that conditions were different in the 1920's since at that time most of the large banks operated security company affiliates (now not allowed) and exchange regulations were not as stringent re speculation as at present. The member opposing listing rejoined that he saw no fundamental difference in the listed stock market between the 1920's and the 1960's. He felt that the stock market was in for a big jolt sometime in the next ten years and believed that it would be in the best interests of the bank not to list its shares at this time.

Another member of the committee opposed to listing was worried that listing might lead to an antitrust suit against the stock exchange which would involve the bank in bad publicity. Rule 394 of the New York Stock Exchange forbids exchange member firms from trading listed stocks in the over-the-counter market. Thus, member firms could not trade shares of Mammoth National with nonmember dealers and brokers. Since bank securities make up about 20% of the entire over-the-counter market, listing of Mammoth National would generate new tensions in a trading sense between the exchange and the unlisted market. This member of the executive committee believed that one or more of these nonmember dealers would bring an antitrust suit against the exchange if they lost their shares of trading Mammoth National Stock. In his opinion, all listing would do would be to transfer commissions from over-the-counter dealers to exchange specialists and floor traders. He could not see how this would benefit the bank or its current stockholders.

A fourth member of the executive committee also opposed listing. He felt that the current system was best since it had worked well for two generations. The over-the-counter market for bank stocks, in his opinion, is both highly competent and well capitalized. He opposed giving this up for an untried experiment on the big board.

The other three members of the executive committee must weigh these arguments and decide on a stand. The decision could not be postponed much longer, because there would be public relations advantages in being one of the first banks to list on the New York Stock Exchange if listing was in the bank's best interest. The committee members assumed that other banks would be considering listing at this time also. They have no knowledge as to what decisions, if any, have been reached by the other big banks.

Case Questions:

1. Evaluate the arguments of the various executive committee members on listing.
2. What other alternatives should be considered?
3. What decision should be made? Why?

Part IV

Special Problems in Managerial Finance

Chapter Nineteen

Leasing—an Alternative to Direct Financing

The purchase of fixed assets by a company usually calls for the procurement of additional debt capital from external sources or additional equity capital from stockholders, old or new, unless the firm has ample retained earnings in the form of excess cash. It is, however, possible for a company to obtain the full use of fixed assets without purchasing them. This alternative is available by means of a lease.

In this chapter, we shall deal only with leasing, which is available as an alternative to purchase. There are many situations in which the company does not have the choice between these alternatives. For example, a national retail chain store organization may desire to open a branch in a shopping center. Unless it cares to purchase the entire center, a rather unlikely and unusual step, it can only lease (i.e., rent) the particular unit that it wants to occupy. The same is true of office space in a building or the use of an entire building in an industrial park. Some manufacturers of potential special-purpose machinery or office equipment may also offer their units for lease only. Quite a few of the larger skyscrapers in New York City, including the entire Rockefeller Center complex and the Empire State Building, were built on land that was only available for long-term leases.

There are, however, many opportunities for a company to negotiate a lease in lieu of purchase and ownership. In these cases, the lease is in fact, although not in form, a substitute for direct financing by the company using the asset. For this reason it is sometimes referred to as *lease financing.*

I. CHARACTERISTICS OF LEASE FINANCING

A lease is a contractual agreement between the owner of the asset (lessor) and the user (lessee) which sets forth in detail the obligations and the rights of the parties. The major provisions deal with the lifetime of the lease, renewal options (if any), the rental, which of the two parties is responsible for maintenance expenses, insurance, and taxes. A lease may also contain a provision giving the lessee the option to purchase the asset at a given price as well as the time when this option may be exercised. Any improvement on the leased asset, which would be shown in the lessee's financial statement on the asset side as "leasehold improvements," accrues to the lessor at the expiration of the lease.

A. Growth

Lease financing has grown at a rapid pace since World War II. Many companies in rapid-growth industries found it either too difficult or too expensive to procure the needed funds in the capital market. On the other hand, insurance companies, pension funds, banks, and other institutional investors have been willing to use a portion of their rapidly expanding funds for the financing of sound lease transactions. In response to this demand-supply situation a new type of institution evolved: the lease-finance company.

The lease-finance company acts as an intermediary between the prospective lessee and the supplier of the funds. Assume that a company wants to acquire the use of a relatively expensive piece of equipment, a special-purpose plant to be constructed to the firm's specifications, or any assets that the firm requires but finds it difficult to purchase. The company will then approach a lease-finance company. The lease-finance company then evaluates the prospective lessee's financial conditions, its credit rating, and other relevant facts. If it is satisfied that the tenant-to-be represents an acceptable credit risk, the lease-finance company will pay the vendor the price for the asset and become the lessor. It procures the funds from one or several of the previously mentioned sources. These sources find the services of the finance company advantageous since the supplier of the funds does not have to make its own investigation and become involved in the negotiations about the terms of the lease and the periodic check-up of the lessee.

Large companies may decide to set up their own lease-finance companies as a separate subsidiary. These subsidiary finance companies usually obtain a substantial portion of their funds from the same type of institutions as the independent lease-finance company.

B. Types of Leases

Lease contracts can be divided into two broad categories: (1) financial leases, and (2) operating leases.

A *financial lease* involves an agreement under which the lessee agrees to make a stipulated series of periodic payments over a span of time which covers the major portion or the entire usable lifetime of the asset. Typically, during this interval, the lessor expects to recover the full price at which the asset would otherwise have been sold plus interest and other costs that the lessor agrees to bear; e.g., insurance, tax, maintenance, etc. A financial lease is usually noncancellable by either party, except for failure to perform in accordance with the agreement.

An *operating lease* is usually for a period of time substantially less than the usable lifetime of the asset. At the expiration of the period, subject to the stipulated advance notice by either party, the lease terminates and the asset reverts to the lessor. During this interval the lessor generally expects to recover less than the full purchase price of the asset. However, he will recover his other costs (e.g., interest, taxes, etc.) and, hopefully, some profit except in case of default by and bankruptcy of the lessee.

A simple illustration of these two types of leases is the case of a truck renting company. A 5-year lease of a truck would exemplify the case of a financial lease. The lease of a truck for a few days or on a monthly basis represents an operational lease.

Short-term or operating leases rather than acquisition, even at the substantially higher cost on a time basis, is especially desirable if the lessee is uncertain about the future need for the asset. This situation is frequently present in defense contracts. The firm that procures an order cannot be sure that it will obtain repeat orders. If the execution of the order calls for equipment that the firm does not presently have and for which it will have no further use unless it obtains repeat orders, it is advantageous to obtain the use of the equipment through an operating lease. Smaller construction firms obtain most, if not all, of their heavy equipment by means of an operating lease. Larger construction firms, in contrast, "own" their heavy equipment through financial leases since they can be reasonably sure of requiring these assets over a period of years and, thus, over the greater portion of the usable lifetime of the equipment.

C. Sale and Leaseback

This new technique of procuring additional funds evolved rapidly after World War II and constitutes an important part of the operations of lease-finance companies. The process involves the simultaneous sale of an asset and its lease by the vendor firm from the lease-finance company. Its effect is to place additional capital rather than additional fixed assets at the immediate disposal of the business firm. The firm is free to use these funds either for working capital, the purchase of fixed assets, or both. The finance company thus becomes the legal owner and lessor of existing assets already operated by the lessee.

Sale and leaseback have also become an important instrument for the investment of funds by educational institutions, tax-free foundations, pension funds, and insurance companies. These purchasers-lessors differ from the lease-finance company in regard to the asset(s) that they will purchase and lease back to the vendor. Whereas the finance company will accept equipment, machinery, trucks, and other durable assets, institutional investors generally confine their transactions to real estate. Since the purchasing institution acquires the real estate, it can pay the full value, in contrast with a mortgage loan that would be for substantially less than the market value of the property. Many states, for example, permit insurance companies to invest up to 5% of their total assets in real estate but generally limit mortgage loans to 75% of the market value.

II. TO BUY OR LEASE

The decision to buy or to lease hinges on the answers to two questions. What are the respective explicit and implicit costs of the two alternatives? What are the auxiliary advantages, if any, that a firm can obtain from a lease or leaseback transaction?

A. Explicit Costs

At the outset, it must be stressed that a financial lease is, in effect, although not in form, equivalent to a purchase of the asset. In entering into a long-term contract, the business firm assumes a fixed obligation to make the specified periodic payments just as if it had issued debt securities. A comparison of the alternative costs therefore calls first for a determination of the expenses involved in obtaining debt capital. These expenses are: (1) the legal costs in preparing the various documents for a securities issue; (2) the payment, if any, of a "finder's fee" to an intermediary between the company and an underwriter; (3) the charges of the underwriter or the investment banker; (4) the discount, if any, from the face value of the debt securities by the purchaser of the debt securities; and (5) last but most important, the effective rate of interest; e.g., the rate of interest paid by the company on the net proceeds from the sale of the debt securities.

In the case of a lease-finance company, the explicit costs involve the stipulated periodic payment which consists of (1) interest on the amount invested by the finance company, and (2) the amortization of the investment. The amortization is a direct payment while its counterpart, in the case of debt capital, is represented by depreciation, which is a book entry, except in the case of a provision for a sinking fund which also calls for actual periodic cash transfers.

The magnitude of the comparative costs is a function of the size of the business firm and its access to the suppliers of long-term capital. A large corporation, for instance, will usually have no difficulty in negotiating directly with an insurance company, an educational institution, or a foundation for the private sale of debt securities. By contrast, a smaller company may find it necessary to utilize the services of an underwriter or an investment banker. Similarly, a large company is not likely to be asked by a bank to maintain a compensating balance in case of an intermediate-term loan, whereas the smaller firm may have to agree to such condition. Finally, the mere size of the funds required by a large corporation often exceeds the resources available to a lease-finance company.

B. Implicit Costs

The Certificate of Indenture, which forms the basis of the debt securities, sets forth terms in addition to those relating to the rate of interest and repayment of the debt. These terms may restrict the dividend policy, the acquisition of additional fixed assets and subsequent loans against these assets (i.e., an after-acquired clause) or they may provide for convertibility of debt securities into common stock. These constraints constitute implicit costs that must be weighed by management after a determination of the explicit costs.

Small companies are frequently not in a position to choose between debt capital and lease financing. Their size and the nature of their business may preclude access to the bond market. Instead, they have the choice between equity capital and lease financing. An issue of additional equity securities then calls for a determination of its impact on the present stockholders in terms of dilution of ownership and control of the company.

C. Special Cost Advantages of Leasing

Companies that are engaged in production under a cost-plus contract, either with a governmental body or private firm, will frequently find a financial lease more advantageous than the purchase of the asset with funds obtained in the capital market. If the company acquires the asset, it can depreciate the asset only at an annual rate spread over its normal usable lifetime. To be sure, it has the alternative of using the accelerated depreciation method which usually depreciates about two-thirds of the purchase price in one-half of the normal life of the asset. This annual depreciation allocation is a tax-deductible cost item.

By using a financial lease rather than purchase, the company can tailor the lifetime of the lease to the anticipated length of the cost-plus contract. The periodic payments under the lease are fully deductible as an operating expense. Let us assume that the asset in question has a usable lifetime of 12 years and that its purchase price is $120,000. If purchased outright, the firm can write off as a tax deductible expense (depreciation) roughly $65,000 in the first five years. Next, let us assume that the effective cost of debt capital would be 8% a year. The cost-plus contract is for four years and the finance company is asking for 16 quarterly payments of $7100 each. A schedule of comparative costs would then show the following:

If purchased:

Cost of asset		$120,000
Depreciation (declining balance) over 4 years	$ 74,100	74,100
Book value at end of 4 years		$ 45,900
Cost of debt capital at 8% per annum[1]	38,400	
	$112,500	

If leased:

16 quarterly payments of $7100		$113,600

[1] Assuming entire amount of debt capital remains outstanding for the four years.

At first glance, it would appear that the purchase offers a slight advantage in cost; about $1100 over the 4-year period. However, the question is whether the company will be able to recover the book value of $45,900 if the contract is not renewed and the asset becomes superfluous. At that time, the firm would have recovered only $74,100 (plus any interest earned on this cash) toward repayment of the debt of $120,000. A forced sale of the asset at the end of 4 years may easily result in a price substantially less than the book value. This difference would have to be added to the cost of $112,500 in order to arrive at the total cost if the asset is purchased. On the other hand, the firm would protect itself against this additional cost if it accepts the terms of the finance company. Conceivably, the finance company may be willing to give the firm a renewal option at substantially less than $7100 per quarter.

The finance company may be in a position to offer terms that are moderately or even substantially less—say, quarterly payments of $6500 which would total $102,000 over the 4-year period—for three reasons. First, the finance company is often in a position to obtain its funds at a lower rate of interest than the business firm, especially if the firm is relatively small. And in the second place, the finance company reduces its debt periodically by the payments received from the firm. Or it reinvests the payments in other leases which yield a return greater than the interest paid by the finance company. Finally, a finance company is frequently in a better position to recover the full book value than the firm. This is especially true if the finance company either specializes in this particular field of business or is a subsidiary of the original producer of the equipment. For example, the larger truck and car leasing companies maintain their own maintenance facilities and, in addition, are able to purchase trucks and cars at special discounts.

1. Realizing Capital Gains The sale-leaseback technique offers a company the opportunity to realize a profit from the appreciation of a fixed asset without losing the use of the asset. Suppose a company owns and occupies a building for which it paid $1 million and which is carried on the books at $600,000 net of depreciation (based on historical cost). As a result of inflation, rising land values, or both, the property has a current fair market value of $1.3 million. By means of a sale and leaseback, the company will obtain $1.3 million in cash, which can then be used for the acquisition of additional assets or to increase its net working capital. The profit of $700,000 (excess of sales price over balance sheet value) is subject to the capital gains tax of 25%.

As a result, the company's equity under the conventional accounting procedure will increase by $525,000 over the presale balance sheet figure.

A similar situation arises if a company has an asset that has been fully depreciated on the books but which is still usable for a number of years. In this case, too, a sale and leaseback offers a source of additional funds and a corresponding increase in net worth on the accountant's balance sheet.

2. Reducing Book Losses   It is quite conceivable that some assets may have decreased in value by an amount greater than the depreciated value shown on the balance sheet. A case in point would be a computer or some other piece of equipment acquired by the company a few years ago that is decidedly inferior to new models selling at the same price as the original cost of the computer. Or the building owned and occupied by the company has decreased in market value, as a result of a deteriorating neighborhood, by much more than the depreciation shown in the balance sheet. If the firm plans to use the equipment or building for several more years, the loss of value cannot be written off against operating profits until the asset is actually sold and a book loss established.

The sale and leaseback provides an opportunity to establish the loss now and write it off against operating profit; i.e., about one-half of the loss could be absorbed by the tax on corporate income. If the present fiscal year is exceptionally profitable, the management may well decide to take the book loss now rather than in some future year when the same loss would cut sharply into a normal rate of operating profit and, thus, have an adverse effect on the (capital) market image of the firm.

However, to qualify as a write-off against the operating profit for income tax purposes, the sale must be negotiated at a reasonable market price and the leaseback cannot exceed 30 years, including renewal options. Furthermore, the leaseback agreement cannot have a repurchase option for the vendor-lessee at a fixed price. It may, however, grant the lessee an option to repurchase the asset at the expiration of the lease at a price equal to any other bid obtained by the lessor at that time.

3. Balance Sheet Advantages   Funds procured from a term loan or from the sale of debt securities appear on the balance sheet as liabilities. The fixed obligations of periodic repayments of interest and principal on term loans, or bond interest and sinking funds, affect the company's credit rating and its ability to procure subsequently additional debt capital. Lease obligations, however, are not generally shown in the financial statements except, perhaps, as a footnote. The ordinary investor, who usually must rely solely on the financial statements in deciding whether to purchase debt securities or stock in the company, is therefore not in a position to determine the reasonable value of the security. The same is true of suppliers and other short-term creditors whose decision tends to be based largely on financial statements.

By contrast, term lenders, underwriters, and investment banks, as well as financial analysts, almost invariably request information and data on lease agreements with an unexpired lifetime of more than 3 years when evaluating a company. However, there exists a wide divergence of views on the analytical treatment of the periodic payments. The difficulty arises from the fact that the payments are fixed obligations, similar to the interest payment on bonds, and therefore enter into the income statement as part of the operating costs. However, unlike bonds, which are shown in the balance sheet as liabilities of the company, leases are not generally identified as such in the liabilities under present accounting practices. Furthermore, the payments under the lease are reflected under operating expenses. Yet, for purposes of determining the effects of lease payments on debt ratio, leverage, and burden coverage, it is important for both management and the financial analyst to determine the impact of these fixed payments on the company.

D. Lease Obligations and Debt Coverage

Interest, sinking fund payments, and the final redemption of bonds constitute a "burden" on the income of the corporation which must be met prior to any distribution of earnings to stockholders. In fact, this burden must be met regardless of whether the firm operates at a profit or loss.

Basically, the same procedure is applicable to the treatment of lease payments. In this instance, however, it is necessary to determine first the value of the asset(s) which are the subject of the lease. This amount then should be treated as an *imputed liability* that is offset by the same entry of an imputed asset equal to the value placed on the leased asset. Let us assume that a corporation shows the balance sheet liabilities in Table 19-1.

Next, suppose that the leased asset has a value of $250,000 and that the annual lease payments amount to $40,000. The adjusted balance sheet and income statements will then be as shown in Table 19-2.

Table 19-1

Long term obligations:	
6% mortgage bonds due 1980	$1,000,000
Stockholders equity:	
Common stock, $10 par value, issued and outstanding 75,000 shares	750,000
Retained earnings	450,000
	$2,200,000
Excerpts from income statement:	
Earnings before interest and taxes	$ 260,000
minus interest on bonds	60,000
Earnings after interest before taxes	$ 200,000
minus taxes (50% of earnings)	100,000
Net earnings	$ 100,000
Calculated ratios:	
Equity ratio ($1,200,000 : $1,000,000)	1.2:1 E
Burden coverage ($260,000 ÷ $60,000)	4.33 B
Trading on equity:	
$(E) \dfrac{(B-1)}{(B)} = \dfrac{(1.2)}{(1.0)} \dfrac{(3.33)}{(4.33)}$	0.92

The adjusted figures in the financial statements clearly reflect the extent to which the lease payments reduce the coverage of the fixed payments by the earnings of the company. They also show that the company is "trading" much heavier on its equity than is indicated by the unadjusted statements. As in the case of the bonds, the company is "locked in" once the lease agreement has been signed. The annual lease payments must be met whether or not the leased asset generates incremental earnings equal to, greater or smaller than the lease payments.

From the viewpoint of financial planning the specific identification of lease payments in the balance sheet and income statement offers several advantages. First, it plays an important role in the decision-making phase whether to buy or to lease. At that juncture, the obligations under the planned lease can be estimated in relation to the balance sheet and the major ratios. These items are bound to play an important role in future negotiations for term loans and new securities issues. Top management must therefore weigh the probable effects of the proposed lease payments on the future credit position of the company.

TABLE 19-2

Long term obligations:		
6% mortgage bonds		$1,000,000
Leasehold value		250,000
Stockholders equity:		
Common stock		750,000
Retained earnings		450,000
		$2,450,000
Income statement:		
Earnings before interest and taxes		$ 300,000[a]
minus interest on bonds	$60,000	
lease payments	40,000	100,000
Earnings before taxes		$ 200,000
Taxes		100,000
Net earnings		$ 100,000
Calculated ratios:		
Equity ratio ($1,200,000:$1,250,000)		0.96:1
Burden coverage ($300,000:$100,000)		3:1
Trading on equity		
$\left[\dfrac{(0.96)}{(1.00)}\dfrac{(2.00)}{(3.00)}\right]$		0.64

[a] Lease payments have been put back into earnings and then charged against these earnings in order to provide the same treatment as interest on the bonds.

Second, if the lease agreement has already been consummated, the adjusted figures and ratios can be taken into consideration in determining the pay-out ratio; i.e., the dividend policy. It is a generally accepted practice—in fact, it is a specific requirement in the typical debenture certificate—that a reasonable portion of the after-tax earnings should be retained as a cushion against a future decline in profits, or actual losses, so that the company can continue to pay its fixed obligations without impairing its capital. Additionally, retained earnings reduce, proportionately, the company's dependence on external sources of funds. By adjusting the income statement and balance sheet top management can see more clearly the extent to which the lease payments added to the interest on other fixed debt obligations require a smaller pay-out ratio.

E. Inflexibility of Lease

Assets that are owned by the company can be sold whenever, in the opinion of management, this action will be either profitable, because of appreciation of value, or minimize losses if the asset can no longer be used profitably in its operations. This alternative is not available under a leasehold. The company is obligated to make the annual lease payments for the entire lifetime of the lease. This inflexibility is reduced by provisions for subleasing. However, if the sublessee does not meet his lease payments, the original lessee is generally liable for them.

This inflexibility does not exist if the company has financed the purchase of an asset by means of debt capital and has no intention of disposing of the asset during its usable lifetime. It still has one alternative available if it has issued debt securities. It can refund (i.e., recast) its debt structure if interest rates should decline during the lifetime of the debt. The company can then sell new debt securities at the prevailing lower rate and use the proceeds to retire the original debt. It is customary for long-term debt securities to have a "callable" provision; i.e., after a specified date in the lifetime of the securities the company has the option to redeem the debt.

The growing practice of leasing and the increased availability of companies offering this service has opened a new option to the firm that does not wish to issue new securities or increase its long-term debt. The continued growth of leasing as an alternative to direct financing will likely lead to changes in current accounting practices to reflect the imputed liability of a lease.

SUMMARY

Leasing makes it possible for a company to obtain the full use of fixed assets without purchasing them. A lease is a contractual agreement between the owner of the asset (lessor) and the user (lessee) which sets forth in detail the obligations and the rights of the parties. The financial manager must know the major provisions of the lease—its lifetime, renewal options, rental rate, responsibility for insurance and taxes, and purchase option.

Lease financing has grown at a rapid pace since World War II. Insurance companies, pension funds, banks, and other institutional investors have been willing to use a portion of their rapidly expanding funds for the financing of sound lease transactions. A new type of institution, the lease-finance company, has evolved to act as an intermediary between the prospective lessee and the supplier of funds.

Lease contracts can be divided into two broad categories: financial leases and operating leases. A financial lease involves an agreement under which the lessee agrees to make a stipulated series of periodic payments over a span of time which covers the major portion or the entire usable lifetime of the asset. An operating lease is usually for a period of time substantially less than the usable lifetime of the assets.

The costs and auxiliary advantages must be considered by the financial manager when he decides whether the firm should buy or lease an asset.

Questions

1. What are the major provisions of a lease?
2. What are the reasons for the increased importance of leasing in recent years?
3. What is the function of a lease finance company?
4. How do financial leases differ from operating leases?
5. What are the advantages to a firm of a sale and leaseback of a fixed asset? The disadvantages?
6. Is the cost of leasing a piece of equipment always more to a firm than the cost of purchase?
7. Why should the financial analyst be interested in adjusting the balance sheet and income statement of a firm to show its lease obligations?

Case: MOLLY CORPORATION

The treasurer of Molly Corporation must decide whether to buy or lease a computer. Molly Corporation generally earns about 14% on its invested capital. The computer can be purchased for $275,000. The computer is expected to have an economic life of 10 years, and will have no scrap value at the end of this period. The $275,000 to purchase the computer can be borrowed from the Third National Bank on the following basis.

1. Interest of 6% per annum on the declining balance of the loan.
2. The loan will be repaid in 10 equal installments and interest plus principal payments would be made at the end of each year.

Alternatively, the computer manufacturer will lease the computer to Molly Corporation on the following basis:

1. The lease will run for 10 years.
2. Annual lease payments will be $38,000 per annum.

The payments will be due at the end of each fiscal year.

Case Questions:

1. Which proposal would be best from a quantitative point of view? (*Hint.* Present value techniques will be helpful to you in your calculations.)
2. What other factors should the treasurer consider before reaching a decision?
3. Which proposal would you recommend to the Board of Directors of Molly Corporation? Why?

~~~~~~

Chapter Twenty

Valuation and Mergers

The determination of the monetary value of the business firm is a matter of financial analysis rather than accounting. To be sure, the statements of the accountant constitute an indispensable basis for this determination. But what is needed—both for short-term and long-term planning—is a valuation of the firm as a *going concern*. This task involves concepts and procedures that lie outside the province of the accountant.

I. OBJECTIVES OF VALUATION

The concept of the "going concern" embraces two distinct sets of elements: (1) the physical assets of the firm; and (2) the invisible assets. The physical assets consist of the several items that appear in the financial statement of the accountant: land, buildings, machinery, furniture, inventory, cash, receivables, etc. The invisible assets, as the term already implies, do not appear in the statement. They involve such items as: trademarks, patents, franchises, goodwill.

Whether an asset is "visible" or "invisible" the determination of its monetary value frequently involves subjective judgment. The only exceptions are cash, marketable securities, and receivables from accounts with an established good credit rating. As for the other assets of the firm, their valuation depends in large measure on the objectives of the person or firm making the evaluation.

1. Liquidation Value In this instance, the valuation is confined primarily to the physical assets. In estimating the liquidation value of a physical asset the premise is that the liquidation will be in the nature of a forced sale. It is readily apparent that a prospective buyer will not pay the full value. The maximum price that this prospective buyer is willing to pay is the market price or value of the specific asset. In practice, however, he will rarely be prepared to pay the "full value." The mere fact that the firm is to be liquidated depresses the price below the market price for comparable items. Liquidation always implies an opportunity for "bargains." As a rule, it calls for a cash transaction. Furthermore, the seller is under a time pressure to liquidate as soon as feasible. In addition, the asset or assets are offered *en bloc;* i.e., in the quantity "as is" rather than in the quantity that the prospective buyer would ordinarily care to purchase.

In a forced or liquidation sale, the valuation placed on the assets by the accountant has little or no bearing on the price offered by a buyer or the price actually realized.

The accountant's value of assets is based on original cost less depreciation or on market value, if it is known to be lower (as is implied in the rule "cost or market, whichever is lower"). In a forced or liquidation sale, the transaction is a one-time sale in which the seller must dispose of his supply. The buyer, on the other hand, is under no compunction to buy these assets. The buyer can select his supply from a variety of sources and can purchase at a time of his convenience. If the buyer decides to purchase assets at a forced sale, he will generally pay less than the current market value of the assets on a going concern basis. The accountant's value of the assets, based on original cost or market value, whichever is lower, will have no relevance to such a buyer's decision since the accountant's valuation will be based on cost of the assets (which may be higher or lower than current value) or on market value on a going concern basis, which will generally be higher than when a forced sale takes place.

As for the "invisible" assets, these usually have no market value for the simple reason that the firm ceases to exist with the liquidation of the assets. Thus, goodwill, trademarks, and franchise have little or no monetary value to a prospective buyer. However, it is sometimes quite conceivable that a prospective purchaser may be more interested in acquiring the invisible assets rather than the visible assets. This is the case if an established business is to be sold because of the death of the owner or as a result of dissension among partners. But in this case, we are not dealing with the liquidation of the firm. Instead, this situation really involves the liquidation of ownership. The firm itself is expected to continue but under new owner(s).

There is little, if anything, that the financial manager can contribute to the final selling price of the physical assets of the firm. The value that he may place on the items is at best a minimum price which the enterprise can hope to realize. However, in the last analysis, liquidation implies a forced sale. Under these circumstances, the firm is under time pressure. Top management will attempt to bargain for the best possible price. But it has little if any choice. It will have to accept the best price offered by whatever prospective purchasers it may be able to attract.

2. Loan Value Suppliers and financial institutions first look at the financial statements as a guide to the value of the firm. However, their second and decisive concern is with the capacity of the firm to generate both earnings and cash flows to insure the repayment of the loan or the payment of the bills, respectively.

To the short-term creditor, the equity or book value of the firm is of subordinate importance. It serves as a margin of safety against the possibility that the firm may not have the liquid funds at the maturity of the obligation. Since the emphasis is on short-term liquidity, the creditors are primarily concerned with the current ratio, the quick or acid-test ratio, and the net working capital of the firm.

By the same token, the term lender stresses the equity value of the firm. Over a period of years the liquidity of the firm, as reflected in the proportion of current assets to current liabilities, is subject to changes as a result of internal and external economic factors. These cannot be predicted with any degree of certainty. Furthermore, the future monetary value of the invisible assets of the firm is equally unpredictable. The only tangible basis is provided by the current book value of the equity; i.e., its value at the time when the loan is granted. Naturally, the creditor hopes, and the debtor firm anticipates, that the projected future profits will enhance the value of the invisible assets and add to the tangible worth of the equity.

In negotiating a loan, the financial officer can and will point out to the lender any undervaluation of assets that may appear in the financial statements. For example, land and buildings may have increased in value very substantially since their acquisition by the firm. This appreciation in values is not reflected in the accountant's figures which, traditionally, are based on original cost less depreciation, or current market value if it is less than original cost less depreciation. This revaluation of the assets may induce the lender to increase the amount of the loan, i.e., applying his customary percentage of say, 70% to the higher base of the financial manager rather than to the lower figure of the accountant. However, in this case, too, the prospective profits and cash flow play a decisive role in determining whether the firm can "carry" the larger obligation.

3. Investment Value   The prospective investor in the securities of a firm focuses primarily on the earnings and dividends of the enterprise. The current and prospective profit constitutes the reservoir from which the firm is expected to divert a portion into interest payments and dividends, if any. The balance retained by the firm adds to the subsequent earning capacity of the enterprise; and, in addition, provides a cushion against temporary adverse developments.

From the viewpoint of the investor, the dividends and retained earnings are the cause, and the price of the security is the effect. The better the prospects of future earnings, the higher will he value the firm and the higher the price that he is prepared to pay for the shares of the corporation. However, the prospects of future earnings and dividends contain a strong element of uncertainty. This uncertainty applies particularly to companies that operate in a competitive market and to firms that are subject to substantial cyclical fluctuations in the demand for their products. As a result, the price-earnings ratio of corporate shares shows a wide range at any given time as well as over a period of time.

The wide range in the price-earnings ratio is clearly reflected in the index of the American Stock Exchange in New York City. The first such index was prepared and published by this Exchange in June 1966. For the more than 950 common stocks traded, it showed a median price-earnings ratio of 13.5. The largest single group, 273 corporate stocks fell in the range 10:1 to 15:1. No less than 186, the second largest group had a ratio between 5:1 and 10:1; while 115 issues sold at a ratio between 15 and 20 to 1. Thus, 574 issues were priced between 5 and 20 times their earnings.

A high price-earnings ratio (e.g., 20:1) indicates that investors anticipate a significant rise in the earnings of the company in the not too distant future. It also generally assumes that the risk of a decline in the earnings is low. Conversely, a low ratio of say, 5:1, reflects the opposite sentiment. In summary, investors, whether individuals or institutional investors, evaluate current and prospective future profits and differences of risk as to profit stability in arriving at their asking and bidding prices.

Investors in fixed-return securities—e.g., nonconvertible bonds and debentures or nonparticipating preferred stock—value such securities similar to the term lender. Their concern is with the prospective capacity of the firm to maintain the agreed-upon interest or fixed dividend payment and the repayment of the principal at maturity. In this case, too, the monetary value of the invisible assets of the firm plays a minor role in the investment decision of the securities purchaser.

4. Mergers   A merger involves the acquisition of the common stock of a corporation by a second corporation through an exchange of shares. For example, in October, 1964, the Norfolk and Western Railway acquired the Nickel Plate (New York, Chicago, and St. Louis Railroad) as a result of an exchange of shares. Some 1,900,000 Norfolk and Western common shares were issued for all the outstanding stock of the Nickel Plate on the basis of 0.45 share of Norfolk and Western for each Nickel Plate share. At the same time, the Norfolk and Western leased the Wabash and acquired several smaller railroads. The merger led to the diversification of freight revenues by combining Norfolk and Western's coal and coke traffic with the industrial and agricultural volume of the Nickel Plate and the Wabash. In addition, the merger resulted in a rail system that transverses 14 states and part of Canada—serving cities from Norfolk, Virginia to Des Moines, Iowa.

The determination of the respective monetary values of the two merging corporations as a basis for the ratio of the respective shares involves a series of qualitative judgments as well as quantitative measurements. In addition, a number of subjective elements frequently enter into the decisive bargaining sessions in which the ratio of exchange of the common stock of the two corporations is negotiated. In these sessions, the financial officers play a central role in assessing the relative value of their respective corporations.

II. REASONS FOR MERGERS

The motivations for a merger play an important role in the determination of the respective values of the two companies that negotiate a possible merger. Basically, the reasons can be classified under two broad headings: (1) economic objectives, and (2) personal motivations. It must be stressed, however, that these are not mutually exclusive. Quite frequently, one or both firms are prompted by more than one single objective. However, in most cases, one particular aim plays a dominant role in the decision of top management to engage in negotiations for a possible merger.

A. Economic Objectives

The economic motivation for a merger is a function of the overall policy of the firm. This policy can be oriented in either one of two basic directions: (1) expansion or (2) growth.

Expansion implies an increase in the *size of the firm*. It corresponds to the concept of the economies of scale. By means of the merger with another company engaged in the same line (manufacturing, wholesaling, retailing) and producing the same products or services, the two firms anticipate savings in costs. These savings could be derived from a reduction in the combined sales personnel, advertising, purchasing or any one of the multiple operations performed by the two enterprises. It may also involve the closing down and the sale of say, a plant or retail outlet and the transfer of its operations to other existing units. The best known examples of mergers for the purpose of increased size and anticipated savings are bank mergers. Railroad mergers (such as the Norfolk and Western merger already discussed and the recent major merger of the Pennsylvania and New York Central) are designed to facilitate substantial cost savings as well as improved services and, thus, increased total revenues.

Growth, by contrast, involves some change in the *field of operations* of the two merging firms. For example, the merger of Martin Company (an aerospace company) and American Marietta Corporation (a construction materials producer) into Martin Marietta in 1961 represented a subtantial change in product and marketing policy. The top management of the merged companies had to shift its perspective from a single objective to two objectives. Moreover, top management had to evolve a new policy and strategy—both marketing and pricing strategy—which encompassed the combined lines of products and operations. New guidelines had to be formulated for selling and pricing, advertising and purchasing, credit extension and borrowing, labor relations, etc. Frequently, top management may decide to permit each of the two merged companies to continue along the path that it had followed prior to the merger. However, this policy is usually only a temporary expedient. The "no-change" decision is intended to gain time until top management can formulate and put into effect a new policy with a minimum of frictions and irritations within the two companies.

The merger of Cities Service Company and the United Nuclear Corporation in 1966 marked the entry of the former into the field of atomic energy. United Nuclear operates uranium mines and has fabricating engineering facilities in Connecticut, New York, Rhode Island, and Missouri. It is one of the few companies engaged in the production of atomic fuel. By means of this merger, Cities Service was the first oil company to enter this field. In a sense, this merger represents an insurance for Cities Service that it will be able to preserve its overall market position in the field of energy if and when nuclear power emerges as a serious competitor to oil as a source of energy.

From the viewpoint of the financial manager, the benefits of expansion (in the same product line) can be quantified and measured more readily than those that accrue from growth through diversification. In the former case, it is possible to estimate with a fair degree of certainty the probable cost savings—and, if necessary, the additional capital investments—which will be attained in the short run as well as in the long run. To make a similar estimate of the benefits of growth through diversification is more difficult. This involves a series of qualitative judgments of future changes in policy and strategy and their respective impact on the merged companies. Some of the potential benefits of the merger can be readily estimated because they involve immediate quantitative decisions. Some positions in top or middle management may be eliminated as soon as the merger is consummated; e.g., one comptroller rather than two or centralization of bookkeeping and billing procedures. Savings in rent may be feasible by transferring some or all manufacturing operations of one merged company into excess space available in the plant of the other company.

The above-discussed broad-gauged economic objectives of a merger are usually reinforced by one or more of the following considerations.

1. Reducing Cyclical Volatility   Every firm is susceptible to the impact of the business cycle in terms of upswing or decline. However, the degree of cyclical change varies widely among industries and differs also between firms in the same line of business. Moreover, enterprises that manufacture producers' goods—such as machinery, tools, etc.—are subject to a greater cyclical volatility than companies that produce consumer goods. Within these two categories—producers' goods versus consumer goods—manufacturers are more susceptible to cyclical influences than retailers in the respective line of business. In macroeconomic theory, this is known as the *accelerator principle*.

By means of a merger with a cyclically less volatile firm, a highly volatile company anticipates several economic benefits. First, the consolidated profit and loss statement of the two merged firms will show a better financial picture in a period of declining economic activity. That is to say, the profits of the relatively stable firm will in part or in whole offset the losses of the volatile enterprise. This in turn facilitates the maintenance of dividend payments, even if at a reduced amount, rather than the omission of dividends. Second, the ability to procure short-term loans in a period of recession is improved since the consolidated statement is more favorable than would otherwise be the case. Third, if the volatile firm has obtained debt capital, it will be able to maintain the payment of interest and principal (sinking fund) out of the consolidated pretax earnings. And last but not least, it will have a more positive cash-flow position than in the absence of a "reservoir" in the more stable company.

It must also be borne in mind that a consumer-oriented firm can stimulate the demand for its products and, thus, its volume of sales through adjustments in price. On the other hand, a price concession is less effective in the case of producers' goods.

2. Seasonal Fluctuations Many lines of business are subject to sharp seasonal fluctuations. Toy manufacturers enjoy their peak season in the period preceding Christmas. Producers of furniture register their high points in the early fall while the makers of air conditioners reach their peak in the late spring and early summer. Manufacturers of building supplies record their biggest monthly sales in the summer season.

A merger of two companies with different seasonal patterns offers several advantages. If the product lines of the two firms are compatible—e.g., plastic toys and plastic beach games; indoor (wood) furniture and garden furniture; calendars and greeting cards—a merger may enable the two companies to utilize more effectively a smaller number of machines, workers, and salesmen on a year-round basis than by separately maintaining a capacity that is geared to the seasonal peak rather than to level monthly production.

As in the previous case, cyclical volatility, the potential benefits can be measured quantitatively by the financial manager. To be sure, top management must also weigh qualitative elements; e.g., the feasibility of integrating the two types of operation, the capacity of management to plan effectively for two distinct markets, the geography of the two markets in which the respective firms operate.

3. Filling the Product Line   It is not unusual for a firm to discover a serious void in its product line. This may be the result of technological developments that bring to the surface new raw materials and/or new products. For example, the development of new synthetic fibres gave rise to a host of new products that served the same purpose as the traditional raw materials. Thus, a firm that has an established firm foothold in the "traditional" product market may want to add the new line of synthetics in order to offer its customers a complete choice.

Rather than start up its own operations in a field in which it lacks experience and technical know-how, it favors a merger with a firm that possesses the technical know-how and which has succeeded in carving for itself a portion of the market. Similarly, a company manufacturing duplicating machines for office use may conclude that the addition of collators is a "natural" complement to its product line. It has a sales organization that could easily handle both lines of products. But the producer of duplicating machines has neither the technical background nor the patents to manufacture collators. Here, too, a merger could prove a "natural" for both firms.

4. Research and Development   For a company that wants to keep ahead of its competitors and insure its growth, a competent research and development staff is often a must. To set up a promising program of research and development involves time and money. A merger with a company that has a well functioning research and development program in the same or in a related field offers, therefore, a shortcut in time and money to the desired goal.

Conversely, the firm that has built up a competent research and development department may lack the know-how and organization for the effective marketing of the products developed by its researchers. By merging with a company that possesses an established market, the firm with the research and development staff may be able to reap greater benefits in a shorter time than by trying to set up its own sales organization.

5. Entry into a Glamour Field   Imaginative top executives of companies are not immune to the potential of newly developing products and technologies even if these occur in fields quite removed from the industries in which these executives are engaged. Through the acquisition of a small promising company in the "industry of tomorrow" by means of merger, a large enterprise hopes to obtain a stake in a potentially highly profitable field. To the owners of the small firm, the merger opens the door to ample capital for rapid expansion, the marketing know-how of the large company and, frequently, the latter's physical and human resources for expanded research and development.

6. Economies of Scale   The anticipated benefits of a merger of two companies engaged in the same line of business have already been discussed in the early part of this section. If the two firms are active on the same level—e.g., manufacturing, wholesaling, or retailing—the merger will yield an additional advantage: reduced competition. That is to say, to the extent to which the two companies had been engaged in price competition against each other, the need for such a policy disappears with the merger.

7. Tax Reasons   The corporation is subject to a corporate income tax. Suppose the tax rate is 48%. However, a corporation may debit its taxable earnings in any one year with a loss suffered in one or two of the preceding years. This is known as the carry-forward provision. Suppose Corporation X had a net operating loss of $250,000 in the year 196x and a loss of $400,000 in the 196x + 1. In 196x + 2 it shows earnings of $750,000. Under the carry-forward provision, the corporation then has a tax liability on $100,000 earnings in 196x + 2 [$750,000 — (250,000 + 400,000)].

Assume that Company ABC has lost $3,000,000 in the past two fiscal years and that its management has little hope of operating in the black in the foreseeable future. Next, assume that Corporation XY shows earnings of five million dollars in its last fiscal year and that its prospects for continued profits are good. If Corporation XY mergers with the deficit firm, it can offset the latter's losses of $3,000,000 against its earnings of five million dollars. It will net a tax saving of $1,440,000.

In spite of the fact that Company ABC has suffered a substantial loss with no prospect of earnings in the years ahead, it has a value of one million dollars or more as a "losing concern" plus whatever value its physical assets may have. By merging with ABC, the profitable Corporation XY can quickly recover the price paid for the tax deductible loss; up to the maximum of $1,440,000.

B. Personal Motivation

Mergers are not always the result of economic objectives on the part of one or both firms. Not infrequently, the dominant reason is to be found in the subjective aims of the top management of one or both corporations.

1. Estate Planning   In a closed corporation—i.e., a corporation owned and operated by a few stockholders-officers—the problem of estate taxes quite often becomes a matter of serious concern to the stockholder(s) who approaches or passes the 60th birthday; sometimes even much earlier. The shares of such a corporation are not traded in the market. In the case of death, the value of the shares for tax purposes is apt to become a matter of serious dispute between the tax authorities and the heirs. The subsequent sale of a portion of the shares to pay the inheritance tax presents a problem to the heirs as well as to the surviving other stockholders.

A merger with a corporation whose shares are traded in the market solves both problems. The value of the estate is readily ascertainable; i.e., the market price of the stock at the time of death. And the heirs can liquidate a portion of the shares in the market in order to pay the inheritance tax.

2. Prestige   This motive can work both ways. The owners-officers of a relatively small corporation become members of top management in a far larger corporation. Usually, they are moved down one or two steps in the organizational hierarchy; e.g., the president of the smaller firm becomes one of several vice-presidents in the larger (merged) corporation, although his compensation may be greater in the merged company. On the other hand, this individual may have an opportunity in the course of time to advance to a higher position and, thus, gain still greater prestige plus the greater compensation paid in the larger company.

At times, a rather large corporation may desire to merge with a smaller firm that enjoys a high prestige in the business world; and, incidentally, also in the community. For example, in 1965 one of America's large corporations merged with a book publishing firm that had established for itself the reputation as a leading publisher of great literary works. In terms of markets, sales organization, and production techniques, the two firms had nothing in common. Even after the merger, each of the two corporations continued to pursue their respective premerger policies. The only change that occurred took place in the personnel of the top management of the publishing firm. The position of president was vacated and given to a vice president of the larger corporation. Parenthetically, the newly appointed president had no previous experience as a book publisher. Among other book publishers, at least, the prevailing opinion was that this assignment was motivated by a desire for prestige on the part of the new president and that this same reason had also played an important role in the merger itself.

3. Empire Builders Bigness in itself has a strong appeal to many entrepreneurs, especially in those instances in which a firm has grown from minute size to a multimillion company in the course of ten or fifteen years. There is a tendency for the rate of expansion to slow down as an enterprise changes from a one-man dominated firm to an organization. The head of this organization is not satisfied with the prospects of continued but slower expansion. To maintain and, if possible, to accelerate the earlier rate of expansion, he will resort to a series of consecutive mergers. The motivation is a mixture of economic objectives and subjective ambitions.

C. Types of Mergers

The "direction" in which a company seeks to increase its size by means of a merger can be (1) horizontal; (2) vertical; (3) unrelated or conglomerate.

1. Horizontal This involves the merger of two companies engaged in the same line of business and operating on the same level. For example, a furniture manufacturer merging with another producer of furniture would constitute a horizontal merger, even if the two companies are making different types of furniture and in different price lines.

2. Vertical A merger between a retailer and a manufacturer who produces some of the items sold by the retailer represents a vertical merger. Other examples of vertical mergers are the merger between an oil refinery and a chain of gasoline stations, between a steel mill and a coal mining company, a motion picture producer and a chain of theaters.

3. Unrelated or Conglomerate In the above two types—horizontal and vertical—we can at least presume an economic rationale for a merger. On the other hand, it is difficult to postulate the economies of scale in a merger of two firms in totally unrelated fields, although the management of the two companies may have found a common cause in a phase of operations that is not readily visible to the outsider.

The merger of the Philadelphia Reading Railroad and the Union Underwear Company is, on the surface at least, an example of an unrelated merger. The same applies to the merger of Charles of the Ritz, a cosmetics producer, and the Venus Pen and Pencil Company. Or between Bigelow-Sanford, a producer of carpets and rugs, and Crestline, Inc., a manufacturer of outboard motors, or between Radio Corporation of America and Hertz Rent-A-Car.

The result of a merger is that the stock of the "merged" corporation is removed from the market. The stockholders of the company receive a stipulated and agreed-on number of shares in the "absorbing" company. Table 20-1 shows the results of mergers of companies listed on the New York Stock Exchange which merged in the year 1965.

III. MERGERS: VALUATION OF FIRMS

When two firms give serious consideration to a possible merger, the financial manager of each company is usually charged with the task of making an initial determination of three values. First, he must estimate the monetary value of his own firm as a "going concern." This figure is intended as the probable minimum asking price by the top management of his company. Second, the financial manager must similarly determine the value of the other firm. This figure, in turn, generally becomes the maximum price that his company will set on the other firm. And finally, the financial manager is expected to evaluate the probable effect of the merger on the future profitability of the consolidated companies. This projection is then compared with the prospective profitability of his firm if there is to be no merger.

Armed with these quantitative tools, the negotiating officers of the two firms can start the bargaining process. This section will analyze the several methods that may be employed by the financial manager in arriving at the respective minimum asking and maximum offering prices. The techniques of the negotiating or bargaining process will be discussed in the next section of this chapter.

1. Book Value   Under this method, the determination of the value of the firm is rather simple. Using the firm's balance sheet as a source, it requires the mere addition of the value shown for the capital stock, both preferred and common, plus the retained earnings plus the capital surplus. If the balance sheet shows reserves for bad debts or contingencies, the excess of these reserves over the actual requirement is added to the above enumerated figures.

The use of book value suffers from several serious defects. Book value does not reflect the current value of the fixed assets. Instead,

Table 20-1.   Mergers and Consolidations in 1965[a]

Name of Company Removed	Date Removed	Stockholders of Original Company Received:	
		Name of Company	Per Common Share
Aldens, Inc.	1/ 4	Gamble-Skogmo, Inc.	1 share $1.60 Conv. Pfd. Stk.
Baldwin-Lima-Hamilton Corp.	7/ 6	Armour & Co.	13/100 share $4.75 Cum. Pfd. Stk. and 1/6 share Common Stk.
Bestwall Gypsum Company	4/30	Georgia-Pacific Corp.	1 share $1.64 Conv. Pfd. Stk.
Drackett Company	8/ 3	Bristol-Myers Co.	46/100 share Common Stk.
Ekco Products Co.	10/ 1	American Home Products Corp.	1 share $2 Conv. Pfd. Stk.
Frito-Lay, Inc.	6/11	PepsiCo. Inc.	⅔ share Capital Stk.
Hewitt-Robins Incorporated	2/25	Litton Industries, Inc.	.35359 share $3 Cum. Conv. Ser. A Pfd. Stk.
Minnesota & Ontario Paper Co.	2/ 1	Boise Cascade Corp.	1 share $1.40 Conv. Pfd. Stk.
Mueller Brass Co.	9/27	U.S. Smelting, Ref. & Mng. Co.	42/100 share $5.50 Cum. Pfd. Stk.
National Castings Company	4/26	Midland-Ross Corp.	45/100 share $4.75 Cum. Conv. Ser. A Pfd. Stk.
Pacific Cement & Aggregates, Inc.	9/ 1	Lone Star Cement Corp.	225/1000 share $4.50 Cum. Conv. Pfd. Stk.
Packaging Corp. of America	6/ 9	Tennessee Gas Transmission Co.	12/10 shares Common Stk.
Penick & Ford Ltd., Inc.	6/10	Reynolds (R. J.) Tobacco Co.	$22 cash
Pfaudler Permutit Inc.	11/ 1	Ritter Pfaudler Corp.	1 share Common Stk.
Pure Oil Company	7/19	Union Oil Co. of Cal.	1 share $2.50 Cum. Conv. Pfd. Stk. and $0.196 cash
Ritter Corporation	11/ 1	Ritter Pfaulder Corp.	1 share Common Stk.
Royal McBee Corp.	3/ 1	Litton Industries, Inc.	.16875 share $3 Cum. Conv. Ser. A Pfd. Stk.
Smith-Douglass Co., Inc.	1/ 5	Borden Company	9/10 share Capital Stk. and $0.12 cash
Spiegel, Inc.	11/ 1	Beneficial Finance Co.	¼ share $430 Div. Cum. Conv. Pfd. Stk. and ⅛ share Common and a cash distribution of $0.086
Towmotor Corporation	11/10	Caterpillar Tractor Co.	1 share Common Stk.

[a] Listed are companies removed from the New York Stock Exchange's trading list, the stockholders of which Companies received securities in other listed companies.
Source: New York Stock Exchange Fact Book, 1966.

it records the original cost minus the amount set up for depreciation. As a result, the book value of fixed assets will rarely correspond to their current value measured by replacement cost minus actual depreciation.

A second deficiency, which is rather frequent among smaller companies, is the tendency on the part of the owners to understate the firm's earnings in order to reduce the tax liability of the firm. This does not imply an intention to evade the tax by illegal methods of accounting. The tax laws permit a firm to charge its expenditures for research and development against current revenues. In a highly profitable year, a company may decide to spend a disproportionate sum on research in the hope of attaining an earlier breakthrough than would otherwise be the case. Or the firm makes major repairs sooner than they would ordinarily be done. Or it spends more money on exhibits and attendance at business shows in the hope of building up its image at a faster pace and "cashing in" the next fiscal year. Another example would be the opening of new branches that will, initially, operate at a loss. In brief, the firm is prepared to divert a portion of its current earnings in order to make larger profits in subsequent years. Whenever such projects are undertaken at an accelerated pace compared with the tempo in normal profit years, the net effect is an understatement of current earnings. The same effect, understatement of earnings, is also attained if the firm is overgenerous in expense allowances for officers and employees.

In the absence of a merger, the diversion and consequent understatement of earnings has no adverse effect on the firm over a period of time. What has been lost in a given year is expected to be recovered in the next year or two. But this anticipation is not visible in the book value shown on the balance sheet.

2. Appraisal Value   This method is designed to rectify the accountant's understatement of the value of the fixed assets. The procedure is fairly simple. Fixed assets are broken down into appropriate subgroups; e.g., undeveloped land, buildings, machinery, equipment, fixtures, etc. Expert appraisers in these various fields are then called in to make an "impartial" appraisal of the current value of the respective groups of fixed assets.

The appraisal value approach has several shortcomings. First, experts do not necessarily agree in the valuation of assets. Furthermore, their appraisal is focused on current value, which usually means replacement cost minus depreciation. It is in the matter of depreciation that substantial differences of opinion are likely to arise. Second, and more important, the appraiser determines the physical value. Most importantly, management is primarily interested in the earning capacity of these assets, both present and future, within the complex called the firm, rather than their replacement cost less depreciation.

3. Market Price of Stock   Under this method, the ratio of the market price of the common shares of the two companies is used in determining the ratio of exchange of stock. If Corporation A has a market price of $75 and Corporation B of $50, the ratio is $1\frac{1}{2}$ shares of B for 1 share of A.

The advocates of this approach argue that market price reflects the valuation of the respective earning power of the two corporations by investors. It therefore represents an objective rational valuation. If this ratio is accepted, the shareholders of Corporation B—assuming that B is to be merged into A—receive for their shares the same price that they would realize if they sold their stock in the market. Thus, the owner of 150 shares could get $7500 if he sold his stock; and he would realize $7500 if he exchanges his 150 shares for 100 shares of A which have a market price of $75.

This line of reasoning has several weaknesses. As far as the market price *per se* goes, it does not measure the value of the entire issue. Usually, only a small portion of a corporation's shares are traded. The market itself may be rather "thin;" i.e., the price would drop very drastically if a major portion of the outstanding stock were thrown on the market. In other instances, the market price may reflect transactions that take place intermittently. Under these circumstances, the market price is highly vulnerable and may change substantialy with even minor changes in supply or demand.

Another important and well-known fact is the instability of market price. We need only look at the daily report of stock prices either on the New York Stock Exchange or on the American Stock Exchange and examine the "high" and "low" for the year. Without exception, it will quickly be seen that the stock prices fluctuate substantially in the course of the year even if the earnings of the corporation remain constant.

Speculation, interest rates, political development at home or abroad, and monetary policy are some of the major external influences that affect the market climate as much or even more than current or prospective earnings of the individual corporation. The so-called "blue chips"— i.e., the shares of large well-established corporations—are not immune to a bearish sentiment in the market. (Optimistic buyers are known as "bulls" while their pessimistic counterparts are labelled "bears.")

4. Capitalization of Earnings Here the stress is entirely on the earnings of the firm. Its value lies in its capacity to generate profit. The earnings of the last year and those of the preceding years are used as a base for the projection of future earnings.

Since earnings serve as the yardstick, the finance manager must frequently reconstruct the profit and loss statements of the firm. Every major expenditure item has to be reviewed and reanalyzed. A determination must be made whether a given expense represented an extraordinary nonrecurring item; or, if a recurring expenditure, whether it would become superfluous after the consummation of the merger. For instance, one of the owner-officers may be close to retirement and no replacement need be planned. Overgenerous travel and other allowances to officers and employees can be "disallowed" in the reconstructed income statement if these expenditures, too, can be eliminated after the merger.

Unusual incidents that affected the sales volume adversely have to be analyzed. A prolonged strike in the plant of a major supplier may have had serious repercussions on the output and sales of the firm. An estimate must be made of the "lost opportunities" and their approximate monetary value, i.e., lost profits. Or the firm may have had some unusual production problems with a new product which were subsequently resolved, but too late in the fiscal year to make up for the earlier losses.

Sales and revenues also must be reanalyzed. Conceivably, the firm found it necessary to make special price concessions in order to penetrate a new market or to introduce a new product in its established market. In brief, the financial manager faces the formidable task of reconstructing an income statement and balance sheet that can be defended as a more realistic picture of the firm's earning capacity than the statements prepared by the accountant. After all, the latter deals with "facts" rather than with the causes which produced the facts. The financial manager must also be prepared to disallow unusual events which generated windfall profits; e.g., the purchase of supplies at an unusual bargain price, a temporary shortage of supply in the market accompanied by a sharp rise in the market price with substantial profit for the firm which had inadvertently carried too large an inventory.

5. Respective Earnings Potential Assuming each of the two companies planning to merge is a going conern, their respective future earnings must be evaluated. The company that can demonstrate a relatively better profit potential—i.e., a higher prospective rate of profit on its net worth—will insist that this factor be given its full weight in arriving at the present value of the firm in relation to the other company. In other words, it will ask for a higher price-earnings ratio compared with the ratio for the other firm. The argument is analogous to valuation in the securities markets in which the present price is affected by potential future earnings.

In estimating the earnings potential of his firm, the financial manager prepares a projection which takes full account of impending product improvements, planned changes in the product mix, new markets and marketing programs, and prospective revenues and costs. The objective is to demonstrate and to substantiate with a reasonable degree of certainty, the extent to which the firm can anticipate a significant rise in its earnings in the absence of a merger. If this should be the case, the firm is in a position to argue for a higher ratio of value to current earnings.

Assume that a company that wishes to merge with our firm has offered to put a 12:1 ratio on our firm's current earnings of, e.g., $100,000 (i.e., to place a value of $1,200,000 on the stock of the firm). Suppose the financial manager of our firm can demonstrate a high probability that the earnings will increase to say, $150,000 in the next fiscal year and rise above that amount in the subsequent years. The management of our firm will then ask for the application of the 12:1 ratio to the prospective future profits as a basis for negotiating the merger.

The evaluation of prospective earnings is clearly a two-way avenue of bargaining. The other company, too, will make its own projection and argue its findings. Both parties to the merger thus evaluate their own prospects first and then weigh the respective probabilities. In the subsequent bargaining process over the respective earnings, potentials play a major role in arriving at the final exchange ratio of the shares.

6. Effect of Merger on Profit　Finally, each of the two companies assesses the probability of an increase in its earnings as a result of the merger. Assume that company A has projected for itself an increase in earnings from $100,000 (current) to $150,000 in each of the next two years without a merger. Company B shows a projected rise from $200,000 (current) to $250,000. Next, assume that Company B has available ample liquid funds which it is prepared to channel into Company A. These funds will enable Company A to expand its facilities substantially beyond the level that its present resources permit. As a result, its earnings as a direct consequence of the proposed merger are estimated to reach $250,000. An increase in profit for Company A as a result of the merger could also be the result of a superior research and development department in Company B, an already established network of distributors, or some other feature that Company A presently lacks.

A comparison of the three profit levels and ratios shows the picture in Table 20-2.

Suppose that Company B refuses to accept an exchange ratio less than 5 shares of A (B is the surviving corporation).

TABLE 20-2. Projected Profit As Result of Merger

	Company A	Company B
Common stock outstanding	100,000	100,000
Earning:		
Last fiscal year	$100,000	$200,000
Ratio of earnings	1 :	2
Ratio of share value	2 :	1
Projected earnings:		
Without merger	$150,000	$250,000
Ratio of earnings	3 :	5
Ratio of share value	5 :	3
Projected earnings:		
As a result of merger	$250,000	$250,000
Ratio of earnings	1 :	1
Ratio of share value	1 :	1

If A accepts this offer and the anticipated gains are realized the effect will be:

	Company A	Company B
Stocks outstanding (A's stock is held by B)		160,000
B's outstanding shares are distributed	60,000	100,000
Total earnings		$500,000
Share in Earnings	$\frac{3}{8}$	$\frac{5}{8}$
in Dollars	$187,500	$312,500

Thus, if A accepts the exchange ratio of 5:3, its share of earnings will be $187,500 or $37,500 more than in the absence of the merger. B's stockholders will have $312,500 or $62,500 more than otherwise. The bargaining area between the two companies lies, therefore, between 2:1 and 1:1. The ratio of 2:1 (two shares of A for 1 of B) reflects the use of current earnings only, while the ratio of 1:1 takes account only of the prospective gains from the merger.

It must be stressed, however, that earnings ratios value, while playing a major role, are not the only factors that determine the position of the two companies in the bargaining sessions. Personal factors often play an appreciable part in the attitudes of the parties; i.e., the holders of large blocks of shares in the two companies. These subjective motivations are essentially the same as those discussed earlier in this chapter.

IV. MERGER: THE NEGOTIATIONS

Like marriage, a merger is a major step in the life of the two companies. However, in a merger there is no divorce if the initial expectations fail to materialize, unless the courts force an annulment of the merger on the ground that it is in violation of the antitrust laws. Otherwise, once the merger has been consummated, there is only one group of stockholders who share the fruits or failures of the union. If the merged company turns out to be a liability and is subsequently "spun off" (i.e., sold or liquidated), its former shareholders have become part-owners of the surviving company and retain their pro rata position in the equity of the surviving firm.

The possible pitfalls of an irrevocable merger are known facts of life. The management and shareholders of the two companies are cognizant of the uncertainty that attends a merger. The decision to seek a merger and the subsequent consent to the terms constitute a major policy act. This section examines the nature and sequence of the several phases or steps through which a merger customarily evolves. The approach will be from the position of the company that is taking the initiative, i.e., actively seeking a merger. To avoid confusion, this company will be identified in the following discussion as the active firm and the other company as the receptive firm.

A. Setting the Stage

The active firm must first choose between a possible merger and other alternatives as a means of growth. In other words, the management of this firm can expand its present facilities by means of buying an existing plant, building, or leasing the desired facilities. Or if the plan calls for growth—i.e., entry into new fields of operation, adding new products, etc.—it can again select between a direct investment in such new facilities or enter into a lease agreement. In either one of these alternatives, the management has full control over the size, operations and policies of the addition to its present scope of facilities.

By contrast, if the management is considering a merger as an alternative course of action, it will have to accept (at least initially) the size, operations, and the established policies of the potential receptive firm. The active firm can, at best, hope to find a receptive firm which, in capacity and actual operation, falls within an acceptable range of the expansion program planned by the active firm. This is obviously less economical than constructing facilities that correspond to the planned expansion. On the other hand, if a receptive firm can be found, this disadvantage may be more than offset by the fact that the active firm may effect a considerable saving in time by acquiring an already existing operation. Furthermore, it may also save time and money that would otherwise have to be expended in the start-up of new facilities; and, in the case of a new product or new field of operation, it will save the costs of getting a foothold in the market. Last, but by no means least, the receptive firm may offer managerial talents that the active firm either does not have or which it cannot spare for the new program.

The real issue before the management is, therefore, to decide as a matter of fundamental policy whether to select a merger or one of the other alternatives. However, it should be noted that the selection of merger as the most desirable alternative does not prevent the company from chosing one of the other alternatives if it does not find a suitable merger deal.

1. Finding a Receptive Firm   Having reached the decision to explore the feasibility of a merger, the next step is to locate a receptive firm of acceptable size and performance record. To accomplish this objective, the firm can avail itself of several alternatives. It can turn the task over to a professional finder; i.e., a consulting firm, an accountant or lawyer who has acquired a reputation of success in this field. Or the firm can enlist the assistance of an investment banker or broker with extensive contacts in the industry in which the active firm is interested. Finally, members of management may assume the task of initiating direct exploratory talks with officers of presumably receptive firms.

The setting of a time limit on the finding of a receptive firm depends on the sense of urgency about expansion. Quite frequently, the active company will have a long-range program which envisages actual expansion several years in the future. In this case, merger is one of the several alternatives, none of which need be decided upon for some time to come. A merger, if the opportunity presents itself, does not require an advance commitment or a rejection of the other alternatives. It is, therefore, the most flexible course of action if time is not of the essence.

2. Exploration In Depth   Suppose that the efforts to find a receptive firm have been fruitful. In the initial meetings of the top officers of the two companies, the immediate objective is to establish whether or not the two firms are within a serious discussion range. That is, the active firm will make a basic price offer which lies below its tentative maximum, while the receptive firm will quote an asking price which is above its tentative minimum price. In arriving at these respective offer and asking prices, the management of each company has made a broad evaluation of the other firm and fixed a tentative value of its own shares in relation to those of the other company.

Assuming that the respective prices are within a range that appears negotiable, the two firms will then proceed with a mutual exploration in depth. Each firm prepares an extensive set of questions which are to be answered by the management of the other company. The objective of these questions is twofold. The answers provide data and information which are rarely made public by management. They enable the officers of the other company to make a realistic appraisal of the strengths and weaknesses of the firm; to ascertain the presence of legal obstacles to merger (e.g., pending lawsuits); to determine the feasibility of an effective integration of all or some operational phases of the two companies. Above all, the desired information is intended to provide a basis for a monetary evaluation of the visible and intangible assets of the other firm. It will provide the answer to the central question: Is the asking or offering price too high, too low, or reasonable?

Typical questions usually embrace the following areas:

Corporate-legal aspects of the firm
Management and Personnel
Accounting and Financial
Selling and Distribution
Research and Development
Manufacturing facilities and Operations.

Each of these subjects is divided into a series of specific questions. The Appendix to this chapter presents a questionnaire that is typical of the types of information usually requested.

Special stress is placed on the financial records and the prospective earning capacity of the questioned firm. The financial officer has a threefold task. He must determine whether or not the annual reports require specific explanations so as to reflect more accurately the performance of the company. For example, appreciation of property values is not shown in the financial statement but has a definite effect on the asset value of the firm. Substantial expenditures for the promotion of new products, sizeable start-up costs for a new plant, branch, or modernization of equipment tend to understate the real earning capacity of the company in the year in which they occurred. A liberal pension program, bonus payment to officers—which are tax deductible expenditures—also reduce the profit as shown in the income statement. In effect, therefore, the financial officer reconstructs the income statement as a new basis for the merger negotiations.

Next, the financial manager is required to prepare a projection of his firm's operations—product mix, income, expenditures, earnings—for the next three to five years. For this purpose, the financial manager utilizes the company's capital budget, projections of product line and sales by major product groups, cost estimates, and other internal data and estimates in making the required yearly projection for say, the next three years.

Finally, the financial manager also prepares for use by the top officer of his own firm an income statement for the past year or two which shows the earnings that his firm would have made if the merger had been consummated at that time. He will also do the same with the projected income statements. The objective of this hypothetical data is to demonstrate the economic value of the firm to the merger. That is, it points up the incremental earnings that can be attributed to the merger. This prospective incremental profit becomes an additional, and at times even major, factor in the bargaining over the exchange ratio of the shares of the two firms.

3. The Bargaining Sessions After analyzing the information provided by the other company as well as the internal evaluation by its own financial officer, each negotiating team prepares what it regards as a realistic maximum ratio (the asking firm) and minimum ratio (the receptive firm). These two sets of figures then become the range within which the negotiators will attempt to reach a compromise. In the initial session, neither firm is likely to state its final figure. Usually, the financial managers of the two companies submit their arguments in support of their respective documents which constitute the basis for the exchange ratios asked or offered.

The actual bargaining over the ratio is the responsibility of the top officer of the firm. He knows the limit that has been set by his board of directors. Assuming that the negotiators reach an agreement on the exchange ratio, its consummation requires the approval of the stockholders of the two companies.

If one or both firms are subject to supervisory authorities—e.g, banks, public utilities, air lines—the merger requires the approval of the appropriate government agency. A merger of two large business firms may be subject to scrutiny under the antitrust laws by the antitrust division of the Department of Justice or the Federal Trade Commission. In the case of the merger of Korvette and Spartan in 1966, the government required Spartan to divest itself of a number of retail outlets. Both companies were cognizant of the fact that failure to comply with this request would subsequently result in legal prosecution to prevent or undo the merger. Thus, while there is no *legal* obligation to obtain advance approval of the merger, it often is sound policy to solicit the views of the antitrust division before merging.

V. EVALUATING A SMALL COMPANY

If the receptive company is a small firm, the determination of its value raises a number of problems that are not present in the case of a large company.

Value of Assets

Undervaluation of fixed assets is found more frequently among small firms than among larger companies. One reason, previously mentioned, is the desire to minimize tax liabilities. The small firm, in which owners and managers are generally identical, will usually take the maximum allowable rate of depreciation. It is also not uncommon for a small firm to divert a part of its skilled labor to the construction of equipment and fixtures. While the cost of labor is charged to current operating expenditures, the equipment and fixtures are not credited to the fixed capital account. It must also be noted that small companies will at times overstate the value of their fixed assets in the expectation of obtaining larger term loans on the basis of the apparently greater net worth of the firm.

Inventory is another asset that is frequently undervalued by a small firm. As in the case of depreciation, the objective is to minimize the tax liability of the company. Similarly, the reserve for bad debts is likely to be rather liberal for the purpose of reducing the taxable income of the business.

Expenditures

Since the owners and officers of a small company are usually identical, the officers' salaries and expense allowances tend to be higher relative to those in larger corporations. The officers need not worry about an adverse reaction from the stockholders since the officers own the stock of the firm. The reverse is also not unusual. In order to show a very favorable operating statement, as a basis for larger credits from banks and suppliers, the officers of a small firm may deliberately fix their compensation and allowances at a substantially lower figure than they would obtain as *bona fide* employees of another company.

Absence of a Reliable Market Price

The common stock of a small firm is generally either not traded or it is traded in the over-the-counter market. In the former case, there is no market price that could be used as one of the yardsticks for a comparison of the value of the shares of the small company with the shares of the larger corporation whose shares are traded on one of the organized security exchanges.

The situation is only moderately better if the shares of the small firm are traded over the counter. The latter is essentially a noncontinuous market. The sporadic, noncontinuous nature of this market lends itself to manipulation of prices. In consequence, the prices of many issues traded there are highly volatile. An offering of a relatively large block of shares in a given company frequently leads to a substantial drop in the price of the stock. Conversely, the price of a particular stock tends to go up sharply even with a relatively moderate increase in the demand. The management of the active company is therefore not likely to attach much importance to the over-the-counter price as a measure of the value of the receptive firm.

Arriving at a Value

In determining the value of the small firm, the financial officer must take the following steps. First, he should examine closely the financial statements with a view to possible overvaluation or undervaluation of assets. Next, he should similarly scrutinize the salaries and expense allowances of the officers. The most difficult task is the evaluation of the projected earnings. By its very nature, the small company generally operates in a highly competitive industry. This factor introduces a high degree of uncertainty into its projection of sales and profits. The central issue then becomes: What profit will the small company be able to realize if it is merged with the larger company? While the management of the small firm will argue for a high potential, the large company will stress that, if this is the case, the small firm cannot capitalize on the large company's role in this potential profit. The difference between the reconstructed past performance record of the small company and its projected earnings then becomes the important bargaining area between the top officers of the two companies. After this issue has been resolved, the bargaining shifts to the question of the appropriate rate of capitalization of the mutually accepted profit projection. The small firm will argue for a price/projected profit ratio that corresponds to the price/earnings ratio of the larger company. In turn, the larger company will point to its size and competitive strength as the major factor in the P/E ratio and therefore offer a smaller P/E ratio for the small firm. The final outcome of these bargaining sessions depends on the relative strength of desire to merge on the part of the two companies.

SUMMARY

The financial manager is primarily interested in the going concern value of a firm for planning purposes. In order to arrive at a going concern value, both the physical assets (and liabilities) and the invisible assets of a firm must be valued.

The firm has different values based on different needs. Liquidation value, loan value, investment value, and merger value are all likely to be different.

The financial manager must be prepared to evaluate in detail the advantages and disadvantages of merger proposals. The economic motivation for a merger is a function of the overall policy of the firm. This policy can be oriented in one of two basic directions: expansion, or growth. Expansion implies an increase in the size of the firm by means of a merger with another company engaged in the same line. Growth, on the other hand, involves some change in the field of operations of the two merging firms. The major reasons for merger include economic objectives—reducing cyclical volatility, reducing seasonal fluctuations, filling the product line, acquiring an adequate research and development staff, entering a glamour field, gaining economies of scale, and tax reasons; and personal objectives—estate planning, prestige, and empire building.

Valuation for a merger may again be made by different methods, e.g., book value, appraisal value, market price of stock, capitalization of earnings, or respective earnings potential.

The active firm must first choose between a possible merger and other alternatives as a means of growth. Having reached the decision to explore the feasibility of a merger, the next step is to find a prospective firm. Once a firm has been found, the possibilities of merger will be explored in depth by the top management of the two firms. Detailed bargaining sessions will be held at which the two negotiating teams bargain over terms. If all goes well and government agencies do not object to the merger, it can be consummated by approval of the boards of directors and the stockholders of each company.

APPENDIX A   QUESTIONS ASKED IN MERGER NEGOTIATIONS

CORPORATE

1. Describe the present legal form of the organization and the legal forms through which it has passed.
2. Describe the classes of stock outstanding.
3. Describe the principal rights and restrictions imposed on management by the outstanding common stock, preferred stock, long- or short-term debt. Describe any outstanding option agreements, warrants, rights, etc.
4. Describe any restrictions on retained earnings.
5. Describe any restrictions in effect on cash use or payment of dividends as a result of debt or other agreements.
6. Describe ownership in subsidiary companies and method of recording income of such companies.
7. Furnish copy of the agreement with Mr. . . . . (the patent owner).
8. What obligations or contracts exist between the company and other persons or companies?

MANAGEMENT AND PERSONNEL

1. Detail the organizational relationship of the officers and key employees. Furnish an organization chart if available.
2. What are the backgrounds of the owners and other key people in the management? (Age, positions held, portion of time devoted to business, other experience and background.)
3. List each of the following for the owners and executives for the preceding five years: salary, bonus/profit-sharing, pension fund contribution, insur-

ance paid, stock options, other current compensation, and other deferred compensation.

4. What obligations exist for the key people in managment and other members of the company?

5. Details and, if practical, copies of compensation plans, management contracts, etc.

6. List any other companies doing business with the subject company in which the management and/or owners have a financial interest, but which are not being acquired.

7. What are the provisions of fringe benefit plans such as medical, retirement, insurance, profit sharing, bonus, vacation, etc., and what are the extent of vested rights in these by any owners or employees?

8. Give number of employees in following groups:
   (a) Officers
   (b) Supervisors
   (c) Other exempt personnel
   (d) Production, skilled and unskilled
   (e) Office and sales employees
   (f) Other

9. What is the total annual payroll?

ACCOUNTING AND FINANCIAL

1. Furnish audited profit and loss statements and balance sheets for each year since the company's beginning. Explain any significant variations in incomes or expenses in past three years.

2. Furnish unaudited interim statements for current year.

3. List any marketable securities and the basis of recording them on the books together with present market values.

4. Furnish most recent aged accounts receivable schedule.

5. Furnish a schedule of individual accounts with a balance exceeding 10% of total receivables.

6. Furnish a schedule of receivables from other than normal trade accounts, such as United States Government, officers, employees, etc.

7. Schedule inventories by type, including items on consignment.

8. Schedule fixed assets by type, indicating original cost or other basis and amount and rates of accumulated depreciation. Indicate whether there are idle or excess assets held and in what amounts.

9. Attach details of any current appraisals or estimates of value of fixed assets and indicate whether the appraisal was for insurance or other purposes.

10. Indicate whether tax basis and book basis of capital assets are identical. If not, schedule major differences.

11. Schedule investments (if any) showing the basis for book amounts and the current market values or underlying equities.

12. Indicate whether company has any intangible or other assets that are not shown in the accounts.

13. Schedule for any unconsolidated subsidiaries the excess of underlying assets and the unrecorded income for the last five years. Indicate clearly the source from which such data are compiled.

14. Record any advances and payables to affiliated companies or unconsolidated subsidiaries.

15. Attach schedule of major items deferred to subsequent periods and the method of write-off or amortization.

16. Schedule major current liabilities being sure to indicate whether company accrues for profit-sharing bonuses, vacations, dismissal indemnities, and pension costs.

17. Show the following information by type of loan: amount, interest rates, due date, liens on assets, advance-payment privileges and penalties, and renewal privileges.

18. Indicate mortgages and other liens.

19. List any major outstanding commitments, particularly in relation to fixed asset purchases; inventory purchases; advertising campaigns; long-term sales agreements to sell civilian products, military products, and guarantees of work or products.

20. Are any contingent liabilities outstanding—particularly lawsuits, and third party endorsements on behalf of customers, officers and employees, affiliates, etc.?

21. Indicate which years are still open for federal and major state taxes.

22. Evaluate the effect of any prior adjustments on the unexamined years and indicate any major items that are apt to be disputed.

23. Schedule major differences between tax and book income for last five years to determine if book income is reasonable and if any unrecorded future tax liabilities exist.

24. Schedule items of significance that have been disallowed in revenue agents' review of prior years' tax returns.

SELLING AND DISTRIBUTION

1. Describe organization of the marketing function and responsibilities of each level.
2. Number of salesmen in the company's three branch offices—supervision—does the branch report directly to the home office or through a regional manager?
3. Net sales in each branch (dollars and units)—identify units by models.
4. Average earnings of salesmen and managers—compensation plan.
5. Cost of distribution and profitability of branch operations compared with dealers.
6. Terms—cash, lease, deferred contract.
7. When was the most recent new model or models introduced? How long has the oldest model in the line been actively sold?
8. What is the detail of any agreements which exist with the dealers, including discounts allowed, responsibilities of both parties, guarantees, advertising, etc.?
9. List of all dealers, territories covered, and number of men who sell products full time and number who sell products part time.
10. Which of them sell other products in addition to your company's products, and what is your assessment of the effectiveness of each dealer.
11. Sales by each model for last five years, domestic and foreign.
12. Furnish prices and costs for each principal model for last five years and profit and loss estimates by product if such are available.
13. What is the estimate of the total annual dollar retail sales volume and your company's share of it for the last five years?
14. Breakdown of domestic sales between Federal Government and other for past five years.
15. What is the advertising budget, media used, and experience in terms of traceable leads?
16. What amount in dollars and type of advertising has been done for each of last five years? What sales training is given to field salesmen? Can we see movie that has been advertised?
17. Who directs service and to what extent is it important in a product of this kind?
18. Describe the service organization in branches and what service is rendered to or for dealers. Is service profitable?
19. What has been the service trouble history of each principal model?

RESEARCH AND DEVELOPMENT

1. What amount has been spent for each of the last five years for research and/or development on new products?
2. What is size of research and development group? What technical qualification do the members of this group have?
3. What are the patents, patent applications, patent rights, or licenses which are held by company; what are the terms and when do they expire?

MANUFACTURING

1. Data for major facilities:
   (a) Locations, tax rates, insurance coverage
   (b) Products manufactured
   (c) Production in recent years
   (d) Dates of construction or purchase of major items of plant and equipment
   (e) Depreciation rates and accumulated reserves
2. How much space is currently used for production and shipping? How much is available? What proportion of work is subcontracted? What type of work is this?
3. Indicate any problems likely to occur in expansion of facilities; availability or condition of land, zoning, adequate streets, sidings, etc., employee parking facilities, etc.
4. Machinery and equipment—list by type, with cost, age, depreciation value, manufacturer.
5. If facilities (land, buildings, equipment) are leased, detail terms of applicable leases.
6. Describe all foreign (including Canada) manufacturing and sales operations and/or agreements, including financial statements for last five years.

Questions

1. What are the principal economic motivations for a merger?
2. How does a horizontal merger differ from a vertical merger?
3. What are the major defects of using book value for purposes of valuation?

4. What are the advantages and disadvantages of using the market price of stock as the basis of valuation?

5. How does a financial manager evaluate the respective earnings potential of two companies which are planning a merger?

6. What are the pros and cons of a possible merger as a method of corporate growth?

7. What adjustments, if any, would you make in net income after taxes, for purposes of valuation as a result of the following events in a large appliance company:
   (a) The company sold an old plant last year at a profit.
   (b) The company wrote off against income $30,000 of obsolete inventory as a result of introduction of a new product line of television sets.
   (c) An unusually wet Spring caused $40,000 of flood damage.
   (d) The company lost use of a major trademark, as a result of litigation.

8. What value may a company have for merger purposes if it has lost money each year for five years and shows little prospect of improvement?

Problems

1. Compare the latest price earnings ratio, dividend yield, book value, and common stock price of General Motors with Chrysler Corporation. Why do the two stocks sell at different levels of market value?

2. The Swift Action Corporation earned $5 million last year, after taxes. It has one million common shares outstanding. The stock is selling at eight times earnings. Dividends are $1.50 per share per year.
   (a) What is the market price of Swift Action stock?
   (b) What is the price/dividend ratio?
   (c) If Swift Action's industry attracted more attention and stocks in the industry began to sell at twelve times earnings, what would be the likely price per share of Swift Action stock?

3. The Thaxton Saxophone Company has sales of $1,500,000 per year. Most musical instrument firms earn, on the average, about 7% on sales after payment of taxes. Conglomorate Industries Incorporated expects to earn at least 15% after taxes on its investments.
   (a) What is the maximum amount Conglomorate should pay to purchase Thaxton on the basis of the above information?
   (b) The financial manager of Conglomerate has just learned that Thaxton has marketable securities not needed in the business with

a market value of $100,000 and a cost value of $65,000. Capital gains taxes can be assumed to be 25 percent. How much more, if any, should Conglomerate be willing to pay for Thaxton?

4. Acme Blackboard Company is considering merging with Central Slate Works. Data on the two companies is as follows:

	Acme Blackboard	Central Slate
Number of common shares outstanding:	125,000	50,000
Earnings, last fiscal year:	$250,000	$75,000

If Acme acquires Central, Acme will purchase all its slate from central at prevailing market prices. This should increase Central's earnings next year to $110,000.

(a) What is the maximum exchange ratio Acme should agree to?

(b) What is the minimum exchange ratio that Central can expect Acme to offer?

Case: PALATKA APPLIANCE CORPORATION

Palatka Appliance Corporation has been a wholesale distributor and service agency for a major manufacturer's white goods appliances in the greater Washington-Baltimore metropolitan area since 1938. In 1967, the corporation acquired 100% of the outstanding capital stock of a Richmond, Virginia appliance distributor. The investment in the subsidiary is carried at cost. The net worth of the subsidiary on June 30, 1966 was $8322. On that date, the subsidiary was indebted to the parent corporation for $83,080, excluding the original investment.

Annual sales volume over recent years has shown good increases. Small losses were incurred in fiscal 1960 and 1962. Operations have been profitable in the last four years. Exhibits 20-1 and 20-2 present financial data for the corporation in recent years.

In July, 1966, Mr. John Palatka, founder and president of the firm, died from a sudden heart attack. The corporation was beneficiary of a $120,000 life insurance policy on Mr. Palatka. Mr. Roger Grayson, executive vice president, was chosen to succeed Mr. Palatka as president of the firm. Upon Mr. Palatka's death, his stock passed to his widow. Mrs. Palatka, now the owner of 20% of the common stock of the corporation, is the largest single stockholder. Most of the remaining common stock is held by employees of the company. The stock has a par value of $1 per share.

Exhibit 20-1. Palatka Appliance Corporation; Comparative Financial Statements (Dollars)

	June 30, 1964	June 30, 1965	June 30, 1966
Assets:			
Cash	15,177	20,015	17,942
Accounts receivable	295,081	342,498	508,448
Inventory	377,752	620,988	615,568
Other current assets	—	5,347	11,661
Total current assets	688,010	988,848	1,153,619
Fixed assets	82,715	76,127	89,470
Prepaid-Def.	4,018	5,680	13,923
Investments and advances to subsidiary	34,663	71,880	96,370
Other assets	(pp) 32,487ᵃ	(pp) 41,647	(pp) 33,369
Total assets	841,893	1,184,182	1,386,751
Liabilities and equity:			
Due bonds	150,000	200,000	212,500
Notes payable	(S) 13,980ᵃ	(S) 20,501	(S) 20,501
Accounts payable	190,908	389,471	512,600
Accrued liabilities	34,432	65,510	39,876
Federal income taxes	7,464	34,370	48,840
Long-term liabilities	16,702	21,739	33,156
Other current liabilities	1,687	1,687	—
Total liabilities	415,173	733,278	867,473
Preferred stock (6%)	45,800	49,800	50,550
Common stockᵇ	349,124	372,177	421,805
Earned surplus	31,796	28,927	46,923
Total liabilities and equity	841,893	1,184,182	1,386,751

ᵃ (pp) partially pledged to secure (S). Accounts receivable less reserves of $10,000. Inventories valued at lower of cost or market. Fixed assets (June 30, 1966) shown net less reserves for depreciation of $73,240.
ᵇ Par value, $1 per share.

The stock has no public market and is traded very infrequently. It is generally traded with the help of the officers of the corporation. The latest trade, for 12,500 shares, took place in March, 1966, upon the resignation of the assistant sales manager, who left to become sales manager of a similar firm in another city. An employee of the corporation purchased these shares at a price of 55 cents per share.

EXHIBIT 20-2.   Palatka Appliance Corporation; Income Statement (Dollars)

	For the Years Ended		
	June 30 1964	June 30 1965	June 30 1966
Sales	2,928,621	3,635,043	4,589,381
Cost of goods sold	2,277,686	2,835,831	3,622,461
Gross profit	650,935	799,212	966,920
Expenses	605,964	705,313	835,666
Net income on sales	44,971	93,899	131,254
Other income	10,851	14,058	17,024
Total operating income	55,922	107,957	148,278
Less other expenses	34,876	34,217	45,814
Net income before taxes	21,046	73,740	102,464
Less federal income taxes	7,566	29,023	48,841
Net income after taxes	13,480	44,717	53,623

Mrs. Palatka has not been active in the business. She would like to sell her shares back to the corporation. The management is willing to use the life insurance proceeds for this purpose. This is why the corporation took out the life insurance on Mr. Palatka in the first place. Mrs. Palatka's attorney believes she is entitled to receive the book value of her shares, since there is no active market in the shares of the corporation.

Management wishes to be fair, especially since this case will set a precedent for future repurchases in the event of the death of other officers who are insured by the corporation. Management also knows that Mrs. Palatka is not required to accept their offer. Management, however, does not want to give Mrs. Palatka any more than what is fairly due her, as this will not be in the interest of the other shareholders of the corporation.

Case Questions:

1. What should management offer Mrs. Palatka for her shares? (State your price on a per share basis.) Why?
2. As an independent appraiser of the corporation, would your price per share be different? Why?
3. As Mrs. Palatka, what factors would you consider in deciding whether or not to accept the company's offer to purchase your stock?

~~~~~~

Chapter Twenty-One

The Impact of Inflation on Financial Policies

Economic theory postulates the proposition that the price level *tends* to go up in a period of expanding economic activity—i.e., during the prosperity phase of the business cycle—and *tends* to decline in the period of recession. This conclusion is based on the explicit assumptions that the market is governed by a reasonably flexible price mechanism; i.e., the absence of "sticky" or rigid prices for most goods and services. Economic theory recognizes the fact that the public authorities can inject into the market a stream of inflationary purchasing power, by means of deficit spending, which either accentuates the upward movement of prices in a period of expansion or neutralizes the downward tendency in a period of economic contraction. For the purposes of the financial manager, we shall assume that inflation refers to a situation in which the price level is influenced in large measure by the injection of purchasing power via deficit spending, although there are other types of inflation. We shall examine in this chapter the impact of inflation on the financial decisions of the firm.

The Record   Chart 21-1 shows the movement of the consumer price index and of wholesale prices in the years 1948 to 1966 and the several periods of recession during this period. Each shaded area in the chart represents the beginning and the end of a recession. The letter *P* indicates the peak of the prosperity phase and *T* indicates the trough of the cycle.

In the period 1948 to 1966, the American economy experienced four relatively short recessions, ranging from 13 months (1953 to 1954) to 9 months (1960 to 1961). In the first of the four recessions, both consumer and wholesale prices showed a decline, with wholesale prices dropping appreciably more than consumer prices. In the next three reces-

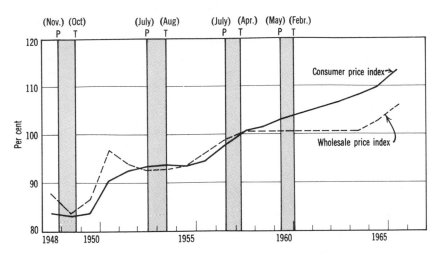

Chart 21-1. Consumer and wholesale price indexes and cyclical recessions, 1948–1966 (1957–1959 = 100).

sion periods, wholesale prices remained fairly stable. Consumer prices were also stable in the 1953–1954 recession but continued to climb in the recessions of 1957–1958 and 1960–1961.

Although both indices show an upward trend over the twenty-year period, it should be noted that there was a significant variance in the wholesale index; i.e., nondurable versus durable goods. Between 1950 and 1964, the wholesale index of durable goods went from 75.9 to 101 or a rise of about one-third. During the same interval, the wholesale price level of nondurable goods increased from 94.9 to 99.1 or a rise of less than 5%. The importance of this variance lies in the fact that the fixed assets of a business firm consist of durable goods. Thus, inflation tends to have a significant impact on the value of a firm's fixed assets over a period of years.

"Built-In" Inflation   Many economists and financial analysts are of the opinion that an inflationary momentum, although at a relatively low annual rate of perhaps 1 or 2%, is a "built-in" feature of our economy which has a long-run tendency to grow. Two factors are regarded as the major force behind the inflationary trend. One is the tendency of the wage structure to move up with the growth in the national output. In the case of goods-producing labor, one can argue, with considerable justification, that the wage increase is equalled or exceeded by rising productivity of labor as a result of advancing technology. The same argument does not apply to the nongoods-producing sectors of our economy (e.g., services, public employees, etc). In these instances, increases in wages and salaries to match those of say, manufacturing industries, tend to have an inflationary effect.

The other factor is the accepted public policy of full employment. Such a policy—desirable as it may be both socially and politically—tends to treat deficit spending as far the lesser of two evils. The other evil being unemployment-recession-political unrest.

To the financial manager, inflation poses two sets of problems. First, do the financial statements, as prepared by the accountant, reflect the real position of the firm? If not, what adjustments should be made in both the interpretation of the statements and company policy? Second, if top management shares the view that the inflationary trend of the past 20 years will continue in the future, what effect will this have on the long-range financial plans of the company?

Historical versus Real Cost   The financial statements prepared by the accountant are invariably expressed in terms of *current* dollars. In his evaluation of fixed assets, the accountant uses as a base the historical cost; i.e., the price paid at the time of purchase. His treatment of depreciation is related directly to the original cost of which a given percentage is written off each year and a corresponding depreciation reserve is set up. At the end of the estimated usable lifetime of the asset, the original investment is expected to have been recovered in the "reserve for depreciation" which at that time, hopefully, will equal the original cost.

This approach ignores completely the loss of purchasing power that may have occurred in the intervening years. On the assumption that "dollar equals dollar," the books are "in balance" although the fully recovered dollar costs may be totally inadequate to replace the used-up asset.

In contrast with the accountant, the economist is primarily concerned with the value of the assets and their financial treatment in terms of constant dollars or the real value of money. Viewed from this perspective, the owners or stockholders have invested a given quantity of purchasing power in the firm. This purchasing power translated into fixed and other assets created a given capacity to produce goods. If, at some future date, the same sum of money will only purchase half of the original capacity, the owners have lost one-half of their purchasing power invested in the original assets.

Many business executives agree with the economist that one of the primary tasks of top management is to preserve the productive capacity

of the firm without diluting the ownership. This is inevitably the case
if the firm must raise additional equity capital to make up the loss
in purchasing power of the depreciation reserve. True, the company
may have accumulated enough profits to make up the deficit in purchasing power of the depreciation reserve. But in this instance, the stockholders have been misled in believing that the firm had been as profitable
as the financial statements appeared to indicate.

At this point, it should be noted that in a number of foreign countries—notably Sweden, France, the Netherlands, West Germany, and
Italy—accountants and business executives have developed various techniques designed to value assets in terms of constant rather than nominal
money units. Some governments have established by law elaborate
methods of revaluing fixed assets for tax purposes and reporting to stockholders.

As far as *published* income statements and balance sheets are concerned, it would appear that literally only a handful of corporations
present price level adjustments in their annual reports.[1] Only five corporations were found to pursue this practice in 1962. However, a substantial number of corporations make such adjustments for internal managerial policies. A study by the National Association of Accountants,
published in 1958, showed that "approximately one-third of the companies participating in this study restate depreciation charges in terms
of the current level [rather than original or historical cost] and use this
information for various managerial purposes."[2]

Areas of Managerial Concern   For purposes of policy decisions,
top management is concerned with the impact of inflation on the following areas:

    I. Short run (income statement)
       A. Inventory
       B. Depreciation
       C. Distribution of earnings (pay-out ratio)
       D. Excess cash
    II. Long run (balance sheet)
       A. Inventory
       B. Plants and equipment

[1] "Inflation and Corporate Accounting," National Industrial Conference Board,
Studies in Business Policy, No. 104, p. 9, (1962).
[2] Research Report No. 33, "Current Practice in Accounting for Depreciation,"
National Association of Accountants.

III. External long-run problems
   A. Debt capital versus equity capital
   B. Sale of assets
   C. Mergers and consolidation

I. THE INCOME STATEMENT

The primary yardstick by which the success of a firm is judged is its record of earnings. This record is reflected in the income statement. To the extent to which inflation affects one or several items in the income statement, the earnings, as shown by the accountant, is not an accurate record of the real earnings in terms of economic values.

A. Inventory

In Chapter Six it was pointed out that the LIFO (last-in-first-out) method of inventory valuation was designed to neutralize some of the effects of inflation on the cost of goods sold. The use of LIFO has been for a number of years a generally accepted accounting procedure and has been allowed for income tax purposes.

But how about that portion of the annual input that was (hypothetically) purchased "first" and at the end of the fiscal year constitutes the "closing inventory?" Under the LIFO method this asset will be recorded and shown in the balance sheet at an *assumed* cost which was the cost of the input in the first operating cycle of the firm. Let us assume for the sake of simplicity, that a firm has four operating cycles of three months each and that its records show the picture of costs and sales in Table 21-1.

TABLE 21-1.

Oper-ating Cycle	Output (in Units)	Input Cost[a] Per Unit ($)	Input Cost[a] Total ($)	Sales Unit Price[b]	Sales Number Sold	Total Revenues ($)
First	100,000	2.00	200,000	3.00	75,000	225,000
Second	175,000	2.10	367,000	3.15	150,000	472,500
Third	150,000	2.10	315,000	3.15	150,000	472,500
Fourth	200,000	2.30	460,000	3.45	150,000	517,500
	625,000				525,000	1,687,500

[a] Only direct labor and materials.
[b] Includes 50% markup for all other costs plus profit.

Under the LIFO method the annual calculation would be:

Produced   625,000 units
Sold   525,000 units
Total revenues from sales $1,687,500
Cost of goods sold (the "last" 525,000 units)
   (Operating cycles 2, 3, 4)   1,142,500
Gross profit $ 545,000

The unsold 100,000 units will then be allocated to "inventory" in the balance sheet at a value of $200,000. Yet a look at the input cost in the fourth operating cycle shows, at that time, an input cost per unit of $2.30 or a current value of $230,000; or $30,000 more than the balance sheet indicates.

From the viewpoint of the accountant who records only historical facts—i.e., from the opening to the closing date of the latest fiscal year—the unsold inventory cost only $200,000. Whether or not the cost will be the same, more, or less in the first operating cycle of the next fiscal year, the sales price thus being $3 (first cycle in last year) or $3.45 (last cycle), is immaterial as far as historical cost and values are concerned.

The financial manager, like top management, is as much if not more concerned with the future as with the past. Looking ahead at say, the first operating cycle of the next fiscal year, the management of the firm believes that costs as well as selling price will not be less than at the end of the last fiscal year. Viewed from this perspective, the 100,000 units in the inventory are "worth" $230,000 and are expected to yield revenues of at least $345,000. Assuming that the current market price of this particular item is "firm" and that there appears no reason to assume a softening in the next operating cycle, the firm will have little trouble in obtaining a loan secured by this inventory from a finance company, factor, or even bank which will be based on a valuation of $230,000 rather than $200,000.

The lender who is willing to make a loan secured by inventory is primarily concerned with the current value of the inventory and its prospective selling price. In fact, the assumption under LIFO that the 100,000 units in the closing inventory were produced in the first operating cycle is not only arbitrary but totally unrealistic. Thus, the sanction of the LIFO method by the tax authorities represents nothing more than a technical (artificial) formula which permits a firm to bring its nominal profit in current dollars closer to its real profit in constant dollars.

If, however, the firm experienced a decrease in its input cost and selling price as a result of deflation in its particular market, the situation will be reversed. Since a firm, once having adopted the LIFO method for tax purposes, must continue to use this method, its profit will be overstated in a period of declining prices. Similarly, the loan value of its closing inventory will be determined by the (lower) current market price rather than by the (higher) price in the early phase of the fiscal year.

B. Depreciation

This item in the income statement is the one most seriously affected by inflation. As pointed out earlier in this chapter, a depreciation reserve based on original cost may restore at the end of the estimated lifetime of the assets the dollar amount invested in the asset; but this dollar amount will not suffice to replace the asset if inflation has raised the replacement cost appreciably.

For internal managerial purposes, the management of the firm must first decide whether it wants to recover the dollar amount or the purchasing power of the original investment in the fixed asset(s). Conceivably, top management may conclude that the dollar figure is adequate because the company financed the purchase of the asset with debt capital only. In this instance, the firm has a fixed dollar obligation that will be met when the depreciation reserve reaches the dollar amount of the debt. If the asset is then replaced by a new asset costing say, 50% more, the company will simply procure new debt capital of a proportionately larger magnitude.

Under the rules of the Internal Revenue Service, a tax deductible depreciation reserve or allowance is allowed only to the extent to which it is based on original cost. The SEC rules provide that the reporting companies must adhere to accepted accounting procedures. The latter, however, do not at present accept replacement cost as a basis for the depreciation reserve or allowance.

However, the management that wants to show, in the balance sheet, depreciation in terms of real purchasing power rather than nominal dollars can solve the problem, at least partially, by setting up a special reserve out of profit. This alternative was suggested in 1952[3] by the Institute of Chartered Accountants in England and Wales:

[3] "Accounting in Relation to Changes in Purchasing Power of Money," *Recommendations on Accounting Principles*, No. 15, The Institute of Chartered Accountants in England and Wales; London, 1952.

"Unless and until a practicable and generally acceptable alternative is available, the council recommends that the accounting principles set out below should continue to be applied:

"(a) Historical cost should continue to be the basis on which annual accounts should be prepared and, in consequence, the basis on which profits shown by such accounts are computed . . .

"Setting amounts aside from profits to reserve in recognition of the effects which changes in the purchasing power of money have had upon the affairs of the business, particularly their effect on the amount of profit which, as a matter of policy, can prudently be regarded as available for distribution."

It must be emphasized that the amount allocated to this special reserve would not be a tax deductible item. It would, therefore, reduce the after-tax profit by a corresponding amount.

On the other hand, top management may decide even in such a situation that the company should use current replacement cost rather than original cost in the annual determination of the depreciation reserve or allowance. Those in favor of using replacement cost argue that the cost, and therefore the selling price, of the product should include full allowance for the real or economic value of the contribution of the fixed asset. The original cost of the asset then becomes irrelevant. If the company acquired the asset(s) at a price that is significantly below the present value of the asset, this differential should accrue to the owners of the firm. The criterion in this case is the same as calculating the selling price of goods on the basis of current cost of labor and materials rather than the lower prices at which labor and material may have been purchased in an earlier operating cycle. In other words, management may decide (for its own purposes) that the principle of the LIFO method should be applied to fixed assets as much as to the goods sold and the closing inventory. In such application, the depreciation policy would be based on the contribution of the fixed assets without regard to the source of funds; e.g., debt capital or equity capital. This treatment would be more consistent with modern capital budgeting theory than the treatment of fixed assets as a special case.

C. Profit

In order for management to obtain an adequate picture of what is really happening in the business, profits must be measured in real dollars rather than nominal dollars. A simple example will illustrate this problem. Suppose the income statement for the latest fiscal year shows an increase in profits from, e.g., $600,000 to $650,000 over the preceding year. How real is this gain of $50,000? The answer depends on (a) the relative sales in the two years and (b) the extent of inflation as measured by the rise in prices. Assume that dollar sales in the latest fiscal year ($11,000,000) were 10% over the preceding year and that the average unit price of the firm's products had increased by 12%, partly as a result of a 10% rise in labor cost and partly as a result of increased material prices, higher local taxes, etc. In this instance, it is evident that the volume of units sold was smaller than in the preceding year; i.e., 99.2 percent. At the same time, the rate of profit—measured by profit per dollar of sales—has decreased from 6¢ per dollar to slightly less than 6¢ per dollar of sales. It is clear in this example that the firm's actual profit performance is overstated by conventional accounting methods.

If management has decided to adopt replacement cost as a basis for its depreciation policy a second problem arises. In this case, management must decide upon an allocation to a special reserve for depreciation (due to inflation). This reserve is taken out of the after-tax profit and the residue is then divided between dividends and retained earnings in the normal manner. Such a reserve dramatizes for management (and the stockholders) the effect of inflation on real profits.

1. A Case Study   In its Research Report, the Conference Board[4] cites the following case. The Reece Corporation, a Massachusetts company, is a manufacturer of special-purpose sewing machines. In 1960, its sales and rental income exceeded $7 million. It had about 1200 shareholders.

The management of this medium-size company had been concerned over the impact of continuing inflation on the adequacy of its depreciation reserve and the failure of the traditional financial statements to reflect the loss of purchasing power of the dollar. Moreover, the management also desired that:

". . . it is important to make the stockholder aware of the true growth, or lack thereof, of the company over the years and to show him why it is necessary to plow back into the business a large portion of the stated earnings.

"Obviously, the publication of price level figures is an educational effort to demonstrate the need for sound economic policy. With only 1,200 stock-

---

[4] Supra, p. 831.

holders, we make a very small splash in a large pond, but we do mail our reports to a number of business schools, professors of economics, accounting firms, members of Congress, and other manufacturing firms."

In determining the effects of inflation, the company applied the Consumer Price Index of the Bureau of Labor Statistics to the individual account balances; i.e., each fixed asset was restated by year of acquisition in constant dollars and similarly the accumulated reserve for depreciation. The adjusted figures were then shown in a separate section of the annual report under the heading "Price Level Study." Thus, the individual stockholder as well as the financial analyst and potential investor was furnished the financial statements prepared in conventional form and another set showing the effects of inflation on the major items in the statements. A series of charts provided also a visual picture of the company's performance measured in current dollars and in constant dollars, as shown in Charts 21-2 and 21-3.

2. Excess Cash   The loss of purchasing power in this situation is clear. This loss may be offset or partly mitigated if the excess funds are invested and produce an income in the form of interest earned. If the rate of interest exceeded the rise in the price level, the firm realized a gain equivalent to the excess. On the other hand, a rise in the price level greater than the rate of interest earned results in a net loss of purchasing power.

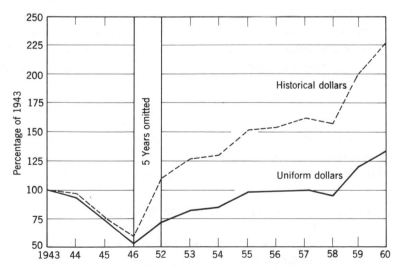

Chart 21-2. Sales volume of Reece Company expressed in uniform and historical dollars.

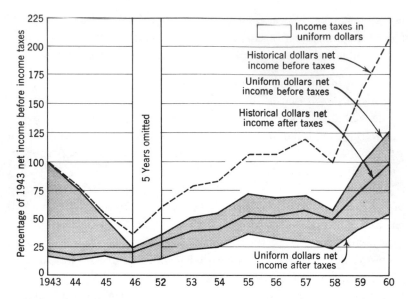

Chart 21-3. Effect of inflation on selected items of financial statement of Reece Company.

The loss of purchasing power of excess cash is of particular concern to management if the company sells debt securities with the intention of subsequently investing the proceeds in fixed assets. Suppose there is a substantial time interval between the receipt of the proceeds from the sale of the securities. It is quite likely that the actual cost of the asset (special machines) or construction of the plant may then be well in excess of the estimates at the time when the securities were offered for sale. The cash plus the earned interest would, in such a situation, be insufficient to provide the anticipated portion of the total cost of the project. The company may then find it necessary to make up the deficiency by diverting the required amount from its liquid equity fund (i.e., net working capital). Or it may sell additional equity securities to make up the difference. In either event, the stockholders bear at least initially the adverse impact of inflation on the excess cash funds.

II. LONG-RUN EFFECTS (BALANCE SHEET)

The discrepancy between nominal and real values becomes progressively greater if inflation continues over a period of years. An advance in the price level of 1 or 2% in the course of a single year is of relatively little significance. However, if the upward trend is sustained over a period of 10, 15, or more years, the discrepancy assumes major proportions.

A. Inventory

The use of the LIFO method over a period of years has the effect of constantly widening the gulf between the book value and the actual value of the inventory. Let us return to the example previously used (p. 608). It will be recalled that the firm had at the end of the fiscal year, a closing inventory of 100,000 units which was valued at $200,000; i.e., the cost in the first operating cycle. Now the "closing inventory" of the last year becomes automatically the "opening inventory" of the next fiscal year. For the sake of simplicity, let us assume that next year cost and prices go up again with the results shown in Table 21-2.

To minimize its taxable profit, the firm will again use the LIFO method. As a matter of fact, the regulations do not permit an arbitrary shift from LIFO to FIFO and back again. Under the LIFO method, the balance sheet will show an inventory valued at $200,000. By this time, current costs are $260,000 and the excess over the first operating cycle in the preceding year is now $60,000. As long as the firm continues to produce the same item—even if there are changes in design—and as long as inflation continues, the balance sheet will show a progressively greater understatement of the value of the inventory.

TABLE 21-2.

| | | Variable Input Cost ($) | | Sales | |
	Output	Per Unit	Total	Price per unit ($)	Number of units sold
Opening inventory	100,000		200,000		
First operating cycle	100,000	2.40	240,000	3.60	150,000
Second operating cycle	175,000	2.40	420,000	3.60	200,000
Third operating cycle	150,000	2.50	375,000	3.75	150,000
Fourth operating cycle	200,000	2.60	520,000	3.90	125,000
Total	725,000				625,000
Closing inventory	100,000				

This process comes to an end whenever the firm "clears" its entire inventory. In this case, the difference between understated book value and the current value makes its appearance in the profit account. Assume that the firm in the above illustration has fixed costs of $0.90 per unit and that the firm "clears" its entire inventory in the following year at a time when the variable costs have reached $2.70 and the product is sold at $4. The books will then show the following for the 100,000 units carried over from the last fiscal year:

Income from sale		$400,000
Cost of goods sold	$200,000	
Overhead	90,000	290,000
Profit before tax		$110,000

By comparison, another 100,000 units produced at a variable unit cost of $2.70 will show a before-tax profit of:

$$100,000 \times \$4.00 - 100,000(\$2.70 + 0.90) = \$40,000.$$

B. Plant and equipment

As in the case of inventory, a depreciation reserve or allowance based on historical or original costs becomes progressively less realistic in a period of inflation as the asset approaches the end of its usable lifetime. But unlike an undervalued inventory which catches up with inflation when the firm clears its inventory, there is no such recovery in the case of the depreciation reserve. By definition, the asset has outlived its usefulness and the reserve is insufficient to replace it with a new asset at the then prevailing inflated price.

True, this adverse impact of inflation is shifted from the stockholders of the company to the extent to which the original purchase had been financed with funds obtained from the buyers of debt securities. These buyers are then paid off with dollars that have less buying power than they had at the time when the creditors supplied the funds. In practice, many corporations—either as a matter of capital budgeting policy or in response to conditions in the capital market—procure debt capital for a lesser amount than the cost of the fixed assets. The difference is provided by equity capital. As a result, the portion of the depreciation reserve that is restored to equity capital has suffered a loss in purchasing power. Furthermore, this dollar figure will not suffice to provide the same percentage of the inflated cost of a new asset. Assume that the firm originally obtained $3 million debt capital in the form of mortgage bonds on assets that cost $4 million. Next suppose that, at the end of the usable lifetime of this asset, its replacement cost is $6 million and that the firm can again raise debt capital equal to 75% of the cost or a total of $4.5 million. However, it has only $1 million in its reserve after redeeming the previous bond issue. The company must then either divert $500,000 from the liquid portion of its equity capital with the effect of reducing its networking capital by the same amount; or it must raise an additional $500,000 in equity capital and, thus, dilute the equity of its shareholders.

III. EXTERNAL LONG-RUN PROBLEMS

Inflation affects not only internal managerial policies but also plays an important role in decisions involving the external relations of the company.

A. Debt Capital versus Equity Capital

From the preceding discussion, it should be evident that the stockholders of a company derive a benefit from the maximum feasible financing of fixed assets by means of debt capital in an inflationary period. To the extent to which the creditor's investment is corroded, the equity capital has been kept relatively at a minimum. Furthermore, if the debt capital reaches maturity prior to the end of the usable lifetime of the asset (in which case the depreciation reserve will usually equal the original total cost), the equity holder has an anti-inflation hedge in the value of the still usable asset. It will be recalled that the company has the option of using accelerated depreciation rather than straight-line depreciation.

Additionally, in a period of continuing inflation, it takes fewer units of output to yield a fixed dollar sum. In consequence, the fixed costs as a portion of total costs tend to go down. This, in turn, increases the leverage for the equity holder since both interest and principal are fixed while the price of output goes up. It should also be noted that, in a period of inflation, the market price of a given product or service tends to be established at or above the total cost level of the least efficient (marginal) firm whose output is needed to establish the balance between the demand and the supply. The least efficient firm is usually, although not necessarily, the firm with the highest fixed cost. This situation is prevalent in capital-oriented industries, with a correspondingly high ratio of fixed cost to variable cost.

B. Sale of Assets

The market value of an asset offered for sale by the company bears no relationship to original cost minus depreciation. A 20-year old plant that cost, say, one million to construct may, at present, be readily saleable for more than the original cost. This may be the consequence of inflated current cost of new construction. Or it may reflect a substantial rise in land values, or a combination of both. If the property is sold at the inflated present value, the company will record a gain in nominal dollars equal to the selling price *plus* depreciation reserve *minus* the original cost. This gain is subject to the capital gains tax at a rate of 25%.

However, this profit is again nominal to the extent to which it is attributable to inflation. Thus, if the asset had been purchased with equity funds, the company suffers a loss in purchasing power since the after-tax nominal profit from the sale is less than the loss of purchasing power. On the other hand, if the asset had been financed largely with debt capital, the net profit may be large enough to more than compensate for the loss of purchasing power on the portion of equity capital invested in the asset.

C. Merger and Consolidation

In determining the value of two companies negotiating a merger, the most important single factor is the relative earning capacity of the two firms. As pointed out in the preceding chapter, the financial statements provide the basis for the determination of past profit performance. However, the use of the statements is predicated on the fact that the respective dollar figures represent equal values. This, however, is not necessarily the case in a period of inflation. Past as well as projected future earnings are easily distorted under the influence of a rising price level. Table 21-3 illustrates the extent to which current dollar figures provide an unrealistic yardstick for the evaluation of two companies.

Table 21-3 shows the condensed balance sheets for the last 3 years of two hypothetical firms and three relevant items from the income statements. One company financed its fixed assets with equity capital while the other procured 70% of the funds for fixed assets from the sale of debt securities. It is assumed that both companies plan to replace

TABLE 21-3. Condensed Financial Statements (in Thousands of Dollars)

	19X1	19X2	19X3	19X4 (Projected)
COMPANY A				
Assets:				
Current assets	7,500	8,500	10,000	6,000
Fixed assets (after depreciation)	750	500	250	7,500
Total	8,250	9,000	10,250	13,500
Liabilities:				
Current liabilities	750	1,300	2,150	3,150
Mortgage bonds (maturing in 19X4)	3,500	3,500	3,500	5,250
Common stock (25,000 shares)	2,500	2,500	2,500	2,500
Retained earnings	1,500	1,700	2,100	2,600
Total	8,250	9,000	10,250	13,500
Net working capital	6,750	7,200	8,850	2,350
Net profit	300	400	600	700
Dividends	200	200	200	200
COMPANY B				
Assets:				
Current assets	10,500	11,500	13,300	5,650
Fixed assets (after depreciation)	1,100	700	400	9,750
Total	11,500	12,200	13,700	15,400
Liabilities:				
Current liabilities	1,500	2,000	3,000	4,000
Common stock (75,000 shares)	7,500	7,500	7,500	7,500
Retained earnings	2,500	2,700	3,200	3,900
Total	11,500	12,200	13,700	15,400
Net working capital	9,000	9,500	10,300	1,650
Net profit	400	500	800	1,000
Dividends	200	300	300	300

their fixed assets in the course of the next fiscal year and that the current price level is 50% higher than at the time the fixed assets were acquired.

Looking first at the earnings of the two companies it appears that Company B has earned in the last three years approximately one-third more than Company A. The retained earnings of B are almost 50% greater than those of A. Also, B has no debt capital outstanding while

A has a mortgage debt of $3.5 million which matures in the next year, coincidental with the end of the usable lifetime of its fixed assets. Finally, the net worth of B is $10.7 million compared with $4.5 million for A. Translated into their respective ratios the values for A and B are as follows:

	Company A	Company B
Profit (in dollars)	3	4
Net worth (equity)	1	2.35
Shares outstanding	1	3
Dividends per share	$8.00	$4.00
Net worth per share	$184.00	$142.50

Assuming next that both companies have about the same relative earnings prospects for the next few years, the bargaining range would be between a ratio of 1 share of A for 2 shares of B—based on dividends—and a ratio of 1 share of A for 1.3 shares of B based on the respective net worth per share.

But now let us look at the effect that inflation has had on the equity capital of the two companies. The last column in Table 21-3 shows the projected conditions of A and B at the end of the next fiscal year. In both cases, the replacement of the fixed assets depletes the net working capital by an amount almost 50% larger than would have been the case if the replacement cost would be equal to original cost. For Company A, the projected ratio of net working capital to current liabilities is 0.75:1. Company B will have a ratio of 0.41:1.

More important is the relative loss of purchasing of the equity capital which is not reflected in the conventionally prepared statements. Company A suffered a loss of purchasing of $750,000 on the $1.5 million of equity funds which it invested in fixed assets. The mortgage bond holders absorbed the balance of the loss of purchasing power, namely $1,750,000. In Company B, the equity capital has to bear the entire loss of purchasing power amounting to $3,250,000. This point will become readily apparent if we set up against retained earnings in the year 19X3 an item "Capital Adjustment (resulting from conversion of historical cost to current cost)"[5] The capital accounts of the two companies in the year 19X3 would then be as follows:

[5] Indiana Telephone Corporation, balance sheet, December 31, 1961. The Sacramento Municipal Utility District used for the same purpose the nomenclature "Accumulated Price-level Depreciation."

	Company A	Company B
	(in thousands)	
Stockholders equity		
Common stock—par value $100	$2,500	$ 7,450
Retained earnings	1,350	—
Capital adjustment to price changes	750	3,250
	$4,600	$10,700

Company A is able to provide for the adjustment by reducing its retained earnings from $2,100 to $1,350. However, Company B has to divert its entire retained earnings plus $50,000 of its capital into the adjustment account.

A Study of Inflation and Financial Statements   In 1955, the American Accounting Association published the results of a study[6] of the effects of inflation on financial statements. This research project, which was directed by Professor Ralph C. Jones of Yale University, had as its objectives:

"1. To develop and test techniques and methods for the preparation of supplementary financial statements expressed in constant-value units, that is, in dollars of uniform purchasing power measured by a general index of prices.

2. To compare the supplementary statements expressed in uniform dollars with the conventional statements expressed in historical dollars in order to measure the effect of inflation on companies of various types and sizes, and to determine the extent to which the conventional financial statements have been affected by the use of an unstable unit of measurement.

3. To present quantitative data which will give business managements, individual accountants, committees of accounting associations, and governmental bodies some basis for judging the need for and the usefulness of figures and statements in dollars of uniform purchasing power."

Among the conclusions[7] reached by Professor Jones, the following are of special interest in view of the fact that inflation has been a persistent element in our economy in the years 1956 to 1968 and there is little likelihood of a change in the foreseeable future:

---

[6] *Price Level Changes and Financial Statements—Case Studies of Four Companies* by Ralph C. Jones, The American Accounting Association, 1955.
[7] The conclusions are reproduced in full in Appendix A.

"The substantial inflation which has cut the purchasing power of the dollar by about half since 1940 has considerably impaired the usefulness of financial statements based entirely on historical costs. It is desirable, therefore, that costs be computed in current dollars and presented to management and others in some form, either as supplementary information or as adjustments of the regular statements. . . .

"The major discrepancy between net income reported on an historical basis and net income computed in current dollars arises from the difference between depreciation on original cost in historical dollars and depreciation on that same original cost measured in current dollars of substantially less purchasing power. . . ."

Financial managers, therefore, must be cognizant of the impact of inflation on financial policies of the firm. The financial manager will find it helpful to prepare revised balance sheets and income statements reflecting changes in the purchasing power of the dollar. These statements are often useful for presentation to the stockholders as well as for internal use. Inflation may markedly influence the financial decisions of the firm. For example, moderate inflation in price levels tends to make debt capital more attractive to the firm in the financing of fixed assets than if price levels remained constant.

SUMMARY

The financial manager is vitally interested in the impact of inflation on the financial decisions of the firm in view of the "built-in" nature of inflation in our current economy. Two factors are regarded as the major forces behind this inflationary trend—the tendency of the wage structure to move up with the growth in the national output and the accepted public policy of full employment.

The accountant's method of preparing financial statements in terms of current dollars is inadequate to meet the needs of the financial manager for planning and measuring purposes because of the effect of changes in purchasing power.

An advance in the price level of 1 or 2% would seem to be of little significance. However, if the advance continues for a period of years (such as 10 years) the discrepancy begins to assume major proportions. Thus management must be concerned with the impact of inflation on both short-run areas, such as plant and equipment, and on external long-run problems, such as mergers, choice of securities, and sale of assets. The financial manager will often find it helpful to prepare revised financial statements reflecting changes in purchasing power.

Appendix A   GENERAL CONCLUSIONS*

These studies have disclosed and attempted to measure some of the major effects of inflation upon the affairs of four different companies—one public utility and three manufacturing companies. The experience of these companies obviously is not unique. All other business enterprises to a greater or less degree have been affected by the same forces. Although the primary purpose of this volume is to present quantitative results, it seems appropriate at this point to state briefly a few general conclusions.

1. The substantial inflation which has cut the purchasing power of the dollar by about half since 1940 has considerably impaired the usefulness of financial statements based entirely on historical costs. It is desirable, therefore, that costs be computed in current dollars and presented to management and others in some form, either as supplementary information or as adjustments of the regular statements. This does not imply that the historical statements are unnecessary or incorrect but rather that the conventions or assumptions on which they rest are not adequate to meet expanding needs for financial and economic information.

2. The conversion of financial statements into uniform current dollars is not a departure from the cost basis of accounting but is rather a recognition of the well-established fact that the basic unit of measurement, the dollar, has changed in value. Since the objective in accounting for inflation is to make adjustments or corrections for changes in the basic unit itself rather than to show current values or replacement costs, a measure of general purchasing power such as the Index of Consumers' Prices of the United States Bureau of Labor Statistics must be used.

3. The major discrepancy between net income reported on an historical basis and net income computed in current dollars arises from the difference between depreciation on original cost in historical dollars and depreciation on that same original cost measured in current dollars of substantially less purchasing power. This seems to be generally true in the aggregate for manufacturing companies as well as for public utilities although manufacturing

* Source: Price Level Changes and Financial Statements—Case Studies of Four Companies, by Ralph C. Jones, American Accounting Association, 1955, pp. 177–179.

companies frequently find the inventory factor temporarily more important during periods of rapidly rising prices.

4. The current economic cost of property exhaustion is not affected by the fact that fixed-dollar obligations such as funded debt and preferred stock form part of the financial structure. This cost is solely a function of the physical properties in use, their service lives, and their original cost measured in current dollars.

5. The limitation of depreciation deductions for income tax purposes to original cost in historical dollars raises real rates of taxation well above statutory rates during and after periods of inflation and thereby discriminates against industries having heavy plant investments. The requirement that inventories be valued at cost in historical dollars for the purpose of computing the cost of goods sold also raises real tax rates above nominal rates when prices are rising. This effect, however, ceases when the rise in prices ends and may sometimes be avoided at least in part by the use of the LIFO method of inventory valuation.

6. The book earning rates of a utility company have little, if any, relevance to the problem of determining the point at which excessive earnings or monopoly profits begin unless they are compared with rates currently earned in unregulated industries rather than with some preconceived standard such as 6% or 8% a year. The reasons for this are: (a) the validity of the preconceived standard rests on an assumption or postulate that the dollars in which revenues, expenses, and capital are measured are commensurable constant-value units and this obviously is not true of book figures in historical dollars; and, (b) the rates of an efficiently managed utility company cannot be regarded as excessive unless they take from consumers something of substance over and above the full economic cost of the services rendered. Earnings or profits which are fictitious and without substance cannot be excessive even if the nominal rates of return rise to fantastic heights as they sometimes do during hyperinflation.

7. A fall in the value of the dollar produces no immediate gain on the principal of debts or the face value of outstanding preferred stocks. Such a gain can be realized only by retiring the outstanding securities and that usually is not feasible during inflation when increased capital requirements normally lead to increases rather than decreases in fixed-dollar obligations. The reduction in the real burden of interest and preferred dividend charges which accompanies a fall in the value of the dollar does, however, constitute an immediate benefit to a corporation and its common stockholders.

Table A. Present Value of One Dollar

Periods until Payment	1%	2%	4%	6%	8%	10%	12%	14%	15%	16%	18%	20%	22%	24%	25%	26%	28%	30%	35%	40%	45%	50%
1	0.990	0.980	0.962	0.943	0.926	0.909	0.893	0.877	0.870	0.862	0.847	0.833	0.820	0.806	0.800	0.794	0.781	0.769	0.741	0.714	0.690	0.667
2	0.980	0.961	0.925	0.890	0.857	0.826	0.797	0.769	0.756	0.743	0.718	0.694	0.672	0.650	0.640	0.630	0.610	0.592	0.549	0.510	0.476	0.444
3	0.971	0.942	0.889	0.840	0.794	0.751	0.717	0.675	0.658	0.641	0.609	0.579	0.551	0.524	0.512	0.500	0.477	0.455	0.406	0.364	0.328	0.296
4	0.961	0.924	0.855	0.792	0.735	0.683	0.636	0.592	0.572	0.552	0.516	0.482	0.451	0.423	0.410	0.397	0.373	0.350	0.301	0.260	0.226	0.198
5	0.951	0.906	0.822	0.747	0.681	0.621	0.567	0.519	0.497	0.476	0.437	0.402	0.370	0.341	0.328	0.315	0.291	0.269	0.223	0.186	0.156	0.132
6	0.942	0.888	0.790	0.705	0.630	0.564	0.507	0.456	0.432	0.410	0.370	0.335	0.303	0.275	0.262	0.250	0.227	0.207	0.165	0.133	0.108	0.088
7	0.933	0.871	0.760	0.665	0.583	0.513	0.452	0.400	0.376	0.354	0.314	0.279	0.249	0.222	0.210	0.198	0.178	0.159	0.122	0.095	0.074	0.059
8	0.923	0.853	0.731	0.627	0.540	0.467	0.404	0.351	0.327	0.305	0.266	0.233	0.204	0.179	0.168	0.157	0.139	0.123	0.091	0.068	0.051	0.039
9	0.914	0.837	0.703	0.592	0.500	0.424	0.361	0.308	0.284	0.263	0.228	0.194	0.167	0.144	0.134	0.125	0.108	0.094	0.067	0.048	0.035	0.026
10	0.905	0.820	0.676	0.558	0.463	0.386	0.322	0.270	0.247	0.227	0.191	0.162	0.137	0.116	0.107	0.099	0.085	0.073	0.050	0.035	0.024	0.017
11	0.896	0.804	0.650	0.527	0.429	0.350	0.287	0.237	0.215	0.195	0.162	0.135	0.112	0.094	0.086	0.079	0.066	0.056	0.037	0.025	0.017	0.012
12	0.887	0.788	0.625	0.497	0.397	0.319	0.257	0.208	0.187	0.168	0.137	0.112	0.092	0.076	0.069	0.062	0.052	0.043	0.027	0.018	0.012	0.008
13	0.879	0.773	0.601	0.469	0.368	0.290	0.229	0.182	0.163	0.145	0.116	0.093	0.075	0.061	0.055	0.050	0.040	0.033	0.020	0.013	0.008	0.005
14	0.870	0.758	0.577	0.442	0.340	0.263	0.205	0.160	0.141	0.125	0.099	0.078	0.062	0.049	0.044	0.039	0.032	0.025	0.015	0.009	0.006	0.003
15	0.861	0.743	0.555	0.417	0.315	0.239	0.183	0.140	0.123	0.108	0.084	0.065	0.051	0.040	0.035	0.031	0.025	0.020	0.011	0.006	0.004	0.002
16	0.853	0.728	0.534	0.394	0.292	0.218	0.163	0.123	0.107	0.093	0.071	0.054	0.042	0.032	0.028	0.025	0.019	0.015	0.008	0.005	0.003	0.002
17	0.844	0.714	0.513	0.371	0.270	0.198	0.146	0.108	0.093	0.080	0.060	0.045	0.034	0.026	0.023	0.020	0.015	0.012	0.006	0.003	0.002	0.001
18	0.836	0.700	0.494	0.350	0.250	0.180	0.130	0.095	0.081	0.069	0.051	0.038	0.028	0.021	0.018	0.016	0.012	0.009	0.005	0.002	0.001	
19	0.828	0.686	0.475	0.331	0.232	0.164	0.116	0.083	0.070	0.060	0.043	0.031	0.023	0.017	0.014	0.012	0.009	0.007	0.003	0.002	0.001	
20	0.820	0.673	0.456	0.312	0.215	0.149	0.104	0.073	0.061	0.051	0.037	0.026	0.019	0.014	0.012	0.010	0.007	0.005	0.002	0.001		
21	0.811	0.660	0.439	0.294	0.199	0.135	0.093	0.064	0.053	0.044	0.031	0.022	0.015	0.011	0.009	0.008	0.006	0.004	0.002	0.001		
22	0.803	0.647	0.422	0.278	0.184	0.123	0.083	0.056	0.046	0.038	0.026	0.018	0.013	0.009	0.007	0.006	0.004	0.003	0.001	0.001		
23	0.795	0.634	0.406	0.262	0.170	0.112	0.074	0.049	0.040	0.033	0.022	0.015	0.010	0.007	0.006	0.005	0.003	0.002	0.001			
24	0.788	0.622	0.390	0.247	0.158	0.102	0.066	0.043	0.035	0.028	0.019	0.013	0.008	0.006	0.005	0.004	0.003	0.002	0.001			
25	0.780	0.610	0.375	0.233	0.146	0.092	0.059	0.038	0.030	0.024	0.016	0.010	0.007	0.005	0.004	0.003	0.003	0.001	0.001			
26	0.772	0.598	0.361	0.220	0.135	0.084	0.053	0.033	0.026	0.021	0.014	0.009	0.006	0.004	0.003	0.002	0.002	0.001				
27	0.764	0.586	0.347	0.207	0.125	0.076	0.047	0.029	0.023	0.018	0.011	0.007	0.005	0.003	0.002	0.002	0.001	0.001				
28	0.757	0.574	0.333	0.196	0.116	0.069	0.042	0.026	0.020	0.016	0.010	0.006	0.004	0.002	0.002	0.001	0.001	0.001				
29	0.749	0.563	0.321	0.185	0.107	0.063	0.037	0.022	0.017	0.014	0.008	0.005	0.003	0.002	0.002	0.001	0.001					
30	0.742	0.552	0.308	0.174	0.099	0.057	0.033	0.020	0.015	0.012	0.007	0.004	0.003	0.002	0.002	0.001	0.001					
40	0.672	0.453	0.208	0.097	0.046	0.022	0.011	0.005	0.004	0.003	0.001	0.001										
50	0.608	0.372	0.141	0.054	0.021	0.009	0.003	0.001	0.001	0.001												

TABLE B.   Present Value of One Dollar Received Annually for N Years

Years (N)	1%	2%	4%	6%	8%	10%	12%	14%	15%	16%	18%	20%	22%	24%	25%	26%	28%	30%	35%	40%	45%	50%
1	0.990	0.980	0.962	0.943	0.926	0.909	0.893	0.877	0.870	0.862	0.847	0.833	0.820	0.806	0.800	0.794	0.781	0.769	0.741	0.714	0.690	0.667
2	1.970	1.942	1.886	1.833	1.783	1.736	1.690	1.647	1.626	1.605	1.566	1.528	1.492	1.457	1.440	1.424	1.392	1.361	1.289	1.224	1.165	1.111
3	2.941	2.884	2.775	2.673	2.577	2.487	2.402	2.322	2.283	2.246	2.174	2.106	2.042	1.981	1.952	1.923	1.868	1.816	1.696	1.589	1.493	1.407
4	3.902	3.808	3.630	3.465	3.312	3.170	3.037	2.914	2.855	2.798	2.690	2.589	2.494	2.404	2.362	2.320	2.241	2.166	1.997	1.849	1.720	1.605
5	4.853	4.713	4.452	4.212	3.993	3.791	3.605	3.433	3.352	3.274	3.127	2.991	2.864	2.745	2.689	2.635	2.532	2.436	2.220	2.035	1.876	1.737
6	5.795	5.601	5.242	4.917	4.623	4.355	4.111	3.889	3.784	3.685	3.498	3.326	3.167	3.020	2.951	2.885	2.759	2.643	2.385	2.168	1.983	1.824
7	6.728	6.472	6.002	5.582	5.206	4.868	4.564	4.288	4.160	4.039	3.812	3.605	3.416	3.242	3.161	3.083	2.937	2.802	2.508	2.263	2.057	1.883
8	7.652	7.325	6.733	6.210	5.747	5.335	4.968	4.639	4.487	4.344	4.078	3.837	3.619	3.421	3.329	3.241	3.076	2.925	2.598	2.331	2.108	1.922
9	8.566	8.162	7.435	6.802	6.247	5.759	5.328	4.946	4.772	4.607	4.303	4.031	3.786	3.566	3.463	3.366	3.184	3.019	2.665	2.379	2.144	1.948
10	9.471	8.983	8.111	7.360	6.710	6.145	5.650	5.216	5.019	4.833	4.494	4.192	3.923	3.682	3.571	3.465	3.269	3.092	2.715	2.414	2.168	1.965
11	10.368	9.787	8.760	7.887	7.139	6.495	5.938	5.453	5.234	5.029	4.656	4.327	4.035	3.776	3.656	3.544	3.335	3.147	2.752	2.438	2.185	1.977
12	11.255	10.575	9.385	8.384	7.536	6.814	6.194	5.660	5.421	5.197	4.793	4.439	4.127	3.851	3.725	3.606	3.387	3.190	2.779	2.456	2.196	1.985
13	12.134	11.343	9.986	8.853	7.904	7.103	6.424	5.842	5.583	5.342	4.910	4.533	4.203	3.912	3.780	3.656	3.427	3.223	2.799	2.468	2.204	1.990
14	13.004	12.106	10.563	9.295	8.244	7.367	6.628	6.002	5.724	5.468	5.008	4.611	4.265	3.962	3.824	3.695	3.459	3.249	2.814	2.477	2.210	1.993
15	13.865	12.849	11.118	9.712	8.559	7.606	6.811	6.142	5.847	5.575	5.092	4.675	4.315	4.001	3.859	3.726	3.483	3.268	2.825	2.484	2.214	1.995
16	14.718	13.578	11.652	10.106	8.851	7.824	6.974	6.265	5.954	5.669	5.162	4.730	4.357	4.033	3.887	3.751	3.503	3.283	2.834	2.489	2.216	1.997
17	15.562	14.292	12.166	10.477	9.122	8.022	7.120	6.373	6.047	5.749	5.222	4.775	4.391	4.059	3.910	3.771	3.518	3.295	2.840	2.492	2.218	1.998
18	16.398	14.992	12.659	10.828	9.372	8.201	7.250	6.467	6.128	5.818	5.273	4.812	4.419	4.080	3.928	3.786	3.529	3.304	2.844	2.494	2.219	1.999
19	17.226	15.678	13.134	11.158	9.604	8.365	7.366	6.550	6.198	5.877	5.316	4.843	4.442	4.097	3.942	3.799	3.539	3.311	2.848	2.496	2.220	1.999
20	18.046	16.351	13.590	11.470	9.818	8.514	7.469	6.623	6.259	5.929	5.353	4.870	4.460	4.110	3.954	3.808	3.546	3.316	2.850	2.497	2.221	1.999
21	18.857	17.011	14.029	11.764	10.017	8.649	7.562	6.687	6.312	5.973	5.384	4.891	4.476	4.121	3.963	3.816	3.551	3.320	2.852	2.498	2.221	2.000
22	19.660	17.658	14.451	12.042	10.201	8.772	7.645	6.743	6.359	6.011	5.410	4.909	4.488	4.130	3.970	3.822	3.556	3.323	2.853	2.498	2.222	2.000
23	20.456	18.292	14.857	12.303	10.371	8.883	7.718	6.792	6.399	6.044	5.432	4.925	4.499	4.137	3.976	3.827	3.559	3.325	2.854	2.499	2.222	2.000
24	21.243	18.914	15.247	12.550	10.529	8.985	7.784	6.835	6.434	6.073	5.451	4.937	4.507	4.143	3.981	3.831	3.562	3.327	2.855	2.499	2.222	2.000
25	22.023	19.523	15.622	12.783	10.675	9.077	7.843	6.873	6.464	6.097	5.467	4.948	4.514	4.147	3.985	3.834	3.564	3.329	2.856	2.499	2.222	2.000
26	22.795	20.121	15.983	13.003	10.810	9.161	7.896	6.906	6.491	6.118	5.480	4.956	4.520	4.151	3.988	3.837	3.566	3.330	2.856	2.500	2.222	2.000
27	23.560	20.707	16.330	13.211	10.935	9.237	7.943	6.935	6.514	6.136	5.492	4.964	4.524	4.154	3.990	3.839	3.567	3.331	2.857	2.500	2.222	2.000
28	24.316	21.281	16.663	13.406	11.051	9.307	7.984	6.961	6.534	6.152	5.502	4.970	4.528	4.157	3.992	3.840	3.568	3.331	2.857	2.500	2.222	2.000
29	25.066	21.844	16.984	13.591	11.158	9.370	8.022	6.983	6.551	6.166	5.510	4.975	4.531	4.159	3.994	3.841	3.569	3.332	2.857	2.500	2.222	2.000
30	25.808	22.396	17.292	13.765	11.258	9.427	8.055	7.003	6.566	6.177	5.517	4.979	4.534	4.160	3.995	3.842	3.569	3.332	2.857	2.500	2.222	2.000
40	32.835	27.355	19.793	15.046	11.925	9.779	8.244	7.105	6.642	6.234	5.548	4.997	4.544	4.166	3.999	3.846	3.571	3.333	2.857	2.500	2.222	2.000
50	39.196	31.424	21.482	15.762	12.233	9.915	8.304	7.133	6.661	6.246	5.554	4.999	4.545	4.167	4.000	3.846	3.571	3.333	2.857	2.500	2.222	2.000

TABLE C. Present Value of $1/12$ Dollar Received Monthly in Year N

Year (N)	1%	2%	4%	6%	8%	10%	12%	14%	15%	16%	18%	20%	22%	24%	25%	26%	28%	30%	35%	40%	45%	50%
1	0.995	0.989	0.979	0.969	0.959	0.950	0.941	0.932	0.928	0.924	0.915	0.907	0.899	0.892	0.888	0.884	0.877	0.870	0.853	0.837	0.822	0.808
2	0.985	0.970	0.941	0.914	0.888	0.864	0.840	0.818	0.807	0.796	0.776	0.756	0.737	0.719	0.710	0.702	0.685	0.669	0.632	0.598	0.567	0.539
3	0.975	0.951	0.905	0.862	0.823	0.785	0.750	0.717	0.702	0.686	0.657	0.630	0.604	0.580	0.568	0.557	0.535	0.515	0.468	0.527	0.391	0.359
4	0.965	0.932	0.870	0.814	0.762	0.714	0.670	0.629	0.610	0.592	0.557	0.525	0.495	0.468	0.455	0.442	0.418	0.396	0.347	0.305	0.270	0.239
5	0.956	0.914	0.837	0.768	0.705	0.649	0.598	0.552	0.531	0.510	0.472	0.438	0.406	0.377	0.364	0.351	0.327	0.305	0.257	0.218	0.186	0.160
6	0.946	0.896	0.805	0.724	0.653	0.590	0.534	0.484	0.461	0.440	0.400	0.365	0.333	0.304	0.291	0.278	0.255	0.234	0.490	0.156	0.128	0.106
7	0.937	0.879	0.774	0.683	0.605	0.536	0.477	0.425	0.401	0.379	0.339	0.304	0.273	0.245	0.233	0.221	0.199	0.180	0.141	0.111	0.088	0.071
8	0.928	0.861	0.744	0.644	0.560	0.488	0.426	0.373	0.349	0.327	0.287	0.253	0.224	0.198	0.186	0.175	0.156	0.139	0.104	0.079	0.061	0.047
9	0.919	0.844	0.715	0.608	0.518	0.443	0.380	0.327	0.303	0.282	0.244	0.211	0.183	0.160	0.149	0.139	0.122	0.107	0.077	0.057	0.042	0.032
10	0.909	0.828	0.688	0.574	0.480	0.403	0.339	0.287	0.264	0.243	0.206	0.176	0.150	0.129	0.119	0.110	0.095	0.082	0.057	0.041	0.029	0.021
11	0.900	0.812	0.661	0.541	0.444	0.366	0.303	0.251	0.229	0.209	0.175	0.147	0.123	0.104	0.095	0.088	0.074	0.063	0.042	0.029	0.020	0.014
12	0.892	0.796	0.636	0.510	0.411	0.323	0.271	0.221	0.199	0.180	0.148	0.122	0.101	0.084	0.076	0.070	0.058	0.049	0.031	0.021	0.014	0.009
13	0.883	0.780	0.612	0.482	0.381	0.303	0.242	0.193	0.173	0.156	0.126	0.102	0.083	0.067	0.061	0.055	0.045	0.037	0.023	0.015	0.010	0.006
14	0.874	0.765	0.588	0.454	0.353	0.275	0.216	0.170	0.151	0.134	0.106	0.085	0.068	0.054	0.049	0.044	0.035	0.028	0.017	0.011	0.007	0.004
15	0.865	0.750	0.565	0.429	0.327	0.250	0.193	0.149	0.131	0.116	0.090	0.071	0.056	0.044	0.039	0.035	0.027	0.022	0.013	0.008	0.005	0.003
16	0.857	0.735	0.544	0.404	0.302	0.227	0.172	0.131	0.114	0.100	0.076	0.059	0.046	0.035	0.031	0.028	0.022	0.017	0.009	0.005	0.003	0.002
17	0.848	0.721	0.523	0.381	0.280	0.207	0.153	0.115	0.099	0.086	0.065	0.049	0.037	0.029	0.025	0.023	0.017	0.013	0.007	0.004	0.002	0.001
18	0.840	0.707	0.503	0.360	0.259	0.188	0.137	0.100	0.086	0.074	0.055	0.041	0.031	0.023	0.020	0.019	0.013	0.010	0.005	0.003	0.001	0.001
19	0.832	0.694	0.483	0.340	0.240	0.171	0.122	0.088	0.075	0.064	0.047	0.034	0.025	0.019	0.016	0.014	0.010	0.008	0.004	0.002	0.001	0.001
20	0.823	0.679	0.465	0.320	0.222	0.155	0.109	0.077	0.065	0.055	0.039	0.028	0.021	0.015	0.013	0.011	0.008	0.006	0.003	0.001		
21	0.815	0.666	0.447	0.302	0.206	0.141	0.098	0.068	0.057	0.047	0.033	0.024	0.017	0.012	0.010	0.009	0.006	0.005	0.002	0.001		
22	0.807	0.653	0.430	0.285	0.191	0.128	0.087	0.060	0.049	0.041	0.028	0.020	0.014	0.010	0.008	0.007	0.005	0.004	0.002	0.001		
23	0.799	0.640	0.413	0.269	0.176	0.117	0.078	0.052	0.043	0.035	0.024	0.016	0.011	0.008	0.007	0.005	0.004	0.003	0.001	0.001		
24	0.791	0.627	0.397	0.254	0.163	0.106	0.069	0.046	0.037	0.030	0.020	0.014	0.009	0.006	0.005	0.004	0.003	0.002	0.001			
25	0.783	0.615	0.382	0.239	0.151	0.096	0.062	0.040	0.032	0.026	0.017	0.011	0.008	0.005	0.004	0.003	0.002	0.002	0.001			
26	0.776	0.603	0.367	0.226	0.140	0.088	0.055	0.035	0.028	0.023	0.015	0.010	0.006	0.004	0.003	0.003	0.002	0.001				
27	0.768	0.591	0.353	0.213	0.130	0.080	0.049	0.031	0.025	0.019	0.012	0.008	0.005	0.003	0.003	0.002	0.001	0.001				
28	0.760	0.580	0.340	0.201	0.120	0.072	0.044	0.027	0.021	0.017	0.010	0.007	0.004	0.003	0.002	0.001	0.001	0.001				
29	0.753	0.568	0.326	0.190	0.111	0.066	0.039	0.024	0.019	0.014	0.009	0.006	0.003	0.002	0.002	0.001	0.001	0.001				
30	0.745	0.557	0.314	0.179	0.103	0.060	0.035	0.021	0.016	0.012	0.008	0.005	0.003	0.002	0.001	0.001	0.001					
40	0.675	0.457	0.212	0.100	0.048	0.023	0.011	0.006	0.004	0.003	0.001	0.001										
50	0.611	0.375	0.143	0.056	0.022	0.009	0.004	0.002	0.001	0.001												

TABLE D. Present Value of $\frac{1}{12}$ Dollar Received Monthly for N Years

Years (N)	1%	2%	4%	6%	8%	10%	12%	14%	15%	16%	18%	20%	22%	24%	25%	26%	28%	30%	35%	40%	45%	50%
1	0.995	0.989	0.979	0.969	0.959	0.950	0.941	0.932	0.928	0.924	0.915	0.907	0.899	0.892	0.888	0.884	0.877	0.870	0.853	0.837	0.822	0.808
2	1.979	1.959	1.920	1.883	1.848	1.814	1.781	1.750	1.735	1.720	1.691	1.663	1.637	1.611	1.598	1.586	1.562	1.539	1.485	1.435	1.390	1.347
3	2.954	2.910	2.826	2.746	2.670	2.599	2.531	2.467	2.436	2.406	2.348	2.293	2.241	2.191	2.167	2.143	2.098	2.054	1.953	1.863	1.781	1.706
4	3.920	3.843	3.696	3.559	3.432	3.313	3.201	3.096	3.046	2.998	2.905	2.818	2.736	2.658	2.621	2.585	2.516	2.450	2.300	2.168	2.050	1.946
5	4.876	4.757	4.533	4.327	4.137	3.962	3.799	3.648	3.577	3.508	3.377	3.256	3.142	3.036	2.985	2.936	2.842	2.755	2.557	2.386	2.236	2.106
6	5.822	5.653	5.338	5.051	4.790	4.551	4.333	4.132	4.038	3.948	3.778	3.620	3.475	3.340	3.276	3.214	3.098	2.989	2.747	2.541	2.365	2.212
7	6.759	6.531	6.111	5.734	5.395	5.088	4.810	4.557	4.439	4.327	4.117	3.924	3.748	3.585	3.509	3.435	3.297	3.169	2.888	2.653	2.453	2.281
8	7.687	7.392	6.855	6.379	5.954	5.575	5.235	4.957	4.788	4.654	4.404	4.177	3.971	3.783	3.695	3.611	3.453	3.308	2.992	2.732	2.514	2.330
9	8.605	8.237	7.571	6.987	6.473	6.018	5.615	5.256	5.091	4.935	4.647	4.388	4.154	3.942	3.844	3.750	3.575	3.414	3.070	2.789	2.556	2.362
10	9.515	9.065	8.259	7.560	6.953	6.421	5.955	5.543	5.355	5.178	4.854	4.564	4.305	4.071	3.963	3.860	3.670	3.497	3.127	2.829	2.585	2.383
11	10.415	9.876	8.920	8.101	7.397	6.788	6.258	5.794	5.584	5.388	5.029	4.711	4.428	4.175	4.058	3.948	3.744	3.560	3.169	2.858	2.605	2.397
12	11.307	10.672	9.556	8.612	7.809	7.121	6.528	6.015	5.784	5.568	5.177	4.833	4.529	4.259	4.135	4.018	3.802	3.608	3.201	2.879	2.619	2.406
13	12.189	11.452	10.167	9.094	8.190	7.423	6.770	6.208	5.957	5.724	5.302	4.935	4.611	4.326	4.196	4.073	3.847	3.646	3.224	2.894	2.629	2.412
14	13.063	12.217	10.755	9.548	8.542	7.699	6.985	6.378	6.108	5.858	5.409	5.019	4.679	4.380	4.245	4.117	3.883	3.674	3.241	2.904	2.635	2.417
15	13.928	12.967	11.321	9.977	8.869	7.949	7.178	6.527	6.239	5.973	5.499	5.090	4.735	4.424	4.284	4.152	3.911	3.696	3.254	2.912	2.640	2.419
16	14.785	13.702	11.864	10.381	9.171	8.176	7.350	6.658	6.353	6.073	5.576	5.149	4.780	4.460	4.315	4.179	3.932	3.713	3.264	2.917	2.643	2.421
17	15.633	14.422	12.387	10.762	9.451	8.383	7.503	6.772	6.452	6.159	5.640	5.198	4.818	4.488	4.340	4.201	3.949	3.726	3.271	2.921	2.645	2.422
18	16.473	15.129	12.890	11.122	9.711	8.571	7.640	6.873	6.539	6.233	5.695	5.239	4.848	4.511	4.360	4.218	3.962	3.736	3.276	2.924	2.647	2.423
19	17.305	15.822	13.373	11.462	9.951	8.742	7.763	6.961	6.614	6.297	5.742	5.273	4.873	4.530	4.376	4.232	3.973	3.744	3.280	2.926	2.648	2.424
20	18.128	16.501	13.838	11.782	10.173	8.897	7.872	7.038	6.679	6.352	5.781	5.301	4.894	4.545	4.389	4.243	3.981	3.750	3.283	2.927	2.648	2.424
21	18.943	17.167	14.285	12.084	10.379	9.038	7.969	7.106	6.735	6.399	5.815	5.325	4.911	4.557	4.399	4.252	3.987	3.755	3.285	2.928	2.649	2.424
22	19.750	17.819	14.714	12.369	10.570	9.167	8.056	7.165	6.785	6.440	5.843	5.345	4.925	4.567	4.407	4.259	3.992	3.758	3.286	2.929	2.649	2.425
23	20.549	18.459	15.127	12.638	10.746	9.283	8.134	7.218	6.828	6.476	5.867	5.361	4.936	4.574	4.414	4.264	3.996	3.761	3.287	2.929	2.649	2.425
24	21.341	19.087	15.525	12.892	10.909	9.389	8.204	7.263	6.865	6.506	5.887	5.375	4.945	4.581	4.419	4.269	3.999	3.763	3.288	2.930	2.650	2.425
25	22.124	19.702	15.906	13.131	11.061	9.486	8.266	7.304	6.897	6.532	5.904	5.386	4.953	4.586	4.423	4.272	4.001	3.765	3.289	2.930	2.650	2.425
26	22.899	20.305	16.274	13.357	11.201	9.574	8.321	7.339	6.926	6.555	5.919	5.396	4.959	4.590	4.426	4.275	4.003	3.766	3.289	2.930	2.650	2.425
27	23.667	20.896	16.627	13.570	11.331	9.653	8.370	7.370	6.950	6.574	5.931	5.404	4.964	4.593	4.429	4.277	4.004	3.767	3.290	2.930	2.650	2.425
28	24.428	21.476	16.966	13.771	11.451	9.726	8.415	7.397	6.971	6.591	5.942	5.410	4.968	4.596	4.431	4.279	4.005	3.768	3.290	2.930	2.650	2.425
29	25.180	22.044	17.293	13.961	11.562	9.792	8.454	7.421	6.990	6.606	5.951	5.416	4.972	4.598	4.433	4.280	4.006	3.768	3.290	2.930	2.650	2.425
30	25.926	22.601	17.607	14.139	11.665	9.852	8.489	7.441	7.006	6.618	5.958	5.420	4.975	4.600	4.434	4.281	4.007	3.769	3.290	2.930	2.650	2.425
40	32.985	27.605	20.153	15.456	12.456	10.220	8.688	7.550	7.087	6.678	5.992	5.440	4.986	4.606	4.439	4.285	4.009	3.770	3.291	2.931	2.650	2.425
50	39.375	31.711	21.873	16.191	12.676	10.361	8.752	7.580	7.107	6.692	5.999	5.443	4.987	4.607	4.440	4.285	4.009	3.770	3.291	2.931	2.650	2.425

8. It is highly unrealistic to assume that investors and others now realize or can ascertain for themselves that as a result of inflation a substantial part of reported earnings based on historical dollars may in fact represent a return of economic capital invested in the enterprise. From this, it follows that company managements and the accountants who audit the financial statements assume a heavy social responsibility when they report earnings on common stock at rates generally regarded as ample or even excessive without either indicating the character of such gains or providing supplementary information which would make it possible for readers to estimate for themselves the amount of inflationary bias.

Questions

1. Contrast the accountant's view of the valuation of a firm's assets with the economist's view.
2. Is the LIFO method of valuing inventory advantageous to a firm in a period of rising prices? Why (not)?
3. Which item in the income statement is most seriously affected by inflation? Why?
4. How can a firm show in its financial statements the effect of inflation on fixed assets?
5. Does the United States Internal Revenue Service permit use of a tax deductible depreciation reserve or allowance on the basis of original cost? On the basis of replacement cost?
6. Why would a firm wish to use replacement cost rather than original cost in the annual determination of the depreciation reserve or allowance?
7. How may a moderate inflation of prices affect a firm's decision on raising debt or equity capital?

Problems

1. Alpha Corporation's net income after taxes in 19X1 was $1,250,000. Net income after taxes was $1,300,000 in 19X2. The Consumer Price Index in 19X2 was 105 in terms of 19X1 dollars. What was Alpha's 19X2 profit in terms of 19X1 dollars?
2. Gamma Company uses the FIFO method of valuing inventory. Production and sales figures for the company's first three years of operations were as shown in Table 21-4.

TABLE 21-4.

Year	Output (in Units)	Cost per Unit Produced[a]	Sales (Unit Price)	Number Sold
19X1	50,000	$10.00	$20.00	40,000
19X2	75,000	11.00	22.50	80,000
19X3	100,000	12.00	25.00	90,000

[a] Only direct labor and materials.

(a) What was the dollar contribution to overhead and profit in each of the three years, using the FIFO method?

(b) If Gamma paid a corporate income tax of 50% and half of the contribution to overhead and profit was profit, how much total taxes (in dollars) would Gamma have paid under FIFO for the three years?

(c) What was the value of the ending inventory (at cost) at the end of 19X3 using the FIFO method?

(d-f) Calculate the answers to the above three questions, if Gamma had used the LIFO method of valuing inventory for the three year period.

Case: NORTHRUP CHEWING GUM COMPANY

The top executive officers of the Northrup Chewing Gum Company are meeting to consider the problem of expected increases in the cost of advertising the company's chewing gum. Between 1946 and 1965 advertising rates increased 47%. In the same period of time, the wholesale price index climbed 55% and the consumer price index climbed 62%. The advertising manager believes advertising rates will probably increase about 2.5% per year on the average in the next 5 to 10 years.

Because of the increasing competition in the candy, gum, and nuts business (150 brands of candy, gum, and nuts in 1950 and 275 in 1963) and the high correlation between the amount of advertising and the volume of sales, management does not believe it possible to reduce the current amount of advertising (per stick of gum sold) to compensate for rising costs. Currently, management is spending 15% of sales (based on the whole-sale price) on advertising. Management does not believe it can raise the traditional retail selling price of 1 cent per stick of gum or increase its wholesale prices, because of the intense competition in the chewing gum market. Currently, the retail price for chewing gum is $1.00 for 100 sticks of gum. The wholesale selling price is 60 cents for 100 sticks of gum. Material, labor, and other costs, excluding advertising, amount to 49 cents per 100 sticks.

Case Questions:

1. If advertising costs increase 2.5% per year (not compounded) as fore-cast, in how many years will the company break even on sales if prices are not raised or advertising expenditures are not reduced?
2. If all costs increase 2.5% per year (not compounded), in how many years will the company break even on sales if prices are not raised and costs are not reduced?
3. What alternatives besides increasing prices or reducing the amount of advertising should management consider?

Index